CRIMINAL PROCEDURE

F I R S T   E D I T I O N

CRIMINAL PROCEDURE

Thomas J. Hickey
Roger Williams University

Boston, Massachusetts   Burr Ridge, Illinois   Dubuque, Iowa
Madison, Wisconsin   New York, New York   San Francisco, California   St. Louis, Missouri

McGraw-Hill

*A Division of The **McGraw·Hill** Companies*

CRIMINAL PROCEDURE

1 2 3 4 5 6 7 8 9 0 DOC/DOC 9 0 9 8 7

ISBN 0-697-32905-4

Editorial director: *Phil Butcher*
Sponsoring editor: *Nancy Blaine/Tom Romaniak*
Marketing manager: *Sally Constable*
Project manager: *Kari Geltemeyer*
Production supervisor: *Karen Thigpen*
Senior designer: *Michael Warrell*
Photo research coordinator: *Sharon Miller*
Compositor: *Shepherd Incorporated*
Typeface: *10/12 Times Roman*
Printer: *R. R. Donnelley & Sons Company*

Library of Congress Cataloging-in-Publication Data

Hickey, Thomas J.
    Criminal procedure / Thomas J. Hickey.
        p.   cm.
    Includes index.
    ISBN 0-697-32905-4 (acid-free paper)
    1. Criminal procedure--United States.   I. Title.
  KF9619.6.H53   1998   97–20450
  345.73'05–dc21   CIP

http://www.mhhe.com

Tom Hickey is a Professor in the School of Justice Studies, Roger Williams University, Bristol, Rhode Island. He received his Bachelor's degree from Providence College, his M.A. and Ph.D. in Criminal Justice from Sam Houston State University, and his J.D. from the University of Oregon School of Law. Tom has received awards for outstanding teaching at the University of Oregon and Penn State Harrisburg. His areas of expertise include criminal law and procedure, constitutional law, administrative law, and the U.S. court system. His recent articles appear in the *Journal of Criminal Justice, the Criminal Law Bulletin,* the *International Journal of Public Administration,* and *Public Administration Quarterly.*

Tom formerly served as a police officer and is a licensed attorney in the Commonwealth of Pennsylvania. He presently lives on Narragansett Bay in Portsmouth, Rhode Island.

To Nancy, Norma, Tom, Sr., Steven, and Roslyn. Thanks for always being there when I need you.

Law and the legal process influence all aspects of life in the United States. The law shapes our social institutions and is at the same time shaped by those same institutions.

Perhaps no single area of law is more interesting to many students than criminal law. The approach that I use in this textbook attempts to convey to students that the study of criminal law is fun and exciting. It is much more than simply memorizing case names and developing the ability to associate cases with particular legal doctrines. Rather, students must be taught to "think legally." To do this, their analytical skills and critical thinking ability must be developed so that they are able to construct sound arguments.

The study of criminal procedure is largely the study of case law. I do not use a "law school case method" to analyze this material. This text uses a modified case law approach to illustrate the various legal principles that comprise the body of criminal procedure. Excerpts from the most important criminal procedure decisions are included within the text and the principles derived from these decisions are developed and explained. Although some texts adopt a highly theoretical approach to the study of criminal procedure, I try to blend the theory and practice of law. Throughout the text, I use examples to show students how legal theory applies in practical situations that they may encounter if they eventually become criminal justice system employees.

I also use an evolutionary perspective to try to provide a sense of how and why these legal principles have developed within our justice system. For example, Chapter 3 discusses the exclusionary rule of evidence. Some students believe that the exclusionary rule represents an abuse of the criminal process—to paraphrase Justice Cardozo, factually guilty criminals are set free because police officers have blundered. More detailed exposure to *Rochin* v. *California, Mapp* v. *Ohio,* and other precedents helps to convince students that the exclusionary rule question is more complex than it first appears to be.

Organizing a criminal procedure text is a difficult task. Some texts use a multiple volume approach that divides a course into pretrial, trial, and post-trial issues. Other works try to integrate the material into a single volume for use in one semester. Although there are compelling reasons for the former approach, particularly in a law school setting, I have adopted the single volume format because this text is designed primarily for use at the undergraduate level.

Each chapter begins with an outline detailing the topics to be considered. Next, key terms are presented to advise students about the most important concepts presented in the chapter. Chapters also contain summaries, review questions, issues for analysis and discussion, and case excerpts. I believe that it is important for students to read actual cases. Therefore, carefully edited case excerpts have been included at the end of each chapter.

Chapter 1 presents an introduction to the study of criminal procedure, which outlines the process that must be followed in police investigations of crimes and in criminal trials. This chapter also discusses introductory concepts in U.S. legal systems, including the nature of an adversary system of justice, U.S. criminal court systems, and the power of judicial review. It concludes with a discussion of how to read and understand a case, how to find a case in a law library, and how to brief a case.

Chapter 2 discusses the stages in the U.S. criminal justice process and begins to explore in greater detail the procedures used in U.S. justice systems. I also consider some basic constitutional protections, including the right to a writ of habeas corpus. Because it is important to develop an appreciation of the historical factors that led to the development of the Bill of Rights, I consider general warrants and writs of assistance. Chapter 2 outlines the provisions in the Bill of Rights that prescribe criminal procedures as well. The provisions in the Fourth, Fifth, Sixth, Eighth, and Fourteenth Amendments that guarantee procedural rights are identified.

Chapter 3 begins a more detailed analysis of procedural law and covers the exclusionary rule of evidence, which may require suppression of evidence obtained through violations of the Fourth, Fifth, or Sixth Amendments. Various exceptions to the exclusionary rule that have been recognized by the Supreme Court are discussed in detail.

Chapter 4 discusses search and arrest warrants. The probable cause standard is considered in detail. The basic elements of a valid warrant and the Fourth Amendment's particularity requirement are discussed.

Chapter 5 considers the law of arrest, searches incident to an arrest, and the use of force by the police, and highlights the emerging issue of domestic violence laws. It contains numerous practical examples of when police may use force to make an arrest.

Chapter 6 discusses stop and frisk practices and investigatory detentions, which may be based on reasonable suspicion that criminal activity is afoot. This rapidly expanding area of criminal procedure is crucial to criminal justice system practitioners. *Terry* v. *Ohio* and other important precedents are analyzed. In addition, police use of drug courier profiles and sobriety checkpoints are examined.

Chapter 7 discusses automobile searches, inventory searches, and consent searches. Students tend to be very interested in the material presented in this chapter. Their most frequent questions involve situations in which they have been stopped by the police for various motor vehicle infractions. Inventory searches and consent searches are considered as well because, although these practices are not limited to automobile stops following traffic offenses, they often occur in this context.

Chapter 8 discusses the plain view doctrine, items found in open fields, and regulatory searches. This chapter uses extensive practical examples to illustrate key concepts.

Moreover, newer legal concepts such as the "plain smell" and "plain touch" doctrines are considered in detail. In addition, this chapter discusses another rapidly expanding area of U.S. law, regulatory searches, which are conducted by government employees for health, safety, or other administrative purposes.

Chapter 9 considers high technology investigation methods and electronic eavesdropping. High-technology investigative methods have developed rapidly in recent years and include techniques such as wiretapping telephones, intercepting wireless communications and cellular telephone transmissions, using infrared cameras to photograph suspicious activities, or even observing suspicious areas with satellites. Recently, some law enforcement agencies have used thermal imaging to detect heat emissions from structures suspected of harboring indoor marijuana growing operations. Chapter 9 concludes the discussion of Fourth Amendment issues.

Chapter 10 is devoted to a discussion of *Miranda* v. *Arizona* and the privilege against self-incrimination. Although there is some reason to believe that *Miranda*'s central thrust has been eroded by the Supreme Court in recent years, it continues to be a seminal criminal case. The most recent empirical evidence on *Miranda*'s effect on criminal cases is analyzed.

Chapter 11 considers pretrial identification procedures and the right to be free from double jeopardy. I also analyze another expanding area of criminal law, property forfeitures and asset seizures. Throughout this text I have made every effort to present material that is completely up-to-date. Cases from the Supreme Court's latest term are included and provide material that should appeal to students and generate classroom discussion. For example, in 1996, *Bennis* v. *Michigan* upheld the seizure of an automobile, which was owned jointly by a husband and wife, because the husband had been convicted of "gross indecency" for consorting with a prostitute.

Chapter 12 shifts the text's focus to a defendant's Sixth Amendment rights at trial. The right to a speedy and public trial, the right to confront and cross-examine adverse witnesses, and the right to counsel are considered in detail.

Chapter 13, which concludes the text, discusses various post-trial processes, including sentencing, appeals, and habeas corpus review.

In addition to attempting to insure that all of the case law included in this text is as current as possible, I have tried to provide the latest external reference material for those who wish to conduct more detailed research into specific areas of criminal procedure. Rather than including a generalized list of "Suggested Additional Readings" at the end of each chapter, I felt that it would be more useful for students and instructors to be able to find materials on precise points of law that are discussed in the text. The endnotes presented at the conclusion of each chapter provide references to recently published materials that discuss in greater detail many of the topics considered in this text.

I used many different resources to develop this text. One of the best sources for conducting research into federal criminal procedure is *The Georgetown Law Journal's Annual Review of Criminal Procedure*. Many of the lower federal court cases that I have used to illustrate various legal doctrines were obtained by using this truly excellent resource.

Two additional resources that have been very helpful to me are Professors Wayne R. LaFave and Jerold H. Israel's *Criminal Procedure* (Second Edition), and Professors

Charles H. Whitebread and Christopher Slobogin's *Criminal Procedure: An Analysis of Cases and Concepts* (Second Edition). Both of these comprehensive works are tremendous contributions to legal literature.

Many individuals have made substantial contributions to this work. Rolando V. del Carmen, my friend and teacher of criminal law, has had a tremendous impact on this text and on my career. Sue Titus Reid, another friend and mentor, taught me how to write a textbook. I will be forever grateful to both of these fine scholars.

The reviewers of this work provided invaluable assistance throughout this project. Listed alphabetically, they include Lincoln D. Barton, Sr., Anna Maria College; Ronald F. Becker, Southwest Texas State University; Charlie E. Chukwudolue, Northern Kentucky University; Jerry L. Dowling, Sam Houston State University; Patrick J. Hopkins, Harrisburg Area Community College; W. Richard Janikowski, University of Memphis; Michael M. Kaune, Radford University; J. Dennis Laster, Central Missouri State University; Daniel F. Ponstingle, Lorain County Community College; Rose P. Rodrigues, Fairfield University; David R. Struckhoff, Loyola University; and Roger D. Turner, Shelby State Community College.

Several other friends and colleagues have also made a significant contribution to this text, including George Porter, Bob Whorf, Richard Janikowski, Pat Shanley, Walter (Buddy) Craddock, Prescott J. Williams, Chris Gontarz, and Bill Monroe. I also thank President Anthony J. Santoro and my colleagues at Roger Williams University for supporting my research. In addition, my research assistant, Colleen Hearn, did an outstanding job helping with legal research and finding highlight materials. I am deeply grateful for the friendship, help, and support of these outstanding individuals.

My family also provided support, love, and encouragement throughout this project. My wife Nancy, mother Norma, father Tom, Sr., brother Steven, and sister Roslyn, are always there when I need them.

Writing a textbook can be an arduous task. However, my editors from McGraw-Hill and Brown & Benchmark made the process an enjoyable one. I thank Nancy Blaine and Tom Romaniak for their patience, perseverance, and good humor throughout this project.

An excellent and comprehensive Instructor's Manual, written by June Speakman, is being published by McGraw-Hill and will be available to those who use this text.

Tom Hickey

BRIEF CONTENTS

C O N T E N T S

13 A Defendant's Rights Following Conviction—Sentencing, Appeals, and Habeas Corpus Review 373

1   An Introduction to the Study of Criminal Procedure

Outline

Key Terms

administrative law,   6

adversary system,   2

appellants,   11

appellate jurisdiction,   9

appellees,   11

beyond a reasonable doubt,   5

Bill of Rights,   7

burden of proof,   5

case briefing,   20

case law,   8

cease and desist order,   6

circuit courts,   17

common law,   8

concurring opinions,   18

court of record,   14

criminal procedure,   5

dissenting opinions,   18

double jeopardy,   12

dual court system,   12

dual sovereignty,   13

felony,   9

inquisitory system,   2

judicial activism,   18

judicial legislation,   18

judicial restraint,   18

judicial review,   11

jurisdiction,   9

magistrates,   16

majority opinion,   18

misdemeanor,   9

The American legal system receives wide publicity. Each day millions of people are exposed to U.S. trials, such as the O. J. Simpson murder case, which the media brings vividly into our living rooms. Highlight 1.1 discusses that case, which is referred to throughout this text.

Often, however, the public's interest in criminal law is mixed with confusion about the procedures that are used in the criminal justice system. Like other criminal cases, the Simpson case raised important procedural questions. For example, why should it matter if Los Angeles police officers had entered O. J. Simpson's home without a search warrant if they found a bloody glove that incriminated Simpson in the murders of Nicole Brown Simpson and Ronald Goldman? Or why should Simpson's seemingly endless staff of attorneys have had the right to cross-examine the prosecution's witnesses for days on end, over minor details? Instead of this lengthy and very costly criminal trial, why not have the defense attorneys and the prosecutors sit down with Judge Lance Ito and determine whether Simpson had committed the crime and, if so, determine a suitable punishment? The purpose of this text is to explore these and other questions about the procedures used in U.S. criminal law systems. Before moving to a more detailed analysis of these issues, however, it is important to discuss several concepts that are crucial to an understanding of the American legal system.

Basic Concepts in U.S. Justice Systems

U.S. criminal justice systems use an **adversary system** to determine a defendant's guilt or innocence. This approach is based on a fundamental assumption: a struggle between two conflicting parties, a defense attorney and a prosecutor, is the best method to determine the truth. The adversary system's roots are found in the ancient practice of **trial by combat,** which assumed that supernatural forces would intervene to assure that the truthful party would prevail in a physical confrontation (often a fight to the death) between two adversaries.

An adversary justice system may be contrasted with an **inquisitory system,** in which the defense and prosecution use a more cooperative approach to determine a

---

Highlight 1.1

The O. J. Simpson Case—An Overview

 His voice sometimes choking with emotion, O. J. Simpson conceded today in a final appearance on the witness stand that he had his share of human frailties, among them womanizing, but he insisted over and over that he had not killed Nicole Brown Simpson and her friend Ronald L. Goldman and instead had done all in his power to help the police catch the killer.

Even when confronted with 30 pictures in which he appeared to be wearing a pair of shoes he had earlier denied ever owning—a pair with soles similar to those that left bloody markings at the murder scene—Mr. Simpson steadfastly denied any guilt.

"I don't think I ever owned shoes like that," he said.

As for a letter written by his wife in which she wrote about his beating her, he said it was nothing more than pre-divorce maneuvering.

Then he took the final question thrown at him in five hard days on the stand, a question asked by his lead lawyer, Robert Baker, and one deliberately intended to sum up dramatically his assertion of innocence in his second trial, this one a wrongful death suit for damages filed by the parents of the two murdered people.

Mr. Baker asked, "Did you, O. J., with your children at home upstairs murder your ex-wife and leave her body where her kids could find it?"

Mr. Simpson, sighing deeply, answered, "No, absolutely not."

Mr. Simpson's court appearance today produced his most detailed courtroom account ever of the days and events surrounding the slashings on June 12, 1994, a recounting immediately challenged on cross-examination.

Not only did he deny any guilt in the slayings, but he said the death of his former wife had so surprised and shocked him that he was left suicidally distraught and almost took his own life after being barred from visiting her freshly closed grave.

Reuters Corbis-Bettmann

"I was in a lot of pain," Mr. Simpson said. "I was missing Nicole," he added, his voice catching. "I just wanted the pain to end. But my mother told me years ago that you couldn't go to Heaven if you committed suicide. So I was totally ashamed of myself right after that."

Mr. Simpson recalled that he had been driven to the cemetery by his close boyhood friend, A. C. Cowlings, and that upon seeing how distraught he was, Mr. Cowlings had told him, "Hey, I'm taking you home."

(Continued)

(Continued)

Much of the return trip was shown on national television because the visit to the cemetery caused Mr. Simpson to be late in turning himself in to the police.

In an effort to counter Mr. Simpson's end-of-trial image of heartfelt concern and angst, an image carefully elicited by Mr. Baker from Mr. Simpson, the main lawyer for the parents, Daniel Petrocelli, not only accused Mr. Simpson of "lying continually" but won the court's permission to enter into the trial record portions of letters and a diary written by Mrs. Simpson that portray her as a woman concerned for her safety.

However, the court ruled that writings could be taken only as an indication of Mrs. Simpson's state of mind, not as pure truth since she could not be called to verify or explain them.

In one passage of a letter, Mrs. Simpson wrote that Mr. Simpson had "beat the holy hell" out of her.

As soon as he began cross-examination, Mr. Petrocelli vigorously attacked Mr. Simpson's veracity, asserting he had a history of lying and dissembling, going all the way back to the days when he began to have extramarital affairs in his first marriage.

"You have been lying throughout your life," he charged.

"No!" Mr. Simpson countered.

At another point, Mr. Petrocelli, leaning toward Mr. Simpson and fixing him with a hard stare, said, "You understand that your credibility is a crucial issue? Yes or no?"

Mr. Simpson hesitated a moment, looked over toward his lawyer, then replied, "I believe it is important for me to be honest to the jury."

Mr. Petrocelli: "Yes or no?"

Mr. Simpson: "I can't answer that the way the question is phrased."

Mr. Petrocelli: "You've been unfaithful to your wife and lied?"

Mr. Simpson: "I don't know that I'd characterize it as a lie. I was morally wrong looking back on it."

Mr. Petrocelli: "You have beaten her in the past and you went to the doctor and lied?"

Mr. Simpson: "No."

Late last year, in the criminal trial that followed Mr. Simpson's arrest several days after the killings, a trial in which racial issues and alleged police misdoing played a major role in the deliberations of a predominantly black, inner-city jury, the former football player, who is black, was acquitted after nine months of testimony. He did not take the stand in that proceeding.

In the current civil trial, before a predominantly white jury, the plaintiffs contend that, regardless of the outcome of the first trial, Mr. Simpson nevertheless committed the murders and should be forced to pay an as-yet-unspecified amount of money.

While being questioned this morning by his own lawyer, Mr. Simpson told the court that his trip to Chicago on the night of the slayings was for previously scheduled business, not an attempt to build an alibi. And he said that upon learning of the slaying he made extraordinary efforts to hurry home, so extraordinary, he went on, that he arrived back hours sooner than anyone expected.

Then, under Mr. Baker's gentle guidance, he told how, upon arrival back in Los Angeles, he immediately volunteered to give the police a blood sample and a statement, unaccompanied by a lawyer. Then, he said, he asked that his trip baggage be inspected and offered to hire special outside investigators to help the Los Angeles police investigators.

Asked by Mr. Baker whether he had hidden or held back anything from investigators at that point, Mr. Simpson, his once-cracking voice now strong and matter-of-fact, replied: "Absolutely nothing. I didn't do anything and I'd do anything to help them."

Mr. Simpson related that before he headed off to Chicago on the night the slayings occurred outside his former wife's condominium, he and Mrs. Simpson and her father, Lou, spent several pleasant hours

(Continued)

(Concluded)

together at a children's recital. As a grainy home video taken at the recital played on a courtroom screen, showing Mr. Simpson having a hearty laugh with Mr. Brown, Mr. Simpson explained the origin of the laughter.

"Lou Brown and I were talking about women and he was teasing me," he said. "I told Lou, 'I've got to stay away from your daughter.' We were kind of teasing."

Source: B. Drummond Ayres, Jr., "Back on Stand, Simpson Again Denies Role in 2 Killings," *The New York Times,* Jan. 14, 1997, Sec. A, p. 10. [Copyright © 1997 by the New York Times Company. Reprinted by permission.]

---

defendant's guilt or innocence. The two approaches may be distinguished in several additional ways. The adversary approach presumes that those accused are innocent. The accused do not have to prove their innocence; rather, the prosecution must carry the **burden of proof**—the prosecution must present evidence that establishes a defendant's guilt. In criminal cases this is a heavy burden because the Supreme Court has held that the prosecution must prove **beyond a reasonable doubt** all elements of a crime with which a defendant is charged.[1] This means that a judge or a jury must be convinced to a moral certainty that the defendant committed the charged offense.[2] In contrast, the inquisitory system eliminates both the presumption of innocence and a presumption of the defendant's guilt. In effect, the defendant and the state begin the case on equal footing. In contrast to an adversary system, an inquisitory system presumes that the defendant and the state will cooperate to reach a proper disposition. The difference between the two approaches is significant: An inquisitory system places a greater emphasis on conviction than on the process by which that conviction is obtained. The adversary approach, in contrast, stresses that proper procedures must be followed, which are designed to protect a suspect's rights.

Criminal law, and more specifically, **criminal procedure,** outlines the process that must be followed when the police investigate crimes and in U.S. criminal trials. This text's remaining chapters will more fully consider the nature of this process. In order to introduce our study of criminal procedure, however, it is instructive to briefly consider the sources of criminal law.

Sources of Criminal Law

There are three main sources of criminal law: statutes, constitutions, and case law.[3] Each of these will be considered separately.

Often, students are given library assignments on various legal topics. One place to start these assignments is among the shelves of libraries' legal collections. This may be a daunting task, however, because of the sheer volume of "laws on the books." In a fully equipped law library it is possible to find thousands of volumes containing the laws of each of the states, all federal laws, and literally millions of administrative regulations. The laws contained in these volumes are termed **statutory laws,** which are laws passed by legislative bodies. Statutes are a primary source of criminal law.

State legislatures enact statutes that become state laws. Congress enacts federal laws, which are binding throughout the United States. State statutes are binding only in the state in which they are passed and they may regulate most kinds of human activity. State laws may not, however, conflict with either the federal constitution, or the state's own constitution. Moreover, state statutes may not conflict with lawful federal statutes because of the U.S. Constitution's Supremacy Clause.[4] For example, the U.S. Constitution and the Oregon Constitution contain a requirement providing that a search warrant must be based upon probable cause if the police wish to enter a person's home to look for evidence of criminal behavior. If the State of Oregon's legislature were to pass a law providing that police officers could make warrantless searches of the homes of persons merely "suspected" of possessing illegal drugs, that law would likely be held unconstitutional because it conflicts with both the U.S. Constitution and the Oregon Constitution. Similarly, because federal law gives the U.S. Postal Service a monopoly on the delivery of first class mail, if a state were to pass a law allowing United Parcel Service (UPS) to deliver first class mail within the state, the law would be invalid because it conflicts with a lawful federal statute.

Statutes that define the procedures that government agents must use to enforce the law are termed **procedural laws.** Most states and the federal government have a separate group of statutes termed the **rules of criminal procedure,** which regulate the criminal trial process. For example, Pennsylvania's Rules of Criminal Procedure state that "no search warrant shall authorize a nighttime search unless the affidavits show reasonable cause for such nighttime search."[5] **Substantive laws,** in contrast, identify the precise behaviors that violate the law.[6] The differences between these types of law are discussed in Chapter 2.

Administrative law, which is derived from statutory law, may also result in criminal charges. Rule-making power is given to state and federal agencies by Congress and state legislatures. For example, state liquor control board officials may be given the authority to make rules that regulate the sale of alcoholic beverages; the Federal Communications Commission is granted the power to create regulations that control the content of radio and television broadcasts. Such rules must be made according to regulations that specify procedures and guidelines. The sheer number of administrative rules that are passed by administrative regulatory agencies is awesome, and, as some colorful media personalities have discovered, may result in the imposition of huge fines. Highlight 1.2 presents a discussion of Howard Stern's recent problems with the Federal Communications Commission (F.C.C.).

In some cases, however, a violation of administrative rules may become a criminal offense. Suppose that a state inspector discovers that a nightclub owner is refilling higher priced liquor bottles with cheaper alternatives. The agency may command the store to stop this practice by issuing a **cease and desist order.** If the nightclub owner violates the order, the administrative agency may get a court order to enforce its cease and desist order. If that order is violated, the nightclub owner may be charged with a criminal offense.[7]

Highlight 1.2

$1.7 Million to End Howard Stern Indecency Case

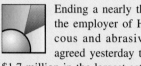 Ending a nearly three-year-long dispute, the employer of Howard Stern, the raucous and abrasive radio disk jockey, agreed yesterday to pay the Government $1.7 million in the largest settlement ever involving accusations of indecent radio broadcasts.

But Mr. Stern's employer, the Infinity Broadcasting Corporation, the nation's largest radio broadcasting company, appeared to act less over concern about the Government's broadcasting standards than over continued obstacles to Infinity's acquisition plans.

Infinity, based in New York, did not admit to any wrongdoing in agreeing to the payment. The $1,715,000 payment is not a fine, but a "voluntary contribution to the U.S. Treasury," according to the Federal Communications Commission, the agency that had sought sanctions against Infinity and Mr Stern. The amount is $9,000 more than the fines the agency had proposed against Infinity.

The Infinity payment far exceeds the $33,000 paid by Evergreen Broadcasting over complaints about excerpts from a Howard Stern show that it broadcast on its Chicago station.

The F.C.C. action that was settled yesterday involved what the agency said were violations dating back to 1992; Infinity also had a dispute with the agency over Mr. Stern in 1987, but that complaint was later dismissed.

AP/Wide World Photos

Excerpts from Anthony Ramirez, "$1.7 Million to End Howard Stern Indecency Case," *The New York Times,* September 2, 1995, Sec. 1, p. 33. [Copyright © 1995 by the New York Times Company. Reprinted by permission.]

Constitutions are an even more basic source of law. The U.S. Constitution contains a **Bill of Rights,** the first ten amendments, which provide individuals with numerous protections against abuses of governmental authority. Additional constitutional rights are provided by state constitutions. Former U.S. Supreme Court Justice William Brennan regards state constitutions as "co-equal guardians of civil rights and liberties."[8] Many readers would be surprised to find that most of the rights contained in the U.S. Constitution were modeled after already existing state constitutional protections. For example, the Massachusetts Declaration of Rights, which was adopted in 1780, seven years before the U.S. Constitution's Fourth Amendment, prohibited "unreasonable searches and seizures."[9]

U.S. Supreme Court decisions are binding on all federal courts and on state courts where federal statutes or rights guaranteed by the U.S. Constitution are involved. When a state supreme court decides a case, its decision is binding on all state courts within that state. Moreover, if a state supreme court decides a case, and bases its decision solely on that state's constitution, it has the final word on the matter and the U.S. Supreme Court lacks the power to overturn that decision.[10] In addition, state constitutions may never give law enforcement officers more power than they have under the U.S. Constitution. State constitutions may be used, however, to expand individual rights beyond those guaranteed by the U.S. Constitution. For example, the U.S. Supreme Court has ruled that without violating the Fourth Amendment, municipal police agencies may operate random sobriety roadblocks to apprehend intoxicated motorists.[11] After the U.S. Supreme Court established this principle, the Michigan Court of Appeals, relying solely on the Michigan Constitution, held that these suspicionless checkpoints violated the Michigan Constitution.[12] Thus, state constitutional law has a significant potential for expanding constitutional rights beyond those guaranteed by the U.S. Constitution.[13]

Two additional sources of criminal law are **common law** and **case law.** When a court decides a case its decision becomes law. Common law is based on the traditions, culture, and social values that courts relied on to decide cases before statutes and constitutions were enacted to regulate behavior. Most common law crimes have been abolished in the United States. These crimes are now regulated by statutes.

Common law developed after William the Conqueror, at the time the Duke of Normandy and later King, invaded England. In 1066, there was no organized system of law and judicial decisions in identical cases in different locales could have completely different results. A central goal of the Normans was to establish a cohesive legal system. Representatives were sent to various parts of the kingdom to gather information about the laws that were used and the judicial decisions in each region. Eventually, the representatives returned with a description of the laws being used that were "common" throughout the land. These laws become known as the "common law of England."[14]

Common law remains relevant today. To illustrate, Pennsylvania substantive law defines burglary as follows: "A person is guilty of burglary if he enters a building or occupied structure, or separately secured or occupied portion thereof, with intent to commit a crime therein, unless the premises are at the time open to the public or the actor is licensed or privileged to enter."[15] Convicting a person of burglary requires proof of these statutorily provided elements: that the defendant entered a building or occupied structure, or a separately secured or occupied portion thereof, and that the defendant intended to commit a crime within that structure. If at the time the incident occurred, the premises were open to the public or the actor was licensed or privileged to enter, he or she would have a statutory defense to the charge of burglary.

What does it mean to "enter" a building or occupied structure? It refers to the requirement of some physical intrusion into the structure. Some courts have interpreted the entry requirement to mean any physical intrusion whatsoever into a structure. At first glance determining whether a physical intrusion into a structure constitutes a burglary appears to be an easy task. The issue may be somewhat complex, however. Assume that a defendant had stolen an apple pie that was cooling on a window ledge. Suppose further that a portion of the pie rested partially on the window ledge and partially outside the structure of the house. The defendant never reached "into," or entered the structure to steal the pie, but still took it from the window ledge. Would this constitute a burglary? Many state burglary statutes do not define the term *entering*, and therefore court decisions would be used to provide a definition. (In some states, taking the pie from the window ledge would satisfy the entry requirement and constitute a burglary of the structure.)

U.S. Criminal Court Systems

In order to understand the operation of U.S. courts, it is necessary to discuss some basic legal terms and concepts. **Jurisdiction** refers to a court's power to hear and decide a legal matter.[16] In the United States the scope of a court's jurisdiction is determined by state and federal constitutions or by statutes. For example, the jurisdiction of the U.S. Supreme Court is provided in Article III of the U.S. Constitution. Likewise, a state supreme court's jurisdiction may be specified in a state's constitution. The jurisdiction of lower courts is specified by statutes. For example, the United States District Courts have jurisdiction in cases involving federal crimes and in certain types of civil cases. Often, state statutes will restrict the jurisdiction of lower state courts to certain types of cases, such as **misdemeanor** or **felony** offenses. In most states, a misdemeanor is a minor crime that is punishable by a fine or by imprisonment for a term not to exceed one year in jail. Likewise, a felony is a more serious crime punishable by death or imprisonment for more than one year in a state or federal penitentiary. Highlight 1.3 illustrates that a state legislature may limit a court's jurisdiction to a particular type of case, such as cases in which a defendant is alleged to have used a firearm when committing a violent crime.

Two different types of jurisdiction are especially relevant for the study of criminal procedure. **Original jurisdiction** refers to a court's power to try the facts of a case. Courts having original jurisdiction are trial courts and determine factual issues, such as whether the defendant actually committed a crime. To illustrate, in the O. J. Simpson murder case the question of whether the defendant was present in California at the time the crime occurred would be a factual issue that a trial court would decide.

Appellate jurisdiction represents a court's power to hear an appeal of a trial court's decision. Appellate courts hear appeals only of legal issues. To illustrate, suppose that a defendant is convicted of murder, based on evidence found at the scene of the crime, after the police had entered his home without a search warrant. An appellate court may be asked to decide whether the trial court had committed an error by admitting the contested evidence that prevented the defendant from receiving a fair trial. On appeal, the defendant is likely to ask the appellate court to declare that the search violated the Fourth Amendment and to require the trial court to exclude any evidence found at the scene. The dispute concerning the search of the defendant's home presents an example of the type of legal issue that an appellate court has the power to consider.

R.I. Gun Court Metes Out Swift Justice

 The fear of crime, especially violent crime, grips the nation. People are particularly afraid of guns. People are afraid of the destruction caused by those who use guns without regard to the deaths and injuries that too often result. And people are afraid that when a gun-toting criminal is finally arrested, he or she will not be kept off the streets long enough.

Where does the trouble begin? It can start with a tough childhood, and today, our country has an increasingly high number of lawless children who carry guns. United States Attorney General Janet Reno stated last year that if government does not increase efforts to fight delinquent crime, citizens will pay the price. "What you see here is a road map of crime. Unless we act now to stop young people from choosing a life of violent crime, the beginning of the 21st century could bring levels of violent crime to our cities that far exceed what we have experienced."

According to a national report, the arrest rate for juvenile crime is likely to double in 15 years. The most frequently cited problems facing our country today are crime and violence. This issue affects our youth in a disturbingly disproportionate manner: called "the young and the ruthless," 83 percent of the inmates in juvenile detention facilities said they owned a gun, and 22 percent of the students attending inner-city high schools said they owned firearms. Moreover, 35 percent of juvenile inmates and 10 percent of the students questioned in the same survey believed it is "okay to shoot a person if that's what it takes to get something you want."

Just as important, juveniles are more likely to be victims of crime today. Attorney General Reno expressed shock at the high murder rate among 14–17-year-olds, which increased 165 percent in the last decade.

These figures make us think: We must find ways of stemming the tide of violent crime, we must find a way to stop the wave of young criminals, because these children will only grow to adults who commit more and more crimes.

And the good news is that Janet Reno just last month issued a report indicating that the rate of juvenile crime is finally coming down. There has been a 15 percent decrease in the number of teenagers arrested for murder from 1994 to 1995.

One reason for this favorable trend is the implementation of new approaches to dealing with crime and punishment. Because our citizens are concerned about the lack of adequate *punishment* for criminals, both young and older, new and more effective ways are being tried to halt rising crime, especially gun crime. "We need a mechanism that ensures swift and certain justice. And now we've got it." So commented the mayor of Providence shortly after the first six months of the nation's first Gun Court.

Under the direction and leadership of Presiding Justice Joseph F. Rodgers, Jr., Rhode Island has established a system for dealing with the problem of rising gun crimes. It is a fast-track, single jurisdiction court within the Rhode Island Superior Court. This special calendar helps crack down on gun crimes by routing all firearms cases to one courtroom and only one judge. As the Washington Post stated, "It has a single judge, a single calendar, and a singular mission: provide swift, serious punishment for all crimes involving guns." The results are very promising.

Last year, we had nearly 6,000 new felonies filed in Rhode Island. This was the highest number in six years, and just under 4,400 of these were in the court division serving our capital city of Providence and nearby communities. In 1994 Parade magazine described Providence as the second-safest city in America, after Honolulu. According to a study conducted by the State Justice Institute, Rhode Island ranks third in the nation in its "felony clearance rate," or the speed with which we are able to resolve felony cases. This was made even more significant by the fact that Rhode Island ranks quite low in the number of judges per capita, with just 3.3 per 100,000 people. But we did not sit back: instead we

(Continued)

(Concluded)

found a way to continue the momentum of improvement in reducing crime: A coalition of police, city officials, state legislators, judges, court personnel and the unlikely combination of the National Rifle Association and gun-control advocates, got together to help put the gun court concept into practice.

How does the new Gun Court work, and what makes it different from the way the normal criminal case is handled? The average criminal case can take as long as two years to go to trial. With the Gun Court calendar, we have reduced that to under four months!

The legislation establishing the Gun Court specifies that cases are to be heard within 60 days of the completion of discovery. Before the court was set up, the average time to disposition in cases involving guns was a lengthy 518 days. Since the start of the program, this time has been drastically reduced to just 118 days. Although the Gun Court judge had estimated that disposition time, according to the legislative mandate, should be approximately 4½ months, it is actually even shorter than that, just over 3½ months, a remarkable accomplishment.

Text of speech delivered by Joseph F. Rodgers to the International Association of Chiefs of Police, October 1995. Reprinted by permission.

A second example should help to clarify the difference between trial and appellate courts. Assume that several defendants are charged with conspiracy to make explosives and with bombing a New York City public building. A trial court would determine issues such as whether the defendants were present in New York City on the day of the bombing and whether they in fact had conspired to make explosives. If the defendants are convicted of these charges, and decide to appeal the trial court's decision, an issue that an appellate court might be asked to decide includes whether the search warrant that the police used to search their homes for evidence of explosives violated the Fourth Amendment. Another potential issue on appeal would be whether the defendants' statements made after they were arrested were obtained in violation of their right to counsel. On appeal, the defendants would be considered the **appellants,** because they filed the appeal with the higher court. The state would be considered the **appellees,** who would be expected to argue that the trial evidence was obtained lawfully and that a new trial should not be granted.

Panels of judges hear cases on appeal.[17] In fact, in most appellate courts the defendants are not present for the lawyers' arguments, although there is usually nothing to prevent defendants from attending appellate arguments.

The Power of Judicial Review

Trial and appellate courts have the power of **judicial review.** This significant power allows courts to review the actions of other branches of government to determine if those acts infringe on rights guaranteed by the state constitutions and by the U.S. Constitution.[18] This power is a strong check against the abuse of power by the legislative and executive branches of government. To cite an extreme example, if Congress were to pass a law that eliminated the Fourth Amendment's search warrant requirement in illegal drug cases, the courts could be expected to declare unconstitutional such an improper expansion of police authority.

U.S. courts view the power of judicial review as an awesome responsibility within the U.S. governmental system and hesitate to exercise this power without a compelling reason. The courts have developed principles designed to prevent themselves from infringing on the authority of the other branches of government. Three such limiting principles are especially relevant to the study of U.S. law. One is the doctrine of **mootness,** which means that the issues in the case have been resolved. If a legal issue is moot, a court will refuse to decide the case. For example, in one case a student who was denied admission to a law school filed a lawsuit against the law school alleging discrimination. A court ordered the school to admit the student while the matter was pending in the courts. By the time the case reached the U.S. Supreme Court, the student had completed the first two years of law school and had started his final year. The Supreme Court dismissed the case because it had become moot—the law school had agreed that even if the student lost the case, he would be allowed to complete his studies and would receive his law degree.[19]

A second doctrine that limits judicial review is called **standing** to sue. Standing requires that a party who brings a lawsuit must have suffered a genuine injury. Moreover, the party bringing the suit must be the injured victim—normally, one cannot file a legal action for another person. For example, suppose that John and Mary become involved in an argument. The argument becomes heated and Mary strikes John. Ron, who witnessed the confrontation, would lack standing to file charges against Mary for striking John. Ron has suffered no injury and has no legally protected interest in the case.

A third concept that limits the power of judicial review is the **political question** doctrine. Courts will refuse to decide a case if the matter should be left to another branch of government. For example, in the 1970s several individuals attempted to challenge the constitutionality of the Vietnam War. The Supreme Court held that this case presented a political question that was better left to Congress.[20]

When courts exercise the power of judicial review they normally abide by the principle of **stare decisis,** which means "let the decision stand." Under this important principle of judicial decision making, courts will abide by previously decided cases, and earlier decisions become precedents for later cases. By providing guidelines for judicial decisions, stare decisis ensures stability in U.S. legal systems. In some instances, however, courts may decide that a new legal rule is needed and overrule a previous decision.[21]

Dual Court System

It is sometimes said that the United States has a **dual court system,** comprised of the state and federal courts,[22] as indicated in Figure 1.1. In reality, there are 50 independent state court systems and one federal court system.

Some acts violate both state and federal law. In these cases a defendant may be tried in both systems for precisely the same crime. There is no violation of the Fifth Amendment protection against **double jeopardy,** which prevents defendants from

FIGURE 1.1

Structure of the U.S. Criminal Court System

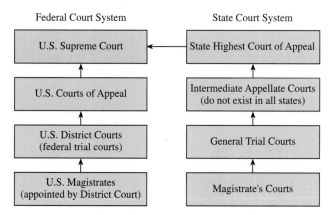

Source: Sue Titus Reid, *Criminal Justice,* 3d ed. Macmillan, (New York, N.Y.: 1993), p. 306.

being tried more than once for the same offense.[23] For example, the crime of bank robbery is a violation of state and federal law. A bank robber could be prosecuted and punished in both federal and state courts for the same conduct. The Supreme Court has permitted such multiple prosecutions under the doctrine of **dual sovereignty,** which provides that when a single crime violates the laws of different independent jurisdictions, each is entitled to prosecute, and upon conviction, punish the offender.[24]

State Courts.   The structure of state criminal court systems varies widely throughout the United States. Due to the highly variable nature of the state court systems, the titles given to state courts may cause some confusion. For example, at the top of most state court systems are their highest appellate courts, usually called the state supreme courts. In New York State, however, the misdemeanor level trial courts are called the New York Supreme Court, while the highest appellate court is called the New York Court of Appeals. While the titles given to various states' courts may be confusing, several generalizations about state court systems are possible. Most state court systems use a hierarchical structure that loosely parallels the federal court system, and may be envisioned as a pyramid. At the top is the state's highest appellate court. In large states an intermediate appellate court often considers appeals of criminal cases from trial courts. In Oregon, for example, this court is called the Court of Appeals. Beneath the intermediate appellate courts are the trial courts. Within state court systems, trial courts are often arranged in a hierarchical fashion. Below a state's appellate court is a felony trial court; beneath that is a misdemeanor court. The lowest level of trial court in most states is sometimes termed a justice of the peace court, which has jurisdiction in petty offense cases and often has limited power to conduct preliminary hearings in more serious cases and to conduct other pretrial proceedings. Figure 1.2 depicts the typical structure of a state court system. The next section presents a general description of each type of state court.

FIGURE 1.2

Structure of State Criminal Court Systems

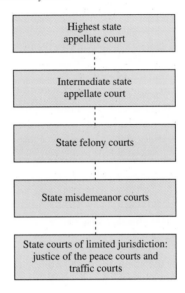

Justice of the Peace Court, Traffic Courts, and City Courts. Justice of the peace courts normally have jurisdiction in non-serious criminal and minor civil matters. There is no constitutional requirement that an individual serving as Justice of the Peace must be an attorney,[25] and the quality of legal work performed by these individuals may vary considerably. While strong arguments support requiring a minimal qualification and education level for justices of the peace, it is doubtful that most states will adopt a requirement that these individuals must be lawyers. In fact, it may be argued persuasively that in minor legal matters the administration of justice is aided by permitting lay members of the community, who are often elected officials, to make commonsense determinations on the merits of particular cases. Moreover, most states do not provide for the right to a jury trial in these cases.

Special traffic courts exist in many states. These courts normally have jurisdiction in cases involving minor traffic offenses and parking tickets. Often, proceedings at this level are quite informal—an individual is asked to "tell his story" to the judge or hearing officer, who then renders a decision.

City courts have been established in many larger cities. These courts typically hear cases involving violations of city ordinances, traffic offenses, or other minor criminal matters. Once again, proceedings in these courts are often less formal than in higher courts.

Justice of the peace courts, traffic courts, and city courts are not normally **courts of record.** This means that no transcript of the proceedings is made that may be used to form the basis for later appeals. If a defendant is convicted of a criminal offense in these lower courts and wishes to appeal the verdict, he or she most often receives a completely new trial in a higher court, a court of record. This is termed a **trial de novo.**

Misdemeanor Courts.   Misdemeanor courts have jurisdiction over minor but non-petty criminal offenses. Moreover, these courts often hear minor civil cases as well as appeals from a state's justice of the peace courts. For example, if Bob was convicted of driving under the influence in a state's justice of the peace court, he would be entitled to appeal the judgment to a misdemeanor court in many states. Bob would receive a trial de novo on the merits of his case at the misdemeanor court level.

Often, a state's misdemeanor courts will serve different geographic regions and are thus sometimes called district courts. Defendants have a constitutional right to a jury trial[26] in these courts if the case charges a criminal offense with a possible term of imprisonment exceeding six months.[27] The titles in various states used to describe misdemeanor courts of record include district courts, circuit courts, and court of common pleas. Because a state's misdemeanor courts are normally courts of record, a judicial decision at this level may be appealed, ordinarily to a felony court.

Felony Courts.   As the name implies, state felony courts have original jurisdiction over felony cases and appellate jurisdiction over cases appealed from misdemeanor courts. Due to the wide variation in state court systems, an appeal taken to a felony court will in some states proceed as a trial de novo. In other states, the felony court would exercise only appellate jurisdiction and determine if the misdemeanor court had committed a legal error. Often, a state will be divided into different judicial districts on a county-by-county basis. These courts are called by a number of different names, including county courts, district courts, and superior courts. Defendants have a constitutional right to a jury trial in all felony cases, as well as a right to appointed counsel if they are indigent.[28]

Felony courts are courts of record. Appeals from felony court proceedings may be taken to the state's appellate courts—either an intermediate court of appeals or the state supreme court.

Court of Appeals.   A minority of state court systems have an intermediate court of appeals between the state's trial courts and its highest appellate court. Intermediate courts of appeals exercise appellate jurisdiction over trial court decisions and may have limited original jurisdiction over certain types of cases.

One advantage to this type of system is that intermediate courts of appeals will reduce caseload congestion within the states' appellate court systems. Theoretically, at least, an intermediate appellate court should help to improve the quality of state supreme court decision making by allowing it to consider only the most important legal matters. For example, in one state without an intermediate appellate court the state's supreme court was required to review a trial court's decision not to allow damages for a plaintiff's emotional distress in a case involving a veterinarian's mistaken use of a flea bath that resulted in a cat's death. Although this case may have had a serious and traumatic impact on the pet's owner, given the congestion in U.S. courts and the scarcity of judicial resources, it is questionable whether a state's supreme court should be considering such cases.

State Supreme Court.   At the top of each state court system is a final appellate court. This is often called a state supreme court, although there are exceptions to this rule. For example, in Maryland the final appellate court in criminal cases is called the Court of Appeals. In most states the highest court has appellate jurisdiction, although in some states it has limited original jurisdiction in certain types of cases, such as attorney disbarment proceedings. If a state's final appellate court decides a case, and its decision is based on an interpretation of a federal statute or the U.S. Constitution, the U.S. Supreme Court may review the state court's judgment. Remember that in the vast majority of cases an appeal taken from a state's final appellate court proceeds immediately to the U.S. Supreme Court and does not move through the lower federal courts.[29] If, however, a state appellate court's decision rests solely on the state's constitution, that decision is final and may not normally be overturned by the U.S. Supreme Court.[30]

Federal Courts.   Federal courts in the United States are part of a unified court system. Consequently, the structure of the federal courts is substantially less confusing than that of many state court systems. At the top of the federal court system is the U.S. Supreme Court. That Court has both original and appellate jurisdiction, although the Supreme Court rarely exercises its original jurisdiction, which is specified in Article III of the U.S. Constitution. The United States Courts of Appeals are the intermediate level court in the federal court system. These courts hear appeals from the trial courts in the federal system, the United States District Courts. At the bottom of the federal court system are the U.S. Magistrates, who are empowered to hear minor federal cases. Each of these courts will be discussed separately.

Magistrates.   U.S. Magistrates are empowered to hear federal cases with the consent of both parties, misdemeanor cases if the defendant consents, and petty offense trials. For example, suppose that Bob is charged with defacing public property for spray-painting graffiti on the restroom walls in a national park (a misdemeanor). If Bob consents, he will be tried by a U.S. Magistrate. Moreover, if he is convicted and wishes to appeal, his case will go to the United States Court of Appeals.

The United States District Court.   The United States District Courts are the trial courts in the federal court system. These courts have original jurisdiction over criminal and civil cases brought under federal law or treaties. United States District Courts do not exercise appellate jurisdiction over state courts. There are 94 U.S. District Courts. At least one exists in each of the 50 states, and many larger states have more than one district. The United States District Courts carry most of the workload in the federal court system. These courts decide more than 600,000 cases per year.[31] Given this heavy caseload, it should not be surprising that delays are common in these courts, although a federal law requires that criminal cases must either be brought to trial within 100 days or be dismissed.[32]

TABLE 1.1   U.S. Court of Appeals Circuits

First Circuit:	Maine, Massachusetts, New Hampshire, Rhode Island, Puerto Rico
Second Circuit:	Connecticut, New York, Vermont
Third Circuit:	Delaware, New Jersey, Pennsylvania, Virgin Islands
Fourth Circuit:	Maryland, North Carolina, South Carolina, Virginia, West Virginia
Fifth Circuit:	Louisiana, Mississippi, Texas
Sixth Circuit:	Kentucky, Michigan, Ohio, Tennessee
Seventh Circuit:	Illinois, Indiana, Wisconsin
Eighth Circuit:	Arkansas, Iowa, Minnesota, Missouri, Nebraska, North Dakota, South Dakota
Ninth Circuit:	Alaska, Arizona, California, Hawaii, Idaho, Montana, Nevada, Oregon, Washington, Guam, Northern Mariana Islands
Tenth Circuit:	Colorado, Kansas, New Mexico, Oklahoma, Utah, Wyoming
Eleventh Circuit:	Alabama, Florida, Georgia

[From *The Judicial Process: An Introductory Analysis of the Courts of the United States,* by Henry J. Abraham. Used by permission of Oxford University Press, Inc.]

The United States Court of Appeals.   The 13 United States Courts of Appeals are often called **circuit courts.** There are 11 different judicial circuits throughout the United States. In addition, one U.S. Court of Appeals is assigned to the District of Columbia, and another exercises jurisdiction over Customs and Patent Appeals. U.S. Courts of Appeals hear appeals of cases from the United States District Courts. Thus, they exercise solely appellate jurisdiction over the United States District Courts and decide approximately 40,000 cases annually.[33] Table 1.1 illustrates the different judicial circuits and the geographic regions each serves.

The United States Supreme Court.   The U.S. Supreme Court is the only court created expressly by the Constitution. There is no constitutional requirement that Supreme Court Justices or other federal judges must be attorneys, although in practice most individuals appointed to these positions have distinguished legal careers. Article III of the U.S. Constitution identifies a few types of cases in which the Supreme Court has original jurisdiction. These include:

1. A lawsuit between the United States and a state;
2. Lawsuits between two or more states;
3. Lawsuits involving foreign ambassadors or other foreign ministers and consuls; and
4. Lawsuits initiated by a state against citizens of another state or against a foreign country.

The vast majority of cases that reach the Supreme Court, however, arrive by way of the Court's appellate jurisdiction, which Congress may regulate by statute. Cases most often reach the Supreme Court if it grants a **writ of certiorari.** A writ is a court order. When the Supreme Court grants a writ of certiorari, it orders that a lower court send up the typed record of the trial, which is termed a **transcript.** Certiorari, however, is granted rarely and only when four Supreme Court Justices vote to hear the case.[34] This is termed the **rule of four.** When the Supreme Court denies certiorari, it does not necessarily mean that it agrees with the decision of the lower court; rather, it simply means that four Justices at the time would not vote to hear the case. If the Court denies certiorari, it refuses to review the case, and the decision of the lower court becomes final. Consequently, because the Supreme Court refuses to hear most cases, state supreme court decisions in state cases, or those of a lower federal court in federal cases, are final and binding on the parties to the case.

If the Supreme Court agrees to hear a case it will normally issue an opinion of the Court. Whenever a simple majority of the nine Supreme Court Justices agree that a case should be decided in a particular way, the Court issues a **majority opinion,** which becomes law and binds parties in similar future cases. Sometimes, however, a majority of the members of the Court will not agree to join a majority opinion. In these cases the Court may issue a **plurality opinion,** in which the Justices decide the case at hand, but for dissimilar reasons. Often, a particular Justice may agree to join the Court's majority opinion, but may wish to write a separate opinion that discusses additional issues or that considers a particular aspect of the case. Such opinions are common and are termed **concurring opinions.** If a Supreme Court Justice disagrees with a majority opinion, he or she may issue a **dissenting opinion.** Unlike majority opinions, concurring and dissenting opinions do not become law and do not bind parties in future cases, although they are still very useful.[35] Smart attorneys (and students) will use these opinions to structure their legal arguments in future cases.

Judicial Activism and Restraint.   The Supreme Court's primary function is to interpret federal laws and the U.S. Constitution. In performing this function of judicial review, the Court is sometimes accused of interpreting the Constitution to create new law. This practice is termed **judicial legislation** or **judicial activism.** Advocates of judicial activism believe that judges must interpret the Constitution in a way that is flexible and will permit it to adapt to the changing needs of modern society.[36]

Opponents of judicial activism believe that the Court should not "find" implied rights in the Constitution.[37] If the Court moves beyond the Constitution's text and "makes law," it is violating the separation of powers principle by performing a legislative function, a power the Constitution assigns to the Congress. Rather, the Supreme Court should try only to determine the framers' original intent when the Constitution was written and frame their decisions in a way that is consistent with the framers' intent. This position is sometimes termed **strict construction,** which is associated with **judicial restraint.**

A problem with judicial activism is that the Supreme Court is a body made up of individuals who are nominated by the President and confirmed by the U.S. Senate. As such, the process of becoming a Supreme Court Justice is a political one. Presidents rarely nominate a potential Justice whose legal and political philosophy differs markedly from their own. If new Supreme Court Justices do not adhere to settled precedents, or are too strongly committed to judicial activism, we may expect a shift in the direction of constitutional precedents toward the political preferences of the Executive branch each time the membership of the Supreme Court changes. This raises constitutional separation of powers questions and creates the possibility that our legal system will become less stable over time.

If the Court is to interpret the Constitution according to the concerns, needs, and aspirations of the day, it will be criticized because these are issues on which reasonable minds may differ. Theoretically, then, the Court does not make, but rather interprets law.

How to Find the Law

When a case is cited, the case name is accompanied by several notations. For instance, the citation for the *Miranda* case is as follows: *Miranda* v. *Arizona,* 384 U.S. 436, 86 S.Ct. 1602, 16 L.Ed.2d 694 (1966). The numbers following the case name mean that *Miranda* v. *Arizona* is found in volume 384 of the *United States Reports,* on page 436. It is found too in volume 86 of the *Supreme Court Reporter,* on page 1602, and in the *Lawyer's Edition,* in volume 16 of the second edition, on page 694. The year in parentheses at the end of the notation indicates the year during which the Court decided the case. Once the Supreme Court decides a case, it may take several years for the decision to be published in the official reporter of Supreme Court decisions, the *United States Reports.* The unofficial reporters, the *Supreme Court Reporter,* and the *Lawyer's Edition,* publish Supreme Court opinions soon after they are handed down. Consequently, for recent opinions it is often necessary to provide the case citation from the *Supreme Court Reporter,* or the *Lawyer's Edition,* rather than the preferred *United States Reports.*

Cases decided by the United States Courts of Appeals are published in the *Federal Reporter.* Cases decided by the United States District Courts are sometimes published in the *Federal Supplement.* These cases may be found by using the same approach used to find U.S. Supreme Court cases, although normally only full service law libraries will have the *Federal Reporter* and *Federal Supplement.* For example, *Hopwood* v. *State of Texas* is found in 78 F.3d 932 (5th Cir. 1996). This means that *Hopwood* v. *State of Texas* is located in volume 78 of the third series of the *Federal Reporter,* on page 932. Such decisions are important because they are binding in future similar cases in the same judicial circuit. When the Fifth Circuit United States Court of Appeals decides a case, its opinion becomes law for that circuit, unless it is overturned by the United States Supreme Court. When a U.S. District Court decides a case, its decision is binding on future cases solely in the district in which it is made.

Cases decided by state supreme courts are published in state reporters, which may be found in well-equipped law libraries. The reports of state cases are important because state supreme court decisions are final unless they are overturned by the U.S. Supreme Court. Thus, when a case is decided by a state supreme court, the decision becomes law and binds future parties in similar cases in that state. Because state court systems are independent, however, a decision of one state's supreme court is not binding in another state, although another state's court may adopt its reasoning if it is found to be persuasive.

There are seven different regional decision reporters that correspond to different geographic regions of the United States. These include the *Atlantic Reporter,* the

TABLE 1.2   Regional Reporters

Atlantic Reporter:	Connecticut, New Hampshire, Delaware, New Jersey, Maine, Pennsylvania, Maryland, Rhode Island, Vermont
Northeastern Reporter:	Illinois, Indiana, Massachusetts, New York, Ohio
Northwestern Reporter:	Iowa, Nebraska, Michigan, North Dakota, Minnesota, South Dakota, Wisconsin
Pacific Reporter:	Arizona, Kansas, Oklahoma, California, Montana, Oregon, Colorado, Nevada, Utah, Indiana, New Mexico, Washington, Wyoming
Southeastern Reporter:	Georgia, South Carolina, North Carolina, Virginia, West Virginia
Southern Reporter:	Alabama, Florida, Louisiana, Mississippi

Northeastern Reporter, the *Northwestern Reporter,* the *Pacific Reporter,* the *Southeastern Reporter,* the *Southwestern Reporter,* and the *Southern Reporter.* Table 1.2 lists each of the states included in the various reporters. It is easy to find state supreme court decisions, once one knows the citation for the case. The *Atlantic Reporter* publishes cases from Connecticut, Massachusetts, New Hampshire, Pennsylvania, Rhode Island, and Vermont. *State of Vermont* v. *Bruyette,* 604 A.2d 1270 (Vt. 1992), is found in volume 604 of the Atlantic Reporter's second series, on page 1270.

Reading and Understanding a Case

Case law is an important aspect of U.S. legal systems. Generally, lawyers will engage in a process called **case briefing,** and professors may recommend this procedure to students as well. Briefing a case enables one to read a case and to state concisely the basic facts, law, holding, and the court's reasoning. Various briefing approaches may be used. The case brief illustration at the end of this chapter uses an approach to case briefing that your instructor may wish to modify to suit his or her preferences.

Summary

Chapter 1 presents an introduction to the study of criminal procedure, which outlines the process that must be followed when the police investigate crimes and in criminal trials. Two different approaches to determining guilt or innocence are adopted in adversary systems and inquisitorial systems of justice. An adversary system is based on the assumption that a struggle between two conflicting parties, a defense attorney and a prosecutor, is the best method to determine the truth. An inquisitorial system uses a more cooperative approach to determine a defendant's guilt or innocence. Moreover, in

an adversary system the prosecution must prove beyond a reasonable doubt all elements of a crime with which a defendant is charged.

The sources of criminal law include statutes, constitutions, case law, and common law. Statutes are a primary source of criminal law. In addition, the Bill of Rights in the U.S. Constitution provides individuals with numerous protections against abuses of governmental authority. Additional protections are provided by state constitutions. Case law is another important source of criminal law. U.S. Supreme Court decisions are binding on all federal courts and on state courts where federal statutes or rights guaranteed by the U.S. Constitution are involved. When a state's highest court decides a case, its decision is binding on that state's courts. Moreover, if a state supreme court decides a case and bases its decision solely on its own state constitution, it has the final word on the matter and the U.S. Supreme Court lacks the power to overturn the decision. Common law is another source of criminal law that may be used to supplement statutory law in many jurisdictions.

This chapter discusses the structure of U.S. criminal court systems. Jurisdiction refers to a court's power to hear and decide a legal matter. Original jurisdiction refers to a court's power to try the facts of a case. Appellate jurisdiction represents the power of a court that may hear an appeal of a trial court's decision.

The power of judicial review allows the courts to review the actions of other branches of government to determine if those acts infringe on constitutional rights. This power is a strong check against the abuse of power by the legislative and executive branches of government. U.S. courts view the power of judicial review as an awesome responsibility and have developed principles designed to prevent themselves from infringing on the authority of the other branches of government. These include the doctrines of mootness and standing to sue. If a case is moot, the issues have been resolved and a court will refuse to hear it. Standing to sue requires that a party who brings a lawsuit must have suffered a genuine injury. A third party is not allowed normally to bring a lawsuit on another person's behalf.

The notion of a dual court system means that the United States has both federal and state court systems; however, in reality there are 50 independent state court systems and one federal system. The chapter also discusses the typical structure of state court systems. While there is substantial variation in the structure of state court systems throughout the United States, most of them are characterized by trial courts and a court of appeal. Some states have intermediate courts of appeal too. The structure of the federal court system consists of a hierarchical system of United States District Courts, United States Courts of Appeals, and the United States Supreme Court. Each of these courts has jurisdiction in different types of cases. The U.S. District Courts are the trial courts in the federal system. The U.S. Courts of Appeals hear appeals from the district courts. The U.S. Supreme Court primarily hears appeals from the U.S. Courts of Appeals and from the highest court in any state when a federal constitutional issue is presented. Moreover, the concepts of judicial restraint and judicial activism are discussed in detail.

Chapter 1 concludes with a discussion of how to read and understand a case, how to find a case in a law library, and how to brief a case. Briefing a case enables one to read a case and to state concisely the basic facts, law, holding, and the court's reasoning.

Review Questions

1. Identify and discuss the following concepts:
   a. adversary system of justice
   b. trial by combat
   c. inquisitory system of justice
   d. burden of proof
   e. proof beyond a reasonable doubt
2. Identify and discuss three main sources of criminal law.
3. Discuss the following concepts:
   a. jurisdiction
   b. appellate jurisdiction
   c. original jurisdiction
4. What does the term "dual court system" imply? Why is the term an inaccurate description of U.S. courts?

5. Describe the typical structure of state court systems. Trace the progression of a misdemeanor offense through a typical state court system to the U.S. Supreme Court.
6. Describe the structure of the federal court system. Identify each court in this system and outline its jurisdiction.
7. Describe the process by which a case reaches the U.S. Supreme Court.

8. Identify the following cases by finding them in your library:
   a. 470 U.S. 753 (1985)
   b. 388 U.S. 218 (1967)
   c. 87 S.Ct. 1926 (1967)
   d. 516 F.2d 594 (1975)
   e. 200 N.E.2d 779 (1964)

Issues for Analysis and Discussion

1. Discuss the power of judicial review. Identify and describe two doctrines that the courts have developed to limit the power of judicial review.
2. Discuss the doctrines of judicial activism and judicial restraint. Which position should judges adopt when deciding cases? Present an argument for an intermediate approach to these judicial decision-making approaches. How does the political process influence the judicial decision-making process?

Case Brief Illustration

1. *Arizona* v. *Evans,* 115 S.Ct. 1185 (1995). (Explanation: This section provides the case name and the case citation. Cases that have been decided recently will not yet have a *U.S. Reports* citation assigned to them. For recent cases, a citation from West's *Supreme Court Reporter* should be provided; however, older cases should provide a *U.S. Reports* citation because it is the "official" reporter of Supreme Court decisions.)

2. *Facts:* In January 1991, a Phoenix police officer observed Evans driving the wrong way on a one-way street. The officer stopped Evans and discovered that his driver's license had been suspended and that there was an outstanding misdemeanor warrant for his arrest. While the officer was placing Evans under arrest, Evans dropped a hand-rolled cigarette that smelled of marijuana. The officer searched Evans's car and discovered a bag of marijuana under the passenger's seat.

The state charged Evans with possession of marijuana. When the police notified the Justice Court that they had arrested Evans, the Court discovered that the arrest warrant issued for Evans's arrest was invalid. At his trial for possession of marijuana, Evans argued that because his arrest was based on an invalid warrant, the marijuana seized incident to the arrest should be suppressed as the fruit of an unlawful arrest. Evans also argued that the good faith exception to the exclusionary rule of evidence was inapplicable because it was police error, not judicial error, which caused the invalid arrest. The trial court granted the motion to suppress because it concluded that the State had been at fault for failing to quash the warrant.

The Arizona Court of Appeals reversed and asserted that the exclusionary rule was not intended to deter the errors of court employees.

The Arizona Supreme Court reversed. The court held that application of the exclusionary rule would serve to improve the efficiency of those who keep records in our criminal justice system.

The U.S. Supreme Court granted certiorari.

(Explanation: This section provides the reader with sufficient information to determine precisely what has happened in the case. By reading a case brief, the reader should know every important detail that the appellate court considered in making its decision.)

3. *Decision of the U.S. Supreme Court:*
   (1) Because the Arizona Supreme Court's decision rested primarily on federal law, the U.S. Supreme Court had jurisdiction to review the case; (2) Evidence seized in violation of the Fourth Amendment following an illegal arrest due to incorrect computer records, which court personnel had failed to update, fell within the good faith exception to the exclusionary rule of evidence and need not be excluded from a defendant's criminal trial. (Explanation: This section relates precisely what the final appellate court decided.)

4. *Issue(s):* (1) Did the U.S. Supreme Court have jurisdiction to review this case? Answer: Yes. (2) Does the exclusionary rule of evidence require suppression of marijuana seized incident to an arrest resulting from an inaccurate computer record? Answer: No.

   (Explanation: This section relates the legal questions that the final appellate court is being asked to decide. Therefore, your issues should always be posed as questions. You must read the entire case carefully in order to determine the issues that the court is deciding.)

5. *Opinion of the Court* (Chief Justice Rehnquist)
   Issue 1:
   a. This court has jurisdiction to review the State Supreme Court's decision. "Under *Michigan* v. *Long,* when a state court decision fairly appears to rest primarily on federal law, or to be interwoven with federal law, and when the adequacy and independence of any possible state law

ground is not clear from the opinion's face, this Court will accept as the most reasonable explanation that the state court decided the case the way it did because it believed that federal law required it to do so."

   b. State courts may interpret state constitutional provisions to accord greater protection to individual rights than do similar provisions of the U.S. Constitution and to serve as experimental laboratories.

   c. In this case, the state Supreme Court based its decision squarely upon its interpretation of federal law when it discussed the appropriateness of applying the exclusionary rule, and it offered no plain statement that its references to federal law were being used only for the purpose of guidance and did not compel the result reached.

   Issue 2:
   a. The exclusionary rule works as a judicially created remedy designed to safeguard against future violations of Fourth Amendment rights through the rule's general deterrent effect. Where it does not result in significant deterrence its use is unwarranted.

   b. In *United States* v. *Leon,* the Court applied these principles to a situation in which a police officer had acted in objectively reasonable reliance on a search warrant, issued by a magistrate, that later was determined to be invalid due to a lack of probable cause. The Court determined that there was no sound reason to apply the exclusionary rule as a means of deterring misconduct on the part of judges who are responsible for issuing warrants. The Court noted that the exclusionary rule was historically designed to deter police misconduct rather than to punish the errors of judges and magistrates.

   c. Applying *Leon*'s reasoning to the facts of this case, the decision of the Arizona Supreme Court must be reversed. If court employees were responsible for the erroneous computer record, the exclusion of evidence at trial would not sufficiently deter future errors so as to warrant such a severe sanction. The exclusionary rule was historically designed as a means of deterring police misconduct, not mistakes by court employees. Evans offered no evidence that court employees are inclined to ignore or subvert the Fourth Amendment or that lawlessness among these individuals requires application of the extreme sanction of exclusion.

d. There is no reason to believe that the arresting officer was not acting objectively reasonably when he relied upon the police computer record. "Application of the *Leon* framework supports a categorical exception to the exclusionary rule for clerical errors of court employees."

(*Concurring* and *Dissenting Opinions:* Brief summaries of concurring and dissenting opinions are optional at the discretion of your instructor.)

6. *Student Comments* (This section presents the student's own view of the case; it may be as extensive or limited as the instructor wishes.)

7. *Principle of Law:* The Supreme Court had jurisdiction to review this case because the Arizona Supreme Court had relied on federal law in reaching its decision. The good faith exception to the exclusionary rule of evidence allows evidence seized incident to an arrest resulting from an inaccurate computer record, which was the fault of court personnel, to be used at trial. (Explanation: This section provides a concise statement of the law established by the case. Hint: An easy way to formulate the principle of law is to state your "issues" as declarative sentences.)

Endnotes

1. *In re Winship,* 397 U.S. 358, 364 (1970).
2. *Victor* v. *Nebraska,* 114 S.Ct. 1239, 1243 (1994).
3. Sue Titus Reid, *Criminal Justice,* 3d ed. (New York, N.Y.: Macmillan, 1993), p. 36.
4. Article VI of the U.S. Constitution contains the Supremacy Clause, which states: "This Constitution, and the Laws of the United States which shall be made in Pursuance thereof; and all Treaties made, or which shall be made, under the Authority of the United States, shall be the Supreme Law of the Land." See *McCullogh* v. *Maryland,* 17 U.S. 316 (1819).
5. Commonwealth of Pennsylvania, *Rules of Criminal Procedure,* Rule 2003 (c), (1996).
6. Reid, supra note 3 at 36.
7. See Reid, supra note 3 at 37.
8. William J. Brennan, Jr., "State Constitutions and the Protection of Individual Rights." 90 *Harvard Law Review* pp. 489–504 (1977).
9. Yale Kamisar, "Does (Did) (Should) the Exclusionary Rule Rest on a 'Principled Basis' Rather than an 'Empirical Proposition?'" 16 *Creighton Law Review* pp. 565–667 (1983).
10. See Thomas J. Hickey and Michael Axline, "Drunk-Driving Roadblocks under State Constitutions: A Reasonable Alternative to *Michigan* v. *Sitz.*" 28 *Criminal Law Bulletin* pp. 195–217 (1992).
11. See *Michigan Department of State Police* v. *Sitz,* 496 U.S. 444 (1990).
12. *Sitz* v. *Michigan Dept. of State Police,* 193 Mich. App. 690, 485 N.W.2d 135 (Mich. Ct. App. 1992).
13. For a more detailed discussion of state constitutional law's impact on suspects' rights in sobriety police roadblock cases, see Thomas J. Hickey and Michael Axline, supra note 10 at 195–217.
14. Reid, supra note 3 at 36.
15. Pennsylvania Annotated Statutes, Title 18, Section 3502 (1994).
16. Henry C. Black, *Black's Law Dictionary With Pronunciations, Abridged,* 5th ed. (St. Paul, Minn.: West, 1983).
17. Reid, supra note 3 at 305.
18. *Marbury* v. *Madison,* 5 U.S. 137 (1803).
19. *DeFunis* v. *Odegaard,* 416 U.S. 312 (1974).

20. See *Massachusetts* v. *Laird,* 400 U.S. 886 (1970).
21. See *United States* v. *Dixon,* 113 S.Ct. 2864 (1993).
22. Reid, supra note 3 at 306.
23. *Blockburger* v. *United States,* 284 U.S. 299 (1932).
24. *Bartkus* v. *Illinois,* 359 U.S. 121 (1959).
25. See *North* v. *Russell,* 427 U.S. 328 (1976).
26. See *Duncan* v. *Louisiana,* 391 U.S. 145 (1968).
27. See *Baldwin* v. *New York,* 399 U.S. 66 (1970).
28. *Gideon* v. *Wainright,* 372 U.S. 335 (1963).
29. One exception to this rule occurs in federal habeas corpus lawsuits in which a convicted state prisoner alleges that a state's criminal proceedings have deprived him or her of a federally protected constitutional right. The current federal habeas corpus statute is found in 28 U.S.C.A. Sections 2241–2255. For an example of a case involving a federal habeas corpus suit brought by a state prisoner, see *Stone* v. *Powell,* 428 U.S. 465 (1976).
30. See *Michigan* v. *Long,* 463 U.S. 1032 (1983).
31. Henry J. Abraham, *The Judicial Process,* 6th ed. (New York, N.Y.: Oxford, 1993), p. 153.
32. See 18 U.S.C. Sections 3161–3174 (1988).
33. Abraham, supra note 31 at p. 162.
34. See Howard Ball, *Courts and Politics: The Federal Judicial System,* 2d ed. (Englewood Cliffs, N.J.: Prentice Hall, 1987), p. 120.
35. For an excellent short discussion of the Supreme Court's decision-making process see Reid, supra note 3, at 316–318.
36. Laurence H. Tribe, *American Constitutional Law,* 2d ed. (Mineola, N.Y.: Foundation Press, 1988), p. 14.
37. See Robert H. Bork, *The Tempting of America: The Political Seduction of the Law* (New York, N.Y.: Free Press, 1990).

2 CRIMINAL JUSTICE PROCESSES IN THE UNITED STATES

Outline

Key Terms

Chapter 1 discussed briefly the nature of procedural law. This chapter will begin to explore in greater detail the procedures used in U.S. criminal justice systems. Some of the procedures are required by the United States Constitution and U.S. Supreme Court cases interpreting constitutional amendments. Additional procedures are required by state constitutions that expand suspects' rights beyond those required by the federal constitution. Still other procedures are required by federal or state statutes, by court rules, or by administrative regulations. A basic issue considered throughout this text concerns why procedures that protect the rights of suspected criminals are necessary. Chapter 2 discusses the historical basis for some of our most important constitutional rights. First, however, it is necessary to present a brief overview of some basic legal concepts and the stages in U.S. criminal justice systems.

The Nature of Criminal Law

Chapter 1 pointed out that there are two primary ways to view U.S. criminal law. This distinction bears repeating because it is essential to developing an understanding of criminal procedure. The first, which may be termed the **substantive aspect of law,** focuses on the specific conduct that the legislature has determined to be a crime. It defines the elements of crimes, rights, and responsibilities imposed by the criminal law. For example, the New York Penal Code defines the crime of harassment as follows: "A person is guilty of harassment in the first degree when he or she intentionally and repeatedly harasses another person by following such person in or about a public place or places or by engaging in a course of conduct or by repeatedly committing acts which places such person in reasonable fear of physical injury."[1] In order to prove that a defendant committed the crime of harassment, the prosecution must prove each of the following elements:

1. intentional and repeated harassment of another person;
2. by following the person in or about a public place;
3. or by repeatedly committing acts;
4. which place the person in reasonable fear of physical injury.

If the State fails to prove each of these elements, it will fail in its harassment prosecution, although it may still convict the defendant of some lesser offense, such as disorderly conduct, which may be easier to prove.

In contrast, the **procedural aspect of law** is concerned with the various procedures that the government must follow when it enforces a law that may result in taking away someone's life, liberty, or property. In the United States there are three possible penalties for committing a crime. The first is the death penalty. A second possible sanction is imprisonment or some other restriction on his or her liberty such as probation, or other types of conditional and restricted freedom, including house arrest or work release. A third punishment, as those of us who have received traffic tickets will attest, is a fine, or taking away his or her property.

Procedural legal questions are common in the American legal system. Examples of these questions include the following: Did a defendant receive his or her *Miranda* warnings before the police questioned him? Did the police have a valid search warrant before they searched a defendant's home? Was the defendant given the opportunity to consult with his or her attorney before being questioned by the police? Did the defendant receive a speedy and public trial? Was a defendant given the opportunity to cross-examine witnesses for the state? These and many other procedural legal issues will be discussed in this text. Before focusing on these questions, however, it is important to consider briefly the procedural steps in U.S. criminal justice systems.

Steps in the Pretrial Criminal Justice Process

Figure 2.1 diagrams the various stages in the U.S. criminal justice process. Each of the stages requires that a defendant be given procedural due process. For example, when a defendant is formally arraigned on criminal charges, if he or she is **indigent,** counsel is appointed. An indigent person is one who cannot afford to retain private counsel. As Herbert Packer once observed, the entire process represents a virtual obstacle course for the state—each of the stages is a separate hurdle that the prosecution must overcome successfully in order to prosecute a defendant in a criminal case.[2] It should not be surprising, then, that many criminal cases never reach the trial stage. This case reduction process has been described as a **funnel effect,**[3] diagrammed in Figure 2.2.

The funnel effect means that the various stages of the criminal justice system act to screen out large numbers of cases. It has been estimated that of 5,000 felonies reported to the police, only 1,500 arrests are made. Approximately 400 of those arrested are juveniles, who are processed through a different judicial system. Formal charges are filed against only 600 of the remaining 1,100 adult arrestees. The number of cases is further reduced because approximately 50 are dismissed by magistrates during early pretrial procedures, and another 50 cases are dropped by the prosecution.[4]

Four hundred of the remaining defendants eventually plead guilty. Therefore, the criminal justice funnel leaves approximately 100 adult defendants who actually go to trial. Of these defendants, approximately 70 percent are convicted. Reid observes that approximately 250 adults are sentenced to terms of confinement out of the 5,000 reported felonies. Many of these individuals are sentenced to short jail terms or probation. Approximately 100 are sentenced to prison.[5]

Reporting a Crime and Filing Charges

Crimes may come to the attention of the police in many different ways. Often, the victim will report the incident to the police. Sometimes the police on patrol, or using

FIGURE 2.1

Institutions and Stages in the American System of Criminal Justice

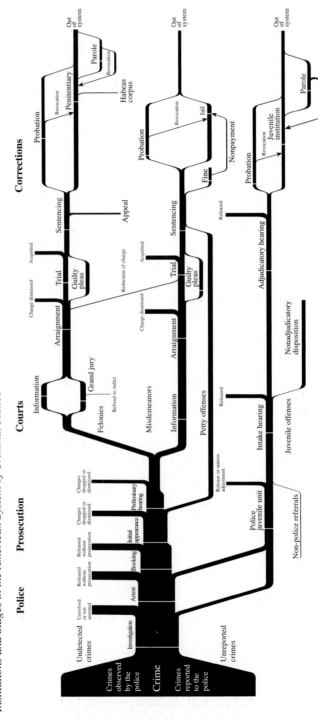

| Police | Prosecution | Courts | Corrections |

Source: "The challenge of Crime in a Free Society" Washington DC: US Govt Printing Office, 1967, pp. 8–9.

FIGURE 2.2

The Criminal Justice Funnel

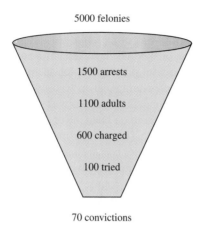

5000 felonies

1500 arrests

1100 adults

600 charged

100 tried

70 convictions

more creative law enforcement strategies, such as posing as prostitutes to lure unsuspecting customers or "johns," discover crimes in progress and make an arrest at the scene of a crime.[6]

Even though police officers may arrest a suspect, a prosecuting attorney may decline to prosecute the case. This may occur for any number of reasons, but happens most often when a case is weak or if a victim is unwilling to file charges.

Regardless of how criminal activities come to the attention of the authorities, persons accused of committing crimes are entitled to procedural safeguards. Such protections apply when a crime is being investigated as well as during the criminal trial process.

Investigation of the Criminal Case

Criminal investigations are a crucial aspect of the U.S. criminal justice process. If investigations are not conducted properly, essential evidence may be lost forever. Murder cases often illustrate the importance that physical evidence, such as blood types, hair specimens, and footprints often plays in a criminal prosecution. Moreover, as any experienced prosecutor will attest, the quality of physical evidence found at a crime scene is often a principal factor in determining if a criminal case will be tried.

During a criminal investigation, police officers often interview prospective witnesses to determine if they can provide evidence. In many cases the information provided by witnesses to the crime is the most critical evidence in the prosecution's case against a defendant.

Police officers' power to investigate crimes is constrained by procedural law, however. For example, officers cannot torture suspects to gain confessions or compel them to incriminate themselves in other ways. That would violate the Fifth Amendment privilege against self-incrimination, which will be discussed in much greater detail later in the text. If the police violate a protected right of the accused, or secure evidence improperly, the evidence may be excluded from trial.[7] This important evidentiary principle is termed the **exclusionary rule of evidence.**

Initial Appearance

Once a suspect is arrested, he or she must be taken before a **magistrate,** an official empowered to conduct certain pretrial procedures, for an **initial appearance.** The initial appearance is for the purpose of ensuring that an accused has been detained lawfully.

Persons may not be held for indefinite periods without criminal charges. Once someone is arrested, if they are not released on bond, he or she must be taken before a magistrate "without unnecessary delay."[8] This usually means that the suspect will be taken before a magistrate on they day of his or her arrest, or on the morning after the arrest.

At the initial appearance defendants are advised of the charges and of their constitutional rights, including the right to counsel. If the defendant is indigent and the charged offense is a misdemeanor that may result in confinement,[9] or a felony,[10] the magistrate will appoint an attorney to represent the suspect. If the defendant is not indigent he or she may retain private defense counsel.

In misdemeanor cases a defendant may enter a plea to the charges at this stage. Felony cases move normally to a preliminary hearing.

Preliminary Hearing

At a **preliminary hearing** a magistrate makes a more detailed examination of the charges against a defendant. There must be at least probable cause to believe that the defendant committed the charged offense. If the charges are not supported by probable cause, a magistrate will dismiss the case. Experienced defense attorneys may use the preliminary hearing to their client's advantage to get an early look at the prosecution's case. At the preliminary hearing the defense has an advantage. The prosecution must divulge enough of its evidence to establish probable cause to believe that the defendant committed the charged offense. The suspect cannot be required to testify, however, and the defense will often decide not to reveal its trial strategy, and so will not contest the charges at this stage.

If probable cause supports the charges, however, the case will move to the next stage in the criminal justice process. If it involves a misdemeanor, it will be set for trial in the state's misdemeanor court. If it involves a felony, many states provide the defendant with the right to a grand jury proceeding.

Grand Jury Proceeding

A **grand jury** is composed of between 12 and 23 private citizens who are chosen to review cases for a designated period of time. Grand juries exercise two primary responsibilities in U.S. justice systems. First, they determine if there is sufficient evidence to bring a case to trial. If so, they will issue an **indictment** which is a formal accusation of a charged offense. Second, in many jurisdictions they may conduct investigations of criminal activity.

In most states grand juries consider only felony offenses. Moreover, because the Supreme Court has not made the right to a grand jury indictment binding on state proceedings, some states have adopted an alternative process, termed an **information.** This process involves a meeting between prosecutors, victims, and witnesses to the crime to decide if the case should be brought to trial.

Grand jury proceedings, which are closed to the public, are the prosecutor's domain. Defendants and their attorneys have no right to appear, to testify, or to present evidence. If a grand jury decides that the evidence supports the charges against a defendant, it issues a **true bill.** If it believes that there is insufficient evidence to permit the charges to go forward, or if it believes that the prosecution is pursuing a case improperly, a grand jury may dismiss the indictment. For example, suppose a loving father is charged with murder for disconnecting a respirator that has kept alive his infant son who became brain dead following an automobile accident. In these circumstances a grand jury may decide not to indict the defendant on murder charges.

A second important function of a grand jury is to conduct criminal investigations. A grand jury's investigations are guided normally by prosecutors. Occasionally, however, a grand jury may initiate an investigation on its own. This is sometimes termed a "runaway" grand jury, because the prosecutor is unable to control the investigation. If members of the grand jury discover criminal activity, they may ask the prosecutor to prepare an indictment against the suspects. This is termed a **presentment.**

Arraignment

The next step in the criminal justice process is an **arraignment.** The judge will read the charges against the defendant and request a plea. The defendant may plead guilty, not guilty, or **nolo contendere.** This plea, which is not normally permitted in felony cases, has the same effect as a guilty plea, with one important difference. A nolo contendere plea may not be used against the defendant in a later civil proceeding.[11] A defendant may elect to stand mute and say nothing when the judge requests a plea to the charges. When this happens a judge will enter a not guilty plea for the defendant.

Pretrial Motions

An important step in the criminal justice process involves the filing of pretrial **motions,** which are written requests to the trial judge for certain action. One common pretrial motion involves a request to prevent the prosecution from using certain evidence because it was obtained improperly. This is termed a motion to suppress evidence. A trial court's ruling on a motion to suppress evidence may be crucial to the case—if important evidence is ruled inadmissible, the state may have no alternative but to discontinue the prosecution.

Another common motion asks the prosecution to inform the defense of the evidence it will use. This process is termed **discovery.** Pretrial discovery rules are designed to prevent a "trial by ambush" and allow a defendant to prepare an effective defense to criminal charges.

The defense may ask the trial judge to move the trial to another location because a defendant is unable to receive a fair trial in a particular locale because the case is so notorious. This is termed a motion for a **change of venue.**[12] This motion asks a trial court to move a criminal trial to a different location because pretrial publicity would prevent a defendant from receiving a fair trial in the original venue. For example, an attorney for Timothy McVeigh, a defendant in the Oklahoma City bombing case, requested that the trial be moved from that city because it would be difficult to get an unbiased jury.

Pretrial Conferences

An important and often informal phase of a criminal trial may be termed a **pretrial conference,** which involves a meeting of the principal actors in the criminal trial process—the judge, the prosecutor, and the defense attorney. Issues that could prove difficult to resolve during trial or that could cause delay are often resolved at pretrial conferences.

Trial judges will sometimes attempt to mediate a settlement of the criminal charges against a defendant during these conferences. Moreover, the judge or one of the attorneys may recommend a reduction in charges or an agreement to a reduced penalty if the defendant will agree to plead guilty. This is termed **plea bargaining,** a process in which a defendant enters a guilty plea in exchange for favorable action by the state. It is estimated that as many as 90 percent of all guilty pleas in the United States result from plea bargaining.[13]

Constitutional Protections in U.S. Justice Systems

The preceding section outlined the normal steps in the pretrial criminal justice process. The conduct of government agents at any of these stages may raise questions about whether a defendant's procedural rights were violated. Before considering the precise nature of these procedural rights, however, it is important to discuss why the framers of the United States Constitution determined that it was essential to give defendants procedural rights in the first place.

The Writ of Habeas Corpus

Suppose that governmental authorities had the power to confine persons indefinitely without charging them with a crime. Such a practice would lead to injustice and would have grave potential for the widespread abuse of citizens' rights. If persons knew they would be held in prison until they confessed, would they not be tempted to confess to avoid further imprisonment, even if they were not guilty of a crime?

One of the most basic rights available to confined persons in this country is the right to be brought before a judge to determine if they are being held lawfully. The right to a **writ of habeas corpus** provides that every person being held by a government agency, or even by a private party, has the right to be taken before a court. The

Highlight 2.1

McNabb v. United States
318 U.S. 332 (1943)

 [The McNabbs were a clan of Tennessee mountaineers who were involved in illicit bootlegging activities living about twelve miles from Chattanooga in a section known as the McNabb Settlement. Federal agents received information that they were planning to sell illegal whiskey. Federal agents planned to raid the McNabb Settlement, and during the raid a revenue agent was shot and killed by one of the suspects. The suspects were arrested and taken to the Federal Building where they were questioned for extended periods without being brought before a magistrate. They made incriminating statements, which were used against them at their trial for second-degree murder, and they were convicted and sentenced to imprisonment for 45 years.]

Mr. Justice Frankfurter delivered the opinion of the Court.

"[T]he evidence elicited from the petitioners in the circumstances disclosed here must be excluded. For in their treatment of the petitioners the arresting officers assumed functions which Congress has explicitly denied them. They subjected the accused to the pressures of a procedure which is wholly incompatible with the vital but very restricted duties of the investigating and arresting officers of the Government and which tends to undermine the integrity of the criminal proceeding. Congress has explicitly commanded that 'It shall be the duty of the marshal, his deputy, or other officer, who may arrest a person charged with any crime or offense, to take the defendant before the nearest United States commissioner or the nearest judicial officer having jurisdiction under existing laws for a hearing, commitment, or taking bail for trial. . . .'

The purpose of this impressively pervasive requirement of criminal procedure is plain: A democratic society, in which respect for the dignity of all men is central, naturally guards against the misuse of the law enforcement process. Zeal in tracking down crime is not in itself an assurance of soberness of judgment. Disinterestedness in law enforcement does not alone prevent disregard of cherished liberties. Experience has therefore counseled that safeguards must be provided against the dangers of the overzealous as well as the despotic. The awful instruments of the criminal law cannot be entrusted to a single functionary. The complicated process of criminal justice is therefore divided into different parts, responsibility for which is separately vested in the various participants upon whom the criminal law relies for its vindication. Legislation such as this, requiring that the police must with reasonable promptness show legal cause for detaining arrested persons, constitutes an important safeguard—not only in assuring protection for the innocent but also in securing conviction of the guilty by methods that commend themselves to a progressive and self-confident society. For this procedural requirement checks resort to those reprehensible practices known as the 'third degree' which, though universally rejected as indefensible, still find their way into use. It aims to avoid all the evil implications of secret interrogation of persons accused of crime. It reflects not a sentimental but a sturdy view of law enforcement. It outlaws easy but self-defeating ways in which brutality is substituted for brains as an instrument of crime detection.

The circumstances in which the statements admitted in evidence against the petitioners were secured reveal a plain disregard of the duty enjoined by Congress upon federal officers. Freeman and Raymond McNabb were arrested in the middle of the night at their home. Instead of being brought before a United States Commissioner or a judicial officer, as the law requires, in order to determine the sufficiency of the justification for their detention, they were put in a barren cell and kept there for fourteen hours. For two

(Continued)

(Concluded)

days they were subjected to unremitting questioning by numerous officers. Benjamin's confession was secured by detaining him unlawfully and questioning him continuously for five or six hours. The McNabbs had to submit to all this without the aid of friends or the benefit of counsel. The record leaves no room for doubt that the questioning of the petitioners took place while they were in the custody of the arresting officers and before any order of commitment was made. Plainly, a conviction resting on evidence secured through such a flagrant disregard of the procedure which Congress has commanded cannot be allowed to stand without making the courts themselves accomplices in willful disobedience of law. Congress has not explicitly forbidden the use of evidence so procured. But to permit such evidence to be made the basis of a conviction in the federal courts would stultify the policy which Congress has enacted into law."

Reversed.

literal meaning of habeas corpus, is "you have the body." Highlight 2.1 presents excerpts from *McNabb* v. *United States*,[14] a case in which the Supreme Court discussed the dangers of incommunicado interrogation and the importance of bringing a suspect before a magistrate "with reasonable promptness."[15]

The right to a writ of habeas corpus is a fundamental right in U.S. justice systems. Its importance is underscored by Highlight 2.2, which contains excerpts from Jacobo Timmerman's *Prisoner Without a Name, Cell Without a Number,* a stark description of Timmerman's confinement in Argentina's military prisons during the 1970s.

The historical origins of the writ of habeas corpus may be traced to the British Magna Carta, but the writ has become a cornerstone of American law as well. The Massachusetts Constitution of 1780 stated, "The privilege and benefit of the writ of habeas corpus shall be enjoyed in this commonwealth, in the most free, easy, cheap, expeditious and ample manner; and shall not be suspended by the legislature, except upon the most urgent and pressing occasions, and for a limited time, not exceeding twelve months."[16] Several years later, the U.S. Constitution stated that "[t]he Privilege of the Writ of Habeas Corpus shall not be suspended, unless when in Cases of Rebellion or Invasion the public Safety may require it."[17]

Former United States Supreme Court Justice Salmon P. Chase described the writ as "the best and only sufficient defence of personal freedom."[18] More recently, former Supreme Court Justice William J. Brennan described the writ of habeas corpus as follows:

> [It is] intertwined with the growth of fundamental rights of personal liberty. For its function has been to provide a prompt and efficacious remedy for whatever society deems to be intolerable restraints. Its root principle is that in a civilized society, government must always be accountable to the judiciary for a man's imprisonment: if the imprisonment cannot be shown to conform with the fundamental requirements of law, the individual is entitled to his immediate release.[19]

The right to a writ of habeas corpus has a longstanding history in the British and American legal systems. Other longstanding constitutional protections restrict the government's power in its dealings with citizens as well. These protections include prohibitions against bills of attainder and ex post facto laws.

Highlight 2.2

Excerpt from Jacobo Timmerman's
Prisoner Without a Name, Cell Without a Number

 "The cell is narrow. When I stand at its center, facing the cell door, I can't extend my arms. But it is long, and when I lie down, I can stretch out my entire body. A stroke of luck, for in the cell I previously occupied—for how long? I was forced to huddle up when seated and keep my knees bent while lying down.

With hands bound behind me and eyes blindfolded, suicide was the only thing that could share the long endless stretch of time, and made up of time and more time, of interrogation and time, of cold and time, of hunger and time, of tears and time.

With hands bound behind me and eyes blindfolded, there was no possibility of suicide. I was transformed from my clandestine prison to the interrogators at police headquarters in the City of La Plata, blindfolded, bound, thrown to the floor in the back of a car, covered with a blanket.

It was early in the morning by the time one of the longer sessions, lasting I think about eighteen hours, was over. Accompanied by two guards, I was leaving La Plata and heading back in the direction of the clandestine prison. They were exhausted but happy: I'd signed a declaration admitting that I was a leftist Zionist. They sat me in back, alone, did not blindfold me or tie me up, and gave me an apple. They said that before reaching the prison, they'd cover me with a blanket so that I wouldn't see the location, which was known in their coded language as the Puesto Vasco. They speeded along the deserted route while I, in absorption, gazed through the window at the road. One of the guards wanted to know what crazy thoughts were passing through my mind as we heard a radio newscast announcing that my wife had presented a new writ of habeas corpus to ascertain my whereabouts. Smiling, I told him I was thinking of opening the door and throwing myself from the car. But he warned me not to attempt this because there obviously wouldn't be enough time—he'd grab me with his hands, and I wouldn't have the strength to move. Again he smiled, and said: 'There were seventeen in this car, Jacobo.' Its for those seventeen faces that I had also to seek haven in the night.

Aside from suicide, there's one other temptation—madness. There are the only two temptations, or rather the only two strong emotions I experienced during my thirty months of imprisonment and beatings. Strong emotions because their repressed violence enables them to overpower time. And time is not an easy enemy."

[From *Prisoner Without a Name, Cell Without a Number* by Jacobo Timmerman, trans., Toby Talbot. Translation Copyright © 1981 by Alfred A. Knopf, Inc. Reprinted by permission of the publisher.]

Bills of Attainder and Ex Post Facto Laws

The U.S. Constitution states that "[n]o bill of attainder or ex post facto Law shall be passed."[20] It prevents the states from passing such laws as well.[21] The right to a writ of habeas corpus, discussed in the preceding section, protects citizens mainly from abuses by the executive branch. The Constitution's protection against bills of attainder and ex post facto laws, in contrast, are intended to protect citizens from abuses by the legislative branch of government.

Originally, a **bill of attainder** was available in the English legislative system to condemn named persons to death or to lesser penalties and to forbid inheritance of their property.[22] More recent U.S. Supreme Court cases suggest that the Constitution's bill of attainder provision forbids any federal or state legislative act that "applies either to named individuals or to easily ascertainable members of a group in such a way as to inflict punishment on them without a judicial trial."[23] This protection is based on the separation of powers doctrine. In the American system of government the judiciary, not the legislature, is entrusted with the responsibility of deciding who should be subjected to punishment.

For example, in 1946 the U.S. Congress's House Un-American Activities Committee passed a bill that forbid the payment of salaries to three named federal employees because they were alleged to be involved in "subversive activities."[24] The Supreme Court held that such a bill was an invalid bill of attainder because it applied to named individuals, and punished them without the benefit of a judicial trial.[25]

Similarly, the Court has held that Congress may not pass a law making it a crime for a member of the Communist Party to become an officer of a labor union.[26] The challenged law specified "in no uncertain terms the persons who possess the feared characteristics and therefore cannot hold union office without incurring criminal liability—members of the Communist Party."[27] Here, the punishment inflicted by the legislature without the benefit of a judicial trial was the ban on becoming a union officer if someone were a member of the Communist Party.

A more current hypothetical application of the Constitution's bill of attainder provision could arise in the aftermath of the Oklahoma City bombing tragedy that resulted in the deaths of many innocent people.[28] Highlight 2.3 presents an overview of that tragedy. Suppose that after investigating the incident, federal law enforcement authorities had concluded that paramilitary militia group members from several different states had helped to plan and execute that bombing. Suppose then that Congress passed a law barring militia group members from employment in any federal government agency. The law imposes severe criminal penalties on anyone who takes a government job while belonging to a paramilitary militia organization. Such a law is likely to be held unconstitutional because it functions as a bill of attainder. It would impose punishment without the benefit of a judicial trial on those belonging to paramilitary militia groups by not allowing them to be employed by federal agencies.

The U.S. Constitution's Article I, Sections 9 and 10 also prohibit **ex post facto laws.** Such laws punish criminal behavior retroactively—behavior which, at the time it originally took place, was not a crime. The U.S. Supreme Court has defined an ex post facto law as one that "retroactively alter[s] the definition of crimes or increase[s] the punishment for criminal acts."[29] The main reason for prohibiting ex post facto laws is based on the idea that the law must give people fair notice that their behavior is criminal. It is unreasonable to punish a person for an act that was not a crime at the time he or she committed it.

For example, assume that Mary, who is not employed as a police officer, goes to a Halloween Party on October 31, 1997, dressed up in a realistic looking police uniform, complete with a badge, nightstick, and plastic handgun. Later that year, in response to a series of bank robberies in which the robbers wore police uniforms, the state legislature passed a law forbidding anyone "not employed by the state, a county, a city or a township as a police officer, from appearing in public dressed in a police uniform." The law provides that a violation of this provision is a misdemeanor punishable by a fine not to exceed $500 and up to 90 days in jail. It is scheduled to take

Highlight 2.3

Oklahoma City Bombing

 The authorities opened an intensive hunt today for whoever bombed a Federal office building in Oklahoma City, and proceeded on the theory that the bombing was a terrorist attack against the Government, law-enforcement officials said.

President Clinton appeared in the White House press room this afternoon and somberly promised that the Government would hunt down the "evil cowards" responsible. "These people are killers," he said, "and must be treated like killers."

Attorney General Janet Reno, speaking to reporters at the White House in early evening, said that casualty figures from the scene were climbing and that of the 550 people who worked in the building, 300 were unaccounted for.

Ms. Reno said Federal prosecutors would seek the death penalty against the bombers. "The death penalty is available," she said, "and we will seek it."

But the authorities said they had no suspects, and questions about the identity of the bombers swirled around the case. The only solid fact was the explosion itself.

Some law-enforcement officials said the bombing might be linked to the second anniversary today of Federal agents' ill-fated assault on the Branch Davidian compound near Waco, Tex., an operation that ended in a fire that killed about 80 people, including many children. Among the offices housed by the Federal building in Oklahoma City was one quartering local agents of the Bureau of Alcohol, Tobacco and Firearms, the agency that Branch Davidians and their sympathizers blamed for the confrontation.

But other officials said that neither the Branch Davidians nor right-wing "militia" groups that have protested the Government's handling of the Davidians were believed to have the technical expertise to engage in bombings like the one today.

Some experts focused on the possibility that the attack had been the work of Islamic militants, like those who bombed the World Trade Center in February 1993.

AP/Wide World Photos

But if so, it was unclear why they would have struck in Oklahoma City. Some Middle Eastern groups have held meetings there, and the city is home to at least three mosques. But of the estimated five million Muslims in the United States, "there's just very, very few out that way," said Imam Muhammad Karoub, director of the Federation of Islamic Associations, based in Redford, Mich., a Detroit suburb.

Several news organizations, including CNN, reported that investigators were seeking to question several men, described as being Middle Eastern in appearance, who had driven away from the building shortly before the blast. There were also reports that the authorities had interviewed employees at a National Car Rental office in Dallas about a recently leased truck.

(Continued)

But Federal officials here said they could not confirm those reports. Indeed, investigators said they did not know whether the bombers were domestic or international terrorists.

The authorities said the bomb had probably been packed in a vehicle parked outside the Alfred P. Murrah Federal Building, where the explosion left a 20-foot-wide, 8-foot-deep crater in the street.

Officials at the Bureau of Alcohol, Tobacco and Firearms said they had not determined the bomb's chemical makeup, which they suspected to be ammonium nitrate and fuel oil, both easily available substances of the type used in the World Trade Center bombing. They said the damage led them to conclude that the bomb, if it was made of ammonium nitrate, might have weighed 1,000 to 1,200 pounds, about the size of the trade center bomb.

From David Johnston, "Terror in Oklahoma City," *The New York Times,* April 20, 1995, Sec. A, p. 1. [Copyright © 1995 by the New York Times Company. Reprinted by permission.]

effect on January 1, 1998. The Constitution's protection against ex post facto laws would clearly protect Mary from being charged with appearing in public dressed as a police officer in October of the previous year.

Criminal Procedures in Colonial America

No discussion of U.S. history during the colonial period would be complete without considering the events leading up to the American Revolution, such as the Boston Tea Party. The practices that led to these "lawless" actions by the colonists, and caused them to revolt against the British Government, led directly to the development of procedural rights in the United States Constitution.

General Warrants and Writs of Assistance

A law enforcement practice that angered colonial Americans, and led directly to the adoption of the U.S. Constitution's First and Fourth Amendments, was the British government's practice of issuing **general warrants.**[30] These warrants allowed law enforcement authorities to search any person or any place for contraband, regardless of whether or not there was a reason to believe that the person had committed a crime, or that a place concealed contraband. Often, the alleged contraband was nothing more than printed materials that criticized the British Government. All such critical materials were considered to be libelous, however, and law enforcement authorities were empowered to seize and destroy them. The founders of our country deeply resented these "search and destroy" missions, which allowed the government to curtail the free exchange of ideas.

A second and equally despised practice in colonial America was the government's use of **writs of assistance.** In response to high taxes that were levied against many different types of common goods, including food and other staples, some colonists became smugglers. A writ of assistance permitted the bearer, often a customs official, to search with unlimited discretion anyone suspected of criminal activity or anything believed to contain contraband. Such writs never expired until the death of the monarch who had issued it, whereas modern search warrants are valid only for a short period of time. Moreover, a writ of assistance did not require law enforcement agents to demonstrate to a judge the existence of probable cause to believe that a person possessed contraband, or that it could be found in a particular place.

Events like the Boston Tea Party were first and foremost a rebellion against the unrestrained exercise of raw governmental power. The early colonists' experience with the British monarchy taught them that limits must be placed on the government's power in a democratic nation. The restraints that were later adopted are contained in our Constitution's Bill of Rights.

The Bill of Rights and the Fourteenth Amendment

The United States Constitution is a document that established the basic structure of the federal government and placed limitations on governmental power. It provides a number of separate protections against the abuse of governmental power. Several of those protections were specifically designed to limit the government's power to conduct criminal investigations. These amendments detail the procedures that the government must follow when it invokes its power to conduct criminal investigations and trials.

Our Constitution's framers considered these rights to be so important that they were embodied in a **Bill of Rights,** the first ten amendments to the U.S. Constitution. Those amendments that prescribe criminal procedures include the Fourth, Fifth, Sixth, and Eighth Amendments. The Fourteenth Amendment too is an essential source of procedural rights because its Due Process Clause has been used to apply provisions in the Bill of Rights to state proceedings.

Fourth Amendment

> The right of the people to be secure in their persons, houses and effects, against unreasonable searches and seizures, shall not be violated, and no Warrants shall issue, but upon probable cause, supported by Oath or affirmation, and particularly describing the place to be searched, and the person or things to be seized.

The Fourth Amendment contains several protections for those suspected of criminal activity. These include:

1. The probable cause requirement: No arrest or search warrant may be issued unless probable cause is established to indicate that a person has committed a crime, or is about to commit a crime, or alternatively, that contraband may be found in a particular place. Probable cause is not easy to define. The Supreme Court has stated that it "is a fluid concept—turning on the assessment of probabilities in particular factual contexts—not readily, or even usefully,

reduced to a neat set of legal rules."[31] For our present purposes, however, probable cause may be regarded as sufficient information to lead a reasonable person to believe that a suspect is committing or has committed a crime or that contraband will be found in a particular place.

2. Supported by Oath or affirmation: A law enforcement officer must present his reasons for believing that probable cause exists to a judge or a magistrate who is empowered by law to issue search or arrest warrants. If the judge agrees that probable cause exists, a warrant may be issued. The officer must swear under penalty of perjury that the information he is presenting to the judge is true to the best of his knowledge.

3. The particularity requirement: The information presented to a judge or a magistrate must be specific as to the location of the place to be searched and the person or things to be seized. Remember that the Constitution's framers were greatly concerned about the abuses that could occur if judges were allowed to issue general warrants.

Fifth Amendment

No person shall be held to answer for a capital, or otherwise infamous crime, unless on a presentment or indictment of a Grand Jury, except in cases arising in the land or naval forces, or in the Militia, when in actual service in time of War or public danger; nor shall any person be subject for the same offence to be twice put in jeopardy of life or limb; nor shall be compelled in any criminal case to be a witness against himself, nor be deprived of life, liberty or property, without due process of law; nor shall private property be taken for public use, without just compensation.

Like the Fourth Amendment, the Fifth Amendment contains several provisions that specify criminal procedures. These include:

1. The right to a grand jury indictment. As you will see in later chapters, the U.S. Supreme Court has not made this right binding on state criminal proceedings. Therefore, the states are free to use alternative procedures in their criminal justice systems.

2. The right to be free from double jeopardy. This right encompasses two separate protections: (1) The right not to be tried more than once for the same offense, and (2) The right not to receive more than one punishment for the same offense.

3. The privilege against self-incrimination.

4. The right not to be deprived of life, liberty, or property without due process of law.

Sixth Amendment

In all criminal prosecutions, the accused shall enjoy the right to a speedy and public trial, by an impartial jury of the State and district wherein the crime shall have been committed, which district shall have been previously ascertained by law, and to be informed of the nature and cause of the accusation; to be confronted with the witnesses against him; to have compulsory process for obtaining Witnesses in his favor, and to have the Assistance of Counsel for his defence.

The Sixth Amendment contains several independent protections for suspects in criminal proceedings. These include:

1. The right to a speedy and public trial;
2. The right to a trial by an impartial jury of the State and district wherein the crimes were committed;
3. The right to be informed of the nature of the charges that the State is bringing;
4. The right to confront adverse witnesses;
5. The right to compel witnesses to appear at trial;
6. The right to defense counsel.

Eighth Amendment

Excessive bail shall not be required, nor excessive fines imposed, nor cruel and unusual punishments inflicted.

Three independent protections are guaranteed by the Eighth Amendment.

1. Courts may not order excessive bail. Like the Fifth Amendment right to a grand jury indictment, however, the Supreme Court has not made this right binding on state proceedings. Therefore, the states are free to set bail at whatever level they deem proper.
2. Courts may not punish offenders with excessive fines.
3. Cruel and unusual punishments may not be imposed on a convicted offender.

Fourteenth Amendment

SECTION 1. All persons born or naturalized in the United States and subject to the jurisdiction thereof, are citizens of the United States and of the State wherein they reside. No State shall make or enforce any law which shall abridge the privileges or immunities of citizens of the United States; nor shall any State deprive any person of life, liberty, or property, without due process of law; nor deny to any person within its jurisdiction the equal protection of the laws.

Three independent protections are provided by Section 1 of the Fourteenth Amendment.

1. A state may not make or enforce any law which shall deny the privileges or immunities of U.S. citizens.
2. A state may not deprive any person of life, liberty, or property, without due process of law.
3. A state may not deny to any person within its jurisdiction the equal protection of the laws.

The Incorporation Debate.   The U.S. Constitution's Bill of Rights limits governmental power. As we observed in Chapter 1, persons are protected by both state constitutions and the federal constitution. Throughout much of U.S. history, however, state constitutions were regarded as the sole source of protections in state criminal proceedings. The federal constitution did not restrict the actions of state officials. In 1833, in *Barron* v. *Baltimore,*[32] the Supreme Court addressed the issue of whether the federal constitution was binding on state officials.

Barron, who owned a wharf in Baltimore, sued the city for diverting the water of several streams, which caused silt to be deposited around his wharf, and caused the wharf to become so shallow that ships were unable to use it to load cargo. Barron claimed that the city had violated the Fifth Amendment to the U.S. Constitution by taking his property without providing him with just compensation. Chief Justice John Marshall asserted that because the Fifth Amendment restricted only federal governmental action, the case did not present a valid federal question. Marshall further implied that the Bill of Rights did not limit state power. State citizens were protected solely by state constitutions.

The principle of law that emerged from this decision became known as the ***Barron* Doctrine,** which asserts that the federal constitution restricts only federal governmental action. The *Barron* Doctrine is associated with a **states' rights** view of federal and state governmental relations. An extreme view of this issue asserts that the U.S. Constitution is not binding on state governments and the federal government is powerless to control state proceedings. The states are free to pursue any policy they wish, even if their law violates a person's federally protected constitutional rights.

Barron v. *Baltimore* was decided in 1833. In the aftermath of the Civil War, however, it became clear that the *Barron* Doctrine was in need of revision. With the passage of the Fourteenth Amendment in 1868, new efforts were made to "nationalize" or "incorporate" the federal Bill of Rights, primarily by using that Amendment's Due Process Clause. These efforts were not immediately successful because the Supreme Court was not yet ready to abandon the *Barron* principle. In fact, it was not until 1925 that the Supreme Court first became willing to apply the protections of the federal Bill of Rights to state proceedings.[33] Even then, the Supreme Court did not adopt a **total incorporation** policy by holding that the entire federal Bill of Rights was binding on state proceedings. Rather, using a **selective incorporation** approach, the Court designated certain "fundamental rights" within the Bill of Rights to be critical to the U.S. governmental system. Fundamental rights were defined by Justice Benjamin Cardozo as those which are "implicit in the concept of ordered liberty."[34] Such rights may not be denied in state proceedings. It was left to the courts to decide which specific rights are fundamental on a case by case basis.

In various cases that have come before the Supreme Court, most of the essential provisions in the Bill of Rights have been made binding on state criminal proceedings through the Fourteenth Amendment's Due Process Clause. These cases are listed in Table 2.1. Some scholars believe that the Supreme Court's willingness, particularly during Chief Justice Earl Warren's tenure from 1952 to 1969, to nationalize provisions of the Bill of Rights resulted in a "Due Process Revolution" in criminal cases. We will consider this issue in greater detail in later chapters.

TABLE 2.1 **Provisions in the Bill of Rights Made Binding on State Proceedings Through the Due Process Clause of the Fourteenth Amendment**

Right	Amendment	Binding on States?	Case
Free from Unreasonable Search and Seizures	4th	Yes	*Wolf* v. *Colorado*, 338 U.S. 25 (1949)
Exclusionary Rule of Evidence	4th	Yes	*Mapp* v. *Ohio*, 367 U.S. 643 (1961)
Privilege Against Self-Incrimination	5th	Yes	*Malloy* v. *Hogan*, 378 U.S. 1 (1964)
Free from Double Jeopardy	5th	Yes	*Benton* v. *Maryland*, 395 U.S. 784 (1969)
Grand Jury Indictment	5th	No	*Hurtado* v. *California*, 110 U.S. 516 (1884)
Trial by Jury	6th	Yes	*Duncan* v. *Louisiana*, 391 U.S. 145 (1968)
Right to Counsel	6th	Yes	*Gideon* v. *Wainright*, 372 U.S. 335 (1963) [felony cases]; *Argersinger* v. *Hamlin*, 407 U.S. 25 (1975) [misdemeanor cases that may result in incarceration]
Speedy Trial	6th	Yes	*Klopfer* v. *North Carolina*, 386 U.S. 213 (1967)
Public Trial	6th	Yes	*In re Oliver*, 330 U.S. 257 (1948)
Confrontation of Adverse Witnesses	6th	Yes	*Pointer* v. *Texas*, 380 U.S. 400 (1965)
Compulsory Process for Obtaining Witnesses	6th	Yes	*Washington* v. *Texas*, 388 U.S. 14 (1967)
Free from Excessive Bail and Fines	8th	No	No case
Free from Cruel and Unusual Punishment	8th	Yes	*Robinson* v. *California*, 370 U.S. 660 (1962)

Summary

Chapter 2 begins with a short overview of basic legal concepts. It discusses the substantive and procedural aspects of criminal law. Procedural law regulates the various processes that the government must follow whenever it enforces the law or tries to take away someone's life, liberty, or property. Procedural legal questions are common in U.S. criminal justice systems. Examples of procedural questions include whether an individual was given proper *Miranda* warnings by the police when he or she was questioned about a crime, whether the police acted with a valid search warrant when they searched someone's home for evidence of a crime, and whether evidence should be excluded from trial because the police acted unlawfully.

The pretrial stages in the American criminal justice process are important and a defendant's procedural rights must be guaranteed. If any of the rights of the accused are violated during arrest, interrogation, investigation, or search and seizure, the evidence secured as a result of those violations may be excluded from the trial. Without the illegally seized evidence, some cases must be dismissed for lack of probable cause. The initial appearance, the preliminary hearing, the grand jury review, and the arraignment all are concerned with the issue of determining whether there is sufficient evidence to continue the case.

The historical basis for some of our most important constitutional rights, including the writ of habeas corpus, which permits anyone that is confined to be brought before a court to determine if they are being held lawfully, is considered too. The constitutional protection against bills of attainder prevents any act by either the federal or state legislatures that applies to named individuals or to easily identifiable members of a group in such a way as to inflict punishment on them without giving them a judicial trial. Likewise, the U.S. Constitution forbids ex post facto laws, which punish criminal behavior in a retroactive manner. General warrants and bills of attainder were additional practices in colonial America that led our nation's founders to adopt Constitutional protections against the abuse of governmental power. General warrants allowed law enforcement authorities to search any person or place for contraband, regardless of whether or not there was a reason to believe that the person had committed a crime or that a place concealed contraband. Writs of assistance permitted government law enforcement agents to search with unlimited discretion anyone suspected of criminal activity or anything believed to contain contraband. These abusive practices led directly to the development of our Constitution's Bill of Rights.

The constitutional amendments that most directly prescribe the criminal procedures that the government must follow include the Fourth, Fifth, Sixth, and Eighth Amendments, as applied to state proceedings through the Fourteenth Amendment's Due Process Clause. This chapter concludes with a discussion of the *Barron* Doctrine and the incorporation controversy and outlines the cases that have applied fundamental rights to state proceedings.

Review Questions

1. Distinguish between the substantive and procedural aspects of criminal law. Use an example to illustrate the distinction.
2. Describe and discuss the funnel effect phenomenon in the American criminal justice process.
3. Describe the main purposes of the initial appearance, preliminary hearing, and arraignment.
4. What is a grand jury review? How does that process differ from a prosecutor's information?

5. What purposes are served by pretrial motions and the discovery process?
6. Discuss the importance of the right to a writ of habeas corpus.
7. Discuss the significance of bills of attainder and ex post facto laws. What protections does the U.S. Constitution provide against these practices?
8. Discuss the significance of general warrants and writs of assistance. What influence did these practices have on the development of our Constitution's Bill of Rights?
9. Outline the essential provisions of the Fourth Amendment to the U.S. Constitution.
10. Outline the essential provisions of the Fifth Amendment to the U.S. Constitution.
11. Outline the essential provisions of the Sixth Amendment to the U.S. Constitution.
12. Outline the essential provisions of the Eighth Amendment to the U.S. Constitution.

Issues for Analysis and Discussion

1. Discuss the "incorporation" doctrine. Why is this doctrine important to an understanding of criminal procedure?
2. Present the basic assumptions of the following terms and concepts:
   a. The *Barron* Doctrine
   b. The "states' rights" perspective on incorporation
   c. The "total incorporation" perspective
   d. "Selective" incorporation
3. Highlight 2.3 presents an overview of the Oklahoma City bombing tragedy. In your opinion, should government law enforcement agencies be given greater power to investigate "subversive groups"? Discuss the potential dangers associated with expanding police power in this way.

Endnotes

1. New York Penal Code, Title N, Section 240.25 *et seq.* (1994).
2. Herbert L. Packer, *The Limits of the Criminal Sanction,* (Palo Alto, Cal.: Stanford University Press, 1968).
3. Sue Titus Reid, *Criminal Justice,* 3d ed. (New York, N.Y.: Macmillan, 1993), p. 391.
4. Id. at 391–392; Wayne R. LaFave and Jerold H. Israel, *Criminal Procedure,* (St. Paul, Minn.: West, 1985) pp. 19–20.
5. Id.
6. See Wayne R. LaFave and Jerold H. Israel, *Criminal Procedure,* 2d ed. (St. Paul, Minn.: West, 1985), pp. 18–29. Portions of the preceeding discussion were taken from this excellent resource.
7. See *Mapp* v. *Ohio,* 367 U.S. 643, 81 S.Ct. 1684 (1961).
8. See *McNabb* v. *United States,* 318 U.S. 332 (1943).
9. See *Argersinger* v. *Hamlin,* 407 U.S. 25 (1972).
10. See *Gideon* v. *Wainright,* 372 U.S. 335 (1963).
11. Reid, supra note 3 at 403.
12. Reid, supra note 3 at 405.
13. See LaFave and Israel, supra note 6 at 899.
14. *McNabb* v. *United States,* 318 U.S. 332 (1943).
15. Id. at 614.
16. Massachusetts Constitution of 1780, Pt. 2, Ch. 6, Art 7.
17. United States Constitution, Article I, Section 9.
18. *Ex Parte Yerger,* 8 U.S. 85, 95 (1868).
19. *Fay* v. *Noia,* 372 U.S. 391, 401–402 (1963).
20. United States Constitution, Article I, Section 9.
21. United States Constitution, Article I, Section 10.

22. See Laurence H. Tribe, *American Constitutional Law,* 2d ed. (Mineola, N.Y.: Foundation, 1988), p. 641.

23. *United States* v. *Lovett,* 328 U.S. 303, 315 (1946).

24. Id.

25. Id. at 318.

26. *United States* v. *Brown,* 381 U.S. 437 (1965).

27. Id. at 450.

28. See "Terror in Oklahoma City: The Investigation." *The New York Times,* April 20, 1995, p. A.1.

29. *Collins* v. *Youngblood,* 497 U.S. 37 (1990), *remanded* 909 F.2d 803 (5th Cir. 1990).

30. For an excellent discussion of the historical development of the Fourth Amendment and the exclusionary rule of evidence, see Potter Stewart, "The Road to *Mapp* v. *Ohio* and Beyond: The Origins, Development and Future of the Exclusionary Rule in Search and Seizure Cases," 83 *Columbia Law Review* pp. 1365–1404 (1983).

31. *Illinois* v. *Gates,* 462 U.S. 213 (1983).

32. *Barron* v. *Baltimore,* 32 U.S. 243 (1833).

33. *Gitlow* v. *New York,* 268 U.S. 652 (1925).

34. *Palko* v. *Connecticut,* 302 U.S. 319 (1937).

3   THE EXCLUSIONARY RULE OF EVIDENCE

Outline

Key Terms

Chapter 2 discussed U.S. criminal justice processes and illustrated the typical progression of a criminal case through the justice systems. The concept of due process of law that is guaranteed to all persons by the Fourteenth Amendment to the U.S. Constitution was discussed. This chapter examines in greater detail the philosophy of due process of law and begins a more detailed analysis of procedural law. An essential aspect of procedural law in U.S. justice systems, the exclusionary rule of evidence, is analyzed in significant detail.

Due Process of Law

The Fifth and Fourteenth Amendments to the Constitution provide that persons shall not be deprived of "life, liberty, or property, without due process of law." The first question one might ask is: Why was it necessary to include two different due process guarantees in the U.S. Constitution? The answer to this question is found in Chapter 2's discussion of the incorporation debate and the nature of federal and state relations in U.S. governmental systems. The Fifth Amendment's clause guarantees that the *federal* government may not deny due process of law to any person. The Fourteenth Amendment's due process clause guards against infringement of procedural safeguards by *state* governments.

A second question concerns the nature of due process. What is due process of law and why is it such a critical aspect of our justice systems? Due process of law expresses the philosophy of fair treatment for all persons upon which our legal systems are based. It has proven difficult to define because it is a fluid concept that changes as society grows and matures. To understand due process of law, it is helpful to consider two related but distinct aspects of this concept.

Substantive Due Process

An immense number of statutory laws have been passed by U.S. legislatures. The vast majority of these laws are valid exercises of legislative authority. What happens, however, if a legislature goes too far and enacts a law that destroys a person's ability to enjoy "life, liberty, or property"? For example, in *Griswold* v. *Connecticut,*[1] the State of Connecticut had passed a law that made it a crime for a person to "use any drug, medicinal article or instrument for the purpose of preventing conception."[2] Anyone violating this statute would be fined not less than $50 or imprisoned not less than 60 days nor more than one year, or both. Another statute made it a crime for any person, including physicians, to provide counseling or assistance to persons seeking to prevent conception.[3] Alan Griswold, Executive Director of the Planned Parenthood League of Connecticut, and David Buxton, a physician who served as Medical Director for Planned Parenthood, were charged with providing counseling and assistance to persons seeking to prevent conception. They were convicted and fined $100 each. Griswold and Buxton appealed, claiming that the Connecticut statutes violated the Fourteenth Amendment's due process guarantee.

The U.S. Supreme Court held that the Connecticut statutes invaded a "zone of privacy created by several fundamental constitutional guarantees."[4] Moreover, the laws were "repulsive to the notions of privacy surrounding the marriage relationship . . . a right of privacy older than the [Constitution]."[5] Consequently, the Connecticut statutes violated the Fourteenth Amendment's due process guarantee.

Griswold v. *Connecticut* illustrates that state laws may not regulate certain aspects of life. There are areas into which a state's laws may not intrude. If the "substance" of a law passed by a state's legislature invades a constitutionally protected zone of privacy, the law will be held to violate the Fourteenth Amendment's due process guarantee.[6] This idea is termed **substantive due process**—state laws may not destroy the basic enjoyment of life, liberty, or property regardless of the fairness of the procedures used to do so.[7]

State legislatures are empowered to pass laws that promote the health, welfare and safety, or morality of its citizens. This broad grant of authority, termed state **police powers,** allows state governments to regulate almost any area of life that may be related to public health or safety.[8] Only rarely do individuals challenge "the substance" of state laws, or a state's authority to pass laws. As a result, substantive due process cases are very rare in the U.S. legal system. The next section considers another aspect of due process of law, however, which is more directly related to our study of criminal procedures.

Procedural Due Process

Many cases decided by the Supreme Court concern procedural due process issues. **Procedural due process** of law involves the processes or procedures that the government must follow whenever it seeks to take someone's life, liberty, or property.[9] For example, in *Goldberg* v. *Kelly,*[10] an administrative law case, a woman's welfare benefits were terminated by New York City officials. The recipient was not given an evidentiary hearing before her benefits were terminated. The U.S. Supreme Court held that the Fourteenth Amendment's due process clause required that she be given such a hearing. Moreover, the Court held that persons facing welfare benefit termination proceedings have the following procedural due process rights:

1. The right to confront and cross-examine opposing witnesses;
2. The right to retain counsel;
3. The right to present oral evidence;
4. The right to an impartial decision-maker; and
5. The right to a decision based solely on the evidence in the record produced at the hearing.

Goldberg v. *Kelly* involved **administrative law,** a body of law that regulates the way administrative agencies must exercise their discretion when dealing with the public. Possible sanctions that an administrative agency may levy against those who have violated its rules include imposing fines, issuing orders commanding persons to cease and desist certain types of behaviors, and terminating benefits. An important conclusion to be derived from *Goldberg* v. *Kelly* is that those facing adverse action by governmental agencies have procedural due process rights, even though the possible sanctions in these proceedings are not as serious as those faced by criminal defendants.[11] Suspects in criminal proceedings receive even more stringent procedural due process safeguards.

The U.S. Constitution provides a number of different procedural due process safeguards in criminal cases. These protections are specifically listed in the Fourth, Fifth, Sixth, and Eighth Amendments. For example, the Fourth Amendment details the procedures that police agencies must follow in order to obtain a valid search warrant. Likewise, the Fifth Amendment provides that persons may not be subjected to double jeopardy. The Sixth Amendment guarantees the right to counsel in criminal cases. Chapter 2 described cases that have incorporated various rights into state criminal proceedings. These cases have provided procedural due process safeguards. One important procedural due process safeguard that has received considerable attention in recent years is the exclusionary rule of evidence. The remainder of this chapter focuses on the history and development of this important procedural safeguard.

The Exclusionary Rule of Evidence

One of the more controversial practices in U.S. criminal justice systems is the **exclusionary rule of evidence.** It provides that evidence obtained in violation of a defendant's constitutionally protected rights may not be used against him or her in a criminal trial.[12]

The exclusionary rule may require the suppression of evidence obtained through a violation of a suspect's Fourth Amendment rights. U.S. courts developed the exclusionary rule to remedy violations of suspects' Fourth Amendment rights; however, violations of suspects' Fifth and Sixth Amendment rights may lead to the suppression or exclusion of evidence in criminal cases as well. To illustrate, if police officers enter someone's home illegally without a search warrant and discover evidence, it may not be used against the homeowner at trial. Likewise, if a suspect is forced by the use of torture to incriminate himself, or is not given the *Miranda* warnings during custodial interrogation, the confession may not be used at trial. In addition, if while being questioned by the police an arrested suspect's request for counsel is denied, any of the suspect's subsequent incriminating statements must be suppressed.

The late Supreme Court Justice Benjamin Cardozo posed the exclusionary rule dilemma as follows: Is the criminal to go free because the constable has blundered?[13] Proponents of the exclusionary rule believe that it is needed to ensure the integrity of our justice system. Exclusionary rule opponents believe that it deprives society of the opportunity to convict guilty people who have violated its laws.[14] Highlight 3.1 provides an overview of the exclusionary rule debate.

The exclusionary rule debate poses difficult questions for U.S. justice systems. In order to present a comprehensive discussion of the exclusionary rule, it is useful to review the purposes and rationales that have been used to support the rule.

Highlight 3.1

The Exclusionary Rule Debate

 ### Arguments Supporting the Exclusionary Rule

Yale Kamisar, 62 *Judicature* (pp. 66–84) (Aug. 1978) (Excerpted, citations omitted).

More than 50 years have passed since the Supreme Court decided the *Weeks* case, barring the use in federal prosecutions of evidence obtained in violation of the Fourth Amendment, and the *Silverthorne* case, invoking what has come to be known as the "fruit of the poisonous tree" doctrine. The justices who decided those cases would, I think, be quite surprised to learn that some day the value of the exclusionary rule would be measured by—and the very life of the rule might depend on—an empirical evaluation of [its ability to deter police misconduct].

A court which admits [illegally obtained evidence] manifests a willingness to tolerate the unconstitutional conduct which produced it. How can the police and the citizenry be expected "to believe that the government truly meant to forbid the conduct in the first place"? Why should the police or the public accept the argument that the available remedies permit the court to admit the evidence without sanctioning the underlying misconduct when the greater possibility of alternative remedies in the "flagrant" or "willful" case does not allow the court to do so?

A court which admits the evidence in a case involving a "run of the mill" Fourth Amendment violation demonstrates an insufficient commitment to the guarantee against unreasonable search and seizure. It demonstrates "the contrast between morality professed by society and immorality practiced on its behalf." It signifies that government officials need not always "be subjected to the same rules of conduct that are commands to the citizens."

Where should the threshold for exclusion be put? At what point should a judge say that the police misconduct is so indefensible or offensive as to warrant throwing out the evidence it produced? To say that

this point is not reached until the police have resorted to violence or brutality or that it is not reached unless they have perpetrated some "gross" or "serious" or "aggravated" violation of the Constitution seems neither a principled nor a manageable way to go about it.

If the line must be drawn somewhere, I can think of no more logical and fitting place to draw it than at unconstitutional police conduct, however "mild," "honest" or "inadvertent" some may label it. Once the court identifies the police action as unconstitutional, that ought to be the end of the matter. There should be no "degrees" of "offensiveness" among different varieties of *unconstitutional* police conduct. A violation of the Constitution ought to be the "bottom line." This is where the *Weeks* and *Mapp* Courts drew the line. This is where it ought to stay.

Arguments Against the Exclusionary Rule

Malcolm Richard Wilkey, "The exclusionary rule: why suppress valid evidence?" 62 *Judicature* p. 214 (Nov. 1978) (Excerpted, citations omitted).

America is now ready to confront frankly and to examine realistically both the achievements and social costs of the policies which have been so hopefully enacted in the past 40 years. That reappraisal has made the most headlines in regard to economic and fiscal matters. It is imperative that this honest reappraisal include the huge social costs which American society—alone in the civilized world—pays as a result of our unique exclusionary rule of evidence in criminal cases.

We can see that huge social cost most clearly in the distressing rate of street crimes—assaults and robberies with deadly weapons, narcotics trafficking, gambling and prostitution—which flourish in no small degree simply because of the exclusionary rule of evidence.

(Continued)

(Concluded)

To this high price we can rightfully add specific, pernicious police conduct and lack of discipline—the very opposite of the objectives of the rule itself.

[The exclusionary rule of evidence must be defended] on one of two grounds, and on that analysis neither is defensible.

First, if Professor Kamisar believes that the Fourth Amendment necessarily mandates the exclusionary rule, then he ought to cite Supreme Court authority for this position. It is undeniable that at no time in the Court's history has a majority in any case ever so held, and I do not believe that any more than two individual justices in the court's history have so expressed themselves. In contrast, numerous justices, both favoring and opposing the rule, have stated that the rule itself is *not* mandated by the Fourth Amendment.

Second, if Professor Kamisar's article is intended only to say that under the Constitution we have a choice of methods to enforce the ban against 'unreasonable searches and seizures,' and that the exclusionary rule is a good choice only because of "the imperative of judicial integrity," then I submit both logic and experience in this country and all other countries refutes this. If the Supreme Court or the Congress has a choice of methods under the Constitution, then it simply will not do to rest the choice of the exclusionary rule solely on the high principle of 'judicial integrity' and to ignore the pragmatic result, the failure to achieve the objective of enforcement and the other pernicious side effects discussed above, which themselves strongly discredit judicial integrity.

If we have a choice, to attempt to justify the continuation of the exclusionary rule on this basis is to be stubbornly blind to 65 years of experience. If we have a choice, to insist on continuing a method of enforcement with as many demonstrated faults as the exclusionary rule is to be blindly stubborn. If we have a choice, let us calmly and carefully consider the available alternatives, draw upon the experience of other nations with systems of justice similar to our own, and by abolishing the rule permit in the laboratories of our 51 jurisdictions the experimentation with various possible alternatives promising far more than the now discredited exclusionary rule.

Excepts from Yale Kamisar, "Is the Exclusionary Rule an 'Illogical' or 'Unnatural' Interpretation of the Fourth Amendment?" *Judicature,* Vol. 62, August 1978, pp. 66–84. Reprinted by permission of the author.

Justifications for the Exclusionary Rule

Since it was first applied to U.S. criminal trials, four rationales for the exclusionary rule of evidence have emerged. The first is termed the **systemic rationale,** which asserts that the use of illegally obtained evidence in a criminal trial compromises the integrity of the entire judicial system.[15] Advocates of this rationale believe that U.S. courts should not become "accomplices in the willful disobedience of a Constitution they are sworn to uphold."[16]

A related justification for the exclusionary rule is the **public trust rationale.** It asserts that in a democratic society people must be able to trust the government. If the government uses unlawfully obtained evidence in criminal cases, it may jeopardize public trust in the court system and undermine popular faith in our governmental system.[17]

A third justification for the exclusionary rule is the **individual rights rationale.** This position asserts that all persons have basic rights that the government violates if the fruits of an illegal search and seizure are used in a criminal trial. The exclusionary rule of evidence is designed to protect those basic rights. In contrast to the systemic rationale, the individual rights perspective does not consider the effect of illegally obtained evidence on governmental institutions. Rather, it maintains that basic individual rights should receive priority in society. Using illegally obtained evidence violates those basic rights.

Another justification for the exclusionary rule is the **deterrence of unlawful police conduct rationale,** which suggests that the exclusionary rule's sole purpose is to deter unlawful police behavior. If excluding evidence at trial will not deter unlawful police conduct, the evidence should be admitted. In *United States* v. *Leon*[18] and numerous other cases,[19] the Supreme Court has voiced strong support for this justification.

The Historical Development of the Exclusionary Rule

The exclusionary rule of evidence has a long history in U.S. justice systems. In 1886, *Boyd* v. *United States*[20] asserted that evidence obtained in violation of the Fourth Amendment should be excluded from federal criminal trials. In 1914, however, *Weeks* v. *United States,*[21] made the exclusionary rule binding in all federal criminal trials. This same protection did not apply to suspects victimized by the unlawful conduct of state officers, however. As Chapter 2 observed, for much of U.S. history the federal Constitution was not viewed as a limitation on state power. The states were not required to follow the federal exclusionary rule and were free to admit unlawfully obtained evidence.

In 1949, in *Wolf* v. *Colorado,*[22] the Supreme Court was asked to determine if evidence obtained in violation of the Fourth Amendment must be excluded in state courts. The Court held that the Fourth Amendment's protection against unlawful searches and seizures applies to the states through the Fourteenth Amendment's due process clause. The states, however, were not required to adopt the exclusionary rule because the victims of illegal searches by state or local law enforcement officers had other remedies. These included tort remedies, "the internal discipline of the police, under the eyes of an alert public,"[23] and a watchful press. A **tort** action is a private civil action for damages, other than a breach of contract, that alleges a breach of some duty owed to a **plaintiff** (the party who is wronged) by a **defendant** (the party who owes the duty). The *Wolf* doctrine was, however, short-lived.

Rochin v. *California,*[24] decided in 1952, presented a compelling case for applying the exclusionary rule to state proceedings. In this case police received "some information" that Rochin was selling narcotics. Three deputy sheriffs entered Rochin's home unlawfully and forced open the door to his bedroom, where they found him sitting partly dressed on the side of the bed. The police observed two capsules on a night table beside the bed. When they asked Rochin, "Whose stuff is this?" he swallowed the capsules. The deputies struggled with Rochin to prevent him from swallowing the capsules; when this failed, they took him to a hospital where at the officers' direction a doctor forced a stomach pumping solution into Rochin's stomach. He vomited the capsules which contained morphine. Rochin was convicted of possessing morphine and was sentenced to 60 days' imprisonment. The primary evidence against him was the two capsules.

The Supreme Court held that the deputies' conduct violated due process of law. Justice Frankfurter stated:

> This is conduct that shocks the conscience. Illegally breaking into the privacy of the petitioner, the struggle to open his mouth and remove what was there, the forcible extraction of his stomach's contents—this course of proceeding by agents of government to obtain evidence is

bound to offend even hardened sensibilities. They are methods too close to the rack and screw to permit of constitutional differentiation.[25]

Rochin represented a qualified expansion of the exclusionary rule's protections in state criminal cases: When state law enforcement agents obtained evidence in a manner that "shock[ed] the conscience," the Fourteenth Amendment's due process clause would bar the evidence at trial. It was left to later cases to expand the scope of the exclusionary rule.

The Silver Platter Doctrine

An important issue that was left unresolved by the early Fourth Amendment exclusionary rule cases involved the **silver platter doctrine,** which allowed evidence obtained unlawfully by state agents to be used in federal trials. *Weeks* v. *United States* held that the exclusionary rule of evidence prevented evidence unlawfully obtained by federal officers from being introduced at federal criminal trials. It did not, however, bar the introduction of evidence unlawfully obtained by state law enforcement officers from the same criminal trials. In such circumstances it proved tempting for state law enforcement authorities to conduct unlawful searches, seize contraband, and provide the evidence to federal prosecutors for use in federal trials.[26] To follow the metaphor, state law enforcement agents, who had obtained evidence illegally, were handing the case to federal authorities on a silver platter. In 1960, *Elkins* v. *United States*[27] rejected the silver platter doctrine because it had undermined state efforts to enforce the Fourth Amendment. By eliminating the silver platter doctrine, the Supreme Court took another step toward adopting a full-fledged exclusionary rule of evidence in Fourth Amendment cases.

The Legacy of **Mapp** *v.* **Ohio**

Mapp v. *Ohio*[28] provided the Supreme Court with an opportunity to reconsider *Wolf* v. *Colorado*'s assertion that police internal discipline and an alert public would prevent state law enforcement authorities from violating suspects' Fourth Amendment rights. By the early 1960s, it had become apparent that a more decisive measure was needed to prevent Fourth Amendment violations. In *Mapp,* Dolree Mapp was convicted of the possession and control of obscene material. The evidence used to convict her was unlawfully obtained by police officers who had forcibly entered her home without a search warrant. The Supreme Court held that "all evidence" obtained in violation of the Fourth Amendment must be excluded in state trials. The Court reasoned that without the exclusionary rule "the assurance against unreasonable . . . searches and seizures would be 'a form of words,' valueless and undeserving of mention in a perpetual charter of inestimable human liberties."[29]

Mapp v. *Ohio* has exerted a substantial impact on the U.S. legal system for several reasons.[30] First, it required state authorities to exclude from trial evidence obtained in violation of defendants' Fourth Amendment rights. In addition, it has led some commentators to suggest that such rules of evidence "handcuff" the police and permit the guilty to go free. Although there is no direct evidence concerning the exclusionary

Highlight 3.2

Empirical Research on the Effects
of the Exclusionary Rule in Fourth Amendment Cases

The greatest contribution of the empirical data on the costs of the exclusionary rule is simply that they expose the erroneous stereotypes that dominate public dialog and demonstrate the need to rethink our expectations about due process standards. Indeed, the available data on the costs of the rule should refocus consideration of the rule's benefits as a deterrent.

For years, the debate over the exclusionary rule has been dominated by the critics' claims that the rule is a weak deterrent *and* results in high costs. Although that combination always seemed improbable, the data showing the low overall cost of the rule should stimulate rethinking of the rule's deterrent function. In addition to deflating the purported costs of the rule to more realistic proportions, the low percentage of arrests lost because of illegal searches also demonstrates the unrealistic nature of the critics' demands that the rule be judged in terms of its ability to deter individual police officers from conducting illegal searches. The data on the effects of the rule suggest that the average police officer is seldom involved in an illegal search that leads to the loss of an arrest. Hence, given that the effects of the rule are seldom experienced by individual officers, it seems clear that the rule operates primarily as a general or systematic deterrent influencing police policies, training, and at-

titudes. The critics' demand that the rule justify itself in specific deterrence terms rather than in broader educative terms has been based on exaggerated perceptions of the rule's costs; since available data consistently show the costs of the rule are modest, the important educative benefits of the rule should be more than sufficient for its justification. Viewed in these terms, the general "deterrent" function of the rule can once again be merged into the principled rationale from which the rule originated—the need for the courts to give substance to the otherwise hollow words of the Fourth Amendment and demonstrate to the police and the citizenry in unambiguous terms that illegal searches are unacceptable.

If the available data on the modest costs of the exclusionary rule receive sufficient attention, perhaps the public dialog can move away from the perception that due process standards and effective law enforcement are necessarily in conflict. Empirical research tells us that the exclusionary rule is neither a panacea to eliminate instances of police lawlessness nor an escape hatch for hordes of hardened criminals. Rather, it is a moderate policy expressing this nation's commitment to values of personal privacy, equality, and the rule of law. In that perspective, the costs of the exclusionary rule are hardly excessive.

(Continued)

rule's impact on the day-to-day operations of the police, there is evidence to suggest that the rule's impact on the U.S. criminal justice system is relatively minimal.[31] Highlight 3.2 presents the results of a 1984 United States Justice Department study on the impact of the exclusionary rule of evidence of criminal prosecutions in California.

Self-Incrimination, Miranda, and the Right to Counsel

The discussion to this point has focused on Fourth Amendment exclusionary rule cases. As stated earlier, however, evidence suppression issues may arise in Fifth or Sixth Amendment cases as well. For example, suppose that a defendant makes incriminating

(Concluded)

Adult Felony Arrests Submitted to California Prosecutors for Complaints, Arrests Rejected for "Illegal Search," and Percentage of Submitted Arrests Rejected for "Illegal Search," 1978–81.

	No. Arrests Presented	No. Arrests Rejected	% Rejected		No. Arrests Presented	No. Arrests Rejected	% Rejected
All Offense Categories				**Burglary**			
1978	123,270	975	0.79	1978	23,126	74	0.32
1979	138,649	1,014	0.73	1979	24,939	35	0.14
1980	154,066	1,311	1.01	1980	27,606	73	0.26
1981	167,284	1,432	0.86	1981	31,220	67	0.21
1982	N.A.	N.A.	N.A.	1982	35,823	75	0.21
Total	N.A.	N.A.	N.A.	Total	142,714	324	0.23
Homicide				**Theft**			
1978	1,116	4	0.36	1978	14,932	63	0.42
1979	1,388	0	...	1979	17,185	71	0.41
1980	1,536	0	...	1980	20,098	119	0.59
1981	2,174	4	0.18	1981	22,788	146	0.64
1982	3,336	0	...	1982	27,719	170	0.61
Total	9,552	8	0.08	Total	102,722	569	0.55
Forcible Rape				**Vehicle Theft**			
1978	1,662	4	0.24	1978	7,007	13	0.19
1979	1,840	2	0.11	1979	7,591	13	0.17
1980	2,402	3	0.12	1980	7,754	11	0.14
1981	2,539	3	0.12	1981	8,201	21	0.26
1982	2,977	1	0.03	1982	7,880	29	0.37
Total	11,420	13	0.11	Total	38,431	87	0.23
Robbery				**Drug Violations**			
1978	8,290	21	0.25	1978	28,181	649	2.30
1979	9,388	27	0.29	1979	31,352	736	2.35
1980	10,456	8	0.08	1980	34,813	938	2.69
1981	12,259	33	0.27	1981	35,669	978	2.79
1982	13,514	28	0.21	1982	38,354	1,352	3.53
Total	53,920	117	0.22	Total	168,369	4,653	2.76
Assault				**Other**			
1978	19,455	52	0.27	1978	19,503	95	0.49
1979	22,447	50	0.22	1979	22,519	80	0.36
1980	24,691	39	0.16	1980	24,697	120	0.49
1981	25,323	24	0.09	1981	27,109	156	0.58
1982	23,122	24	0.10	1982	N.A.	N.A.	N.A.
Total	115,038	189	0.16	Total	N.A.	N.A.	N.A.

Excerpt from Thomas Y. Davies, "A Hard Look at What We Know . . ." *American Bar Foundation Research Journal,* No. 611, 1983. [Reprinted by permission of the American Bar Foundation.]

statements following an illegal arrest. This case involves both Fourth and Fifth Amendment evidence suppression issues. Likewise, suppose a defendant who is not given the *Miranda* warnings is not allowed to have counsel present. Such a case would present Fifth and Sixth Amendment evidence suppression issues. The point is that evidence suppression issues are often difficult to categorize, and that Fourth, Fifth, and Sixth Amendment rights function as complementary protections in U.S. justice systems.

Exceptions to the Exclusionary Rule

The U.S. Supreme Court has identified five different situations in which U.S. courts may admit illegally obtained evidence: (1) a "good-faith exception"—when police officers act in good-faith reliance on an apparently valid search warrant, on a law permitting the challenged search, or when the search results from an invalid arrest caused by the errors of court personnel; (2) a "purged taint" exception—when the connection between the unlawful police conduct and the unlawful evidence is sufficiently broken so that it cures the "illegal" nature of the evidence; (3) an independent source exception—when evidence is obtained from an independent source, even if the police had engaged in misconduct; (4) an "inevitable discovery" exception—when the evidence inevitably would have been discovered by proper means; and (5) when "impeaching" a defendant's trial testimony.

The Good-Faith Exception

During Earl Warren's tenure as chief justice of the U.S. Supreme Court from 1952 to 1969, the U.S. legal system witnessed what has been called a **due process revolution** in criminal proceedings. This means that during this period most of the provisions in the Constitution's Bill of Rights were incorporated, or made binding on state criminal proceedings through the Fourteenth Amendment's due process clause.

When Chief Justice Warren retired from the Court in 1969, Warren Burger was appointed by President Richard M. Nixon to replace him. From 1970 to 1981, five Supreme Court justices retired, allowing the Executive Branch to appoint new Supreme Court justices. Some of the new justices' judicial philosophies differed markedly from their Warren Court predecessors. While the Burger Court declined to reverse many of the most important Warren Court criminal procedure decisions, including *Mapp* v. *Ohio,* the new Court adopted a more conservative law-and-order judicial philosophy.

In a dissenting opinion in 1971, Chief Justice Warren Burger suggested a new approach to Fourth Amendment exclusionary rule issues.[32] Burger maintained that a statutory alternative to the rule should be developed that would permit the victims of Fourth Amendment violations to sue the government for damages. In 1976, Justice Byron White stated a similar view. White asserted that the exclusionary rule should be changed "to prevent its application in those many circumstances where the evidence at issue was seized by an officer acting in the good-faith belief that his conduct comported" with current law.[33] This is because in such circumstances the exclusionary rule would not have deterred police misconduct.

In *United States* v. *Leon,*[34] a Supreme Court majority developed a **good-faith exception** to the exclusionary rule. This exception permits evidence to be used at trial despite a violation of a suspect's constitutional rights if the police were acting in good faith when the error was committed. In *Leon,* police officers who were preparing a search warrant affidavit used information from an informant as well as information obtained through their own investigation. A **search warrant affidavit** is a document presented to a magistrate by a police officer listing the reasons for believing that probable cause exists to search a particular place for a particular thing. A judge had issued the search warrant, and unlawful drugs were found at the premises specified in the warrant. The trial court concluded that the original probable cause affidavit was deficient and failed to establish probable cause because it did not show that the informant was credible and because it had relied on **stale information.** Such information is no longer valid because it is outdated.

Sanctioning the good-faith exception to the exclusionary rule, Justice Byron White stated that the exclusionary rule is not required by the U.S. Constitution in Fourth Amendment cases and is not a personal constitutional right of an accused. Rather, the exclusionary rule is a "judicially created" safeguard "designed to deter police misconduct rather than to punish the errors of judges and magistrates."[35] The *Leon* majority used a balancing test to determine whether the exclusionary rule should apply. On one side of the scale the Court placed the costs of excluding evidence, including the fact that "some guilty defendants may go free."[36] This important social interest was balanced with the benefits of the rule in cases in which the police act with a **facially valid search warrant.** This means that a reasonably competent police officer would not recognize that the warrant is defective. The Court concluded that when the police act in good faith reliance on a search warrant, the costs of the exclusionary rule clearly outweigh its benefits, because punishing "the police officer for the magistrate's error, rather than his own, cannot logically contribute to the deterrence of Fourth Amendment violations."[37]

The Supreme Court extended *Leon's* reasoning in *Massachusetts* v. *Sheppard.*[38] In *Sheppard,* a police search warrant affidavit demonstrated probable cause to conduct a search for evidence in a murder case. The affidavit was prepared on an improper form, however, and the judge approved a form normally reserved to apply for search warrants in unlawful drug cases. The judge assured the officer that he would make the needed changes to make the warrant proper, but he failed to do so completely. The judge did not change the part of the warrant that authorized a search only for unlawful narcotics. Acting with the defective warrant, the police officers seized evidence that was used later to convict Sheppard of murder. On appeal, Justice Byron White, writing for the Court, held that this case fell within *Leon's* good-faith exception to the exclusionary rule because "there was an objectively reasonable basis for the officers' mistaken belief" in the validity of their search warrant.[39]

The Supreme Court has held that the *Leon* exception applies to situations in which police officers act in reasonable reliance on a state law that authorizes a challenged search but where the statute is determined subsequently to be unconstitutional. In *Illinois* v. *Krull,*[40] an Illinois law allowed a warrantless search of the premises of persons dealing in the sale of used automotive parts. After the police conducted a search based on this statute, the defendant was arrested for failing to keep transaction records as required by law. The Supreme Court used the deterrence rationale to support its conclusion that the *Leon* exception should apply to these cases—no deterrent effect would be realized by excluding evidence when the police reasonably rely upon a statute. The officers could not have known that the statute would later be declared unconstitutional. Moreover, there was no evidence to indicate that applying the rule to statutes would deter legislators from passing unconstitutional laws.

The *Leon* exception cases suggest that there are "exceptions to exceptions." In other words, *Leon* does not mean that the good-faith exception will apply to all defective search warrant cases. In fact, *Leon* does not apply to any case in which a police officer's reliance on a search warrant was not reasonable. This may occur in several different situations: first, if the warrant was issued based on an affidavit that is intentionally falsified;[41] second, if a magistrate abandons his or her neutral judicial role and begins to behave as a prosecutor;[42] third, if an affidavit supporting issuance of a warrant is so lacking in its indication of probable cause as to render the magistrate's "belief in its existence entirely unreasonable";[43] and finally, when the warrant itself is so facially deficient that a reasonable police officer would not have believed that it was valid.[44] Moreover, several state supreme courts have refused to follow *Leon,* holding that their state constitutions do not permit adoption of the good-faith exception.[45]

In 1995, the Supreme Court further expanded the scope of the good-faith exception to the exclusionary rule. In *Arizona* v. *Evans,*[46] the Court held that the good-faith exception applied to evidence seized following a court clerical employee's error that failed to cancel an outstanding arrest warrant. Evans, who was arrested by police under the faulty warrant, was charged with possession of marijuana following a search of his vehicle. At a pretrial suppression hearing he moved to suppress the evidence as the fruit of the unlawful arrest. On appeal, the Supreme Court held that *United States* v. *Leon,* "supports a categorical exception to the exclusionary rule for clerical errors of court employees."[47] This is because the exclusionary rule was historically designed as a means of deterring police misconduct, not mistakes by court employees. Chief Justice Rehnquist stated:

> [T]here is no basis for believing that application of the exclusionary rule in these circumstances will have a significant effect on court employees responsible for informing the police that a warrant has been quashed . . . The threat of exclusion of evidence could not be expected to deter such individuals from failing to inform police officials that a warrant has been quashed.[48]

Expanding the Good-Faith Exception. The preceding discussion illustrates that the *Leon* exception to the exclusionary rule applies to searches where police officers execute faulty search warrants that have been approved by judges or magistrates. In addition, evidence need not be excluded if it is found after an arrest based on an unconstitutional statute or a court employee's failure to cancel an outstanding arrest warrant. An important question concerns whether in the future the good-faith exception will be expanded to include situations where police officers acting *without* a search warrant violate the Constitution.[49] A reviewing court's analysis in such circumstances may be limited to determining if police behavior was "objectively reasonable." If so, any evidence could be admitted. A proposed crime-control law introduced into the United States House of Representatives contains a section that would allow evidence obtained by police officers who had acted in good faith, but without a search warrant, to be used in criminal proceedings. This law would apply solely to federal law enforcement officers; however, states may decide to model similar statutes after the federal law. Excerpts from that proposed law are presented in Highlight 3.3.

The implications of recognizing such an approach to the exclusionary rule are substantial for U.S. justice systems—fewer instances of unlawful police behavior could be successfully challenged in court. Proponents of a modified exclusionary rule continue to point to alternative measures for controlling unlawful police behavior. As U.S. justice systems learned, however, after *Wolf* v. *Colorado,* such measures may fail to strike the proper balance between citizens' rights and governmental efforts to control criminal behavior.

The Fruit of the Poisonous Tree Doctrine

The exclusionary rule bars evidence that has been obtained by police as the result of a direct violation of a defendant's constitutional rights. What happens, however, when the police indirectly obtain evidence after a defendant's rights are violated? In *Nardone* v. *United States,*[50] the Supreme Court described such indirect evidence as the "fruit of the poisonous tree." The Supreme Court has held that the exclusionary rule bars indirect, derivative evidence in addition to the more direct use of unlawfully obtained evidence. To follow the Supreme Court's biblical metaphor, the poisonous tree is usually an unlawful arrest or an illegal confession. The question is whether the fruit from the poisonous tree, such as incriminating statements made by a suspect after he or she was illegally arrested, must be excluded at trial. Figure 3.1 depicts the fruit of the poisonous tree doctrine. The Supreme Court has held that if the illegally obtained evidence is somehow purged of its original taint, the evidence may be used. If the evidence is not purged, it is barred from use at trial. The next section presents a more complete discussion of the purged taint exception to the exclusionary rule.

The Purged Taint Exception

A second exception to the exclusionary rule of evidence occurs when the connection is broken between unlawful police conduct and the tainted evidence. In these circumstances the taint caused by the unlawful police behavior is said to have been purged. To determine if tainted evidence has been purged, a court must scrutinize the circumstances of the particular case and decide if the evidence was gained by exploiting the improper search or arrest or by other means that would permit the taint to be purged.[51]

In *Brown* v. *Illinois,*[52] police officers acting without a warrant and without probable cause forced their way into Brown's apartment and arrested him. After giving Brown his *Miranda* warnings, police interrogated him and he made several incriminating statements. The Illinois Supreme Court held that giving Brown the *Miranda* warnings automatically purged the taint caused by the illegal arrest, and allowed the statements to be admitted because they were made voluntarily. The U.S. Supreme Court disagreed and

Highlight 3.3

Recently Proposed "Exclusionary Rule Reform Act of 1995" HR 666 Referred in the United States Senate February 9, 1995

 This proposed bill was defeated and was not passed into law by the United States Congress; it is included solely for illustrative purposes.

An Act

To control crime by exclusionary rule reform.

Be it enacted by the Senate and House of Representatives of the United States of America in Congress assembled,
SECTION 1.

This Act may be cited as the 'Exclusionary Rule Reform Act of 1995'.
Sec. 2.
A IN GENERAL—Chapter 223 of title 18, United States Code, is amended by adding at the end of the following:
Sec. 3510. Admissibility of evidence obtained by search or seizure

(a) EVIDENCE OBTAINED BY OBJECTIVELY REASONABLE SEARCH OR SEIZURE—Evidence which is obtained as a result of a search or seizure shall not be excluded in a proceeding in a court of the United States on the ground that the search or seizure was in violation of the fourth amendment to the Constitution of the United States, if the search or seizure was carried out in circumstances justifying an objectively reasonable belief that is was in conformity with the fourth amendment. The fact that evidence was obtained pursuant to and within the scope of a warrant constitutes prima facie evidence of the existence of such circumstances.

(b) EVIDENCE NOT EXCLUDABLE BY STATUTE OR RULE—

(1) GENERALLY—Evidence shall not be excluded in a proceeding in a court of the United States on the ground that it was obtained in violation of a statute, an administrative rule or regulation, or a rule of procedure unless exclusion is expressly authorized by statute or by a rule prescribed by the Supreme Court pursuant to statutory authority.

(2) SPECIAL RULE RELATING TO OBJECTIVELY REASONABLE SEARCHES AND SEIZURES—Evidence which is otherwise excludable under paragraph (1) shall not be excluded if the search or seizure was carried out in circumstances justifying an objectively reasonable belief that the search or seizure was in conformity with the statute, administrative rule or regulation, or rule of procedure, the violation of which occasioned its being excludable.

(c) RULES OF CONSTRUCTION—This section shall not be construed to require or authorize the exclusion of evidence in any proceeding. Nothing in this section shall be construed so as to violate the fourth article of amendments to the Constitution of the United States.

(d) LIMITATION—This section shall not apply with respect to a search or seizure carried out by, or under the authority of, the Bureau of Alcohol, Tobacco and Firearms.

(e) LIMITATION—This section shall not apply with respect to a search or seizure carried out by, or under the authority of, the Internal Revenue Service.
B CLERICAL AMENDMENT—The table of sections at the beginning of chapter 223 of title 18, United States Code, is amended by adding at the end the following: .3510. Admissibility of evidence obtained by search or seizure.'. Passed the House of Representatives February 8, 1995.
Attest: ROBIN H. CARLE,
Clerk.

FIGURE 3.1

The Fruit of the Poisonous Tree Doctrine

Unlawful arrest or confession   The evidence is poisoned

fashioned a three-pronged test to be used to determine if tainted evidence has been purged: (1) the length of time that has passed between the illegal police behavior and obtaining the evidence; (2) whether other circumstances have intervened that would help to purge the tainted evidence; (3) the degree and seriousness of police misconduct.[53]

To illustrate how the *Brown* test works, suppose that a suspect is arrested unlawfully. At the time of the arrest, he is given the *Miranda* warnings. Later, the suspect is taken to the police station where he is questioned and he makes incriminating statements. Under the *Brown* test, providing *Miranda* warnings by themselves would not purge the tainted confession. The statements could not be used against the suspect at trial. Suppose further, however, that after releasing the suspect, police officers approach him on the street two days later and, after again giving him the *Miranda* warnings, conduct an interrogation. If the suspect makes incriminating statements at this second meeting must these statements be excluded from trial? A court is likely to admit these later statements.[54] The lapse of time between the original unlawful arrest and the incriminating statements is likely to be sufficient to purge the taint from the original unlawful arrest.

Moreover, the fact that police officers at the second encounter had provided the suspect with *Miranda* warnings would be considered an intervening circumstance that would help to purge any taint resulting from the initial unlawful arrest. The court would consider, too, whether the police officers' misconduct was flagrant. If the same officers had used torture to extract a confession from the suspect during their first encounter, it is doubtful that the passage of two days and providing the suspect with *Miranda* warnings would be sufficient to purge the resulting taint.[55] The suspect likely would continue to be influenced by the earlier encounter and fear for his or her safety. In these circumstances, incriminating statements resulting from such serious police misconduct could not be used at trial.

The Effect of *Miranda* Warnings.   Giving a suspect the *Miranda* warnings does not dissipate the taint caused by an unlawful arrest. In *Dunaway* v. *New York*,[56] police officers received information from an informant that implicated Dunaway in a murder.

Police did not have probable cause to arrest Dunaway. Nevertheless, Dunaway was arrested and taken to the police station, where he made incriminating statements and provided other evidence. The Supreme Court held that Dunaway's confession was not admissible because providing the *Miranda* warnings did not purge the taint caused by the unlawful arrest. Providing the *Miranda* warnings is simply one factor to be used to determine whether a confession is voluntarily given after an illegal arrest.

On the other hand, suppose that a lawfully arrested suspect confessed at different times to a crime. The first confession was obtained before he or she was given the *Miranda* warnings. Clearly, that confession should be excluded at trial. Suppose further, however, that three minutes after the suspect's first confession, the police gave the suspect the required warnings. Again, the suspect made incriminating statements. Must these later statements be excluded due to the police officers' failure to provide the *Miranda* warnings before the first confession? Under similar circumstances, the Supreme Court in *Oregon* v. *Elstad*[57] held that if the first confession was voluntary, later *Miranda* warnings may purge the first confession's taint. In *Elstad,* the defendant who was first given inadequate *Miranda* warnings made incriminating statements. Police officers then gave him the proper warnings and he again confessed. The Supreme Court held that because the first confession was made voluntarily (no coercion was used by the police), the second confession could be used at trial. If the first confession had been involuntary, however, the trial court would have been required to use the *Brown* test to determine whether the taint from the first confession required suppression of all later statements.[58]

The Independent Untainted Source Exception

The **independent untainted source exception** to the exclusionary rule is based on the assumption that even if the police obtain evidence through unlawful means, other relevant information may be used at trial if it was obtained from a source that was not associated with the original illegal actions.

For example, in *Segura* v. *United States,*[59] police officers properly arrested Segura for various drug crimes. Even though the police had probable cause to search his apartment, however, they failed to obtain a search warrant. The officers entered the apartment and saw drug paraphernalia, but a search warrant was not obtained for approximately 20 hours. Agents had guarded the apartment while the warrant was being obtained to prevent evidence from being removed or destroyed. Once the officers obtained the search warrant they seized illegal drugs and drug paraphernalia. Segura argued that because the agents entered and remained in the apartment illegally, the evidence seized with the search warrant was the fruit of the poisonous unlawful entry.

The Supreme Court held that because the agents had probable cause, they could have obtained a search warrant and seized the evidence. Therefore, they had an "independent source" of knowledge about the evidence and it could be used at trial.

The Supreme Court expanded the independent source exception further in 1988. In *Murray* v. *United States,*[60] police officers entered a storage warehouse illegally and without a search warrant. They found numerous bales wrapped in burlap, which later proved to contain marijuana. The officers left the warehouse without searching the bales, but kept it under surveillance, until they could obtain a search warrant. When

Highlight 3.4

Murray v. *United States*, 487 U.S. 533 (1988)

In these consolidated cases we are faced with the question whether, assuming evidence obtained pursuant to an independently obtained search warrant, the portion of such evidence that had been observed in plain view at the time of a prior illegal entry must be suppressed. . . .

Both cases arise out of the conviction of petitioner Michael F. Murray, petitioner James D. Carter, and others for conspiracy to possess and distribute illegal drugs. Based on information received from informants, federal law enforcement agents had been surveilling petitioner Murray and several of his co-conspirators. At about 1:45 P.M. on April 6, 1983, they observed Murray drive a truck and Carter a green camper, into a warehouse in South Boston. When petitioners drove the vehicles out about 20 minutes later, the surveilling agents saw within the warehouse two individuals and a tractor-trailer rig bearing a long, dark container. Murray and Carter later turned over the truck and camper to other drivers, who were in turn followed and ultimately arrested, and the vehicles lawfully seized. Both vehicles were found to contain marijuana.

After receiving this information, several of the agents converged on the South Boston warehouse and forced entry. They found the warehouse unoccupied, but observed in plain view numerous burlap-wrapped bales that were later found to contain marijuana. They left without disturbing the bales, kept the warehouse under surveillance, and did not re-enter it until they had a search warrant. In applying for the warrant, the agents did not mention the prior entry, and did not rely on any observations made during that entry. When the warrant was issued at 10:40 P.M., approximately 8 hours after the initial entry, the agents immediately reentered the warehouse and seized 270 bales of marijuana and notebooks listing customers for whom the bales were destined. Before trial, petitioners moved to suppress the evidence found in the warehouse. The District Court denied the motion, rejecting petitioners' arguments that the warrant was invalid because the agents did not inform the magistrate about their prior warrantless entry, and that the warrant was tainted by that entry. Murray and Carter have filed petitions for certiorari which are now consolidated and limited to the Fourth Amendment question. . . .

Our cases that have used the concept of independent source in a general sense identify all evidence acquired in a fashion untainted by the illegal evidence-gathering activity. Thus, where an unlawful entry has given investigators knowledge of facts x and y, but fact z has been learned by other means, fact z can be said to be admissible because derived from an 'independent source.'

[In this case] knowledge that the marijuana was in the warehouse was assuredly acquired at the time of the unlawful entry—but it was also acquired at the time of the entry pursuant to the warrant, and if that later acquisition was not the result of the earlier entry, there is no reason why the independent source doctrine should not apply. Invoking the exclusionary rule would not put the police (and society) in the same position they would have occupied if no violation occurred, but in a worse one. . . .

We vacate the judgment and remand these cases to the Court of Appeals with instructions that it remand to the District Court for determination whether the warrant-authorized search of the warehouse was an independent source of challenged evidence in the sense we have described.

they applied for the warrant, the officers did not inform the judge that they had entered the warehouse illegally. They used other evidence to establish probable cause for the issuance of the warrant. The officers did not rely in any way on their illegal observations in order to get the warrant. The Supreme Court held that the marijuana evidence could be admitted because it was obtained independently of the illegal entry.[61]

Segura and *Murray* indicate that the independent source exception to the exclusionary rule may be used to admit unlawfully obtained evidence if three requirements are met:

1. the police unlawfully enter the place where the questioned search occurs when they first discover the evidence;

2. probable cause exists for the issuance of a search warrant *before* the unlawful entry is made;

3. the police show that they would have applied for a search warrant eventually, despite the unlawful entry.

The Inevitable Discovery Exception

The inevitable discovery exception to the exclusionary rule is similar to the independent source exception. Under the inevitable discovery exception, a trial court may admit illegally obtained evidence if other independent and lawful means would have produced the same evidence at a later time.[62] This exception was established in *Nix* v. *Williams*.[63] This was the second time that this rather exceptional case reached the U.S. Supreme Court. A detailed review of the facts of this case is necessary to understand the inevitable discovery exception to the exclusionary rule. Robert Williams, who had recently escaped from a mental hospital, was charged with murdering a ten-year-old girl, whom Williams had kidnapped from a Y.M.C.A. in Des Moines, Iowa. Two days later an attorney informed members of the Des Moines Police Department that he had received a telephone call from Williams, and that he told Williams to turn himself in to the Davenport, Iowa, police. Williams surrendered that morning to the police in Davenport. The Davenport officers telephoned their counterparts in Des Moines and informed them that Williams had surrendered. The attorney was at the Des Moines police headquarters and spoke with Williams on the telephone. In the presence of the Chief of Police and a police detective named Leaming, the lawyer advised Williams that Des Moines police officers would be driving to Davenport to pick him up, that the officers would not interrogate or mistreat him, and that Williams was not to talk to the officers about the missing child until after consulting with the lawyer upon his return to Des Moines. As a result of these conversations, it was agreed between the lawyer and the Des Moines police officers that Detective Leaming and another officer would drive to Davenport to pick up Williams, that they would bring him directly back to Des Moines, and that they would not question him during the trip.

In the meantime Williams was arraigned before a judge in Davenport. The judge advised him of his *Miranda* rights and committed him to jail. Before leaving the courtroom, Williams conferred with a lawyer, who advised him not to make any statements until consulting with his attorney in Des Moines.

Soon after their arrival in Davenport, Detective Leaming and the other officer met with Williams and his attorney. Detective Leaming repeated the *Miranda* warnings and told Williams:

> [W]e both know that you're being represented here by [Attorney] Kelly and you're being represented by Mr. McKnight in Des Moines, and . . . I want you to remember this because we'll be visiting between here and Des Moines.

Williams conferred again with Attorney Kelly alone, and after this conference Kelly repeated to Detective Leaming that Williams was not to be questioned about the disappearance of the child until after he had consulted with Attorney McKnight in Des Moines. When Leaming expressed some reservations, Kelly stated firmly that the agreement with McKnight was to be carried out: there was to be no interrogation of Williams during the trip back to Des Moines.

The two detectives left Davenport with Williams on their trip back to Des Moines. At no time during the trip did Williams express a willingness to be interrogated in the absence of his attorneys. In fact, he stated several times that "[w]hen I get to Des Moines and see Mr. McKnight, I am going to tell you the whole story." Detective Leaming knew that Williams was a former mental patient and knew also that he was very religious.

Detective Leaming and Williams began a conversation covering a variety of topics, including the subject of religion. Not long after leaving Davenport, Detective Leaming delivered what has been referred to as the "Christian burial speech." Addressing Williams as "Reverend," the Detective said:

> I want to give you something to think about while we're traveling down the road. . . . Number one, I want you to observe the weather conditions, it's raining, it's sleeting, it's freezing, driving is very treacherous, visibility is poor, it's going to be dark early this evening. They are predicting several inches of snow for tonight, and I feel that you yourself are the only person that knows where this little girl's body is, that you yourself have only been there once, and if you get a snow on top of it you yourself may be unable to find it. And, since we will be going right past the area on the way into Des Moines, I feel that we could stop and locate the body, that the parents of this little girl should be entitled to a Christian burial for the little girl who was snatched away from them on Christmas Eve and murdered. And I feel we should stop and locate it on the way in rather than waiting until morning and trying to come back out after a snowstorm and possibly not being able to find it at all.

Williams asked Detective Leaming why he thought their route to Des Moines would be taking them past the girl's body, and Leaming responded that he knew the body was in the area of Mitchellville—a town they would be passing on the way to Des Moines. Leaming then stated: "I do not want you to answer me. I don't want to discuss it further. Just think about it as we're riding down the road."

As the car approached Grinnell, Iowa, Williams asked whether the police had found the victim's shoes. When Detective Leaming replied that he was unsure, Williams directed the officers to a service station where he said he had left the shoes; however, a search for them was unsuccessful. As they continued towards Des Moines, Williams asked whether the police had found the blanket that he had used to cover the child. He then directed the officers to a rest area where he said he had disposed of the blanket. Nothing was found. The car continued towards Des Moines, and as it approached Mitchellville, Williams said that he would show the officers where the body was. He then directed the police to the child's body.

At trial, the judge admitted the evidence resulting from the statements made to the police during the ride. The judge concluded that although an agreement had been reached between Williams's attorneys and the police officers that Williams would not be questioned during the ride, Williams had waived his rights before giving the information.

In a federal *habeas corpus* proceeding, the U.S. District Court concluded that the evidence of the child's body had been admitted improperly at Williams's trial. This conclusion was based on three independent grounds: (1) that Williams had been denied his constitutional right to the assistance of counsel; (2) that he had been denied his *Miranda* rights; and (3) that in any event, the statements had been made involuntarily. The U.S. Court of Appeals appeared to have affirmed the judgment on the first two grounds.[64]

The U.S. Supreme Court held in *Brewer* v. *Williams* that the defendant's right to counsel had been violated. Therefore, the trial court had erred by admitting evidence of the child's body.

Several years later, Williams was charged again with the child's murder. A later chapter will discuss why a second trial in these circumstances does not violate the Fifth Amendment's double jeopardy clause. In *Nix* v. *Williams*,[65] evidence of the child's body was used again. The trial judge accepted the State's argument that despite Williams's tainted statements to the police, the body would have been discovered inevitably by a systematic search made by 200 volunteers near the area where the body was found. Williams was again convicted of the child's murder.

The U.S. Supreme Court held that because the body would have been inevitably discovered without Williams's assistance, it could be used as evidence because excluding the body would have left the prosecution in a more disadvantaged position than if the police had not questioned Williams. The Court reasoned that the exclusionary rule's deterrence rationale does not support this result.

Nix v. *Williams* is a restriction of the exclusionary rule's protections. This case may be criticized on several different grounds.[66] First, the Court's assertion that the child's body would have been discovered inevitably following a diligent search is questionable. How could the Court know that the searchers would have conducted the search in a diligent manner? Second, excluding the evidence of the child's body would have served the exclusionary rule's objective of deterring unlawful police conduct. Therefore, although it is clearly good social policy to confine a child's murderer, the legal basis of *Nix* v. *Williams* is open to criticism, but illustrates the legal principle, "hard cases make bad law."

Impeaching a Defendant's Trial Testimony

Suppose a confession is taken from a defendant who is not given his *Miranda* warnings. Normally, the exclusionary rule of evidence will bar the incriminating statements at trial. Suppose further, however, that the defendant testifies in his or her own defense and contradicts the prior statements given to the police. In these circumstances, the prosecution may use these prior statements to try to show that the defendant is lying. This is termed **impeaching a defendant's testimony.**

The Supreme Court has held that a defendant's right to testify in his or her own defense does not include the right to commit perjury.[67] The Court has stated that "truth is a fundamental goal of our legal system . . . when defendants testify, they must testify truthfully or suffer the consequences" of their perjured testimony.[68] Consequently, if, after providing a tainted statement to police officers, a defendant's testimony contradicts the earlier statement, it may be used to impeach the trial testimony, as long as the tainted statements were made voluntarily.[69]

The Exclusionary Rule in Non-Trial Criminal Proceedings

Not all proceedings in the U.S. justice system involve trials. Chapter 2 discussed the various stages in the U.S. criminal justice process. The exclusionary rule of evidence does not apply with equal force to the various pretrial and posttrial phases of the justice process. Table 3.1 summarizes the case law in this area.

Searches by Private Persons

The exclusionary rule of evidence does not apply to unlawful searches conducted by persons who are not police officers or agents of the government. The rationale for this principle is that the U.S. Constitution was intended to operate solely as a restraint on governmental power. To apply the exclusionary rule to searches conducted by private persons would not serve this limited objective.

Alternatives to the Exclusionary Rule

Highlight 3.1 presents the debate about the exclusionary rule of evidence. Application of the exclusionary rule exacts a cost—reliable evidence is sometimes lost if suspects' constitutional rights are violated. In fact, this is one of the principal objections to the exclusionary rule. It may deprive society of an opportunity to convict truly guilty people.

A question that arises frequently in the debate about the exclusionary rule asks whether there are viable alternatives to excluding trustworthy evidence at trial.[70] Some of the suggested alternative methods include:

1. *Adoption of the Former British Model.* In England, for many years illegally obtained evidence could be used at trial; however, the police officers who obtained the evidence were subject to internal departmental discipline. This method of trying to assure compliance with constitutional safeguards designed to protect suspects' rights is of questionable value. More recently, British law has been changed to give judges the discretion to refuse to admit illegally obtained evidence. Moreover, one need only scrutinize police conduct in the Rodney King case to realize that internal departmental regulations, by themselves, may not ensure proper police behavior.

2. *Civil Tort Lawsuits Against the Police.* Civil tort lawsuits are designed to compensate injured persons. In theory, those who have harmed the victim should be forced

TABLE 3.1 Non-Trial Proceedings and the Exclusionary Rule

Case	Type of Proceeding	Does the ER apply?
U.S. v. *Calandra*[71]	Grand Jury	No
U.S. v. *Janis*[72]	Civil	No
	Sentencing	Undecided*
	Parole Revocation	Undecided**
In re Gault[73]	Juvenile Proceedings	Undecided***
INS v. *Lopez-Mendoza*[74]	Immigration Proceedings	No

* The Supreme Court has not decided whether the exclusionary rule applies to sentencing proceedings. A majority of lower courts have held that it does not apply to such hearings.

** The Supreme Court has not decided whether the exclusionary rule applies to parole revocation hearings. A majority of lower courts have held that it does not apply in these circumstances.

*** The Supreme Court has not decided whether the exclusionary rule applies to juvenile delinquency proceedings. A majority of lower courts have held that the exclusionary rule applies to juvenile court proceedings that may result in a minor's institutional confinement. Many of these courts have based their decision on *In re Gault,* which provides minors with significant due process safeguards in juvenile court proceedings.

to "make the injured party whole" by providing them with financial compensation. Those who advocate this alternative to the exclusionary rule believe that the victims of illegal police behavior should be allowed to pursue a civil remedy against officers whose unlawful behavior produces the evidence.[75]

One type of tort lawsuit against those who violate persons' civil rights is termed a **1983 action.** 1983 cases arise under Section 1983, Chapter 42, of the United States Code (42 U.S.C. Section 1983). 1983 actions provide a federal civil remedy for persons whose rights guaranteed by the Constitution or by federal law have been violated by those acting under color of state law. According to Professor Rolando del Carmen, there are two basic requirements of a Section 1983 lawsuit:

1. A defendant must be acting under color of law (he or she misuses power possessed by virtue of law the authority of the state possesses; and
2. There must be a violation of a constitutional or statutory federally protected right.[76]

Although there is some reason to believe that the threat of Section 1983 actions has exerted a positive impact on police conduct, state tort actions appear to be of limited value for several reasons. First, as any experienced attorney knows well, it is extremely difficult to successfully sue the police. Sometimes the "blue code of silence" prevents officers who witness misconduct from testifying in court. Second, as the old saying goes, "you can't get water from a stone." Police officers are notoriously underpaid. Is it realistic to expect an officer who behaves unlawfully to be able to pay a civil judgment?

3. *Use of Civilian Review Panels.* Civilian review panels are composed of citizens who examine alleged instances of police misconduct. Such panels have proved unpopular with police agencies, however, because many officers believe that panel members have unrealistic expectations for the police and are unable to appreciate just

how difficult it is to enforce the law. In the future the use of civilian review panels may contribute to the development of more positive relationships between the police and the communities they serve. Because they have been rejected by some law enforcement agencies, however, there is little room for optimism that they will become an effective alternative to the exclusionary rule of evidence.

The Doctrine of Standing to Assert the Exclusionary Rule

Article III of the U.S. Constitution is termed the "judicial article" because it establishes and limits the powers of U.S. courts. One important limitation on judicial power is that courts may only hear and decide cases involving real disputes between actual parties to the case. This is sometimes termed Article III's "case and controversy" requirement. Courts will not decide hypothetical disputes or become involved in academic exercises.[77]

The doctrine of **legal standing** is a judicially created doctrine designed to enforce the case or controversy requirement. It is concerned with identifying the persons who may raise legal claims in court.[78] There are two main aspects to the doctrine of legal standing. First, in order to raise a legal claim, a person must have suffered an actual injury. Second, a person must assert his or her own legal rights and interests—a claim cannot be based on the rights of a third party. An example should help to clarify this important legal doctrine. Suppose that John and Mary, who are domestic partners, were involved in a violent argument. During the argument Mary struck John with a textbook and he suffered a bruised left arm. Based on this incident, John would have standing to bring legal actions, in all likelihood both criminal and civil claims, against Mary. This is because John suffered an actual injury. Moreover, John would be asserting his own legal rights and interests. Suppose further that John declined to ask a prosecutor to file criminal charges, or to pursue a civil action against Mary in this case. Jane, who witnessed the incident, and is an advocate for victims of domestic violence, believes that it is important to sanction all those who commit domestic abuse. She therefore tries to file a civil lawsuit for battery against Mary on John's behalf. Unless a state's domestic violence laws specifically permit third party standing, Jane would not be able to bring a civil suit in this case—she suffered no injury and is attempting to assert another person's legal rights and interests.

The U.S. Supreme Court has held that persons must have standing to assert the exclusionary rule of evidence. Just as, in the example above, John would have had to demonstrate that he had suffered injury and that he was asserting his own legal rights, a suspect attempting to exclude relevant evidence must demonstrate that he or she was injured by unlawful police behavior and that the unlawful actions violated his or her own legally protected interests.

Fifth and Sixth Amendment Standing

Evidence suppression standing questions may arise in Fourth, Fifth, or Sixth Amendment cases. In one case, a defendant alleged that his Fifth Amendment privilege against self-incrimination was violated by the state's use of a business partner's records at the defendant's trial. The Supreme Court held, however, that there was no violation of the defendant's Fifth Amendment privilege against self-incrimination because standing in Fifth Amendment cases is strictly a personal right that cannot be gained by virtue of a business association with another person. Therefore, the defendant was not allowed to assert his former partner's privilege against self-incrimination to bar admission of the records at trial.[79]

Similarly, the standing doctrine requires that defendants alleging a violation of their Sixth Amendment right to counsel must demonstrate that their own rights were violated by the police. For example, a defendant may not assert his or her Sixth Amendment right to counsel to exclude evidence obtained in violation of a co-conspirator's right to counsel.[80] The above discussion illustrates how the standing doctrine in Fifth and Sixth Amendment cases will permit illegally obtained evidence to be used at trial unless the defendant can demonstrate that his or her personal rights were violated by the police. The standing doctrine, however, has been most fully developed in Fourth Amendment cases.

Fourth Amendment Standing

One case with significant implications for the development of Fourth Amendment law was *Katz* v. *United States*.[81] Katz was convicted of transmitting bets and wagering information between states by telephone. At trial, the prosecution was allowed, over objection, to admit evidence of Katz's telephone conversations recorded by F.B.I. agents who had attached an electronic listening and recording device to the exterior of a public telephone booth. Katz was convicted. On appeal, the U.S. Supreme Court held that "[n]o less than an individual in a business office, in a friend's apartment, or in a taxicab, a person in a telephone booth may rely upon the protection of the Fourth Amendment."[82] *Katz* illustrates that the right to claim Fourth Amendment protection depends on whether the area being searched is one in which an individual has "a reasonable expectation of privacy" from governmental intrusion.[83] It established, too, a two-part rule in Fourth Amendment exclusionary rule cases: In order to claim the exclusionary rule's protection, a suspect must demonstrate (1) that he or she had an actual (subjective) expectation of privacy; and (2) that the expectation of privacy is one that society is prepared to recognize as reasonable.[84]

In recent years the U.S. Supreme Court has used the two-part *Katz* test to restrict a defendant's ability to claim the protection of the exclusionary rule.[85] For example, suppose that someone is riding in an automobile that he or she does not own. Suppose further that the police illegally search the vehicle. May a person who is riding in the vehicle but who does not own it assert that evidence that is discovered in the vehicle after the illegal stop should be excluded? The U.S. Supreme Court answered this question in 1978. In *Rakas* v. *Illinois*,[86] the defendant was convicted on armed robbery. At trial the prosecution had introduced into evidence a sawed-off rifle and rifle shells that were seized by police during a search of an automobile in which Rakas had been riding. Rakas neither owned the automobile nor asserted that he owned the rifle or shells. The prosecution challenged Rakas's standing to object to the automobile search because he did not own the car and did not claim that he owned the rifle and shells. Justice William

Rehnquist stated that Rakas had no legitimate expectation of privacy in the automobile. Therefore, Rakas lacked standing to use the exclusionary rule to bar the admission of the evidence.

The Supreme Court has ruled, too, that a defendant lacks standing to object to a search of another person's purse. In *Rawlings* v. *Kentucky,*[87] several police officers attempting to serve an arrest warrant went to a suspect's home. While unsuccessfully searching for the suspect in the house, the officers smelled marijuana smoke and saw marijuana seeds. Two of the officers then left to obtain a warrant to search the house, while the remaining officers detained the occupants, including Rawlings, allowing the occupants to leave only if they consented to a body search. Upon returning with the warrant approximately 45 minutes later, the officers showed the warrant to the occupants, gave them the *Miranda* warnings, and ordered one of the occupants, Ms. Cox, to empty her purse onto the table. When Cox emptied her purse, she told Rawlings to "take what was his" and Rawlings immediately claimed ownership of 1,800 L.S.D. tablets. Rawlings was convicted. On appeal, the U.S. Supreme Court upheld the trial court's ruling that Rawlings lacked standing to object to the search of the purse because he had failed to satisfy the burden of establishing that he had a reasonable expectation of privacy in Cox's purse.

Rakas v. *Illinois* and *Rawlings* v. *Kentucky* illustrate that standing to assert the protection of the exclusionary rule is a *personal* right. In order to have standing to exclude illegally obtained evidence a defendant must show that his or her own rights were violated by the police. Standing may not be gained by associating with others. Just how far the Supreme Court is willing to extend this principle remains to be determined. Suppose that in *Rawlings* v. *Kentucky,* Rawlings and Cox had been married. Would the fact of their marriage have given Rawlings a reasonable expectation of privacy in Cox's purse? That question remains unanswered. As you will see, however, the Supreme Court has not been inclined to expand defendants' rights through the law of Fourth Amendment standing. In fact, most of the recent cases curtail the application of the exclusionary rule in Fourth Amendment cases.

Open Fields, Overflights, and Searches of Garbage.   The Supreme Court has used the *Katz* two-part test to restrict defendants' rights in several different types of cases. In *Oliver* v. *United States,*[88] the Supreme Court upheld the defendant's conviction for growing marijuana, despite the fact that police officers had climbed fences and trespassed on his property to look for evidence. Using the first part of the *Katz* test, the Court held that a defendant has no reasonable expectation of privacy in open fields, in this case property that he owned near his home that was not immediately adjacent to the main house. The Court held that "an individual may not legitimately demand privacy for activities conducted out of doors in fields, except in the area immediately surrounding the home."[89]

The Supreme Court has used the second part of the *Katz* test to limit a homeowner's standing to object to police officers' use of aerial surveillance of his backyard to gain evidence. In *California* v. *Ciraolo,*[90] the police had received an anonymous tip that marijuana was growing in the defendant's backyard. They were unable to observe the yard from the ground because Ciraolo had erected a six-foot-high outer fence and a ten-foot-high inner fence around the yard. Police officers obtained an airplane and flew over the yard at an altitude of 1,000 feet and observed and photographed marijuana plants growing in a garden area. Based on their observations and photographs, they obtained a search warrant and seized numerous marijuana plants. The trial court denied Ciraolo's motion to suppress the evidence and Ciraolo was convicted.

The Supreme Court affirmed his conviction and held that Ciraolo's motion to suppress should not have been granted because society was not prepared to recognize that he had a reasonable expectation of privacy in his fenced backyard. See the sample motions to suppress in Figures 3.2 and 3.3. The Court held that "[a]ny member of the public flying in this airspace who glanced down could have seen everything that these officers observed."[91] Therefore, Ciraolo's "expectation that his garden was protected from such observations is unreasonable and is not an expectation that society is prepared to honor."[92] More recently, the Supreme Court has extended *Ciraolo's* holding to helicopter surveillance conducted by the police at an altitude of 400 feet.[93]

Using the same *Katz* privacy expectation test, the Supreme Court has sanctioned, too, warrantless searches of garbage left on the curb for trash collection. In *California v. Greenwood,*[94] another case involving illegal drugs, police officers acting without a warrant searched Greenwood's trash, discovered evidence that indicated illegal drug use, and obtained a warrant to search his home. The Supreme Court held that the warrantless search did not violate Greenwood's expectation of privacy in his trash.[95] The Court stated:

> It is common knowledge that plastic garbage bags left on or at the side of a public street are readily accessible to animals, children, scavengers, snoops, and other members of the public. Moreover, [Greenwood] placed [his] refuse at the curb for the express purpose of conveying it to a third party, the trash collector, who might himself have sorted through [the] trash or permitted others, such as the police, to do so. Accordingly, . . . [Greenwood] could have no reasonable expectation of privacy in the inculpatory items he discarded.[96]

To summarize, the U.S. Supreme Court has used the law of Fourth Amendment standing to restrict a defendant's ability to claim the protection of the exclusionary rule of evidence. Whether or not this is a positive development depends on one's perspective on law enforcement and crime control: Should the police be given more freedom to enforce the law? Or, conversely, should due process safeguards be given priority in our criminal justice system? These are difficult questions to answer. Before we leave this section, however, it may be instructive to consider a final issue.

An "Illegal Drug Case" Exception to the Exclusionary Rule

Many of the exclusionary rule cases discussed in this chapter involved the use, sale, or distribution of illegal drugs. We have seen that the Supreme Court has sanctioned a good-faith exception and has made it more difficult to claim the protection of the exclusionary rule in Fourth Amendment cases by changing the law of standing. Some commentators have suggested that the Supreme Court has intentionally changed the law in this area to facilitate the government's interest in prosecuting illegal drug users.[97] While there is substantial room for debate, there appears to be some merit to this conclusion.

FIGURE 3.2

Sample Motion to Suppress Evidence

STATE OF RHODE ISLAND   SUPERIOR COURT
NEWPORT, SC.

STATE OF RHODE ISLAND

      vs.   C.A. NO. N2/94-402A

    JOHN JAMES
      Defendant

<u>MOTION TO SUPPRESS SEARCH</u>

    Now comes the Defendant, in the above-entitled matter and respectfully requests this Honorable Court to suppress the search of the defendant's vehicle by the Newport Police Department on June 15, 1994. In support of said motion, the Defendant cites Article I, Section 6 of the Rhode Island Constitution, *State v Leavitt*, 237 A2. 309 (1968) and the Fourth Amendment of the United States Constitution, *State v Belcourt*, 425 A2. 1224 (1981), and Rhode Island General Laws § 9-19-25.

              by his attorney,

           ————————————————
           Christopher S. Gontarz, Esq.
           UPDEGROVE & GONTARZ, LTD.
           314 Oliphant Lane
           Middletown, Rhode Island 02842
           #3124

<u>CERTIFICATE OF SERVICE</u>

    I hereby certify that on the ____ day of October, 1994, I did hand-deliver a copy of the within Motion to the Department of Attorney General, Newport County Courthouse, Newport, Rhode Island 02840

           ————————————————

FIGURE 3.3

Sample Motion to Suppress Statements

STATE OF RHODE ISLAND   SUPERIOR COURT
PROVIDENCE, SC.

STATE OF RHODE ISLAND

        vs.   P2/96-1857GB

    Jane Jones

MOTION TO SUPPRESS STATEMENTS

Now comes the Defendant, in the above-captioned matter and hereby moves to suppress any written or oral statement made to the East Providence Police on or about April 9, 1996 and for her reason states:

That the statements taken by the said East Providence Police were taken from defendant as a result of promises and inducements made by said police departments against her will and without having apprised the defendant of her constitutional rights; that there was no probable cause to arrest the defendant and that the taking of said statement was illegal and void and denied the defendant her rights under U.S.Cnst. Amends. IV, V, VI and XIV and R.I. Cnst. Art. 1, Sections 6, 10, 15.

        by his attorney,

        _____

        Anne P. Smith
        123 Main Street
        Chicago, IL

CERTIFICATION

I hereby certify that on the _____ day of June, 1996 I mailed/hand-delivered a copy of the foregoing Motion to the Department of Attorney General, 150 South Main Street, Providence, RI 02903

        _____

Summary

Chapter 3 begins with a discussion of the nature of due process of law. The Fifth Amendment's due process clause, which protects persons from infringement of due process rights by the federal government, and the Fourteenth Amendment's due process clause, which prevents infringement of due process rights by state governments are considered. The distinction between the substantive and procedural aspects of due process are discussed. The substantive due process doctrine asks whether the government may legitimately regulate certain areas of life. The procedural due process doctrine, in contrast, asks whether the government has followed the proper procedures when it is attempting to deprive someone of their life, liberty, or property.

Chapter 3's major focus is on the exclusionary rule of evidence, an issue that has generated significant controversy in the U.S. legal system. Evidence obtained in violation of a defendant's constitutionally protected rights may not be used against him or her in a criminal trial. The rule may require the suppression of evidence obtained through violations of the Fourth, Fifth, or Sixth Amendments. The exclusionary rule debate is highlighted and the various justifications supporting an exclusionary rule are highlighted. These justifications include a systemic rationale, a public trust rationale, an individual rights rationale, and a deterrence of unlawful police conduct rationale.

The historical development of the exclusionary rule of evidence is discussed as well. The various cases that have developed the exclusionary rule are presented and *Mapp* v. *Ohio's* legacy is considered in detail. Quantitative research on the effect of the exclusionary rule is highlighted in this chapter.

Chapter 3 discusses several different circumstances in which the exclusionary rule does not apply. These include: (1) a "good-faith exception" —when police officers act in good-faith reliance on an apparently valid search warrant or on a law permitting the challenged search; (2) a "purged taint" exception—when the connection between the unlawful police conduct and the evidence is sufficiently broken so that it cures the "illegal" nature of the evidence; (3) an "independent source" exception—when evidence is obtained from an independent source, even if the police had engaged in misconduct; (4) an "inevitable discovery" exception—when the evidence inevitably would have been discovered by proper means; and (5) when "impeaching" a defendant's trial testimony. Considered, too, are the exclusionary rule's effects in non-trial criminal proceedings as well as its effect on searches conducted by private persons.

Additional issues related to the exclusionary rule are discussed in detail. These include the doctrine of standing to assert the exclusionary rule in Fourth, Fifth, and Sixth Amendment cases. Moreover, this chapter briefly considers whether the U.S. Supreme Court has effectively developed an "illegal drug case" exception to the exclusionary rule.

Review Questions

1. What is meant by due process of law? How do the Fifth and Fourteenth Amendment due process clauses differ?
2. Distinguish between the substantive and procedural aspects of due process.
3. Present the Supreme Court's holding in *Goldberg* v. *Kelly*. Why would one expect the protections a defendant receives in criminal proceedings to be even greater than those given to persons facing adverse action by an administrative agency?
4. Describe the exclusionary rule of evidence.
5. Exclusionary rule issues may arise in Fourth, Fifth, or Sixth Amendment cases. Which rights provided in these Amendments may give rise to exclusionary rule questions?

6. Present arguments for and against the exclusionary rule of evidence.
7. Discuss the historical development of the exclusionary rule of evidence. Be sure to cite relevant case law in completing your answer.
8. Discuss the following exceptions to the exclusionary rule of evidence:
   a. the "good-faith" exception
   b. the "purged taint" exception
   c. the "independent source" exception
   d. the "inevitable discovery" exception
   e. the "impeached testimony" exception
9. Does the exclusionary rule of evidence apply to non-trial proceedings? Be sure to cite relevant case law in completing your answer.
10. Discuss the doctrine of standing to assert the exclusionary rule.
11. Use case law discussed in this chapter to develop arguments: (1) that the U.S. Supreme Court has developed an "illegal drug case" exception to the exclusionary rule; and (2) that such an exception has not been created.

Issues for Analysis and Discussion

1. Present several different philosophical justifications for the exclusionary rule that the U.S. courts have used at various times in our history.
   a. How has the Supreme Court used the "deterrence" justification for the exclusionary rule to restrict its application in criminal cases? (Be sure to present the Court's specific language in *Mapp* v. *Ohio, United States* v. *Leon,* and *Arizona* v. *Evans* to formulate your answer.)
2. In *United States* v. *Leon,* Justice Byron White asserted that the central purpose of the exclusionary rule is to deter police misconduct. In contrast, Justice William Brennan, dissenting, suggested that the exclusionary rule "restrains the power of the government as a whole; it does not specify only a particular agency and exempt all others. The judiciary is responsible, no less than the executive, for ensuring that constitutional rights are respected." Discuss the implications of these differing positions for the development of the exclusionary rule of evidence?

CASE EXCERPT: *MAPP V. OHIO*
SUPREME COURT OF THE UNITED STATES (1961)
367 U.S. 643

On May 23, 1957, three Cleveland police officers arrived at Mapp's residence pursuant to information that a bombing suspect was hiding in her home and that there was a large amount of paraphernalia hidden there. The officers knocked on the door and demanded entry but Mapp, after telephoning her attorney, refused to admit them without a search warrant. The officers again sought entrance three hours later when four or more additional officers arrived on the scene. When Ms. Mapp did not come to the door immediately, the door to the house was forcibly opened and the police gained admittance. When the officers entered the home, Ms. Mapp demanded to see the search warrant. A paper, claimed to be a warrant, was held up by one of the officers. She grabbed the "warrant" and placed it in her bosom. A struggle ensued in which the officers recovered the piece of paper and as a result of which they handcuffed Mapp because she had been "belligerent" in resisting their official rescue of the "warrant" from her person. The officers searched the entire house including her bedroom where they searched a dresser, a chest of drawers, a closet and some suitcases. They also looked into a photo album and through Mapp's personal papers. The basement of the building and a trunk was also searched. The obscene materials for possession of which she was ultimately convicted were discovered in the course of that widespread search. At trial no search warrant was produced by the prosecution, nor was the failure to produce one explained or accounted for. The Ohio Supreme Court upheld Mapp's conviction for possession of obscene materials and the U.S. Supreme Court granted certiorari.

Mr. Justice Clark delivered the opinion of the Court.

* * *

The State says that even if the search were made without authority or otherwise unreasonably, it is not prevented from using the unconstitutionally seized evidence at trial, citing *Wolf* v. *People of the State of Colorado*. On this appeal . . . it is urged once again that we review that holding.

* * *

[In *Wolf*] after declaring that the "security of one's privacy against arbitrary intrusion by the police" is "implicit in 'the concept of ordered liberty' and as such enforceable against the States through the Due Process Clause," and announcing that it "stoutly adhere[d]" to the *Weeks* decision, the Court decided that the *Weeks* exclusionary rule would not then be imposed upon the States as "an essential ingredient of the right."

* * *

Since the Fourth Amendment's right of privacy has been declared enforceable against the States through the Due Process Clause of the Fourteenth, it is enforceable against them by the same sanction of exclusion as is used against the Federal Government. Were it otherwise, then just as without the *Weeks* rule the assurance against unreasonable federal searches and seizures would be "a form of words," valueless and undeserving of mention in a perpetual charter of inestimable human liberties, so too, without that rule the freedom from all brutish means of coercing evidence as not to merit this Court's high regard as a freedom "implicit in 'the concept of ordered liberty.'" At the time that the Court held in *Wolf* that the Amendment was applicable to the States through the Due Process Clause, the cases of this Court, as we have seen, had steadfastly held that as to federal officers the Fourth Amendment included the exclusion of evidence seized in violation of its provisions. Even *Wolf* "stoutly adhered" to that proposition. The right to privacy, when conceded operatively enforceable against the States, was not susceptible of destruction by avulsion of the sanction upon which its protection and enjoyment had always been deemed dependent under the earlier case law. Therefore, in extending the substantive protections of due process to all constitutionally unreasonable searches—state or federal—it was logically and constitutionally necessary that the exclusion doctrine—an essential part of the right to privacy—be also insisted upon as an essential ingredient of the right newly recognized by the *Wolf* case. In short, the admission of the new constitutional right by *Wolf* could not consistently tolerate denial of its most important constitutional privilege, namely, the exclusion of the evidence which an accused had been forced to give by reason of the unlawful seizure. To hold otherwise is to grant the right but in reality to withhold its privilege and enjoyment. Only last year the Court itself recognized that the purpose of the exclusionary rule "is to deter—to compel respect for the constitutional guaranty in the only effective available way—by removing the incentive to disregard it."

* * *

Moreover, our holding that the exclusionary rule is an essential part of both the Fourth and Fourteenth Amendments is not only the logical dictate of prior cases, but it also makes very good sense. There is no war between the Constitution and common sense. Presently, a federal prosecutor may make no use of evidence illegally seized, but a State's attorney across the street may, although he supposedly is operating under the enforceable prohibitions of the same Amendment. Thus the State, by admitting evidence unlawfully seized, served to encourage disobedience to the Federal Constitution which it is bound to uphold.

* * *

There are those who say, as did Justice Cardoza, that under our constitutional exclusionary doctrine "[t]he criminal is to go free because the constable has blundered." In some cases this will undoubtedly be the result. But as was said in *Elkins,* "there is another consideration—the imperative of judicial integrity." The criminal goes free, if he must, but it is the law that sets him free. Nothing can destroy a government more quickly than its failure to observe its own laws, or worse, its disregard of the charter of its own existence. As Mr. Justice Brandeis, dissenting, said in *Olmstead* v. *United States:* "Our government is the potent, the omnipresent teacher. For good or ill, it teaches the whole people by its example. . . . If

the government becomes a lawbreaker, it breeds contempt for law; it invites every man to become a law unto himself; it invites anarchy." Nor can it lightly be assumed that, as a practical matter, adoption of the exclusionary rule fetters law enforcement. Only last year this Court expressly considered that contention and found that "pragmatic evidence of a sort" to the contrary was not wanting. The Court noted that "The federal courts themselves have operated under the exclusionary rule of *Weeks* for almost half a century; yet it has not been suggested either that the Federal Bureau of Investigation has thereby been rendered ineffective, or that the administration of criminal justice in the federal courts has thereby been disrupted. Moreover, the experience of the states has been impressive . . . The movement towards the rule of exclusion has been halting but seemingly inexorable."

The ignoble shortcut to conviction left open to the States tends to destroy the entire system of constitutional restraints on which the liberties of the people rest. Having once recognized that the right to privacy embodied in the Fourth Amendment is enforceable against the States, and that the right to be secure against rude invasions of privacy by state officers is, therefore, constitutional in origin, we can no longer permit that right to remain an empty promise. Because it is enforceable in the same manner and to like effect as other basic rights secured by the Due Process Clause, we can no longer permit it to be revocable at the whim of any police officer who, in the name of law enforcement itself, chooses to suspend its enjoyment. Our decision, founded on reason and truth, gives to the individual no more than that which the Constitution guarantees him, to the police officer no less than that to which honest law enforcement is entitled, and, to the courts, that judicial integrity so necessary in the true administration of justice.

Reversed and remanded.

CASE EXCERPT: *UNITED STATES V. LEON*
SUPREME COURT OF THE UNITED STATES (1984)
468 U.S. 897

Acting on the basis of information from a confidential informant, a police officer prepared a search warrant affidavit, and a search warrant was obtained from a state judge. It indicated that two individuals were selling illegal drugs from their home and that the informant had witnessed several sales. Police officers who observed the house revealed that individuals who frequented the home had been convicted previously for selling illegal drugs. A search warrant affidavit was prepared by an experienced police officer and was reviewed by several assistant district attorneys. A federal trial court held that although the officers had acted in good faith reliance on the search warrant, the affidavit supporting it was inadequate because it did not establish the informant's reliability or probable cause to believe that illegal drug sales had occurred. The U.S. Court of Appeals affirmed and the U.S. Supreme Court granted certiorari.

Mr. Justice White delivered the opinion of the Court.

* * *

This case presents the question whether the Fourth Amendment exclusionary rule should be modified so as not to bar the use in the prosecution's case in chief of evidence obtained by officers acting in reasonable reliance on a search warrant issued by a detached and neutral magistrate but ultimately found to be unsupported by probable cause.

* * *

We have concluded that, in the Fourth Amendment context, the exclusionary rule can be modified somewhat without jeopardizing its ability to perform its intended functions.

* * *

The Fourth Amendment contains no provision expressly precluding the use of evidence obtained in violation of its commands, and an examination of its origin and purposes makes clear that the use of fruits of a past unlawful search or seizure "work[s] no new Fourth Amendment wrong." The wrong condemned by the Amendment is "fully accomplished" by the unlawful

search or seizure itself, and the exclusionary rule is neither intended nor able to "cure the invasion of the defendant's rights which he has already suffered." The rule thus operates as "a judicially created remedy designed to safeguard Fourth Amendment rights generally through its deterrent effect, rather than a personal constitutional right of the party aggrieved."

* * *

The substantial social costs exacted by the exclusionary rule for the vindication of Fourth Amendment rights have long been a source of concern. "Our cases have consistently recognized that unbending application of the exclusionary sanction to enforce ideals of governmental rectitude would impede unacceptably the truth-finding functions of judge and jury . . . Particularly when law enforcement officers have acted in objective good faith or their transgressions have been minor, the magnitude of the benefit conferred on such guilty defendants offends basic concepts of the criminal justice system. Indiscriminate application of the exclusionary rule, therefore, may well "generat[e] disrespect for the law and administration of justice." Accordingly, "[a]s with any remedial device, the application of the rule has been restricted to those areas where its remedial objectives are thought most efficaciously served."

* * *

[T]he balancing approach that has evolved in various contexts—including criminal trials—"forcefully suggest[s] that the exclusionary rule be more generally modified to permit the introduction of evidence obtained in the reasonable good-faith belief that a search or seizure was in accord with the Fourth Amendment."

* * *

As yet, we have not recognized any form of good-faith exception to the Fourth Amendment exclusionary rule. But the balancing approach that has evolved during the years of experience with the rule provides strong support for the modification currently urged upon us . . . [O]ur evaluation of the costs and benefits of suppressing reliable physical evidence seized by officers reasonably relying on a warrant issued by a detached and neutral magistrate leads to the conclusion that such evidence should be admissible in the prosecution's case in chief.

* * *

If the exclusion of evidence obtained pursuant to a subsequently invalidated warrant is to have any deterrent effect, therefore, it must alter the behavior of individual law enforcement officers or the policies of their departments.

* * *

We have frequently questioned whether the exclusionary rule can have any deterrent effect when the offending officers acted in the objectively reasonably belief that their conduct did not violate the Fourth Amendment . . . But even assuming that the rule effectively deters some police misconduct and provides incentives for the law enforcement profession as a whole to conduct itself in accord with the Fourth Amendment, it cannot be expected, and should not be applied to deter objectively reasonable law enforcement activity.

* * *

Nevertheless, the officer's reliance on the magistrate's probable-cause determination and on the technical sufficiency of the warrant he issues must be objectively reasonable, and it is clear that in some circumstances the officer will have no reasonable grounds for believing that the warrant was properly issued.

* * *

In the absence of an allegation that the magistrate abandoned his detached and neutral role, suppression is appropriate only if the officers were dishonest or reckless in preparing their affidavit or could not have harbored an objectively reasonable belief in the existence of probable cause . . . Under [the circumstances in this case], the officers' reliance on the magistrate's determination of probable cause was objectively reasonable, and application of the extreme sanction of exclusion is inappropriate.

Accordingly, the judgment of the Court of Appeals is Reversed.

Endnotes

1. *Griswold* v. *Connecticut,* 381 U.S. 479 (1965).
2. General Statutes of Connecticut, Section 53–32.
3. General Statutes of Connecticut, Section 54–196.
4. *Griswold* v. *Connecticut,* 381 U.S. 479, 486 (1965).
5. Id.
6. See Russell W. Galloway, Jr., "Basic Substantive Due Process Analysis." 26 *University of San Francisco Law Review* pp. 625–666 (1992).

7. Peter Lewis and Kenneth Peoples, *The Supreme Court and the Criminal Process—Cases and Comments* (Philadelphia, Pa.: W.B. Saunders Company, 1978), p. 92.

8. Id.

9. See Amy L. Ficklin, "Dumping Drug Dealers off the Dole: An Examination of the Procedural Due Process Implications of Pre-Hearing Seizures of Public Housing Leaseholds From Tenants Involved in Drug Trafficking." 26 *Indiana Law Review* pp. 89–115 (1992).

10. *Goldberg* v. *Kelly,* 397 U.S. 294 (1970).

11. See Sylvia A. Law, "Reflections on *Goldberg* v. *Kelly* at Twenty Years." 56 *Brooklyn Law Review* pp. 805–830 (1990).

12. See Yale Kamisar, "The Warren Court and Criminal Justice: A Quarter Century Retrospective." 31 *Tulane Law Journal* pp. 1–55 (1995).

13. *People* v. *Defore,* 150 N.E. 585, 587 (1926).

14. See Christine M. D'Elia, "The Exclusionary Rule: Who Does it Punish?" 5 *Seton Hall Constitutional Law Journal* pp. 563–607 (1995).

15. See *Elkins* v. *United States,* 364 U.S. 206 (1960).

16. Id. at 223.

17. *United States* v. *Calandra,* 414 U.S. 338 (1974).

18. *United States* v. *Leon,* 468 U.S. 897 (1984).

19. See *United States* v. *Calandra,* 414 U.S. 338 (1974)(a grand jury witness may not refuse to answer questions when they are derived from illegally seized evidence because such a rule would not achieve a deterrent effect).

20. *Boyd* v. *United States,* 116 U.S. 616 (1886).

21. *Weeks* v. *United States,* 232 U.S. 383 (1914).

22. *Wolf* v. *Colorado,* 338 U.S. 25 (1949).

23. Id. at 31.

24. *Rochin* v. *California,* 342 U.S. 165 (1952).

25. Id. at 172.

26. See *Byars* v. *United States,* 273 U.S. 28 (1927).

27. *Elkins* v. *United States,* 364 U.S. 206 (1960).

28. *Mapp* v. *Ohio,* 367 U.S. 643 (1961).

29. Id. at 655.

30. See Wayne R. LaFave, "Mapp Revisited: Shakespeare, J., and Other Fourth Amendment Poets." 47 *Stanford Law Review* pp. 261–268 (1995).

31. See Craig D. Uchida, Timothy S. Bynum, Dennis Rogan, and Donna M. Murasky, "Acting in Good Faith: The Effects of *U.S.* v. *Leon* on the Police and the Courts." 30 *Arizona Law Review* pp. 467–495 (1988).

32. *Bivens* v. *Six Unknown Agents,* 403 U.S. 388 (1971).

33. *Stone* v. *Powell,* 428 U.S. 465, 540 (1976).

34. *United States* v. *Leon,* 468 U.S. 897 (1984).

35. Id. at 898.

36. Id. at 907.

37. Id. at 898.

38. *Massachusetts* v. *Sheppard,* 468 U.S. 981 (1984).

39. Id. at 988.

40. *Illinois* v. *Krull,* 480 U.S. 340 (1987).

41. See *Franks* v. *Delaware,* 438 U.S. 154 (1978).

42. See *Lo-Ji Sales, Inc.* v. *New York,* 442 U.S. 319 (1979).

43. *Leon,* 468 U.S. at 923.

44. Id.; Anne Clark, "The Exclusionary Rule." *The Geo L.J. Twenty-Fifth Annual Review of C.P.* 84 pp. 877–878 (1996).

45. Leigh A. Morrissey, "State Courts Reject Leon on State Constitutional Grounds." 47 *Vanderbilt Law Review* pp. 917–941 (1994).

46. *Arizona* v. *Evans,* 115 S.Ct. 1185 (1995).

47. Id. at 1194.

48. Id. at 1193.

49. See Joseph H. Palmer, Jr., "Expanding the Good Faith Exception to the Exclusionary Rule." 29 *Creighton Law Review* pp. 903–937 (1996).

50. *Nardone* v. *United States,* 308 U.S. 338 (1939).

51. *Wong Sun* v. *United States,* 371 U.S. 471 (1963).

52. *Brown* v. *Illinois,* 422 U.S. 590 (1975).

53. See Aaron C. Yarcusko, "Brown to Payton to Harris: A Fourth Amendment Double Play by the Supreme Court." 43 *Case Western Reserve Law Review* pp. 253–286 (1992).

54. For an excellent discussion of these issues see Clark, supra note 44 at 879–880. See *United States* v. *Daniel,* 932 F.2d 517 (6th Cir.), cert denied, 502 U.S. 890 (1991).

55. See *United States* v. *Bradley,* 922 F.2d 1290 (6th Cir. 1991).

56. *Dunaway* v. *New York,* 442 U.S. 200 (1979).

57. *Oregon* v. *Elstad,* 470 U.S. 298 (1985).

58. See Clark, supra note 44 at 881.

59. *Segura* v. *United States,* 468 U.S. 796 (1984).

60. *Murray* v. *United States,* 487 U.S. 533 (1988).

61. Id.

62. Clark, supra note 44 at 882–883.

63. *Nix* v. *Williams,* 467 U.S. 431 (1984).

64. *Brewer* v. *Williams,* 700 F.2d 1164 (1983).

65. Supra note 63.

66. See Jessica Forbes, "The Inevitable Discovery Exception, Primary Evidence, and the Emasculation of the Fourth Amendment." 55 *Fordham Law Review* pp. 1221–1238 (1987).
67. *Harris* v. *New York,* 401 U.S. 222 (1971).
68. *Oregon* v. *Hass,* 420 U.S. 714 (1975).
69. Supra note 66 at 1227.
70. See Milt Hirsch, "Alternatives to the Exclusionary Rule." 13 *Search and Seizure Law Report* pp. 65–70 (1986); Donald MacDougall, "The Exclusionary Rule and its Alternatives—Remedies for Constitutional Violations in Canada and the United States." 76 *Journal of Criminal Law and Criminology* pp. 608–655 (1985).
71. *United States* v. *Calandra,* 414 U.S. 338 (1974).
72. *United States* v. *Janis,* 428 U.S. 433 (1976).
73. *In re Gault,* 387 U.S. 1 (1967).
74. *INS* v. *Lopez-Mendoza,* 468 U.S. 1032 (1984).
75. See Harvey Berkman, "Bill: Illegal Evidence Just a Tort." 17 *The National Law Journal* p. A14 (February 20, 1995).
76. Rolando V. del Carmen, *Civil Liabilities in American Policing* (Englewood Cliffs, NJ: Prentice Hall, Inc., 1991), p. 31. A comprehensive discussion of Section 1983 lawsuits is beyond the scope of this text; see del Carmen for an excellent treatment of this subject.
77. See *Rakas* v. *Illinois,* 439 U.S. 128 (1978).
78. Lawrence H. Tribe, *American Constitutional Law,* 2d ed. (Mineola, N.Y.: The Foundation Press, 1988), p. 107.
79. *Bellis* v. *United States,* 417 U.S. 85 (1974); Clark, supra note 44 at 874.
80. See *United States* v. *Sims,* 845 F.2d 1564 (11th Cir.), cert denied, 488 U.S. 957 (1988).
81. *Katz* v. *United States,* 389 U.S. 347 (1967).
82. Id. at 348.
83. Id.
84. *Katz* v. *United States,* 389 U.S. 347, 361 (1967) (Harlan, J., concurring).
85. See Eulis Simien, Jr., "The Interrelationship of the Scope of the Fourth Amendment and Standing to Object to Unreasonable Searches." 41 *Arkansas Law Review* pp. 487–583 (1988).
86. *Rakas* v. *Illinois,* 439 U.S. 128 (1978).
87. *Rawlings* v. *Kentucky,* 448 U.S. 98 (1980).
88. *Oliver* v. *United States,* 466 U.S. 170 (1984).
89. Id. at 178.
90. *California* v. *Ciraolo,* 476 U.S. 206 (1986).
91. Id. at 213.
92. Id. at 214.
93. *Florida* v. *Riley,* 109 S.Ct. 693 (1989).
94. *California* v. *Greenwood,* 108 S.Ct. 1625 (1988).
95. See Jon E. Lemole, "From Katz to Greenwood: Abandonment Gets Recycled from the Trash Pile—Can our Garbage be Saved from the Court's Rummaging Hands?" *Case Western Reserve Law Review* pp. 581–612 (1991).
96. Supra note 94 at 1625, 1628–1629.
97. See, e.g., Thomas J. Hickey and Rolando v. del Carmen, "The Evolution of Standing in Search and Seizure Cases." 27 *Criminal Law Bulletin* pp. 134–158 (1991).

4 THE LAW OF SEARCH AND SEIZURE—SEARCH AND ARREST WARRANTS

Outline

Key Terms

Chapter 3 discussed the exclusionary rule of evidence and observed that exclusionary rule questions may arise in Fourth, Fifth, or Sixth Amendment cases. This chapter focuses more directly on search and seizure issues arising under the Fourth Amendment. The Fourth Amendment provides:

> The right of the people to be secure in their persons, houses, papers, and effects, against unreasonable searches and seizures, shall not be violated, and no Warrants shall issue, but upon probable cause, supported by Oath or affirmation, and particularly describing the place to be searched, and the persons or things to be seized.

The Probable Cause Standard

One of the Fourth Amendment's most important provisions is the probable cause requirement. **Probable cause** is defined as a set of facts or circumstances that would lead a reasonable person to believe that a person committed a crime, or that contraband may be found in a particular place. **Contraband** is property that is unlawful to possess.

Probable cause is a restriction on arbitrary government conduct or the abuse of governmental authority—police officers may not subject someone to a search or arrest him or her simply because they may "feel like it." To subject someone to these processes, there must be an objective reason to believe that the individual has violated the law.

In recent years, the probable cause inquiry has become less complex.[1] The Supreme Court has held that the probable cause showing is an objective one. An officer's subjective belief about whether he or she had probable cause in a particular situation is not the focus of the inquiry; rather, because it is an objective inquiry, the test focuses on whether or not a reasonable person would have believed that probable cause existed in a particular situation.[2] A police officer's knowledge, experience, and training, however, are considered by a court in determining whether or not probable cause supported a particular action.[3] Moreover, the probable cause determination must be based upon articulable facts and circumstances that give rise to an officer's belief that crime is afoot. The officer must be prepared to testify in court about the objective facts and circumstances that led him or her to believe that a crime was occurring. An unconfirmed "hunch" or "feeling" that someone is involved in criminal activity is never enough to satisfy the probable cause requirement.

Many different standards of proof are used in the U.S. legal system. Probable cause is one of these standards. Table 4.1 illustrates several of the different standards that are used in different situations and proceedings.

As the term implies, probable cause requires the showing of a probability that a crime has taken place, or that contraband may be found in a certain place. It does not require certainty. The U.S. Supreme Court has stated:

> In dealing with probable cause . . . as the very name implies, we deal with probabilities. These are not technical; they are the factual and practical considerations of everyday life on which reasonable and prudent men, not legal technicians, act.[4]

Probable cause must be established with facts. The Supreme Court has not established the precise level of probability required to establish probable cause. It is clear that

---

TABLE **4.1**   **Levels of Proof in the U.S. Legal System**

Type of Proceeding	Level of Proof Required
Civil investigations	No suspicion
Stop and frisk investigation	Reasonable suspicion of suspicious activity
Arrest with a warrant	Probable cause
Arrest without a warrant	Probable cause
Search and seizure with a warrant	Probable cause
Search and seizure without a warrant	Probable cause
Administrative hearings	Substantial evidence in the record as a whole
Civil trials	Clear and convincing evidence
Civil trials	A preponderance of the evidence*
Criminal trials	Proof beyond a reasonable doubt

*The standard of proof required in different types of civil cases sometimes varies among different states.

probable cause requires more than mere suspicion of wrongdoing. A number of the Supreme Court's earlier decisions appeared to adopt a more-probable-than-not test for determining probable cause.[5] More recent decisions seem to require an even less demanding standard. In *Illinois* v. *Gates*,[6] a case involving a search for unlawful drugs conducted with a warrant, the Court asserted that the probable cause requirement was satisfied by demonstrating a "fair probability" that contraband could be found in a particular place.[7]

The case law appears to indicate that there may be a slight difference in the probable cause showing required when the police act with a warrant, and when they act without one. On numerous occasions the Supreme Court has signaled a preference for the use of warrants. In *United States* v. *Ventresca*,[8] the Court stated that in a case where probable cause was questionable, a search with a warrant may be upheld, whereas a search without one would be unlawful.

U.S. Supreme Court interpretations of the Fourth Amendment have indicated that probable cause is required in four[9] different situations:

1. When the police search for and seize evidence with a warrant;[10]
2. When an arrest is made with a warrant;[11]
3. When the police search for and seize evidence without a warrant;[12]
4. When the police make an arrest without a warrant.[13]

Establishing Probable Cause

Four types of information may be used by a police officer to establish probable cause:

1. Facts obtained from criminal, unidentified or anonymous informants, including hearsay evidence;
2. Facts obtained from criminal, unidentified or anonymous informants plus corroborative (follow-up) police investigation;

3. Facts obtained from identified non-criminal informants, including witnesses;
4. Facts obtained by police officers with their own senses, including information about a suspect's past criminal record.

The next section will discuss how to establish probable cause with each of these types of information.

Informants.   Police informants may be persons of questionable reputation and character. In fact, many are criminals or associates of criminals, who overhear statements and sometimes solicit information about crimes on behalf of the police. The information that informants provide to police, however, is often invaluable.[14] Highlight 4.1 provides a brief description of an informant's role in the trial of Sheik Abdul Rahman and his followers, who were recently convicted of various federal crimes for conspiring to destroy various U.S. properties.

Informants may provide information to the police that they have obtained through direct observation of criminal behavior. Sometimes the information may be a less direct indication of criminal activity such as rumors, or conversations that have been overheard, which incriminate particular individuals. Such information may be **hearsay evidence,** which is an out-of-court statement that is offered to prove a matter in court made by a person who is not testifying at trial.[15] The following example illustrates hearsay evidence. Suppose that an informant overheard a conversation between two women in a barroom, which indicated that John, a suspect in a criminal homicide, was involved in a fight with Joe, who died later that same night. If the informant tried to testify at John's manslaughter trial that he heard the women say that John was involved in a fight with Joe, the statement would not be admissible because it is hearsay evidence. The rationale for excluding hearsay evidence is that it may be unreliable. There is no opportunity to question the person who made the statement originally because he or she is not present at trial. The same information may be used by the police, however, to help establish probable cause to obtain a warrant to search John's home for evidence of his involvement in Joe's death.[16]

In *McCray* v. *Illinois,*[17] the Supreme Court held that criminal defendants are not always entitled to be advised of an informant's identity. In these circumstances it is more difficult to establish probable cause to obtain a warrant. In general it is much easier to obtain a warrant with information obtained by a police officer through his or her own senses. The following examples illustrate this point. Suppose that an experienced police patrol officer drives by Debbie's house and sees a marijuana plant growing on the window ledge. The officer completes a search warrant affidavit attesting to his or her observation, which he or she takes to a judge. A judge is likely to issue the warrant based on the officer's observation. Suppose, however, that Mark, a police informant who has been arrested for various crimes on many occasions, tells a police officer that Debbie is growing marijuana in her home. Unless a judge is provided with some additional information, he or she is unlikely to issue a search warrant based solely on these facts.

A Test for Analyzing Informants and Their Information.   In 1964, in *Aguilar* v. *Texas,*[18] the U.S. Supreme Court formulated a test to determine if information obtained

----
Highlight 4.1

World Trade Center Bombing Suspect Denies Conspiracy

Sheik Omar Abdul Rahman says he is not a conspirator, even though he's been charged with spearheading a group allegedly bent on waging a war of terrorism against the U.S. government. 'We preach the word of Allah,' says the fiery, blind Egyptian cleric, 'but we do not conspire.' Abdul Rahman, with his lawyer and his own translator present, refused to answer most specifics about the case, which is expected to go to trial next year in this federal courthouse. 'How can we conspire against America while the American people were very generous to us and they accepted us here?' the sheik insists.

From Abdul Rahman's point of view, Egypt pushed Washington into arresting and charging him with the alleged plot. The Egyptian regime just ordered and the American government just rushed to obey, says the Muslim fundamentalist cleric, but says Rahman, Washington got an extra push from U.S. Senator Alfonse D'Amato, who lobbied Attorney Janet Reno to place the Sheik under arrest. Both Senator D'Amato and Egyptian President Hosni Mubarak were, according to investigators, targeted for assassination by Sheik Abdul Rahman and his alleged associates.

In his off-camera interview with CNN and other news organizations, Abdul Rahman seemed in good shape, despite his diabetes and his claim of poor prison conditions. 'The constitution has taken a vacation,' says the sheik, speaking of conditions in the pre-trial detention center. Last week, two defendants in the World Trade Center bombing case apparently tried to kill themselves, their lawyers say because of conditions in the federal jail.

On other matters, the Sheik says Emad Salem, the FBI informant who helped break the case against him, was a double agent for Egyptian intelligence,

AP/Wide World Photos

although he offered no proof. The sheik denied again he ever worked for the U.S. Central Intelligence Agency and says the war in Afghanistan, for which he reportedly helped recruit Muslim fighters, was dictated by the Koran, the Islamic holy book.

from an informant established probable cause for the issuance of a search warrant. In this famous case the search warrant affidavit stated:

> Affiants have received reliable information from a credible person and do believe that heroin, marijuana, barbiturates, and other narcotics and narcotic paraphernalia are being kept at the above described premises for the purpose of sale and use contrary to the provisions of the law.

The Supreme Court held that the information presented in the affidavit failed to establish probable cause for several reasons. First, it did not inform the magistrate of some of the underlying circumstances from which the informant had concluded that the illegal drugs were where he claimed they were. In addition, it failed to indicate why the police had concluded that the informant was "credible" or why his information was "reliable." The problem with such an affidavit was that it would not allow the judge to function as a "neutral and detached magistrate," as the Fourth Amendment requires. Rather, such a bare-bones affidavit would permit police officers who are "engaged in the often competitive enterprise of ferreting out crime," to draw inferences about whether there is probable cause to conduct a search.[19]

The *Aguilar* test has become known as the **two-pronged test.** It is used to determine if information obtained from an informant establishes probable cause for the issuance of a search warrant.[20] The two-pronged test is summarized as follows:

> **Prong 1:** Focuses on the informant's basis of knowledge. Under this prong facts must be shown that allow a judge to make a determination about whether the informant had sufficient grounds for his or her belief that a suspect was involved in criminal behavior, or that contraband could be found in a particular place.
>
> **Prong 2:** Focuses on the informant's truthfulness. Under the "veracity" prong, adequate information had to be provided to allow a judge to determine the informant's credibility or the information's reliability.[21]

In 1969, *Spinelli* v. *United States*[22] helped to clarify the meaning of the two-pronged test. As Justice Byron White explained:

> If [a search warrant affidavit is based] on hearsay—an informant's report—what is necessary under *Aguilar* is one of two things: the informant must declare either (1) that he has himself seen or perceived the fact or facts asserted; or (2) that his information is hearsay, but there is good reason for believing it.[23]

Spinelli demonstrated that the basis of an informant's knowledge could be shown by providing substantial detail about the criminal activity as well.[24] The type of detail that would satisfy the *Aguilar-Spinelli* test was illustrated in *Draper* v. *United States*.[25] Federal agents were told by a previously reliable informant that Draper, who was selling illegal drugs to several addicts in Denver, would arrive from Chicago by train on a particular morning, bringing with him a quantity of heroin. The informant stated that Draper, whom the agent did not know, would be wearing certain clothing and would carry a tan zipper bag. Moreover, the informant provided a very detailed description of Draper. On the specified morning, a federal agent and a Denver police officer observed a person with the precise physical attributes and wearing the exact clothing described by the informant leave a train and walk toward the exit. The suspect was carrying a tan zipper bag. At that point the officers arrested Draper and during a search of the bag, discovered heroin.

The Supreme Court held that the facts in this case were sufficient to establish probable cause to arrest Draper and to seize the heroin. Because the informant's description of Draper and his activities was so precise, it followed that the police had "probable cause and reasonable grounds" to believe that he was violating the law.

Following *Aguilar* and *Spinelli,* U.S. courts used the two-pronged test to determine if an informant's information established probable cause for issuance of a search warrant. Both parts of the test were regarded as separate and distinct, and each part had to be satisfied to establish probable cause for issuing a search warrant. In 1983, the Supreme Court developed a new test for probable cause that did not treat both parts of the *Aguilar* test as separate inquiries.

A Totality of Circumstances Probable Cause Test.   The two-pronged test was an effective but relatively complex way to determine if probable cause supported issuing a search warrant. In 1983, however, the Supreme Court rejected that test and developed a new standard for determining if an informant's information establishes probable cause for issuing a search warrant. In *Illinois* v. *Gates,*[26] police officers received an anonymous letter, which is presented in Highlight 4.2, stating that Lance and Sue Gates were drug dealers. The anonymous letter contained detailed information about the Gates's drug-selling practices. The letter was sent to the chief of police of the Bloomingdale, Illinois, Police Department, who referred the letter to his detective division. Detective Mader, who conducted a follow-up investigation, learned that Lance Gates had made a reservation on a flight to West Palm Beach, Florida, on May 5, at 4:15 PM. Mader then made arrangements with an agent of the Drug Enforcement Administration (DEA) for surveillance of the flight. The agent later informed Mader that Gates had boarded the flight and that federal agents in Florida had observed him arrive in Florida and take a taxi to the nearby Holiday Inn. In addition, they reported that Gates went to a room registered to Susan Gates and that at 7:00 AM the next morning, Gates and a woman left the motel in a Mercury bearing Illinois license plates and headed north on an interstate often used by travelers to the Chicago area. The DEA agent informed Mader that the car's license plate number indicated that Gates owned the vehicle. The agent also informed Mader that the driving time between West Palm Beach and Bloomingdale, Illinois, was approximately 22 to 24 hours.

Mader signed an affidavit setting forth the foregoing facts and submitted it with a copy of the anonymous letter to a judge. The judge issued a search warrant for the Gates's residence and for their car.

At 5:15 AM on May 7, Lance and Sue Gates returned to their home in Bloomingdale, driving the car in which they had left West Palm Beach. The Bloomingdale Police were waiting for them, searched the trunk of the car, and found approximately 350 pounds of marijuana, weapons, and other contraband. A search of the Gates's home revealed marijuana, weapons, and other contraband. An Illinois circuit court ordered suppression of all the evidence, because the affidavit submitted to the judge who issued the search warrant failed to establish probable cause to believe that the Gates's automobile and home contained the contraband in question. The Illinois Supreme

Highlight 4.2

Anonymous letter in *Illinois* v. *Gates,* 462 U.S. 213 (1983)

 This letter is to inform you that you have a couple in your town who strictly make their living on selling drugs. They are Sue and Lance Gates, they live on Greenway, off Bloomingdale Rd. in the condominiums. Most of their buys are done in Florida. Sue his wife drives their car to Florida, where she leaves it to be loaded with drugs, then Lance flys [sic] down and drives it back. Sue flys [sic] back after she drops the car off in Florida. May 3 she is driving down there again and Lance will be flying down in a few days to drive it back. At the time Lance drives the car back

he has the trunk loaded with over $100,000.00 in drugs. Presently they have over $100,000.00 worth of drugs in their basement.

They brag about the fact they never have to work, and make their entire living on pushers.

I guarantee if you watch them carefully you will make a big catch. They are friends with some big drug dealers, who visit their house often.

Lance & Susan Gates
Greenway
in Condominiums

Court affirmed the suppression order, but the U.S. Supreme Court concluded that the search warrant affidavit established probable cause.

In applying the *Aguilar* two-pronged test to the search warrant affidavit in *Gates,* the Illinois Supreme Court believed that the anonymous letter had to satisfy both parts of the test. Accordingly, the letter as supplemented by detective Mader's corroborating evidence, had to show the letter writer's basis of knowledge, or the particular means by which he or she received the information given in the letter. Second, it had to provide facts sufficiently establishing either the informant's veracity, or, alternatively, the reliability of the informant's report.

The Illinois Supreme Court decided that the veracity prong was not satisfied because there was no basis for concluding that the anonymous letter writer was credible. In addition, the letter gave no indication of the basis of its writer's knowledge of Gates's activities. The Illinois court believed also that the letter failed to provide sufficient detail to permit the inference that the letter writer had a reliable basis for his statements. Therefore, the court concluded that the search warrant affidavit failed to establish probable cause.

A majority of the U.S. Supreme Court justices disagreed.[27] The Court abandoned the *Aguilar* test, which required that both prongs be satisfied independently. The Court asserted that the *Aguilar* test was excessively technical, rigid, and at odds with common-sense notions of probable cause. Rather, the Supreme Court held that the two parts should be examined as part of a **totality of circumstances test** for determining probable cause. This standard asks a reviewing judge or magistrate to examine all of the circumstances in a case and make a common-sense determination of whether probable cause exists to support a search. Under the totality of circumstances test a deficiency in one part of the two-pronged test may be compensated for "by a strong showing as to the other, or by some other" indication of reliability. The key factor is the reliability of the information used to make the probable cause determination. The Supreme Court concluded:

> The task of the issuing magistrate is simply to make a practical, common-sense decision whether, given all the circumstances set forth in the affidavit before him, including the "veracity" and "basis of knowledge" of persons supplying hearsay information, there is a fair probability that contraband or evidence of a crime will be found in a particular place. And the duty of a reviewing court is simply to ensure that the magistrate had a "substantial basis for . . . conclud[ing]" that probable cause existed.[28]

***The Use of Anonymous Tips after* Illinois *v.* Gates.**   The *Gates* probable cause test permits anonymous tips from informants to be used to establish probable cause. When anonymous tips are used to formulate probable cause it is essential for police officers to corroborate the informant's information. In *Gates,* the anonymous informant was accurate in his or her prediction of Lance and Sue Gates's actions. Even though the acts of flying and driving to Florida and returning to Illinois were not criminal acts, these details provided a reason to conclude that the informant had reliable information. Therefore, although the tip by itself did not establish probable cause, an examination of the totality of circumstances indicated that probable cause existed to search the Gates's home and car. Such detailed corroboration is necessary whenever the police attempt to get a warrant based upon an anonymous informant's tip.

Illinois v. *Gates* makes it easier to establish probable cause for the issuance of a search warrant.[29] The danger of this approach is that unethical police officers could fabricate anonymous tips to assist them in obtaining search warrants. If, however, it is shown that such practices begin to occur with some frequency, the Supreme Court may mandate a return to a more technical approach for determining probable cause. It is a good law enforcement practice to continue to follow the *Aguilar* two-pronged test. If a search warrant affidavit satisfies the two-pronged test, it is on solid legal ground and will satisfy the *Gates* totality of circumstances test. Moreover, some state supreme courts using state constitutions have rejected the *Gates* totality of circumstances approach in favor of *Aguilar's* more stringent probable cause test.

Information from an Identified Victim.   When compared to the process of obtaining a search warrant with information from a criminal or anonymous source, it is much easier to get a search warrant with information from a victim or a witness. When a criminal informant or an anonymous source provides information to the police, there is always a question about the source's credibility. When a victim or a witness provides the information used to formulate probable cause, however, the informant's credibility may be presumed. In these situations a judge or a magistrate will use the *Gates* totality of circumstances test to review a search warrant affidavit to ensure that the source's information presents a sufficient indication of probable cause. A police officer must present information that satisfies the Fourth Amendment's particularity requirement. If the information that is presented to the judge or magistrate is highly specific it will provide an adequate basis for issuance of a search or an arrest warrant.

Information from Law Enforcement Sources.   A final source of information to establish probable cause is direct observation by police, which may be more reliable than other types of information. If, however, police officers receive information about criminal activity as a result of their own observations or from other law enforcement officers they must still present their evidence to a judge or a magistrate for a probable cause determination. In these circumstances the information is presumed to be reliable,[30] and it is easier to obtain a search warrant. For example, suppose a police patrol officer passes by a home in a residential area of the city. He is informed by neighborhood residents that the persons who reside in the home are involved in manufacturing and selling methamphetamine (speed). The officer decides to investigate further and approaches the garage next to the house, which adjoins a city park. He smells a very strong and peculiar odor emanating from the garage and knows from experience that this type of odor is often associated with the manufacture of methamphetamine. This information would provide a sufficient basis for a judge or a magistrate to issue a search warrant for the premises.

The Use of Warrants in U.S. Justice Systems

This section focuses primarily on search warrants. Chapter 5 will present a much more detailed treatment of the law of arrest. Many of the general principles considered here, however, apply equally to search warrants and arrest warrants. A **search warrant** is a court order issued by a judge or a magistrate that directs a law enforcement officer to search for and seize contraband or any evidence of a crime. An **arrest warrant** is an order that directs a peace officer to bring someone before the court to face criminal charges. Because search warrants are used more frequently in U.S. justice systems, this discussion focuses on them.

A judge or a magistrate may issue a search or an arrest warrant only if he or she is presented with a sworn statement, termed an **affidavit,** which establishes probable cause to believe that the contraband is present in a specific place or that a specified person committed a crime. The U.S. Supreme Court has held that warrantless searches are presumed to be "unreasonable under the Fourth Amendment subject only to a few specifically established and well-delineated exceptions."[31] A sample search warrant affidavit is featured in Figure 4.1. The numerous exceptions to the warrant requirement are considered in later chapters.

Reasons for Obtaining Warrants

If time permits and there is no immediate reason to arrest a suspect or to conduct a search for contraband, police officers are advised to obtain a search warrant or an arrest warrant. There are several reasons for this. First, the Supreme Court has indicated a strong preference for warrants. This is because a warrant places an impartial party, a judge or a magistrate, between the police and the person suspected of criminal activity. A judge should be able to provide a more informed decision on the issue of whether probable cause supports a particular police action.[32]

FIGURE 4.1

Sample Search Warrent Affidavit

State of Rhode Island and Providence Plantations
Complaint To Search and Seize Property/or Person

TO .... Justice of the Supreme, Superior Court,
or Judge of the District Court of the State of Rhode Island

a) .... Chief, Deputy Chief, Captain, of Police,

Sheriff, Deputy Sheriff of ...., Member of the Division of the State Police

b) .... a person authorized by law to bring complaints for violation
of the law which it is my responsibility to enforce/a person who has a right to possession of the property stolen, embezzled, or obtained by
false pretense or pretenses:

ON OATH COMPLAINS THAT:

(1) Certain property has been stolen or embezzled, or obtained by false pretense, or pretenses, with intent to cheat or defraud within
this state or elsewhere;

(2) Certain property has been kept, suffered to be kept, concealed, deposited, or possessed in violation of law, or for the purpose of
violating the law;

(3) Certain property is designed or intended for use, or is or has been used in violation of law, or as a means of committing a violation of law;

(4)

and prays that a warrant to search for and seize said property/person be issued and if the same be subject to forfeiture, that
the property be forfeited.

The person/property or articles to be searched for and/or seized is described as follows:

The name of the owner or keeper, thereof (if known) is:

The place or person to be searched is described as follows:

Your complainant prays that said warrant may be served in the nighttime for the reason that:

Subscribed and sworn to before me:

....
Date

....
Judge/Justice

....
Complainant

FIGURE **4.1** (*continued*)

AFFIDAVIT

Your affiant upon oath states that he has reason to believe and does believe that grounds for such warrant exist and states the following facts on which such belief is founded on the following affidavit.

....
Date   Affiant

...., Sc.   In .... this

.... day of ...., 19 ...., before me personally came

.... and made oath to the truth of the foregoing.

....
Judge of the Di   Court
Justice of the '   e/Superior Court

Second, the officer may need less evidence to establish probable cause if he or she obtains a warrant.[33] A court reviewing the initial determination of probable cause will defer to the issuing judge's findings unless it is very clear that the application for the warrant lacked probable cause.[34] In fact, there is a presumption that probable cause supported the search or arrest. If, however, the police officer acting without a warrant determines that probable cause exists, that presumption disappears. The probable cause determination should be scrutinized carefully by defense attorneys to ensure that the officer was acting properly. If probable cause did not exist, the evidence seized during the search should be barred from use at the trial. In addition, as Chapter 3 indicated, even if a police officer acts with a facially valid search warrant that is determined subsequently not to have been supported by probable cause, any evidence seized may still be admitted at trial under the good-faith exception to the exclusionary rule.[35]

Third, obtaining a warrant will help shield police officers from potential civil liability. The United States has witnessed a litigation explosion in recent years. Law enforcement officers are hardly immune from civil lawsuits. If, however, a police officer acting in good faith relies on a search or an arrest warrant, it will provide him or her with a measure of protection. For example, suppose that a police officer with a valid warrant arrests a suspect in a highly publicized murder case. Later, the suspect, who was found not guilty at trial, may file a civil lawsuit against the officer alleging false arrest. The fact that the officer relied upon a valid arrest warrant will give protection against civil liability. Figure 4.2 reproduces a search warrant.

The Judge's Role in the Warrant Process

Judges and magistrates play a crucial role in the warrant process. The Supreme Court has stated that the Fourth Amendment's "protection consists in requiring that [inferences about whether or not probable cause exists should] be drawn by a neutral and detached magistrate instead of being judged by [a police officer] engaged in the often competitive enterprise of ferreting out crime."[36]

Valid arrest warrants and search warrants may be obtained only from a judge or a magistrate. To get either type of warrant, police officers must demonstrate to the judge that they have probable cause. The amount of proof that investigators who are seeking an arrest warrant or a search warrant must present to a judge or a magistrate is presumed to be the same. Establishing probable cause in these varying situations requires a somewhat different showing, however, and the facts establishing probable cause for issuing a search warrant do not necessarily establish probable cause for an arrest (or vice versa). Officers applying for a search warrant must demonstrate that the contraband or other evidence sought is connected with a crime, and that it will be found in the particular place to be searched. Officers seeking an arrest warrant must show that a crime has been committed, and it is likely that the suspect to be arrested committed it.

FIGURE 4.2

Sample Search Warrant

𝕾𝖊𝖆𝖗𝖈𝖍 𝖂𝖆𝖗𝖗𝖆𝖓𝖙

State Ex rel	City/Town	County
vs Respondent		TO: An Officer authorized by law to execute the within warrant,

Complaint and affidavit having been made to me under oath,   and as I am satisfied that there is probable cause for the belief therein set forth that grounds for issuing a search warrant exist, you are hereby commanded diligently to search the place or person herein described for the property specified and to bring such property or articles, and to summon the owner, or keeper thereof, if any be named in the complaint, if to be found by you, to appear before the District Court in the district where such property shall have been seized, namely the .... Division of the District Court of Rhode Island.

Place or person to be searched:

Property or articles to be searched for:

Name of owner, or keeper, thereof if known to complainant:

Said warrant shall be served in the daytime — may be served in the nighttime — within seven (7) days fom the issuance hereof, AND IF NOT SERVED WITHIN SAID TIME TO BE RETURNED FORTHWITH TO A JUDGE SITTING IN THE ABOVE NAMED COURT.

Property seized by you hereunder shall be safely kept by you under the direction of the Court so long as may be necessary for the purpose of being used as evidence in any case. As soon as may be thereafter, if the same be subject to forfeiture, such further proceedings shall be had thereon for forfeiture as is prescribed by law.

Hereof fail not and MAKE TRUE RETURN PROMPTLY OF THIS WARRANT TO A JUDGE THERE SITTING with your doings thereon, accompanied by a written inventory of any property taken to a judge sitting in the above named court.

Issued at .... in the county of .... this

.... day of ...., A. D. 19............

....
Judge of the District Court
Justice of the Supreme/Superior Court

ACKNOWLEDGMENT OF RETURN

Warrant received on .... day of ...., 19..........., from

.... **at** ....

....
RIDC 002CA (4-74)   **Judge**

FIGURE 4.2 (*continued*)

RETURN OF SERVICE

STATE OF RHODE ISLAND AND PROVIDENCE PLANTATIONS

...., Sc.

At ....
(place)   (date)

A. D. 19............, pursuant to the within warrant I have made search during the daytime — during the nighttime — as commanded and submit herewith a written inventory of property taken:

I have also summoned ....

named in said Complaint, as commanded to appear before the .... Division of the

District Court in .... at 9:30 o'clock in the forenoon,

on .... A. D. 19............

I have also given to ....

the person from whom — from whose premises said property was taken — a copy of the within warrant — I have left a
copy of the within warrant at — on the place from which said property was taken —I did not find the person from whose
premises said property was taken but left a copy of said warrant at — on the place from which the property was taken.

....

Authorized Officer

Basic Elements of a Valid Search Warrant

The Fourth Amendment requires that a valid search or arrest warrant be based on probable cause accompanied by an affidavit detailing the reasons for believing that probable cause exists. The affidavit must describe specifically the place(s) to be searched and/or the person or things to be seized. This is termed the **particularity requirement.**

The Particularity Requirement

The particularity requirement demands specificity. Police officers must describe precisely the place to be searched or the person or things to be seized.[37] This requirement, which prevents the police from engaging in general fishing expeditions for evidence, expresses the founding fathers' distaste for general warrants that did not limit the discretion of the king's agents.[38]

Description of the Place to Be Searched.   To satisfy the Fourth Amendment's particularity requirement, the affiant's description of the place to be searched must be reasonably precise. The test is whether the description enables the officer "with reasonable effort [to] ascertain and identify the place intended."[39] Furthermore, the Supreme Court has stated that the warrant should be sufficiently precise as to leave nothing "to the discretion of the officer executing the warrant."[40] This standard, however, is flexible. In *Maryland* v. *Garrison,*[41] the Supreme Court upheld a search warrant's validity even though it was later demonstrated that the warrant affidavit was insufficiently particular. Police officers had obtained a warrant to search "premises known as 2036 Park Avenue third floor apartment." While they were executing the warrant, the officers discovered two separate apartments on the third floor and mistakenly entered Garrison's apartment rather than that of the individual specified in the warrant. They found drugs belonging to Garrison. The Court held that this evidence should not be suppressed because the officers neither knew nor should have known that there were two apartments on the third floor.

Additional examples should help to clarify these issues. A warrant that authorizes the police to search for illegal drugs contains the following description of the house to be searched:

> A white colonial-style house with blue shutters, located at 75 Apple Lane, at the intersection of Apple Lane and Spring Road, Houston, Texas, which is known by agents to be the residence of John Doe.

This description of the place to be searched is sufficiently particular to satisfy the Fourth Amendment.

A second warrant that authorizes the police to search for evidence in a murder case contains the following description of a room in a boardinghouse, in which the murder suspect, John Doe lives:

> Room 12 in the Happy Day Room and Boarding House, the present residence of John Doe, located at 25 Apple Lane, Houston, Texas.

This description of the place to be searched is sufficiently particular to satisfy the Fourth Amendment. Further, the description may be sufficiently particular to support the search even if the police had mistakenly identified the room number in their description. To illustrate, suppose that John Doe resides in Room 10 rather than Room 12 at the Happy Day Room and Boardinghouse. When the police arrive at the scene to serve the search warrant, they realize their mistake after speaking with the owner of the Boarding House. They search Room 10. The search based upon the warrant is likely to be upheld by a reviewing court, despite the mistaken description.[42]

Finally, a third warrant authorizes the police to search for stolen property and contains the following description of an apartment to be searched:

> An upstairs apartment belonging to John Doe in an apartment complex located on Spring Road, Houston, Texas.

If there are different apartment complexes located on Spring Road, this description will not be sufficiently particular. Any evidence obtained from a search of John Doe's apartment with this warrant should be suppressed by a reviewing court.

Description of the Persons or Things to Be Seized.   The Fourth Amendment's language permits search warrants to be issued either for persons, or for evidence of a crime. For example, if police officers have probable cause to believe that the victim of a recent kidnapping is being held in a particular house, or a fugitive is hiding in a residence, they may obtain search warrants for the premises. The Fourth Amendment requires, however, that if a search warrant is to be issued, the person or things to be seized with a search warrant be described with sufficient particularity.

What constitutes a sufficiently particular description of the persons or things to be seized varies considerably with the type of evidence or contraband sought by the police. For example, federal agents were conducting a racketeering and mail fraud investigation involving several nightclubs, peep shows, movie theaters, and adult bookstores in Boston's Combat Zone (an adult entertainment district). The agents believed that probable cause existed to support the issuance of a search warrant for the second floor offices belonging to the owner of several of these establishments, located at 671 Washington Street, Boston, Massachusetts. In the search warrant affidavit the agents described the materials to be seized as follows:

> [R]ecords, documents, notes and physical objects which constitute evidence of and instrumentalities of violations of 18 U.S.C. Sections 1961(c) and (d) (i.e., conducting and participating in the affairs of an enterprise, and agreeing to do so, through a pattern of racketeering activity consisting of multiple acts of bribery and mail fraud, Title 18, U.S.C. S 1341, and Title 18 U.S.C. S 371), and, in particular, records documents, notes and physical objects evidencing the ownership or control of businesses in the Combat Zone in Boston . . . and the payment of bribes to public officials with regulatory authority over such licensed premises; said records, documents, notes and physical objects to include licenses or copies thereof, personnel records and payroll records, a list of employees, checkbooks and check stubs, accounting books and ledgers, invoices, corporate books and records, including stock ledgers, documents bearing the names and/or telephone numbers of police officers or other municipal officials, citations, incident reports, correspondence, and supplies and objects used in the operation of the listed businesses, including peep show tokens and automatic amusement devices.

Source: Spencer Grant/Stock Boston

This description of the items to be seized was held to be sufficiently particular to support issuance of a search warrant for the defendant's business premises.[43]

Another example should help to further clarify the particularity requirement when police seek a search warrant for evidence of a crime. Suppose that officers have probable cause to believe that a suspect's residence contained evidence of numerous illegal drug transactions. A warrant authorizes law enforcement agents to search for and seize the following items:

> All money, financial instruments, his and her matching gold Rolex watches, gold and diamond rings, controlled substances, [and] drug paraphernalia.

This description of the items to be seized with the search warrant was held to be sufficiently particular when an affidavit contained probable cause to believe that the defendant's home contained evidence of various illegal drug crimes.[44]

A third warrant authorizes federal agents to search a specified office at a particular location for evidence of medicare fraud. In the search warrant affidavit the agents described the materials to be seized as follows:

> [A]ll medical records in the offices of Dr. Smith.

This description does not satisfy the Fourth Amendment's particularity requirement.[45]

Items That May Be Seized with a Search Warrant

Several categories of items may be seized by police officers acting with a search warrant:[46]

1. mere evidence of a crime, including a suspect's personal belongings;
2. fruits of a crime;

3. instrumentalities of a crime;

4. other contraband.

In federal criminal cases a warrant may be issued to search and seize

1. property that constitutes evidence of the commission of a criminal offense; or

2. contraband, the fruits of crime, or things otherwise criminally possessed; or

3. property designed or intended for use or which is or has been used as the means of committing a criminal offense; or

4. persons for whose arrest there is probable cause, or who is unlawfully restrained.[47]

A fact pattern illustrates these categories of items that may be seized. Jack and Jill, a married couple, plan and execute an almost-perfect bank robbery in Portland, Oregon. After the successful robbery, which nets $40,000 in cash and the bank manager's gold Rolex wristwatch, the police have probable cause to believe that Jack and Jill committed the crime. They obtain a valid search warrant for the suspects' home. While executing the search warrant, police seize numerous items.

1. *Mere evidence of the crime* is any evidence, including for example, personal property and papers, clothing, and copies of personal records that would implicate Jack and Jill in the robbery. At one time the rule was that police officers were permitted to seize only the fruits and instrumentalities of a crime, not mere evidence. The modern rule is that any type of property may be seized with a search warrant. Possible evidence that could be seized may include the masks and camouflage clothing worn by the robbers, hair samples to be used for comparison with evidence left at the crime scene, Jack's personal diary, and the maps and photographs used to plan the robbery.

2. *Fruits of the crime* include the loot Jack and Jill obtained from the bank. The $40,000 and the gold Rolex wrist watch would be considered fruits of this crime and could be seized with the search warrant.

3. *Instrumentalities of the crime* include anything that was an aid in committing the crime, such as the gun that was pointed at the bank tellers, the getaway vehicle, maps or diagrams of the area, or a pocket police scanner used to track the police.

4. *Other contraband* such as illegal marijuana plants growing in plain view on the kitchen window ledge inside the home may be seized.

Additional Requirements of a Valid Search Warrant

Case law, statutes, and police department administrative rules impose additional requirements that must be satisfied to obtain a valid search warrant. These include

1. **A neutral and detached judge or magistrate who must issue and sign the search warrant:** This is designed to ensure that the judge or magistrate will make a fair determination as to whether probable cause supports the issuance of a warrant. Law enforcement officers may never issue search or arrest warrants. In *Coolidge* v. *New Hampshire*,[48] the Supreme Court held that the attorney general of New Hampshire, as

the state's chief law enforcement officer, was not a neutral and detached magistrate. Therefore a search warrant that he had issued was invalid. In addition, judges or magistrates may not be paid according to the number of warrants they issue. That would give them a financial incentive to issue more warrants, some of which may be invalid.[49] Judges or magistrates should never accompany the police when they serve a warrant or otherwise participate in the law enforcement process.[50]

2. **Oath or affirmation:** Police officers should present all of the information in their possession that would justify a finding that probable cause supports a search or seizure. If police officers have additional information that is not presented to the judge or magistrate in the affidavit, this evidence may not be used later to support a deficient warrant.[51] The oath or affirmation requirement does not mandate, however, that information be presented to the judge or magistrate in written form. A few states, including California and Arizona, allow police officers to apply for search warrants by telephone. An **oral search warrant** application must be supported by the officer's sworn statement detailing his or her reasons for believing that probable cause exists.

3. **"Fresh information":** The affidavit supporting the warrant must indicate to the judge or magistrate that the evidence or contraband is present in the place to be searched. A warrant is invalid if it is based on stale information. Precisely what constitutes stale information depends upon the nature of the crimes involved, but the facts in an affidavit supporting a search warrant must be sufficiently fresh to allow a judge to conclude that probable cause will exist when the search is to be conducted.[52] For example, in a prohibition era case, the Supreme Court held that probable cause to search a hotel room did not exist when a search warrant affidavit stated that an informant had purchased illegal liquor there three weeks earlier.[53]

4. **A statement detailing when the search warrant is to be served:** Some states require that a warrant must normally be served during the daytime unless there is a valid reason for serving it at night. For example, the rules that govern federal law enforcement agents state: "[A] warrant shall be served in the daytime, unless the issuing authority, by appropriate provision in the warrant, and for reasonable cause shown, authorizes its execution at times other than daytime."[54] When the premises described in a warrant are searched, the warrant is executed. Once the person, property, or contraband described in the warrant have been seized, the search must cease. The rationale for the daylight service rule is that serving a warrant during the daytime is likely to minimize the chances of a violent encounter between police officers and those whose home is being searched.

5. **A statement that the search warrant is to be executed within a certain time period:** In federal cases, a search warrant must be executed within ten days of its issuance.[55] Many states follow this rule as well; however, at least one state requires that a search warrant must be executed within 48 hours of its issuance. This requirement is designed to prevent the probable cause that justified issuing the warrant from becoming stale.

6. **An inventory of seized items and a receipt for seized property:** After a search with a warrant has been completed, federal law[56] and the laws of most states require police officers to complete an inventory of seized items and return a copy of the inventory and a copy of the search warrant to the judge who issued it originally. Police officers must give a receipt for all seized property to the person whose property is searched.

No Knock Searches

Before entering a structure to execute a search warrant, police officers are normally required to announce their identity and their purpose. They may enter a structure forcibly only if they are denied admittance. There are two reasons for this requirement. First, it decreases the possibility that the person who is subjected to the search will react in a violent manner. Second, it limits property damage by giving an occupant the opportunity to allow the police to enter voluntarily.[57] A **no knock entry** occurs when the police do not announce their presence before entering a structure. If police officers fail to comply with the "knock and announce" requirement, any evidence seized once they have entered the premises may be suppressed.[58]

There is an important exception to the **knock and announce rule,** which requires police officers to knock and announce their presence before entering a home to serve a search warrant. In *Ker* v. *California,*[59] the U.S. Supreme Court held that if announcing their presence would permit the occupant to destroy evidence, the police may enter a structure forcibly without identifying themselves. The knock and announce rule is not intended to make law enforcement a more dangerous profession. Therefore, when police officers would face greater danger if they announced their presence before entering a structure, the knock and announce rule may be waived.

The Supreme Court reaffirmed the knock and announce rule in 1995. In *Wilson* v. *Arkansas,*[60] the Court held that if a police officer fails to knock and announce his or her intention to serve a warrant, a resulting search may be unreasonable under the Fourth Amendment and any evidence found may be excluded. If, however, important law enforcement interests are likely to be jeopardized by complying with the rule, officers will not be required to knock and announce their presence. These interests include increased danger to the officers or the possibility that evidence will be destroyed. In 1997, the Supreme Court again upheld the knock and announce rule. At issue was a Wisconsin Supreme Court ruling that allowed police officers attempting to serve warrants in illegal drug cases to enter the home of suspects without knocking and announcing their presence because such cases are inherently dangerous. In *Richards* v. *Wisconsin,*[61] the U.S. Supreme Court held that the Fourth Amendment does not support a blanket exception to the knock and announce rule. The Court further stated, however, that dispensing with the knock and announce requirement is a reasonable police procedure if doing so would pose a danger to officers or would inhibit the investigation.

Anticipatory Search Warrants

An **anticipatory search warrant** is one that is issued by a judge in the absence of probable cause when there is reason to believe that probable cause will exist at some future time.[62] Anticipatory search warrants are rarely issued, and the supporting affidavit must contain facts that outline clearly the triggering event, such as the delivery of a package containing illegal drugs to a specified residence. The Supreme Court has not yet ruled on the constitutionality of issuing anticipatory search warrants; however, a number of lower courts have upheld this practice. The constitutional problem with these warrants is the Fourth Amendment's requirement that no warrant shall be issued without probable cause. Most often, no probable cause has been established when police officers apply for an anticipatory search warrant; rather, probable cause comes into being once the events described in the anticipatory search warrant begin to unfold.

For example, suppose that police officers have a substantial reason to believe (but not probable cause to believe) that a drug dealer plans to deliver a package of marijuana to a certain home. They apply for a search warrant of the house in anticipation of the delivery. This search warrant is likely to be upheld by a reviewing court if service of the warrant is made contingent upon delivery of the package to the residence.[63]

Searches of Persons Present When a Search Warrant Is Executed

A search warrant may describe not only the place to be searched or the items to be seized but also persons expected to be found on the premises, although execution of a search warrant does not provide automatic grounds for arresting them. If the police have probable cause to believe that a person has the objects named in the warrant in his or her possession, they may search that person. Officers may frisk someone for weapons if they have a reasonable belief that the person presents a danger. In addition, even without grounds to arrest, the police may detain persons found at the scene if they reside at the premises and if the warrant authorizes a search for contraband.[64] If, however, a person at the premises does not appear to be connected to the criminal activity described in the warrant, he or she may not be searched.[65]

The Scope of a Search with a Warrant

If the police have a search warrant for a specified structure, they may search the entire area described in the warrant. For example, if the search warrant specifies a house at 25 Maple Street, the house, the yard, and the buildings within the home's curtilage may be searched. Police officers wishing to search a vehicle on the premises should specify the vehicle in the warrant.[66]

When the police are executing a search warrant at a particular location, the nature of what they are searching for determines the precise areas that may be searched. For example, if a warrant specifies a search for a stolen automobile, police may not search in a desk drawer. A search of areas that could not have concealed the object(s) of the search is unlawful. If, however, the warrant specifies a search for illegal drugs, searching a desk drawer would be permissible, as those items may be concealed almost anywhere within the specified structure.

Seizure of Items in Plain View

The **plain view doctrine** is an exception to the search warrant requirement. It provides that "objects falling in the plain view of an officer who has a right to be in the position to have that view" may be seized and introduced into evidence.[67] This plain view doctrine will be discussed in greater detail in Chapter 8, but these issues arise often when the police are serving search warrants. While executing a warrant, the police may seize items of "incriminating character" that are in plain view if there is probable cause to believe that the materials were involved in a crime.

Arrest Warrants

Arrest warrants play a somewhat different role in U.S. justice systems than search warrants. The courts have held that in many circumstances arrest warrants are not required by the U.S. Constitution, even when police officers have time to obtain them.[68] Some states require the police to obtain an arrest warrant whenever possible, however. In contrast to search warrants, which are valid only for a short time period (10 days in many jurisdictions), once an arrest warrant is issued it remains in effect until the suspect is arrested and brought before the court. At least one state requires an arrest warrant to be executed within 180 days or it becomes invalid.

The Fourth Amendment's particularity requirement is satisfied more easily in arrest warrant cases than in those involving search warrants. In some circumstances, a court will issue an arrest warrant for an unnamed person if there is probable cause to believe that he or she had engaged or is engaging in criminal activity. This is termed a **John Doe warrant.** If police officers are seeking a John Doe warrant, they must provide a description of the individual to be arrested with reasonable particularity. Just as the courts will not issue general search warrants, they will not permit police officers to use arrest warrants to conduct general fishing expeditions for suspects. For example, Jon Morrisey alias Jack the Blade, escaped from police custody following his conviction on aggravated assault charges. The arrest warrant affidavit must state only his name, the crime with which Morrisey is charged, and contain the issuing judge's signature.

In a second example, police officers have probable cause to believe that a drug courier will arrive on a flight from Miami to Los Angeles. An anonymous letter, which did not provide the suspect's name, specified the date and time he would arrive and the flight on which he would arrive. It stated, too, that he was traveling under a false name. In addition, it described the individual as follows:

> He has blond hair and blue eyes; he will be wearing a blue blazer and blue jeans; he will walk fast and carry an expensive black leather briefcase, containing two kilograms of cocaine; he will be met by a limousine operated by Briar's Limousine Service.

The preceding facts contain a sufficiently detailed description of the suspect to support the issuance of a John Doe arrest warrant.[69] See a sample arrest warrant in Figure 4.3.

FIGURE 4.3

Sample Arrest Warrant

001W 5-80

STATE OF
RHODE ISLAND
AND
PROVIDENCE
PLANTATIONS

AFFIDAVIT AND ARREST WARRANT

AFFIDAVIT

AFFIANT	AGENT OF

DEFENDANT	ADDRESS	NO.	STREET	CITY/TOWN	STATE

AFFIDAVIT

Your affiant upon oath states that he has reason to believe and does believe that grounds for issuance of an arrest warrant exists and states the following facts on which such belief is founded:

IF SPACE IS NOT SUFFICIENT,
CHECK (X) HERE AND
☐ ATTACH ADDITIONAL
INFORMATION

AFFIANT

X

SUBSCRIBED AND SWORN TO BEFORE ME AT (CITY/TOWN)	DATE	JUDGE OR DISTRICT COURT, JUSTICE OF SUPERIOR COURT OR ANY OTHER AUTHORIZED OFFICER X

ARREST WARRANT

STATE, EX REL	CITY/TOWN	COUNTY	DATE OF BIRTH	DIVISION RHODE ISLAND DISTRICT COURT	WARRANT DATE
VS. DEFENDANT		ADDRESS	NO.	STREET	CITY/TOWN	STATE

TO ANY AUTHORIZED OFFICER: Affidavit (and complaint) having been made to me under oath, and as I am satisfied that there is probable cause for the belief therein set forth that grounds for issuing an arrest warrant exists, you are hereby commanded to arrest the defendant forthwith and to bring him before a judge of this court without unnecessary delay.

BAIL $	SURETY ☐ with ☐ without	DATE SIGNED	JUDGE OR DISTRICT COURT, JUSTICE SUPERIOR COURT OR ANY AUTHORIZED OFFICER X

RETURN OF SERVICE

I have apprehended the within named defendant and have presented him/her before the court as herein commanded.

SERVICE $	MILEAGE $	DATE OF RETURN	AUTHORIZED OFFICER X

WHITE COPY—COURT   YELLOW COPY—POLICE

Summary

Chapter 4 begins with a discussion of the Fourth Amendment's probable cause standard. It considers precisely what constitutes probable cause and discuss the various situations in which it is required. These include (1) search and seizure with a warrant; (2) search and seizure without a warrant; (3) arrest with a warrant; and (4) arrest without a warrant. Because the police often use informants to gain information, we discuss the process of obtaining warrants with information from these individuals.

This chapter distinguishes, too, between search and arrest warrants. Many of the general principles considered here apply with equal force to search and arrest warrants. A search warrant is a court order, issued by a judge or a magistrate, which directs a law enforcement officer to search for and seize contraband or any evidence of a crime. Similarly, an arrest warrant is an order that directs a peace officer to bring someone before the court to face criminal charges.

It is advisable for a police officer to obtain a warrant whenever possible. First, the courts have indicated a strong preference for warrants. Second, the officer may need less evidence to establish probable cause when he or she obtains a warrant. Third, obtaining a warrant will help to shield a police officer from potential civil liability.

The types of items that may be seized with a search warrant are considered as well. These include evidence of a crime, fruits of a crime, instrumentalities of a crime and other contraband.

The basic elements of a valid warrant are presented and the Fourth Amendment's particularity requirement is considered in detail. Numerous additional requirements of a valid search warrant are discussed, including that of a neutral and detached judge or magistrate. In addition, several important issues regarding the execution of warrants are considered including no knock searches, anticipatory search warrants, and searches of persons on the premises when a search warrant is executed. The scope of a search with a warrant, seizure of items in plain view, and the types of information that may be used to establish probable cause are considered as well.

The tests that have been used by the U.S. Supreme Court to determine if probable cause supported issuance of a warrant are discussed in detail. The two-pronged test and the totality of circumstances test are contrasted. The newer totality of circumstances test, which permits the police to use anonymous tips to establish probable cause for the issuance of a search warrant, is a less demanding standard. The danger of this approach, however, is that an unethical police officer could fabricate anonymous tips to assist him or her in obtaining warrants.

Review Questions

1. What is probable cause?
2. Distinguish between the different levels of proof that are used in the U.S. legal system.
3. Identify four situations in which the police must have probable cause.
4. Distinguish between a search warrant and an arrest warrant.
5. List and discuss several reasons police officers conducting criminal investigations should obtain warrants whenever possible.
6. Discuss and illustrate four different types of items that may be seized with a search warrant.
7. Discuss the basic elements of a valid search warrant.
   a. How particular must a search warrant be?
8. Discuss the following requirements of a valid search warrant:
   a. The neutral and detached magistrate requirement
   b. The oath or affirmation requirement

   c. The fresh information requirement
   d. The time of day requirement
9. Discuss the following concepts:
   a. No knock searches
   b. Anticipatory search warrants
10. When may the police search someone found at the premises when a search warrant is executed?

11. What is the scope of a search with a warrant?
12. Under present law, when may police officers use anonymous tips from informants to obtain search warrants? What dangers may arise from using anonymous tips to establish probable cause?

Issues for Analysis and Discussion

1. Discuss the two-pronged test for determining probable cause. How may corroboration help the police to establish probable cause?
2. In *Illinois* v. *Gates,* the Supreme Court formulated a totality of circumstances test for determining probable cause. How does this test differ from the two-pronged test? Discuss

Justice Rehnquist's rationale for abandoning the two-pronged test in favor of the totality of circumstances test.
3. Consider the facts in *Spinelli* v. *United States.* Would the circumstances in that case be likely to establish probable cause under the totality of circumstances test? Present your rationale.

CASE EXCERPT: *ILLINOIS* V. *GATES*
SUPREME COURT OF THE UNITED STATES (1983)
462 U.S. 213

On May 3, 1978, the Police Department of Bloomingdale, Illinois, received an anonymous letter which included statements that Lance and Sue Gates were engaged in selling drugs; that Sue Gates would drive their car to Florida on May 3 to be loaded with drugs, and Lance Gates would fly down in a few days to drive the car back. The letter further stated that the car's trunk would be loaded with drugs and that the defendants presently had over $100,000 worth of drugs in their basement. Acting on the tip, a police officer determined the defendants' address and learned that Lance Gates had made a reservation on a May 5 flight to Florida. Arrangements for surveillance of the flight were made with an agent of the Drug Enforcement Administration (DEA), and the surveillance disclosed that Lance Gates took the flight, stayed overnight in a motel room registered in Sue Gates' name, and left the following morning with a woman in a car bearing an Illinois license plate issued to Lance Gates. The car traveled north on an interstate highway used by travelers to the Bloomingdale area. A search warrant for the defendants' home and automobile was obtained from a state judge based on the anonymous letter and the corroborative investigation. When the defendants arrived at their home, the police were waiting and discovered marijuana and other contraband in the defendants' car trunk and home. Prior to the defendants' trial on charges of violating state drug laws, the trial court ordered suppression of all the items seized, and the Illinois Appellate Court and Illinois Supreme Court affirmed. The Illinois Supreme Court held that the letter and affidavit were inadequate to sustain a determination of probable cause for issuance of a search warrant because they failed to satisfy the "two-pronged" test of (1) revealing the informant's basis of knowledge and (2) providing sufficient facts to establish either the informant's "veracity" or the "reliability" of the informant's information.

Mr. Justice Rehnquist delivered the Opinion of the Court.

* * *

We granted certiorari to consider the application of the Fourth Amendment to a magistrate's issuance of a search warrant on the basis of a partially corroborated anonymous informant's tip.

* * *

In holding that the affidavit [that supported the issuance of the search warrant] did not contain sufficient additional information to sustain a determination of probable cause, the Illinois Court applied a "two-pronged test," derived from our decision in *Spinelli* v. *United States.* The Illinois Supreme Court, like some others, apparently understood Spinelli as requiring that the anonymous letter satisfy each of two independent requirements before it could be relied on . . . The Illinois court, alluding to an elaborate set of legal rules that have developed among various lower courts to enforce the "two-pronged test" found that the test had not been satisfied.

* * *

We agree with the Illinois Supreme Court that an informant's "veracity," "reliability," and "basis of knowledge" are all highly relevant in determining the value of his report. We do not agree, however, that these elements should be understood as entirely separate and independent requirements to be rigidly exacted in every case.

* * *

[The] totality-of-the-circumstances approach is far more consistent with our prior treatment of probable cause . . . Perhaps the central teaching of our decisions bearing on the probable cause standard is that it is a "practical, nontechnical conception."

* * *

Probable cause is a fluid concept—turning on the assessment of probabilities in particular factual contexts—not readily, or even usefully, reduced to a neat set of legal rules . . . Unlike a totality-of-the-circumstances analysis, which permits a balanced assessment of the relative weights of all the various indicia of reliability (and unreliability) attending an informant's tip, the "two-pronged test" had encouraged an excessively technical dissection of informants' tips, with undue attention being focused on isolated issues that cannot sensibly be divorced from the other facts presented to the magistrate.

* * *

[T]he traditional standard for review of an issuing magistrate's probable cause determination has been that so long as the magistrate had a "substantial basis for . . . conclud[ing] that a search would uncover evidence of wrongdoing, the Fourth Amendment requires no more. We think reaffirmation of this standard better serves the purpose of encouraging recourse to the warrant procedure and is more consistent with our traditional deference to the probable cause determination of magistrates than is the two-pronged test.

* * *

[P]robable cause does not demand the certainty we associate with formal trials. It is enough that there was a fair probability that the writer of the anonymous letter had obtained his entire story either from the Gateses or someone they trusted. And corroboration of major portions of the letter's predictions provides just this probability. It is apparent, therefore, that the judge issuing the warrant had a "substantial basis for . . . concluding that probable cause to search the Gateses' home and car existed."

The judgment of the Supreme Court of Illinois therefore must be Reversed.

Case Excerpt: *Spinelli v. United States*
Supreme Court of the United States (1964)
394 U.S. 410

The F.B.I. had kept track of Spinelli's movements on five days during the month of August 1965. On four of these occasions, Spinelli was seen crossing one of two bridges leading from Illinois into St. Louis, Missouri, between 11 AM and 12:15 PM. On four of the five days, Spinelli was also seen parking his car in a lot used by residents of an apartment house at 1108 Indian Circle Drive in St. Louis, between 3:30 PM and 4:45 PM. On one day, Spinelli was followed further and seen to enter a particular apartment in the building. An F.B.I. check with the telephone company revealed that this apartment contained two telephones listed under the name of Grace P. Hagen, and carrying the numbers WYdown 4-0029 and WYdown 4-0136. The application stated that William Spinelli is known to this affiant and to federal law enforcement agents as a bookmaker, an associate of bookmakers, a gambler, and an associate of gamblers. Finally, it was stated that the F.B.I. "has been informed by a confidential reliable informant that William Spinelli is operating a handbook and accepting wagers and disseminating wagering information by means of the telephones which have been assigned the numbers WYdown 4-0029 and WYdown 4-0136." Spinelli was convicted of various federal gambling violations and he challenged the constitutionality of the warrant used to obtain the evidence in this case.

Mr. Justice Harlan delivered the Opinion of the Court.

* * *

There can be no question that the . . . informant's tip has a fundamental place in this warrant application. Without it, probable cause could not be established. The first two items reflect only innocent-seeming activity and data. Spinelli's travels to and from the apartment building and his entry into a particular apartment on one occasion could hardly be taken as bespeaking gambling activity; and there is surely nothing unusual about an apartment containing two separate telephones. Many a householder indulges himself in this petty luxury. Finally, the allegation that Spinelli was "known" to the affiant and to other federal and local law enforcement officers as a gambler and an associate of gamblers is but a bald and unilluminating assertion of suspicion that is entitled to no weight in appraising the magistrate's decision.

* * *

The informer's report must first be measured against *Aguilar's* standards so that its probative value can be assessed. If the tip is found inadequate under *Aguilar,* the other allegations which corroborate the information contained in the hearsay report should then be considered . . . A magistrate cannot be said to have properly discharged his constitutional duty if he relies on an informer's tip which—even when partially corroborated—is not as reliable as one which passes *Aguilar's* requirements when standing alone.

Applying these principles to the present case, we first consider the weight to be given the informer's tip when it is considered apart from the rest of the affidavit. It is clear that a Commissioner could not credit it without abdicating his constitutional function. Though the affiant swore that his confidant was "reliable," he offered the magistrate no reason in support of this conclusion. Perhaps even more important is the fact that Aguilar's other test has not been satisfied. The tip does not contain a sufficient statement of the underlying circumstances from which the informer concluded that Spinelli was running a bookmaking operation.

* * *

We conclude, then, that in the present case the informant's tip—even when corroborated to the extent indicated—was not sufficient to provide the basis for a finding of probable cause. This is not to say that the tip was so insubstantial that it could not properly have counted in the magistrate's determination. Rather, it needed some further support. When we look to the other parts of the application, however, we find nothing alleged which would permit the suspicions engendered by the informant's report to ripen into a judgment that a crime was probably being committed.

* * *

[W]e cannot sustain this warrant without diluting important safeguards that assure that the judgment of a disinterested judicial officer will interpose itself between the police and the citizenry.

The judgment of the Court of Appeals is reversed and the case is remanded to that court for further proceedings consistent with this opinion.

It is so ordered.

Reversed and remanded.

Endnotes

1. See *Illinois* v. *Gates,* 462 U.S. 213 (1983).
2. *Beck* v. *Ohio,* 379 U.S. 89 (1964); see Thomas K. Clancy, "The Role of Individualized Suspicion in Assessing the Reasonableness of Searches and Seizures." 25 *The University of Memphis Law Review* pp. 483–635 (1995).
3. See *Johnson* v. *United States,* 333 U.S. 10 (1948).
4. *Brinegar* v. *United States,* 338 U.S. 160 (1949).
5. Wayne R. LaFave and Jerold H. Israel, *Criminal Procedure,* 2d ed. (St. Paul, Minn.: West, 1992), p. 134.
6. Supra note 1.
7. See id. at 237.
8. *United States* v. *Ventresca,* 380 U.S. 102 (1965); LaFave and Israel supra note 5 at 138.
9. Rolando V. del Carmen, *Criminal Procedure: Law and Practice,* 3d ed. (Belmont, Calif.: Wadsworth, 1995), p. 89.
10. See *United States* v. *Leon,* 468 U.S. 897 (1984).
11. See *United States* v. *Watson,* 423 U.S. 411 (1976).
12. See *Chimel* v. *California,* 395 U.S. 752 (1969).
13. See *Gerstein* v. *Pugh,* 420 U.S. 103 (1975).
14. For excellent discussions of these issues see Thomas A. Mauet, "Informant Disclosure and Production: A Second Look at Paid Informants." 37 *Arizona Law Review* pp. 563–576 (1995); Clifford S. Zimmerman, "Toward a New Vision of Informants: A History of Abuses and Suggestions for Reform." 22 *Hastings Constitutional Law Quarterly* pp. 81–178 (1994).

15. See Christopher B. Mueller and Laird C. Kirkpatrick, *Evidence Under The Rules: Text, Cases, and Problems,* (Boston, Mass.: Little, Brown and Co., 1988).

16. See *Brinegar* v. *United States,* 338 U.S. 160 (1949).

17. *McCray* v. *Illinois,* 386 U.S. 300 (1967).

18. *Aguilar* v. *Texas,* 378 U.S. 108 (1964).

19. LaFave and Israel, supra note 5, at 142.

20. *McCray* v. *Illinois,* 386 U.S. 300 (1967), later applied the two-pronged test to situations in which the police claimed that probable cause supported a warrantless arrest or a search.

21. LaFave and Israel, supra note 5 at 142–143.

22. *Spinelli* v. *United States,* 394 U.S. 410 (1964).

23. Id.

24. LaFave and Israel, supra note 5 at 146.

25. *Draper* v. *United States,* 358 U.S. 307 (1959).

26. *Illinois* v. *Gates,* 462 U.S. 213 (1983).

27. Associate Justice Byron R. White, concurring in the judgment, felt that the facts recited in the *Gates* search warrant affidavit were sufficient to establish probable cause under the *Aguilar* test.

28. Supra note 26 at 237.

29. See Roger S. Hanson, "The Aftermath of *Illinois* v. *Gates* and *United States* v. *Leon:* A Comprehensive Evaluation of Their Impact upon the Litigation of Search Warrant Validity." 15 *Western State University Law Review* pp. 393–575 (1988).

30. See *United States* v. *Ventresca,* 380 U.S. 102 (1965).

31. *Katz* v. *United States,* 389 U.S. 347 (1967).

32. See *Aguilar* v. *Texas,* 378 U.S. 108 (1964).

33. *United States* v. *Ventresca,* 380 U.S. 102 (1965).

34. See *Massachusetts* v. *Upton,* 466 U.S. 727 (1983).

35. *United States* v. *Leon,* 468 U.S. 897 (1984).

36. *Johnson* v. *United States,* 333 U.S. 10 (1948).

37. See John M. Burkoff, "Search Warrant Particularity: Places to be Searched." 16 *Search and Seizure Law Report* pp. 113–120 (1989).

38. See *Maryland* v. *Garrison,* 480 U.S. 79 (1987).

39. *Steele* v. *United States,* 267 U.S. 498 (1925); Brian J. Telpner, "The Warrant Requirement." 84 *The Georgetown Law Journal Twenty-fifth Annual Review of Criminal Procedure* pp. 733 (1996).

40. *Andresen* v. *Maryland,* 427 U.S. 463, 480 (1976).

41. *Maryland* v. *Garrison,* 480 U.S. 79 (1987).

42. See *United States* v. *Bentley,* 825 F.2d 1104 (7th Cir.), cert. denied, 494 U.S. 901 (1987); many of the federal cases cited as examples in this chapter were obtained using Telpner supra note 39.

43. *United States* v. *Bucuvalas,* 970 F.2d 937 (1st Cir. 1992).

44. *United States* v. *Webster,* 734 F.2d 1048 (5th Cir.), *cert denied,* 114 S.Ct. 1084 (1994).

45. See *United States* v. *Abrams,* 615 F.2d 541 (1st Cir. 1980).

46. See *Warden* v. *Hayden,* 387 U.S. 294 (1967).

47. Fed. R. Crim. Pro. 41(b).

48. *Coolidge* v. *New Hampshire,* 403 U.S. 443 (1971).

49. See *Connally* v. *Georgia,* 429 U.S. 245 (1977).

50. *Lo-Ji Sales, Inc.* v. *New York,* 442 U.S. 319 (1979).

51. *Whiteley* v. *Warden,* 401 U.S. 560 (1971).

52. *United States* v. *Wagner,* 989 F.2d 69 (2nd Cir. 1993).

53. *Sgro* v. *United States,* 287 U.S. 206 (1932).

54. Fed. R. Crim. Pro. 41(c); see Telpner supra note 39, at 743.

55. Fed. R. Crim. Pro. 41(c).

56. Fed. Rule Crim. Pro. 41(d).

57. See LaFave and Israel, supra note 5 at 163.

58. See Thomas M. Lockney, "Probable Cause for Nighttime No-Knock Searches: The Illusion of Judicial Control in North Dakota." 69 *North Dakota Law Review* pp. 613–626 (1993).

59. *Ker* v. *California,* 374 U.S. 23 (1963).

60. *Wilson* v. *Arkansas,* 115 S.Ct. 1914 (1995).

61. *Richards* v. *Wisconsin,* 117 S.Ct. 1416 (1997).

62. See David P. Mitchell, "Anticipatory Search Warrants: The Supreme Court's Opportunity to Reexamine the Framework of the Fourth Amendment." 44 *Vanderbilt Law Review* pp. 1387–1407 (1991).

63. See *United States* v. *Bieri,* 21 F.3d 811 (8th Cir.), cert denied, 115 U.S. 208 (1994).

64. *Michigan* v. *Summers,* 452 U.S. 692 (1981).

65. *Ybarra* v. *Illinois,* 444 U.S. 85 (1979).

66. See *Coolidge* v. *New Hampshire,* 403 U.S. 443 (1971); see LaFave and Israel supra note 5 at 165.

67. *Harris* v. *United States,* 390 U.S. 234 (1968).

68. See *United States* v. *Watson,* 423 U.S. 411 (1976).

69. See *Draper* v. *United States,* 358 U.S. 307 (1959).

5　THE LAW OF ARREST

Key Terms

Chapter 4 discussed the role of search and arrest warrants in U.S. justice systems. *Katz v. United States*,[1] which was considered in detail, cited a familiar criminal law principle: warrantless searches and seizures are "unreasonable under the Fourth Amendment subject only to a few specifically established and well-delineated exceptions."[2] U.S. criminal procedure has developed considerably since *Katz* was decided in 1967. The "few specifically established and well-delineated exceptions" have evolved into a large body of case law containing many different exceptions to the warrant requirement. These include warrantless arrests, searches incident to arrest, exigent circumstances searches, hot pursuit, stop and frisk, investigatory detentions, inventory searches, consent searches, border searches, automobile searches, administrative searches, seizure of contraband or other evidence in plain view, and searches where the special needs of law enforcement make obtaining a warrant impractical. The next three chapters will focus on these exceptions to the warrant requirement. First, however, it is important to define two concepts that are basic to understanding many of the principles considered in this chapter.

Searches and Seizures Contrasted

In the U.S. legal system, governmental searches of a person or his or her property, and seizures of evidence or contraband are governed by the Fourth Amendment. Searches and seizures are different processes, however. A **search** is a governmental intrusion into any area in which a person has a reasonable expectation of privacy.[3]

A **seizure,** in contrast, is defined as a governmental interference with an individual's interest in property. *Black's Law Dictionary* defines a seizure as:

> The act of taking possession of property, e.g., for a violation of law or by virtue of [the operation of law] . . . Seizure of an individual . . . connotes the taking of one physically or constructively into custody and detaining him, thus causing a deprivation of his freedom in a significant way, with real interruption of his liberty of movement.[4]

Whereas a search is designed to produce evidence for a criminal prosecution, a seizure involves the exercise of dominion and control over a person or his or her property by the government. If the government seizes a person in order to bring criminal charges against him or her, the process is termed an arrest.

The Law of Arrest

An **arrest:**

> Deprive[s] a person of his liberty by legal authority. [It requires] taking, under real or assumed authority, custody of another for the purpose of holding or detaining him to answer a criminal charge or civil demand.[5]

Elements of A Lawful Arrest

All valid arrests have four common elements:[6]

1. **Authority** to arrest, which is governed by statutes that define when police officers and members of the general public may arrest those who have violated the law.

2. **Intention** to arrest, which may be either implied or expressed. A police officer may tell someone that he or she is under arrest. If the officer puts handcuffs on someone, however, and places the suspect in a patrol car, it is also clear that the officer intended to arrest the individual.

3. **Seizure** and **detention** of the person to be arrested. This may involve the **actual seizure** of the arrestee, for example, by handcuffing him or her or by some other type of physical touching; or a **constructive seizure,** which involves the suspect's willing submission to the police officer's authority.

4. **Understanding** by the arrestee that he or she is being arrested. In most circumstances an arrestee will know and understand that he or she is being arrested. If, however, a suspect is severely intoxicated or unconscious, he or she may be incapable of understanding what has occurred.

Felony Arrests

The vast majority of arrests in the United States are made without an arrest warrant. The Supreme Court has held that the Fourth Amendment does not require an arrest warrant to make arrests in public places even when the police could obtain one without any inconvenience or without jeopardizing the arrest.[7] At common law the police were permitted, without a warrant, to arrest someone whenever there was probable cause to believe that the individual had committed a felony. This continues to be the rule in all states. In addition, if police officers arrest someone without a warrant in either a felony or a misdemeanor case, the Supreme Court has held that the Fourth Amendment requires a hearing so that a judge or a magistrate may make a formal determination of whether probable cause supported the arrest. This is termed a **Gerstein hearing.**[8] Such a hearing should be conducted as soon as possible after an arrest, and must normally occur within 48 hours.[9]

Warrantless Felony Arrests at a Suspect's Home.   The U.S. Supreme Court has consistently held that one of the core values that the Fourth Amendment is intended to protect is the sanctity and privacy of the home. Unless there is an emergency such as the fear of immediate destruction of evidence, or a threat to public safety or to the police, officers wishing to arrest someone may not enter the suspect's home without an arrest warrant. In *Payton* v. *New York,* the Court held that "the Fourth Amendment has drawn a fine line at the entrance to a house."[10] If police officers without an arrest warrant enter a suspect's home in order to make a routine felony arrest, any evidence obtained during the arrest will be inadmissible.[11] The suspect will not be relieved of criminal charges, however, in these circumstances. Police officers may obtain a proper warrant and arrest the suspect at a later time.

Warrantless Felony Arrests at a Third Party's Home.   The Supreme Court has held that an arrest warrant does not give police officers the right to enter a third person's home to search for a suspect, even when there is probable cause to believe that the person named in the warrant is present. This rule assumes that no emergency exists, which could justify an immediate entry by the police. In *Steagald* v. *United States*,[12] the Supreme Court held that a search warrant is required in order to enter a third party's home to serve an arrest warrant.[13]

Exigent Circumstances.   In emergency situations police officers may be required to act quickly to arrest a suspect, preserve evidence, or to prevent harm to a suspect or to others. These situations, which are termed **exigent circumstances,** justify immediate action by the police because it is not feasible to for the police to delay a search or seizure until they get a search or arrest warrant.[14] Some of the factors that a reviewing court will consider in determining if exigent circumstances support police officers' actions include:

1. The seriousness of the offense;
2. Whether there is a reasonable belief that the suspect has a weapon;
3. If it is clear that there is probable cause to believe that a defendant committed a crime;
4. If there is a strong indication that the suspect is present in a particular location;
5. If there is a strong likelihood that the suspect will escape if not arrested immediately;
6. If the officers' entry is made without the use of force;
7. If the officers' entry is made at night.[15]

For example, assume that a police officer receives a report that an intoxicated driver, who struck and killed a pedestrian, has left the scene of an accident. Approximately five minutes later, eyewitnesses at the scene provide the police with the license plate number of the suspect's vehicle, and a detailed description of the car and the driver. Police officers immediately trace the car's license number to Edward J. Smith, of 101 Jones Road, Greenville, North Carolina. When the officers arrive at Smith's residence they see a car that matches the description of the vehicle involved in the homicide parked in the driveway. Upon entering the home without a warrant, the police find Smith sleeping in a second floor bedroom. Smith is placed under arrest and taken to the hospital where a doctor extracts a blood sample from him in order to conduct a blood alcohol analysis.

In these circumstances, the police officers' warrantless entry of Smith's home and his warrantless arrest is likely to be held lawful by a reviewing court. Because this case involved a serious crime and the evidence of Smith's intoxication would have disappeared if the police failed to act quickly, exigent circumstances would support this action.

Another example of an exigent circumstances search occurred in the O. J. Simpson trial. One important issue considered by a state court at a hearing before the trial began was whether certain items found on Simpson's Brentwood estate could be admitted into evidence.[16] Police Officers testified that upon discovering that Nicole

Source: Owne T.B./Black Star

Brown Simpson and Ronald Goldman had been murdered, they immediately went to Simpson's home in order to guarantee his safety. When they discovered that the gates were locked, an officer scaled the walls surrounding the estate and found evidence linking Simpson to the murders, including blood stains in his Ford Bronco, and a blood-stained glove. Photo 5.1 depicts several of the evidentiary items found during the search of Simpson's home and vehicle.

At the hearing on a motion to suppress this evidence, the prosecution argued that exigent circumstances justified the officers' entry into the estate. The emergency that permitted the entry was alleged to be the officers' concern that whomever had killed Nicole Brown Simpson and Ronald Goldman may have presented a threat to O. J. Simpson's life as well. Defense attorneys argued that the evidence found at the estate should be suppressed because the officers' entry onto the estate was merely a pretext to conduct a warrantless search. The court held that the officers' entry onto the estate was justified by exigent circumstances—a legitimate concern for O. J. Simpson's safety.

Three Types of Exigent Circumstances.   U.S. courts have identified three situations in which search or arrest warrants are not required due to exigent circumstances:

1. Where it is likely that evidence will be destroyed if police officers do not act immediately;[17]

2. When the police are in immediate pursuit of a felon and he or she enters a dwelling. **Hot pursuit laws,** which most states have adopted, permit a police officer to continue pursuing suspects across jurisdictional boundaries, such as city or state boundary lines, if he or she is in fresh, immediate pursuit of a felon;

3. When investigators are at the scene of a fire.

Searches if Evidence Is Likely to Be Destroyed.   If police officers must act quickly to prevent evidence from being destroyed, exigent circumstances will justify an immediate search and seizure. In *Cupp* v. *Murphy,*[18] police officers at the station house were questioning a suspect about his wife's murder. During the conversation, they noticed a dark spot on the suspect's finger, which they believed to be dried blood. Over the suspect's protests and without a warrant, the officers took scrapings from his fingernails, which were later used to convict him of murder. The Supreme Court held that due to the limited nature of the intrusion and the ready destructibility of the evidence, the search did not violate the Fourth Amendment.

Hot Pursuit.   If police officers are in fresh, immediate pursuit of a felon, they may continue pursuing suspects across jurisdictional boundaries such as city or state boundary lines. Moreover, if a suspect who is fleeing from the police takes refuge in a building or a home, officers may enter and search for the individual.[19] In addition, if officers searching for the suspect discover evidence or contraband, it may be seized without a warrant and admitted at trial.[20]

An Investigation at the Scene of a Fire.   The Supreme Court has held that when investigators are present at the scene of a fire they may remain there for a reasonable time to investigate the causes of the fire. In *Michigan* v. *Tyler,*[21] the Court held that even though investigators had left the scene of the fire and returned approximately three hours later, during daylight hours, the warrantless search of the premises was lawful. The Court further held, however, that a warrantless search of the same premises approximately three weeks later violated the Fourth Amendment.

No General Murder Scene Exception.   Murder cases are among the most serious cases in the U.S. legal system. The Supreme Court has held, however, that despite the grave nature of these cases there is no general murder scene exception to the search warrant requirement.[22] In *Mincey* v. *Arizona,*[23] a defendant, in his own home, shot and killed an undercover police officer. Following his arrest, police officers conducted a warrantless search of the home that lasted for four days. The Supreme Court refused, however, to recognize a general murder scene exception to the warrant requirement and held that the Arizona statute that allowed these searches was unconstitutional. The Court further held that because there was no emergency present that would threaten the officers, exigent circumstances did not justify this search.

Misdemeanor Arrests

At common law, police officers were permitted to arrest for a misdemeanor only with an arrest warrant or, in cases involving a breach of the peace, if the crime occurred in the officer's presence. The law regulating misdemeanor arrests in most places has been changed over time to allow the police to arrest for any misdemeanor that occurs in the officer's presence.[24] In addition, most states have adopted exceptions to this rule and presently allow the police to arrest someone for a misdemeanor committed outside their presence under certain conditions, including:

1. When there is reason to believe that the suspect will flee the jurisdiction unless arrested immediately;
2. To prevent the destruction of evidence;
3. To prevent harm to the suspect or to others;
4. When there is probable cause to make an arrest.

Warrantless Arrests at a Suspect's Home.   Unless police officers have a warrant or consent, they should not enter a suspect's home to make an arrest for a minor offense. The courts are likely to hold that such an arrest is unreasonable, even where exigent circumstances are present. For example, in *Welsh* v. *Wisconsin,* the defendant, who was intoxicated, was arrested in his own home by police officers acting without a warrant, several minutes after a witness had observed him drive his car off the roadway and into a field. The Supreme Court held that "an important factor to be considered when determining whether any exigency exists is the gravity of the underlying offense for which the arrest is being made."[25] Application of the exigent circumstances exception to the warrant requirement will rarely be upheld when there is probable cause to believe that only a minor offense has occurred, such as driving under the influence of alcohol not involving injury or significant property damage.

The facts of *Welsh* v. *Wisconsin* may be contrasted with an example used in a previous chapter. Suppose that Paul, who had recently driven away from a drinking establishment and appeared to be highly intoxicated, struck and killed a pedestrian who was crossing the street. Assume further that Paul fled immediately from the scene of the accident; however, several witnesses reported observing Paul drive away from the scene, and gave police a description of his vehicle and his license plate number. In these circumstances an immediate warrantless entry of Paul's home by police officers to make an arrest would be permitted under the exigent circumstances exception to the warrant requirement. If officers failed to act quickly, crucial evidence of Paul's blood alcohol content would be lost.

The Special Problem of Domestic Violence.   In recent years many states have recognized that domestic violence presents a unique problem. Numerous states have passed special domestic violence statutes that require police officers to make an arrest if there is probable cause to believe that someone has committed a domestic assault, even if the assault does not constitute a felony.[26] Highlight 5.1 presents the State of Oregon's domestic violence statute, which requires police officers to arrest suspects whenever there is probable cause to believe that a domestic assault has taken place. Figure 5.1 presents a copy of a form used by police officers in Rhode Island in domestic violence cases. Such forms may ensure that these cases are investigated effectively and help to minimize police liability in domestic violence cases.

Police officers must remain acutely aware of developments in this area of the law. Archaic attitudes that once viewed women as the personal property of their husbands

Highlight 5.1

The State of Oregon's Domestic Assault Statute
O.R.S. 133.055 (2), (3)

(2) [W]hen a peace officer is at the scene of a domestic disturbance and has probable cause to believe that an assault has occurred between spouses, former spouses or adult persons related by blood or marriage or persons of opposite sex residing together or who formerly resided together, or to believe that one such person has placed the other in fear of imminent serious physical injury, the officer shall arrest and take into custody the alleged assailant or potential assailant.

(3) Whenever any peace officer has reason to believe that a family or household member has been abused . . . that officer shall use all reasonable means to prevent further abuse, including advising each person of the availability of a shelter or other services in the community and giving each person immediate notice of the legal rights and remedies available. The notice shall consist of handing each person a copy of the following statement:

"IF YOU ARE THE VICTIM OF DOMESTIC VIOLENCE, you can ask the district attorney to file a criminal complaint. You also have the right to go to the circuit court and file a petition requesting any of the following orders for relief: (a) An order restraining your attacker from abusing you; (b) an order directing your attacker to leave your household; (c) an order preventing your attacker from entering your residence, school, business or place of employment; (d) an order awarding you or the other parent custody of or visitation with a minor child or children; (e) an order restraining your attacker from molesting or interfering with minor children in your custody; (f) an order directing the party not granted custody to pay support of minor children, or for support of the other party if that party has a legal obligation to do so.

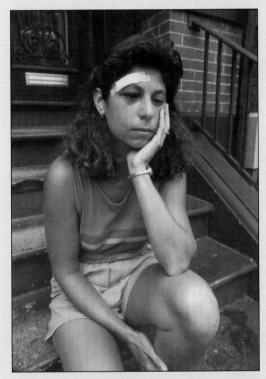

Mike Mazzaschi/Stock Boston

You also have the right to sue for losses suffered as a result of the abuse, including medical and moving expenses, loss of earnings or support, and other out-of-pocket expenses for injuries sustained and damage to your property. This can be done without an attorney in small claims court if the total amount claimed is under $700."

FIGURE 5.1

Form Used by RI Police Departments in Domestic Violence Cases

(revised May 10, 1996)

DOMESTIC VIOLENCE/SEXUAL ASSAULT REPORTING FORM

POLICE CASE #

DV/SA-1

A. INCIDENT INFORMATION

LOCATION: (street address) _____

CITY: _____
ZIP: _____

○ PUBLIC PLACE/INDOORS
○ PUBLIC PLACE/OUTDOORS
○ DWELLING   ○ VEHICLE
○ OTHER (SPECIFY)_____

TIME: _____
DATE: _____

WHO CALLED POLICE?

○ VICTIM   ○ HOSPITAL   ○ NEIGHBOR   ○ FAMILY MEMBER
○ OTHER (SPECIFY)_____

CALLER'S NAME:

TELEPHONE #:_____

IN YOUR OPINION. WAS ALCOHOL INVOLVED?
  ○ YES   ○ NO   ○ UNKNOWN
BY WHOM?   ○ VICTIM   ○ SUSPECT   ○ BOTH

IN YOUR OPINION. WERE DRUGS INVOLVED?
  ○ YES   ○ NO   ○ UNKNOWN
BY WHOM?   ○ VICTIM   ○ SUSPECT   ○ BOTH

B. VICTIM INFORMATION

NAME:_____   DOB:_____
ADDRESS:_____   GENDER   F ○ M ○
CITY:_____ STATE:_____ ZIP:_____
HOME PH#_____ WORK PH#_____

PH# WHERE CURRENTLY STAYING
(WHITE OUT NUMBER FOR DISCOVERY)
_____

IF VICTIM WAS A **MINOR**, WAS DCYF NOTIFIED?	IF VICTIM WAS **60 YEARS OR OLDER**, WAS DEA NOTIFIED?
○ YES ○ NO 1-800-RI CHILD	○ YES ○ NO 1-800-322-2889

ETHNIC BACKGROUND:

○ WH ○ BL   ○ ASIAN   ○ NAT AMER ○ OTHER_____
HISPANIC?   ○ YES   ○ NO

VICTIM WAS: (MARK ALL APPROPRIATE CIRCLES)
○ TEARFUL/CRYING   ○ HYSTERICAL ○ AFRAID
○ SHAKING/TREMBLING   ○ ANGRY   ○ NERVOUS
○ OTHER _____

C. SUSPECT INFORMATION

NAME:_____   DOB:_____
ADDRESS:_____   GENDER   F ○ M ○
CITY:_____ STATE:_____ ZIP:_____

(MARK ALL APPROPRIATE CIRCLES)

○ FAMILY MEMBER (SPECIFY) _____
○ MARRIED   ○ FORMERLY MARRIED   ○ COHABITANT
○ INTIMATE PARTNER   ○ FORMER INTIMATE PARTNER
○ CHILD IN COMMON   ○ ACQUAINTANCE
○ DATE   ○ FRIEND
VICTIM/SUSPECT **CURRENTLY** LIVING TOGETHER? ○ YES ○ NO
ETHNIC BACKGROUND:
○ WH ○ BL   ○ ASIAN   ○ NAT AMER ○ OTHER_____
HISPANIC?   ○ YES   ○ NO

C. SUSPECT *(continued)*

• IS SUSPECT ON PROBATION?   ○ YES   ○ NO
    WHERE? _____ NAME, PROB. OFF.:_____
• DOES SUSPECT **POSSESS FIREARMS?**   ○ YES   ○ NO
  SUSPECT WAS: (MARK ALL APPROPRIATE CIRCLES)
  ○ APOLOGETIC   ○ CALM   ○ BELLIGERENT
  ○ THREATENING   ○ ANGRY   ○ NERVOUS
  ○ OTHER_____

D. ARREST INFORMATION

• DID **PROBABLE CAUSE** EXIST FOR YOU TO BELIEVE
  A **DOMESTIC VIOLENCE** CRIME OCCURED?   ○ YES ○ NO
• DID **PROBABLE CAUSE** EXIST FOR YOU TO BELIEVE
  A **SEXUAL ASSAULT** CRIME OCCURRED?   ○ YES ○ NO
• WAS AN **ARREST** MADE?   ○ YES ○ NO
• WAS **PICTURE** TAKEN OF **VICTIM?**   ○ YES ○ NO
• WAS **PICTURE** TAKEN OF **CRIME SCENE?**   ○ YES ○ NO
• WAS **OTHER PHYSICAL EVIDENCE** COLLECTED?   ○ YES ○ NO
• WAS CRIMINAL **NO CONTACT ORDER** ISSUED?   ○ YES ○ NO
• WAS A **WARRANT ISSUED** ON ARREST?   ○ YES ○ NO
• WAS **ARREST** MADE AFTER WARRANT?   ○ YES ○ NO
• WAS **FOLLOW-UP PHOTO TAKEN?** (3-4 DAYS LATER) ○ YES ○ NO

E. ASSAULT INFORMATION

• WAS VICTIM **PHYSICALLY** ASSAULTED?   ○ YES ○ NO
• WAS VICTIM **SEXUALLY** ASSAULTED?   ○ YES ○ NO
• WAS WEAPON OR OBJECT USED?   ○ YES ○ NO
  IF YES, DESCRIBE _____
• DID VICTIM SUSTAIN PHYSICAL INJURIES?   ○ YES ○ NO

MARK APPROPRIATE CIRCLES TO DESCRIBE WHAT OCCURRED:

○ THROWING OBJECTS   ○ GRABBING   ○ BITING
○ PUSHING/SHOVING   ○ KICKING   ○ CHOKING
○ HITTING W/FISTS   ○ SLAPPING   ○ BEATING
○ THREAT W/WEAPON   ○ USE WEAPON ○ BURNING
○ PREVENTED FROM LEAVING ○ STALKING   ○ TOUCHING
○ THREAT OF PHYSICAL VIOLENCE
○ THREAT OF SEXUAL VIOLENCE
○ SEXUAL CONTACT   ○ VAGINAL PENETRATION
○ ANAL PENETRATION   ○ ORAL PENETRATION

• WERE ALL INJURIES CAUSED BY SUSPECT?   ○ YES ○ NO
  IF NO. EXPLAIN _____
• HAS SUSPECT ASSAULTED VICTIM BEFORE?   ○ YES ○ NO
  IF YES. WHEN _____
• WERE THREATS MADE BY SUSPECT?   ○ YES ○ NO
  IF YES. TO WHOM? _____
  WHAT WAS SAID? _____
• IS VICTIM IN PAIN NOW?   ○ YES ○ NO
• DID VICTIM REQUIRE MEDICAL ATTENTION?   ○ YES ○ NO
• IF YES. WHAT MEDICAL FACILITY? _____
• WAS FORENSIC SEXUAL ASSAULT EXAM DONE?   ○ YES ○ NO
• ANYONE ELSE ASSAULTED BY SUSPECT?   ○ YES ○ NO

  IF YES. WHO? _____

INSTRUCTIONS FOR DISPOSITION OF THIS FORM:
1. FAX COPY TO 273-8940 / ATTORNEY GENERAL'S DV/SA UNIT (PROVIDENCE)
2. MAIL ORIGINAL OR LEGIBLE COPY TO: DOMESTIC VIOLENCE UNIT, 4800 TOWER HILL ROAD, WAKEFIELD, RI 02879

have given way to a more enlightened approach to the problems associated with domestic assault.[27] Officers failing to comply with the arrest provisions of domestic violence laws may be subjected to personal civil liability.[28] Supervising officers may be liable for the failure to properly train subordinates to ensure compliance with these laws. Highlight 5.2 presents the case of *Calloway* v. *Kunkelaar,*[29] and illustrates that police officers who fail to enforce domestic assault laws will be held liable in civil proceedings.

Using Force to Make an Arrest

An arrest involves a governmental seizure of a person suspected of a crime. If a police officer uses excessive force to arrest someone, the seizure is unreasonable. Thus, even when the police have probable cause to arrest, the Fourth Amendment places restrictions on how it may be accomplished. First, an officer must act in a reasonable manner and may not use **excessive force** to make an arrest. Excessive force is defined as any force beyond that which is immediately necessary to overcome a suspect's resistance.

The use of excessive force by police officers is to be discouraged for both moral and practical reasons. First, even beyond the basic humanitarian principle that it is simply wrong to brutalize another person, the use of excessive force by the police may jeopardize the criminal case against the suspect. For example, if a defendant has been beaten, it is easy for a defense attorney to argue that any incriminating statements that the defendant made were coerced or involuntary. Second, police officers who use excessive force are subject to criminal charges and may be held liable for compensatory and punitive damages in civil lawsuits.[30] Moreover, police officers who use excessive force may jeopardize their departments' reputations and create feelings of public hostility.

Analyzing the Amount of Force Used to Make an Arrest.   The amount of force that a police officer may lawfully use to make an arrest is directly related to the amount of resistance he or she encounters from a suspect during the arrest process. An officer is privileged to use sufficient force to overcome a suspect's resistance. This is termed the **rule of proportionate force.** Unfortunately, this rule cannot be reduced to a simple mechanical formula to guide law enforcement officers. The Supreme Court has held, however, that police use of force must be judged by using an **objective reasonableness test.** In *Graham* v. *Connor,*[31] excerpted in Highlight 5.3, the Supreme Court described this test as one that must be applied from the perspective of a reasonable officer at the scene. A reviewing court is to consider all of the circumstances surrounding the officer's decision to use force, including the time frame in which the officer had to act. The Supreme Court asserted that a reviewing court should not take the role of a Monday morning quarterback regarding an officer's use of force. Rather, the court must focus on what a reasonable police officer would have done in the same position. This is an effective standard for judging use of force cases that strikes a proper balance between police officers' rights and those of criminal suspects.

The Use of Deadly Force to Make an Arrest.   The common-law rule regarding the use of deadly force to make an arrest was a simple one: Law enforcement officers were permitted to use deadly force to stop and arrest a fleeing felon.[32] Long ago, this rule

---
Highlight 5.2

Calloway v. *Kinkelaar,* 659 N.E.2d 1322 (1995).

Calloway, who had obtained a civil protection order against her husband, sued the county and the county sheriff, alleging willful and wanton conduct for failing to prevent her abduction by her husband.

In the case at bar, plaintiff's complaint is premised on the provisions of the Domestic Violence Act of 1986, which the General Assembly intended to be 'liberally construed and applied to promote its underlying purposes.'

* * *

Article III of the Act enumerates the responsibilities of law enforcement officers, which include 'making an arrest without warrant if the officer has probable cause to believe that the person has committed or is committing any crime, including but not limited to violation of an order of protection, . . . even if the crime was not committed in the presence of the officer.'

In the case at bar, potential governmental liability derives from the statutory scheme created by the Domestic Violence Act, which identifies a specially protected class of individuals to whom statutorily mandated duties are owed. These duties are expressed in Section 304, which states that law enforcement officers having reason to know of the abuse 'shall immediately use all reasonable means to prevent further abuse,' including the arrest of the abuser and physically transporting the victim to safety.

* * *

To give effect to the legislature's purposes and intent in enacting the Domestic Violence Act, we believe judicial recognition of a right of action for civil damages is necessary, provided that the injured party can establish that he or she is a person in need of protection under the Act, the statutory law enforcement duties owed to him or her were breached by the willful and wanton acts or omissions of law enforcement officers and such conduct proximately cause plaintiff's injuries.

* * *

In the case at bar, defendants were informed that Calloway had a gun and was making threats to plaintiff, but did nothing to enforce the order of protection or to intervene after being informed of Calloway's continuing abuse. The Act imposed a duty upon defendants to promptly undertake all reasonable steps to assist plaintiff, a 'person protected' by the Act, when they learned of Calloway's threatening conduct and ongoing violation of the order of protection. Whether defendants breached this legal duty by willful and wanton misconduct that proximately caused plaintiff's injury is a question of fact for the jury to determine at trial.

Highlight 5.3

Excerpt from *Graham* v. *Connor,* 490 U.S. 386, 386 (1989)

 The "reasonableness" of a particular use of force must be judged from the perspective of a reasonable officer on the scene, rather than with the 20/20 vision of hindsight. The Fourth Amendment is not violated by an arrest based on probable cause, even though the wrong person is arrested, nor by the mistaken execution of a valid search warrant on the wrong premises. With respect to a claim of excessive force, the same standard of reasonableness at the moment applies: "Not every push or shove, even if it may later seem unnecessary in the peace of a judge's chambers" violates the Fourth Amendment. The calculus of reasonableness must embody allowance for the fact that police officers are often forced to make split-second judgments—in circumstances that are tense, uncertain, and rapidly evolving—about the amount of force that is necessary in a particular situation. As in other Fourth Amendment contexts, however, the "reasonableness" inquiry in an excessive force case is an objective one: the question is whether the officers' actions are "objectively reasonable" in light of the facts and circumstances confronting them, without regard to their underlying intent or motivation. An officer's evil intentions will not make a Fourth Amendment violation out of an objectively reasonable use of force; nor will an officer's good intentions make an objectively unreasonable use of force constitutional.

made sense—most common law crimes were punishable by death. In modern times when very few crimes are punishable by death, it makes little sense to allow police officers to use deadly force against persons whose crimes involve relatively minor offenses.

***The Rule of* Tennessee *v.* Garner.**   *Tennessee* v. *Garner*[33] is perhaps the most important U.S. Supreme Court decision concerning the use of deadly force by the police. In *Garner,* the police received a report of a nighttime burglary at a private home. An officer observed a fleeing suspect, who refused to stop. The officer shot the suspect in the back, killing him. The officer had shot Garner under the authority of a Tennessee statute providing that if a suspect flees after being notified of an officer's intention to arrest, "the officer may use all the necessary means to effect the arrest." The suspect had not displayed a weapon and did not present a threat to the officer. In Garner's possession were ten dollars and a purse taken from the burglarized home. The Supreme Court held that the Tennessee law was unconstitutional because the use of deadly force to stop a fleeing felon may be unreasonable under the Fourth Amendment. The Court stated:

> The use of deadly force to prevent the escape of all felony suspects, whatever the circumstances, is constitutionally unreasonable. It is not better that all felony suspects die than

that they escape. Where the suspect poses no immediate threat to the officer and no threat to others, the harm resulting from failing to apprehend him does not justify the use of deadly force to do so . . . Where the officer has probable cause to believe that the suspect poses a threat of serious physical harm, either to the officer or to others, it is not constitutionally unreasonable to prevent escape by using deadly force.[34]

Tennessee v. *Garner* established a clear Fourth Amendment rule in cases involving the use of deadly force: If a suspect poses no immediate threat to a police officer, or to others, deadly force may not be used.[35] If, however, there is probable cause to believe that the suspect poses a threat of serious physical harm, either to the officer or to other persons, it is not unreasonable to prevent escape by using deadly force.

A number of state and local police departments have been criticized for their use of deadly force. State and local police departments are not the only agencies that have receive criticism for their use of force. Federal law enforcement agencies, too, have come under increased scrutiny as a result of two highly publicized incidents involving the use of deadly force. In 1993, members of the U.S. Bureau of Alcohol, Tobacco, and Firearms (ATF) raided the Branch Davidian compound in Waco, Texas, following a long standoff. Numerous people were killed.[36] In another incident near Ruby Ridge, Idaho, Federal Bureau of Investigation (FBI) agents shot and killed two persons while attempting to arrest Randy Weaver for federal firearms violations.[37] These incidents have led federal authorities to develop a new policy on the use of deadly force by federal law enforcement agents. One law enforcement agency's use of deadly force policy is presented in Highlight 5.4. The Weaver case illustrates that law enforcement agents may be held liable in civil proceedings for an excessive use of force.

Several examples should help to clarify when police officers may use deadly force lawfully to stop a fleeing suspect. First, assume that at 3:30 AM on a Tuesday, a Chicago police officer observes a juvenile driving a stolen car. At this time of night the streets are virtually deserted. When the officer stops the vehicle, the juvenile flees from the car and runs into a dark alley. There is no indication that the suspect is armed or that he represents a threat to others. Because the suspect poses no threat of serious physical harm, either to the officer or to other persons, deadly force should not be used. It is easy to change our example into a situation that would permit an officer to use deadly force, however. Assume that in the case presented above the juvenile who was running away had turned and fired several pistol shots at the pursuing officer. Because the suspect poses a significant threat of physical harm, the officer may use deadly force.

Two additional examples will help to clarify the permissible scope of the use of deadly force. Suppose that at 3:30 PM on a Tuesday, a mugger grabs a woman's purse from her and runs down a dark alley. A police officer who observed the incident chases the suspect, but determines that she will not be able to catch the mugger, who is young and a very fast runner. Because the suspect no longer poses a threat of serious physical harm to the officer, or to others, deadly force may not be used.

In a final example, assume that at 3:30 PM on a Tuesday, a bank robbery suspect is running away from several New York City police officers on a crowded sidewalk. The suspect is reasonably believed to be carrying a handgun but has not fired at the officers or at other persons. This case presents a more difficult call. Because of the potential

---

Highlight 5.4

Portsmouth Police Department Portsmouth, RI

 Use of Force

Purpose. Society recognizes the need for law enforcement officers to use physical force to carry out their peacekeeping and law enforcement responsibilities. These duties may include effecting an arrest, defending themselves against bodily injury or death, protecting citizens from bodily injury or death, preventing suicide or self-inflicted injury, and preserving the peace. It is commonly held by the courts that an officer may use the amount of force necessary to perform his/her duties, given the facts and circumstances known to the officer or which should be known by the officer at the time of the incident. Generally, a reasonable amount of force is considered to be the minimum amount necessary under the circumstances of the incident.

The decision to use or escalate force is contingent on many factors. Among the factors to be considered are:

1. The nature of the crime, (infraction, misdemeanor, felony);
2. The degree of resistance being offered;
3. Whether any weapons are involved and the nature of those weapons;
4. The size differential between the officer and the persona against whom force is being used;
5. The number of persons involved in the incident;
6. The availability of back-up officers;
7. The feasibility of alternative actions by the officer.

It is the policy of the Portsmouth Police Department that only the minimum amount of force be used to accomplish the tasks of law enforcement.

Definitions.

Deadly force: Force resulting from the use of a firearm or other weapon likely to cause serious physical injury or death with its intended use.

Nondeadly force: Force likely to cause less than serious physical injury with its intended use.

Serious physical injury: Injury that creates a substantial risk of death or causes protracted loss or impairment of the function of any bodily part, member, or organ, or cause serious permanent disfigurement.

Use of force continuum: Escalating levels of force through which a Department can effect an arrest, beginning with verbal communication and culminating with the use of deadly force.

Policy. It is the policy of the Portsmouth Police Department that a Department member shall use the lowest level of force necessary under the existing circumstances to perform their lawful duties.

The use of deadly force: Deadly force may be used only where the officer has probable cause to believe that a criminal suspect poses a threat of serious physical injury to the officer or to others. If the suspect threatens the officer with a weapon of where there is probable cause to believe that the suspect has committed a crime involving the infliction or threatened infliction of serious physical harm or death, deadly force may be used if necessary to effect the arrest or to prevent escape. Prior to the use of deadly force, some warning must be given, if it is feasible under the circumstance.

The use of non-deadly force: Non-deadly force may be used by an officer in the performance of his duty in the following situations:

1. When necessary to preserve the peace, prevent commission of a crime, or prevent suicide of self-inflicted injury;
2. When necessary to overcome resistance to a lawful arrest, search and seizure, and to prevent escapes from custody;
3. When in self-defense or in defense of another officer or citizen against unlawful violence to his person or property.

(Continued)

Minimum force necessary: An officer may only use the minimum force necessary to perform his duties. The amount of force used is to be reasonable as judged by the particular facts and circumstances of the incident known to the officer at the time of the incident. The force will start at the lowest level of the use of force continuum as practical at the time. The use of force continuum is listed below in ascending order, from the least severe to the most drastic:

1. Verbal communication;
2. Restraining devices (handcuffs, etc.);
3. Physical strength and skill;
4. Department approved chemical agent (Placed after soft empty hand controls within physical strength and skills);
5. Department approved impact weapons;
6. Deadly force.

Use of Deadly Force

Policy.   It is the policy of the Portsmouth Police Department to consider the value of human life to be immeasurable. The basic responsibility of the police is to protect life and property and to apprehend offenders of the criminal laws. The protection of property and the apprehension of criminal offenders must, at all times, be subservient to the protection of life, including the life of the offender. The use of deadly force is in final step on the use of force continuum and is to be employed only when other measures are either exhausted or unreasonable.

No set of guidelines for the use of deadly force can cover every situation that might arise. The officer is expected to respond to any emergency decisively and with the highest level of good judgment and professional competence.

Procedure.   Deadly force may be used only where the officer has probable cause to believe that a criminal suspect poses a threat of serious injury to the officer or to others. *If the suspect threatens the officer or another person with a weapon, deadly force may be used if necessary for self-defense or the defense of another person. Where the officer has probable cause to believe that the suspect has committed a crime involving the infliction or threatened infliction of serious physical injury or death and the suspect's continued freedom represents an imminent threat of death or serious bodily injury to members of the community, deadly force may be used if necessary to effect the arrest or to prevent the escape of the suspect.* Flight in and of itself is not necessarily evidence of the commission of a crime and is insufficient justification to use deadly force. *Prior to the use of deadly force, some warning must be given, if it is feasible under the circumstances.*

Deadly force may be used under the above conditions only after the officer has exhausted all other reasonable means for apprehension and control. Officers will exercise the utmost restraint in using deadly force. The use of a firearm or other means of deadly force is never to be considered a routine method of apprehension or control.

No officer shall be disciplined for failing to use deadly force if its use may threaten the life or safety of another officer or an innocent person or if the use is not clearly warranted by the policy and rules of the Portsmouth Police Department.

Examples of deadly force: Deadly force has been defined as force resulting from the use of a firearm or other weapon likely to cause serious bodily injury or death with its intended use. Two key factors regarding deadly force are that the force will *foreseeably* result in death or serious bodily injury and that the force must be *intentionally applied.*

The use of a firearm is the use of deadly force when it is force intentionally applied to a suspect. This includes circumstances in which the officer intended to wound rather than kill a suspect. The accidental discharge of a firearm may be considered to not be the use of deadly force because the element of intentionality is missing.

Other methods of force which have been considered deadly force include: the use of an impact weapon in a manner likely to cause serious injury— i.e., a strike on the head; the intentional ramming of

(Continued)

(Concluded)

a suspect vehicle by a police vehicle; the use of a roadblock, set up in such a manner likely to cause a collision. This list is intended merely to illustrate examples and is not to be considered exhaustive.

Firearms: The discharge of a firearm is the most obvious use of deadly force by a police officer. The following rules are intended to guide officers in all cases involving the use of firearms consistent with the general use of deadly force procedure. These rules are applicable in both on-duty and off-duty situations and to the use of any firearm.

1. Officers shall not discharge a firearm except for self-defense or the defense of another, or to effect an arrest or prevent the escape of a suspect who poses an imminent threat of death or serious physical injury to the community.

2. Officers shall not discharge their firearms when doing so may endanger innocent persons, unless that force is necessary for self-defense or the defense of another.

3. Officers shall not discharge their firearms to subdue persons whose actions are destructive to property or injurious to themselves and do not represent a threat of death or serious injury to the officer or others.

4. Officers shall not discharge their firearms at or from a moving vehicle unless it is absolutely necessary in defense of themselves or others. Officers shall not discharge a firearm with the intent to disable a moving vehicle. The discharge of a firearm at a moving vehicle shall be allowed only when the vehicle is being used as a dangerous weapon or the suspect(s) is using lethal force against the officer or others, when the officer has reasonable belief that the lives of innocent persons will not be endangered by the action, and when the officer has a clear shot at the suspect(s) in the vehicle and a reasonable expectation of hitting the suspect(s).

5. Officers shall not fire warning shots, as they pose a danger to officers and citizens alike.

6. Officers shall not draw or display their firearms to effect an arrest for a misdemeanor, unless necessary for the self-defense of the officer.

7. Officers shall not unnecessarily draw or display their firearms unless there is justification for its use to accomplish a proper police purpose. Firearms shall not be drawn for intimidation or a show of force, but only when there is reasonable suspicion of a threat of death or serious physical injury by the suspect(s). A firearm shall never be pointed at a suspect unless there is justification for its use, in accordance with this policy. In responding to any potentially dangerous situation (i.e., position where it can be used speedily and effectively if needed). The decision to draw a firearm in such situations shall be based on the officer's reasonable suspicion that there is a substantial risk that the situation may escalate to a point where deadly force may be justified. When it is determined that deadly force is not necessary, the officer shall, as soon as practical, holster or otherwise secure the firearm.

8. Officers may discharge a firearm to kill a dangerous animal or animal so badly injured that the humane treatment is to remove it from further suffering. This shall be done in accordance with the department's Animal Control Policy.

danger to innocent bystanders, however, and the fact that the suspect has not demonstrated a significant threat to the officers or to other persons, deadly force should not be used.

Searches Incident to Lawful Arrests

One of the most widely used exceptions to the Fourth Amendment warrant requirement is a **search incident to a lawful arrest.** This exception allows police officers who have made a lawful custodial arrest to conduct a warrantless search of the suspect's person and property without probable cause or reasonable suspicion to believe that the suspect has weapons or any type of contraband.[38] If, however, an arrest is later determined to be unlawful due to an absence of probable cause, any evidence found during a search incident to the arrest will be suppressed, unless another exception to the warrant requirement allows it to be introduced. Searches incident to arrests are permitted in order to protect the suspect and the arresting police officers as well as to promote the government's interest in preserving evidence of criminal behavior.

The Scope of a Search Incident to a Lawful Arrest

If the police arrest a suspect lawfully, they may search the physical area within a suspect's "immediate control." The Supreme Court has interpreted this phrase to mean the area into which a suspect could reach to obtain a weapon or to destroy evidence. This rule, established in *Chimel* v. *California*,[39] applies even if a suspect is restrained or handcuffed, and even if officers present at the scene could easily prevent the suspect from obtaining a weapon or destroying evidence. The *Chimel* rule applies too when there is no suspicion that weapons or evidence will be found. A search incident to a lawful arrest, however, may not be so widespread that it goes beyond the area within a suspect's immediate control and becomes a general search for evidence.[40]

Two examples should help to clarify the scope of a search incident to a lawful arrest. First, assume that a suspect is arrested for driving under the influence of alcohol. The interior of the suspect's vehicle may be searched incident to a lawful arrest. The vehicle's trunk may not be searched lawfully in this case because it is outside of the area into which the suspect could reach for a weapon or to destroy evidence. Second, assume that a suspect is arrested for possession of marijuana. A locked suitcase that the suspect was carrying at the time of the arrest may be searched incident to a lawful arrest.

The Protective Sweep Doctrine.   An exception to the rule that incident to a lawful arrest the police may search only the area within the suspect's immediate control was established in *Maryland* v. *Buie*.[41] In *Buie*, police officers executing an arrest warrant went to the suspect's home and searched the first and second floors. When one of the officers shouted for persons in the basement to come upstairs, Buie came out of the basement and was immediately arrested. An officer then went into the basement to determine if other persons were present. During the search the officer found evidence that was used to convict Buie of robbery. The issue on appeal to the Supreme Court was whether the evidence should have been excluded because it was discovered in an area beyond the suspect's immediate control. The Court held that when an arrest occurs in a suspect's home, the officers may conduct a protective sweep of the house. A **protective sweep** is defined as a limited search of a house, incident to an arrest, that is designed to protect the arresting officers. It is limited in scope, permits only a cursory inspection of the areas, and may include only those places in which a person could be found. In order to justify a protective sweep, however, the police must have a reasonable belief based on objective facts that another person who could present a danger to the officers may be present.[42]

Time Constraints and Searches Incident to Arrest

A valid search incident to an arrest may sometimes occur before the suspect is arrested. What is found, however, may not then be used to establish probable cause for the arrest itself. To illustrate, in *Smith* v. *Ohio*,[43] police officers arrested the defendant after finding drug paraphernalia following a warrantless search of a paper bag that he was holding. At a pretrial suppression hearing, the prosecution argued that although probable cause to arrest Smith did not exist before the police searched the paper bag, it had developed once the drug paraphernalia had been found. Therefore, although the initial search and seizure was not supported by probable cause, the arrest itself was lawful. The Supreme Court held that a search incident to arrest may not precede the arrest and serve as part of its justification.

A search incident to an arrest must occur normally at or near the time a suspect is arrested. Even if a search does not immediately follow an arrest, however, the police may search items in the defendant's possession at the time of the arrest.

A Search Immediately Preceding an Arrest. In *Rawlings* v. *Kentucky*,[44] Rawlings admitted ownership of approximately 1800 L.S.D. tablets that were found in his friend's purse. When police officers searched Rawlings they discovered a knife and $4,500 in cash, and he was arrested. On an appeal of his conviction, Rawlings argued that because the search that revealed the L.S.D. tablets occurred *before* his arrest, it could not be justified as a search incident to a lawful arrest. The Supreme Court held that because the police had probable cause to arrest Rawlings, it was immaterial that the search was conducted before his actual arrest. Moreover, because Rawlings had no reasonable expectation of privacy in his friend's purse, he lacked standing to challenge the lawfulness of the search and seizure of the evidence.

Searches Following an Arrest. As *Rawlings* indicates, a search incident to a lawful arrest may occur after an arrest has been made. Even when a suspect is arrested for a relatively minor crime, such as a traffic offense, a search incident to the arrest may extend to a suspect's body and any items in his or her possession. In *United States* v. *Robinson*,[45] a police officer observed Robinson driving an automobile in Washington, D.C. As a result of previous encounters with the suspect, the officer knew that Robinson's driver's license had been revoked. This was an offense in the District of Columbia that carried a mandatory jail term and a fine. When the officer stopped the car, Robinson was placed under arrest for driving with a revoked driver's license. The officer then began to search Robinson. As the officer was "patting him down," he felt an object in Robinson's left breast pocket, but testified that he "couldn't tell what it was." The officer then reached into the pocket and pulled out a "crumpled up cigarette package," which proved to contain heroin.

The Supreme Court held that the search of Robinson's body and his possessions was lawful and established a longstanding rule in cases involving custodial arrests: "In the case of a lawful custodial arrest, a full search of the person is not only an exception to the warrant requirement, but is also a 'reasonable' search under that amendment."[46]

Searches of a Suspect at the Jail. Once a suspect has been arrested and transported to jail, he or she may be subjected to a search. In *United States* v. *Edwards,*[47] the Supreme Court held that if a search and seizure could have been conducted lawfully at the scene when the suspect was arrested, it may be conducted later when the person arrives at the jail. No additional showing of probable cause to conduct the search is needed—the arrest itself is sufficient to justify the search of the suspect at the jail. The justification for this type of search is protection of the police and the suspect as well as the preservation of any evidence or contraband that the defendant may possess.

Under *Edwards,* a search of the arrestee's possessions need not occur immediately after the suspect is brought to the jail. In *Edwards,* the defendant's clothing was searched by police officers approximately 24 hours after he was arrested and brought to jail on burglary charges. The Supreme Court held that no search warrant was required to search the clothing.

Moreover, when a suspect is arrested and taken to jail, police officers without a warrant may conduct a thorough inventory search of his or her possessions. Inventory searches, which are often considered part of a police officer's routine administrative caretaking duties, are justified by the need to protect the suspect's property and prevent false claims against the police. Chapter 7 presents a more detailed treatment of these issues.

Accompanying an Arrested Suspect. A police officer has a right to accompany a suspect incident to a lawful arrest. In *Washington* v. *Chrisman,*[48] a minor student, Overdahl, was arrested for possession of liquor. When the officer asked Overdahl for identification, he indicated that it was in his dormitory room and asked to be allowed to return to the room to obtain it. The officer accompanied Overdahl to the room and observed seeds and a marijuana pipe on a desk. The officer then arrested Overdahl's roommate, Chrisman, for possession of the items. Chrisman moved to suppress the evidence because the officer's entry into the room was not justified by exigent circumstances. The Supreme Court held that once a police officer makes a lawful arrest he is permitted to remain with the suspect at all times. Therefore, anything the officer observed in plain view while accompanying the suspect could be properly seized without a search warrant.

Intrusive Searches Following an Arrest. Any significant intrusion into a suspect's body requires a search warrant, unless exigent circumstances demand immediate action to preserve evidence or to prevent harm to the individual or the police. Moreover, any intrusion into a suspect's body must be accomplished in a reasonable manner. To determine whether the search is reasonable, the courts will use a balancing test in which an "individual's interests in privacy and security are weighed against society's interests in conducting the procedure."[49] Types of bodily searches include blood tests, fingernail scrapings, bullet removal, stomach pumping, and strip and body cavity searches.

1. Blood Tests. A blood test is a minor intrusion into a person's body, which may be conducted with a warrant, or without a warrant if exigent circumstances exist.[50] In *Schmerber* v. *California,*[51] the defendant, who was charged with driving under the influence of alcohol, was arrested at a hospital while receiving treatment for injuries suffered in an automobile accident. At the direction of police officers and without a warrant, a doctor extracted a sample of Schmerber's blood in order to conduct a blood-alcohol analysis. The results were used to convict him of driving under the influence of alcohol. On appeal, Schmerber maintained that taking his blood without his consent was an unreasonable search and seizure under the Fourth Amendment. The Supreme Court held that this search was conducted in a reasonable manner. Schmerber's Fourth Amendment rights were not violated because the blood sample "was taken by a physician in a hospital environment according to accepted medical practices." Moreover, in these circumstances the warrant requirement did not apply because if the police had failed to act immediately the evidence would have dissipated.

2. Fingernail Scrapings. In *Cupp* v. *Murphy,*[52] discussed earlier in this chapter, the Supreme Court held that there was no Fourth Amendment violation when police officers who were investigating a murder took scrapings from the defendant's fingernails without a warrant. The scrapings involved only a limited intrusion on the individual's privacy and the evidence would have been destroyed if the police had not acted quickly.

3. Bullet Removal. The Fourth Amendment will not allow police officers to require that suspects submit to more intrusive procedures in order to obtain evidence. In *Winston* v. *Lee,*[53] the Supreme Court held that a robbery suspect was not required to submit to surgery to remove a bullet. Using a balancing test, the Court concluded that the surgery, which would have required the use of a general anesthetic, was an extensive intrusion on the defendant's personal privacy. Moreover, the state's need for the bullet to prove its case was not substantial because there was additional persuasive evidence that the defendant had committed the crime. The courts have declined to develop a clear rule in bullet-removal cases; rather, *Winston's* balancing test will be used to analyze the facts of the particular case and determine whether the intrusion on personal privacy is outweighed by the state's need for the evidence.[54]

4. Stomach Pumping. Pumping a suspect's stomach without a warrant in order to obtain evidence is a significant governmental intrusion into an area in which a suspect has a reasonable expectation of privacy.[55] In *Rochin* v. *California,*[56] police officers, without probable cause and without a search warrant, entered Rochin's home and forced open the door to his bedroom. When Rochin saw the officers, he swallowed some capsules that were on a table next to his bed. The officers took the suspect to a hospital where they pumped his stomach and found the capsules, which contained morphine. Following Rochin's conviction for possession of morphine, the Supreme Court

held that the police officers' behavior amounted to "conduct that shocks the conscience." It therefore violated the due process clause of the Fourteenth Amendment.

The general rule in cases involving intrusive searches into a suspect's body is that the government must first obtain a search warrant. Thus, police officers must have probable cause to support the issuance of a warrant in these cases.

5. Strip Searches and Body Cavity Searches. Strip and body cavity searches following an arrest are not always lawful and may expose police officers to civil liability.[57] Police department policies that authorize strip and body cavity searches of all arrested suspects are clearly unconstitutional. In order to conduct a lawful strip or body cavity search, officers must have reasonable suspicion to believe that a suspect is concealing a weapon or contraband, or that he or she is dangerous.[58]

For example, in one case a motorist, Wachtler, was arrested by a New York state trooper when he refused to identify himself after being stopped for a traffic violation. Upon their arrival at the county jail, Wachtler was strip searched by a male guard. The suspect filed suit in the United States District Court under 42 U.S.C. Section 1983, alleging that the county's strip search policy violated his civil rights. The U.S. District Court dismissed the lawsuit. The U.S. Court of Appeals held, however, that Wachtler should have been allowed to prove his claim against the county. The Court stated:

> The Fourth Amendment precludes prison officials from performing strip/body cavity searches of arrestees charged with misdemeanors or other minor offenses unless the officials have a reasonable suspicion that the arrestee is concealing weapons or other contraband based on the crime charged, the particular characteristics of the arrestee, and/or the circumstances of the arrest.[59]

This case illustrates that reasonable suspicion does not arise from the mere fact that a suspect has been arrested.[60] In contrast, jail inmates who are awaiting trial may be subjected to routine strip and body cavity searches following contact visits with persons from outside the institution.[61]

Searches of Closed Containers in a Suspect's Possession.   Based on *Chimel* v. *California,* and *United States* v. *Robinson,* when a suspect is arrested searches of containers in his or her possession or reach are lawful because they are in his or her "immediate control." Such items would include a wallet, a purse, or a package.[62] For example, assume that police arrest Jane, who is carrying a purse, for disorderly conduct during a sidewalk demonstration. When a police officer searched Jane's purse, he discovered two "joints" (hand-rolled marijuana cigarettes). Jane may be charged with possession of marijuana. Likewise, assume that police officers have arrested a suspected terrorist who is carrying a sealed package and they have probable cause to believe that the suspect is involved in a plot to bomb historical landmarks in New York City. The package resembles those that have been used in similar bombings. This example illustrates a familiar principle in U.S. criminal procedure: in many cases, more than one exception to the warrant requirement may be used to justify a warrantless search and seizure. In this example, either exigent circumstances, or a search incident to a lawful arrest would justify an immediate search of the package by the police department's bomb squad. If the package were found to contain heroin, instead of a bomb, the heroin would be admissible at trial.

Searches of Closed Containers in Police Custody.   Once a suspect is arrested and police officers gain exclusive control over items in his or her possession, they should obtain a search warrant for closed containers. In *United States* v. *Chadwick,*[63] the defendant, who was suspected of smuggling drugs, was arrested standing next to an open automobile trunk. He had just placed a double-locked footlocker, which federal agents believed to contain marijuana, into the car's trunk. After the agents took the suspect and the footlocker to the federal building, they searched it without a search warrant. The Supreme Court held that this search could not be justified as a search incident to a lawful arrest because there was no possibility that Chadwick could gain access to the locker to obtain a weapon or to destroy evidence. Moreover, the agents had exclusive control of the locker and had sufficient time to obtain a search warrant.

Similarly, in *Arkansas* v. *Sanders,*[64] the Supreme Court held that a search warrant is required for opening a closed suitcase found during a search of a vehicle. More recently, however, the Supreme Court has rejected the *Sanders* rule.[65]

Searches of Closed Containers Found in Automobiles.   In *New York* v. *Belton,*[66] the Supreme Court established the following rule: If a suspect is arrested in an automobile, the entire passenger compartment, including closed containers, may be searched incident to the arrest.[67] Initially, this rule did not include items found in the trunk. In a more recent case, however, the Supreme Court held that if police officers have probable cause, they may search without a warrant a vehicle's trunk and any containers found within it.[68]

In 1991, the Court further extended the *Belton* rule. In *California* v. *Acevedo,*[69] police officers observed the defendant leaving his home with a brown paper bag, which they believed to contain marijuana. Acevedo placed the bag in his car's trunk and started to drive down the street. The officers stopped Acevedo and searched the car's trunk, despite the fact that they did not have probable cause to stop the car and did not have a search warrant. The Supreme Court held that when police officers have probable cause to suspect that a container contains contraband, they may wait until the container is placed inside the car and then stop the car and open the container, without a search warrant. This rule applies even when no exigent circumstances would justify an immediate search of the vehicle or the container.[70] The automobile exception to the search warrant requirement will be considered in much greater detail in later chapters.

Summary

Chapter 5 discusses the law of arrest and begins to consider exceptions to the Fourth Amendment warrant requirement, including searches incident to arrest and exigent circumstances searches. The discussion of the law of arrest includes a consideration of the elements of an arrest including authority, intention, seizure and detention of the suspect, and understanding.

The differences between felony and misdemeanor arrests are considered. At common law, peace officers were empowered to arrest someone for a felony whenever there was probable cause to believe that a crime had been committed and that the suspect was the perpetrator. This continues to be the rule in all states. The Supreme Court has held, however, that unless there is an emergency such as the fear of immediate destruction of evidence, or a threat to public safety or to the police, officers may not enter a suspect's home without an arrest warrant. Moreover, in order to enter a third party's home to make an arrest, police officers must have probable cause to believe that the suspect is present in the home and obtain a search warrant to enter the home and arrest the suspect.

Searches and arrests made in emergency situations are considered in this chapter. Such situations, which are termed exigent circumstances, occur whenever police officers must act quickly to arrest a suspect, preserve evidence, or to prevent harm to a suspect or to others. In these circumstances it is impractical to obtain a search or an arrest warrant. Two applications of the exigent circumstances exception to the warrant requirement are discussed: (1) searches that must be conducted immediately because evidence will be destroyed if police officers do not act quickly; and (2) searches made by police officers who are in hot pursuit of a fleeing suspect.

Chapter 5 discusses the law of misdemeanor arrests. At common law, police officers were permitted to arrest for a misdemeanor only with an arrest warrant or, in cases involving a breach of the peace, if the crime occurred in the officer's presence. The law regulating misdemeanor arrests has changed over time in most places to allow the police to arrest for any misdemeanor that occurs in the officer's presence. In recent years laws designed to prevent domestic violence, which require police officers to make an arrest whenever there is evidence of a domestic assault, have been adopted in many states.

The use of force in making an arrest is discussed as well. An arrest involves a governmental seizure of a person suspected of a crime. Under the Fourth Amendment, if a police officer uses excessive force to arrest someone, the seizure is unreasonable. The standard used to determine if a police officer has used excessive force is an objective one—would a reasonable police officer under the circumstances have used the same amount of force that the officer did in this case? Police use of deadly force is discussed at length. The Supreme Court has developed a clear rule to guide the police in cases involving the use of deadly force: If a suspect poses no immediate threat to police officers or to others, deadly force may not be used.

Exceptions to the warrant requirement are considered. One very important exception is a search that is conducted incident to a lawful arrest. Once police officers have made a lawful custodial arrest, they may conduct a warrantless search of the suspect's person and property without probable cause or reasonable suspicion to believe that the suspect has weapons or any type of contraband. In addition, police officers may search the physical area within a suspect's immediate control and, if they are executing an arrest warrant, may conduct a protective sweep of a home that is designed to protect the arresting officers.

More intrusive searches of an arrested person are discussed in some detail. These searches include blood tests, fingernail scrapings, bullet removal, and stomach pumping. In these cases, the courts will use a balancing test to assess whether the intrusion on personal privacy is outweighed by the state's need for the evidence. An arrestee may often be subjected to a jailhouse strip or body cavity searches; however, police department policies authorizing strip and body cavity searches of all arrested suspects are unconstitutional.

Review Questions

1. Distinguish between a search and a seizure.
2. What is an arrest? Present and describe the major elements of a lawful arrest.
3. Present and discuss the law regarding felony and misdemeanor arrests.
4. Discuss the exigent circumstances exception to the Fourth Amendment warrant requirement.

List several of the factors that a reviewing court will consider in determining if exigent circumstances support police officers' actions.

5. Discuss the development of domestic violence laws. Describe a typical domestic assault law. Why does the enforcement of domestic violence laws present an area of potential liability for law enforcement personnel?

6. How much force may a police officer use to make an arrest? What constitutes excessive force and how will a court determine if excessive force has been used? Present *Tennessee* v. *Garner's* rule regarding police officers' use of deadly force.

7. Describe the search incident to a lawful arrest exception to the Fourth Amendment warrant requirement. What is the scope of a search incident to a lawful arrest? What is the protective sweep doctrine?

8. Present and discuss the law regarding strip searches and body cavity searches following an arrest.

Issues for Analysis and Discussion

1. In *United States* v. *Robinson,* the Supreme Court held that a search incident to a lawful arrest is a traditional exception to the Fourth Amendment's search warrant requirement. Describe Justice Rehnquist's justifications for this exception. Are these justifications convincing?

2. *Maryland* v. *Buie* held that in order to determine the reasonableness of a search an seizure, the Supreme Court will balance an individual's Fourth Amendment interests against its promotion of legitimate governmental interests. From the cases you have read in this chapter, do you feel that the Supreme Court's balancing analysis is a proper way of determining if an individual's Fourth Amendment rights have been violated? Is the Supreme Court's scale "tilted" toward producing convictions, or is it likely to result in an inappropriate expansion of defendants' Fourth Amendment rights? (Be sure to cite relevant case law in completing your answer.)

Case Excerpt: *United States v. Robinson*
The Supreme Court of the United States (1973)
414 U.S. 218

On April 23, 1968, at approximately 11:00 PM, Officer Richard Jenks, a 15-year veteran of the District of Columbia Metropolitan Police Department, observed Robinson driving his car on a public highway. Jenks, as a result of previous investigation following a check of Robinson's operator's permit four days earlier, determined there was reason to believe that Robinson was operating a vehicle after the revocation of his license. This is an offense defined by statute in the District of Columbia which carries a mandatory minimum jail term, a mandatory minimum fine, or both. Jenks stopped Robinson's vehicle and placed him under arrest. In line with procedures established in police department regulations, Jenks conducted a search of Robinson. During the patdown, Jenks felt an object in the left breast pocket of the heavy coat Robinson was wearing, but testified that he "couldn't tell what it was." Jenks then reached into the pocket and pulled out the object, which turned out to be a "crumpled up cigarette package." Jenks later testified that he still could not tell what was inside the package and opened it and found 14 gelatin capsules containing heroin. The heroin was admitted into evidence at trial and resulted in Robinson's conviction. Following an appeal to the U.S. Court of Appeals, the United States Supreme Court granted certiorari.

Mr. Justice Rehnquist delivered the Opinion of the Court.

* * *

It is well settled that a search incident to a lawful arrest is a traditional exception to the warrant requirement of the Fourth Amendment. This general exception has historically been formulated into two distinct propositions. The first is that a search may be made of the *person* of the arrestee by virtue of the lawful arrest. The second is that a search may be made of the area within the control of the arrestee.

* * *

Terry v. *Ohio* did not involve an arrest for probable cause, and it made quite clear that the "protective frisk" for weapons which it approved might be conducted without probable cause. This Court's opinion explicitly recognized that there is a "distinction in purpose, character, and extent between a search incident to an arrest and a limited search for weapons."

"The former, although justified in part by the acknowledged necessity to protect the arresting officer from assault with a concealed weapon, is also justified on other grounds, and can therefore involve a relatively extensive exploration of the person." A search for weapons in the absence of probable cause to arrest, however, must, like any other search be strictly circumscribed by the exigencies which justify its initiation.

* * *

The justification or reason for the authority to search incident to a lawful arrest rests quite as much on the need to disarm the suspect in order to take him into custody as it does on the need to preserve evidence on his person for later use at trial. The standards traditionally governing a search incident to lawful arrest are not, therefore, commuted to the stricter *Terry* standards by the absence of probable fruits or further evidence of the particular crime for which the arrest is made.

Nor are we inclined, on the basis of what seems to us to be a rather speculative judgment, to qualify the breadth of the general authority to search incident to a lawful custodial arrest on an assumption that person arrested for the offense of driving while their licenses have been revoked are less likely to possess dangerous weapons than are those arrested for other crimes. It is scarcely open to doubt that the danger to an officer is far greater in the case of the extended exposure which follows the taking of a suspect into custody and transporting him to the police station than in the case of the relatively fleeting contact resulting from the typical *Terry*-type stop. This is an adequate basis for treating all custodial arrests alike for purposes of search justification.

* * *

A police officer's determination as to how and where to search the person of a suspect whom he has arrested is necessarily a quick ad hoc judgment which the Fourth Amendment does not require to be broken down in each instance into an analysis of each step in the search. The authority to search the person incident to a lawful custodial arrest, while based upon the need to disarm and to discover evidence, does not depend on what a court may later decide was the probability in a particular arrest situation that weapons or evidence would in fact be found upon the person of the suspect. A custodial arrest of a suspect based on probable cause is a reasonable intrusion under the Fourth Amendment; that intrusion being lawful, a search incident to the arrest requires no additional justification. It is the fact of the lawful arrest which establishes the authority to search, and we hold that in the case of a lawful custodial arrest a full search of the person is not only an exception to the warrant requirement of the Fourth Amendment, but is also a "reasonable" search under that Amendment.

The search of respondent's person conducted by Officer Jenks in this case and the seizure from him of the heroin, were permissible under established Fourth Amendment law. While none of the extreme or patently abusive characteristics which were held to violate the Due Process Clause of the Fourteenth Amendment in *Rochin* v. *California*. Since it is the fact of custodial arrest which gives rise to the authority to search, it is of no moment that Jenks did not indicate any subjective fear of the respondent or that he did not himself suspect that the respondent was armed. Having in the course of a lawful search come upon the crumpled package of cigarettes, he was entitled to inspect it; and when his inspection revealed the heroin capsules, he was entitled to seize them as "fruits, instrumentalities, or contraband" probative of criminal conduct. The judgment of the Court of Appeals holding otherwise is Reversed.

Case Excerpt: *Maryland v. Buie*
The Supreme Court of the United States (1990)
494 U.S. 325

Following a Maryland armed robbery by two men, one of whom was wearing a red running suit, police obtained arrest warrants for Buie and his suspected accomplice. They executed the warrant for Buie at his house. After Buie was arrested upon emerging from the basement, one of the officers entered the basement "in case there was someone else" there and seized a red running suit lying in plain view. The trial court denied Buie's motion to suppress the running suit, the suit was introduced into evidence, and Buie was convicted of armed robbery and a weapons offense. An appellate court affirmed the denial of the suppression motion, but the State Court of Appeals reversed, ruling that the running suit was inadmissible because the officer who conducted the "protected sweep" of the basement did not have probable cause to believe that a serious and demonstrable potentiality for danger existed. The U.S. Supreme Court granted certiorari.

Mr. Justice White delivered the Opinion of the Court.

* * *

A "protective sweep" is a quick and limited search of premises, incident to an arrest and conducted to protect the safety of police officers or others. It is narrowly confined to a cursory visual inspection of those places in which a person might be hiding. In this case we must decide what level of justification is required by the Fourth and Fourteenth Amendments before police officers, while effecting the arrest of a suspect in his home pursuant to an arrest warrant, may conduct a warrantless protective sweep of all or part of the premises. The Court of Appeals of Maryland held that a running suit seized in plain view during such a protective sweep should have been suppressed at respondent's armed robbery trial because the officer who conducted the sweep did not have probable cause to believe that a serious and demonstrable potentiality for danger existed. We conclude that the Fourth Amendment would permit the protective sweep undertaken here if the searching officer "possesse[d] a reasonable belief based on 'specific and articulable facts which, taken together with the rational inferences from those facts, reasonably warrant[ed]' the officer in believing" that the area harbored an individual posing a danger to the officer or others. We accordingly vacate the judgement below and remand for application of this standard.

* * *

It goes without saying that the Fourth Amendment bars only unreasonable searches and seizures. Our cases show that in determining reasonableness, we have balanced the intrusion on the individual's Fourth Amendment interests against its promotion of legitimate governmental interests. Under this test, a search of the house or office is generally not reasonable without a warrant issued on probable cause. There are other contexts, however, where the public interest is such that neither a warrant nor probable cause is required.

* * *

The ingredients to apply the balance struck in *Terry* [v. *Ohio*] and [*Michigan* v.] *Long* are pre-sent in this case. Possessing an arrest warrant and probable cause to believe Buie was in his home, the officers were entitled to enter and to search anywhere in the house in which Buie might be found. Once he was found, however, the search for him was over, and there was no longer that particular justification for entering any rooms that had not yet been searched.

That Buie had an expectation of privacy in those remaining areas of his house, however, does not mean such rooms were immune from entry. In *Terry* and *Long* we were concerned with the immediate interest of the police officers in taking steps to assure themselves that the persons with whom they were dealing were not armed with, or able to gain immediate control of, a weapon that could unexpectedly and fatally be used against them. In the instant case, there is an analogous interest of the officers in taking steps to assure themselves that the house in which a suspect is being, or has just been, arrested is not harboring other persons who are dangerous and who could unexpectedly launch an attack. The risk of danger in the context of an arrest in the home is as great as, if not greater than, it is in an on-the-street or roadside investigatory encounter. A *Terry* or *Long* frisk occurs before a police-citizen confrontation has escalated to the point of arrest. A protective sweep, in contrast, occurs as a adjunct to the serious step of taking a person into custody for the purpose of prosecuting him for a crime. Moreover, unlike an encounter on the street or along a highway, an in-home arrest puts the officer at the disadvantage of being on his adversary's "turf." An ambush in a confined setting of unknown configuration is more to be feared than it is in open, more familiar surroundings.

We agree with the State, as did the court below, that a warrant was not required. We also hold that as an incident to the arrest the officers could, as a precautionary matter and without probable cause or reasonable suspicion, look in closets and other spaces immediately adjoining the place of arrest from which an attack could be immediately launched. Beyond that, however, we hold that there must be articulable facts which, taken together with the rational inferences from those facts, would warrant a reasonably prudent officer in believing that the area to be swept harbors an individual posing a danger to those on the arrest scene. This is no more and no less than was required in *Terry* and *Long,* and as in those cases, we think this balance is the proper one.

We should emphasize that such a protective sweep, aimed a protecting the arresting officers, if justified by the circumstances, is nevertheless not a full search of the premises, but may extend only to a cursory inspection of those spaces where a person may be found. The sweep lasts no longer than is necessary to dispel the reasonable suspicion of danger and in any event no longer than it takes to complete the arrest and depart the premises.

* * *

We therefore vacate the judgment below and remand this case to the Court of Appeals of Maryland for further proceedings not inconsistent with this opinion.

It is so ordered.

Endnotes

1. *Katz* v. *United States,* 389 U.S. 347 (1967).
2. Id. at 357.
3. *Oliver* v. *United States,* 466 U.S. 170 (1984).
4. Entry defining "seizure," [Reprinted from *Black's Law Dictionary,* Copyright © 1992, with permission of the West Publishing Corporation.]
5. Id. at 57.
6. See Rolando del Carmen, *Criminal Procedure Law and Practice,* 3d ed. (Belmont, Cal: Wadsworth, 1995), pp. 137–141.
7. *United States* v. *Watson,* 423 U.S. 411 (1976).
8. See *Gerstein* v. *Pugh,* 420 U.S. 103 (1975).
9. See *County of Riverside* v. *McLaughlin,* 111 S.Ct. 1661 (1991).
10. *Payton* v. *New York,* 445 U.S. 573 (1980).
11. See Alan C. Yarcusko, "From Brown to Payton to Harris: A Fourth Amendment Double Play by the Supreme Court." 43 *Case Western Reserve Law Review* pp. 253–286 (1992).
12. *Steagald* v. *United States,* 451 U.S. 204 (1981).
13. See Beverly A. Patterson, "Search Warrant Required to Search Third Party's Home When Serving an Arrest Warrant." 59 *Washington University Law Quarterly* pp. 1409–1424 (1982).
14. See Amy B. Beller, "The Exigent Circumstances Exception and the Erosion of the Fourth Amendment." 20 *Hofstra Law Review* pp. 407–428 (1991); many of the case examples used in this chapter were taken from Elise B. Clarke et al., "Warrants, Searches and Seizures" 84 *The Georgetown Law Journal 25th Annual Review of Criminal Procedure* (1996).
15. See *Dorman* v. *United States,* 435 F.2d 385 (D.C. Cir. 1970).
16. See Michael D. Harris, "Simpson Search Passes Muster Prosecutors Say; 'Exigent Circumstances.'" 107 *The Los Angeles Daily Journal* p. 1 (July 6, 1994).
17. See *Cupp* v. *Murphy,* 412 U.S. 291 (1973); *Vale* v. *Louisiana,* 399 U.S. 30 (1970).
18. *Cupp* v. *Murphy,* 412 U.S. 291 (1973).
19. See *Warden* v. *Hayden,* 387 U.S. 294 (1967).
20. See *United States* v. *Santana,* 427 U.S. 38 (1976).
21. *Michigan* v. *Tyler,* 436 U.S. 499 (1978).
22. See Bruce D. Hausknect, "The 'Homicide Scene' Exception to the Fourth Amendment Warrant Requirement: A Dead Issue?" 71 *Journal of Criminal Law and Criminology* pp. 289–329 (1980).
23. *Mincey* v. *Arizona,* 437 U.S. 385 (1978).
24. See William A. Schroeder, "Warrantless Misdemeanor Arrests and the Fourth Amendment." *Missouri Law Review* pp. 771–853 (1993).
25. *Welsh* v. *Wisconsin,* 466 U.S. 740 (1984).
26. Lawrence W. Sherman, "The Influence of Criminology on Criminal Law: Evaluating Arrests for Misdemeanor Domestic Violence." 83 *Journal of Criminal Law and Criminology* pp. 1–45 (1992).
27. See Loretta J. Stalans and Arthur J. Leurigo, "Public Preferences for the Court's Handling of Domestic Violence Situations." 41 *Crime and Delinquency* pp. 399–413 (1995).
28. Margo L. Ely, "High Court Ruling on Domestic Violence Expands Police Liability." 142 *Chicago Daily Law Bulletin* p. 6 (January 15, 1996).

29. *Calloway* v. *Kunkelaar,* No. 77391 (Ill. Sup. Ct. 12/21/95).

30. See Mark S. Binder, "When Police Use Excessive Force: Choosing a Constitutional Threshold of Liability." 62 *St. John's Law Review* pp. 735–750 (1988); Victor E. Kappeler, Stephen F. Kappeler and Rolondo v. del Carmen, "A Content Analysis of Police Civil Liability Cases: Decisions of the Federal District Courts, 1978–1990." 21 *Journal of Criminal Justice* pp. 325–337 (1993); Michael S. Vaughn and Lisa F. Coomes, "Police Civil Liability Under Section 1983: When Do Police Officers Act Under Color of Law?" 23 *Journal of Criminal Justice* pp. 395–415 (1995).

31. *Graham* v. *Connor,* 490 U.S. 386 (1989).

32. See John Simon, "The Fleeing Felon Rule." 30 *St. Johns University Law Journal* pp. 1259–1277 (1986).

33. *Tennessee* v. *Garner,* 471 U.S. 1 (1985).

34. Id. at 9.

35. See R. Wilson Freyermuth, "Rethinking Excessive Force." *Duke Law Journal* (1987) 692–711 (1987).

36. See Gary Taylor, "Waco Siege Raises Vexing Issues." 15 *The National Law Journal* p. 15 (March 29, 1993).

37. See Editorial, "Justice in Ruby Ridge." 108 *The Los Angeles Daily Journal* p. 6 (August 31, 1995).

38. See Stephen Gibbs, "In Search of Straightforward Rules: The Burger Court's Expansion of the Search Incident to Arrest Exception to the Warrant Requirement." 22 *Santa Clara Law Review* pp. 1087–1107 (1993).

39. *Chimel* v. *California,* 395 U.S. 752 (1969).

40. See Thomas R. Canham, "Expanding the Scope of a Search Incident to an Arrest: Efficiency at the Expense of Fourth Amendment Rights." 31 *De Paul Law Review* pp. 581–605 (1982).

41. *Maryland* v. *Buie,* 494 U.S. 325 (1990).

42. See Mark A. Cuthbertson, "The Supreme Court's Protective Sweep Doctrine Runs Rings Around the Arrestee." 56 *Albany Law Review* pp. 159–195 (1992); Mark J. Sifferlin, "Fourth Amendment Protective Sweep Doctrine: When Does the Fourth Amendment allow Police Officers to Search the Home Incident to a Lawful Arrest?" 81 *Journal of Criminal Law and Criminology* pp. 862–882 (1991).

43. *Smith* v. *Ohio,* 494 U.S. 541 (1990).

44. *Rawlings* v. *Kentucky,* 448 U.S. 98 (1980).

45. *United States* v. *Robinson,* 414 U.S. 218 (1973).

46. Id. at 235.

47. *United States* v. *Edwards,* 415 U.S. 800 (1974).

48. *Washington* v. *Chrisman,* 455 U.S. 1 (1982).

49. *Winston* v. *Lee,* 470 U.S. 753 (1985).

50. See *Breithaupt* v. *Abram,* 352 U.S. 432 (1957).

51. *Schmerber* v. *California,* 384 U.S. 757 (1966).

52. *Cupp* v. *Murphy,* 412 U.S. 291 (1973).

53. *Winston* v. *Lee,* 470 U.S. 753 (1985).

54. See Edward D. Tolley and N. E. H. Hall, "Court Ordered Surgery to Retrieve Evidence in Georgia in Light of the United States Supreme Court's Decision in Winston v. Lee." *Mercer Law Review* pp. 1005–1018 (1986).

55. See *Breithaupt* v. *Abram,* 352 U.S. 432 (1957).

56. *Rochin* v. *California,* 342 U.S. 165 (1952).

57. See Rolando v. del Carmen, *Civil Liability In American Policing: A Text For Law Enforcement Personnel* (Englewood Cliffs, N.J.: Prentice Hall, 1991).

58. See Barbara C. Stief, "Body Packers and the Fourth Amendment: A Hard Case to Swallow." 1 *San Diego Justice Journal* pp. 207–225 (1993).

59. *Wachtler* v. *County of Herkimer,* 35 F. 3d 77, 81 (2nd Cir. 1994).

60. See Jonathan A. Koff, "Searches Incident to Arrest: Exposing the Unconstitutionality of Chicago's Strip Search Policy." 33 *De Paul Law Review* pp. 575–594 (1984).

61. *Bell* v. *Wolfish,* 414 U.S. 520 (1979); see Tracy McMath, "Do Prison Inmates Retain Any Fourth Amendment Protection From Body Cavity Searches?" 56 *University of Cincinnati Law Review* pp. 739–755 (1987).

62. For an excellent discussion of these issues, see LaFave & Israel, *Criminal Procedure, Second Edition* (1992), at 178–179.

63. *United States* v. *Chadwick,* 433 U.S. 1 (1977).

64. *Arkansas* v. *Sanders,* 442 U.S. 753 (1979).

65. See *United States* v. *Ross,* 456 U.S. 798 (1982).

66. *New York* v. *Belton,* 453 U.S. 454 (1981).

67. See Michael Tudzin, "Closed Container in Your Car? Contraband and Carriers Beware!" 56 *Whittier Law Review* pp. 979–1007 (1992).

68. See *United States* v. *Ross,* 456 U.S. 798 (1982).

69. *California* v. *Acevedo,* 500 U.S. 565 (1991).

70. See Stephen J. Bogacz, "Bright Lines and Opaque Containers: Searching for Reasonable Rules in Automobile Cases." 10 *Touro Law Review* pp. 679–704 (1994).

6 STOP AND FRISK AND INVESTIGATORY DETENTIONS

Outline

Key Terms

Chapter 5 considered the law of arrest and searches incident to an arrest. The general rule is that persons may be arrested only upon a showing of probable cause. Likewise, most searches conducted by police officers must be supported by probable cause. However, a person may be engaged in suspicious activity that does not rise to the level of probable cause for a search. For many years this type of case presented a difficulty for law enforcement officers: If they investigated suspicious persons without probable cause, any evidence that was found could be excluded at trial. If officers failed to investigate suspicious activity, however, their safety as well as that of the public might be jeopardized. The United States Supreme Court recognized this difficulty, and in *Terry* v. *Ohio,*[1] sanctioned a **stop and frisk** procedure. A **stop** occurs when the police temporarily detain someone for questioning. The Supreme Court has held that such a detention is a seizure under the Fourth Amendment. A **frisk** is a pat-down of the detained person's outer clothing to detect the presence of weapons.

In *Terry* v. *Ohio,* the Supreme Court allowed the police to stop, question, and frisk someone without probable cause if there was reasonable suspicion to believe that he or she was involved in criminal activity. Although the *Terry* doctrine was developed originally as a way to protect police officers and the public from physical harm, in recent years it has evolved into an investigatory tool as well.[2] This chapter will focus on police stop and frisk practices and more recent cases that permit the police to detain people or seize property for investigation based on reasonable suspicion of criminal activity. It is first necessary, however, to present a detailed treatment of the basic stop and frisk procedure.

Terry v. *Ohio* and Stop and Frisk Practices

In *Terry* v. *Ohio,* an experienced police detective, Martin McFadden, observed two men on a street corner in Cleveland, Ohio, at approximately 2:30 PM. Detective McFadden believed that the men were "casing" a store for a robbery attempt. The men had walked up and down in front of the building, staring into the store window, and they both returned to the same corner to talk. A few minutes later, a third man joined the other two, and then left the scene. When McFadden saw the two men meet the other man a few blocks away, he approached them, identified himself as a police officer, and asked them for identification. When McFadden received a mumbled response, he frisked the men. The pat-down revealed that Terry and another man were carrying handguns, and they were arrested for carrying concealed weapons. After their conviction in an Ohio state court, the defendants appealed and the Supreme Court granted certiorari.

The issue in *Terry* was whether it is always unreasonable for a police officer to seize a person and subject him to a limited search for weapons unless there is probable cause for an arrest.[3] The defendants asserted that because Officer McFadden lacked probable cause for the stop, which constituted an arrest, the frisk was an illegal search. Therefore the weapons seized as a result of the unlawful arrest should have been excluded at trial. The Supreme Court did not agree. Although Chief Justice Earl Warren, who authored the opinion of the Court, agreed that stopping someone on the street was a sufficient intrusion to constitute a Fourth Amendment seizure, and that a frisk

Source: UPI/Corbis Bettmann

involved a search, Officer McFadden's behavior in this case was lawful. Moreover, the stop and frisk practice did not require probable cause. Chief Justice Warren stated:

> When an officer is justified in believing that the individual whose suspicious behavior he is investigating at close range is armed and presently dangerous to the officer or to others, it would appear to be clearly unreasonable to deny the officer the power to take necessary measures to determine whether the person is in fact carrying a weapon and to neutralize the threat of physical harm.[4]

Warren further observed that the justification for a search in these circumstances is the protection of the police officer and the public. "[I]t must therefore be confined in scope to an intrusion reasonably designed to discover guns, knives, clubs, or other hidden instruments for the assault of the police officer."[5] In addition, in order to conduct a stop and frisk, an officer must have a reasonable suspicion that criminal activity is taking place. The rule of *Terry* v. *Ohio* is summarized in Highlight 6.1.

The Scope of a Stop and Frisk

A stop occurs when police officers deprive someone of his or her liberty in a meaningful way. The distinction between a stop and an arrest is often unclear, and the Supreme Court has refused to develop a bright-line rule to determine when a *Terry*-type encounter becomes an arrest.[6] The case law, however, permits two important observations. First, a stop is a temporary detention, whereas an **arrest** is a more intrusive and

---

Highlight 6.1

Excerpt from *Terry* v. *Ohio,* 392 U.S. 1, 30 (1967)

"[W]here a police officer observes unusual conduct which leads him reasonably to conclude in light of his experience that criminal activity may be afoot and that the person with whom he is dealing may be armed and dangerous, where in the course of investigating this behavior he identifies himself as a policeman and makes reasonable inquiries, and where nothing in the initial stages of the encounter serves to dispel his reasonable fear for his own or others' safety, he is entitled for the protection of himself and others in the area to conduct a carefully limited search of the outer clothing of such persons in an attempt to discover weapons which might be used to assault him."

---

lengthy interference with a suspect's liberty interest.[7] Second, a police officer may stop a person based upon reasonable suspicion of criminal activity. An arrest must be based upon probable cause. If a suspect is arrested without probable cause, any evidence obtained as a result of the arrest will be excluded at trial. For example, in *Dunaway* v. *New York,*[8] the defendant was taken into police custody for investigation of a murder. During interrogation, the defendant confessed. The Supreme Court held that because the police lacked probable cause to arrest Dunaway, the confession was inadmissible at trial.

Whether a suspect is under arrest or simply detained during a *Terry*-type encounter is significant because a search incident to an arrest is designed to protect the police *and* produce evidence of criminal activity, whereas a stop and frisk justifies a pat-down search of a suspect's outer clothing solely for weapons.[9] If, after frisking someone, a police officer in a *Terry*-type encounter reaches into the suspect's pocket and retrieves evidence that did not appear to be a weapon, normally the evidence must be excluded at trial. If, however, the suspect had been placed under arrest, the officer could have lawfully searched the suspect's pockets for evidence of a crime.

Distinguishing Probable Cause from Reasonable Suspicion

Chapter 4 defined **probable cause** as a set of facts or circumstances that would lead a reasonable person to believe that a person committed a crime or that contraband may be found in a particular place. Probable cause is needed whenever the police wish to make an arrest or search for contraband. In *Terry* v. *Ohio*, however, the Supreme Court asserted that reasonable suspicion will justify a stop in some circumstances.

The distinction between probable cause and reasonable suspicion is not always clear. In 1996, the Supreme Court discussed the relationship between probable cause and reasonable suspicion in *Ornelas* v. *United States.*[10] Excerpts from that decision are presented in Highlight 6.2. The Court held that defining precisely what these concepts mean is not possible. Rather, "[t]hey are instead fluid concepts that take their

Highlight 6.2

Ornelas v. *United States*, 134 L.Ed. 2d 911, 918–919 (1996)

"Articulating precisely what 'reasonable suspicion' and 'probable cause' mean is not possible. They are common sense, nontechnical conceptions that deal with 'the factual and practical considerations of everyday life on which reasonable and prudent men, not legal technicians, act.' As such, the standards are 'not readily, or even usefully, reduced to a neat set of legal rules.' We have described reasonable suspicion simply as 'a particularized and objective basis' for suspecting the person stopped of criminal activity, and probable cause to search as existing where the known facts and circumstances are sufficient to warrant a man of reasonable prudence in the belief that contraband or

evidence of a crime will be found. We have cautioned that these two legal principles are not 'finely-tuned standards,' comparable to the standards of proof beyond a reasonable doubt or of proof by a preponderance of the evidence. They are instead fluid concepts that take their substantive content from the particular contexts in which the standards are being assessed.

The principal components of a determination of reasonable suspicion or probable cause will be the events which occurred leading up to the stop or search, and then the decision whether these historical facts, viewed from the standpoint of an objectively reasonable police officer, amount to reasonable suspicion or to probable cause.

substantive content from the particular contexts in which the standards are being assessed."[11] It is safe to say, however, that probable cause is more difficult to establish than reasonable suspicion because it requires a higher degree of certainty that a crime has been committed or that contraband may be found in a certain place.[12]

Although **reasonable suspicion** requires a lesser degree of certainty than probable cause, an officer must be able to point to specific objective facts that give rise to his or her suspicion.[13] This is termed **articulable suspicion.** A police officer's knowledge and experience will be considered in determining if reasonable suspicion supports a stop, because an experienced officer may become suspicious when he or she observes activity that appears innocent to a less experienced officer or to a member of the public.[14]

General suspicion is not enough to satisfy the *Terry* standard. For example, in *Brown* v. *Texas*,[15] a suspect was stopped because he was present in an area where illegal drugs were often sold. Police officers stated that he looked suspicious and that he had not been observed by the officers in that area in the past. The Supreme Court held that a stop based on *Terry* v. *Ohio* requires "specific, objective facts indicating that society's legitimate interests require the seizure of the particular individual, or that the seizure must be carried out pursuant to a plan embodying explicit, neutral limitations on the conduct of the individual officers."[16]

Supreme Court precedents make it clear that the reasonable suspicion standard "requires considerably less than proof by a preponderance of the evidence."[17] This means that the reasonable suspicion standard will be satisfied by something significantly less than a more-probable-than-not standard of proof. This standard will not be satisfied by a police officer's mere inarticulable hunch or a guess that criminal activity is occurring. For example, in one case a police officer's hunch that a driver who would not look at his patrol car was involved in drug trafficking did not satisfy the reasonable suspicion standard.[18]

Stop and Frisk—A Two-Stage Inquiry

In *Terry*, the Supreme Court established that police officers who wish to stop and frisk those suspected of criminal activity must engage in a two-part analysis. First, the officer must have reasonable suspicion to stop and question the individual. If, after questioning the suspect, the officer's fears are resolved, a frisk need not be conducted. If, however, the officer is not satisfied with the suspect's responses, or receives a "mumbled response" to questions, *and* the officer has reasonable suspicion to believe that the suspect may be armed, a pat-down frisk of the suspect's outer clothing may be conducted. Police may frisk only a suspect's outer clothing to determine if weapons are present. If the officer feels a weapon he or she may retrieve it; however, a pat-down frisk is *not* a full-scale search for evidence of criminal activity.

It is important to emphasize that the two parts of the stop and frisk analysis are usually dependent—only when a suspect's responses to the officer's questions are inadequate and the officer has reason to fear for his or her safety will a frisk of the suspect's outer clothing be lawful. The Supreme Court has held, however, that in limited circumstances a police officer may, without first questioning a suspect, conduct a frisk when the officer fears for his or her safety and has reasonable suspicion to believe that the individual is armed. In *Adams* v. *Williams*,[19] an informant told a police officer that a person sitting in a parked car had a pistol tucked into his belt. The officer approached the car and when the window was rolled down reached in his waistband and removed a handgun. A search incident to the suspect's arrest revealed illegal drugs. The Supreme Court held that the seizure of the handgun and illegal drugs was lawful because the officer justifiably feared for his safety and the drugs were discovered as the result of a valid search incident to the suspect's arrest.

An example should help to further clarify these concepts. Suppose that in response to a series of recent burglaries at a local college, police officers are asked to conduct a surveillance of a particular college dormitory. At approximately 3:30 AM, officers observe a shadowy figure crouching near a doorway to the dormitory. When officers approach the individual and ask what she is doing, she identifies herself to the officers' satisfaction as the college's Dean of Students, who is conducting her own investigation of the burglaries. The officers would not be justified in frisking the Dean—their suspicions were allayed by the Dean's responses to their questions and a reasonable officer would not fear for his or her safety. Suppose, in contrast, that in similar circumstances the officers approach the individual, who has no identification and when asked what he is doing in the area, states: "I was just out for a walk, man; what are you hassling me for?" Moreover, the weather that night is clear and the temperature outside is approximately 78 degrees, but the individual is wearing a long trench coat. In these circumstances, the officers would have reasonable suspicion to believe that the suspect may be armed and present a threat to their safety. A frisk in these circumstances is clearly justified.

Terry v. *Ohio* is an important Fourth Amendment case for several reasons. First, it established that for Fourth Amendment purposes a stop was a seizure and a frisk was a search. For the first time, however, the Supreme Court allowed the police to conduct searches and seizures without probable cause. A stop and frisk encounter could be based on reasonable suspicion, which is a less demanding standard of proof. Second, *Terry* was an effective accommodation between competing interests—citizens' privacy interests and protection of the police and the public. In order to determine which interest had priority, the Supreme Court used a test that balanced a suspect's privacy interest with society's need to conduct the challenged search. The Supreme Court has used this test often in the years since *Terry* to determine the lawfulness of challenged searches and seizures.[20]

The Nature of a Stop

In *Terry* v. *Ohio* the Supreme Court did not determine precisely what constitutes a stop. That task was left to later cases. In *United States* v. *Mendenhall*,[21] federal drug enforcement agents stopped a suspect as she was walking through an airport. They requested her identification, and asked to see her airline ticket. The name on her ticket did not match the name on her driver's license. The agents asked Mendenhall if she would return to the airport's Drug Enforcement Administration (DEA) office for additional questioning. She accompanied the agents and later consented to a search, which revealed that she was carrying illegal drugs. At trial she was convicted of narcotics possession. The U.S. Court of Appeals held, however, that the evidence should have been excluded because it resulted from Mendenhall's illegal detention.[22]

The U.S. Supreme Court reversed and held that Mendenhall was not seized within the meaning of the Fourth Amendment. The test developed by the Court was whether "in view of all the circumstances surrounding the incident, a reasonable person would have believed that he was not free to leave."[23] The Court identified several factors to be considered to determine whether a person has been seized, even if he or she did not attempt to leave:

1. whether there was a threatening presence of several officers;
2. whether the officers displayed a weapon;
3. whether there was a physical touching of the person by an officer;
4. whether the officer used language or a tone of voice indicating that compliance with his or her request might be compelled.[24]

Florida v. *Royer*[25] provided additional Supreme Court guidance about precisely what constitutes a stop or a seizure in Fourth Amendment cases. Detectives at an airport believed Royer was carrying illegal drugs and approached him and asked to see his airline ticket and driver's license. When the names on the ticket and the driver's license did not match, the officers, who had retained the ticket and the license, asked Royer to accompany them to a nearby office. Using the *Mendenhall* test, the Court held that under these circumstances the show of official authority was such that a reasonable person would have believed he was not free to leave and reversed his conviction.

The Supreme Court has sanctioned brief detentions aboard commercial passenger buses that permit police officers to investigate persons suspected of carrying illegal drugs. This investigatory practice, which is termed "working the buses" by one police agency,[26] allows officers to board commercial passenger buses in order to conduct random drug sweeps. In *Florida* v. *Bostick*,[27] during a stopover in Fort Lauderdale, two police officers boarded a bus bound from Miami to Atlanta. After observing the passengers, the officers, without articulable suspicion, asked to see the defendant's identification and bus ticket. The ticket matched Bostick's identification and both were immediately returned to him. The police officers then explained their presence as narcotics agents looking for illegal drugs. They requested the defendant's consent to search his luggage. Although Bostick testified that he had consented to a search of the first bag, there was a conflict at trial about whether he had consented to the search of the second bag in which the contraband was found. A search of Bostick's luggage revealed cocaine and at trial he was convicted of various drug offenses.

On appeal to the Supreme Court, the issue was whether such a police encounter aboard a bus constitutes a Fourth Amendment seizure. If Bostick had been seized and the seizure was not supported by probable cause or reasonable suspicion, the evidence should have been suppressed at trial because it was the product of an unlawful seizure. The Supreme Court used a freedom of movement test to determine whether a Fourth Amendment seizure has occurred when police officers board a bus to search for drugs. That test asks whether a reasonable person would feel free to terminate the encounter with the officers. The Court stated: "So long as a reasonable person would feel free 'to disregard the police and go about his business, . . . the encounter is consensual and no reasonable suspicion is required."[28] Based on the trial record, the Court was unable to determine whether Bostick would have felt free to terminate the encounter with the police. It therefore remanded the case to the trial court.

Florida v. *Bostick* is an important Fourth Amendment case. It establishes that police officers may, without reasonable suspicion to believe that a person is involved in criminal conduct, encounter the individual within the confines of a closed bus, ask questions, and request consent to search his luggage.[29] The nature of this type of encounter does not automatically render invalid the individual's consent to search.

The Supreme Court further clarified the issue of when a Fourth Amendment seizure occurs in *California* v. *Hodari D.*[30] In this case police officers observed several youths acting suspiciously near a parked car. The juveniles saw the police officers and began to run away. One of the officers chased Hodari D., who tossed away a small package that contained crack cocaine. At trial, Hodari D. argued that the cocaine should be suppressed because he was seized without probable cause when the officer began to chase him. The state maintained that Hodari D. was not seized until the officer actually caught him. Moreover, because Hodari D. had abandoned the drugs, they were admissible against him. The Supreme Court upheld Hodari D.'s conviction because he had voluntarily abandoned the property before he was placed under arrest.[31]

Time Restrictions and Investigatory Detentions

The Supreme Court has consistently refused to create a bright-line rule establishing the permissible length of a *Terry*-type stop. This is because "common sense and ordinary human experience must govern over rigid criteria"[32] in determining whether the length of a *Terry*-type encounter is reasonable. Therefore, to determine whether a stop has become an arrest the courts will use a case-by-case analysis. The case law, however, provides some general guidance. In *United States* v. *Sharpe,*[33] police officers detained for 20 minutes a driver who had attempted to evade them. Because the police officers had conducted their investigation in a diligent manner, which means that they completed the inquiry designed to dispel their suspicion as rapidly as possible under the circumstances, the Supreme Court held that the stop was reasonable. The 20-minute standard, however, is not a bright-line rule. The courts will scrutinize the circumstances of each case to determine whether the length of a stop is reasonable. It is possible that a stop lasting less than 20 minutes would be held unreasonable if police officers failed to complete their investigation in a diligent manner. In contrast, a stop lasting more than 20 minutes may be reasonable if police officers pursue their investigation diligently. The United States Court of Appeals for the Eighth Circuit has held that a stop that lasted 40 minutes while a driver was waiting in a police car for a warning ticket to be issued was unreasonable.[34] Moreover, in *United States* v. *Place,*[35] discussed later in this chapter, a 90-minute investigatory detention of a suspect's luggage was found to be unreasonable.

Justifications for a Stop

Over the years the Supreme Court has approved several different justifications for stopping a suspect when the police have reasonable suspicion that he or she may be involved in criminal behavior. The following sections will discuss each of these justifications.

Information from an Informant

Terry v. *Ohio* held that reasonable suspicion for a stop could be established through a police officer's personal observations. A few years after *Terry* v. *Ohio* was decided, the Court expanded this basic principle in *Adams* v. *Williams.*[36] The Court held that reasonable suspicion for a stop and frisk may also be established by using an informant's tip.

Likewise, in *Alabama* v. *White,*[37] the Court upheld a stop after an anonymous informant had given police officers information that accurately described White's vehicle, the time of his departure, and his destination.[38] The Court asserted that as in search warrant cases, an anonymous informant's information may be supplemented with corroborative police investigation.[39]

Drug Courier Profiles

A **drug courier profile** is an investigatory device used to identify individuals who may be transporting illegal drugs.[40] Such profiles are used often at major transportation centers such as airports, train stations, or bus terminals. The fact that an individual may exhibit behaviors that match a drug courier profile does not by itself constitute reasonable suspicion to stop and question a person. Such profiles may be used, however, as *part* of the information that police officers consider to determine if reasonable suspicion exists to justify stopping and detaining a traveler for investigation.

Some of the factors used to identify potential drug couriers include:

1. paying for airline tickets with large amounts of cash;
2. traveling under a false name;
3. traveling from a destination that is known as a **source city** for illegal drugs (a source city is one known by law enforcement officials to constitute a distribution center for unlawful drugs);
4. staying at a destination for a short period of time;
5. the suspect's nervous appearance at the transportation center or during the trip.[41]

An individual's race or ethnicity should not be listed as a factor in a drug courier profile. Such discriminatory enforcement practices are likely to be held unconstitutional.[42]

The Supreme Court has held that the reasonable suspicion standard is not satisfied by isolated examples of innocent conduct. Therefore, standing alone, any single factor listed in a drug courier profile will not be held to constitute reasonable suspicion. For example, in *Reid* v. *Georgia*[43] the Court held that drug agents lacked reasonable suspicion to stop someone who had arrived on an early morning flight from a source city for illegal drugs and who had looked at another passenger on several different occasions. If, however, police observe suspicious behavior and several of the factors in the profile are present it may give rise to a reasonable suspicion of criminal activity. In *United States* v. *Sokolow*,[44] the Court held that federal drug agents had reasonable suspicion to stop and question the defendant because his behavior was suspicious. Moreover, Sokolow exhibited the five characteristics described above.[45]

Information Provided in Police Flyers

Information provided in a police flyer may provide an officer with reasonable suspicion to believe that a suspect has been involved in criminal activity. In *United States* v. *Hensley,*[46] a police officer was alerted by a flyer indicating that the driver of a car was wanted for investigation of an armed robbery, was armed, and should be considered dangerous. The officer stopped and approached the car with his service revolver drawn, discovered a handgun in the car, and took the suspect into custody. At his trial for illegal weapons possession, the defendant asserted that the stop was illegal; therefore, the evidence should be excluded. The Supreme Court upheld the conviction and asserted that police officers may stop and detain a suspect who is wanted by another jurisdiction.[47]

The Scope of a Stop and Frisk

The general rule is that the scope of a stop and frisk is limited to a pat-down of a suspect's outer clothing to determine the presence of weapons. If the encounter develops into a full-scale search, it must be supported by probable cause, or any evidence seized may be excluded at trial. Recently, however, the Supreme Court has recognized an important exception to this principle, which may be termed the plain touch doctrine.

A Plain Touch Doctrine

An exception to the general rule regarding the scope of a search in a stop and frisk encounter arises when a police officer feels an object in a suspect's possession and has probable cause to believe that it is contraband. In *Minnesota* v. *Dickerson,*[48] police officers observed a suspect leaving a building where drugs were sold. Once Dickerson left the "crack house," he began to behave in a suspicious manner, although the police did not have probable cause to stop or arrest him. The police officers stopped Dickerson and conducted a frisk, which revealed a lump in his jacket. Although the officers realized that the lump was probably not a weapon, they squeezed and manipulated it extensively in an effort to determine what it was. They subsequently removed a lump of crack cocaine from Dickerson's pocket and he was convicted of possession of crack cocaine. On appeal to the Supreme Court, Dickerson contended that the cocaine should have been excluded because when the police officers squeezed and manipulated the crack cocaine they exceeded the permitted scope of a *Terry*-type frisk. The Supreme Court reiterated its commitment to the *Terry* doctrine, which permits a pat-down to determine the presence of weapons. Once the officers realized that the lump was not a weapon, however, they should have stopped. Because the officers had manipulated the lump extensively in an effort to determine what it was, the frisk in this case had become a search for evidence, which must be supported by probable cause. Therefore, because the police lacked probable cause for the search the evidence should have been suppressed.

Despite the fact that the evidence was held inadmissible in *Dickerson,* the Supreme Court for the first time recognized the **plain touch doctrine.** Under this doctrine, a police officer who is conducting a *Terry*-type frisk for weapons may expand a search and seize an object if he or she feels something and there is probable cause to believe it is contraband.[49] The plain touch doctrine's requirements are similar to those of the plain view doctrine:

1. The police officer must lawfully be in the position in which he or she feels the suspicious object;
2. Its incriminating nature must be immediately apparent when it is touched;
3. The police officer must have a lawful right to seize the object.[50]

In *Minnesota* v. *Dickerson* the defendant was charged with possession of crack cocaine. This highly potent form of cocaine continues to present a major challenge to law enforcement authorities in major U.S. cities, especially in inner city neighborhoods. Because its use has become so prevalent, a number of legislatures have passed laws making the penalties for possession and distribution of crack cocaine even more severe than for other types of illegal drugs. Recently, the U.S. Supreme Court was asked to determine whether crack cocaine laws discriminated against African-Americans.[51] Highlight 6.3 presents excerpts from that case.

Automobile Searches Based on Reasonable Suspicion

Terry v. *Ohio* allowed only a pat-down search of a suspect's outer clothing for the purpose of detecting weapons. In the years since *Terry* was decided the Supreme Court has expanded substantially the scope of permissible searches based on reasonable suspicion. In *Michigan* v. *Long,*[52] two deputy sheriffs observed a car drive into a ditch. Long, who had been driving the car, met the officers at the rear of the car and handed them his driver's license. When he went back to the car to retrieve his automobile's registration, the deputies saw a large hunting knife on the floor. Long was frisked, and a deputy discovered a pouch containing marijuana beneath an armrest. The evidence was admitted against Long, who was convicted of possession of marijuana. The Supreme Court upheld the search of Long's car based on *Terry* v. *Ohio*. The Court ruled that police officers may search a car's passenger compartment under two conditions: (1) if they have a reasonable belief that he is dangerous and could gain control of weapons in the car; and (2) the officers search only in places within the passenger compartment where weapons may be hidden.[53] Moreover, if while searching the passenger compartment for weapons, the police discover illegal contraband, they may seize that evidence under the plain view doctrine. In *Long,* the Supreme Court accepted the trial court's finding that a weapon may have been concealed in the leather pouch.

In addition, if police officers based upon reasonable suspicion stop a motorist they may order the driver to exit the car. In *Pennsylvania* v. *Mimms,*[54] the Supreme Court held that ordering a driver to leave the car is an appropriate measure designed to insure the safety of police officers.

Likewise, in *Maryland* v. *Wilson,*[55] the Supreme Court held recently that police officers may automatically order passengers to exit a car during a routine traffic stop because such an order is a minimal intrusion on a passenger's privacy interests, which is outweighed by governmental interests in public safety.

Roadblocks

Roadblocks are a form of seizure under the Fourth Amendment. In *Brower* v. *Inyo County,*[56] Brower, who was fleeing from police, was allegedly killed when police officers moved an 18-wheel tractor-trailer across the lanes of travel around the bend on a highway. The Supreme Court held that such a practice would constitute a Fourth Amendment seizure, which they defined as a "governmental termination of freedom of movement through means intentionally applied."[57] Therefore, a roadblock must meet the Fourth Amendment's reasonableness standards. Moreover, if police

Highlight 6.3

United States v. *Armstrong*, 116 S.Ct. 1480 (1996)

 [Armstrong was indicted in U.S. District Court on charges of violating federal firearms laws and on drug conspiracy charges involving his alleged distribution of crack cocaine. At trial and on appeal, the defendant argued that he had been selected for prosecution because he was an African-American.]

"In this case, we consider the showing necessary for a defendant to be entitled to discovery on a claim that the prosecuting attorney singled him out for prosecution on the basis of race. We conclude that respondents failed to satisfy the threshold showing: They failed to show that the Government declined to prosecute similarly situated suspects of other races . . .

The requirements for a selective prosecution claim draw on ordinary equal protection standards. The claimant must demonstrate that the federal prosecutorial policy 'had a discriminatory effect and that it was motivated by a discriminatory purpose.' To establish a discriminatory effect in a race case, the claimant must show that similarly situated individuals of a different race were not prosecuted. . . . We think the required threshold—a credible showing of different treatment of similarly situated persons— adequately balances the Government's interest in vigorous prosecution and the defendant's interest in avoiding selective prosecution.

In the case before us, respondent's 'study' did not constitute 'some evidence tending to show the existence of the essential elements of' a selective prosecution claim. The study failed to identify individuals who were not black, could have been prosecuted for the offenses for which respondents were charged, but were not so prosecuted. This omission was not remedied by respondents' evidence in opposition to the Government's motion for reconsideration. The newspaper article, which discussed the discriminatory effect of federal drug sentencing laws, was not relevant to an allegation of discrimination in decisions to prosecute. Respondents' affidavits, which recounted one attorney's conversation with a drug treatment center employee and the experience of another attorney defending drug prosecutions in state court, recounted hearsay and reported personal conclusions based on anecdotal evidence. The judgment of the Court of Appeals is therefore reversed, and the case is remanded for proceedings consistent with this opinion."

officers use roadblocks that are unsafe and cause injury or death, they may be subjected to civil liability.

The Supreme Court has not yet determined the lawfulness of police use of roadblocks to stop all vehicles moving on the roadways to search for the perpetrators of a recent crime. Two prominent legal scholars, Professors Wayne R. LaFave and Jerold H. Israel, suggest that police use of roadblocks are different from an ordinary *Terry* stop and should be allowed only when:

1. there is a reliable report of a crime, and not merely suspicion that a crime has been committed;
2. the alleged crime is a serious one, which gives rise to a strong public interest in prompt apprehension of the offender;
3. the roadblock is placed in a location that is reasonably likely to result in the apprehension of the offender.[58]

Source: UPI/Corbis Bettmann

Sobriety Roadblock Checkpoints.   Intoxicated drivers have long represented a major threat to society. In the 1970s and 1980s in response to public demands to get tough with drunk drivers, many police agencies sought alternative ways to enforce impaired operator laws.[59] The constitutionality of state laws permitting police agencies to employ drunk-driving roadblocks remained unsettled, however, until 1990.

Michigan Department of State Police v. *Sitz,*[60] involved a police program in which all vehicles passing through a checkpoint were stopped and their drivers examined briefly for signs of intoxication. Before the program began officially, Sitz sought a ruling from a Michigan court that the program was unconstitutional. In *Brown* v. *Texas,*[61] the Supreme Court had developed a balancing test for determining the reasonableness of a Fourth Amendment seizure. This test required a trial court to balance "the gravity of the public concerns served by the seizure, the degree to which the seizure advances the public interest, and the severity of the interference with individual liberty."[62] Using this test, the Michigan Court of Appeals held in *Sitz* that the police checkpoints violated the Fourth Amendment. Its analysis concluded that the state had a "grave and legitimate" interest in preventing drunk driving; that sobriety checkpoint programs were generally ineffective, and therefore did not further significantly the state's interest; and that the checkpoint's intrusion on individual liberties was substantial.[63]

The U.S. Supreme Court upheld the constitutionality of the sobriety checkpoints, ruling that the Michigan Court of Appeals had misapplied the *Brown* balancing test. The Court balanced the seriousness of the U.S. drunk-driving problem and the state's interest in curtailing it, with the intrusion on individual rights caused by the sobriety checkpoints. The Court held that the seriousness of the drunk driving problem in the U.S. outweighed substantially the "minimal" intrusion on individual rights caused by the sobriety checkpoints. Moreover, the Michigan State Police's sobriety checkpoint

Source: Spencer Grant/ Photo Researchers

program was developed according to properly formulated administrative rules that restricted police officer discretion and provided appropriate safeguards for the public. The Supreme Court's scale tilted in favor of Michigan's sobriety checkpoint program.

In the aftermath of *Michigan Department of State Police* v. *Sitz,* some state courts have rejected sobriety checkpoint programs as a violation of their state constitutions.[64] For example, in *Pimental* v. *Department of Transportation*[65] the Rhode Island Supreme Court held that drunk-driving roadblocks violate Article 1, Section 6, of the Rhode Island Constitution. The Court stated:

> We believe that allowing such roadblocks would diminish the guarantees against unreasonable searches and seizures contained in the Rhode Island Constitution. It is illogical to permit law enforcement officers to stop fifty or a hundred vehicles on the speculative chance that one or two may be driven by a person violating the law against intoxication. We therefore hold that roadblocks or checkpoints, established to apprehend persons violating the law against driving under the influence of intoxicating beverages or drugs, operate without probable cause or reasonable suspicion and violate the Rhode Island Constitution.[66]

Likewise, in *State* v. *Henderson,*[67] the Idaho Supreme Court rejected drunk-driving roadblocks under the Idaho Constitution. Highlight 6.4 presents excerpts from that decision.

Highlight 6.4

To summarize, drunk-driving roadblocks are lawful in a majority of the states. The Supreme Court has held that this practice does not violate the Fourth Amendment because roadblocks involve only a minor intrusion on individual liberty, which is outweighed by the magnitude of the drunk-driving problem.[68]

Other Types of Investigatory Detentions

The Supreme Court has considered several additional types of detentions for investigatory purposes. These include detentions of luggage at airports, detentions of suspects for fingerprinting, and detentions at U.S. borders. Each of these will be discussed separately.

Detentions of Property at Airports

When the Supreme Court decided *Terry* v. *Ohio*, the sole justification for a stop and frisk was the safety of police officers and members of the public. More recently, the Court has expanded the *Terry* doctrine to allow the police to seize and hold property to investigate possible crimes.

In *United States* v. *Place,*[69] Miami police officers, who had observed Place in the Miami International Airport, suspected that he might be carrying illegal drugs to New York City. They contacted Drug Enforcement Administration (DEA) agents, who were waiting for Place when he arrived in New York. The agents identified themselves and asked Place for identification and for permission to search his luggage. Place provided identification but refused to grant permission to search his bags. The agents seized the bags and took them to another airport where trained drug detection dogs sniffed the bags. When the dogs reacted positively to one of the bags, agents obtained a search warrant and conducted a search during which cocaine was discovered. The entire process took approximately 90 minutes. At trial, Place was convicted of possession of cocaine with intent to distribute in violation of federal law.

The Supreme Court held that the seizure of the bags was not lawful under *Terry* v. *Ohio.*[70] The Court asserted that although persons traveling through airports have a

Source: AP/Wide World Photos

diminished expectation of privacy in their activities, this property detention lasted too long. Property detentions are allowed under *Terry* only for a brief period "to investigate the circumstances that aroused [a law enforcement officer's] suspicion, provided that the investigative detention is properly limited in scope."[71] The Court declined, however, to determine precisely how much time such an investigation could take under *Terry*. Moreover, in *Place* the Court decided that the police may without probable cause or reasonable suspicion use trained dogs to sniff luggage. Such procedures do not violate the Fourth Amendment because dog sniffs are so relatively unobtrusive that they are not searches.[72] In addition, a positive response by trained dogs may be used to establish probable cause to search for illegal drugs.

Place suggests that to determine the reasonableness of a property seizure for investigation the courts will consider the following factors:

1. whether the police conducted the investigation in a diligent manner;
2. how long the property seizure lasted; and
3. whether the seized property was taken to a different location for further scrutiny.[73]

For example, one court has held that a detention of an airline passenger's luggage for 35 minutes was reasonable because law enforcement officers diligently pursued their investigation and, once they established probable cause to search, obtained a warrant as soon as possible.[74] Moreover, another court has held that a detention of a suspect's luggage for 10 hours was reasonable because it was seized late at night and officers diligently pursued a search warrant.[75]

Detentions of Suspects for Fingerprinting

Terry v. *Ohio* does not allow the police to detain a suspect and transport him to the police station for fingerprinting. In *Davis* v. *Mississippi*,[76] police officers investigating a crime conducted a round-up of all black males in a small Mississippi town and transported them to the police station for fingerprinting. Such investigatory practices were held to violate the Fourth Amendment.[77] The Court indicated, however, that it may be permissible to detain suspects and take their fingerprints in the field. A more recent Supreme Court case suggests that a detention for fingerprinting may be permitted in the following circumstances:

1. if there is reasonable suspicion that a suspect has committed a crime;
2. if there is a reasonable basis for believing that fingerprinting will establish or negate the suspect's connection to the crime;
3. if the fingerprinting procedure is carried out quickly.[78]

Detentions at U.S. Borders

Persons have a diminished expectation of privacy in airports. Personal expectations of privacy are diminished to an even greater extent when a passenger returns to the United States from an international journey. The rule is that customs agents or immigration officials may conduct routine suspicionless searches of a person's baggage or vehicle.[79] These searches may be conducted without probable cause or reasonable suspicion to believe that a traveler is violating the law.[80] A more intrusive search, such as a strip search or a body cavity search, must be supported by reasonable suspicion. In *United States* v. *Montoya de Hernandez*,[81] a suspect who spoke no English had made eight recent trips to Los Angeles and Miami. She told agents that she had no friends or family in the United States but was attempting to purchase merchandise for her husband's store in Bogota, Colombia. The suspect carried $5,000 in cash but no credit cards and had no hotel reservations, little luggage, and could not explain how her airline ticket was purchased. Customs agents, who suspected that she was smuggling cocaine in her alimentary canal, gave her the choice of submitting to an X-ray examination or being detained until she had a bowel movement. The suspect declined to be taken to a hospital for an X-ray examination and was held for 16 hours. When the suspect would not eat or drink anything and had not produced a bowel movement after 16 hours, the agents sought a court order for an X-ray and rectal examination to be conducted by a physician. The examination, which occurred approximately 24 hours after the suspect's flight had arrived, disclosed a balloon containing cocaine. She was placed under arrest.

The Supreme Court held that the suspect's detention was permissible because it was based upon reasonable suspicion that she was carrying illegal drugs. Although the detention exceeded any other detention the Court had approved under reasonable suspicion, the difficulty in detecting alimentary canal drug smuggling made the delay a reasonable one.[82] Moreover, because the defendant had made active "efforts to resist the call of nature"[83] the lengthy detention was reasonable under the circumstances.

Summary

Chapter 6 considers stop and frisk, investigatory detentions, and several additional forms of investigatory activity. Unlike an arrest, which must be supported by probable cause, a stop and frisk may be based upon reasonable and articulable suspicion that criminal activity is afoot. *Terry* v. *Ohio*, is a seminal case that permits police to stop and frisk those reasonably suspected of criminal activity.

The permitted scope of a stop and frisk encounter is discussed as well. The line between a stop and frisk and an arrest is often unclear because the Supreme Court has refused to develop a bright-line rule to determine precisely when a *Terry*-type stop becomes an arrest. The case law permits two important observations. First, a stop is a temporary detention, whereas an arrest is a more intrusive and lengthy interference with a suspect's liberty. Second, a police officer may stop a person based upon reasonable suspicion of criminal activity, whereas an arrest must be supported by probable cause. Whether a suspect is under arrest or simply detained during a *Terry*-type encounter is significant because a search incident to an arrest is designed to produce evidence of criminal activity, whereas a stop and frisk justifies solely a pat-down search of a suspect's outer clothing for weapons.

A stop and frisk encounter involves two stages. First, an officer must stop and question an individual. Second, if the officer is not satisfied with the suspect's responses, a pat-down frisk of the suspect's outer clothing may be conducted. A frisk is justified by important social interests in protecting the police and members of the public.

The Supreme Court has held that a stop is a Fourth Amendment seizure. It has clarified the issue of precisely what constitutes a stop in several cases since *Terry* v. *Ohio*. One test emphasizes whether "in view of all the circumstances surrounding the incident, a reasonable person would have believed that he was not free to leave." Some of the factors that a court will consider in determining if a Fourth Amendment seizure has occurred include: (1) the threatening presence of several officers; (2) the display of a weapon by the police; (3) some physical touching of the person by an officer; (4) the use of language or tone suggesting that compliance with an officer's request might be compelled.

Time restrictions on investigatory detentions are another important issue. The Supreme Court has refused to create a bright-line rule establishing the permissible length of a *Terry*-type stop. Therefore, the courts will determine whether a stop has become an arrest on a case-by-case basis. The case law provides some general guidance and suggests that if police officers pursue their investigation in a diligent manner, a 20-minute detention is not unreasonable.

Police officers may use different types of information to justify a stop and frisk. One type is information obtained from an informant, which may be supplemented with corroborative police investigation. In addition, the police may use drug courier profiles. Still another source of information for a stop and frisk is data contained in flyers from various law enforcement agencies.

A relatively recent modification of a *Terry*-type frisk is termed the plain touch doctrine. As originally formulated in *Terry*, a frisk permitted only a pat-down of a suspect's outer clothing to determine the presence of weapons. Under the plain touch doctrine, a police officer who is conducting a frisk may expand a search and seize an object if he or she feels something in the suspect's clothing and there is probable cause to believe that it is contraband.

Another modification of the *Terry* doctrine allows police officers to search the passenger compartment of a car upon two conditions. First, they must reasonably believe that an occupant is dangerous and could gain control of weapons. Second, the officers may search only in places within the passenger compartment where weapons may be hidden.

Chapter 6 considers sobriety roadblock check-points. The Supreme Court has upheld the constitutionality of this practice under the Fourth Amendment. Several state supreme courts have held that drunk-driving roadblocks violate state constitutional protections. Moreover, property detentions at airports are permitted only for a brief period to investigate the circumstances that aroused a law enforcement officer's suspicion, provided that it is properly limited in scope.

Police officers are not permitted to conduct dragnet detentions of suspects for fingerprinting.

Recent case law suggests, however, that it may be permissible to detain suspects and take their fingerprints in the field.

Law enforcement officers may detain persons at U.S. borders and may conduct routine suspicionless searches of luggage or vehicles. Strip searches or body cavity searches, however, must be supported by reasonable suspicion. If there is reasonable suspicion to believe that a suspect is carrying drugs inside his or her body, the suspect may be detained for investigation by law enforcement officers for an extended period.

Review Questions

1. What is a stop and frisk procedure? How does it differ from an arrest?
2. Distinguish between probable cause and reasonable suspicion. Why is the difference important?
3. Identify the two-stage inquiry developed by the Supreme Court in *Terry* v. *Ohio*.
4. What is a "stop"? Identify several factors a trial court would examine to determine if a person was seized by police lawfully.
5. What are the time limitations on a *Terry*-type detention?
6. Discuss how the police may use the following to justify stopping someone for investigatory purposes:
   a. information from an informant
   b. drug courier profiles
   c. information contained in police flyers
7. What is the "plain touch" doctrine. Has the Supreme Court imposed any limitations on this practice?
8. When may police officers search an automobile based solely upon reasonable suspicion?
9. Discuss the present constitutional status of drunk-driving roadblocks.
10. Discuss the present constitutional status of the following police investigatory practices:
   a. detentions of property at airports
   b. drug detection dog sniffs of a passenger's luggage
   c. detentions of suspects for fingerprinting
   d. detentions of persons at U.S. borders

Issues for Analysis and Discussion

1. In *Terry* v. *Ohio*, the Supreme Court for the first time allowed police officers with reasonable suspicion to stop and frisk suspicious individuals. Compare the Court's rationale for allowing the police to conduct stop and frisk practices with its rationale in *United States* v. *Robinson* (in Chapter 5) for allowing the police to search an individual incident to a lawful arrest. Is the Supreme Court's reasoning in these cases consistent?

2. In *United States* v. *Mendenhall,* the Supreme Court held that the defendant had not been

"seized" for Fourth Amendment purposes when government narcotics agents asked her for her airline ticket and requested that she accompany them to the DEA office. The Court concluded that a person is "seized" only if, "in view of all of the circumstances surrounding the incident, a reasonable person would have believed that he was not free to leave." Using the *Mendenhall* facts, write a "dissenting opinion" arguing that she had in fact been "seized" for Fourth Amendment purposes by the government agents.

CASE EXCERPT: *TERRY V. OHIO*
SUPREME COURT OF THE UNITED STATES (1967)
392 U.S. 1

While on patrol, a Cleveland police officer, Detective McFadden, saw two men on a street in downtown Cleveland at approximately 2:30 PM, on October 31, 1963. The two men were acting suspiciously because they walked back and forth looking into the store window, and then both returned to the corner to confer. Later, another man joined the two. Detective McFadden approached the men, informed them that he was a police officer, and asked who they were. When McFadden received a mumbled response, he conducted a pat-down search of all three men. The frisk determined that Terry and one of the other two men were carrying pistols and they were both convicted of carrying concealed weapons. The Court of Appeals for the Eighth Judicial District, affirmed the conviction and the Ohio Supreme Court dismissed the appeal. The U.S. Supreme Court granted certiorari.

Mr. Chief Justice Warren delivered the Opinion of the Court.

* * *

The Fourth Amendment provides that "the right of the people to be secure in their persons, houses, papers, and effects, against unreasonable searches and seizures, shall not be violated . . ." This inestimable right of personal security belongs as much to the citizen on the streets of our cities as to the homeowner closeted in his study to dispose of his secret affairs . . .

We have recently held that "the Fourth Amendment protects people, not places," and wherever an individual may harbor a reasonable "expectation of privacy," he is entitled to be free from unreasonable governmental intrusion. Of course, the specific content and incidents of this right must be shaped by the context in which it is asserted. For "what the Constitution forbids is not all searches and seizures, but unreasonable searches and seizures." Unquestionably petitioner was entitled to the protection of the Fourth Amendment as he walked down the street in Cleveland. The question is whether in all the circumstances of this on-the-street encounter, his right to personal security was violated by an unreasonable search and seizure.

We would be less than candid if we did not acknowledge that this question thrusts to the fore difficult and troublesome issues regarding a sensitive area of police activity—issues which have never before been squarely presented to this Court. Reflective of the tensions involved are the practical and constitutional arguments pressed with great vigor on both sides of the public debate over the power of the police to "stop and frisk"—as it is sometimes euphemistically termed—suspicious persons.

One the one hand, it is frequently argued that in dealing with the rapidly unfolding and often dangerous situations on city streets the police are in need of an escalating set of flexible responses, graduated in relation to the amount of information they possess. For this purpose it is urged that distinctions should be made between a "stop" and an "arrest" (or a seizure of a person), and the police should be allowed to "stop" a person and detain him briefly for questioning upon suspicion that he may be connected with criminal activity. Upon suspicion that the person may be armed, the police should have the power to "frisk" him for weapons. If the "stop" and the "frisk" give rise to probable cause to believe that the suspect has committed a crime, then the police should be empowered to make a formal "arrest," and a full incident "search" of the person. This scheme is justified in part upon the notion that a "stop" and a "frisk" amount to a mere "minor inconvenience and petty indignity," which can properly be imposed upon the citizen in the interest of effective law enforcement on the basis of a police officer's suspicion.

On the other side the argument is made that the authority of the police must be strictly circumscribed by the law of arrest and search as it has developed to date in the traditional jurisprudence of the Fourth Amendment. It is contended with some force that there is not—and cannot be—a variety of police activity which does not depend solely upon the voluntary cooperation of the citizen an yet which stops short of an arrest based upon probable cause to make such an arrest. The heart of the Fourth Amendment, the argument runs, is a severe requirement of specific justification for any intrusion upon protected personal security, coupled with a highly developed system of judicial controls to enforce upon the agents of the State the commands of the Constitution. Acquiescence by the

courts in the compulsion inherent in the field interrogation practices at issue here, it is urged, would constitute an abdication of judicial control over, and indeed an encouragement of, substantial interference with liberty and personal security by police officers whose judgment is necessarily colored by their primary involvement in "the often competitive enterprise of ferreting out crime." This, it is argued, can only serve to exacerbate police-community tensions in the crowded centers of our Nation's cities.

* * *

Proper adjudication of cases in which the exclusionary rule is invoked demands a constant awareness of [its] limitations. The wholesale harassment by certain elements of the police community, of which minority groups, particularly Negroes, frequently complain, will not be stopped by the exclusion of any evidence from any evidence from any criminal trial. Yet a rigid and unthinking application of the exclusionary rule, in futile protest against practices which it can never be used effectively to control, may exact a high toll in human injury and frustration of efforts to prevent crime. No judicial opinion can comprehend the protean variety of the street encounter, and we can only judge the facts of the case before us.

* * *

Having thus roughly sketched the perimeters of the constitutional debate over the limits on police investigative conduct in general and the background against which this case presents itself, we turn our attention to the quite narrow question posed by the facts before us: whether it is always unreasonable for a policeman to seize a person and subject him to a limited search for weapons unless there is probable cause for an arrest.

* * *

"Search" and "seizure" are not talismans. We therefore reject the notions that the Fourth

Amendment does not come into play at all as a limitation upon police conduct if the officers stop short of something called a "technical arrest" or a "full-blown search."

In this case there can be no question, then, that Officer McFadden "seized" petitioner and subjected him to a "search" when he took hold of him and patted down the outer surfaces of his clothing. We must decide whether at that point it was reasonable for Officer McFadden to have interfered with petitioner's security as he did. And in determining whether the seizure and search were "unreasonable" our inquiry is a dual one—whether the officer's action was justified at its inception, and whether it was reasonably related in scope to the circumstances which justified the interference in the first place.

If this case involved police conduct subject to the Warrant Clause of the Fourth Amendment, we would have to ascertain whether "probable cause" existed to justify the search and seizure which took place. However, that is not the case. We do not retreat from our holdings that the police must, whenever practicable obtain advance judicial approval of searches and seizures. . . But we deal here with an entire rubric of police conduct—necessarily swift action predicated upon the on-the-spot observations of the officer on the beat—which historically has not been, and as a practical matter could not be, subjected to the warrant procedure. Instead, the conduct involved in this case must be tested by the Fourth Amendment's general proscription against unreasonable searches and seizures.

* * *

Our evaluation of the proper balance that has to be struck in this type of case leads us to conclude that there must be a narrowly drawn authority to permit a reasonable search for weapons for the protection of the police officer, where he has reason to believe that he is dealing with an armed and dangerous individual, regardless of whether he has probable cause to arrest the individual for a crime. The officer need not be absolutely certain that the individual is armed; the issue is whether a reasonably prudent man in the circumstances would be warranted in the belief that his safety or that of others was in danger. And in determining whether the officer acted reasonably in such circumstances, due weight must be given, not to his inchoate and unparticularized suspicion or "hunch," but to the specific reasonable inferences which he is entitled to draw from the facts in light of his experience.

* * *

We conclude that the revolver seized from Terry was properly admitted in evidence against him. At the time he seized Petitioner and searched him for weapons, Officer McFadden had reasonable grounds to believe that petitioner was armed and dangerous, and it was necessary for the protection of himself and others to take swift measures to discover the true facts and neutralize the threat of harm if it materialized. The policeman carefully restricted his search to what was appropriate to the discovery of the particular items which he sought. Each case of this sort will, of course, have to be decided on its own facts. We merely hold today that where a police officer observes unusual conduct which leads him reasonably to conclude in light of his experience that criminal activity may be afoot and that the persons with whom he is dealing may be armed and presently dangerous, where in the course of investigating this behavior he identifies himself as a policeman and makes reasonable inquiries, and where nothing in the initial stages of the encounter serves to dispel his reasonable fear for his own or others' safety, he is entitled for the protection of himself and others in the area to conduct a carefully limited search of the outer clothing of such persons in an attempt to discover weapons which might be used to assault him. Such a search is a reasonable search under the Fourth Amendment, and any weapons seized may properly be introduced in evidence against the person from whom they were taken. Affirmed.

CASE EXCERPT: *UNITED STATES V. MENDENHALL*
SUPREME COURT OF THE UNITED STATES (1979)
446 U.S. 544

Mendenhall was tried in United States District Court on a charge of possessing heroin with intent to distribute. At trial the evidence indicated that she had arrived at the Detroit Metropolitan Airport on a commercial flight from Los Angeles. As she left the plane, she was observed by two DEA agents, who were at the airport for the purpose of detecting unlawful narcotics. After observing Mendenhall's conduct, which appeared to the agents to be characteristic of persons unlawfully carrying narcotics, the agents approached her as she was walking through the concourse, identified themselves as DEA agents, and asked to see her identification and airline ticket. Mendenhall produced her driver's license. Her airline ticket, however, was issued in the name of "Annette Ford." When asked why the ticket bore a name different from her own, Mendenhall stated that she "just felt like using that name."

After returning the airline ticket and driver's license to her, the agents asked Mendenhall if she would accompany him to the airport DEA office for further questions. She did so and at the office an agent asked her if she would allow a search of her person and handbag and told her that she had the right to decline the search. Mendenhall responded: "Go ahead." When a policewoman conducted a strip search of Mendenhall, the officer discovered two small packages, one of which appeared to contain heroin. The agents arrested Mendenhall for possession of heroin.

The trial court held that the search of Mendenhall was lawful based on *Terry* v. *Ohio* and subsequent case law. The Court of Appeals reversed, because of the agents' reliance on a "drug courier profile," and held that the agents could not reasonably have suspected that Mendenhall was engaged in criminal activity because her activities were consistent with innocent behavior. The U.S. Supreme Court granted certiorari.

Mr. Justice Stewart delivered the Opinion of the Court.

* * *

The Fourth Amendment's requirement that searches and seizures be founded upon an objective justification, governing all seizures of the person, "including seizures that involve only a brief detention short of traditional arrest. Accordingly, if the respondent was "seized" when the DEA agents approached her on the concourse and asked questions of her, the agents' conduct in doing so was constitutional only if they reasonably suspected the respondent of wrongdoing. But "[o]bviously, not all personal intercourse between policemen and citizens involves 'seizures' of persons. Only when the officer, by means of physical force or show of authority, has in some way restrained the liberty of a citizen may we conclude that a 'seizure' has occurred."

* * *

We adhere to the view that a person is "seized" only by means of physical force or a show of authority when his freedom of movement is restrained. Only when such restraint is imposed is there any foundation whatever for invoking constitutional safeguards. The purpose of the

Fourth Amendment is not to eliminate all contact between the police and the citizenry, but "to prevent arbitrary and oppressive interference by enforcement officials with the privacy and personal security of individuals. As long as the person to whom questions are put remains free to disregard the questions and walk away, there has been no intrusion upon that person's liberty of privacy as would under the Constitution require some particularized and objective justification.

Moreover, characterizing every street encounter between a citizen and the police as a "seizure," while not enhancing any interest secured by the Fourth Amendment, would impose wholly unrealistic restrictions upon a wide variety of legitimate law enforcement practices. The Court has on other occasions referred to the acknowledged need for police questioning as a tool in the effective enforcement of the criminal laws. "Without such investigation, those who were innocent might be falsely accused, those who were guilty might wholly escape prosecution, and many crimes would go unsolved. In short, the security of all would be diminished.

We conclude that a person has been "seized" within the meaning of the Fourth Amendment only if, in view of all of the circumstances surrounding the incident, a reasonable person would have believed that he was not free to leave. Examples of circumstances that might indicate a seizure, even where the person did not attempt to leave, would be the threatening presence of several officers, the display of a weapon by an officer, some physical touching of the person on the citizen, or the use of language or tone of voice indicating that compliance with the officer's request might be compelled.

* * *

On the facts of this case, no "seizure" of the respondent occurred. The events took place in the public realm. The agents wore no uniforms and displayed no weapons. They did not summon the respondent to their presence, and instead approached her and identified themselves as DEA agents. They requested, but did not demand to see respondent's identification and ticket. Such conduct, without more, did not amount to an intrusion upon any constitutionally protected interest. The respondent was not seized simply by reason of the fact that the agents approached her and asked her if she would show them her ticket and identify herself and posed to her a few questions.

* * *

Although we have concluded that the initial encounter between the DEA agents and the respondent on the concourse at the Detroit Airport did not constitute and unlawful seizure, it is still arguable that the respondent's Fourth Amendment protections were violated when she went from the concourse to the DEA office. Such a violation might in turn infect a subsequent search of the respondent's person.

* * *

The question of whether the respondent's consent to accompany the agents was in fact voluntary or was the product of duress of coercion, express or implied, is to be determined by the totality of all the circumstances, and is a matter which the Government has the burden of proving. The respondent did not testify at the hearing. The Government's evidence showed that the respondent was not told that she had to go to the office, but was simply asked if she would accompany the officers. There were neither threats nor any show of force. The respondent had been questioned only briefly, and her ticket and identification were returned to her before she was asked to accompany the officers.

* * *

We conclude that the District Court's determination that the respondent consented to the search of her person . . . was sustained by the evidence and that the Court of Appeals was, therefore, in error in setting it aside. Accordingly, the judgment of the Court of Appeals is reversed, and the case is remanded to that court for further proceedings. It is so ordered.

Endnotes

1. *Terry* v. *Ohio,* 392 U.S. 1 (1968).
2. See Rachel K. Laser, "Unreasonable Suspicion: Relying on Refusals to Support Terry Stops." 62 *University of Chicago Law Review* pp. 1161–1185 (1995); Kathryn R. Urbanya, "Dangerous Misperceptions: Protecting Police Officers, Society, and the Fourth Amendment Right to Personal Security." 22 *Hastings Constitutional Law Quarterly* pp. 623–706 (1995).
3. *Terry* v. *Ohio,* 392 U.S. 1, 8 (1968).
4. Id. at 29.
5. Id.
6. *United States* v. *Sharpe,* 470 U.S. 675 (1985).
7. See *Dunaway* v. *New York,* 442 U.S. 200 (1979).
8. Id.
9. See *United States* v. *Robinson,* 485 U.S. 25 (1973).
10. *Ornelas* v. *United States,* 134 L.Ed. 2d 911 (1996).
11. Id. at 918.
12. *Alabama* v. *White,* 496 U.S. 325 (1990).
13. David A. Harris, "Factors for Reasonable Suspicion: When Black and Poor Means Stopped and Frisked." 69 *Indiana Law Journal* pp. 659–688 (1994).
14. *United States* v. *Cortez,* 449 U.S. 411, 418 (1981).
15. *Brown* v. *Texas,* 443 U.S. 47 (1979).
16. Id. at 51.
17. *United States* v. *Cortez,* 449 U.S. 411, 418 (1981).
18. *United States* v. *Smith,* 799 F.2d 704 (11th Cir. 1986).
19. *Adams* v. *Williams,* 407 U.S. 143 (1972).
20. See *United States* v. *Leon,* 468 U.S. 897 (1984); *California* v. *Greenwood,* 486 U.S. 35 (1989).
21. *United States* v. *Mendenhall,* 446 U.S. 544 (1980).
22. Id. at 549.
23. Id. at 554.
24. Id.
25. *Florida* v. *Royer,* 460 U.S. 491 (1983).
26. See *Florida* v. *Bostick,* 501 U.S. 429 (1991).
27. Id.
28. Id. at 434.
29. See Matthew I. Farmer, "Go Greyhound and Leave the Fourth Amendment to Us." 23 *Loyola University of Chicago Law Journal* pp. 533–555 (1992); Natasha L. Golding, "The Deconstruction of the Fourth Amendment." 27 *University of San Francisco Law Review* pp. 699–735 (1993).
30. *California* v. *Hodari D.,* 499 U.S. 621 (1991).
31. See Ronald J. Bacigal, "The Right of the People to be Secure." 82 *The Kentucky Law Journal* pp. 145–218 (1993).
32. *United States* v. *Sharpe,* 470 U.S. 675, 685 (1985).
33. Id.
34. *United States* v. *Ramos,* 20 F.3d 348 (8th Cir. 1994).
35. *United States* v. *Place,* 462 U.S. 696 (1983).
36. *Adams* v. *Williams,* 407 U.S. 143 (1972).
37. *Alabama* v. *White,* 496 U.S. 325 (1990).
38. See David S. Rudstein, "White on White: Anonymous Tips, Reasonable Suspicion, and the Constitution." 19 *Search and Seizure Law Report* pp. 25–31 (1992).
39. See Martin K. Berks, "Anonymous Tip Held Sufficient Basis for Investigatory Stop Under the Fourth Amendment." 24 *John Marshall Law Review* pp. 909–926 (1991).
40. See Monique D. Boham and Roger S. Hanson, "The Drug Courier Profile: The Unwritten Catch 22 in the Drug Enforcement Agency Dragnet." 18 *Southern University Law Review* pp. 233–254 (1991).
41. See *United States* v. *Sokolow,* 490 U.S. 1 (1989).
42. See *United States* v. *Brignoni-Ponce,* 422 U.S. 873 (1975).
43. *Reid* v. *Georgia,* 448 U.S. 438 (1990).
44. *United States* v. *Sokolow,* 490 U.S. 1 (1989).
45. See Steven K. Bernstein, "Fourth Amendment— Using the Drug Courier Profile to Fight the War on Drugs." 80 *Journal of Criminal Law and Criminology* pp. 996–1017 (1990).
46. *United States* v. *Hensley,* 469 U.S. 221 (1985).
47. See Jolene D. Pettis, "Fourth Amendment—the Expansion of the Terry Doctrine to Completed Felonies." 76 *Journal of Criminal Law and Criminology* pp. 986–1002 (1985).
48. *Minnesota* v. *Dickerson,* 113 S.Ct. 2130 (1993).
49. Lawrence J. Wadsack, "The Plain Touch Doctrine and Confusion Following United States v. Dickerson: The Terry Frisk Needs an Expansion." 39 *St. Louis University Law Journal* pp. 1053–1098 (1995).
50. *Minnesota* v. *Dickerson,* 113 S.Ct. 2130, 2136–37 (1993).
51. See also *United States* v. *Armstrong,* 116 S.Ct. 1480 (1996). (Holding that crack cocaine laws do

not discriminate against African-Americans, even though they may have a harsh effect on that group.)

52. *Michigan* v. *Long,* 463 U.S. 1032 (1983).
53. See James R. Salisbury, "Criminal Procedure—Due Process: Towards More Effective Law Enforcement—Utilization of Collective Knowledge to Sustain a Reasonable Suspicion Inquiry." 71 *North Dakota Law Review* pp. 797–820 (1995).
54. *Pennsylvania* v. *Mimms,* 434 U.S. 106 (1977).
55. *Maryland* v. *Wilson,* 117 S.Ct. 882 (1997).
56. *Brower* v. *Inyo County,* 489 U.S. 593 (1989).
57. Id. at 597.
58. Wayne R. LaFave and Jerold H. Israel, *Criminal Procedure,* 2d ed. (St. Paul, Minn.: West, 1992), p. 214.
59. See Eustace T. Francis, "Combating the Drunk Driver Menace: Conditioning the Use of Public Highways on Consent to Sobriety Checkpoint Seizures—the Constitutionality of a Model Consent Seizure Statute." 59 *Albany Law Review* pp. 599–670 (1995).
60. *Michigan Department of State Police* v. *Sitz,* 496 U.S. 444 (1990).
61. *Brown* v. *Texas,* 443 U.S. 47 (1979).
62. Id. at 51.
63. *Sitz* v. *Michigan Department of State Police,* 429 N.W. 2d 180, 185 (1990).
64. For a detailed discussion of this issue see Thomas J. Hickey and Michael Axline, "Drunk-Driving Roadblocks Under State Constitutions: A Reasonable Alternative to Michigan v. Sitz." 28 *Criminal Law Bulletin* pp. 195–217 (1992).
65. *Pimental* v. *Department of Transportation,* 561 A.2d 1348 (R.I. 1989).
66. Id. at 1352.
67. *State* v. *Henderson,* 756 P.2d 1057 (Idaho Sup. Ct.) (1988).
68. See H. Laurence Ross, "Sobriety Checkpoints, American Style." 22 *Journal of Criminal Justice* pp. 437–444 (1994).
69. *United States* v. *Place,* 462 U.S. 696 (1983).
70. See Patrick K. Emerson, "The Terry Balancing Test and Independent Seizures of Airport Luggage." 2 *Cooley Law Review* pp. 399–418 (1984).
71. *United States* v. *Place,* 462 U.S. 696, 709 (1983).
72. See Hope W. Hall, "Sniffing Out the Fourth Amendment—Dog Sniffs—Ten Years Later." 46 *Maine Law Review* pp. 151–188 (1994).
73. Greg Knopp, et. al, "Twenty-Fourth Annual Review of Criminal Procedure: United States Supreme Court and Courts of Appeals 1993–1994," 83 *Georgetown Law Journal* pp. 692–768 (1995).
74. *United States* v. *Cooper,* 873 F.2d 269 (11th Cir.), *cert denied,* 493 U.S. 837 (1989); see id for an excellent case law analysis of these issues.
75. *United States* v. *Respress,* 9 F.3d 483 (6th Cir. 1993).
76. *Davis* v. *Mississippi,* 394 U.S. 721 (1969).
77. See Mark P. Asselta, "The Constitutionality of Compulsory Identification Procedures on Less Than Probably Cause: Reassessing the Davis Dictum." 89 *Dickenson Law Review* pp. 501–525 (1985).
78. *Hayes* v. *Florida,* 470 U.S. 811, 818 (1985).
79. See *Almeida-Sanchez* v. *United States,* 413 U.S. 266 (1973).
80. See Arthur J. Kyrazis and Harry M. Caldwell, "Unchecked Discretion, the Buck Stops Here: Is There a Fourth Amendment at the International Borders of the United States?" 14 *Whittier Law Review* pp. 613–638 (1993).
81. *United States* v. *Montoya de Hernandez,* 473 U.S. 531 (1985).
82. See Michael G. Rogers, "Bodily Intrusions in Search of Evidence: A Study in Fourth Amendment Decisionmaking." 62 *Indiana Law Journal* pp. 1181–1207 (1987).
83. *United States* v. *Montoya de Hernandez,* 437 U.S. 531, 535 (1985).

7 AUTOMOBILE SEARCHES, INVENTORY SEARCHES, AND CONSENT SEARCHES

Outline

Key Terms

Chapters 5 and 6 have considered several exemptions to the Fourth Amendment's warrant requirement. This chapter considers additional important exemptions: the automobile exception, inventory searches of personal property, and consent searches. Ever since Henry Ford made the automobile affordable for millions of people, it has occupied a special place in the American consciousness. Americans love the automobile and the freedom and mobility it brings. With so many vehicles on U.S. highways, it should not be surprising that a substantial body of procedural law has developed to regulate automobile stops and searches. In fact, as many criminal law professors will attest, the questions that students ask most often involve situations where they were stopped by the police for various motor vehicle infractions. This chapter analyzes the body of procedural law that regulates automobile stops and searches. Inventory searches and consent searches are considered too because, although these practices are not limited to automobile stops following motor vehicle infractions, they often take place in this context.

The *Carroll* Doctrine

The automobile exception to the Fourth Amendment's warrant requirement is often referred to as the ***Carroll* doctrine,** which was first established in *Carroll* v. *United States,*[1] a case decided long ago that involved the transportation of bootlegged whiskey. *Carroll* provides that a police officer may conduct a warrantless search of a motor vehicle stopped on a public highway if he or she has probable cause to believe that it contains contraband or other evidence of a crime.

The first consideration in most automobile search cases is whether the police have probable cause to believe that the vehicle contains contraband.[2] If evidence that is not supported by probable cause is seized during a search of a vehicle, it must be excluded at trial.[3]

A person has a lesser expectation of privacy in an automobile than in a home. The Supreme Court has consistently held that the home receives special protection under the Fourth Amendment.[4] Persons traveling in automobiles on public highways do not receive the same degree of protection under the Fourth Amendment's search warrant clause for three reasons. First, an automobile's inherent mobility often makes it impractical to obtain a search warrant. By the time a police officer obtains a search warrant, the operator of the vehicle could leave the area or evidence could be destroyed.[5] Second, automobiles are extensively regulated by state laws.[6] Third, the occupants of a motor vehicle are readily visible from the outside. These last two factors serve to diminish an occupant's reasonable expectation of privacy.[7] The result is that people who leave items in an automobile enjoy substantially less Fourth Amendment protection than those leaving property in a house.

Probable Cause and Reasonable Suspicion for Vehicle Stops

A motor vehicle stop is a seizure under the Fourth Amendment.[8] Therefore, if a police officer stops someone's vehicle he or she must be able to point to objective facts to justify the stop. Police officers may not stop someone simply because there was nothing better to

Source: UPI/Corbis Bettmann

do at the time. In *Delaware* v. *Prouse,*[9] a police officer arrested Prouse for possession of marijuana, which the officer observed in plain view after stopping Prouse's vehicle. The officer testified that prior to stopping the vehicle he had not observed traffic or equipment violations or any suspicious activity and that he made the stop only in order to check the driver's license and registration. The officer stated that he "saw the car in the area and wasn't answering any complaints, so I decided to pull them off."[10] The Supreme Court held that stopping Prouse's vehicle violated the Fourth Amendment and that the trial court correctly suppressed the evidence. The Court held that in order to justify a vehicle stop there must be "at least articulable and reasonable suspicion that a motorist is unlicenced or that an automobile is not registered, or that either the vehicle or an occupant is otherwise subject to seizure for violation of law."[11] The Court suggested, however, that other less intrusive means of conducting license and registration checks, which do not give police officers unlimited discretion, may be permissible under the Fourth Amendment. This may include questioning all oncoming traffic at a roadblock-type stop.[12]

Prouse establishes that police officers must have at least reasonable suspicion to believe that a vehicle's occupants are involved in criminal activity or have committed some type of offense to justify a stop. An example may help to clarify this rule. Suppose that a police officer observes a vehicle at 3:00 AM moving slowly through an area of a city known for illegal drug activity. The officer watches the suspect stop his car, speak briefly with someone standing on a street corner, and exchange something with another person. The officer would have reasonable suspicion to justify stopping the vehicle for a further investigation.

Police officers who observe a traffic violation have a lawful justification for stopping a vehicle. This is true even if a reasonable officer would not have stopped the vehicle under the circumstances, and the officer actually has an ulterior motive for the stop, such as to search for illegal drugs. As long as a traffic violation has occurred a police officer may lawfully stop the motorist—his or her subjective motivation for the stop plays no role in determining whether the stop was lawful.

In *Whren* v. *United States,*[13] a police officer observed the Whren's Pathfinder truck stopped at an intersection for more than 20 seconds in an area of Washington, D.C., known for illegal drug activity. When the police car made a U-turn in order to head back toward the truck, the Pathfinder turned suddenly to its right, without signaling, and sped off at an "unreasonable" speed. A short time later the police pulled up alongside the truck at a traffic light and an officer stepped out and approached the driver's door. When the officer approached the window, he observed two large plastic bags of what appeared to be crack cocaine in Whren's hands. Whren was convicted of violating federal drug laws. On appeal, Whren argued that the stop of his vehicle was not justified by probable cause or reasonable suspicion to believe that he was engaged in illegal drug activity. Moreover, he argued that the officer's asserted ground for approaching the vehicle—to give the driver a warning concerning traffic violations—was pretextual. Whren asserted that the real reason the officer approached the vehicle was that he wished to investigate illegal drug activity and that the officer lacked probable cause to do so. Therefore, the evidence should have been suppressed.

The Supreme Court disagreed. Justice Antonin Scalia stated: "As a general matter, the decision to stop an automobile is reasonable where the police have probable cause to believe that a traffic violation has occurred."[14] *Whren* indicates that an officer's subjective beliefs that the occupants of an automobile *may* be engaging in some other illegal behavior are irrelevant if the officer could have stopped the vehicle for a suspected traffic violation.

Automobile Searches

Law enforcement officers may conduct two different types of automobile searches. The first type occurs when a vehicle is stopped on a public highway and is searched by officers at the scene. The second type of automobile search occurs when a vehicle is immobilized and is in police custody. The rules for conducting a lawful search of the vehicle vary somewhat in these different situations.

Searches on Public Highways

If the police stop an automobile on a public highway and have probable cause to believe that it contains contraband, they may conduct a warrantless search of the vehicle.

The search may extend to *any* area of the vehicle in which the contraband may be hidden. Moreover, police officers may search the automobile just as thoroughly as if they had obtained a search warrant. The Supreme Court established this rule in *United States* v. *Ross,*[15] in which police officers lawfully stopped an automobile and had probable cause to believe that it contained illegal drugs. In an ensuing search of the car's trunk, officers discovered and opened a closed brown paper bag and a zippered leather pouch, and found money in the pouch and heroin in the bag. The defendant appealed his conviction to the Supreme Court. In upholding the search and seizure of the car and the containers inside the trunk, the Court stated:

> The scope of a warrantless search based on probable cause is no narrower—and no broader—than the scope of a search authorized by a warrant supported by probable cause. Only the prior approval of the magistrate is waived; the search otherwise is as the magistrate could authorize.[16]

The Court in *Ross* clarified the permissible scope of an automobile search based upon probable cause. The scope of an automobile search is not defined by the type of container in which contraband is hidden.[17] "Rather, it is defined by the object of the search and the places in which there is probable cause to believe that it may be found."[18] This means that the scope of an automobile search is determined by the type of evidence that the police are searching for. If there is probable cause to search a vehicle for illegal drugs, the search may extend to any part of the vehicle and any container within the vehicle that may contain the contraband.[19] If, however, police officers are searching a truck for a stolen large screen television set, they may not lawfully search the glove compartment because it could not possibly contain the object of the search.

Moreover, in some automobile search cases a police officer may not know precisely what he or she is looking for. For example, suppose that police officers, who have just received a radio broadcast providing the description of a car that had fled the scene of a bank robbery, stop the vehicle after a brief high-speed chase and arrest its two occupants. Assume that the entire incident took approximately two minutes from the time the officers received the broadcast until the time the suspects were arrested. The officers would be permitted to conduct a warrantless search of the vehicle, even though they may not be completely sure about exactly what loot or evidence they are looking for. In these circumstances, the officers may not yet know what type of weapon was used to commit the robbery, whether the suspects wore particular disguises, or even if any money or other types of loot were taken. Any relevant evidence found during a search of the vehicle incident to the arrest of the suspects may be used, however.

The Supreme Court has held too that the *Ross* principle applies to mobile homes. In *California* v. *Carney,*[20] the Court upheld the warrantless search of a stationary mobile home that was parked in a public parking lot. Such a search was legitimate if a reasonable person could believe that the mobile home was being used as a vehicle rather than a home.[21]

Searching a Vehicle's Interior Based on Reasonable Suspicion.   Chapter 6 considered *Terry* v. *Ohio,* which allowed police officers to stop and frisk an individual based on reasonable suspicion that he or she was engaging in criminal activity. The Supreme Court's original justification for allowing a stop and frisk was to protect police officers and members of the public from potential harm. In 1983, the Supreme Court in *Michigan* v. *Long*[22] expanded *Terry* to permit a search for weapons inside a vehicle's passenger compartment, in spite of the fact that the suspect was no longer in the vehicle. In *Long,* sheriff's deputies observed the defendant drive his vehicle into a ditch. Long stepped out of the car and met the deputies, who suspected Long of driving under the influence of alcohol, near the rear of the vehicle. After Long fumbled to produce his driver's license, he went back to his car, although he had not been placed under arrest, and the officers observed a large knife on the vehicle's floor. The officers then subjected Long to a frisk for weapons, but found none. An officer then shined a flashlight into the car, to search for weapons, and observed a pouch partially concealed under the armrest. When the officer opened the pouch he found marijuana, and Long was convicted of possession. On appeal, a central issue was whether the search of the car's passenger compartment was justified under *Terry* v. *Ohio.* The Supreme Court held that two conditions may justify a search of a vehicle's passenger compartment based on *Terry:* (1) the officers must have reasonable suspicion based upon objective and articulable facts that the suspect is dangerous and may obtain control of a weapon if it is in the vehicle; and (2) the search is limited to those portions of the vehicle's passenger compartment that may conceal a weapon. Moreover, if during such a search police discover evidence or contraband in plain view, it may be seized. The Supreme Court upheld the search of the pouch in Long's car because it was possible that it contained a weapon.

Michigan v. *Long* is an important expansion of *Terry* v. *Ohio. Long* indicates that if a police officer stops a vehicle and has reasonable suspicion to believe that the operator poses a threat, he or she may search the automobile's interior for weapons. If, during the course of that search, contraband is discovered in plain view, it may be seized. In addition, if an officer discovers a container that may conceal a weapon, it too may be searched and, if contraband is discovered, used against a defendant.

Examining a Vehicle Identification Number

Police officers may reach inside a lawfully stopped vehicle and move items that obscure a vehicle identification number (VIN) panel. In *New York* v. *Class*[23] a police officer had stopped Class for a routine traffic violation. A New York statute required that the vehicle's VIN must be visible from the outside. Because some papers obscured the VIN panel on the dashboard, the officer reached into the car and moved the papers and discovered a handgun. The Supreme Court held that Class had no reasonable expectation of privacy of the VIN and that the intrusion into the vehicle was minimal. Therefore, moving the papers was a reasonable search and the handgun was properly admitted into evidence.[24] *Class* appears to be a narrow ruling that applies strictly to moving papers that obscure a VIN.

Monitoring Vehicles Traveling on Public Highways

Police officers may use electronic tracking devices to monitor vehicles traveling on public highways. In *United States* v. *Knotts*[25] representatives of the 3M Company notified police officers that a former employee of the company had stolen chemicals that could be used to manufacture illegal drugs. Drug agents learned that after Knotts had left the company he began to purchase the chemicals from the Hawkins Chemical Company. With 3M's consent, agents installed an electronic beeper in a five-gallon container of the chemical. A second defendant purchased the chemical and transported it by automobile to Knotts's secluded cabin in another state. Officers monitored the automobile until it arrived at its destination and, after three days of watching the cabin, obtained a search warrant and discovered illegal drugs. Knotts moved to suppress the evidence, asserting that the warrantless monitoring of the beeper violated the Fourth Amendment. The Supreme Court held that monitoring the beeper did not violate Knotts's reasonable expectation of privacy. This was because "[a] person traveling in an automobile on public thoroughfares has no reasonable expectation of privacy in his movements from one place to another."[26]

Knotts is a significant case that restricts Fourth Amendment protections for persons traveling in automobiles.[27] In addition, a case decided one year after *Knotts,* *United States* v. *Karo,*[28] held that the warrantless use and monitoring of an electronic beeper inside a private residence violated the Fourth Amendment. *Karo* illustrates an important principle suggested earlier in this chapter: the Fourth Amendment provides greater protection for persons in homes than for those traveling in automobiles.[29]

Probable Cause to Search Containers within a Vehicle

The Supreme Court furthered the scope of a permissible automobile search in *California* v. *Acevedo.*[30] In *Acevedo,* marijuana seized by federal narcotics agents in a shipment from Hawaii was sent to members of the Santa Ana, California, Police Department so that they could arrange a controlled delivery. Jamie Daza, who picked up the package from the local Federal Express office, was followed to his apartment. Shortly thereafter, Daza left the apartment and dropped the marijuana's packaging into a trash container. An officer then left the scene to obtain a search warrant. While he was gone other officers watched Richard St. George leave the apartment with a partially full knapsack. The officers stopped St. George as he was driving away and discovered 1.5 pounds of marijuana in the knapsack.

Several minutes later, Charles Acevedo arrived at the apartment. He stayed for about 10 minutes, and left with a brown paper bag that appeared to be full. The officers noted that the bag was approximately the size of one of the wrapped marijuana packages sent from Hawaii. Acevedo placed the bag in the trunk of his car and began to drive away. Fearing the loss of evidence, officers in a marked patrol car stopped him. When they opened the trunk and the bag they discovered marijuana.

The California Court of Appeals held that the marijuana should have been suppressed at Acevedo's trial. The court asserted that because there was probable cause to search the bag but not the vehicle, the officers should have obtained a search warrant. The Court of Appeals distinguished this case from *United States* v. *Ross.* That case allowed the police to search an entire vehicle and the closed containers found within it. Here, however, the officers' probable cause was directed specifically at the bag, not the entire vehicle.

The Supreme Court reversed the California Court of Appeals and held that the Fourth Amendment does not require police officers to obtain a warrant to search a closed container in a movable vehicle simply because they lack probable cause to search the entire car.[31] *California* v. *Acevedo* is a significant expansion of *Ross,* which had not answered the question of whether police officers should obtain a warrant when there is probable cause to believe that closed containers inside a car contain contraband.[32] The rule that emerges from this case is that whenever police officers have probable cause to search a vehicle or containers inside it, they may conduct a search that is as complete as if they had a valid search warrant.

A Time Lapse in Completing the Search

If there is probable cause to search a vehicle, *United States* v. *Ross* will permit a search of a closed container within it, even if there is a substantial time lapse between the original stop and the search.[33] In *United States* v. *Johns,*[34] U.S. Customs Agents stopped two trucks suspected of carrying marijuana. Several packages believed to contain marijuana were seized and placed in a government storage area. Three days later, agents opened the packages without a search warrant and discovered marijuana. Following the rule established in *Ross,* the Supreme Court upheld the search, despite the three-day delay. Based on earlier vehicle search cases, the Court asserted that a delay in searching a vehicle that is seized under an exception to the Fourth Amendment's warrant requirement is permissible.

Searching a Vehicle in Police Custody

If police officers have seized a vehicle and have a lawful justification to search it, they are not required to conduct the search at the scene. For many reasons, officers may wish to search the vehicle at the police station or at a secured storage area rather than searching it in public. In these circumstances there is no need to obtain a search warrant if the officers had a lawful justification for searching the vehicle at the scene.[35] In *Chambers* v. *Maroney,*[36] the Supreme Court held that the police may search an immobilized vehicle if, at the point of the original stop, exigent circumstances would have allowed an immediate search. This rule applies even if there is time to obtain a search warrant while the vehicle is in police custody. Moreover, in *Cardwell* v. *Lewis*[37] the Court held that police officers could lawfully take paint scrapings from the exterior of a car that was used in a crime because such a search did not infringe on the owner's legitimate expectation of privacy.

If time permits, police officers should obtain a search warrant for a vehicle before it is stopped if there is probable cause to believe that it contains contraband or evidence of a crime. If they fail to procure a warrant, the *Chambers* principle will not apply and may result in the exclusion of important evidence. For example, in *Coolidge* v. *New Hampshire,*[38] police officers investigating a murder focused on Coolidge and obtained a warrant from the attorney general of New Hampshire, to search Coolidge's automobile. The search uncovered evidence that was used to convict Coolidge of murder. The Supreme Court held that the search warrant was invalid because it was issued by New Hampshire's attorney general, who was not a neutral and detached magistrate.

Once the warrant was declared invalid, the prosecution attempted to justify the search of the vehicle by asserting that the search fell within the automobile exception to the warrant requirement. The Supreme Court held that the exception did not apply in this case. It distinguished *Coolidge* from *Chambers* v. *Maroney* because the Chambers vehicle had been stopped on a public street and was still essentially mobile.[39] In contrast, Coolidge's vehicle was immobile because it was parked in the driveway of his home and was being guarded by police officers. Therefore, the automobile exception to the warrant requirement did not apply.

The Plain View Doctrine and Automobile Searches

Chapter Eight presents a detailed discussion of the **plain view doctrine,** which provides that police officers may seize evidence or contraband in plain view without a warrant or probable cause. In order to seize evidence or contraband in plain view, the following requirements must be met:

1. the officer must be legally present in the place where the sighting is made;
2. the item(s) must be immediately recognizable as contraband;
3. the items must be plainly visible to the officer.[40]

Plain view doctrine issues arise frequently in the context of motor vehicle stops. For example, suppose a police officer stops someone for a motor vehicle violation and sees marijuana and drug paraphernalia in plain view inside the vehicle. The plain view doctrine will permit seizure of the evidence.

Inventory Searches

When police officers **impound** a vehicle, which means that they have seized and taken it into custody for a lawful reason, they may search and inventory its contents. Police officers may lawfully impound a vehicle for a number of different reasons, including the arrest of its occupants for a crime, seizing it for nonpayment of parking violations, or holding it for later forfeiture proceedings.

Although police officers often conduct **inventory searches** of lawfully impounded vehicles, any type of personal property may be subjected to an inventory search. An inventory search occurs when police officers enter a lawfully impounded vehicle or inspect another type of container such as a briefcase or suitcase to determine its contents. The Supreme Court has held that inventory searches are justified for three reasons: (1) to protect the owner's property while it is impounded; (2) to protect the police against claims of lost or stolen property; and (3) to protect the police from possible danger.[41]

Inventory Searches of Vehicles

Often, police officers impound vehicles for any number of reasons that may have little or nothing to do with criminal activity. To illustrate, suppose that someone's car is parked illegally in an airport one-hour parking zone for a three-day period. Most owners would not be surprised if they returned to discover that their car had been towed and taken to a police department impoundment lot. In these circumstances there is no reason to believe that the vehicle had been involved in criminal activity. The operator of the vehicle violated existing parking regulations and that justified towing the car. Police officers may conduct an administrative inventory of the vehicle, however, which may have the same effect as a search for evidence of a crime.

To inventory lawfully impounded vehicles, a police department must develop administrative policies that standardize departmental procedures and restrict officer discretion. In *Florida* v. *Wells*,[42] the Supreme Court identified specific procedures that could satisfy an administrative policy requirement involving closed container searches.[43] These may include a policy of opening all closed containers found in impounded vehicles; a policy of opening no closed containers found in impounded vehicles; or a policy of opening closed containers whose contents cannot be determined from the outside.[44] Figure 7.1 provides an illustration of one police department's vehicle inventory report. The central purpose of requiring police departments to develop administrative policies is to ensure that all persons whose vehicles are impounded are treated fairly. Moreover, police officers may not use inventory practices to justify suspicionless fishing expeditions for evidence when there is no probable cause to believe that a vehicle contains contraband.

The Supreme Court has upheld impounded vehicle inventory searches on several occasions in which a police department's administrative policies contain proper safeguards. For example, in *South Dakota* v. *Opperman*,[45] the defendant's unoccupied car was parked in a restricted zone. It was taken to a police department impoundment lot when it received two parking tickets in one morning. Police officers observed valuable items of personal property in plain view inside the car. The car was locked but officers gained entry and conducted an inventory of the vehicle's contents. In the glove compartment of the vehicle officers found a plastic bag that contained marijuana. When Opperman arrived at the police station to claim the vehicle, he was charged with possession of marijuana.

The Supreme Court upheld Opperman's conviction. The Court held that police agencies do not need a warrant or probable cause to conduct routine inventory procedures on impounded vehicles. *South Dakota* v. *Opperman* establishes that a police agency may inventory any lawfully impounded vehicle without probable cause.

Later cases have expanded *Opperman* and suggest that an inventory procedure may extend to any part of a vehicle and to all closed containers found within it. In *Colorado* v. *Bertine*,[46] the defendant was arrested for driving under the influence of alcohol. After Bertine was taken into custody and before the arrival of a tow truck to take the van to a police department impoundment lot, an officer inventoried the contents of the van. The officer opened a closed backpack and discovered illegal drugs, cocaine paraphernalia, and a large amount of cash. Bertine asserted that the evidence was seized without probable cause and moved to exclude it. The Supreme Court held that the probable cause standard does not apply when police officers conduct inventory searches:

> The standard of probable cause is peculiarly related to criminal investigations, not routine, noncriminal procedures. . . . The probable cause approach is unhelpful when analysis centers upon the reasonableness of routine caretaking functions, particularly when no claim is made that the protective procedures are a subterfuge for criminal investigations.[47]

Figure 7.1

Sample police department inventory report

<u>Inventory Report</u>

DATE: _____   CCR. _____

VEHICLE OWNER: _____ ADDRESS _____

VEHICLE OPERATOR _____ ADDRESS
_____

VEHICLE REG. _____ STATE ___. ___. VEHICLE MAKE _____ MODEL _____

VEHICLE VIN. _____ VEHICLE COLOR _____

Reason for vehicle impoundment _____

_____ Location of vehicle _____

Exterior Check—Damages _____

_____Wheel Covers _____

Interior contents: Radio _____ CB _____ Tape/Player _____

Other _____ Glove Compartment: Locked _____ Unlocked _____

Contents of Glove Compartment _____

Items removed from interior of vehicle for safe keeping _____

_____

Location stored _____

Trunk: Locked _____ Unlocked _____ Spare Tire _____ Jack _____ Other _____

Contents: _____

Notes: _____

_____

_____

                                        Officer Doing the Inventory

Witness: _____   _____

The reason the probable cause standard does not apply to inventory searches is that they are designed to guarantee the safety of the police and protect the vehicle owner's property.[48]

Inventory Searches of Other Types of Personal Property

If, after a lawful arrest, police officers take a suspect into custody, they may inventory personal property such as a wallet, purse, or briefcase. If officers discover contraband during an inventory, the owner may be charged with a crime. An inventory of personal property is permitted for the same reasons that justify vehicle inventories, as illustrated by *Illinois* v. *Layfayette.*[49] In *Layfayette,* the defendant was arrested for disturbing the peace and was taken to the police station. While searching Layfayette at the station, officers ordered him to empty his pockets. A police officer removed the contents of Layfayette's shoulder bag and found ten amphetamine tablets wrapped inside the plastic wrap of a cigarette package. Layfayette was convicted of possession of a controlled substance. On appeal, Layfayette asserted that the search of his bag violated the Fourth Amendment. The Supreme Court described this search as "an incidental administrative step following arrest and preceding incarceration."[50] In such circumstances it is reasonable for police to search a person's personal effects "and any container or article in his possession" as part of the routine administrative procedure at a police station house incident to booking and jailing the suspect.[51]

Searches with Consent

Another important exception to the Fourth Amendment's search warrant requirement is one based on a suspect's consent. A **consent search** is one that a suspect agrees to allow the police to conduct. It need not be supported by probable cause. The rule is that if a suspect consents to a search by police officers without a warrant or probable cause, any evidence or contraband discovered may be seized and used against the suspect. The consent to a search waives Fourth Amendment rights, provided it is made knowingly and voluntarily by a competent person. The waiver of Fourth Amendment rights may be express or implied. An **express waiver** occurs when suspects give police officers some affirmative indication that they are permitted to search. For example, if John, a suspected burglar, tells police officers to "go ahead and search my car," he has expressly waived his Fourth Amendment rights. Likewise, if John signs a consent-to-search form he has expressly waived his rights. An **implied waiver** occurs when persons do not expressly waive their rights, but their conduct indicates an agreement to allow the police to search. For example, if, after police officers have asked Sue if they may search her car, she offers to unlock the trunk, she has implicitly waived her Fourth Amendment rights.

Consent search issues may arise during any type of encounter between police officers and members of the public. Recently, however, these issues have received substantial publicity in the context of motor vehicle stops for various traffic infractions.[52] Highlight 7.1 presents excerpts from a newspaper article that discusses the increasing prevalence of consent searches during motor vehicle stops.

Highlight 7.1

The Improper Use of Forfeiture Laws

 On April 24, 1990, Selena Washington and her cousin were traveling on Interstate 95 through Volusia County, Florida. At 3:15 AM, a Volusia County Sheriff's officer, a member of the Volusia County Selective Enforcement Team, stopped Ms. Washington for driving seven miles over the speed limit. The officer gave Ms. Washington a warning and asked permission to search her car. After Ms. Washington consented, the officer searched the car and found $19,000 in cash. Ms. Washington explained that her Charleston, South Carolina, home had been damaged by Hurricane Hugo. Because the cost of building materials needed to repair her home had skyrocketed in South Carolina, Ms. Washington said, she was traveling to Miami to purchase the materials. The officer seized Ms. Washington's $19,000, claiming it was "drug money."

Ms. Washington, a forty-three-year-old African-American who had no criminal history, hired an attorney to get her money back. She also provided canceled checks and sworn affidavits to verify that her cash was not "drug money." The paperwork showed that the cash was from loans she obtained from a friend and two relatives while she was waiting for an insurance settlement for property damaged by Hurricane Hugo. Volusia Country gave her the option of having $15,000 of the $19,000 returned to her or challenging the forfeiture in court. Because Florida law at the time gave her little chance of recovering her costs and attorneys fees, her attorney advised her that it would be less expensive to accept the county's offer than to pay the expenses involved in contesting the seizure in Florida state courts. Accepting the advice, she signed an agreement with Volusia County, receiving $15,000 of the $19,000 taken, and paid her attorney $1000.

Selena Washington's story is merely one example of the abusive application of civil asset forfeiture. In fact, the Volusia County Sheriff's Office has repeatedly used the Florida forfeiture statutes to seize cash from apparently innocent I-95 minority motorists, such as Selena Washington. Unfortunately, the potential for abuse is not limited to local law enforcement. Federal authorities also are susceptible to similar misapplica-

tions because the same temptation for cash seizure is present under the federal Controlled Substances Act. Given the possibility of abuse, there remains one critical question: What constitutional protection does an innocent minority motorist, who happens to be carrying cash, have against the immense power of law enforcement agencies?

The Fifth Amendment to the United States Constitution prohibits the federal government from depriving an individual of property without due process of law. The Fourteenth Amendment makes that due process guarantee applicable against state action and prohibits a state from denying "equal protection of the laws." Guided by these amendments, the role of the courts has been to safeguard the individual's constitutional rights by reviewing allegedly unconstitutional actions of public officials. In *Tumey* v. *Ohio* and *Ward* v. *Monroeville,* the Supreme Court held that the defendants' due process right had been violated because of the "possible temptation" of the mayor/judge to convict when pecuniary benefits would flow from the conviction.

The pecuniary benefits flowing to law enforcement officers under state and federal forfeiture statutes are similar to those flowing to the mayor/judge in *Ward.* Like the officials in *Ward,* police departments are allowed to retain a portion of the proceeds seized through asset forfeiture. The ability to share the proceeds of civils forfeitures may create an incentive for police officers to overzealously and, perhaps, unconstitutionally apply local seizure laws. Although judges are aware of this "possible temptation," federal and Florida courts seem unwilling to afford minority motorists any pre-seizure protection. Until the legislative branch amends the forfeiture statutes to better protect the innocent motorist who chooses to travel with large amounts of cash, minority motorists like Selena Washington are protected only by adverse publicity and lawsuits under 42 U.S.C. § 1983.

From Carol M. Bast, "Symposium: What Price Civil Forfeiture?" [Reprinted by permission of the *New York Law Review* from 39 N.Y.L. SCH. L. REV. 49, 49–53 (1994).]

One of the main objections to consent searches involves a suspect's knowledge of a right to refuse a police officer's request to search. Should individuals be informed of a right to refuse to consent to a search by police officers? Some persons may be intimidated by police officers or simply not know that they have a right to refuse a request to search.[53] Or, to be candid, would a rational person consent voluntarily to a search if he or she possessed contraband and knew of a right to refuse?

A consent search is even more questionable when the person asked to consent to a search does not have a strong command of the English language or does not fully comprehend what is happening. Some persons may have immigrated from countries with a long tradition of authoritarian police behavior and may presume that police officers have unlimited authority. In view of these problems, should police officers be required to advise persons that they have a right to refuse to consent to a search? The Supreme Court has declined to impose such a rule. When police officers obtain evidence as a result of a consent search, however, the prosecution must demonstrate that the consent was given voluntarily. Officers may not use coercive tactics to gain a suspect's consent to search. For example, police officers may not tell a suspect that if he or she does not consent to a search they will obtain a search warrant and search the property anyway. In *Schneckloth* v. *Bustamonte* the Court held:

> [W]hen a subject of a search is not in custody and the State attempts to justify a search on the basis of his consent, the Fourth and Fourteenth Amendments require that it demonstrate that the consent was in fact voluntarily given, and not the result of duress or coercion, express or implied. Voluntariness is a question of fact to be determined from all the circumstances, and while the subject's knowledge of a right to refuse is a factor to be taken into account, the prosecution is not required to demonstrate such knowledge as a prerequisite to establishing a voluntary consent.[54]

The factors that a court will use to determine whether a suspect's consent to search was voluntary include:

1. knowledge of a right to refuse consent;
2. intelligence, age, and education;
3. whether the suspect believed it was likely that contraband would be found;
4. how long the suspect is detained and the nature of questioning by police officers; and
5. whether the police behaved in a coercive manner.[55]

One technique that many police departments have used to document that consent to search is voluntarily given is to ask the individual to sign a consent to search form, which contains an explicit waiver of his or her Fourth Amendment rights. A consent to search form is presented in Figure 7.2. Signing a consent to search form does not, by itself, establish that a suspect's consent was given voluntarily. A reviewing court will consider other relevant factors, such as those listed above. A signed consent to search form, however, provides a strong indication that a suspect was aware of his or her Fourth Amendment rights and waived them voluntarily.

Recently, the Supreme Court reaffirmed this approach to determining if an individual's consent to search is given voluntarily. In *Robinette* v. *Ohio,*[56] the Supreme Court

Figure 7.2

Consent to search form

DATE _____

TIME _____

PLACE _____

<u>Consent to Search</u>

I, _____, having been informed of my right not to have a search made of the premises and/or vehicle described below without a search warrant and of my right to refuse to consent to such a search, do authorize _____, of the _____ Police Department to conduct a complete search of my premises and/or vehicle described as _____. I give my consent to this search knowing that if any incriminating evidence is found it can be used against me in Court.

The police officer(s) named above has my permission to take any letters, papers, or other property from my premises and/or vehicle.

I give this written permission to the police officer(s) named above voluntarily and without threats or promises of any kind.

_____
Signed

Witnesses: _____

_____

held that when police officers stop motorists for traffic violations, they are not required to tell the motorists that they are free to go before questioning them or asking for consent to search their cars. Rather, to determine if an individual's consent to search is voluntary, trial courts must use a totality of circumstances test, which analyzes all of the circumstances surrounding an encounter between the police and the motorist.

The Scope of Consent to Search

If police officers receive consent to search a particular area or container, their search must be accordingly limited. Moreover, an individual may withdraw his or her consent to search. For example, an individual's consent to a search of his or her car does not ordinarily give an officer the right to dismantle it. If, however, during the course of a search with consent an officer discovers additional facts, such as a loose door panel, that generates probable cause to believe that illegal drugs are being concealed, the officer may search further.[57]

In *Florida* v. *Jimeno,*[58] the Supreme Court held that a suspect's general consent to search his vehicle implied consent to search containers found within it. The Court stated that trial courts must use a **reasonable person test** to determine the scope of a suspect's consent.[59] That test asks whether a reasonable person would have believed that the suspect consented to the extent of the conducted search.

Trial courts must apply the reasonable person test on a case-by-case basis, and it is difficult to state a clear rule about how far a consent search may go. In fact, lower courts have been unclear about this issue. For example, one court has held that a suspect's consent to search his car implied consent to search a duffel bag within the trunk for illegal drugs.[60] In contrast, the United States Court of Appeals for the Seventh Circuit has held that a suspect's consent to search his car did not permit police officers to pry open the door panels to search for drugs.[61] Similarly, another court has held that a suspect's consent to search his car did not authorize dismantling it at a service station.[62]

Given the lack of clear guidance from the lower courts and the Supreme Court about the scope of consent searches, the best course appears to be a cautious one. A police officer should attempt to obtain from a suspect a clear indication of consent to search a particular area or container. This will avoid later search and seizure problems at trial.

Third Party Consent to Search

Suppose that you own a home and rent a room to a tenant. One evening police officers come to your door and ask you if they may search the tenant's room for illegal drugs. May you give lawful consent to search the property? This hypothetical situation presents a third party consent-to-search issue. A **third party consent-to-search** case arises whenever someone other than one who has lawful control of property is asked for permission to search it. For example, a parent may be asked for permission to search a child's room. Or, conversely, a child whose parents are not at home may be asked for permission to search the parents' room.

The general rule is that anyone who has a reasonable expectation of privacy in the place being searched may consent to a warrantless search of the property.[63] In *United States* v. *Matlock,* the Supreme Court held that a warrantless entry and search by law enforcement officers does not violate the Fourth Amendment's proscription of unreasonable searches and seizures if the officers have obtained the consent of a third party who possesses common authority over the premises.[64] Therefore, any co-owner, co-tenant, roommate, parent, or other occupant with a common right to use the property may consent to a warrantless search. The Supreme Court has held that if a person shares property with someone else, he or she assumes the risk that the other party will allow police officers to search it.[65] If one occupant has the right to the exclusive use of a certain part of a dwelling or other premises, however, a co-occupant may not give valid consent to search that area.[66] The prosecution has the burden of proving that a third party who consented to a search had common authority over the property.[67]

In some circumstances a third party may have **apparent authority** to permit a search. This means that a reasonable police officer would be justified in believing that the person was authorized to permit a search of the premises. If a third party has apparent authority to allow a search, and it is later established that he or she did not have actual authority to permit a search, any evidence discovered is admissible.[68] *Illinois* v. *Rodriguez*[69] presented this dilemma. Police officers were called to a residence and were met by a woman who showed signs of a severe beating. She told officers that she had been assaulted by Rodriguez earlier that day at another apartment in a different location. She stated that Rodriguez was asleep in the apartment, and she agreed to accompany officers to that location and open the door with her key so that they could arrest him. During the conversation with the officers, the woman referred to the apartment as "our" apartment, and stated that she had clothes and furniture there.

The officers and the woman drove to the apartment but the officers did not obtain an arrest warrant for Rodriguez, nor did they seek a search warrant for the apartment. When they arrived, the woman unlocked the door with her key and gave the officers permission to enter. Officers observed in plain view drug paraphernalia and containers filled with cocaine. They proceeded to the bedroom, where they found Rodriguez asleep and discovered additional containers of cocaine in two open briefcases. The officers arrested Rodriguez and seized the drugs and drug paraphernalia, and he was convicted in state court.

On appeal to the Supreme Court the issue was whether a warrantless entry is lawful when based upon the consent of a third party whom the police, at the time of entry, reasonably believe to possess common authority over the premises, but who in fact does not have such authority. The Court held that the test to be applied was an objective one—would the facts available to the officer at the scene "warrant a man of reasonable caution in the belief that the consenting party had authority over the premises?"[70] On these facts the Court held that the officers' belief that the woman could properly consent to a search of the apartment was a reasonable one. Therefore, the evidence was properly admitted at Rodriguez's trial.

A substantial body of case law has developed regarding the issue of third party consent to search in various circumstances. The law of third party consent is summarized in Table 7.1.

TABLE 7.1   The Law of Third Party Consent

1. May one spouse consent to a search of his or her spouse's shared living quarters?

   Answer: Yes

   Case: *United States* v. *Matlock*[71]

2. May a parent consent to a search of a minor child's living quarters or bedroom?

   Answer: Probably, if the parent has access to the area and the child does not pay rent. If, however, the child pays rent and the area to be searched is reserved for the child's exclusive use and control, parental consent to search may not be valid.

   Case: *United States* v. *Whitfield*[72]

3. May a child consent to a search of a parent's living quarters or bedroom?

   Answer: Probably, if the child has routine access to the area.

   Case: *United States* v. *Clutter*[73]

4. May a roommate consent to a search of another roommate's shared living quarters?

   Answer: Yes, a roommate may consent to a search of shared living quarters such as a kitchen or a living room. If, however, both roommates are paying rent and an area is reserved for one person's exclusive use, the other roommate may not give lawful consent to search that area.

   Case: *Illinois* v. *Rodriguez*[74]

5. May a hotel clerk consent to a search of a hotel guest's room?

   Answer: No.

   Case: *Stoner* v. *California*[75]

6. May a landlord consent to a search of a tenant's apartment?

   Answer: Probably not. If a landlord has only limited authority to enter an apartment to make repairs, he or she may not consent to a search of a tenant's living quarters if the rent is paid and the apartment is not abandoned. If, however, the premises have been abandoned, or if the rental period has expired, a landlord may give valid consent to search.[76]

   Case: *United States* v. *Warner*[77]

Summary

Chapter 7 discusses automobile searches, inventory searches, and consent searches, which are important exceptions to the Fourth Amendment's warrant requirement. The automobile exception, which is often termed the *Carroll* doctrine, provides that a police officer may conduct a warrantless search of a motor vehicle stopped on a public highway if he or she has probable cause to believe that it contains contraband. If evidence is seized during a search of a vehicle that is not supported by probable cause it must be excluded at trial.

When compared with searches of homes, the probable cause standard is somewhat different in automobile search cases. The Supreme Court has consistently held that the home receives special protection under the Fourth Amendment. Persons traveling in automobiles do not receive the same degree of protection. The result is that people who leave items in an automobile enjoy substantially less Fourth Amendment protection than those leaving property in a house.

The probable cause standard in automobile search cases is discussed in detail. The general rule is that if the police stop an automobile on a public highway and have probable cause to believe that it contains contraband, they may conduct a warrantless search of the vehicle. The search may extend to any area of the vehicle in which the contraband might be hidden. The scope of an automobile search is determined by the type of evidence that the police are searching for. Police officers with probable cause may search, without a warrant, closed containers inside a vehicle.

Police officers may search vehicles that are in lawful custody at a police garage or other impoundment area as well. There is no need to obtain a search warrant if the officers had a lawful justification for searching the vehicle at the scene.

Inventory searches of vehicles or other types of property in police custody are permitted if police departments develop administrative policies that standardize procedures and restrict officer discretion. Police officers do not need probable cause or any level of suspicion to inventory a suspect's possessions. If, during the course of an inventory

search the police discover contraband, it may be used as evidence.

A search with consent is another exception to the Fourth Amendment search warrant requirement. The rule is that if a suspect consents to a search by police officers acting without a warrant or probable cause, any evidence or contraband discovered may be seized and used against him. The Supreme Court has held that police officers need not advise a suspect of a right to refuse a request to search. Moreover, in some circumstances a third party may give lawful consent to search someone's property. Anyone who has a reasonable expectation of privacy in the place or property being searched may consent to a warrantless search.

Review Questions

1. Discuss the *Carroll* doctrine. Why do persons traveling in automobiles on public highways enjoy less Fourth Amendment protection than persons in homes?
2. How did *Michigan* v. *Long* modify *Terry* v. *Ohio,* in the context of automobile searches?
3. Discuss the significance of *United States* v. *Ross.* How did *California* v. *Acevedo* modify the *Ross* principle?
4. When may the police search a vehicle in lawful custody under the automobile exception to the Fourth Amendment search warrant requirement? Why should police officers obtain a search warrant to search an automobile whenever possible?
5. What is an inventory search? Discuss the scope of an inventory search of a suspect's automobile or other type of personal property that is in lawful police custody.
6. Why has the Supreme Court required that police departments develop standardized administrative procedures in order to conduct inventory searches of a person's vehicle or other type of property?

7. What is a consent search? Distinguish between express and implied consent to search.
8. What is the scope of a consent search? Identify several factors that a court will consider to determine if a suspect's consent to search is given voluntarily.
9. When may a third party give lawful consent to search another person's property? Discuss whether the consent to search given by the following individuals is lawful:
   a. A spouse who consents to a search of another spouse's shared living quarters.
   b. A parent who consents to a search of a minor child's bedroom.
   c. A child who consents to a search of a parent's bedroom.
   d. A roommate who consents to a search of another roommate's shared living quarters.
   e. A hotel clerk who consents to a search of a guest's room.
   f. A landlord who consents to a search of a tenant's apartment.

Issues for Analysis and Discussion

1. In *United States* v. *Ross,* the Supreme Court held that "[t]he scope of a warrantless search of an automobile thus is not defined by the nature of the container in which the contraband is secreted." Discuss the implications of this statement for the law of automobile searches.

2. In *Schneckloth* v. *Bustamonte,* the Supreme Court held that "[w]hile knowledge of the right to refuse consent is one factor to be taken into account [in determining the voluntariness of a suspect's consent to search in a Fourth Amendment case], the government need not establish such knowledge as the [hallmark] of an effective consent." Present an argument that police officers who ask a suspect for consent to search should be required to inform him or her of a right to refuse.

CASE EXCERPT: *UNITED STATES* V. *ROSS*
SUPREME COURT OF THE UNITED STATES (1982)
456 U.S. 798

Acting on information from an informant that a described individual was selling narcotics kept in the trunk of a certain car parked at a specified location, District of Columbia police officers immediately drove to the location, found the car there, and a short while later stopped the car and arrested the driver, who matched the informant's description. One of the officers opened the car's trunk, found a closed brown paper bag, and after opening the bag, discovered glassine bags containing white powder that was later determined to be heroin. The officer then drove the car to headquarters, where another warrantless search of the trunk revealed a zippered leather pouch containing cash. Ross was subsequently convicted of possession of heroin with intent to distribute after his motion to suppress the evidence had been denied. The Court of Appeals reversed, holding that while the officers had probable cause to stop and search the defendant's car, including its trunk, without a warrant, they should not have opened either the paper bag or the leather pouch found in the trunk without first obtaining a warrant. The United States Supreme Court granted certiorari.

Mr. Justice Stevens delivered the Opinion of the Court.

* * *

In *Carroll* v. *United States,* 267 U.S. 132, the Court held that a warrantless search of an automobile stopped by police officers who had probable cause to believe the vehicle contained contraband was not unreasonable within the meaning of the Fourth Amendment. The Court in *Carroll* did not explicitly address the scope of the search that is permissible. In this case, we consider the extent to which police officers—who have legitimately stopped an automobile and who have probable cause to believe that contraband is concealed somewhere within it—may conduct a probing search of compartments and containers within the vehicle whose contents are not in plain view. We hold that they may conduct a search of the vehicle that is as thorough as a magistrate could authorize in a warrant "particularly describing the place to be searched."

* * *

In defining the nature of this "exception" to the general rule that "[i]n cases where the securing of a warrant is reasonably practicable, it must be used," the Court in *Carroll* emphasized the importance of the requirement that officers have probable cause to believe that the vehicle contains contraband . . . Moreover, the probable-cause determination must be based on objective facts that could justify the issuance of a warrant by a magistrate and not merely on the subjective good faith of the police officers. "As we have seen, good faith is not enough to constitute probable cause. That faith must be grounded on facts within knowledge of the [officer], which in the judgment of the court would make his faith reasonable."

In short, the exception to the warrant requirement established in *Carroll*—the scope of which we consider in this case—applies only to searches of vehicles that are supported by probable cause. In this class of cases, a search is not unreasonable if based on facts that would justify the issuance of a warrant, even though a warrant has not actually been obtained.

* * *

As Justice Stewart stated in *Robbins* [v. *California*], the Fourth Amendment provides protection to the owner of every container that conceals its contents from plain view. But the protection afforded by the Amendment varies in different settings. The luggage carried by a traveler entering the country may be searched at random by a customs officer; the luggage may be searched no matter how great the traveler's desire to conceal the contents may be. A container carried at the time of arrest often may be searched without a warrant and even without any specific suspicion concerning its contents. A container that may conceal the object of a search authorized by a warrant may be opened immediately; the individual's interest in privacy must give way to the magistrate's official determination of probable cause.

In the same manner, an individual's expectation of privacy in a vehicle and its contents may not survive if probable cause is given to believe that the vehicle is transporting contraband. Certainly the privacy interests in a car's trunk or glove compartment may be no less than those in a movable container. An individual undoubtedly has a significant interest that the upholstery of his automobile will not be ripped or a hidden compartment within it opened. These interests must yield to the authority of a search, however, which in light of *Carroll*— does not require the prior approval of a magistrate. The scope of a warrantless search based on probable cause is no narrower—and no broader—than the scope of a search authorized by a warrant supported by probable cause. Only the prior approval of the magistrate is waived; the search otherwise is as the magistrate could authorize.

The scope of a warrantless search of an automobile thus is not defined by the nature of the container in which the contraband is secreted. Rather, it is defined by the object of the search and the places in which there is probable cause to believe it may be found. Just as probable cause to believe that a stolen lawnmower may be found in a garage will not support a warrant to search an upstairs bedroom, probable cause to believe that undocumented aliens are being transported in a van will not justify a warrantless search of a suitcase. Probable cause to believe that a container placed in the trunk of a taxi contains contraband or evidence does not justify a search of the entire cab.

* * *

We reaffirm the basic rule of Fourth Amendment jurisprudence stated by Justice Stewart for a unanimous Court in *Mincey* v. *Arizona,* 437 U.S. 385, 390:

> "The Fourth Amendment proscribes all unreasonable searches and seizures, and it is a cardinal principle that 'searches conducted outside the judicial process, without prior approval by judge or

magistrate, are per se unreasonable under the Fourth Amendment—subject only to a few specifically established and well-delineated exceptions.'"

The exception recognized in *Carroll* is unquestionably one that is "specifically established and well delineated." We hold that the scope of the warrantless search authorized by that exception is no broader and no narrower than a magistrate could legitimately authorize by warrant. If probable cause justifies the search of a lawfully stopped vehicle, it justifies the search of every part of the vehicle and its contents that may conceal the object of the search.

The judgment of the Court of Appeals is reversed. The case is remanded for further proceedings consistent with this opinion. It is so ordered.

CASE EXCERPT: *SCHNECKLOTH* V. *BUSTAMONTE*
SUPREME COURT OF THE UNITED STATES (1973)
412 U.S. 218

While on routine patrol in Sunnyvale, California, at approximately 2:40 in the morning, a police officer stopped an automobile when he observed that one headlight and its license plate light were burned out. Six men were in the vehicle. Joe Alcala and the respondent, Robert Bustamonte, were in the front seat with Joe Gonzales, the driver. Three other men were seated in the rear. When, in response to the policeman's questions, Gonzales could not produce a driver's license, the officer asked if any of the other five had any evidence of identification. Only Alcala produced a license, and he explained that the car was his brother's. After the six occupants had stepped out of the car at the officer's request and after two additional policemen had arrived, an officer asked Alcala if he could search the car. Alcala replied, "Sure, go ahead." Prior to the search no one was threatened with arrest and, according to an officer's uncontradicted testimony, it "was all very congenial at this time." Gonzales testified that Alcala actually helped in the search of the car, by opening the trunk and glove compartment. Wadded up under the left rear seat, the police officers found three checks that had previously been stolen from a car wash.

The judge denied the motion to suppress the evidence, and the checks were admitted in evidence at Bustamonte's trial. On the basis of this and other evidence he was convicted and the California Court of Appeals affirmed. The Supreme Court granted certiorari.

Mr. Justice Stewart delivered the Opinion of the Court.

* * *

It is well settled under the Fourth and Fourteenth Amendments that a search conducted without a warrant issued upon probable cause is "per se unreasonable . . . subject only to a few specifically established and well-delineated exceptions." It is equally well settled that one of the specifically established exceptions to the requirements of both a warrant and probable cause is a search that is conducted pursuant to consent. The constitutional question in the present case concerns the definition of "consent" in this Fourth and Fourteenth Amendment context.

It is important to make it clear at the outset what is not involved in this case. The respondent concedes that a search conducted pursuant to a valid consent is constitutionally permissible. . . And similarly the State concedes that "[w]hen a prosecutor seeks to rely upon consent to justify the lawfulness of a search, he has the burden of proving that the consent was, in fact, freely and voluntarily given."

The precise question in this case, then, is what must the prosecution prove to demonstrate that a consent was "voluntarily" given. And upon that question there is a square conflict of views between the state and federal courts that have reviewed the search involved in the case before us. The Court of Appeals for the Ninth Circuit concluded that it is an essential part of the State's initial burden to prove that a person knows he has a right to refuse consent. The California courts have followed the rule that voluntariness is a question of fact to be determined from the totality of all the circumstances, and that the state of a defendant's knowledge is only one factor to be taken into account in assessing the voluntariness of a consent.

* * *

"[V]oluntariness" has reflected an accommodation of the complex of values implicated in police questioning of a suspect. At one end of the spectrum is the acknowledged need for police questioning as a tool for the effective enforcement of criminal laws. Without such investigation, those who were innocent might be falsely accused, those who were guilty might wholly escape prosecution, and many crimes would go unsolved. In short, the security of all would be diminished. At the other end of the spectrum is . . . society's deeply felt belief that the criminal law cannot be used as an instrument of unfairness, and that the possibility of unfair and even brutal police tactics poses a real and serious threat to civilized notions of justice.

* * *

[We] agree with the courts of California that the question whether a consent to a search was in fact "voluntary" or was the product of duress or coercion, express or implied, is a question of fact to be determined from the totality of all the circumstances. While knowledge of the right to refuse consent is one factor to be taken into account, the government need not establish such knowledge as the sine qua non of an effective consent. As with police questioning, two competing concerns must be accommodated in determining the meaning of a "voluntary" consent—the legitimate need for such searches and the equally important requirement of assuring the absence of coercion.

In situations where the police have some evidence of illicit activity, but lack probable cause to arrest or search, a search authorized by a valid consent may be the only means of obtaining important and reliable evidence. In the present case for example, while the police had reason to stop the car for traffic violations, the State does not contend that there was probable cause to search the vehicle or that the search was incident to a valid arrest of any of the occupants. Yet, the search yielded tangible evidence that served as a basis for a prosecution, and provided some assurance that others, wholly innocent of the crime, were not mistakenly brought to trial. And in those cases where there is probable cause to arrest or search, but where the police lack a warrant, a consent search may still be valuable. If the search is conducted and proves fruitless, that in itself may convince the police that an arrest with its possible stigma and embarrassment is unnecessary, or that a far more extensive search pursuant to a warrant is not justified. In short, a search pursuant to consent may result in considerably less inconvenience for the subject of the search, and, properly conducted, is a constitutionally permissible and wholly legitimate aspect of effective police activity.

But the Fourth and Fourteenth Amendments require that a consent not be coerced, by explicit or implicit means, by implied threat or covert force. For no matter how subtly the coercion was applied, the resulting "consent" would be no more than a pretext for the unjustified police intrusion against which the Fourth Amendment is directed.

* * *

Our decision today is a narrow one. We hold only that when the subject of a search is not in custody and the State attempts to justify a search on the basis of his consent, the Fourth and Fourteenth Amendments require that it demonstrate that the consent was in fact voluntarily given, and not the result of duress or coercion, express or implied. Voluntariness is a question of fact to be determined from all the circumstances, and while the subject's knowledge of a right to refuse is a factor to be taken into account, the prosecution is not required to demonstrate such knowledge as a prerequisite to establishing a voluntary consent. Because the California court followed these principles in affirming the respondent's conviction, and because the Court of Appeals for the Ninth Circuit in remanding for an evidentiary hearing required more, its judgment must be reversed. It is so ordered.

Endnotes

1. *Carroll* v. *United States,* 267 U.S.132 (1925).
2. See James Podgers, "Poisoned Fruit: The Quest Continues for a Consistent Rule on Searches Following Traffic Stops." 81 *American Bar Association Journal* pp. 50–52 (1995).
3. See *Dyke* v. *Taylor Implement Company, Inc.,* 391 U.S. 216 (1967).
4. See *United States* v. *Karo,* 468 U.S. 705 (1984).
5. See *California* v. *Acevedo,* 500 U.S. 565 (1991).
6. See *New York* v. *Class,* 475 U.S. 106 (1986).
7. See *California* v. *Carney,* 471 U.S. 386 (1985).
8. See Andrew J. Pulliam, "Developing a Meaningful Fourth Amendment Approach to Investigative Stops." 47 *Vanderbilt Law Review* pp. 477–533 (1994).
9. *Delaware* v. *Prouse,* 440 U.S. 648 (1979).
10. Id. at 650–651.
11. Id. at 663.
12. See Christopher S. Gontarz, "Delaware v. Prouse: Guidelines for Drunk Driver Roadblocks." 12 *Journal of Police Science and Administration* pp. 177–185 (1984).
13. *Whren* v. *United States,* 135 L.Ed. 2d 89 (1996).
14. Id. at 95.
15. *United States* v. *Ross,* 456 U.S. 798 (1982).
16. Id at 823.
17. See Myron A. Schreck, "California v. Acevedo: The Supreme Court Reconsiders the Chadwick-Ross Dichotomy As to Warrantless Searches of Containers Located in Vehicles." 18 *Search and Seizure Law Report* pp. 105–112 (1991).
18. *United States* v. *Ross,* 456 U.S. 798, 824 (1982).
19. See Steven J. McHugh, "Containers, Automobiles, and the Law of Search and Seizure." 5 *The University of Hawaii Law Review* pp. 349–360 (1983).
20. *California* v. *Carney,* 471 U.S. 386 (1985).
21. See Jamel A. Hill, "The Automobile Exception and Mobile Homes." 27 *Arizona Law Review* pp. 899–912 (1985).
22. *Michigan* v. *Long,* 463 U.S. 1032 (1983).
23. *New York* v. *Class,* 475 U.S. 106 (1986).
24. See Tracey Maclin, "New York v. Class: A Little-Noticed Case with Disturbing Implications." 78 *Journal of Criminal Law and Criminology* pp. 1–86 (1987).
25. *United States* v. *Knotts,* 460 U.S. 276 (1983).
26. Id. at 281.
27. See Richard H. McAdams, "Tying Privacy in Knotts: Beeper Monitoring and Collective Fourth

Amendment Rights." 71 *Virginia Law Review* pp. 297–341 (1985); Janice E. Oakes, "Criminal Procedure—Search and Seizure—Beeper Monitoring and the Fourth Amendment: What Has Knotts Wrought?" 58 *Tulane Law Review* pp. 849–862 (1984).

28. *United States* v. *Karo,* 468 U.S. 705 (1984).
29. See Clifford S. Fishman, "Electronic Tracking Devices and the Fourth Amendment: Knotts, Karo, and the Questions Still Unanswered." 34 *Catholic University Law Review* pp. 277–395 (1985).
30. *California* v. *Acevedo,* 500 U.S. 565 (1991).
31. Id. at 580.
32. See Stephen J. Bogacz, "Bright Lines and Opaque Containers: Searching for Reasonable Rules in Automobile Cases." 10 *Touro Law Review* pp. 679–704 (1994); Craig M. Bradley, "The Court's 'Two Model' Approach to the Fourth Amendment: Carpe Diem." 84 *Journal of Criminal Law and Criminology* pp. 429–461 (1993).
33. See Lewis R. Katz, "The Automobile Exception Transformed: The rise of a Public Place Exception to the Warrant Requirement." 36 *Case Western Reserve Law Review* pp. 375–430 (1986).
34. *United States* v. *Johns,* 469 U.S. 478 (1985).
35. See Carlos A. Esqueda, "Automobile Inventory Searches of Closed Containers: The Waning Right of Privacy." 13 *Journal of Contemporary Law* pp. 365–382 (1987).
36. *Chambers* v. *Maroney,* 399 U.S. 42 (1970).
37. *Cardwell* v. *Lewis,* 417 U.S. 583 (1974).
38. *Coolidge* v. *New Hampshire,* 403 U.S. 443 (1971).
39. Id. at 447.
40. Id. at 465–466.
41. *Colorado* v. *Bertine,* 479 U.S. 367 (1987); Elise B. Clare et al., "Inventory Searches." 84 *The Georgetown Law Journal 25th Annual Review of Criminal Procedure* pp. 797 (1996).
42. *Florida* v. *Wells,* 495 U.S. 1 (1990).
43. See Brent A. Rogers, "The Supreme Court Bypasses an Opportunity to Protect Motorists From Abuses of Police Discretion." 77 *Iowa Law Review* pp. 347–370 (1991).
44. *Florida* v. *Wells,* 495 U.S. 1, 4 (1990).
45. *South Dakota* v. *Opperman,* 428 U.S. 364 (1976).
46. *Colorado* v. *Bertine,* 479 U.S. 367 (1987).
47. Id. at 371, quoting *South Dakota* v. *Opperman,* 428 U.S. 364, 370 (1976).

48. See Lawrence T. King, "The Inventory Exception to the Fourth Amendment Warrant Requirement: Why the Last in Should be the First Out—or, Putting Opperman and Bertine in Their Place." 12 *American Journal of Trial Advocacy* pp. 273–295 (1988).
49. *Illinois* v. *Layfayette,* 462 U.S. 640 (1983).
50. Id. at 644.
51. Id. at 648; see Philip Popper, "Has the Fourth Amendment Vanished in the Face of Administrative Expediency?" 21 *Case Western Reserve Law Review* pp. 218–235 (1984).
52. See George S. Locchead, "Fourth Amendment—Expanding the Scope of Automobile Consent Searches." 82 *Journal of Criminal Law and Criminology* pp. 773–796 (1992).
53. See Robert H. Whorf, "Coercive Ambiguity Stops." 30 *Suffolk University Law Review* pp. 379–412 (1996).
54. *Schneckloth* v. *Bustamonte,* 412 U.S. 218, 248–249 (1973).
55. Greg Knopp et al., "Consent Searches." 83 *The Georgetown Law Journal Twenty-Fourth Annual Review of Criminal Procedure* pp. 692–768 (1995).
56. *Robinette* v. *Ohio* (117 S.Ct. 417)(1996).
57. See *Ornelas* v. *United States,* 116 S.Ct. 1657 (1996).
58. *Florida* v. *Jimeno,* 500 U.S. 248 (1991).
59. See Marc L. Edmonson, "Scope of Consent Searches: Are Police Officers and Judges Misguided by the Objective Reasonableness Test?" 57 *Missouri Law Review* pp. 1057–1076 (1992).
60. *United States* v. *Zapata,* 18 F.3d 971 (1st Cir. 1994). For an excellent review of federal case law in this area see Knopp, supra note 55 at 738–739.
61. *United States* v. *Garcia,* 897 F.2d 1413 (7th Cir. 1990); id.
62. *United States* v. *Rivera,* 867 F.2d 1261 (10th Cir. 1989); id.
63. Knopp, supra note 55 at 692–768; see Dorothy K. Kagehiro, Ralph B. Taylor, and Alan T. Harland, "Reasonable Expectation of Privacy and Third Party Consent Searches." (Special Issue: Social Science and the U.S. Constitution). 15 *Law and Human Behavior* pp. 121–138 (1991).
64. *United States* v. *Matlock,* 415 U.S. 164 (1974).
65. Id. at 171.
66. See *United States* v. *Whitfield,* 939 F.2d 1071, 1074–1075 (D.C. Cir. 1991).

67. *Illinois* v. *Rodriguez,* 497 U.S. 177, 181 (1990).
68. See Tammy Campbell, "Should Apparent Authority Validate Third Party Consent Searches?" 63 *University of Colorado Law Review* pp. 481–500 (1992).
69. *Illinois* v. *Rodriguez,* 497 U.S. 177 (1990).
70. Id. at 188; see Michael C. Wieber, "The Theory and Practice of Illinois v. Rodriguez: Why an Officer's Reasonable Belief About a Third Party's Authority to Consent Does Not Protect a Criminal Suspect's Rights." 84 *Journal of Criminal Law and Criminology* pp. 604–641 (1993).
71. *United States* v. *Matlock,* 415 U.S. 164 (1974).
72. *United States* v. *Whitfield,* 939 F.2d 1071 (D.C. Cir. 1990). For an excellent review of federal case law on third party consent see Clare et al., supra note 41 at 788–790.
73. *United States* v. *Clutter,* 914 F.2d 775 (6th Cir. 1990), *cert denied,* 499 U.S. 947 (1991).
74. *Illinois* v. *Rodriguez,* 497 U.S. 177 (1990).
75. *Stoner* v. *California,* 376 U.S. 483 (1964).
76. See *United States* v. *Rambo,* 789 F.2d 1289 (8th Cir. 1986).
77. *United States* v. *Warner,* 843 F.2d 401 (9th Cir. 1988).

8　The Plain View Doctrine, Items Found in Open Fields, Abandoned Property, and Regulatory Searches

Outline

Key Terms

Chapter 7 discussed the automobile exception to the Fourth Amendment's search warrant requirement. Chapter 8 discusses three additional exceptions to that requirement: the plain view doctrine, abandoned property, and property found in open fields. If contraband is discovered in plain view by a police officer, the Fourth Amendment's search warrant requirement does not apply because a person does not have a reasonable expectation of privacy in items that are displayed to the public. Likewise, if property is abandoned, no person has a reasonable expectation of privacy in it. Moreover, persons do not enjoy a reasonable expectation of privacy in open fields because they are accessible to the public. Chapter 8 considers these increasingly important exceptions to the search warrant requirement. In addition, regulatory searches, a rapidly expanding area of Fourth Amendment law, are considered in detail.

The Plain View Doctrine

Contraband or other evidence that police officers find in plain view may be used at trial. In *Coolidge* v. *New Hampshire*,[1] the Supreme Court held that a warrantless seizure by police of an item that comes within plain view during a lawful search of a private area may be reasonable under the Fourth Amendment. The **plain view doctrine** provides that police officers who observe evidence or contraband in plain sight may seize it without a warrant and without probable cause. If officers observe evidence or contraband in plain view, their observation does not constitute a Fourth Amendment search. Chapter 7 observed that in order to seize evidence or contraband found in plain view, the following requirements must be met:

1. the officer must be lawfully present in the place where the sighting is made;
2. the item(s) must be immediately recognizable as contraband;
3. the item(s) must be plainly visible to the officer.

It is instructive to consider briefly each of these requirements.

Lawful Presence

A police officer may not violate the Fourth Amendment to gain entry to the place from which he or she sees contraband or other evidence. For example, if a police officer enters a home illegally, contraband or other evidence discovered in plain view may not be seized. If, however, the officer is serving an arrest warrant, search warrant, or is otherwise present lawfully in a particular area, the plain view doctrine may permit the seizure of contraband or other evidence. For example, if a police officer stops someone for committing a motor vehicle violation, the officer is present lawfully when standing on the street outside of the suspect's vehicle. If the officer observes contraband or other evidence in within the suspect's vehicle, the evidence may be seized if the plain view doctrine's requirements are met. If, however, the stop was unlawful—it was not supported by reasonable suspicion or probable cause—any evidence or contraband observed in plain view would be suppressed at trial.

Items Immediately Recognizable as Contraband

A second requirement of the plain view doctrine is that the items must be immediately recognizable as evidence or contraband. This means that the incriminating nature of the evidence or contraband must be readily apparent[2]—there must be probable cause to believe that an item in plain view is subject to seizure.[3] In order to satisfy this requirement, police officers must demonstrate that by observing the item, they can determine that it is incriminating evidence or contraband. They are not permitted to manipulate or move the item to gain a better viewpoint or to observe areas that could not be seen without manipulating it. In *Arizona* v. *Hicks,*[4] police officers entered an apartment to search for a person who had shot a bullet through the floor, injuring someone in the unit below. They seized three weapons, including a sawed-off rifle. One officer noticed two sets of expensive stereo components, which appeared out of place in the dingy apartment. Believing that they were stolen, he read and recorded their serial numbers, moving some of the components in order to do so. The Supreme Court held that because the serial numbers were not in plain view, the search for the numbers required probable cause to believe that the items were stolen. Therefore, the items were not admissible at Hicks's trial for armed robbery.

Items Plainly Visible to the Officer

Finally, an item to be seized under the plain view doctrine must be within the officer's plain sight. With one exception, which we will consider shortly, the Supreme Court has not permitted the seizure of evidence or contraband based upon the officer's use of any senses other than sight. For example, if a police officer who is lawfully serving an arrest warrant sees a bag containing marijuana on a kitchen table, the contraband may be seized under the plain view doctrine. If, however, the officer in the same circumstances were to look under a living room sofa and discover a bag of marijuana, the plain view doctrine could not be used to justify the seizure.

Moreover, a police officer may use a flashlight to illuminate an item. In *Texas* v. *Brown,*[5] a police officer, who had stopped Brown's vehicle at night, used a flashlight to illuminate the car's interior and observed a balloon that contained illegal drugs. The Supreme Court held that the contraband could be seized under the plain view doctrine.

Texas v. *Brown* held too that a police officer may shift his or her own physical position to try to gain a better look at suspected contraband. Once the officer has shifted position, if he or she is then able to recognize an item as incriminating evidence or contraband, it may be seized under the plain view doctrine.[6]

An Inadvertent Discovery Requirement No Longer Applies

Until 1990, the Supreme Court had required that a discovery of contraband under the plain view doctrine had to be inadvertent—officers may not have had prior knowledge that the contraband was likely to be present. In *Horton* v. *California,*[7] however, the Court rejected this requirement and allowed evidence in plain view to be seized even when police officers had prior knowledge that it was likely to be present.

The plain view doctrine should not be viewed as an independent exception to the Fourth Amendment's warrant requirement. Under the plain view doctrine, evidence in plain view does not constitute a Fourth Amendment *search*. Simply because police officers observe evidence in plain view, however, does not automatically give them the lawful right to *seize* it without a warrant. In order to seize the evidence or contraband, police officers must have a search warrant, an arrest warrant, or a formally recognized exception to the warrant requirement must apply.[8] For example, suppose that a police officer passes by John's house and sees a marijuana plant growing on the window ledge. In these circumstances the plain view doctrine would not permit the officer to enter the house to seize the marijuana plant. To determine whether the plain view doctrine will allow incriminating evidence or contraband to be seized without a warrant, it is best to review that doctrine's requirements:

1. *Lawful presence:* In this example, the officer was present lawfully in the place where the sighting was made. She was driving her patrol car on a public street when she saw the marijuana plant. The problem in this case, however, is that the officer has no lawful right to enter the premises to seize the marijuana plant. She has no arrest warrant or search warrant and, on the facts presented, no exception to the warrant requirement would apply to permit her to enter the home. This requirement of the plain view doctrine is not satisfied.

2. *Items immediately recognizable as contraband:* If the officer has had experience or training, possibly including a police academy training course that included instruction on what marijuana plants look like, that would give rise to a reasonable belief that the plant on the window ledge was marijuana. This requirement of the plain view doctrine is satisfied.

3. *Items plainly visible to the officer:* Because the officer observed the marijuana with her sense of sight, this requirement of the plain view doctrine is satisfied.

To take our hypothetical example one step further, police officers who see through a window that marijuana plants are growing inside a home should obtain a search warrant for the residence. An officer's observation of the plants would weigh heavily in a judge or a magistrate's determination of whether probable cause supported a search of the home.

It is easy, however, to change our example to a plain view doctrine situation that would permit the seizure of contraband found within a home. Suppose a police officer had received a report of a domestic disturbance at the same home. When the officer arrives at the scene, he or she is invited into the living room by one of the residents. During a conversation with one of the residents, the officer sees the marijuana plant growing on the window ledge in the living room. The plain view doctrine would permit the evidence to be seized. Again, in order to analyze this case it is best to review the plain view doctrine's essential requirements:

1. *Lawful presence:* The officer was lawfully present in the place where he or she observed the marijuana plant. He or she was invited into the living room by one of the residents. This requirement of the plain view doctrine is satisfied.

Source: UPI/Corbis Bettmann

2. *Items immediately recognizable as contraband:* If the officer has had experience or training that would give rise to a reasonable belief that the plant on the window ledge was marijuana, this requirement is satisfied.

3. *Items plainly visible to the officer:* In this example, the officer would have the right to immediately seize the marijuana because it was within his or her plain sight.

The Plain Touch Doctrine

Chapter 6 considered *Terry* v. *Ohio,*[9] which permitted police officers to stop and frisk suspects based upon reasonable suspicion of criminal activity. This procedure was originally intended to be a limited pat-down search of a suspect's outer clothing to determine if he or she possessed a weapon. The **plain touch doctrine** represents an extension of this principle: if a police officer who is frisking someone feels an object that is immediately recognized as contraband, it too may be seized. In *Minnesota* v. *Dickerson,*[10] the Supreme Court held that if a police officer is conducting a pat-down search and has probable cause to believe that something he or she feels in a suspect's possession is contraband, it may be seized without a warrant. Highlight 8.1 presents an excerpt from that decision. Police officers are not, however, permitted to extensively manipulate the item to determine its nature. In *Dickerson,* the suspect was frisked and officers found a lump in his jacket. The problem was that when they realized that the lump was probably not a weapon, they squeezed and manipulated it extensively in an effort to determine what it was. They then removed a lump of crack cocaine from Dickerson's pocket and he was convicted of possession of illegal drugs. On appeal, the Supreme Court restated its commitment to *Terry* v. *Ohio,* which permits a pat-down search if the police have reasonable suspicion to believe that someone may possess a weapon. The Court stated, however, that once the officers realized the lump was not a weapon, the investigation should have ended. Because the officers had extensively manipulated the lump in an effort to determine what it was, the frisk in this case had become a search for evidence that required probable cause. Because there was no probable cause, the evidence was suppressed.

For the plain touch doctrine to apply, two requirements of the plain view doctrine and one additional requirement must be met:

1. the officer must be lawfully present in the place where he or she feels the contraband;
2. when it is felt the item must be immediately recognizable as contraband;
3. the officer must use his or her sense of touch to determine the nature of the contraband.[11]

The officer need not be able to view the contraband, however, so that the plain view doctrine's visibility requirement need not be met.

Although it is a relatively new development, the plain touch doctrine is likely to have a significant impact on stop and frisk practices.[12] For example, one federal court has upheld the warrantless seizure of lock-picking tools under the plain touch doctrine when a police officer serving an arrest warrant was able to immediately determine the nature of the items when he touched their case.[13]

Highlight 8.1

Minnesota v. *Dickerson,* 113 S.Ct. 2130 (1993)

 We have already held that police officers, at least under certain circumstances, may seize contraband detected during the lawful execution of a *Terry* search. . . .

If a police officer lawfully pats down a suspect's outer clothing and feels an object whose contour or mass makes its identity immediately apparent, there has been no invasion of the suspect's privacy beyond that already authorized by the officer's search for weapons; if the object is contraband, its warrantless seizure would be justified by the same practical considerations that inhere in the plain view context. . . .

[T]he police officer in this case overstepped the bounds of the 'strictly circumscribed' search for weapons allowed under *Terry.* Where, as here, 'an officer who is executing a valid search for one item seizes a different item,' this Court rightly 'has been sensitive to the danger . . . that officers will enlarge a specific authorization, furnished by a warrant or an exigency, into the equivalent of a general warrant to rummage and seize at will.' Here, the officer's continued exploration of respondent's pocket after having concluded that it contained no weapon was unrelated to '[t]he sole justification of the search [under *Terry*:] the protection of the police officer and others nearby.' It therefore amounted to the sort of evidentiary search that *Terry* expressly refused to authorize, and that we have condemned in subsequent cases. . . .

Although the officer was lawfully in a position to feel the lump in respondent's pocket, because *Terry* entitled him to place his hands upon respondent's jacket, the court below determined that the incriminating character of the object was not immediately apparent to him. Rather, the officer determined that the item was contraband only after conducting a further search, one not authorized by *Terry* or by any other exception to the warrant requirement. Because this further search of respondent's pocket was constitutionally invalid, the seizure of the cocaine that followed is likewise unconstitutional.

The Plain Smell Doctrine

The **plain smell doctrine** represents still another possible expansion of the plain view doctrine: If a police officer who is lawfully present in a particular place smells something that is immediately recognized as contraband, it may be seized. The Supreme Court has not yet sanctioned this doctrine, although several lower courts have approved it. The basic requirements of the plain view doctrine apply with equal force to plain smell cases:

1. the officer must be lawfully present in the place where the odor is smelled;
2. the odor must be immediately recognizable as emanating from contraband;
3. the officer must use his or her sense of smell to discover the suspected evidence or contraband.

For example, one federal court has upheld the warrantless seizure of illegal drugs after a police officer had stopped a motorist for a traffic violation and smelled the strong odor of burned marijuana.[14] Likewise, another court has upheld the warrantless seizure of laboratory equipment used to make methamphetamine (speed) when a police officer approached the defendant's car in a public place and smelled the strong odor of chemicals used to manufacture the drug.[15]

The above discussion pertains to police officers who smell unlawful contraband. Trained dog sniffs, however, are a different matter. In *United States* v. *Place,*[16] the Supreme Court held that using trained dogs to detect contraband does not constitute a Fourth Amendment search. Therefore, police officers do not need a search warrant, probable cause, or even reasonable suspicion to expose property to a sniff by a trained dog.[17] Moreover, if a trained dog exhibits a positive reaction to an item of property, that reaction may be used to establish probable cause to search a suspect for unlawful drugs.[18] Excerpts from *United States* v. *Place* are presented in Highlight 8.2.

In contrast, the Supreme Court has not yet decided whether the warrantless use of trained dogs to sniff people for illegal drugs violates the Fourth Amendment. At least one court has held that such law enforcement practices violate the Fourth Amendment.[19]

Items Found in Open Fields

Chapter 3 discussed Fourth Amendment standing. To briefly review that concept, a person has standing to assert the protection of the Fourth Amendment if he or she has a reasonable expectation of privacy in the area being searched that society is prepared to recognize. This privacy expectation formula was developed by Justice John Marshall Harlan in a concurring opinion in *Katz* v. *United States.*[20] *Katz* established too that a person may have a reasonable expectation of privacy in a public area because "the Fourth Amendment protects people, not places."[21]

The Fourth Amendment standing inquiry is closely related to the open fields doctrine. A person may not claim Fourth Amendment protection for items that are found in open fields because in those areas he or she has no reasonable expectation of privacy that society is prepared to recognize. In 1924, in *Hester* v. *United States,*[22] federal law enforcement agents seized bottles of moonshine that were thrown into a field. The Supreme Court ruled that the evidence was not protected by the Fourth Amendment.

For Fourth Amendment purposes, an **open field** is defined as any area in which an individual has no reasonable expectation of privacy. The term open field does not necessarily imply a field, wooded area, or other uninhabited place. An open field may include parking lots, public streets, waterways, or any number of public or semi-private places, even if they are posted with "no trespassing" signs. Because a person has no Fourth Amendment protection in an open field, any evidence or contraband discovered there may be seized and used at trial.

Open fields may be contrasted with areas that are closely associated with a person's home. The Fourth Amendment's core protection revolves around the home. Areas closely associated with the home receive special Fourth Amendment protection and are defined as **curtilage.** Within these areas, an individual has a reasonable expectation of privacy. Normally, police officers may not enter these areas without a search warrant. Areas outside of a home's curtilage often do not qualify for Fourth Amendment protection.

Highlight 8.2

United States v. *Place,* 462 U.S. 696 (1982)

 [W]e conclude that when an officer's observations lead him reasonably to believe that a traveler is carrying luggage that contains narcotics, the principles of *Terry* and its progeny would permit the officer to detain the luggage briefly to investigate the circumstances that aroused his suspicion, provided that the investigative detention is properly limited in scope.

The purpose for which respondent's luggage was seized, of course, was to arrange its exposure to a narcotics detection dog. Obviously, if this investigative procedure is itself a search requiring probable cause, the initial seizure of respondent's luggage for the purpose of subjecting it to the sniff test—no matter how brief—could not be justified on less than probable cause.

The Fourth Amendment "protects people from unreasonable government intrusions into their legitimate expectations of privacy." We have affirmed that a person possesses a privacy interest in the contents of personal luggage that is protected by the Fourth Amendment. A "canine sniff" by a well-trained narcotics detection dog, however, does not require opening the luggage. It does not expose contraband items that otherwise would remain hidden from public view, as does, for example, an officer's rummaging through the contents of luggage. Thus, the manner in which information is obtained through this investigative technique is much less intrusive than a typical search. Moreover, the sniff discloses only the presence or absence of narcotics, a contraband item. Thus, despite the fact that the sniff tells the authorities something about the contents of the luggage, the information obtained is limited. This limited disclosure also ensures that the owner of the property is not subjected to the embarrassment and inconvenience entailed in less discriminate and more intrusive investigative methods.

* * *

We are aware of no other investigative procedure that is so limited both in the manner in which the information is obtained and in the content of the information revealed by the procedure. Therefore, we conclude that the particular course of investigation that the agents intended to pursue here—exposure of respondent's luggage, which was located in a public place, to a trained canine—did not constitute a "search" within the meaning of the Fourth Amendment.

The Supreme Court has expanded the open fields concept in recent years to include even a suspect's private property that is not within his home's curtilage. In *Oliver* v. *United States*,[23] police officers without search warrants entered the defendant's property, which was heavily wooded, and discovered marijuana plants. The land had been posted with "no trespassing" signs, and although it was located approximately one mile from the defendant's home, it was protected by a fence and a locked gate. Oliver was convicted of cultivating marijuana, and he appealed, asserting that the conduct of the police had violated the Fourth Amendment.

The central question was whether Oliver had a constitutionally protected reasonable expectation of privacy in the area that was searched. The Supreme Court held that Oliver had no expectation of privacy in that area because "an individual may not legitimately demand privacy for activities conducted out of doors in fields, except in the area immediately surrounding the home."[24] The rule of law that emerges from *Oliver* is that areas outside of a home's curtilage do not receive Fourth Amendment protection. A search may be upheld even if law enforcement agents commit a trespass to gain access to the property, although this factor will be considered by a reviewing court in determining reasonableness of police behavior. *Oliver,* however, left an important question unanswered: What precisely is the scope of a home's curtilage? That question was answered three years later.

United States v. *Dunn*[25] involved a suspect who was manufacturing methamphetamine (speed). In *Dunn,* drug enforcement agents crossed over three fences and trespassed onto Dunn's property. When the agents looked into a barn located approximately 60 yards from Dunn's house, which was enclosed by a fence, they observed materials used to manufacture methamphetamine. Based on their observations, the agents obtained a search warrant for Dunn's property. Dunn was convicted of manufacturing illegal drugs. On appeal, the issue was whether the barn was within the curtilage of Dunn's home. The Supreme Court developed a four-factor test to be used to determine if a building is a part of a home's curtilage:

1. the home's proximity to the area that is searched;
2. whether the area is included within an enclosure surrounding the home;
3. the area's normal uses; and
4. the steps taken by the resident to protect the area from observation by people passing by.[26]

The Court held that the building was not part of the curtilage of Dunn's home, because:

1. the building was located 60 yards from the house;
2. it was outside a fence surrounding the house;
3. it was not being used for the intimate activities of the home;
4. the building was not protected from view from those standing in open fields adjacent to it.[27]

United States v. *Dunn* suggests that buildings and other areas located a significant distance from a house may not receive substantial Fourth Amendment protection. Moreover, police officers may not violate the Fourth Amendment even if they commit a trespass in order to view areas outside of a home's curtilage, because a person may have no reasonable expectation of privacy in those areas.[28]

Using Airplanes and Helicopters to View Curtilage

The use of airplanes, helicopters, and other high technology equipment by law enforcement agents has increased substantially in recent years. Not surprisingly, questions about the lawfulness of law enforcement officers' aerial surveillance of suspects' property have arisen. The general rule that has emerged from the Supreme Court's decisions is that even if police officers may not lawfully enter a private area from the

Source: AP/Wide World Photos

ground, they may view it from public airspace.[29] This appears to be true even if the area is located within a home's curtilage.

In *California* v. *Ciraolo,*[30] police officers, acting on a tip, inspected the fenced backyard of a house while flying in an airplane at an altitude of approximately 1,000 feet. The officers observed what they believed to be marijuana plants and, based on their observations, obtained a search warrant. The Supreme Court held that the aerial observation was not a Fourth Amendment search. Although Ciraolo had a reasonable expectation of privacy in his backyard, it was not one that society was prepared to honor because "any member of the public flying in this airspace who glanced down could have seen everything that these officers observed."[31] The Court concluded:

> In an age where private and commercial flight in the public airways is routine, it is unreasonable for [Ciraolo] to expect that his marijuana plants were constitutionally protected from being observed with the naked eye from an altitude of 1,000 feet. The Fourth Amendment simply does not require the police traveling in the public airways at this altitude to obtain a warrant to observe what is visible to the naked eye.[32]

Likewise, in *Florida* v. *Riley,*[33] the Supreme Court held that the surveillance of the interior of a partially covered greenhouse in a residential backyard from a helicopter flying 400 feet above it did not require a search warrant. Relying on its reasoning in *California* v. *Ciraolo,* the Court held that society was not prepared to honor Riley's privacy expectation because any member of the public could have viewed the interior of his greenhouse from public airspace.

Taken together, *Ciraolo* and *Riley* indicate that police officers are permitted to observe a home's curtilage from public airspace without a search warrant because such actions do not constitute a Fourth Amendment search.[34]

Abandoned Property

Abandoned property is property that has been given up voluntarily and completely or to such an extent that its examination by another person is not unlikely.[35] It does not receive Fourth Amendment protection because persons do not have a reasonable expectation of privacy in abandoned property.[36] For example, if a guest checks out of a hotel room and had discarded property in the wastebasket, that property is considered abandoned.[37] Likewise, if someone is walking down the street and places a parcel in a roadside trash container, that property too would be abandoned.

Experienced police officers will attest that a common practice of illegal drug users is to discard their unlawful stashes if they are about to be stopped and questioned. If a container of unlawful drugs is discarded, it is considered abandoned property and may be used as evidence against a suspect because he or she no longer has a reasonable expectation of privacy in its contents. If, however, the original reason for stopping a suspect is unlawful, the evidence may be excluded under the fruit of the poisonous tree doctrine. In *California* v. *Hodari D.,*[38] two police officers were on patrol in a high-crime area of Oakland, California. They were dressed in street clothes and wearing jackets that identified them as police officers. As they rounded a corner in an unmarked police car, they saw several youths, including Hodari D., huddled around a small red car parked at the curb. When the youths saw the officers' car approaching, they began to flee. One officer chased Hodari D. on foot. During the chase, Hodari D. threw away what appeared to be a small rock. The officer tackled Hodari D., handcuffed him, and radioed for assistance. The rock Hodari D. discarded was found to be crack cocaine. Hodari D. moved to suppress the evidence at a juvenile hearing but the motion was denied by the juvenile court. An appellate court held, however, that the evidence should have been suppressed because Hodari D. had been seized when the officer started to run toward him, that this seizure was unreasonable, and therefore the cocaine evidence was suppressed because it was the fruit of an unlawful seizure. On appeal to the U.S. Supreme Court the issue was whether Hodari D. was seized for Fourth Amendment purposes when the officer began the chase. The Supreme Court held that the Hodari D. was not seized when the chase began, that the officer's pursuit of Hodari D. was lawful, and that the cocaine evidence, which Hodari D. had abandoned when he threw it during the pursuit, was not the fruit of an unlawful seizure. Rather, it was abandoned property that could be admitted into evidence at the juvenile proceeding.

Police Searches of Trash Containers

A person does not have a reasonable expectation of privacy in the contents of trash that is left outside a home's curtilage for curbside collection.[39] In *California* v. *Greenwood,*[40] presented in Highlight 8.3, the Supreme Court held that a person has no

---

Highlight 8.3

California v. Greenwood, 486 U.S. 35 (1988)

The warrantless search and seizure of the garbage bags left at the curb outside the Greenwood house would violate the Fourth Amendment only if respondents manifested a subjective expectation of privacy that society accepts as objectively reasonable. Respondents do not disagree with this standard.

They assert, however, that they had, and exhibited, an expectation of privacy with respect to the trash that was searched by the police: The trash, which was placed on the street for collection at a fixed time, was contained in opaque plastic bags, which the garbage collector was expected to pick up, mingle with the trash of others, and deposit at the garbage dump. The trash was only temporarily on the street, and there was little likelihood that it would be inspected by anyone.

It may well be that respondents did not expect that the contents of their garbage bags would become known to the police or other members of the public. An expectation of privacy does not give rise to

Fourth Amendment protection, however, unless society is prepared to accept that expectation as objectively reasonable.

Here, we conclude that respondents exposed their garbage to the public sufficiently to defeat their claim to Fourth Amendment protection. It is common knowledge that plastic garbage bags left on or at the side of a public street are readily accessible to animals, children, scavengers, snoops, and other members of the public. Moreover, respondents placed their refuse at the curb for the express purpose of conveying it to a third party, the trash collector, who might himself have sorted through respondents' trash or permitted others, such as the police, to do so. Accordingly, having deposited their garbage "in an area particularly suited for public inspection and, in a manner of speaking, public consumption, for the express purpose of having strangers take it," respondents could have had no reasonable expectation of privacy in the inculpatory items that they discarded.

---

reasonable expectation of privacy in the contents of trash left for curbside collection. This is because once the trash collector has the property, he or she is free to rummage through it, or to give it to someone else. Moreover, one federal court has held that a person does not have a reasonable expectation of privacy in the contents of his income tax returns that were left for collection outside his home's curtilage, even when the materials retrieved from the trash had been shredded.[41]

The issue of precisely where a person's trash is left for collection may be an important one, however. In *Greenwood,* the trash was left on the curbside, outside of the curtilage to the home. At least one federal court has held that a police officer's warrantless search of trash and seizure of shredded documents that had been left within a home's curtilage violated the homeowner's reasonable expectation of privacy.[42]

The Supreme Court has not yet considered the issue of whether a homeowner has a reasonable expectation of privacy in trash left for collection within a home's curtilage. The Court will, however, use the two-part privacy expectation test developed in *Katz* v. *United States* to analyze the issue. That test asks whether a person has a reasonable expectation of privacy in a place that is searched and whether society is prepared to accept that expectation as a reasonable one. It is interesting to speculate about how the Supreme Court would decide the issue. On one hand, a home receives stringent Fourth Amendment protection. Therefore, items located within its curtilage, including trash left for later collection, should be protected from scrutiny by police officers. On the other hand, when the trash collector removes the garbage from the curtilage, he or she is free to rummage through it or to give it to someone else, including a police officer. Therefore, the person who previously owned the trash would not have had a reasonable expectation of privacy in its contents. It is presently unclear how the Supreme Court would decide this case.

Regulatory Searches and Inspections

A **regulatory search** is an inspection conducted by government employees for health, safety, or other regulatory purposes. Most of these inspections do not involve criminal justice processes and therefore do not require strict Fourth Amendment protections, such as probable cause or a search warrant. For example, building inspectors examine new homes to ensure that they conform to housing codes, or agents from the United States Department of Agriculture (U.S.D.A.) inspect food processing plants to insure that meat and poultry are being processed safely.

The importance of such regulatory inspections is difficult to overestimate because they affect the health and well-being of enormous numbers of people. The Supreme Court has expanded the scope of regulatory searches in recent years to include searches of homes destroyed by fire, searches at U.S. borders, business searches, and searches of probationers and parolees.

Administrative Search Warrants

In *Camara* v. *Municipal Court,*[43] the Supreme Court established that the Fourth Amendment did not allow city building inspectors to conduct nonconsensual safety inspections of dwellings without a search warrant. The type of warrant needed to conduct such a safety inspection is, however, much easier to obtain than a traditional search warrant used in a criminal case. Such a "watered-down" search warrant, which may be termed an **administrative search warrant,** does not require that an inspector show probable cause to believe that a particular home violates the city's building code. Rather, he or she must show only that the inspection is part of a regulatory plan designed to detect unsafe conditions. These searches may be conducted if the procedures used to conduct them do not give inspectors unlimited discretion to conduct searches and are not enforced in an arbitrary manner. The Supreme Court has held that a balancing test should be used to determine the reasonableness of a regulatory search. Such a test asks whether the particular type of search has "a long history of judicial and public acceptance," if the practice is necessary to regulate the particular area, and whether the type of search involves a "relatively limited" invasion of privacy.[44] The Supreme Court has used this test on many different occasions to determine whether regulatory searches are permitted under the Fourth Amendment.[45]

Source: Cary Wolinsky/Stock Boston

Warrantless Administrative Searches of Businesses

In general, a regulatory inspection of a business is easier to support than a similar inspection of a dwelling. Whether a government inspector is required to obtain a search warrant to inspect a business depends on the nature of the particular business.[46] If a business is licensed by the federal government, a state, or a local government it is easier to justify a warrantless regulatory inspection. This is because the owner of a regulated business has a diminished expectation of privacy due to the fact of governmental regulation of his or her business. In *New York* v. *Burger,*[47] the Supreme Court established a three-part test for determining the lawfulness of a warrantless administrative search of a closely regulated business. This test asks (1) whether there is a substantial state interest behind the regulatory scheme supporting the search, (2) whether the search is necessary to further that scheme, and (3) whether the statute authorizing the search is an adequate substitute for a warrant in providing notice to owners and restricting the discretion of those conducting the search.[48] For example, in *United States* v. *Biswell,*[49] the Supreme Court upheld the warrantless inspection of a firearms dealer by a federal agent because the dealer voluntarily chose to participate in a business subject to strict federal licensing standards that could only be enforced by unannounced inspections. In contrast, the Court ruled in *Marshall* v. *Barlow's, Inc.,*[50] that an inspection by the Occupational Safety and Health Administration (OSHA) must be supported by an administrative search warrant. The Court distinguished this case from *Biswell* by noting that the statute allowing OSHA inspectors to conduct warrantless inspections was very broad, whereas *Biswell* involved a search of a "closely regulated industry."[51] These cases illustrate that if a business is closely regulated by the government, such as those involved in firearms or alcohol sales,[52] it will be easier for inspectors to justify warrantless regulatory inspections of their records and business premises.

Searches of Homes Destroyed by Fire

Police and fire personnel may conduct a warrantless search of property that has been destroyed by fire. It would be ridiculous to require firefighters to obtain a warrant to enter a burning building to extinguish the fire. Even when the circumstances of a fire are suspicious, however, a homeowner may still retain a reasonable expectation of privacy in the property. In *Michigan* v. *Tyler,* the Supreme Court held that when a fire occurs, officials may "remain in a building for a reasonable time to investigate the cause of a blaze after it has been extinguished."[53] If police officers or fire marshals wish to return at a later time to investigate the fire, however, they must first obtain a search warrant.

Michigan v. *Clifford,*[54] decided in 1984, suggests that authorities need only an administrative search warrant to return to the scene of a fire to determine its cause. To obtain the warrant, inspectors must show that a fire of undetermined origin has occurred, that the scope of the proposed search is reasonable, and that the search will be "executed at a reasonable and convenient time."[55] If, however, investigators already present at the scene of a fire discover evidence of possible arson and wish to return to the scene to conduct an additional investigation at a later time, they must obtain a traditional criminal search warrant. Moreover, a home owner may retain a reasonable expectation of privacy in an area damaged by fire. This could be shown by the owner's efforts to secure the premises after the fire or the continued presence of the owner's personal belongings at the scene. Therefore, law enforcement officers should obtain a search warrant before returning to the scene of a suspicious fire, especially if they had previously discovered evidence indicating that arson may have caused it.

Border Searches

Searches of persons or property at U.S. borders receive little Fourth Amendment protection. This principle applies equally to those persons entering, leaving, or traveling through the U.S. The Supreme Court has consistently held that such searches may be routinely conducted without a warrant, probable cause, or any suspicion of criminal activity.[56] In *Almeida-Sanchez* v. *United States,*[57] the Supreme Court held that "national self-protection" justifies searching travelers crossing an international boundary into the United States. Certain types of searches at the border may, however, require customs officials to demonstrate some degree of suspicion. The Supreme Court has not been completely clear about precisely what level of suspicion is required for customs officials to conduct these investigative practices. A review of the case law, however, permits several observations. A strip search requires reasonable suspicion based upon articulable facts to indicate that a suspect is concealing contraband.[58] Likewise, X-ray examinations require reasonable suspicion.[59] Body cavity searches, however,

Highlight 8.4

United States v. *Montoya de Hernandez,* 473 U.S. 531 (1985)

 Consistently, therefore, with Congress's power to protect the nation by stopping and examining persons entering this country, the Fourth Amendment's balance of reasonableness is qualitatively different at the international border than in the interior. Routine searches of the persons and effects of entrants are not subject to any requirement of reasonable suspicion, probable cause, or warrant, and first-class mail may be opened without a warrant on less than probable cause.

* * *

[Our] cases reflect longstanding concern for the protection of the integrity of the border. This concern is, if anything, heightened by the veritable national crisis in law enforcement caused by smuggling of illicit narcotics, and in particular by the increasing utilization of alimentary canal smuggling. This desperate practice appears to be a relatively recent addition to the smugglers' repertoire of deceptive practices, and it also appears to be exceedingly difficult to detect.

* * *

We hold that the detention of a traveler at the border, beyond the scope of a routine customs search and inspection is justified at its inception if customs agents, considering all the facts surrounding the traveler and her trip, reasonably suspect that the traveler is smuggling contraband in her alimentary canal.

---

require a higher degree of suspicion and a "clear indication" of smuggling activity.[60] Moreover, if customs agents have reason to believe that a suspect is carrying unlawful drugs in his or her alimentary canal, the individual may be detained until he or she has a bowel movement.[61] Excerpts from such a case, *United States* v. *Montoya de Hernandez,*[62] are presented in Highlight 8.4.

Roadway Patrols and Fixed Roadblocks

In *Almeida-Sanchez* v. *United States,*[63] the Supreme Court considered the issue of moving patrols designed to stop and search vehicles on the highways for illegal aliens. A **moving patrol** is a mobile search by immigration officials for illegal aliens that is not set up at a fixed checkpoint. The Court held that unless there was probable cause or a search warrant, such stops violate the Fourth Amendment. Moreover, in *United States* v. *Brignoni-Ponce,*[64] it held that "a roving patrol may [not] stop a vehicle in an area near the border and question its occupants when the only ground for suspicion is that the occupants appear to be of Mexican ancestry."[65] Rather, immigration officials may stop vehicles only upon reasonable suspicion that they contain illegal aliens.

At **fixed roadblocks,** which are set up some distance from the border, immigration officials stop all vehicles traveling on a particular roadway to search for illegal aliens. When such a checkpoint is used to question a vehicle's occupants briefly, it does not require a search warrant and does not violate the Fourth Amendment.[66] Officials may question the occupants about their citizenship, immigration status, and any suspicious circumstances. In *United States* v. *Martinez-Fuerte,*[67] the Court held that once the vehicle is stopped and customs officials suspect that it contains illegal aliens, it may be sent to a secondary inspection area. If officials have probable cause, they may then search the entire vehicle.

Factory Surveys

A **factory survey** is a technique used by immigration officials to discover illegal aliens whereby agents, with the employer's consent or with a search warrant, conduct unannounced inspections of businesses and question employees to determine their immigration status. In *Immigration and Naturalization Service* v. *Delgado,*[68] the Supreme Court held that such surveys do not normally constitute a Fourth Amendment seizure of a worker. This is because a reasonable person would feel that he was free to discontinue the conversation and leave the area. In general, then, factory surveys to determine residency status are lawful and do not violate the Fourth Amendment.

Special Needs Searches

A **special needs search** is one that is justified by special circumstances, outside the ordinary needs of law enforcement. In such circumstances government agents may conduct searches without a warrant or probable cause. To this point, the Court has identified five situations in which the special needs exception to the search warrant requirement may apply: a search of a probationer's home under a state regulation that permitted such searches; a search of a public employee's work area; a search of a high school student's purse by school authorities; suspicionless testing of high school athletes for drug use; and suspicionless drug testing of government employees. Moreover, although the Supreme Court did not specifically utilize the special needs exception to the warrant requirement, it has used a similar rationale to uphold the unannounced searches of prison inmates' cells. We will consider separately each of these exceptions.

Searches of Probationers' and Parolees' Homes

Although probationers and parolees retain some expectation of privacy in their homes, it is diminished because of their status.[69] In *Griffin* v. *Wisconsin,*[70] the Supreme Court upheld a probation officer's warrantless search of a probationer's home based on a state regulation that permitted such searches. The Court held that the special needs of the probation system supported such a rule. Requiring a search warrant or probable cause would reduce the deterrent effect of probation and "[a] probation agency must be able to act based upon a lesser degree of certainty than the Fourth Amendment would otherwise require in order to intervene before a probationer does damage to himself or society."[71] Although *Griffin* v. *Wisconsin* involved the warrantless search of a probationer's home, there is every reason to believe that its principle would apply with equal force to warrantless searches of a parolee's home.[72]

Searches of Public Employees' Work Areas

The Supreme Court has made it clear that public employees have little Fourth Amendment protection in their work areas. In *O'Connor* v. *Ortega*,[73] the Court upheld the warrantless search of a doctor's office by his supervisors at a public hospital, who were investigating work-related misconduct. It held that although the doctor had a reasonable expectation of privacy in his desk and file cabinets, that expectation had to be balanced against the employer's interests in maintaining an efficient work environment. Here, the employer's interest prevailed because requiring search warrants or a probable cause requirement would impose an unworkable burden. Moreover, the Court asserted that a search of a public employee's work area should be judged using an **objective reasonableness test.** This test asks whether, considering all the circumstances in a particular case, an objective person would find the employer's actions to be reasonable.

Searches of Students

School authorities are often permitted to search students without a warrant or probable cause.[74] In *New Jersey* v. *T.L.O.*,[75] a public high school teacher discovered a 14-year-old high school student smoking in a lavatory in violation of school rules. When a vice-principal ordered the student to open her purse, he discovered a pack of cigarettes and a package of rolling papers. A small amount of marijuana, a pipe, plastic bags, several one-dollar bills, an index card with a list of students who owed her money, and two letters that indicated that T.L.O. was selling marijuana were discovered too. The evidence was admitted into juvenile delinquency proceedings but the New Jersey Supreme Court held that it should have been suppressed because the search violated the Fourth Amendment. On appeal, the U.S. Supreme Court held that to determine the lawfulness of this search required a "balancing of the need to search against the invasion which the search entails."[76] Here, the Court balanced the child's interest in privacy with "the substantial interest of teachers and administrators in maintaining discipline in the classroom and on school grounds."[77] The Court upheld the lawfulness of the search because the school's interest in maintaining order and discipline were special needs that justified the warrantless search of T.L.O.'s purse. In addition, the Court held that in ordinary circumstances, a search of a student by a teacher or school official is justified:

> when there are reasonable grounds for suspecting that the search will turn up evidence that
> the student has violated or is violating either the law or the rules of the school. Such a
> search will be permissible in scope when the measures adopted are reasonably related to
> the objectives of the search and not excessively intrusive in light of the age and sex of the
> student and the nature of the infraction.[78]

Although the Supreme Court has not yet settled the issue of searches of student lockers and desks, it appears that these practices would be upheld as well.[79] School officials are not, however, permitted to conduct strip searches or to "round up" a group of students and search them without reasonable suspicion. Such a search would violate the Fourth Amendment. Moreover, it is unclear whether *T.L.O's* rationale would apply to searches of high school students if a search is requested by a law enforcement officer.

Another issue that the Supreme Court has not resolved is the precise reach of *T.L.O.,* which involved a search of a young public high school student. The Court's opinion in that case rested partially on the fact that high school administrators are expected to act in the place of a student's parents. Many college students are adults. It is therefore doubtful that the Court would extend *T.L.O's* rationale to searches by college administrators of students, their possessions, or their dormitory rooms. One technique that some colleges use to permit warrantless searches of students' dormitory rooms is to require students to sign contracts, in which they expressly agree to allow college officials to enter and examine dormitory rooms as a condition of residence on campus.

Testing High School Students for Drug Use

New Jersey v. *T.L.O.'s* rationale has been extended to other activities conducted on high school grounds. Recently, in *Veronia School District 47J* v. *Acton,*[80] the Supreme Court upheld the warrantless and suspicionless urinalysis testing of high school athletes because of the school's interest in maintaining order and discipline, and because students who voluntarily participate in high school athletic programs have a diminished expectation of privacy.[81]

Suspicionless Urinalysis Testing of Customs Officials

In 1989, the Supreme Court decided two important cases that involved employee drug testing. In *Skinner* v. *Railway Labor Executives' Association,*[82] a federal regulation required railroad administrators to conduct mandatory blood and urine tests of employees involved in serious train accidents. The Court held that although these tests were Fourth Amendment searches, they were lawful because the government's interest in public safety outweighed the employees' privacy interests.

Likewise, in *National Treasury Employees Union* v. *Von Raab,*[83] the Supreme Court upheld a random urinalysis drug testing program that the U.S. Customs Service had developed for many of its employees. The Court held that the government's special need to ensure that agents involved in drug interdiction are "physically fit, and have unimpeachable integrity and judgment," outweighed the employees' privacy interests. Unlike *Skinner,* where substantial evidence of railroad employee drug and alcohol use was documented, *Von Raab* presented scant evidence of unlawful drug use by Customs agents. Justice Antonin Scalia noted this difference between these cases and issued a scathing dissenting opinion in *Von Raab.* Excerpts from his opinion are presented in Highlight 8.5.

A two-part rule emerges from examining numerous drug testing cases involving government employees: (1) drug testing is permitted if it is based on reasonable suspicion of a particular employee's drug use; and (2) mandatory random drug testing is lawful if an employee holds a sensitive position in which he or she is responsible for ensuring public safety. Moreover, many courts have upheld mandatory random drug testing programs developed by state and local law enforcement and corrections agencies as well as those based upon reasonable suspicion of a particular employee's illegal drug usage.[84] In addition, the majority of U.S. courts that have considered the issue have approved private employers' drug testing programs for their employees.[85] Fourth

---

Highlight 8.5

National Treasury Employees Union v. *Von Raab,* 489 U.S. 656 (1989)

(Justice Antonin Scalia, Dissenting)

The issue in this case is not whether Customs Service employees can constitutionally be denied promotion, or even dismissed, for a single instance of unlawful drug use, at home or at work. They assuredly can. The issue here is what steps can constitutionally be taken to *detect* such drug use. The Government asserts it can demand that employees perform "an excretory function traditionally shielded by great privacy," while "a monitor of the same sex . . . remains close at hand to listen for the normal sounds," and that the excretion thus produced be turned over to the Government for chemical analysis. The Court agrees that this constitutes a search for purposes of the Fourth Amendment—and I think it is a type of search particularly destructive of privacy and offensive to personal dignity.

* * *

Those who lose because of the lack of understanding that begot the present exercise in symbolism are not just the Customs Service employees, whose dignity is thus offended, but all of us—who suffer a coarsening of our national manners that ultimately give the Fourth Amendment its content, and who become subject to the administration of federal officials whose respect for our privacy can hardly be greater than the small respect they have been taught to have for their own.

Amendment concerns are generally not implicated in these cases because the actions of a private employer are at issue and no *governmental* conduct is involved.

Searches of Prison Inmates' Cells

Managing a prison is a difficult task. Prison inmates have found ingenious ways to hide weapons, drugs, and other contraband from correctional authorities.

Due to correctional administrators' need to maintain order and institutional security, authorities may conduct routine unannounced searches of inmates' cells.[86] A prison inmate has no reasonable expectation of privacy in his or her cell or other living quarters. In *Hudson* v. *Palmer,*[87] the Supreme Court asserted that the administration of a prison is a difficult undertaking. Furthermore,

> it would be literally impossible to accomplish the prison objectives . . . if inmates retained a right of privacy in their cells. Virtually the only place inmates can conceal weapons, drugs, and other contraband is in their cells. Unfettered access to these cells by prison officials, thus, is imperative if drugs and contraband are to be ferreted out and sanitary surroundings are to be maintained.[88]

Hudson v. *Palmer* held that *prison* inmates have no legitimate expectation of privacy in their cells. Likewise, the Court has held that *jail* inmates, including those who have not been convicted of an offense and are awaiting trial, have no Fourth Amendment right to privacy in their cells. In *Bell* v. *Wolfish,*[89] the Court held too that prison authorities are free to impose further restrictions that are needed to maintain order and institutional security. In addition to unannounced cell searches, such restrictions may include searching all parcels sent to inmates and conducting strip and body cavity searches of jail inmates following contact visits with outsiders.

Summary

Under the plain view doctrine, contraband or other evidence that police officers find in plain view may be seized without a search warrant and without probable cause. The requirements of this doctrine include: (1) the officer must be lawfully present in the place where the sighting is made; (2) the item(s) must be immediately recognizable as contraband; (3) the item(s) must be plainly visible to the officer.

The plain touch doctrine, which the Supreme Court developed recently, is discussed as well. This doctrine expands the plain view principle and asserts that if a police officer who is frisking someone feels an object that is immediately recognizable as contraband, it may be seized without a warrant. Even more recently, some courts have recognized another extension of the plain view principle, the plain smell doctrine.

The seizure of evidence or contraband found in open fields is considered. An open field is defined as any area in which an individual has no reasonable expectation of privacy. It may include a parking lot, public street, waterways, or any number of public or semi-private places, even if they are posted with "no trespassing" signs. Because a person has no reasonable expectation of privacy in an open field, any evidence or contraband discovered may be seized and used at trial. The Supreme Court has developed a test to be used to determine if an area to be searched is located within a home's curtilage. This test assesses: (1) the home's proximity to the area; (2) whether the area is included within an enclosure surrounding the home; (3) what the area is normally used for; and (4) the

steps taken by the resident to protect the area from observation by people passing by.

Law enforcement agents may use airplanes, helicopters, and other high technology equipment to view private areas from public airspace. Moreover, Supreme Court precedents indicate that police officers are permitted to observe a home's curtilage from public airspace without a search warrant because such actions do not constitute a Fourth Amendment search.

Abandoned property has been given up voluntarily and completely or to such an extent that its examination by another person is not unlikely. It does not receive Fourth Amendment protection because persons do not have a reasonable expectation of privacy in property that has been abandoned. The Supreme Court has held that a person has no reasonable expectation of privacy in the contents of trash left for curbside collection because a defendant has no reasonable expectation of privacy in it that society is prepared to recognize.

Regulatory searches and inspections are discussed. Many types of government inspections occur each day that do not involve criminal justice processes. The Supreme Court has recognized that such searches do not require full Fourth Amendment protections, such as probable cause or a search warrant. The Court has expanded the scope of regulatory searches in recent years to include searches of homes destroyed by fire, searches at U.S. borders, business searches, and searches of probationers and parolees. Administrative search warrants as well as warrantless administrative searches are discussed in detail.

Special needs searches, wherein governmental interests extend beyond the normal needs of law enforcement, may allow police to conduct searches without a warrant or probable cause. The Court has identified at least five situations in which the special needs exception to the search warrant requirement may apply: a search of a probationer's home under a state regulation that permitted such searches; a search of a public employee's work area; a search of a high school student's purse by school authorities; suspicionless testing of high school student athletes for drug use and suspicionless drug testing of certain government employees. The Supreme Court has upheld routine unannounced searches of inmates' cells under a similar rationale.

Review Questions

1. Discuss the plain view doctrine. Identify and describe the essential requirements of this doctrine.

2. Discuss the present status of the "inadvertent discovery" requirement of the plain view doctrine.

3. Discuss the present status of the "plain touch" doctrine. What is the present status of the "plain smell" doctrine?

4. What is an open field? Why may contraband or other evidence found in open fields be used at trial? How has the Supreme Court expanded the open fields doctrine in recent years?

5. Identify and discuss a test that the courts will use to determine if a building is within a home's curtilage. Discuss the present status of law enforcement agents' use of airplanes and helicopters to view a suspect's property.

6. What is abandoned property? May such property be used at trial against someone accused of committing a crime? Discuss the present status of trash container searches by law enforcement officers.

7. What is an administrative search warrant? Must an administrative official demonstrate probable cause in order to obtain an administrative search warrant? What is the reason for this rule?

8. May administrative officials conduct warrantless searches of businesses? Describe a test that may be used to determine the lawfulness of such a search. Identify several types of businesses that may be searched by administrative officials without a warrant.

9. Searches of persons and property at U.S. borders receive little Fourth Amendment protection. Describe the level of suspicion that customs officials must establish in order to conduct the following types of searches:
   a. automobile searches at the border
   b. strip searches
   c. x-ray examinations
   d. body cavity searches
   e. alimentary canal searches

10. Discuss the lawfulness of moving patrols, fixed checkpoint roadblocks, and factory surveys that are designed to apprehend illegal immigrants.

11. Discuss the special needs exception to the Fourth Amendment's search warrant requirement in the following situations:
   a. a search of a probationer's home
   b. a search of a public employee's work area
   c. a search of a high school student's purse by school officials
   d. suspicionless drug testing of government employees

12. Discuss the status of a prison inmate's right to privacy in his or her cell. What is the rationale for this rule?

Issues for Analysis and Discussion

1. In *Oliver* v. *United States,* the Supreme Court stated "we reject the suggestion that steps taken to protect privacy establish that expectations of privacy in an open field are legitimate." Discuss this statement fully. Do you agree with the Court's position? If you were a U.S. Supreme Court Justice deciding a case with facts similar to those in Oliver, what significance, if any, would you attach to a law enforcement officer's trespass onto private property to observe evidence of criminal activity?

2. In *New Jersey* v. *T.L.O.,* the Supreme Court held that "school officials need not obtain a warrant before searching a student who is under their authority." Present and discuss the Supreme Court's justification for this rule. Do you agree with this rule? Using the Supreme Court's privacy expectation language, present an argument that college students at a public college should have a greater expectation of privacy than the students in *T.L.O.* Should the same principle apply to college students at a private college?

CASE EXCERPT: *OLIVER* v. *UNITED STATES*
SUPREME COURT OF THE UNITED STATES, 1984
466 U.S. 170

Acting on reports that marijuana was being grown on Oliver's farm, Kentucky State Police Officers went to investigate. The officers drove past Oliver's house to a locked gate with a "No Trespassing" sign, but with a path along one side. The officers went around the gate and found a field of marijuana over a mile from Oliver's house. Oliver was charged with manufacturing a controlled substance in violation of federal law. The U.S. District Court suppressed the evidence and asserted that Oliver had a reasonable expectation of privacy because the area in which the marijuana was found was not an open field. The U.S. Court of Appeals reversed, holding that the open fields doctrine allowed the officers to enter and search the area without a warrant. The U.S. Supreme Court granted certiorari. [This case was consolidated with another case, *Maine* v. *Thornton,* which presented an almost identical question.]

Mr. Justice Powell delivered the opinion of the Court.

* * *

The "open fields" doctrine, first enunciated by this Court in *Hester* v. *United States,* permits police officers to enter and search a field without a warrant. We granted certiorari in these cases to clarify confusion that has arisen as to the continued vitality of the doctrine.

* * *

As Justice Holmes explained for the Court in his characteristically laconic style: "[T]he special protection accorded by the Fourth Amendment to the people in their 'persons, houses, papers, and effects,' is not extended to the open fields. The distinction between the latter and the house is as old as the common law." Nor are open fields "effects" within the meaning of the Fourth Amendment. . . . [T]he term "effects" is less inclusive than "property" and cannot be said to encompass open fields. We conclude, as did the Court in deciding *Hester* v. *United States,* that the government's intrusion upon the open fields is not one of those "unreasonable searches" proscribed by the text of the Fourth Amendment.

This interpretation of the Fourth Amendment's language is consistent with the understanding of the right to privacy expressed in our Fourth Amendment jurisprudence. Since *Katz* v. *United States,* the touchstone of Amendment analysis has been the question whether a person has a "constitutionally protected reasonable expectation of privacy." The Amendment does not protect the merely subjective expectation of privacy, but only those "expectation[s] that society is prepared to recognize as reasonable."

No single factor determines whether an individual legitimately may claim under the Fourth Amendment that a place should be free of government intrusion not authorized by warrant. In assessing the degree to which a search infringes upon individual privacy, the Court has given weight to such factors as the intention of the Framers of the Fourth Amendment, the uses to which the individual has put a location, and our societal understanding that certain areas deserve the most scrupulous protection from government invasion. These factors are equally relevant to determining whether the government's intrusion upon open fields without a warrant or probable cause violates reasonable expectations of privacy and is therefore a search proscribed by the Amendment.

In this light, the rule of *Hester* v. *United States,* that we affirm today, may be understood as providing that an individual may not legitimately demand privacy for activities conducted out of doors in fields, except in the area immediately surrounding the home. . . . [O]pen fields do not provide the setting for those intimate activ-

ities that the Amendment is intended to shelter from government interference or surveillance. There is no societal interest in protecting the privacy of those activities such as the cultivation of crops, that occur in open fields. Moreover, as a practical matter these lands usually are accessible to the public and the police in ways that a home, an office, or commercial structure would not be. It is not generally true that fences or "No Trespassing" signs effectively bar the public from viewing open fields in rural areas. . . . For these reasons, the asserted expectation of privacy in open fields is not an expectation that "society recognizes as reasonable."

At common law, the curtilage is the area to which extends the intimate activity associated with the "sanctity of a man's home and the privacies of life," and therefore has been considered part of the home itself for Fourth Amendment purposes. Thus, courts have extended Fourth Amendment protection to the curtilage, as did the common law, by reference to the factors that determine whether an individual reasonably may expect that an area immediately adjacent to the home will remain private. Conversely, the common law implies, as we reaffirm today, that no expectation of privacy legitimately attaches to open fields.

[W]e reject the suggestion that steps taken to protect privacy establish that expectations of privacy in an open field are legitimate. It is true, of course, that petitioner Oliver and respondent Thornton, in order to conceal their criminal activities, planted the marijuana upon secluded land and erected fences and "No Trespassing" signs around the property. And it may be that because of such precautions, few members of the public stumbled upon the marijuana crops seized by the police. Neither of these suppositions demonstrates, however, that the expectation of privacy was *legitimate* in the sense required by the Fourth Amendment. The test of legitimacy is not whether the individual chooses to conceal assertedly "private" activity. Rather, the correct inquiry is whether the government's intrusion infringes upon the personal and societal values protected by the Fourth Amendment. As we have explained, we find no basis for concluding that a police inspection of open fields accomplishes such an infringement.

Nor is the government's intrusion upon an open field a "search" in the constitutional sense because that intrusion is a trespass at common law. The existence of a property right is but one element in determining whether expectations of privacy are legitimate. "[E]ven a property interest in premises may not be sufficient to establish a legitimate expectation of privacy with respect to partic-

ular items located on the premises or activity conducted thereon." . . . The law of trespass, however, forbids intrusions upon land that the Fourth Amendment would not proscribe. For trespass law extends to instances where the exercise of the right to exclude vindicates no legitimate privacy interest. Thus, in the case of open fields, the general rights of property protected by the common law of trespass have little or no relevance to the applicability of the Fourth Amendment.

Affirmed.

Case Excerpt: *New Jersey* v. *T.L.O.*
Supreme Court of the United States (1985)
469 U.S. 325

A teacher at a New Jersey high school, upon discovering T.L.O., then a 14-year-old freshman, smoking a cigarette in a school lavatory in violation of a school rule, took her to the Principal's office. T.L.O., in response to an Assistant Vice Principal's questioning, denied that she had been smoking and claimed that she did not smoke at all. The Assistant Vice Principal demanded to see her purse, and upon opening it found a pack of cigarettes and a package of cigarette rolling papers commonly used to roll marijuana joints. He then searched the purse thoroughly and found marijuana, a pipe, plastic bags, a fairly substantial amount of money, an index card containing a list of students who owed T.L.O. money, and two letters that implicated her in selling marijuana. The State brought delinquency charges against T.L.O. in the Juvenile Court, which admitted the evidence and held that while the Fourth Amendment applies to searches by school officials, the search of T.L.O.'s purse was a reasonable one. The New Jersey Supreme Court reversed the conviction, holding that the search of the purse violated the Fourth Amendment.

Mr. Justice White delivered the Opinion of the Court.

* * *

We granted certiorari in this case to examine the appropriateness of the exclusionary rule as a remedy for searches carried out in violation of the Fourth Amendment by public school authorities. Our consideration of the proper application of the Fourth Amendment to the public

schools, however, has led us to conclude that the search that gave rise to the case now before us did not violate the Fourth Amendment. Accordingly, we here address only the questions of the proper standard for assessing the legality of searches conducted by public school officials and the application of that standard to the facts of this case.

* * *

In determining whether the search at issue in this case violated the Fourth Amendment, we are faced initially with the question whether that Amendment's prohibition on unreasonable searches and seizures applies to searches conducted by public school officials. We hold that it does.

* * *

Today's public school officials do not merely exercise authority voluntarily conferred on them by individual parents; rather they act in furtherance of publicly mandated educational and disciplinary policies. In carrying out searches and other disciplinary functions pursuant to such policies, school officials act as representatives of the State, not merely as surrogates for the parents, and they cannot claim the parents' immunity from the strictures of the Fourth Amendment.

To hold that the Fourth Amendment applies to searches conducted by school authorities is only to begin the inquiry into the standards governing such searches. Although the underlying command of the Fourth Amendment is always that searches and seizures be reasonable, what is reasonable depends on the context within which a search takes place. The determination of the standard of reasonableness governing any specific class of searches requires "balancing the need to search against the invasion which the search entails." On one side of the balance are arrayed the individual's legitimate expectations of privacy and personal security; on the other the government's need for effective methods to deal with breaches of public order.

* * *

Although this Court may take notice of the difficulty of maintaining discipline in the public schools today, the situation is not so dire that students in the schools may claim no legitimate expectation of privacy. We have recently recognized that the need to maintain order in a prison

is such that prisoners retain no legitimate expectations of privacy in their cells, but it goes almost without saying that "[t]he prisoner and the schoolchild stand in wholly different circumstances, separated by the harsh facts of criminal conviction and incarceration."

* * *

Nor does the State's suggestion that children have no legitimate need to bring personal property into the schools seem well anchored in reality. Students at a minimum must bring to school not only the supplies needed for their studies, but also keys, money, and the necessaries of personal hygiene and grooming. In addition, students may carry on their persons or in purses or wallets such nondisruptive yet highly personal items as photographs, letters, and diaries.

* * *

Against the child's interest in privacy must be set the substantial interest of teachers and administrators in maintaining discipline in the classroom and on school grounds. Maintaining order in the classroom has never been easy, but in recent years, school disorder has often taken particularly ugly forms: drug use and violent crime in the schools have become major health problems. Even in schools that have been spared the most severe disciplinary problems, the preservation of order and a proper educational environment requires close supervision of schoolchildren, as well as the enforcement of rules against conduct that would be perfectly permissible if undertaken by an adult.

* * *

How, then, should we strike the balance between the schoolchild's legitimate expectations of privacy and the school's equally legitimate need to maintain an environment in which learning can take place? It is evident that the school setting requires some easing of the restrictions to which searches by public authorities are ordinarily subject. The warrant requirement, in particular, is unsuited to the school environment: requiring a teacher to obtain a warrant before searching a child suspected of an infraction of school rules (or of the criminal law) would unduly interfere with the maintenance of swift and informal disciplinary procedures needed in the schools. Just as we have in other cases dispensed with the warrant requirement when "the burden of obtaining a warrant is likely to frustrate the governmental purpose behind the search," we hold today that school officials need not obtain a warrant before searching a student who is under their authority.

The school setting also requires some modification of the level of suspicion of illicit activity needed to justify a search. Ordinarily, a search— even one that may permissibly be carried out without a warrant—must be based upon "probable cause" to believe that a violation of the law has occurred. However, "probable cause" is not an irreducible requirement of a valid search. The fundamental command of the Fourth Amendment is that searches and seizures be reasonable, and although "both the concept of probable cause and the requirement of a warrant bear on the reasonableness of a search, . . . in certain limited circumstances neither is required.

* * *

We join the majority of courts that have examined this issue in concluding that the accommodation of the privacy interests of schoolchildren with the substantial need of teachers and administrators for freedom to maintain order in the schools does not require strict adherence to the requirement that searches be based on probable cause to believe that the subject of the search has violated or is violating the law. Rather, the legality of a search of a student should depend simply on the reasonableness, under all the circumstances, of the search. Determining the reasonableess of any search involves a twofold inquiry: first, one must consider "whether the . . . action was justified at its inception;" second, one must determine whether the search as actually conducted "was reasonably related in scope to the circumstances which justified the interference in the first place." Under ordinary circumstances, a search of a student by a teacher or other school official will be "justified at its inception" when there are reasonable grounds for suspecting that the search will turn up evidence that the student has violated or is violating either the law or the rules of the school. Such a search will be permissible in its scope when the measures adopted are reasonably related to the objectives of the search and not excessively intrusive in light of the age and sex of the student and the nature of the infraction.

* * *

Because the search resulting in the discovery of the evidence of marijuana dealing by T.L.O. was reasonable, the New Jersey Supreme Court's decision to exclude that evidence from T.L.O.'s juvenile delinquency proceedings on Fourth Amendment grounds was erroneous. Accordingly, the judgment of the Supreme Court of New Jersey is *Reversed.*

Endnotes

1. *Coolidge* v. *New Hampshire,* 403 U.S. 325 (1975).
2. *Horton* v. *California,* 496 U.S. 128 (1990).
3. *Minnesota* v. *Dickerson,* 113 S.Ct. 2130 (1993).
4. *Arizona* v. *Hicks,* 480 U.S. 321 (1987).
5. *Texas* v. *Brown,* 460 U.S. 730 (1983).
6. Id. at 740.
7. *Horton* v. *California,* 496 U.S. 128 (1990).
8. Elise B. Clare et al., "Seizure of Items in Plain View." 84 *The Georgetown Law Journal Twenty-Fifth Annual Review of Criminal Procedure* pp. 767–768 (1996).
9. *Terry* v. *Ohio,* 392 U.S. 1 (1968).
10. Supra note 3.
11. Greg Knopp et al., "Seizure of Items in Plain View." 83 *The Georgetown Law Journal Twenty-Fourth Annual Review of Criminal Procedure* pp. 714–718 (1995).

12. See Brett Harvey, "The Plain Touch Doctrine: A Proposal to Preserve Fourth Amendment Liberties During Investigatory Stops." 58 *Albany Law Review* pp. 871–915 (1995).

13. *United States* v. *Grubczak,* 793 F.2d 458 (2d Cir. 1986); for a comprehension review of federal case law in this area, see Knopp, supra note 11.

14. *United States* v. *Haley,* 669 F.2d 201 (4th Cir.) *cert denied,* 457 U.S. 1117 (1982); see Knopp, supra note 11.

15. *United States* v. *Miller,* 812 F.2d 1206 (9th Cir. 1987).

16. *United States* v. *Place,* 462 U.S. 696 (1983).

17. See Lina Shahin, "The Constitutional Posture of Canine Sniffs." 9 *Touro Law Review* pp. 645–697 (1993).

18. See *United States* v. *Dixon,* 51 F.3d 1376 (8th Cir. 1995).

19. *United States* v. *Beale,* 736 F.2d 1289, *cert denied,* 469 U.S. 1072 (1984); for a review of the federal case law in this area see Knopp, supra note 11.

20. *Katz* v. *United States,* 389 U.S. 347, 361 (1967). Justice Harlan's concurring opinion developed a two-part test for determining if a person may assert the protection of the Fourth Amendment, which asserts:
    1. a person must have an actual (subjective) expectation of privacy;
    2. the expectation must be one that society is prepared to recognize as reasonable.

21. Id. at 351.

22. *Hester* v. *United States,* 265 U.S. 57 (1924).

23. *Oliver* v. *United States,* 466 U.S. 170 (1984).

24. Id. at 178.

25. *United States* v. *Dunn,* 480 U.S. 294 (1987).

26. Id. at 301.

27. Id. at 302–303.

28. See Clifford S. Fishman, "Police Trespass and the Fourth Amendment: A Wall in Need of Mending." 22 *John Marshall Law Review* pp. 795–824 (1989).

29. See Neil McCable, "From Open Fields to Open Skies: The Constitutionality of Aerial Surveillance." 16 *Search and Seizure Law Report,* pp. 153–159 (1989).

30. *California* v. *Ciraolo,* 476 U.S. 207, 213 (1986).

31. Id. at 213–214.

32. Id. at 215.

33. *Florida* v. *Riley,* 488 U.S. 445 (1989).

34. See Jon Gavenman, "The Descent of Fourth Amendment Protections in Aerial Surveillance Cases." 17 *Hastings Constitutional Law Quarterly* pp. 725–757 (1990).

35. Wayne R. LaFave and Jerold H. Israel, *Criminal Procedure,* 2d ed. (St. Paul, Minn.: West, 1992), p. 134.

36. See C. Edward Nicholson, "Abandonment of Property Under the Fourth Amendment." 10 *Search and Seizure Law Report* pp. 97–102 (1983).

37. *Abel* v. *United States,* 362 U.S. 217 (1960).

38. *California* v. *Hodari D.,* 499 U.S. 621 (1991).

39. See Jon E. Lamella, "From Katz to Greenwood: Abandonment Gets Recycled from the Trash Pile—Can Our Garbage be Saved from the Court's Rummaging Hands?" 41 *Case Western Reserve Law Review* pp. 581–612 (1991).

40. *California* v. *Greenwood,* 486 U.S. 35 (1988).

41. *United States* v. *Scott,* 975 F.2d 927 (1st Cir. 1992).

42. *United States* v. *Certain Real Property Located at 987 Fisher Road,* 719 F. Supp. 1396 (E.D. Mich. 1989). For a review of the federal case law in this area see Jonathon R. Freeman, "Conduct Constituting a Search or a Seizure." 84 *The Georgetown Law Journal Twenty-Fifth Annual Review of Criminal Procedure* pp. 721 (1996).

43. *Camara* v. *Municipal Court,* 387 U.S. 523 (1967).

44. Id. at 537.

45. See Geoffrey G. Hemphill, "The Administrative Search Doctrine: Isn't This Exactly What the Framers Were Trying to Avoid?" 5 *Regents University Law Review* pp. 215–259 (1995).

46. *See* v. *City of Seattle,* 387 U.S. 541 (1967).

47. *New York* v. *Burger,* 482 U.S. 691 (1987).

48. Knopp et al., supra note 11, at 762.

49. *United States* v. *Biswell,* 406 U.S. 311 (1972).

50. *Marshall* v. *Barlow's, Inc.,* 436 U.S. 307 (1978).

51. Id. at 313.

52. See *Colonnade Catering Corp.* v. *United States,* 397 U.S. 72 (1970).

53. *Michigan* v. *Tyler,* 436 U.S. 499, 510 (1978).

54. *Michigan* v. *Clifford,* 464 U.S. 287 (1984).

55. Id. at 294.

56. See Katherine Auchincolss-Lorr, "Police Encounters of the Third Kind: The Role of Immigration Law and Policy in the Pre-Seizure Interrogation Strategies." 3 *Search and Seizure Law Report* pp. 105–112 (1993).

57. *Almeida-Sanchez* v. *United States,* 413 U.S. 266 (1973).

58. See *United States* v. *Adekunle,* 980 F.2d 985 (5th Cir. 1992), *cert. denied,* 113 S.Ct. 2380 (1993). For a review of the case law in this area see Knopp, supra note 11 at 750.

59. See *United States* v. *Oyekan,* 786 F.2d 832 (8th Cir. 1986).

60. See *United States* v. *Handy,* 788 F.2d 1357 (11th Cir. 1984).

61. *United States* v. *Montoya de Hernandez,* 473 U.S. 531 (1985).

62. Id.

63. *Almeida-Sanchez* v. *United States,* 413 U.S. 266 (1973).

64. *United States* v. *Brignoni-Ponce,* 422 U.S. 873 (1975).

65. Id. at 884.

66. *United States* v. *Ortiz,* 422 U.S. 891 (1975).

67. *United States* v. *Martinez-Fuerte,* 428 U.S. 543 (1976).

68. *Immigration and Naturalization Service* v. *Delgado,* 466 U.S. 210 (1984).

69. See Edward W. Lewis, "Searches of Probationers and Parolees After Griffin v. Wisconsin." 15 *Search and Seizure Law Report* pp. 25–32 (1988).

70. *Griffin* v. *Wisconsin,* 483 U.S. 868 (1987).

71. Id. at 879.

72. See *Morrissey* v. *Brewer,* 408 U.S. 471 (1972).

73. *O'Connor* v. *Ortega,* 480 U.S. 709 (1987).

74. See Dale Edward and F. T. Zane, "School Searches Under the Fourth Amendment." 72 *Cornell Law Review* pp. 368-396 (1987); and Ann L. Majestic, "Principles of Search and Seizure in the Public Schools." 18 *School Law Bulletin,* pp. 15–27 (1987).

75. *New Jersey* v. *T.L.O.,* 469 U.S. 325 (1985).

76. Id. at 337.

77. Id. at 339.

78. Id. at 469.

79. See *Cason* v. *Cook,* 810 F.2d 188 (8th Cir.), *cert denied,* 482 U.S. 930 (1987); see Knopp, supra note 11 at 764.

80. *Veronia School District 47J,* v. *Acton,* 115 S.Ct. 2386 (1995).

81. See Robert C. Farley, Jr., "Suspicionless, Random Urinalysis: The Unreasonable Search of the Student Athlete." *Temple Law Review* pp. 439–459 (Spring 1995); and Anita Richardson, "The Ever Widening Drug Exception to the Fourth Amendment." 22 *Search and Seizure Law Report* pp. 153–158 (1995).

82. *Skinner* v. *Railway Labor Executives Association,* 489 U.S. 602 (1989).

83. *National Treasury Employees Union* v. *Von Raab,* 489 U.S. 656 (1989).

84. See Thomas J. Hickey and Sue Titus Reid, "Testing Law Enforcement and Corrections Officers for Illegal Drug Use After Skinner and Von Raab." 19 *Public Administration Quarterly* pp. 26–41 (1995).

85. See John N. Norwood, "Drug Testing in the Private Sector and its Impact on Employees' Right to Privacy." *Labor Law Journal* pp. 731–748 (December 1994).

86. See Stephen D. Ellis, "Prisons and the Fourth Amendment Behind the Constitutional Iron Curtain." 38 *Rutgers Law Review* pp. 303–340 (1986).

87. *Hudson* v. *Palmer,* 468 U.S. 517 (1984).

88. Id. at 527.

89. *Bell* v. *Wolfish,* 441 U.S. 520 (1979).

9 HIGH TECHNOLOGY INVESTIGATION METHODS, ELECTRONIC EAVESDROPPING, AND RECORDING CONVERSATIONS

Outline

Key Terms

Chapter 8 considered several different exceptions to the Fourth Amendment's search warrant requirement. Chapter 9 concludes the text's discussion of Fourth Amendment issues. It analyzes the use of high technology, electronic surveillance, and other methods of sensory enhancement used by law enforcement officers to investigate crimes. High technology investigative methods have developed rapidly in recent years and include techniques such as wiretapping telephones, intercepting wireless communications and cellular telephone transmissions, using infrared cameras to photograph suspicious activities, or even observing suspicious areas with satellites. These methods of gathering evidence have generated substantial controversy and may lead to more debate as technology continues to improve. The benefits of using enhanced technology in the investigatory process include more effective criminal prosecutions. Some critics have suggested, however, that people may not be willing to sacrifice their personal privacy to improve the efficiency of the law enforcement process. The use of high technology by law enforcement officers may even conjure Orwellian images of the government acting as "Big Brother," by prying into the most sensitive areas of life. Highlight 9.1 presents an excerpt from Orwell's *1984.*

Both the congress and the courts have sought to strike a balance between the use of electronic monitoring by law enforcement officers and individual privacy interests. This has not always been an easy task.

The Use of Electronic Surveillance by Law Enforcement Agents

The use of electronic surveillance methods by law enforcement officers to monitor behavior is a twentieth century phenomenon. Our Constitution's framers could not have envisioned that orbiting satellites, infrared cameras, spike microphones, and sensitive sound recording devices would be developed to allow government agents access to even the most private conversations. Thus, unlike cases involving issues such as whether a search warrant affidavit is overly general, the law in this area of electronic surveillance is of a relatively recent vintage. The photograph on page 234 shows some of the devices that are used by law enforcement agents to conduct electronic surveillance.

The early cases on electronic surveillance and eavesdropping advanced a central proposition: unless government agents had committed a physical trespass into a constitutionally protected area when they conducted an electronic investigation, no violation of the Fourth Amendment had occurred.[1] In recent years, however, the Supreme Court has held that the issue of physical trespass has little bearing on whether a suspect's Fourth Amendment rights were violated by government agents using electronic surveillance. Rather, the central inquiry is whether a suspect has a justifiable expectation of privacy that society is prepared to recognize, regardless of where the surveillance occurs.[2]

Telephone Wiretapping and Electronic Surveillance

Telephone wiretapping techniques have existed since the 1920s. One of the early cases to reach the U.S. Supreme Court that confronted the issue of the legality of wiretapping was *Olmstead* v. *United States,*[3] where federal agents, acting without a search warrant,

Highlight 9.1

Excerpt from Orwell's *1984*

I understand HOW: I do not understand WHY.

He picked up the children's history book and looked at the portrait of Big Brother which formed its frontispiece. The hypnotic eyes gazed into his own. It was as though some huge force were pressing down upon you—something that penetrated inside your skull, battering against your brain, frightening you out of your beliefs, persuading you, almost, to deny the evidence of your senses. In the end the Party would announce that two and two made five, and you would have to believe it. It was inevitable that they should make that claim sooner or later: the logic of their position demanded it. Not merely the validity of experience, but the very existence of external reality was tacitly denied by their philosophy. The heresy of heresies was common sense. And what was terrifying was not that they would kill you for thinking otherwise, but that they might be right. For, after all, how do we know that two and two make four? Or that the force of gravity works? Or that the past is unchangeable? If both the past and the external world exist only in the mind, and if the mind itself is controllable—what then?

But no! His courage seemed suddenly to stiffen of its own accord. The face of O'Brien, not called up by any obvious association, had floated into his mind. He knew, with more certainty than before, that O'Brien was on his side. He was writing the diary for O'Brien—*to* O'Brien; it was like an interminable letter which no one would ever read, but which was addressed to a particular person and took its color from that fact.

The Party told you to reject the evidence of your eyes and ears. It was their final, most essential command. His heart sank as he thought of the enormous power arrayed against him, the ease with which any Party intellectual would overthrow him in debate, the subtle arguments which he would not be able to understand, much less answer. And yet he was in the right! They were wrong and he was right. The obvious, the silly, and the true had got to be defended. Truisms are true, hold on to that! The solid world exists, its laws do not change. Stones are hard, water is wet, objects unsupported fall toward the earth's center. With the feeling that he was speaking to O'Brien, and also that he was setting forth an important axiom, he wrote:

Freedom is the freedom to say that two plus two make four. If that is granted, all else follows.

[Excerpt from *Nineteen Eighty-Four*, by George Orwell, © 1944 by Harcourt Brace & Company and renewed 1977 by Sonia Brownell Orwell and Martin Secker and Warburg Ltd. Reprinted by permission of the publishers.]

had placed a wiretap on Olmstead's telephone lines and recorded his conversations. The Supreme Court ruled that the wiretap was lawful because the agents had not trespassed to install the listening device. This became known as the ***Olmstead* doctrine.** More recently, however, the Supreme Court has abandoned *Olmstead*'s reasoning.

The Modern Standard: **Katz v. United States**

In *Katz,* F.B.I. agents attached an electronic eavesdropping device to the exterior of a public telephone booth. This enabled them to intercept and record Katz's transmission of bets and wagers. Katz was convicted in U.S. District Court of using a telephone to transmit gambling information between different states in violation of federal gambling

Source: Jean Pierre Laffont/SYGMA

laws. On appeal to the Supreme Court the issue was whether the electronic eavesdropping violated the Fourth Amendment. The government argued that its agents had acted lawfully because they did not begin the electronic surveillance until a corroborative investigation had established a strong probability that Katz had used the telephone to transmit interstate wagering information. In addition, the surveillance was limited and did not intrude upon other parties' conversations. Further, the government argued that although the interior of the telephone booth may have been a private area, its agents had not intruded *into* that area. The recorded conversations should be admitted into evidence because the listening and recording device was attached to the *exterior* of the booth.

The Supreme Court overturned Katz's conviction because the F.B.I. had failed to obtain prior judicial authorization in the form of a search warrant before conducting the surveillance. Moreover, *Katz* v. *United States* rejected *Olmstead*'s trespass doctrine, stating:

> The government stresses the fact that the telephone booth from which the petitioner made his calls was constructed partly of glass, so that he was as visible after he entered it as he would have been if he had remained outside. But what he sought to exclude when he

entered the booth was not the intruding eye—it was the uninvited ear. He did not shed his right to do so, simply because he made his calls from a place where he might be seen. No less than an individual in a business office, in a friend's apartment, or in a taxicab, a person in a telephone booth may rely upon the protection of the Fourth Amendment. One who occupies it, shuts the door behind him, and pays the toll that permits him to place a call, is surely entitled to assume that the words he utters into the mouthpiece will not be broadcast to the world. To read the Constitution more narrowly is to ignore the vital role that the public telephone has come to play in private communication.[4]

Katz, therefore, established an important principle in Fourth Amendment law, including the law of electronic surveillance: government agents may not intrude into a private area (one in which a person has a justifiable expectation of privacy) without a search warrant to conduct criminal investigations. *Katz* makes it clear that two conditions must be satisfied in order for government agents to intercept lawful telephone communications or to conduct other types of electronic eavesdropping:

1. a statute that authorizes the eavesdropping in the circumstances of the particular case; and
2. prior magisterial authorization in the form of a search warrant.

Persons may retain their privacy rights even in areas readily accessible to the public, including telephone booths, public restrooms, and facilities owned by the government. To use the Supreme Court's language, this is because "[t]he Fourth Amendment protects people, not places."[5] This principle is termed the ***Katz* doctrine.**

The next section considers *Katz*'s first requirement, a statute that permits electronic eavesdropping in specified types of cases. Title III of the Omnibus Crime Control and Safe Streets Act of 1968 is a federal statute that regulates the interception of telephone communications and electronic eavesdropping.

Statutory Regulation of Wiretapping and Electronic Eavesdropping

The Supreme Court decided *Katz* in 1967. That same year, the Court reviewed the provisions of a New York State law that allowed electronic eavesdropping. In *Berger* v. *New York,*[6] the Court held that the challenged statute was unconstitutional for two reasons:

1. It contained a vague probable cause standard and the warrant was authorized for 60 days and permitted lengthy extensions. Search warrants could be issued without showing that a particular offense had been or was being committed and without describing specifically the conversations to be intercepted. Moreover, the 60 day authorization period was "the equivalent of a series of intrusions"[7] under a single showing of probable cause. Further, extensions of the warrant could be granted without an additional showing of probable cause.
2. It placed no restriction on when the wiretaps had to be concluded once the intended conversations had been intercepted.

Title III of the Omnibus Crime Control and Safe Streets Act of 1968

In response to *Berger* v. *New York,* the U.S. Congress passed the Omnibus Crime Control and Safe Streets Act of 1968.[8] This statute enables selected employees of the U.S. Justice Department to apply to a federal judge for a warrant to permit wiretapping or electronic eavesdropping. In Title III cases, an application for a warrant is termed a **surveillance application.** The warrant itself is termed a **surveillance order.** A surveillance application under Title III must contain all the following information:

1. A full and complete statement of the suspected offense.
2. A description of the facilities where the communications are to be intercepted.
3. A particular description of the communications sought to be seized.
4. The identity of the persons whose communications are to be intercepted and who are suspected of committing the offense.
5. A comprehensive statement of whether alternative investigative techniques have been tried and failed or why they appear unlikely to succeed or are too dangerous.
6. A statement of the time period for which the interception is to be conducted.[9]

A court may issue a warrant under Title III to intercept communications if it determines that probable cause supports an inference that:

1. a suspect is committing one of the crimes specified in Title III (these crimes include most felonies);
2. communications about the alleged offense will be intercepted with the intended interception; and
3. the location from which the communications are to be intercepted are being used for the commission of the offense.[10]

In addition, the court must find that in the circumstances of the case traditional investigative methods are not likely to succeed or would be too dangerous.[11] Moreover, an interception order is valid solely for the communications specified in the application. If agents overhear and wish to use new evidence of an incriminating nature, they must first obtain a new court order as soon as possible.

Title III provides that any person who by electronic means intentionally intercepts a conversation, except as allowed by the statute, is guilty of a crime.[12] A violation of this section is punishable by a fine or imprisonment for not more than five years or both.[13] Moreover, Title III provides a civil remedy for those whose communications are intercepted in violation of the statute. Damages may include the victim's actual damages as well as punitive damages, or statutory damages of $100 per day or $10,000.[14] In addition, Title III allows state or county prosecutors to apply to a state judge for a warrant in specified cases.[15]

Law enforcement agents may enter a structure to install and/or remove a listening device under a warrant allowed by Title III. In *Dalia* v. *United States,*[16] members of the F.B.I. entered an office to install and later remove a small listening device (a "bug") under a warrant that permitted them to intercept all oral communications at that office regarding an ongoing conspiracy. The warrant did not, however, expressly allow them to enter the office to install or remove the bug. The Supreme Court held that nothing in the Fourth Amendment or in Title III requires that search warrants must specify "the precise manner in which they are to be executed. On the contrary, it is generally left to the discretion of the executing officers to determine the details of how best to proceed with the performance of a search authorized by warrant . . ."[17]

Intercepting Communications under Title III without Prior Judicial Approval

A designated government agent may intercept communications under Title III without prior judicial approval in certain emergency situations, which include:

1. immediate danger of death or serious physical injury to any person,
2. conspiratorial activities threatening the national security interest, or
3. conspiratorial activities characteristic of organized crime that requires a wire, oral, or electronic communication to be intercepted before an order authorizing such interception can be obtained, and there are grounds upon which an order could be entered.[18]

Whenever Title III's emergency provision is used, the government agent must apply within 48 hours for a court order authorizing the interception, and it must terminate when the communication sought is obtained. In addition, if the national security is threatened by a foreign power, Title III does not restrict the Constitutional power of the President to take such measures as he deems necessary to protect the nation.[19]

As this discussion of Title III indicates, Congress intentionally made it difficult for law enforcement authorities to obtain court orders to allow them to wiretap telephone lines or to intercept other forms of communication. This is because free speech and unrestricted communication are the cornerstones of a democratic society, and individuals should be able to rely on the privacy of their conversations.

Title III regulates wiretapping and other electronic means of intercepting communications. It does not regulate the use of listening and recording devices or **wires** that may be worn by one party to a conversation without another party's knowledge. A wire is a small transmitter that may be used to broadcast conversations to government agents who then record the information. Neither the U.S. Congress, state legislatures, or the U.S. Supreme Court have demonstrated a substantial willingness to place restrictions similar to those contained in Title III on these important law enforcement investigatory tools.

Taping a Conversation with the Consent of One Party

You may recall that the *Katz* doctrine operates to protect a person's privacy from a governmental surveillance whenever he or she has a justifiable expectation of privacy. This principle applies regardless of whether the surveillance occurs in a traditionally private area or in a public place. When someone communicates with another, however, there is always a risk that the second party will reveal the contents of the communication. For example, suppose that Joe and Bob are both government employees. One morning, Joe makes a telephone call to Bob to discuss problems with their boss. Without telling Bob, Joe is actually soliciting information for the boss and records Bob's responses to several questions about their work environment. He then gives the recordings to the boss. In these circumstances, Bob has given up his privacy expectation in the information because he revealed it to someone else. He took the risk that Joe would not reveal it to others, such as the boss. Likewise, a person who reveals information that is relevant to a criminal investigation takes the risk that a second person will not reveal it to the police. There is no violation of Title III because, by virtue of revealing the information to another, the communicator has lost his or her justifiable expectation of privacy in the information. For example, if Mary telephones John to ask him to purchase cocaine, she takes the risk that John is a government informant who will tape record the conversation and give it to the police. It does not matter whether John or Mary initiated the telephone call. In most states, either party could lawfully tape record the conversation and disclose its contents without telling the other that the conversation was being recorded. Highlight 9.2, a Florida law regulating privacy rights, demonstrates that state legislatures consider the interception of electronic communications to be a very serious matter.

Despite Florida's law, the majority of states have a less restrictive rule for taping conversations—if one party to a communication decides to record it, or allows another to do so, there is no violation of the first party's justifiable expectation of privacy. The recording may be given to the police and may be used as evidence at a criminal trial. Moreover, if a law enforcement officer is a party to a conversation and records it without obtaining a warrant, it too is admissible at trial.[20]

A different situation is presented, however, when governmental agents acting without prior judicial approval tape record private communications between persons who have not consented to the taping. Highlight 9.3 presents a newspaper description of a case involving the government's electronic monitoring and taping of a prisoner's private jailhouse confession to a priest. Neither the prisoner nor the priest had consented to the taping. Incredibly enough, the county's district attorney had approved the surreptitious taping in advance.

Use of Secret Informants by Law Enforcement Agents

Anyone who has watched television programs or movies about U.S. law enforcement officers is aware of the important role played by informants, who are often themselves criminals. Chapters 3 and 4 presented a detailed discussion of the use of informants by law enforcement officers. For purposes of the present discussion of electronic surveillance, it is important to note that informants are frequently asked to wear wires when they obtain information from suspected criminals. The conversations are then broadcast to government agents in nearby locations who record the information. Transcripts and/or the actual recordings of the conversations are often introduced as evidence. Such recordings may provide riveting courtroom evidence that can sometimes seal a defendant's conviction.

Highlight 9.2

Florida Law Regulating Privacy Rights

§ 906. State constitutional right to privacy
Title 47

Except as otherwise provided by the Florida Constitution, every natural person has the right to be let alone and free from governmental intrusion into his private life. This right ensures that individuals are able to determine when, how, and to what extent information about them is communicated to others and to provide a zone of privacy into which not even government may intrude without invitation or consent.

The right of privacy demands that individuals be free from uninvited observation of or interference in those aspects of their lives that fall within the ambit of this zone of privacy unless the intrusion is warranted by the necessity of a compelling state interest. A legitimate, ongoing criminal investigation will satisfy the state's burden of demonstrating a compelling state interest when it establishes a clear connection between the illegal activity and the person whose privacy would be invaded. Thus, for example, when the state seeks to install a pen register it must show a reasonable founded suspicion that the targeted telephone line was being used for a criminal purpose.

The state also must demonstrate that the least intrusive means have been employed to accomplish its goal. In analyzing whether the least intrusive means were utilized, one must consider procedural safeguards in conjunction with the extent of the actual intrusion into privacy.

The portions of the statutes governing the security of communications that authorize interception of wire or oral communications are statutory exceptions to federal and state constitutional rights of privacy, and as such, must be strictly construed.

The general rule is that if a government informant agrees to wear a wire and speak with a suspect, any evidence recorded is admissible at a criminal trial. The process is not regulated by Title III because that statute exempts communications intercepted with the consent of a party to the conversation. In *On Lee* v. *United States,*[21] a government agent who was wearing a wire entered the defendant's business and attempted to solicit incriminating statements from him. The conversation was recorded by government agents outside the business. The Supreme Court held that the statements solicited by the undercover agent were admissible at On Lee's trial because the agent did not physically trespass onto On Lee's property. Because there was no physical trespass, there was no Fourth Amendment violation.

On Lee, like the pre-*Katz* cases involving other forms of electronic monitoring, used a physical trespass standard for determining whether a Fourth Amendment violation had occurred. *Katz,* however, changed the focus of the Fourth Amendment inquiry from whether government agents had physically trespassed to one that focuses on whether they had violated the defendant's justifiable expectation of privacy. *United*

Highlight 9.3

Judge: Jail Conversation a Sacrament

 A secretly tape-recorded conversation between a Catholic priest and an inmate of the Lane County Jail was a religious sacrament, a judge has ruled.

U.S. District Judge Owen Panner said Monday that although Conan Hale is not a Catholic, he was baptized a Christian, and the Rev. Timothy Mockaitis had gone to the jail with the intent of administering to him the sacrament of reconciliation.

Their jailhouse meeting April 22 was recorded by authorities.

The Catholic Church is seeking the destruction of the tape, calling it an ongoing violation of the constitutional guarantees of religious freedom.

The Rev. Michael Maslowsky, lawyer for the Archdiocese of Portland, said Monday's ruling in Portland is important because it recognizes the nature of the recording based solely on the statements of the individuals who were recorded.

It also recognized a longstanding legal tradition that blocks judges from deciding for an individual what is or is not religious, Maslowsky said. He said Panner did not listen to the tape before issuing his ruling.

Lane County District Attorney Doug Harcleroad publicly apologized in May for authorizing the taping. Harcleroad also pledged not to use it to persecute Hale, and turned it over to the court for safekeeping.

However, a Lane County judge decided last week to allow Hale's defense lawyers to listen to the tapes. Hale's defense lawyer, Terri Wood of Eugene, argued she needed to know what prosecutors learned from the tape so she can determine whether the contents might have any bearing on her case.

"Judge: Jail Conversation a Sacrament," *Bulletin,* August 6, 1996. Reprinted with permission.

States v. *White*[22] applied the *Katz* principle to cases involving the government's use of agents who are wired for sound. The rule that emerged from this case is that when a person places his trust in another he or she takes the risk that the second person will reveal the contents of the conversation.

The Entrapment Defense.   Persons who are arrested by undercover police officers sometimes use a defense to criminal charges termed **entrapment,** which occurs when police cause an individual to commit a crime that he or she did not contemplate and was not predisposed to commit. Street corner "wisdom" suggests that it is easy to establish an entrapment defense to criminal charges. This is patently false. There is no constitutional right to an entrapment defense and it is a very difficult defense to use successfully. In general, cases that successfully plead entrapment must demonstrate that the conduct of government agents went beyond acceptable limits, or that they "implant[ed] in an innocent person's mind the disposition to commit a criminal act, and then induce[d] commission of the crime so that the government [could] prosecute."[23] A defendant pleading entrapment faces an uphill battle under this heavy burden.

Two Tests for Determining Entrapment. Two primary tests have been used in the United States to determine if government agents have entrapped an unsuspecting person. Most states and the federal government have adopted the **subjective test,** which focuses on the defendant's predisposition to commit the charged offense, not on the conduct of government agents. This test was formulated by the Supreme Court in *Sherman* v. *United States.*[24] Under the subjective test, if the target of the investigation was predisposed to commit an offense, the entrapment defense will fail. As you might expect, a defendant's criminal record and prior conduct is relevant evidence to show his or her predisposition in jurisdictions using the subjective test. For example, suppose that Paul is charged with cultivating marijuana. Paul decides to use an entrapment defense and claims that Bill, a police undercover agent, encouraged him to plant the marijuana, gave him some seeds, and helped him to water the plants. Paul, however, was convicted on two previous occasions of possessing marijuana. In a jurisdiction using the subjective approach, Paul's defense is likely to fail because it would be easy for the prosecution to show that he was predisposed to commit the offense. If Paul had not used an entrapment defense, the prosecution would have been unable to introduce evidence of his prior convictions unless he testified at trial or in other unusual circumstances.

A second test for entrapment used in several states is termed the **objective test,** which focuses on the behavior of law enforcement agents. Under this test, the entrapment defense is established if police officers go too far to encourage a suspect to commit a crime. It is easy to see why this approach to determining entrapment is more appealing to criminal defendants. In the example above, if Bill, the police undercover agent, had supplied the marijuana seeds and helped to water the plants, it is quite possible that an entrapment defense would succeed. A jury could well conclude that the officer went too far to encourage Paul to commit the offense.

Case Law on the Entrapment Defense. A brief discussion of three Supreme Court precedents will help to illustrate the entrapment defense. In *United States* v. *Russell,*[25] the defendant was convicted in U.S. District Court for unlawfully manufacturing and selling methamphetamine (speed). Russell claimed that he was entrapped by a federal undercover agent who had provided an essential chemical ingredient for making methamphetamine. Without this chemical the drug could not have been made. On appeal, the U.S. Supreme Court, using the subjective test, upheld Russell's conviction because he was predisposed to commit the offense.

Hampton v. *United States*[26] presented the issue of whether a defendant may be convicted for the sale of heroin that he bought from a government agent. A Drug Enforcement Administration (D.E.A.) informant and Hampton were playing pool when he observed needle marks on the informant's arm. Hampton told the informant that he needed money and knew where he could obtain heroin. The informant stated that he could find a buyer for the heroin and contacted D.E.A. agents and arranged a sale. Hampton then sold the heroin to the D.E.A. agents. The Supreme Court sustained Hampton's conviction because he was predisposed to commit the offense and "the police, the government informer, and the defendant acted in concert with one another."[27] Moreover, the court asserted that if "the police engage in illegal activity in concert with a defendant beyond the scope of their duties the remedy lies, not in freeing the equally culpable defendant, but in prosecuting the police under the applicable provisions of state or federal law."[28]

More recently, the defendant in *Jacobson* v. *United States*[29] used an entrapment defense to defend successfully against child pornography charges. In 1984, the defendant had ordered two magazines, which contained nude photographs of teenage boys, from a California adult bookstore. Receiving these publications was not a violation of federal or state law at the time. A few months later, however, Congress passed a law making it illegal to use the mails to receive sexually explicit depictions of children. That same month, postal inspectors found Jacobson's name on the mailing list of the California bookstore that had mailed him the two magazines. Over the next two years, government agents made repeated efforts, through five fictitious organizations and a bogus pen pal, to determine whether Jacobson would break the new law by ordering sexually explicit photographs of children. After many such efforts, Jacobson responded and was charged and convicted with receiving child pornography.

The Supreme Court held that the government had failed to prove that Jacobson's predisposition to commit the offense "was independent and not the product of the attention that the Government had directed at [him] since January 1985."[30] Moreover, "[w]hen the Government's quest for conviction leads to the apprehension of an otherwise law-abiding citizen who, if left to his own devices, likely would have never run afoul of the law, the courts should intervene."[31] Jacobson's conviction was therefore reversed.

The above cases illustrate that entrapment is a very difficult defense to establish in criminal cases. Moreover, when law enforcement agents use electronic surveillance or recording it is often even more difficult for a defendant to establish an entrapment defense. It is hard to argue that a defendant was not predisposed to commit a crime if there is a clear record of his or her willing participation.

Other Types of Electronic Surveillance

The discussion of electronic surveillance and bugging to this point has focused on highly intrusive forms of electronic monitoring, including telephone wiretapping and recording personal conversations. It is clear that substantial Fourth Amendment concerns are raised by these types of governmental investigatory techniques. In recent years, however, the Supreme Court appears to have drawn a Fourth Amendment line between these highly intrusive electronic monitoring techniques and electronic investigations that are less intrusive. The rule that emerges from these cases is that some less intrusive forms of warrantless sensory enhancement by government agents do not constitute Fourth Amendment searches and therefore are subject to little or no constitutional restriction. The decisions have approved several different types of less intrusive forms of sensory enhancement by government agents. Each will be considered separately.

Flashlights.   As early as 1927, the Supreme Court held that a U.S. Coast Guard ship's use of a searchlight to view another ship was not a Fourth Amendment search.[32] More recently, in *United States* v. *Dunn*,[33] the Court held that a law enforcement officer's use of a flashlight to allow him to look inside a defendant's barn did not constitute an unlawful search. The rule is that a law enforcement officer's use of a flashlight to illuminate darkened areas is not a Fourth Amendment search.

X-Rays.   The general rule is that an X-ray of the human body is a highly intrusive search that may not be conducted unless officers first obtain a search warrant. In some limited circumstances, however, it appears that law enforcement officers without a search warrant may use X-rays to investigate criminal activity.[34] For example, if law enforcement agents at a U.S. border have reasonable suspicion to believe that a suspect is attempting to smuggle drugs, an X-ray examination is likely to be upheld.[35]

You may recall that persons have a substantially diminished expectation of privacy at U.S. borders. The case law does not indicate that police officers will be permitted to conduct routine warrantless X-ray searches of suspects in locations removed from the border.

Electronic Tracking Devices/Beepers.   Suppose that a person suspected of carrying a large quantity of illegal drugs is driving a car headed north on an interstate highway in Texas. The trip originated in Houston and the suspect appears to be headed to Dallas. May police officers acting without a search warrant follow and monitor the suspect's movements? Clearly, the answer is yes. Suppose further, however, that police officers without a search warrant decide to secretly attach an electronic tracking device or a beeper to the suspect's vehicle. Would this violate the suspect's Fourth Amendment rights? The courts are very likely to hold that it does not.

In *United States* v. *Knotts,*[36] representatives of a chemical manufacturing company notified law enforcement officials that Knotts, a former employee, had stolen chemicals that could be used to manufacture methamphetamine (speed). Agents learned that after Knotts had left the company he began to purchase the same chemicals from the Hawkins Chemical Company. With the company's consent, agents installed an electronic beeper in a five-gallon container of the chemical that was to be sold to Knotts. A co-defendant purchased the chemical and transported it by automobile to Knotts's secluded cabin in another state. Agents monitored the vehicle until it arrived at its destination and, after three days of surveillance, obtained a search warrant for the cabin and found evidence used to convict the defendants of manufacturing unlawful drugs. At trial, Knotts moved to suppress the evidence found at the cabin, asserting that the agents' warrantless monitoring of the electronic beeper violated the Fourth Amendment.

The Supreme Court held that monitoring the beeper did not violate Knotts's reasonable expectation of privacy. Chief Justice Rehnquist asserted that the beeper simply enabled the agents to monitor efficiently a vehicle traveling on the open roadway. According to Rehnquist, law enforcement efficiency should not be equated with unconstitutionality and "nothing in the Fourth Amendment prohibits the police from augmenting the sensory faculties bestowed upon them at birth with such enhancement as science and technology afforded them in this case."[37] Moreover, "a person traveling in an automobile on public thoroughfares has no reasonable expectation of privacy in his movements from one place to another."[38]

Knotts established an important Fourth Amendment principle in electronic monitoring cases involving vehicles traveling on public roadways: if police officers use electronic devices to enhance their ability to conduct a surveillance in a public area, the Fourth Amendment is not violated because the same results could have been attained by ordinary surveillance. You should bear in mind, however, that *Knotts* involved a police surveillance of a vehicle traveling in plain sight on a public highway. Later cases indicate that when an electronic investigation intrudes into an area that has received historically a greater degree of protection, the *Knotts* principle may yield to important Fourth Amendment interests.

United States v. *Karo,*[39] decided one year after *Knotts,* helped to clarify the issue of electronic beeper monitoring by law enforcement agents. *Karo* presented the issue of whether governmental monitoring of an electronic beeper in a private residence violates the Fourth Amendment rights of those who have a legitimate interest in the privacy of the home. The Court held that the warrantless use of an electronic beeper by government agents to obtain information they could not have obtained from outside the house violated the Fourth Amendment.

Pen Registers and Bank Records.   A **pen register** is an electronic device that records the telephone numbers that are dialed from a particular telephone. Pen registers do not record telephone conversations. They may, however, provide valuable evidence in criminal cases. For example, suppose that in a case charging several defendants with a **criminal conspiracy,** a common enterprise involving two or more people for criminal purposes, for plotting to blow up famous U.S. landmarks, the prosecution shows that one defendant had telephoned the other defendants on many different occasions during a two-week period. This fact is **circumstantial evidence** that may lead a jury to conclude that the defendants were involved in a criminal conspiracy. Circumstantial evidence is all evidence other than eyewitness testimony that does not prove directly that a suspect committed a crime, but may provide an inference that he or she did so.

In *New York* v. *New York Telephone Co.,*[40] the Supreme Court held that Title III does not govern the use of pen registers because these devices do not record the contents of telephone conversations. Moreover, a U.S. District Court judge may compel a telephone company to assist government agents in the installation of such a device. In a later case the Supreme Court went even further. In *Smith* v. *Maryland,*[41] it held that the use of pen registers by government agents does not constitute a Fourth Amendment search and seizure. Furthermore, a person who uses a telephone has no legitimate expectation of privacy in the numbers dialed because by dialing the telephone he or she voluntarily discloses the numbers to the telephone company. The telephone company, in turn, may choose to disclose the numbers to law enforcement officials. In 1986, however, Congress passed a law that requires law enforcement officers to obtain a court order before installing a pen register on a telephone.[42]

In 1976, the Supreme Court extended its reasoning in pen register cases to a suspect's banking records. In *United States* v. *Miller,*[43] the Court held that a defendant had no reasonable expectation of privacy in checks, deposit slips, and account statements that were given to his bank. This is because the "Fourth Amendment does not prohibit the obtaining of information revealed to a third party and conveyed by him to government authorities, even if that information is revealed on the assumption that it will be used only for a limited purpose and the confidence placed in the third party will not be betrayed."[44]

The preceding cases further emphasize an important Fourth Amendment principle: if a person knowingly exposes something to the public it will not receive Fourth Amendment protection and law enforcement agents may gain access to the information without a search warrant.

Aerial Surveillance.   Law enforcement agents may use airplanes and helicopters to conduct aerial surveillance of suspected criminal activities. In *California* v. *Ciraolo*,[45] police officers, who suspected that Ciraolo was growing marijuana, used a small airplane flying at 1,000 feet to look into his yard. A search warrant was obtained based on their observations and marijuana plants were discovered. Although Ciraolo had a subjective expectation of privacy in the yard, the "expectation that his garden was protected from such observation is unreasonable and is not an expectation that society is prepared to honor."[46] Further,

> In an age where private and commercial flight in the public airways is routine, it is unreasonable for [Ciraolo] to expect that his marijuana plants were constitutionally protected from being observed with the naked eye from an altitude of 1,000 feet. The Fourth Amendment simply does not require the police traveling in the public airways at this altitude to obtain a warrant in order to observe what is visible to the naked eye. . . .[47]

The rule that emerged from this case is that police officers flying in navigable airspace do not need a search warrant to conduct aerial surveillance. If they observe suspected criminal activity as a result of an aerial surveillance, they may use their information to obtain a warrant to search the area.

This rule received additional support in *Florida* v. *Riley*,[48] where police officers flying in a helicopter at an altitude of 400 feet observed marijuana plants growing in Riley's partially open greenhouse. The Supreme Court held that the aerial surveillance did not violate the Fourth Amendment because "[a]ny member of the public could legally have been flying over Riley's property in a helicopter at an altitude of 400 feet and could have observed Riley's greenhouse. The police officer did no more."[49]

Telescopic Cameras, Satellite Surveillance, and Thermal Imagery.   A police officer's use of a camera with a traditional telephoto lens to photograph suspected criminal activity does not violate the Fourth Amendment. In *Dow Chemical Company* v. *United States*[50] law enforcement agents used a sophisticated $22,000 aerial surveillance camera to photograph the defendant's property. The Supreme Court held that neither the use of an airplane to fly over the defendant's property, nor the use of the specialized surveillance camera violated the defendant's reasonable expectation of privacy. Therefore, the agents were not required to obtain a search warrant before photographing the area.

The Supreme Court has not ruled, however, on whether law enforcement agents are required to obtain a search warrant in cases involving extremely sophisticated telescopic equipment or satellite technology. *Dow Chemical* suggests that in such cases a defendant's privacy expectation *may* be protected against warrantless surveillance. One writer has recently stated that the use of satellite technology by law enforcement agents may seriously threaten Fourth Amendment privacy rights. Although the courts have not yet decided this issue, which will become even more important as technology continues to develop, she asserts that law enforcement agents should be required to obtain a search warrant before conducting a satellite surveillance.[51]

Thermal imagery is a process that uses electronic sensors to identify and produce a graphic image of radiant heat energy. It was first developed by the U.S. Army for use in locating enemy tanks and other vehicles during combat.[52] Some law enforcement agencies have used thermal imagery recently to detect the heat emissions from the grow lights in buildings housing indoor marijuana-growing operations. The information is then used to help establish probable cause for the issuance of a search warrant. The U.S. Supreme Court has not yet determined whether a law enforcement agency's warrantless use of thermal imagery violates the Fourth Amendment. Several lower courts have split on the issue.

In *United States* v. *Ishmael,*[53] the Fifth Circuit U.S. Court of Appeals, using the *Katz* test, held that although a person has a subjective expectation of privacy in his home, he or she has no objective privacy expectation because it is not one that society is prepared to accept as reasonable. It therefore held that the warrantless use of thermal imagery by law enforcement agents to conduct a surveillance of the exterior of defendant's home did not violate the Fourth Amendment. Likewise, the Arizona Court of Appeals has held that the use of thermal imagery by law enforcement agents does not violate a defendant's Fourth Amendment rights.[54] The Washington Court of Appeals, in contrast, has held that a law enforcement agency's use of thermal imagery to survey a defendant's home is a violation of the Washington State Constitution.[55]

The Supreme Court's most recent decisions involving law enforcement officers' use of high technology for investigating crimes suggest that the warrantless use of thermal imaging techniques, which survey a home's exterior for heat emissions, may well be permitted. Thermal imaging cases may be readily distinguished from *U.S.* v. *Karo,* where the Supreme Court held that monitoring an electronic beeper taken inside a suspect's home violated the Fourth Amendment. Until this issue is finally settled, however, it is a good law enforcement practice to obtain a search warrant to conduct a thermal scan whenever possible.

Electronic Mail (E-mail).   Electronic mail has become an important aspect of modern life in the United States. Each day billions of electronic messages are sent, read, and routinely discarded. Although many people would like to believe that their messages are private, in a legal sense this issue remains unresolved. Some cases suggest that a person has no reasonable expectation of privacy in the contents of his or her E-mail transmissions.[56] Moreover, as Highlight 9.4 indicates, employers, associates, or law enforcement agents may access the information contained in E-mail transmissions.[57]

Highlight 9.4

E-mail as Evidence

 When a Massachusetts bank learned it had just bought a piece of land with hazardous waste buried on it, lawyers filed suit and sifted through the seller's records to learn if knowledge of the dump had been hidden during the transaction.

But it was not until a computer sleuth, John Jessen, armed with a court order, tapped into the selling company's computer files that they found the proverbial smoking gun, in the form of an electronic message between the broker and a company official.

"Eric, the papers have been signed and the bank is now the owner of Parcel 13," the e-mail read. "We made it through the whole process without alerting them of the waste site on the northeast corner."

More and more, computer-savvy lawyers are demanding that such computer files, especially e-mail correspondences, be part of discoverable evidence in lawsuits over trade secrets, sex and race discrimination, and questionable dismissals, as if the words were pulled from a cabinet file drawer rather than a computer disc.

For many companies and the employees within them, Jessen's arrival marks a worst-case scenario. He has the seemingly magical ability to resurrect years' worth of e-mail and deleted files that computer users wishfully assumed had been zapped from the system long ago.

Such ability of Jessen and a few others has sparked a furious debate in legal circles, and has raised a host of questions among corporate computer users, most notably, isn't an e-mail correspondence between two workers private? The answer, in a nutshell: no.

"People are stunned to learn it," said Michael Patrick, a Palo Alto, Calif., lawyer who wrote a book on the use of computer files in court suits. "Their jaws drop. I tell in-house lawyers that they have to get people to realize that this is for real. Paint a picture: 'Look, folks, next time you are sending an e-mail message, repeat the mantra that a lawyer outside of the company will look at this and show it to a judge.'"

Jessen, owner of Seattle-based Electronic Evidence Discovery, one of only two companies in the country that specialize in computer sleuthing, said a personal computer isn't actually personal, not when it's at a company, and the delete button rarely means delete, not when there are little-known backup tapes running all hours of the day that store old files and e-mail messages for weeks, months and even years at a time. It's just that few people, even experts, can manipulate them, he said.

Typically, Jessen will arrive at a company with a court order giving him access to the computer system so he can search for potential evidence in a lawsuit. Invariably, lawyers are especially interested in deleted files and e-mail correspondences, the latter because that is where people let down their guard and write thoughts they might never publicly speak or commit to paper.

"People just don't use the same level of care when they are putting things into the computer," said Jessen, sitting in his Seattle office. "They have this false sense of privacy. These are not personal computers."

Said Joan Feldman, owner of Seattle-based Computer Forensics Inc., the rival company: "E-mail is where people are honest, it is where they are joking, and it's where they are using their creativity—what your lawyer would hate but my client would love."

Time and again, such e-mail has yielded the smoking gun in lawsuits, with the result being enormous judgments in favor of the plaintiff.

In one particular redlining case, Jessen said he found an e-mail message from a bank official that said, "We're not going to approve of anything in that part of town."

In his searches, Jessen often comes across company employees using their computers for extracurricular purposes. One employee of a Philadelphia

(Continued)

(Concluded)

media company was spending an average of six hours a day downloading pornography into his computer system, repackaging it and then selling it at computer fairs, Jessen said. Accountants are constantly found doing the books of other companies.

"One lawyer told me one day, 'If other people write the same garbage in e-mail that I do, I want to see it,'" Jessen said.

Lawyers in the nation's computer corridors are increasingly turning to this kind of discovery, specialists said. Jessen and Feldman routinely spend days and even weeks at a time on the road, much of it in Boston, Philadelphia, New York, Washington and Silicon Valley, Calif., and both are often hired by companies to seek advice on how they can protect themselves from a rival's foray into their computer systems in a court suit. Still, most lawyers, especially older ones, have yet to turn to computer files for discovery.

"Lawyers are not as savvy as the technical people, the people who know what's available electronically," said Jean Pechette, a lawyer with the Chicago firm Pattishall, McAuliffe, Newbury, Hilliard & Geraldson, and a specialist in computer evidence. "They tend to be behind the times. . . . But more and more, lawyers are waking up to the notion of seeking electronic based discovery in their motions."

Within legal circles, a debate is raging about how public expectations over e-mail privacy do not match the law, and whether the law should be changed. Most workers think their own firm cannot even peruse their e-mail. But unless that company has led them to expect that their mail is off limits, it is fair game.

"The law hasn't caught up yet with the expectations of employees," Patrick said. "Lots of employees think there is more privacy."

Until then, there will be boom times for the likes of Jessen and Feldman, and Feldman is about to open a second office in Washington. Jessen alone is amid 118 litigations now, and advises 18 Fortune 500 companies how to quickly dispose of their computer data.

One case Jessen was called in on was particularly pointed. A high-level executive with a Manhattan health company had a new technology that allows users to tape themselves with a tiny camera built into their monitor, send it through the system and have it appear on the recipient's screen as a talking, moving image.

One night, arriving at her hotel, she flipped open her portable computer and began recording such a message. Sitting before her laptop in the privacy of her room, she teasingly disrobed, performed what a corporate lawyer would later describe as a "shimmy," and purred to the intended recipient, a fellow married colleague, "Hurry to the hotel and here's what you get tonight."

Problem is, she struck the wrong button on her computer, and the video flashed on the screens of more than 400 employees throughout her health company—subordinates, bosses and people who had never met her before.

Jessen was asked to come in and do damage control and educate workers on the dangers of e-mail. Shortly after the video message was distributed around the company, bootleg versions showed up on floppy discs and were sold at computer fairs.

"It was like the dance that wouldn't die," he said.

From Brian McGrory, "E-mail as Evidence," *The Boston Globe,* October 19,1995, p. 1. {Reprinted courtesy of The Boston Globe.]

Cordless Telephones, Cellular Transmissions, and Electronic Paging Devices.   Privacy in wireless communications may be the Fourth Amendment problem of the decade.[58] Wireless communication devices such as cellular telephones, cordless telephones, and automated pagers use the public airwaves and may be intercepted easily.[59] In fact, in 1984, radio operators even intercepted President Ronald Reagan's secret communications aboard Air Force One.[60]

In 1986, the U.S. Congress passed the Electronic Communications Privacy Act (ECPA).[61] This law was designed as a civil counterpart to Title III that is intended to protect the privacy of wire and oral communications. It provides a civil remedy to any person "whose wire, oral, or electronic communication is intercepted, disclosed, or intentionally used in violation" of the Act. It prohibits the intentional interception of *cellular* mobile telephone and automated paging devices. Title III does not protect the radio transmissions from a cordless telephone.[62]

The U.S. Supreme Court has not considered the issue of whether a warrantless *cordless* telephone transmission interception by law enforcement agents violates the Fourth Amendment. At least one state court has held, however, that cordless telephone users have no reasonable expectation of privacy in the contents of their communications. In *State* v. *Delaurier,*[63] a child playing with a standard radio overheard Delaurier's cordless telephone conversations. The child's mother informed the police that she had heard a conversation involving an unlawful drug sale. Police officers tuned into the same frequency and recorded Delaurier's conversations without a search warrant and Delaurier was convicted of selling unlawful drugs. On appeal, the State Supreme Court upheld Delaurier's conviction and rejected his contention that the officers' interception of the telephone transmissions violated the Fourth Amendment and the state constitution.

Cellular telephone users are protected by Title III and the ECPA because cellular transmissions are specifically included as "wired" communications under the Act. Therefore, a cellular telephone user has a reasonable expectation of privacy and is protected against the warrantless interception of his or her cellular communications.[64] The general rule is that a person who communicates over public radio waves has no reasonable expectation of privacy in the contents of his or her communication. Likewise, paging devices that use tonal sounds are not protected by Title III or the ECPA and may be intercepted by law enforcement agents acting without a search warrant.[65] Voice and digital display pagers do appear to be protected by Title III because they are considered forms of "wired" communications.[66] If you are somewhat confused at this point about precisely what types of communications are protected from interception, you are not alone. This unsettled area of the law awaits clarification by the courts. Until this happens, as one writer has pointed out, "many wireless users will have to guess whether they have the right to expect privacy."[67]

A Right to Privacy on the Internet and in Personal Computer Files?   Communications on the information superhighway, the Internet, are a fact of modern life. Millions of people access the Internet on a daily basis. The information superhighway is, however, a two-way street, as incidents of computer hacking illustrate. Using widely available computer technology, law enforcement officials may be able to access information contained on the hard disc-drives of millions of internet users. Because this area is at the cutting edge of U.S. law, it is interesting to speculate about whether U.S. courts would recognize a constitutional right to privacy on the Internet and in personal computer files. One writer has stated:

> As we enter a new age . . . in which it may be possible for the authorities to scan broadly for evidence of illegal conduct without learning anything else, we must ask whether a

freedom from such surveillance is not part of the "right of the people to be secure in their persons, houses, papers and effects, against unreasonable searches and seizures.[68]

For example, suppose that law enforcement agents decide to conduct a warrantless search for pornographic materials through hundreds of millions of computer files located on hard disk drives owned by private citizens throughout the United States. Would such a warrantless intrusion violate the Fourth Amendment? There is at present no clear answer to this question.

Opponents of such computerized searches are likely to point out that the computers being searched are located most often inside of homes and should therefore be accorded the most stringent Fourth Amendment protection. As in *United States* v. *Karo,* where an electronic beeper allowed police officers to monitor activities inside a private residence, these searches may violate the homeowner's subjective expectation of privacy.

Computer search advocates are likely to maintain that the Internet is a vast public forum. Once material is placed on the Internet it is part of the public domain and may be accessed by millions of people. Therefore, using the Fourth Amendment test established in *Katz,* persons have no subjective privacy expectation that society is prepared to recognize. In any event, in the next several years U.S. courts will have the opportunity to decide novel and fascinating cases that will dramatically affect the quality of life in the information age.

Summary

Chapter 9 concludes the text's discussion of Fourth Amendment issues and analyzes the use of high technology, electronic surveillance, and other means of sensory enhancement by law enforcement officers to investigate crimes. High technology investigative methods have developed rapidly in recent years and include techniques such as wiretapping telephones, using infrared cameras to photograph suspicious activities, or even observing suspicious areas with satellites.

The early cases held that unless government agents had committed a physical trespass into a constitutionally protected area, no violation of the Fourth Amendment had occurred. More recently the Supreme Court has held that the issue of physical trespass has little bearing on whether a suspect's Fourth Amendment rights were violated by government agents using electronic surveillance. The central inquiry is whether a suspect has a justifiable expectation of privacy that society is prepared to recognize, regardless of where the surveillance occurs.

The modern standard for electronic surveillance was established in *United States* v. *Katz,* which concluded that government agents may not intrude into a private area without a search warrant to conduct criminal investigations. Therefore, persons may retain their privacy rights even in areas traditionally accessible to the public.

Wiretapping and electronic eavesdropping is controlled by Title III of the Omnibus Crime Control and Safe Streets Act of 1968. The requirements for obtaining a search warrant under Title III are quite demanding, however, and require a strong showing of probable cause. Title III provides that any person who by electronic means intercepts a conversation, except as allowed by the statute, is guilty of a crime. A violation of this statute is punishable by a fine or imprisonment for not more than five years or both.

When persons communicate there is always a risk that someone will reveal the contents of a communication. In most states, either party to a conversation may lawfully tape record a conversation and disclose its contents without telling the other party that the conversation was being recorded. A minority of states have passed laws, however, that prohibit one-party taping of private communications.

Wires are electronic transmitting devices that may be worn by police informants to obtain information from suspected criminals. The conversations may be broadcast to government agents in nearby locations who record the information and use it as evidence. If a government informant agrees to wear a wire and speak with a suspect, any evidence recorded is admissible at a criminal trial.

Entrapment defense issues arise often in cases involving secret government informants. Entrapment occurs when government agents implant in an innocent person's mind the disposition to commit a criminal act, and then induce commission of the crime so that the government may prosecute. Two tests have been developed to determine if government agents have entrapped an unsuspecting person. Most states have adopted the subjective test, which focuses on the defendant's predisposition to commit the charged offense, not on the conduct of government agents. A second test used in some states is termed the objective test, which focuses on the conduct of law enforcement agents, and asks if they went too far to encourage a suspect to commit a crime.

Less intrusive forms of electronic monitoring often do not require a search warrant. A police officer's use of a flashlight during the nighttime to examine a suspect's property does not violate the Fourth Amendment. Likewise, placing an electronic beeper on an automobile to allow its movements to be monitored on a public roadway is lawful. In contrast, placing a similar device on a parcel that was taken into a private residence violates the Fourth Amendment privacy rights of those with a legitimate interest in the privacy of the home. The Supreme Court has held that government agents may use pen registers that record the telephone numbers dialed from a particular telephone without a warrant because these devices do not record the contents of telephone conversations. A person who uses a telephone has no legitimate expectation of privacy in the numbers dialed because by dialing the telephone he or she voluntarily discloses them to the telephone company. The Supreme Court has extended this same proposition to a suspect's banking records, including checks, deposit slips, and account statements. If such materials are given voluntarily to a bank, bank officials may convey the information to law enforcement agents.

The Supreme Court has held that suspects have little privacy expectation in areas that may be viewed without a search warrant by law enforcement officers using airplanes and helicopters. Likewise, officers without a search warrant may use high-powered cameras to survey a defendant's property. Several lower courts have held that law enforcement agencies may without a warrant use thermal imagery techniques to try to detect indoor marijuana growing operations.

E-mail, cordless telephones, cellular transmissions, and electronic paging devices are considered as well. Most cases suggest that a person has no reasonable expectation of privacy in the contents of his or her E-mail transmissions. Similarly, it is doubtful that the courts will recognize a right to privacy in *cordless* telephone transmissions because these devices use radio waves that are easily accessible to the public. *Cellular* telephone users, however, are protected by Title III and the Electronic Communications Privacy Act (ECPA). These areas of law are new and await clarification by the courts.

The Internet is a two-way street that may eventually allow law enforcement officials to access personal computer files. U.S. courts will be asked in the future to decide whether there is a reasonable expectation of privacy in computer files and on information presented on the Internet.

Review Questions

1. Discuss the early standard (the *Olmstead* doctrine) for the government's use of electronic surveillance. How did *Katz* v. *United States* change that standard?

2. Discuss Title III of the Omnibus Crime Control and Safe Streets Act of 1964.
   a. Present the requirements for a warrant application under Title III.
   b. What must a court find in order to issue a wiretap order under Title III?

3. Hypothetical situation: Joe makes a telephone call to Bob to discuss a possible marijuana sale. Unknown to Bob, Joe tape records the conversation and gives it to the police who then give it to prosecutors to use in Bob's trial for conspiracy to sell marijuana. Before trial, Bob's lawyer moves to suppress the recorded conversations. How is the trial court likely to rule on this motion? Why?

4. Discuss the state of the law involving the use of informants who wear listening devices and record conversations with suspected criminals. Are such recorded conversations likely to be admitted into evidence at a criminal trial? Why?

5. Discuss the entrapment defense to criminal charges. Distinguish between two tests that courts may use to determine if a defendant was entrapped by law enforcement agents. Why is it so difficult to establish an entrapment defense? (Use relevant case law to illustrate your answer.)

6. Discuss the legality of the following law enforcement investigatory techniques:
   a.. The use of electronic beepers to follow automobiles on public roadways.
   b. The use of electronic beepers to monitor activities inside a private residence.
   c. The use of pen registers.
   d. Examining a suspect's banking records.

7. Discuss the lawfulness of the use of aerial surveillance by law enforcement officers.

8. Discuss the current state of the law involving the following law enforcement investigatory techniques:
   a. Telescopic cameras.
   b. Highly sophisticated telescopic equipment or satellite technology.
   c. Thermal imagery.

9. Discuss whether a person has a reasonable expectation of privacy in the following types of communications:
   a. Electronic mail (E-mail).
   b. Cordless telephone transmissions.
   c. Cellular telephone transmissions.

Issues for Analysis and Discussion

1. "The Fourth Amendment protects people, not places." Discuss the importance of this assertion for the development of Fourth Amendment protections.

2. Present arguments regarding whether persons should have a reasonable expectation of privacy in the contents of information communicated on the Internet information superhighway and in the contents of personal computer files.

3. In *United States* v. *Ishmael,* the Fifth Circuit U.S. Court of Appeals stated that a thermal imager "poses no greater intrusion on one's privacy than a precise mapping camera, an electronic beeper, or a pen register." Do you agree with the Court's holding in this case? Use the Court's "privacy expectation" method of analysis to develop an argument that law enforcement agents' use of thermal imagery constitutes a highly significant intrusion on a person's privacy.

CASE EXCERPT: *UNITED STATES V. ISHMAEL*
UNITED STATES COURT OF APPEALS, FIFTH CIRCUIT (1995)
48 F.3d 850

In 1992, a confidential source informed D.E.A. Agent Paul Black that he had delivered numerous truck loads of concrete to the Ishmaels' secluded property. The defendants took inordinate measures to conceal the need for the concrete. Black entered the property and saw two mobile homes and a trailer, however, he did not witness any illegal activity. After examining Rohn Ishmael's criminal record, Black found at least four separate marijuana-related incidents, several of which involved the cultivation of marijuana. After observing the area from the air, Black suspected that the Ishmaels were cultivating marijuana in a structure beneath a steel building. The D.E.A. then used a helicopter with a thermal imager and flew over the property at approximately 500 to 1,000 feet. The D.E.A. used the thermal imager's readings, along with extensive information gathered by Agent Black, to obtain a warrant to search the steel building and its substructure on the Ishmael's property. The officers executed the warrant and discovered 770 marijuana plants and several firearms. After being indicted in October 1993, the Ishmaels moved to suppress the evidence. They argued that the readings from the thermal imager constituted an unconstitutional search and that, without those readings, the D.E.A. did not have probable cause to obtain a warrant. The U.S. District Court granted the motion to suppress.

Mr. Justice DeMoss delivered the opinion of the Court.

* * *

In reviewing a district court's ruling on a motion to suppress, we review the court's conclusions of law de novo and its findings of fact for clear error. Furthermore, we view the evidence in a light most favorable to the prevailing party, which in this case is the Ishmaels.

The warrantless use of thermal imagers by the police has spawned a fair amount of search and seizure jurisprudence over the last several years. Though the Fifth Circuit has yet to squarely address this issue, three of our sister circuits have, and each has concluded that such use is not a "search" proscribed by the Fourth Amendment. We now hold that the warrantless use of a thermal imager in an "open field" does not violate the Fourth Amendment.

The Fourth Amendment provides in part: "The right of the people to be secure in their persons, houses, papers, and effects, against unreasonable searches and seizures, shall not be violated." As in any Fourth Amendment surveillance case, our analysis begins with *Katz* v. *United States.* The Supreme Court in *Katz* enunciated its two-prong test for determining whether a warrantless search violated a defendant's legitimate expectation of privacy: the defendant must have exhibited a subjective expectation of privacy, and that expectation must be one society is prepared to recognize as reasonable. With regard to the first prong, the government maintains that the Ishmaels did not exhibit a subjective expectation of privacy because they made no effort to conceal the heat emanating from the building.

* * *

[U]nless we intend to render *Katz*'s first prong meaningless, we must conclude that the Ishmaels exhibited a subjective expectation that their hydroponic laboratory would remain private. Though the Ishmaels did not—indeed, could not—take every precaution against the detection of the hydroponic laboratory, the balance of the evidence demonstrates that the Ishmaels exhibited a subjective expectation of privacy.

We now must address whether the government's intrusion on the Ishmael's subjective expectation of privacy with a thermal imager was a reasonable one. It is at this point in the analysis that the use of technology, and its degree of sophistication, becomes an issue, because more sophisticated forms of technology increase the likelihood that their warrantless use will constitute an unreasonable intrusion.

* * *

[T]he mere fact that the police have employed relatively sophisticated forms of technological surveillance does not render the surveillance unconstitutional. While technology certainly gives law enforcement a leg up on crime, the Supreme Court has "never equated police efficiency with unconstitutionality." The crucial inquiry, as in any search and seizure analysis, is whether the technology reveals "intimate details."

A thermal imager, according to the government, is no more intrusive than the other animate and inanimate means of surveillance that the Supreme Court has concluded does not offend the Fourth Amendment. That is, like the trained canine in *Place* or the precise mapping camera in *Dow Chemical,* a thermal imager is an acceptable surveillance technique because it does not reveal intimate details within the structure being scanned. . . . The Ishmaels contend, however, that a thermal imager is the functional equivalent of an X-ray machine in that it allows officers to "see" within a structure what it otherwise cannot see with the naked eye. Specifically, they argue, a thermal imager measures heat that is generated *within* a structure and, to that extent, constitutes an unreasonable intrusion on one's Fourth Amendment privacy. The Ishmaels . . . argue that a thermal imager is the type of "sophisticated technology" that the Court in *Dow Chemical* warned law enforcement officials not to use without a warrant.

The Ishmaels overstate the device's capabilities. The device "does not intrude in any way into the privacy and sanctity of a home." It "is a passive, non-intrusive instrument" in that "[i]t does not send any beams or rays into the area on which it is fixed or in any way penetrate structures within that area." . . . The device, in other words, poses no greater intrusion on one's privacy than a precise mapping camera, an electronic beeper, or a pen register.

The *manner* in which a thermal imager was used in this case is equally significant in assessing the reasonableness of the intrusion. When the DEA performed its pre-dawn thermal readings in this case, the officers never *physically* invaded the Ishmael's residential or commercial curtilage.

* * *

[A thermal imager], when used in an "open field" does not offend the Fourth Amendment because it is passive and non-intrusive. The sanctity of one's home or business is undisturbed. We therefore conclude that the D.E.A.'s warrantless use of a thermal imager in this case was not an unconstitutional search.

CASE EXCERPT: *UNITED STATES V. KARO*
SUPREME COURT OF THE UNITED STATES (1984)
486 U.S. 705 (1984)

After a Drug Enforcement Administration (D.E.A.) Agent learned that respondents Karo, Horton, and Harley had ordered 50 gallons of ether from a Government informant, who had told the agent that the ether was to be used to extract cocaine from clothing that had been imported into the United States, the Government obtained a court order authorizing the installation and monitoring of a beeper in one of the cans of ether. With the informant's consent, D.E.A. agents substituted their own can containing a beeper for one of the cans in the shipment. Thereafter, agents saw Karo pick up the ether from the informant, followed Karo to his house, and determined by using the beeper that the ether was inside the house where it was then monitored. The ether then moved in succession to two other houses, including Horton's, before it was moved first to a locker in one commercial storage facility and then to a locker in another such facility. Both lockers were rented jointly by Horton and Harley. Finally, the ether was removed from the second storage facility by Rhodes and an unidentified woman and transported in Horton's truck, first to Rhodes' house and then to a house rented by Horton, Harley, and respondent Steele. Using the beeper monitor, agents determined that the beeper can was inside the house and obtained a warrant to search the house based in part on the information derived through use of the beeper. The warrant was executed and Horton, Harley, Steele, Roth, and Karo were arrested, and cocaine was seized. The defendants were charged with various drug offenses. The U.S. District Court granted their pretrial motion to suppress the seized evidence. The U.S. Court of Appeals affirmed, holding that a warrant was required to install the beeper in the can of ether and to monitor it in private dwellings. The U.S. Supreme Court granted certiorari.

Mr. Justice White delivered the opinion of the Court.

* * *

We granted the Government's petition for certiorari, which raised the question whether a warrant was required to authorize either the installation of the beeper or its subsequent monitoring. We deal with each contention in turn.

* * *

Because the judgment below in favor of Karo rested in major part on the conclusion that the installation violated his Fourth Amendment rights and that any information obtained from monitoring the beeper was tainted by the initial illegality,

we must deal with the legality of the warrantless installation. It is clear that the actual placement of the beeper into the can violated no one's Fourth Amendment rights. The can into which the beeper was placed belonged at the time to the DEA, and by no stretch of the imagination could it be said that respondents then had any legitimate expectation of privacy in it. The ether and the original 10 cans, on the other hand, belonged to, and were in the possession of [the government's informant], who had given his consent to any invasion of those items that occurred. Thus, even if there had been no substitution of cans and the agents had placed the beeper into one of the original 10 cans, [the informant's] consent was sufficient to validate the placement of the beeper in the can.

The Court of Appeals acknowledged that before Karo took control of the ether "the DEA and [the informant] presumably could do with the can and ether whatever they liked without violating Karo's rights." It did not hold that the actual placement of the beeper into the ether can violated the Fourth Amendment. Instead, it held that the violation occurred at the time the beeper-laden can was transferred to Karo.

* * *

Not surprisingly, the Court of Appeals did not describe the transfer as either a "search" or a "seizure," for plainly it is neither. A "search" occurs "when an expectation of privacy that society is prepared to consider reasonable is infringed." The mere transfer to Karo of a can containing an unmonitored beeper infringed no privacy interest. It conveyed no information that Karo wished to keep private, for it conveyed no information at all. To be sure, it created a potential for an invasion of privacy, but we have never held that potential, as opposed to actual, invasions of privacy constitute searches for purposes of the Fourth Amendment. A holding to that effect would mean that policemen walking down the street carrying a parabolic microphone capable of picking up conversations in nearby homes would be engaging in a search even if the microphone were not turned on. It is the exploitation of technological advances that implicates the Fourth Amendment, not their mere existence.

We likewise do not believe that the transfer of the container constituted a seizure. A "seizure" of property occurs when "there is some meaningful interference with an individual's possessory interests in that property." Although the can may have contained an unknown and unwanted foreign object, it cannot be said that anyone's possessory interest was interfered with in a meaningful way. At most, there was a technical trespass on the space occupied by the beeper.

The existence of a physical trespass is only marginally relevant to the question of whether the Fourth Amendment has been violated, however, for an actual trespass is neither necessary nor sufficient to establish a constitutional violation.

* * *

We conclude that no Fourth Amendment interest of Karo or of any other respondent was infringed by the installation of the beeper. Rather, any impairment of their privacy interests that may have occurred was occasioned by the monitoring of the beeper.

* * *

This case [also] presents the question whether the monitoring of a beeper in a private residence, a location not open to visual surveillance, violates the Fourth Amendment rights of those who have a justifiable interest in the privacy of the residence. Contrary to the submission of the United States, we think that it does.

At the risk of belaboring the obvious, private residences are places in which the individual normally expects privacy free of governmental intrusion not authorized by a warrant, and that expectation is plainly one that society is prepared to recognize as justifiable. Our cases have not deviated from this basic Fourth Amendment principle. Searches and seizures inside a home without a warrant are presumptively unreasonable absent exigent circumstances. In this case, had a DEA agent thought it useful to enter the residence to verify that the ether was actually in the house and had he done so surreptitiously and without a warrant, there is little doubt that he would have engaged in an unreasonable search within the meaning of the Fourth Amendment. For purposes of the Amendment, the result is the same where, without a warrant, the Government surreptitiously employs an electronic device to obtain information that it could not have obtained by observation from outside the curtilage of the house. The beeper tells the agent that a particular article is actually located at a particular time in the private residence and is in the possession of the person or persons whose residence is being watched. Even if visual surveillance has revealed that the article to which the beeper is attached has entered the house, the later monitoring not only verifies the officers' observations but also establishes that the article remains on the premises. Here, for example, the beeper was monitored for a significant period after the arrival of the ether . . . and before the application for a warrant to search.

The monitoring of an electronic device such as a beeper is, of course, less intrusive than a full-scale search, but it does reveal a critical fact about the interior of the premises that the Government is extremely interested in knowing and that it could not have otherwise obtained without a warrant. . . . Indiscriminate monitoring of property that has been withdrawn from public view would present far too serious a threat to privacy interests in the home to escape entirely some sort of Fourth Amendment oversight.

We also reject the Government's contention that it should be able to monitor beepers in private residences without a warrant if there is the requisite justification in the facts for believing that a crimes is being or will be committed and that monitoring the beeper wherever it goes is likely to produce evidence of criminal activity. Warrantless searches are presumptively unreasonable, though the Court has recognized a few limited exceptions to this general rule. . . . The primary reason for the warrant requirement is to interpose a "neutral and detached magistrate" between the citizen and "the officer engaged in the often competitive enterprise of ferreting out crime." Those suspected of drug offenses are no less entitled to that protection than those suspected of nondrug offenses. Requiring a warrant will have the salutary effect of ensuring that use of beepers is not abused, by imposing upon agents the requirement that they demonstrate in advance their justification for the desired search.

Endnotes

1. See *Olmstead* v. *United States,* 277 U.S. 438 (1928).
2. See *Katz* v. *United States,* 389 U.S. 347 (1967).
3. Supra, note 1.
4. Supra, note 2 at 352.
5. Id. at 359.
6. *Berger* v. *New York,* 388 U.S. 41 (1967).
7. Id. at 57.
8. 18 U.S.C.A. Sections 2510–2520; 18 U.S.C.A. Sections 2701–2710.
9. For an excellent discussion of electronic surveillance, see Geoffrey C. Mason, "Twenty-Fifth Annual Review of Criminal Procedure." 84 *The Georgetown Law Journal* pp. 825–826 (1996).
10. Id. at 826–827.
11. Id. at 827.
12. 18 U.S.C.A. Section 2511(1).
13. 18 U.S.C.A. Section 2511(4)(a).
14. 18 U.S.C.A. Section 2520.
15. These offenses include: murder, kidnapping, gambling, robbery, bribery, extortion, or dealing in narcotic drugs, marijuana or other dangerous drugs, or other crime dangerous to life, limb, or property, and punishable by imprisonment for more than one year.
16. *Dalia* v. *United States,* 441 U.S. 238 (1979).
17. Id. at 257.
18. 18 U.S.C.A. Section 2518(7); Wayne R. LaFave and Jerold H. Israel, *Criminal Procedure,* 2d ed. (St. Paul, Minn.: West, 1992), p. 249.
19. 18 U.S.C.A. Section 2511(3).
20. LaFave and Israel, supra note 18; *United States* v. *White,* 401 U.S. 745 (1971).
21. *On Lee* v. *United States,* 343 U.S. 747 (1952).
22. *United States* v. *White,* 401 U.S. 745 (1971).
23. *Jacobson* v. *United States,* 503 U.S. 540, 548 (1992).
24. *Sherman* v. *United States,* 356 U.S. 369 (1958).
25. *United States* v. *Russell,* 411 U.S. 423 (1973).
26. *Hampton* v. *United States,* 425 U.S. 484 (1976).
27. Id. at 490.
28. Id.
29. Supra, note 23.
30. Id. at 550.

31. Id. at 553–554.
32. *United States* v. *Lee,* 274 U.S. 599 (1927).
33. *United States* v. *Dunn,* 480 U.S. 294 (1987); see *Minnesota* v. *Dickerson,* 113 S.Ct. 2130 (1993).
34. *U.S.* v. *Montoya de Hernandez,* 473 U.S. 531 (1985).
35. See id. at 541 note 4 (Stevens, J. Concurring).
36. *United States* v. *Knotts,* 460 U.S. 276 (1983).
37. Id. at 282.
38. Id. at 281.
39. *United States* v. *Karo,* 468 U.S. 705 (1984).
40. *New York* v. *New York Telephone Co.,* 434 U.S. 159 (1977).
41. *Smith* v. *Maryland,* 442 U.S. 735 (1979).
42. 18 U.S.C. Section 312 (1986).
43. *United States* v. *Miller,* 425 U.S. 435 (1976).
44. Id.
45. *California* v. *Ciraolo,* 476 U.S. 207 (1986).
46. Id. at 214.
47. Id. at 215.
48. *Florida* v. *Riley,* 488 U.S. 445 (1989).
49. Id. at 451.
50. *Dow Chemical Company* v. *United States,* 476 U.S. 227 (1986).
51. Krysten C. Kelly, "Warrantless Satellite Surveillance: Will Our Privacy Rights be Lost in Space?" 13 *The John Marshall Journal of Computer & Information Law* pp. 729–762 (1995).
52. Mindy G. Wilson, "The Prewarrant Use of Thermal Imagery: Has this Technological Advance in the War on Drugs Come at the Expense of Fourth Amendment Protections Against Unreasonable Searches and Seizures?" 83 *The Kentucky Law Journal* pp. 891–914 (1995).
53. *United States* v. *Ishmael,* 48 F.3d 850 (5th Cir. 1995); accord, *United States* v. *Ford,* 34 F.3d 992 (11th Cir. 1994).
54. *State* v. *Cramer,* 851 P.2d 147 (Ariz. Ct. App. 1992).
55. *State* v. *Johnson,* 879 P.2d 984 (Wash. Ct. App. 1994).
56. See *Steve Jackson Games, Inc.* v. *United States Secret Service,* 36 F.3d 457 (5th Cir. 1994); *Smyth* v. *Pillsbury Co.,* 914 F. Supp. 97 (E.D. Pa. 1996).
57. See Alan Cohen, "E-Mail Users: Caveat Sender." 18 *American Lawyer* pp. 95–97 (1996).
58. Charlene L. Lu, "Seeking Privacy in Wireless Communications: Balancing the Right of Individual Privacy With the Need for Effective Law Enforcement." 17 *Hastings Communication & Entertainment Law Journal* pp. 531–556 (1995).
59. See Lisa Horvath, "Cellular and Cordless Phone Privacy: An Oxymoron." 14 *Preventive Law Reporter* pp. 7–10 (1995).
60. Lu, supra note 58 at 534.
61. Pub. L. No. 99-508, 100 Stat. 1848 (1946).
62. See 18 U.S.C. Section 2510(1); see also *In re Askin,* 47 F.3d 100 (4th Cir.)(Title III is not implicated by the interception of the radio wave portion of a cordless telephone transmission), *cert. denied,* 116 S.Ct. 382 (1995); see Mason, supra note 9 at 842.
63. *State* v. *Delaurier,* 488 A.2d 688 (R.I. 1985).
64. Lu, supra note 49 at 538.
65. 18 U.S.C. Section 2510(12)(c)(1988).
66. Lu, supra note 58 at 539.
67. Id. at 539
68. Michael Adler, "Cyberspace, General Searches, and Digital Contraband: The Fourth Amendment and the Net-Wide Search." 105 *The Yale Law Journal* pp. 1093–1120 (1996).

10 *MIRANDA* v. *ARIZONA* AND THE PRIVILEGE AGAINST SELF-INCRIMINATION

Outline

Key Terms

Earlier chapters have discussed individual rights under the Fourth Amendment to the United States Constitution. Chapter 10 shifts the focus of our study to constitutional rights under the Fifth and Sixth Amendments. In 1964, the Supreme Court applied the privilege against self-incrimination to state criminal proceedings in *Malloy* v. *Hogan.*[1] That same year it decided *Escobedo* v. *Illinois,*[2] which held that a suspect had the right to consult with an attorney about his privilege against self-incrimination. Counsel's main reason for being present during an interrogation is to protect the suspect's privilege against self-incrimination.

Two years later the Supreme Court decided *Miranda* v. *Arizona,*[3] one of the most important criminal procedure cases in U.S. history. Although there is some reason to believe that *Miranda*'s central thrust has been eroded by the Supreme Court in recent years, it continues to be a seminal criminal case.[4] *Miranda* is more than just a self-incrimination decision. It represents an interaction of different but dependent constitutional provisions—the Fifth Amendment privilege against self-incrimination and the Sixth Amendment right to counsel. In *Miranda,* the Court stated: "[W]e hold that an individual held for interrogation must be clearly informed that he has the right to consult with a lawyer and to have the lawyer with him during interrogation under the system for protecting the privilege we delineate today."[5] That is why *Miranda* v. *Arizona* is sometimes described as a case that resulted in the **marriage of the Fifth Amendment privilege against self-incrimination and the Sixth Amendment right to counsel.** The importance of this interaction will become more apparent as the discussion of *Miranda* continues.

The Development of the Privilege Against Self-Incrimination

During the Middle Ages, those suspected of offenses against the church or the state were tortured in the normal course of judicial proceedings in an effort to extract confessions of criminal or sinful behavior. The authorities presumed that such confessions originated solely from a sense of guilt and they were regarded as conclusive proof, even when they were extracted through the use of the most heinous forms of torture.[6] The problem is that confessions obtained in this manner are unreliable—almost any rational person would confess to avoid the pain of further torture. To prevent such abuses the framers of the U.S. Constitution developed the Fifth Amendment privilege against self-incrimination.

The Pre-*Miranda* Standard—A Voluntariness Test

Before the Supreme Court decided *Miranda* v. *Arizona* there was one main requirement for using a confession in a criminal case: it must have been a product of a defendant's exercise of free will. This is termed the **voluntariness requirement.** The voluntariness test uses a **totality of circumstances** approach for evaluating a confession—a court will consider factors including a defendant's education, understanding of the English language, emotional stability, and where and when the police interrogation occurred.[7]

The voluntariness test continues to be relevant in post-*Miranda* cases, because even if a suspect is given the *Miranda* warnings, the confession must still be voluntary. For example, suppose that police officers have probable cause to believe that someone has murdered a child. After the suspect is arrested and taken to the police station, officers advise him of his rights, and he declines to speak. Due to the heinous nature of the crime, however, the officers insist on interrogating him and beat him with a rubber hose until he confesses. A confession extracted in this manner is inadmissible at trial, even though the suspect was provided with the *Miranda* warnings, because it was involuntary.

Although cases involving the use of torture are now rare in U.S. legal systems, some of the early cases involved police misconduct that was even more outrageous than that portrayed in the example above. In *Brown* v. *Mississippi,*[8] three African-American defendants were tortured by sheriff deputies until they confessed to a murder. Portions of this case are presented in Highlight 10.1. The confessions were admitted into evidence and the defendants were convicted of murder in Mississippi State Court, over a defense objection that the confessions were involuntary.

The U.S. Supreme Court held that the State violated the Due Process Clause of the Fourteenth Amendment by using the confessions. Chief Justice Hughes stated:

> It would be difficult to conceive of methods more revolting to the sense of justice than those taken to procure the confessions of these petitioners, and the use of the confessions thus obtained as the basis for conviction and sentence was a clear denial of due process.[9]

Brown v. *Mississippi* established that confessions obtained through the use of physical torture may not be used in state proceedings. Such confessions clearly violate due process of law and the voluntariness rule and are inadmissible.

The Supreme Court later held that confessions may not be admitted into evidence if police officers use mental coercion. In *Spano* v. *New York,*[10] the defendant was charged with murder for shooting a man who had beaten him and stolen his money. Spano, who had retained an attorney, surrendered to police and was interrogated for approximately five hours, outside the presence of counsel. The attorney had instructed Spano, who had a history of emotional problems, to say nothing to the officers. During the interrogation Spano had made several requests to speak with his lawyer. After Spano was given refreshments, he was questioned by a new police officer named Bruno, who had once been his close friend. Senior officers instructed Bruno to elicit sympathy from Spano by informing him that higher-ranking police officers blamed Bruno for what Spano had done and that his job was in jeopardy because of Spano's failure to confess. Bruno questioned Spano several times and he eventually made incriminating statements that were used to convict him of murder in state court. The U.S. Supreme Court held that Spano's confession was involuntary and his privilege against self-incrimination was violated by the police officers who had used mental coercion.[11]

Determining if a Confession is Voluntary

In order to admit a defendant's incriminating statements at trial they must "truly be the product of his free choice."[12] In *Colorado* v. *Connelly,*[13] the Supreme Court held that a suspect's incriminating statements that are made voluntarily in the absence of custodial

Highlight 10.1

Brown v. *Mississippi,* 297 U.S. 278 (1936)

Mr. Chief Justice Hughes delivered the opinion of the court.

The question in this case is whether convictions, which rest solely upon confessions shown to have been extorted by officers of the State by brutality and violence, are consistent with the due process of law required by the Fourteenth Amendment of the Constitution of the United States.

Petitioners were indicted for the murder of one Raymond Stewart, whose death occurred on March 30, 1934. They were indicted on April 4, 1934, and were then arraigned and pleaded not guilty. Counsel were appointed by the court to defend them. Trial was begun the next morning and was concluded on the following day, when they were found guilty and sentenced to death.

Aside from the confessions, there was no evidence sufficient to warrant the submission of the case to the jury. After a preliminary inquiry, testimony as to the confessions was received over the objection of defendants' counsel. Defendants then testified that the confessions were false and had been procured by physical torture. The case went to the jury with instructions, upon the request of defendants' counsel, that if the jury had reasonable doubt as to the confessions having resulted from coercion, and that they were not true, they were not to be considered as evidence. On their appeal to the Supreme Court of the State, defendants assigned as error the inadmissibility of the confessions. The judgment was affirmed. 158 So. 339.

Defendants then moved in the Supreme Court of the State to arrest the judgment and for a new trial on the ground that all the evidence against them was obtained by coercion and brutality known to the court and to the district attorney, and that defendants had been denied the benefit of counsel or opportunity to confer with counsel in a reasonable manner. The motion was supported by affidavits. At about the same time, defendants filed in the Supreme Court a "suggestion of error" explicitly challenging the proceedings of the trial, in the use of the confessions and with respect to the alleged denial of representation by counsel, as violating the due process clause of the Fourteenth Amendment of the Constitution of the United States. The state court entertained the suggestion of error, considered the federal question, and decided it against defendants' contentions. 161 So. 465. Two judges dissented. *Id.,* p. 470. We granted a writ of certiorari.

The grounds of the decision were (1) that immunity from self-incrimination is not essential to due process of law, and (2) that the failure of the trial court to exclude the confessions after the introduction of evidence showing their incompetency, in the absence of a request for such exclusion, did not deprive the defendants of life or liberty without due process of law; and that even if the trial court had erroneously overruled a motion to exclude the confessions, the ruling would have been mere error reversible on appeal, but not a violation of constitutional right. *Id.,* p. 468.

The opinion of the state court did not set forth the evidence as to the circumstances in which the confessions were procured. That the evidence established that they were procured by coercion was not questioned. The state court said: "After the state closed its case on the merits, the appellants, for the first time, introduced evidence from which it appears that the confessions were not made voluntarily but were coerced." *Id.,* p. 466. There is no dispute as to the facts upon this point and as they are clearly and adequately stated in the dissenting opinion of Judge Griffith (with whom Judge Anderson concurred)—showing both the extreme brutality of the measures

(Continued)

to extort the confessions and the participation of the state authorities—we quote this part of his opinion in full, as follows (*Id.,* pp. 470, 471):

"The crime with which these defendants, all ignorant negroes, are charged, was discovered about one o'clock p.m. on Friday, March 30, 1934. On that night one Dial, a deputy sheriff, accompanied by others, came to the home of Ellington, one of the defendants, and requested him to accompany them to the house of the deceased, and there a number of white men were gathered, who began to accuse the defendant of the crime. Upon his denial they seized him, and with the participation of the deputy they hanged him by a rope to the limb of a tree, and having let him down, they hung him again, and when he was let down the second time, and he still protested his innocence, he was tied to a tree and whipped, and still declining to accede to the demands that he confess, he was finally released and he returned with some difficulty to his home, suffering intense pain and agony. The record of the testimony shows that the signs of the rope on his neck were plainly visible during the so-called trial. A day or two thereafter the said deputy, accompanied by another, returned to the home of the said defendant and arrested him, and departed with the prisoner towards the jail in an adjoining county, but went by a route which led into the State of Alabama; and while on the way, in that State, the deputy stopped and again severely whipped the defendant, declaring that he would continue the whipping until he confessed, and the defendant then agreed to confess to such a statement as the deputy would dictate, and he did so, after which he was delivered to jail.

"The other two defendants, Ed Brown and Henry Shields, were also arrested and taken to the same jail. On Sunday night, April 1, 1934, the same deputy, accompanied by a number of white men, one of whom was also an officer, and by the jailer, came to the jail, and the two last named defendants were made to strip and they were laid over chairs and their backs were cut to pieces with a leather strap with buckles on it, and they were likewise made by the said deputy definitely to understand that the whipping would be continued unless and until they confessed, and not only confessed, but confessed in every matter of detail as demanded by those present;

and in this manner the defendants confessed the crime, and as the whippings progressed and were repeated, they changed or adjusted their confession in all particulars of detail so as to conform to the demands of their torturers. When the confessions had been obtained in the exact form and contents as desired by the mob, they left with the parting admonition and warning that, if the defendants changed their story at any time in any respect from that last stated, the perpetrators of the outrage would administer the same or equally effective treatment.

"Further details of the brutal treatment to which these helpless prisoners were subjected need not be pursued. It is sufficient to say that in pertinent respects the transcript reads more like pages torn from some medieval account, than a record made within the confines of a modern civilization which aspires to an enlightened constitutional government.

"All this having been accomplished, on the next day, that is, on Monday, April 2, when the defendants had been given time to recuperate somewhat from the tortures to which they had been subjected, the two sheriffs, one of the county where the crime was committed, and the other of the county of the jail in which the prisoners were confined, came to the jail, accompanied by eight other persons, some of them deputies, there to hear the free and voluntary confession of these miserable and abject defendants. The sheriff of the county of the crime admitted that he had heard of the whipping, but averred that he had no personal knowledge of it. He admitted that one of the defendants, when brought before him to confess, was limping and did not sit down, and that this particular defendant then and there stated that he had been strapped so severely that he could not sit down, and as already stated, the signs of the rope on the neck of another of the defendants were plainly visible to all. Nevertheless the solemn farce of hearing the free and voluntary confessions was gone through with, and these two sheriffs and one other person then present were the three witnesses used in court to establish the so-called confessions, which were received by the court and admitted in evidence over the objections of the defendants duly entered of record as each of the said three witnesses delivered their alleged testimony. There was thus enough before the court when these confessions were first offered to

Highlight 10.1

Brown v. *Mississippi—continued*

make known to the court that they were not, beyond all reasonable doubt, free and voluntary; and the failure of the court then to exclude the confessions is sufficient to reverse the judgment, under every rule of procedure that has heretofore been prescribed, and hence it was not necessary subsequently to renew the objections by motion or otherwise.

"The spurious confessions having been obtained—and the farce last mentioned having been gone through with on Monday, April 2d—the court, then in session, on the following day, Tuesday, April 3, 1934, ordered the grand jury to reassemble on the succeeding day, April 4, 1934, at nine o'clock, and on the morning of the day last mentioned the grand jury returned an indictment against the defendants for murder. Late that afternoon the defendants were brought from the jail in the adjoining county and arraigned, when one or more of them offered to plead guilty, which the court declined to accept, and, upon inquiry whether they had or desired counsel, they stated that they had none, and did not suppose that counsel could be of any assistance to them. The court thereupon appointed counsel, and set the case for trial for the following morning at nine o'clock, and the defendants were returned to the jail in the adjoining county about thirty miles away.

"The defendants were brought to the courthouse of the county of the following morning, April 5th, and the so-called trial was opened, and was concluded on the next day, April 6, 1934, and resulted in a pretended conviction with death sentences. The evidence upon which the conviction was obtained was the so-called confessions. Without this evidence a peremptory instruction to find for the defendants would have been inescapable. The defendants were put on the stand, and by their testimony the facts and the details thereof as to the manner by which the confessions were extorted from them were fully developed, and it is further disclosed by the record that the same deputy, Dial, under whose guiding hand and active participation the tortures to coerce the confessions were administered, was actively in the

performance of the supposed duties of a court deputy in the courthouse and in the presence of the prisoners during what is denominated, in complimentary terms, the trial of these defendants. This deputy was put on the stand by the state in rebuttal, and admitted the whippings. It is interesting to note that in his testimony with reference to the whipping of the defendant Ellington, and in response to the inquiry as to how severely he was whipped, the deputy stated, 'Not too much for a negro; not as much as I would have done if it were left to me.' Two others who had participated in these whippings were introduced and admitted it—not a single witness was introduced who denied it. The facts are not only undisputed, they are admitted, and admitted to have been done by officers of the state, in conjunction with other participants, and all this was definitely well known to everybody connected with the trial, and during the trial, including the state's prosecuting attorney and the trial judge presiding."

1. The state stresses the statement in *Twining* v. *New Jersey,* 211 U.S. 78, 114, that "exemption from compulsory self-incrimination in the courts of the States is not secured by any part of the Federal Constitution," and the statement in *Snyder* v. *Massachusetts,* 291 U.S. 97, 105, that "the privilege against self-incrimination may be withdrawn and the accused put upon the stand as a witness for the State." But the question of the right of the State to withdraw the privilege against self-incrimination is not here involved. The compulsion to which the quoted statements refer is that of the processes of justice by which the accused may be called as a witness and required to testify. Compulsion by torture to extort a confession is a different matter.

The State is free to regulate the procedure of its courts in accordance with its own conceptions of policy, unless in so doing it "offends some principle of justice so rooted in the traditions and conscience of our people as to be ranked as fundamental." The

(Continued)

State may abolish trial by jury. It may dispense with indictment by a grand jury and substitute complaint or information. But the freedom of the State in establishing its policy is the freedom of constitutional government and is limited by the requirement of due process of law. Because a State may dispense with a jury trial, it does not follow that it may substitute trial by ordeal. The rack and torture chamber may not be substituted for the witness stand. The State may not permit an accused to be hurried to conviction under mob domination—where the whole proceeding is but a mask—without supplying corrective process. The State may not deny to the accused the aid of counsel. Nor may a State, through the action of its officers, contrive a conviction through the pretense of a trial which in truth is "but used as a means of depriving a defendant of liberty through a deliberate deception of court and jury by the presentation of testimony known to be perjured." And the trial equally is a mere pretense where the state authorities have contrived a conviction resting solely upon confessions obtained by violence. The due process clause requires "that state action, whether through one agency or another, shall be consistent with the fundamental principles of liberty and justice which lie at the base of all our civil and political institutions." It would be difficult to conceive of methods more revolting to the sense of justice than those taken to procure the confessions of these petitioners, and the use of the confessions thus obtained as the basis for conviction and sentence was a clear denial of due process.

2. It is in this view that the further contention of the State must be considered. That contention rests upon the failure of counsel for the accused, who had objected to the admissibility of the confessions, to move for their exclusion after they had been introduced and the fact of coercion had been proved. It is a contention which proceeds upon a misconception of the nature of petitioners' complaint. That complaint is not of the commission of mere error, but of a wrong

so fundamental that it made the whole proceeding a mere pretense of a trial and rendered the conviction and sentence wholly void. We are not concerned with a mere question of state practice, or whether counsel assigned to petitioners were competent or mistakenly assumed that their first objections were sufficient. In an earlier case the Supreme Court of the State had recognized the duty of the court to supply corrective process where due process of law had been denied. In *Fisher* v. *State,* 145 Miss. 116, 134; 110 So. 361, 365, the court said: "Coercing the supposed state's criminals into confessions and using such confessions so coerced from them against them in trials has been the curse of all countries. It was the chief inequity, the crowning infamy of the Star Chamber, and the Inquisition, and other similar institutions. The constitution recognized the evils that lay behind these practices and prohibited them in this country. . . . The duty of maintaining constitutional rights of a person on trial for his life rises above mere rules of procedure and wherever the court is clearly satisfied that such violations exist, it will refuse to sanction such violations and will apply the corrective."

In the instant case, trial court was fully advised by the undisputed evidence of the way in which the confessions had been procured. The trial court knew that there was no other evidence upon which conviction and sentence could be based. Yet it proceeded to permit conviction and to pronounce sentence. The conviction and sentence were void for want of the essential elements of due process, and the proceeding thus vitiated could be challenged in any appropriate manner. It was challenged before the Supreme Court of the State by the express invocation of the Fourteenth Amendment. That court entertained the challenge, considered the federal question thus presented, but declined to enforce petitioners' constitutional right. The court thus denied a federal right fully established and specially set up and claimed and the judgment must be

Reversed.

interrogation are admissible at trial. To determine if a confession is voluntary the courts will use a totality of circumstances test, and ask whether the suspect was in custody and whether the police used interrogation tactics that were designed to overcome the suspect's will.[14] A reviewing court will consider the following factors:

1. where the questioning takes place;
2. whether *Miranda* warnings have been given;
3. whether the police or the accused initiated the questioning.[15]

In addition, a court will consider a suspect's personal characteristics, including age, drug addiction, psychological problems, physical condition, and lack of experience with the criminal justice system.[16] For example, in *Mincey* v. *Arizona,*[17] a police officer was killed during a drug raid on Mincey's home. Mincey was brought to the hospital after the shooting and taken to the emergency room where he was treated for injuries, and was later admitted to the intensive care unit (ICU). Later that evening a police officer came to the ICU to interrogate Mincey but could not speak with him because feeding tubes had been inserted into his mouth. The detective insisted on interrogating Mincey, however, and after giving Mincey the *Miranda* warnings, wrote various questions on a piece of paper. Although Mincey asked repeatedly that the interrogation stop until he could get a lawyer, the questioning continued for approximately four hours. Mincey was convicted in state court of murder and various drug charges. The Supreme Court held that the test to be used to determine if Mincey's statements were admissible was whether they were "the product of a rational intellect and a free will."[18] Because "[i]t [was] hard to imagine a situation less conducive to the exercise of a 'rational intellect and a free will' than Mincey's,"[19] the Court reversed his conviction for murder.

The case law suggests several additional factors that will render a defendant's confession involuntary, including:

1. The use of physical compulsion.
2. The use of mental coercion.
3. Prolonged detention of the suspect.
4. Prolonged questioning designed to wear down the suspect's resistance.[20]
5. A refusal to permit a suspect to communicate with counsel.

Even if a defendant's confession is found by an appellate court to be involuntary, there is still a chance that the conviction may stand. If the appellate court concludes that the effect of admitting the involuntary confession at trial was harmless and did not prejudice the defendant's rights, the conviction will be upheld.[21] This is termed the **harmless error doctrine.** The reason for the rule is to avoid overturning criminal convictions for small trial errors that may not have impacted the result of the trial. The prosecution must carry the burden of proving that the error was harmless beyond a reasonable doubt. Appellate courts apply harmless error analysis if evidence at a criminal trial is admitted in violation of a defendant's Fourth Amendment rights, as well as some Fifth and Sixth Amendment rights.

In *Arizona* v. *Fulminante,*[22] the Supreme Court applied the harmless error rule to a defendant's involuntary confession, which had been admitted at trial. It held that although it is difficult for the prosecution to prove beyond a reasonable doubt that the admission of a defendant's involuntary confession is harmless error, it may be possible in some cases to do so. For example, suppose that a defendant is arrested for murder after he shoots another person in front of several witnesses. After his arrest he confesses to police officers, but is not allowed to speak with an attorney. The trial court mistakenly admits the confession into evidence. In addition to the confession, however, there is overwhelming evidence in the trial record that the defendant committed the murder, including the testimony of five witnesses to the shooting. Based on the trial record an appellate court may conclude that admitting the confession was harmless error and allow the defendant's conviction to stand.

The Supreme Court has identified several types of constitutional violations that never constitute harmless error and always require the automatic reversal of a defendant's conviction. This is termed the **automatic reversal rule.** These include the following violations of a defendant's rights:

1. The right to counsel.
2. The right to an impartial judge.
3. The right to a public trial.
4. The right to represent oneself in a criminal case.

To summarize, the early self-incrimination cases used solely a voluntariness test to determine the admissibility of a defendant's confession. In *Miranda* v. *Arizona,* however, the Supreme Court added a second requirement and developed a clear rule for determining whether a defendant's incriminating statements are admissible—has the suspect been given the *Miranda* warnings?[23] It would be difficult to overstate *Miranda* v. *Arizona*'s importance. Highlight 10.2 discusses the impact of this seminal case and describes Ernesto Miranda's criminal career and death at an early age.

Miranda v. *Arizona,* 384 U.S. 436 (1966)

Those of us who have watched police shows on television at one time or another know well the familiar *Miranda* warnings that are given as a matter of routine to suspects when they are held for **custodial interrogation.** Custodial interrogation occurs whenever the police question someone who is taken into custody about a crime. This is an essential aspect of *Miranda*—if a defendant is either not exposed to interrogation by officers *or* is free to leave and terminate an encounter with the police, then *Miranda* warnings are not required. The *Miranda* warnings were designed to protect the privilege against self-incrimination because custodial interrogation in a "police-dominated atmosphere" is inherently coercive. They should be given to a suspect regardless of the severity of the charged offense.[24]

The *Miranda* warnings include the following statements:

1. You have the right to remain silent.
2. Anything you say can and will be used against you.

Highlight 10.2

Ernesto Miranda, for whom the landmark Miranda decision was named—requiring police to inform arrested persons of their rights—was stabbed to death yesterday in what police said appeared to be a bar fight.

Miranda, 34, received numerous stab wounds and was pronounced dead at a Phoenix hospital, police said. They said no one had been arrested and there were no other details available immediately.

The decision involving Miranda was issued by the U.S. Supreme Court in 1966 after the justices overturned his conviction for rape and kidnapping on grounds that he was not advised of his rights at the time of his arrest.

Miranda was later retried, convicted and resentenced to 20 to 30 years in prison for the 1963 crimes. He also served a consecutive term for an unrelated $8 robbery of a housewife.

Miranda was paroled in 1972. In July, 1974, he was arrested on a charge of possession of a firearm while on parole. The arrest came after he was stopped for a routine traffic violation. That charge was later dropped.

When he was arrested in 1963, Miranda was 23 years old and had just rented a house in Phoenix.

He said officers promised to drop robbery charges if he would confess to a kidnapping.

"So I made the statement," Miranda said.

But when he got to court he was told he was still charged with robbery. Miranda said he repeatedly asked for a lawyer but was denied one. Eventually an attorney was appointed by the Court.

Miranda was convicted of robbery, then was brought to trial for kidnapping and rape, for which he also was convicted.

Unknown to Miranda, his case had caught the eye of other Phoenix lawyers. His case was argued before the U.S. Supreme Court by John Flynn, who thought the crux of the case rested on a violation of the Fifth Amendment, which guarantees the right to remain silent.

He also argued that the Sixth Amendment, the right to counsel, had been violated.

On June 13, 1966, the Supreme Court in a 5–4 decision, upheld the Fifth and Sixth Amendment rights of Miranda and other prisoners in other states.

By chance, Miranda's name was the first on the list.

Article from *The Kansas City Star*, February 1, 1976. Reprinted by permission of the Associated Press.

---

3. You have the right to an attorney during questioning.

4. If you cannot afford an attorney, one will be provided for you.

Even if the warnings are not stated exactly as described above, an officer may still comply with *Miranda*,[25] as long as the suspect is informed of the right to be free from self-incrimination and the right to counsel.[26] For example, in *Duckworth* v. *Eagan*[27] the Supreme Court held that the following warnings were adequate, even though they were less than perfectly clear:

> "You have a right to talk to a lawyer for advice before we ask you any questions, and to have him with you during questioning. You have the right to the advice and presence of a lawyer even if you cannot afford to hire one. We have no way of giving you a lawyer, but one will be appointed for you, if you wish, if and when you go to court."[28]

To repeat, *Miranda* requires both custody *and* interrogation—if either element is missing, the rule will not apply to bar a suspect's incriminating statements at trial.

Highlight 10.3

Miranda **v.** *Arizona,* **384 U.S. 436 (1966)**

"[W]hen an individual is taken into custody or otherwise deprived of his freedom by the authorities in a significant way and is subjected to questioning, the privilege against self-incrimination is jeopardized. Procedural safeguards must be employed . . . and unless other fully effective means are adopted to notify the person of his right of silence and to ensure that the exercise of the right will be scrupulously honored, the following measures are required. He must be warned prior to any questioning that he has the right to remain silent, that anything he says can be used against him in a court of law, that he has the right to the presence of an attorney, and that if he cannot afford an attorney one will be appointed for him prior to any questioning if he so desires. After such warnings have been given, and such opportunity afforded him, the individual may knowingly and intelligently waive these rights and agree to answer questions or make a statement. But unless and until such warnings and waiver are demonstrated, no evidence obtained as a result of interrogation can be used against him."

Two examples should help to clarify this point. Suppose that Mary encounters a police officer on a street corner in Madison, Wisconsin. Before the officer says anything, Mary tells him that she has just committed a bank robbery. Mary's statement would be admissible at trial because she was neither in custody nor interrogated by the officer.

Likewise, suppose that John is arrested by a police officer who has probable cause to believe that he committed a bank robbery. John is placed in a police cruiser for transportation to the county jail but he is not given the *Miranda* warnings. During the ride to the jail, the officer says nothing to John. John, however, states: "My family will be devastated. I must have been crazy to get involved in something like this." This statement is likely to be admitted at John's trial for bank robbery because although John was in police custody, he was not being interrogated. Again, both custody and interrogation must be present for *Miranda* to apply.

A defendant exposed to custodial interrogation need not be informed of the particular crime being investigated.[29] This is true even when a suspect thinks that police officers are investigating a minor crime, when in reality, they are seeking information about a much more serious crime.[30] A suspect may, however, exercise his or her rights at any time during the interrogation process and questioning must cease. Highlight 10.3 presents an excerpt from *Miranda* v. *Arizona* that illustrates this point. Furthermore, the *Miranda* warnings must be given to the suspect, even if police officers believe that the suspect is fully aware of his or her constitutional rights. Police officers often arrest the same individuals on numerous occasions for different offenses. Even though a suspect may be as familiar with the *Miranda* warnings as the investigating police officer, he or she must still be provided with the warnings.

Reading the **Miranda** *Warnings*

Many experienced police officers carry small cards that contain a written statement of the *Miranda* warnings, which they will *read* to a suspect prior to conducting a custodial interrogation. This is a good practice because it will help to ensure that any statements made by the suspect are admissible at trial. Figure 10.1 presents a copy of a *Miranda* warning card used presently by one police department. If an officer reads the warnings directly from a card, it reduces the possibility that he or she may fail to properly advise the suspect. A favorite tactic of experienced defense attorneys is to ask a police officer if he or she had given the defendant the *Miranda* warnings before asking questions. When the officer says "yes," the attorney will then ask whether he or she recited the warnings from memory. If so, the attorney will ask the officer to recite them on the witness stand. If the officer (who is under very great pressure in an important case) forgets to recite any important piece of the warnings, the attorney will move to suppress the defendant's incriminating statements. Therefore, because it reduces the possibility of error, it is always a good practice for a police officer to *read* the *Miranda* warnings directly from a card.

A suspect may waive his or her constitutional rights and agree to answer questions. The burden of proving that an accused waived his or her constitutional rights lies with the prosecution. This means that the prosecution must be able to demonstrate that the suspect understood the *Miranda* warnings, and that he or she voluntarily and intelligently agreed to answer questions. Before considering these issues, however, it is important to discuss more fully *Miranda*'s two cornerstones, custody and interrogation.

Custody

Understanding what **custody** means is one key to understanding *Miranda* v. *Arizona.* A suspect is in police custody for *Miranda* purposes whenever he or she is deprived of the freedom of action in a significant way. If a suspect is in police custody and is interrogated by officers, he or she must be given *Miranda* warnings in order for any statements to be admissible at trial.

To determine if a suspect was in police custody a court will use an **objective test**—it will ask whether a reasonable person in the defendant's circumstances would have felt free to terminate the encounter and leave.[31] In *Stansbury* v. *California,*[32] the Supreme Court held that this test focuses on what a hypothetically reasonable person would believe in the particular situation, not on the subjective beliefs of the particular suspect or on the police officers' intentions, unless they are communicated to the defendant. Moreover, a court will use a totality of circumstances test on a case-by-case basis to determine if a reasonable person would have felt free to leave. This means that a court will examine numerous factors, such as where the questioning takes place. The general rule is that custody is more likely to occur when a suspect is placed in unfamiliar or potentially hostile surroundings.

An earlier section of this Chapter observed that the Supreme Court has eroded *Miranda*'s principle to some extent in recent years. One way that the Court has done so is by taking a restrictive view of what constitutes custody.

FIGURE 10.1

Copy of Miranda *warning card*

Rights of Accused Under Fifth Amendment ("*Miranda* Warning")	Waiver
1. You have the right to remain silent. 2. Anything you say can and will be used against you in a court of law. 3. You have the right to talk to a lawyer and have him present with you while you are being questioned. 4. If you cannot afford to hire a lawyer, one will be appointed to represent you before any questioning, if you wish one.	After the warning is given and in order to secure a waiver, the following questions should be asked and an affirmative reply secured to each question. 1. Do you understand each of these rights I have explained to you? 2. Having these rights in mind, do you wish to talk to us now?

Questioning at the Police Station.   Simply because a suspect is questioned at the police station does not mean that he or she is in custody and must be given the *Miranda* warnings. In *California* v. *Beheler,*[33] the Court held that *Miranda* warnings were not required when a suspect who was not under arrest voluntarily accompanied police officers to headquarters, talked with them for approximately 30 minutes, and was then permitted to leave.

Oregon v. *Mathiason*[34] presented another station house interrogation. A state police officer investigating a burglary tried unsuccessfully several times to contact Mathiason, who was a parolee. After about 25 days, the officer left his card at Mathiason's apartment with a note asking him to call because "I'd like to discuss something with you." The next day Mathiason called the officer, who asked him where it would be convenient to meet. Mathiason had no preference, so the officer asked if he would meet him at the police station. The officer met Mathiason in the hallway, shook hands and took him into an office. Mathiason was told that he was not under arrest, the door was closed, and they sat across a desk. The officer told Mathiason that he wanted to discuss a burglary and that his truthfulness would possibly be considered by the district attorney or judge. The officer further told Mathiason that the police believed that he was involved in the burglary and falsely stated that Mathiason's fingerprints were found at the scene. Mathiason admitted taking the property. The officer then advised Mathiason of his constitutional rights and took a taped confession. The defendant's confession was crucial to the prosecution's case, and at trial he was convicted of burglary. The Supreme Court of Oregon held that the interrogation took place in a coercive environment and reversed Mathiason's conviction. The U.S. Supreme Court held, however, that the confession was properly admitted into evidence because no *custodial* interrogation had occurred. Although the officer had interrogated Mathiason, he was not in custody, even though the encounter had taken place in the police station.

The rule that emerges from these cases is that a suspect's incriminating statements made in response to questioning in the absence of *Miranda* warnings at the police station may be used as evidence when the individual is not deprived of his or her freedom. If a suspect is arrested and transported to the police station and questioned, or if a reasonable person would not feel free to terminate the encounter and leave, any incriminating statements will be suppressed unless they are preceded by the *Miranda* warnings. Consequently, it is a good police practice to advise suspects of their constitutional rights whenever they are brought to the police station for questioning.

Questioning in a Police Vehicle.   Police officers interrogating suspects in police vehicles should provide them with the *Miranda* warnings. If a suspect is locked behind a screen in a police car, a court is likely to hold that the suspect had been placed in an inherently coercive environment. For example, suppose two suspects are handcuffed and placed in a police cruiser, but the officer says nothing to them. The circumstances suggest that the individuals have been placed under arrest. If the officer then asks questions and the suspects make incriminating statements, a court is likely to hold that custodial interrogation had occurred. Their statements may be used at trial only if the *Miranda* warnings were provided.

General On-the-Scene Questioning.   In general, police officers need not give persons *Miranda* warnings during general conversations on the street. For example, suppose that a police officer received a call to respond to a traffic accident at a particular intersection. When the officer arrived at the scene, several people were standing around a car that had just apparently struck a telephone pole. The officer got out of the police car and asked: "What happened?" One person in the group responded: "I was driving toward Centerville and I fell asleep and hit this pole." This statement may be used at trial because general on-the-scene questioning does not require the *Miranda* warnings.

A slight change in the above example may result in a different outcome, however. Suppose that when the officer arrives at the scene he or she sees a single individual standing next to the car that had just struck the telephone pole. The individual is staggering, bleeding profusely from the head, and reeks of the smell of intoxicating liquor. Moreover, the person is holding a bottle of Jack Daniels whiskey in his right hand. The suspect should be given the *Miranda* warnings before any questioning takes place. Simply because a criminal investigation has focused on a suspect does not mean that the police must give him or her the *Miranda* warnings. In this example, however, it is highly unlikely that the police officer would have allowed the suspect to leave. *Miranda* warnings are required if a reasonable person in the suspect's position would have been likely to realize that he or she was not free to leave.

Stop and Frisk Encounters.   An individual is not automatically entitled to the *Miranda* warnings whenever a police officer who has reasonable suspicion to believe that the suspect is involved in criminal activity conducts a stop and frisk. In fact, *Miranda* warnings are not required in *most* stop and frisk encounters.[35] In *Berkemer*

v. *McCarty,*[36] the Court stated that there is no "suggestion in our opinions that *Terry* stops are subject to the dictates of *Miranda.*"[37] You should bear in mind, however, that if a suspect is arrested following a stop and frisk encounter, he or she must be given the *Miranda* warnings before any questioning.

Stops for Traffic Violations.   A motorist stopped for a routine traffic violation is not entitled to the *Miranda* warnings. In most traffic encounters a reasonable motorist would believe that he or she was free to leave after a ticket is issued. In *Berkemer* v. *McCarty,*[38] the Supreme Court held that the *Miranda* warnings need not be given to motorists in an ordinary traffic stop situation. Even when a motorist is suspected of driving under the influence of alcohol, no *Miranda* warnings are necessary before an officer orders the suspect to perform sobriety tests, including dexterity tests, at the scene. The Court held that although suspects in these circumstances are "seized" for Fourth Amendment purposes, the relatively "nonthreatening character" of such stops supported a rule that such persons were not "in custody" and do not require the *Miranda* warnings.[39] An individual suspected of driving under the influence of alcohol must be given the *Miranda* warnings, however, once he or she is arrested and interrogated by police officers. Moreover, the Court in *Berkemer* emphasized that a suspect must be given the *Miranda* warnings whenever he or she is exposed to custodial interrogation, regardless of the seriousness of the offense.

Questioning at a Defendant's Home.   A person may be entitled to the *Miranda* warnings even if an interrogation occurs in the suspect's own home. In *Orozco* v. *Texas,*[40] the Supreme Court held that a police officer's questioning of a murder suspect who was at home in bed at 4:00 AM was custodial interrogation. Orozco was surrounded by police officers, one of whom later testified that Orozco was under arrest and not free to leave. In these circumstances there was an intimidating atmosphere and a potential for compulsion. Therefore, Orozco should have been given the *Miranda* warnings, and his conviction was reversed. *Orozco* illustrates that custodial interrogation may occur anywhere. Even in familiar and comfortable surroundings, police officers must still give a suspect the *Miranda* warnings if he or she is questioned and, considering all the circumstances surrounding the encounter, a reasonable person would not feel free to leave.

Police officers need not give *Miranda* warnings, however, if they question a suspect at home in a noncoercive atmosphere and there is no custodial interrogation. It is interesting to compare *Orozco* with *Beckwith* v. *United States.*[41] In *Beckwith,* Internal Revenue Service agents, who suspected Beckwith of tax evasion, questioned him at his home for three hours. Beckwith, who was not in custody and was informed that he was free to discontinue the interview at any time, made incriminating statements. At trial, Beckwith argued that his statements should be suppressed because the investigation had focused upon him and he was not given the *Miranda* warnings, even though he was not exposed to custodial interrogation. The Supreme Court held that because Beckwith was not in custody, he was not entitled to the *Miranda* warnings.

A central difference between *Orozco* and *Beckwith* is that the environment in which the questioning occurred in *Orozco* was inherently coercive. Officers had questioned Orozco at 4:00 AM and he was not free to leave. In *Beckwith,* the questioning did not occur in an inherently coercive environment. He was not in custody and was questioned at his home at 8:00 AM In these circumstances, Beckwith was not entitled to the *Miranda* warnings.

Questioning at a Jail and Questioning Probationers.   A jail or a prison is a highly coercive environment. Consequently, if police officers question a suspect at a jail or a prison, the individual should be given the *Miranda* warnings.[42] In *Mathis* v. *United States,*[43] the Supreme Court held that an Internal Revenue Service investigator's failure to provide Mathis with the *Miranda* warnings at a state prison where Mathis was incarcerated for an unrelated offense violated the Fifth Amendment.

Probation officers are not required to give the *Miranda* warnings to probationers during required meetings. *Minnesota* v. *Murphy*[44] held that a probationer was not entitled to the *Miranda* warnings when he admitted to a probation officer that he had committed a rape and murder several years earlier.

Interrogation

Interrogation is *Miranda* v. *Arizona*'s second cornerstone. Clearly, "express questioning"[45] is one form of interrogation. *Rhode Island* v. *Innis* held that police practices that are the "functional equivalent"[46] of express questioning are forms of interrogation as well. This includes actions or words by the police that are reasonably likely to result in a suspect's incriminating response. *Miranda*'s protections extend only to persons who are interrogated once they are in police custody. Precisely what constitutes interrogation, however, may be a tricky question.[47]

In *Rhode Island* v. *Innis,* Innis was arrested at approximately 4:30 AM, for suspicion of robbing a taxicab driver and murdering him with a shotgun blast to the back of the head. Innis was unarmed at the time of his arrest. Within minutes a police sergeant and a captain arrived at the scene. The captain gave Innis the *Miranda* warnings, and Innis asked to speak with an attorney. The captain then directed that Innis be placed in a police cruiser and taken to the station. Three officers accompanied Innis. During the ride to the station two of the officers began to discuss the missing murder weapon. One of the officers later testified: "At this point, I was talking back and forth with Patrolman McKenna stating that I frequent this area while on patrol and [that because a school for handicapped children is located nearby,] there's a lot of handicapped children running around in this area, and God forbid one of them might find a weapon with shells and they might hurt themselves." The other patrolman agreed that they should continue to search for the weapon. Innis then interrupted the conversation, stating that he would direct the officers to the missing gun. The officers returned to the scene of the arrest where other officers were searching for the weapon. The captain again advised Innis of his rights. Innis indicated that he understood his rights, but "wanted to get the gun out of the way because of the kids in the area in the school." Innis then led the officers to a field, where they discovered the shotgun hidden under some rocks. At trial, the judge admitted the shotgun and Innis's statements into evidence and he was convicted of murder. The Rhode Island Supreme Court overturned the conviction and held that the officers had "interrogated" Innis without a valid waiver of his right to counsel, and held too that the conversation in the police cruiser amounted to "subtle coercion" that was the equivalent of interrogation. The U.S. Supreme Court held that *Miranda* safeguards:

> "[C]ome into play whenever a person in custody is subjected to either express questioning or its functional equivalent. . . . [W]e conclude that [Innis] was not "interrogated" within the meaning of *Miranda.* It is undisputed that the first prong of the definition of "interrogation" was not satisfied, for the conversation [between the officers] included no express questioning. . . . Rather, that conversation was, at least in form, nothing more than a dialogue between the two officers to which no response from the respondent was invited."[48]

The Court held too that the conversation between the officers was not the "functional equivalent" of questioning because it involved a brief conversation and the officers could not have known that Innis "would suddenly be moved to make a self-incriminating response."[49]

On its face, *Rhode Island* v. *Innis* appears to present an issue that is similar to one decided in *Brewer* v. *Williams,* the "proper Christian burial speech" case, considered in detail in Chapter 3.[50] *Brewer,* however, was a Sixth Amendment right to counsel case, whereas *Innis* presented a Fifth Amendment self-incrimination issue. *Innis* held that the two types of issues are conceptually distinct, because "the policies underlying the two constitutional protections are quite different."[51]

Rhode Island v. *Innis* takes a restrictive view of what constitutes interrogation under *Miranda.* One could argue that the conversation between the officers in that case was a psychological ploy, a "guilt trip" designed to elicit an incriminating response from Innis. In *Innis,* the Supreme Court did not accept this argument.

Later cases have asserted, however, that police officers may go too far in trying to manipulate a situation in order to elicit an incriminating response. For example, if police officers were to falsely tell a suspect that they would harm the suspect's family unless he or she confessed to a crime, a reviewing court is likely to hold their actions to be the functional equivalent of interrogation.[52] In *Arizona* v. *Mauro,*[53] however, the Court held that police officers' creation of a situation that led to the increased likelihood that a suspect would confess did not constitute interrogation. Mauro had informed officers that he did not want to speak with them without counsel. Mauro's wife came to police headquarters, however, and the police allowed her to speak with her husband in the presence of an officer with a tape recorder in plain sight on a desk. During the conversation, Mauro made incriminating statements, which were admitted into evidence at trial. The Supreme Court held that the police practices here did not constitute interrogation. There was no evidence that the meeting between Mauro and his wife had been designed to produce incriminating statements—the wife had requested the meeting, and the police initially attempted to discourage it.

Taken together, *Innis* and *Mauro* appear to indicate that only highly deceptive police behavior that is designed to elicit a suspect's incriminating response will be held to constitute "interrogation" or its "functional equivalent" under *Miranda.* Some types of questioning do not constitute interrogation, however, under *Miranda.* These include questioning by private persons, routine booking questions, questions asked by officials at U.S. borders, general on-the-scene questioning, and questions asked by police officers at a meeting requested by a defendant.[54] In *Estelle* v. *Smith,*[55] the Court held, however, that defendants undergoing court-ordered psychiatric evaluations are exposed to interrogation and must be given the *Miranda* warnings.

Questioning by Private Persons.   *Miranda* is designed to prevent *government* agents from making suspects incriminate themselves. Therefore, questioning by a private person, including the victim of a crime, does not require the *Miranda* warnings.

Routine Booking Procedures.   When suspects are arrested they are normally taken to a police station or a jail where they are processed. Typical procedures include taking their fingerprints, taking photographs, and recording general biographical information. These processes are termed *routine booking procedures.* In *Pennsylvania* v. *Muniz,*[56] a plurality of four Supreme Court Justices stated that police officers need not provide a suspect with the *Miranda* warnings when they ask questions designed to elicit information for routine booking procedures. If the suspect's response contains incriminating information that was not requested by the question, the information is considered to have been given voluntarily, and it may be used as evidence. This is because such questions are not designed to produce incriminating responses, *Miranda*'s chief concern; rather, routine booking questions are a reasonable part of an administrative record-keeping process.

Questioning at U.S. Borders.   Chapter 6 discussed searches conducted at U.S. borders and indicated that persons entering or leaving the country have a diminished expectation of privacy. Law enforcement agents need not give persons the *Miranda* warnings when questioning them at U.S. borders.[57] Typical questions may inquire about a person's place of birth, age, citizenship, and state of residence. If, however, law enforcement agents have reason to believe that a suspect is committing a crime, they must provide him or her with the *Miranda* warnings before asking questions that are designed to elicit an incriminating response.

General On-the-Scene Questioning.   The earlier discussion of what constitutes custody under *Miranda* v. *Arizona* indicated that police officers conducting general on-the-scene questioning need not provide individuals with *Miranda* warnings. One reason for this rule is that when a police officer first arrives at the scene of an incident, often no suspect has been placed in custody. For example, suppose that a police officer receives a report of a traffic accident at a particular intersection. When the officer arrives at the scene, he or she sees several people standing around. The officer approaches them and asks "what happened?" Such questioning is an illustration of general on-the-scene questioning that would not require the *Miranda* warnings. In addition, if one person had responded, "I guess I had a little too much to drink," the statement is likely to be admissible at trial if the person is later charged with driving under the influence of alcohol.

Meetings Requested by a Suspect.   *Miranda* warnings are not required if a suspect requests a meeting with the police and makes incriminating statements.[58] A reviewing court is likely to consider such statements by a defendant to have been made voluntarily.

Questioning During Grand Jury Proceedings. Although the U.S. Supreme Court has not conclusively decided the issue, a number of courts have held that a suspect need not be given the *Miranda* warnings at a grand jury proceeding. In *United States* v. *Mandujano,*[59] the Supreme Court held that an indigent suspect need not be advised of his right to appointed counsel or his right to discontinue questioning at a grand jury proceeding. The rationale for this rule is that the grand jury's need for information during the investigatory process outweighs the defendant's need for counsel in this setting.

Asserting a Suspect's Constitutional Rights

Suppose a suspect is taken into custody and is given the *Miranda* warnings at the police station. He then agrees to answer police officers' questions about a recent series of burglaries. Two minutes into the questioning, however, the suspect suddenly decides to stop answering questions and says that he wishes to speak with an attorney. Police officers must stop the questioning as soon as the suspect asserts his or her constitutional rights. An individual may assert constitutional rights either by clearly indicating that he or she has decided to remain silent or wishes to speak with an attorney. This example presents a clear instance of someone asserting his or her constitutional rights. Many cases that present these issues are not so clear, however, and have led to numerous appeals of criminal convictions. Because the courts decide these issues on a case-by-case basis, it is important to develop a working knowledge of the case law in this area.

Ambiguous Assertions of a Right to Counsel. In order to assert his or her constitutional rights, a suspect's request for counsel or statement of a desire to remain silent must be clear and unambiguous. If during custodial interrogation a suspect asserts a desire to speak with counsel, police officers must cease all questioning until an attorney is provided. In *McNeil* v. *Wisconsin,*[60] the Supreme Court stated that this second level of *Miranda*'s protections is "designed to prevent police from badgering a defendant into waiving his previously asserted Miranda rights."[61] A suspect's request for counsel, however, must be sufficiently clear to apprise a reasonable police officer that he or she is requesting an attorney. If the request is ambiguous, and the suspect continues to make incriminating statements, they may be used as evidence.[62] For example, in *Davis* v. *United States,*[63] the suspect waived his constitutional rights and began to answer police officers' questions. Davis stated later, however, "Maybe I should talk to a lawyer."[64] He continued to answer questions, however, and made incriminating statements. The Supreme Court held that the statements could be admitted into evidence because Davis's request for counsel was ambiguous.

Moreover, if a defendant makes a request for counsel at his or her arraignment, police officers may not question the individual until counsel is provided. In *Michigan* v. *Jackson,*[65] the Supreme Court held that if the police initiate such post-arraignment questioning, the defendant's incriminating statements are inadmissible.

The Rule of *Edwards* v. *Arizona.* If a suspect makes a clear request for counsel, police officers must cease questioning until the attorney is provided. In *Edwards* v. *Arizona*[66] the defendant was charged with robbery, burglary, and murder and was arrested at his home. He was taken to the police station where he was advised of his constitutional rights. Edwards stated that he understood his rights and agreed to submit to questioning. Police officers told Edwards that another suspect already in custody had implicated him in the crime; however, he denied any involvement. After making a brief statement he sought to "make a deal." The interrogating officer told Edwards that he wanted a statement, but that he did not have the authority to negotiate a deal. Edwards told the officer: "I want an attorney before making a deal." At this point questioning ceased and Edwards was taken to jail.

The next morning two detectives came to the jail and asked to see Edwards. When the detention officer told Edwards that the detectives wished to speak with him, he stated that he did not want to talk with anyone. The guard told him that "he had" to talk and took him to meet with the detectives. The officers identified themselves and informed him of his *Miranda* warnings. Edwards was willing to talk, but first he wanted to hear the taped statement of the alleged accomplice who had implicated him. After listening to the tape for several minutes, Edwards implicated himself in the crime.

Prior to trial, Edwards moved to suppress his confession on the ground that his rights were violated when the officers returned to question him after he had invoked his right to counsel. The motion was denied and his confession was admitted into evidence. On appeal, the U.S. Supreme Court held that the confession was inadmissible because it was obtained in violation of Edwards's right to counsel. The Court stated:

> We think it clear that Edwards was subjected to custodial interrogation . . . within the meaning of *Rhode Island* v. *Innis,* and that this occurred at the instance of authorities. His statement, made without having had access to counsel, did not amount to a valid waiver and hence was inadmissible.[67]

Edwards makes it clear that if a suspect makes an unambiguous request for counsel, he or she must be given an attorney before interrogation may resume. This is termed the ***Edwards* rule.** If, however, the accused "himself initiates further communication, exchanges, or conversations with the police" any incriminating statements may be used at trial.[68] Once an accused retains counsel, however, the attorney must be allowed to be present when interrogation resumes. This principle was established in *Minnick* v. *Mississippi,*[69] where the Supreme Court held that a defendant who had invoked his right to counsel and had retained an attorney could not later be interrogated by police officers outside the lawyer's presence.

Under *Miranda,* however, an accused has no right to see someone other than a lawyer. In *Fare* v. *Michael C.,*[70] a juvenile asked to see his probation officer but the police refused. The suspect then agreed to speak with the police and made incriminating statements. The Supreme Court held that this request was not the equivalent of a request for an attorney and his request for the probation officer was only one factor to be used to determine if he had waived his rights.

Conversation Initiated by a Suspect.   In *Oregon* v. *Bradshaw,*[71] the defendant, who was intoxicated and involved in a fatal accident, was suspected of manslaughter. While he was being transported to the police station he asked an officer: "What is going to happen to me now?" The officer informed Bradshaw that he was not required to speak and that because he had requested a lawyer, any additional conversation had to be completely voluntary. Bradshaw indicated that he understood and the officer suggested that Bradshaw might help himself by taking a polygraph test. He took the test and, after failing it, confessed to the crime. The Supreme Court held in a plurality opinion that because Bradshaw had initiated the conversation with the officer, there was no violation of his constitutional rights.

Questioning a Suspect About an Unrelated Crime. The *Edwards* rule applies too when a suspect invokes his or her right to counsel during an initial interrogation and police officers return later to interrogate the suspect at a different time about an unrelated crime. In *Arizona* v. *Roberson,*[72] the defendant was arrested at the scene of a burglary and told officers that he wanted counsel before answering questions. Three days later, a second police officer who was unaware that Robertson had requested counsel gave him the *Miranda* warnings, asked him about a different burglary, and Robertson made incriminating statements. The Supreme Court held that the *Edwards* rule prevented Robertson's statements from being used as evidence because the new *Miranda* warnings did not overcome the presumption of government coercion created by the lengthy period of confinement.

The *Massiah* Doctrine. *Massiah* v. *United States*[73] was an early case involving an indicted defendant who had retained counsel, was out on bail, and whose remarks were solicited by a police undercover agent. The ***Massiah* doctrine** asserts that once a suspect has been indicted, is formally charged with a crime, has retained counsel, and is released from custody (usually on bail), any statements he or she makes to an undercover agent who tries to elicit a confession are inadmissible at trial. Evidence obtained in this manner violates the defendant's right to counsel. *Maine* v. *Moulton*[74] reaffirmed this principle, although it held that any information an informant obtains about crimes other than the one charged in the defendant's original indictment may be used as evidence.

Using Police Informants to Get Confessions. The Supreme Court has ruled that the police may not plant an informant in a jail cell to interrogate a suspect about whether he or she committed the charged crime. *United States* v. *Henry,*[75] overturned a defendant's conviction when police officers planted an informant who asked Henry incriminating questions in jail. Such questioning violated Henry's right to counsel. In *Kuhlman* v. *Wilson,*[76] however, the Court held that prosecutors may use a defendant's statements to a police informant in a jail if the informant simply listens and does not actively question the individual.

Waiver of Constitutional Rights

A suspect may waive his or her constitutional rights and agree to answer questions during custodial interrogation. The prosecution, however, bears the substantial burden of proving that a waiver of constitutional rights was voluntary and intelligent. A reviewing court will use a totality of circumstances approach to determine if a waiver was valid and examine a defendant's personal characteristics, including intelligence, experience, and age.[77] A waiver of constitutional rights need not be "wise to be intelligent," however, and even if a defendant's ability to make rational choices is affected by a mental disease, he may validly waive his rights.[78] For example, in *Colorado* v. *Connelly*[79] the Supreme Court held that the chief evil that *Miranda* is designed to guard against is government coercion. The fact that Connelly was suffering from psychosis when he waived his constitutional rights did not prevent the state from using his incriminating statements in the absence of police coercion.

Moreover, even juveniles may waive their constitutional rights. *Fare* v. *Michael C.*[80] held that the juvenile's age, experience, and other relevant factors must be considered using a totality of circumstances test to determine whether a waiver is valid. Many states have passed laws, however, that will permit a juvenile to waive his or her constitutional rights only in the presence of a parent, lawful guardian, or an attorney.

Written Waiver. A waiver of constitutional rights need not be in writing, although obtaining a written waiver is a good law enforcement practice. Figure 10.2 contains a copy of a standard written waiver form used by many law enforcement agencies. In *North Carolina* v. *Butler,*[81] the defendant indicated that he was willing to talk with F.B.I. agents but he refused to sign a written waiver form. Butler did not say anything when he was advised of his right to counsel and later made incriminating statements. The Supreme Court held that a waiver of constitutional rights may sometimes be "inferred from the actions and words of the person interrogated."[82] Likewise, in *Connecticut* v. *Barrett*[83] the Supreme Court held that if a defendant refuses to sign a written waiver form outside the presence of counsel, his oral responses to questions may be admitted at trial. A valid waiver may not, however, be presumed because a defendant decides to remain silent.

Events that occur outside a suspect's presence that he or she is not aware of do not affect the ability to waive constitutional rights. In *Moran* v. *Burbine,*[84] after being informed of his constitutional rights, and after executing a series of written waivers, Burbine confessed to the murder of a young woman. At no point during the interrogation did he request counsel. While he was in police custody, his sister attempted to retain a lawyer to represent him. The attorney telephoned the police station and received assurances that Burbine would not be questioned further until the next day. In fact, the interrogation session that resulted in the incriminating statements began later that evening. The question that reached the Supreme Court was whether the conduct of the police, or Burbine's ignorance of the attorney's efforts to reach him, tainted the validity of the waivers. The Supreme Court held that the confessions could be admitted into evidence.

Exceptions to the *Miranda* Rule

The Supreme Court in recent years has restricted *Miranda*'s impact by recognizing several exceptions. Table 10.1 summarizes these exceptions. Each of these will be discussed separately.

Figure 10.2

Copy of standard Miranda *waiver form*

RIGHTS

TIME _____   STATEMENT TAKEN BY _____

DATE _____

OFFICE OF _____

I, _____, having been informed that

I am a suspect in the crime of _____,

voluntarily, without threats or promises on the part of the police, make the following statement to

members of the _____ Police Department

after having been advised that:

      1.   I do not have to give a statement.

      2.   I have the right to remain silent.

      3.   Anything I say can and will be used against me in a court of law.

      4.   I have the right to the presence of an attorney prior to and during any questioning by the police.

      5.   I have the right to the presence of an attorney during a lineup or of witnesses, if any line-up or such confrontation takes place.

      6.   If I cannot afford an attorney, one will be appointed for me prior to any questioning, if I so desire.

I further admit and agree that:

      7.   After having been informed of my constitutional rights, I do understand these rights, and I agree to give a statement at this time.

      8.   I do not want an attorney called or appointed for me at this time.

WITNESSES: _____

              _____

                                          _____

SIGNATURE

TABLE 10.1   **Recognized Exceptions to *Miranda* v. *Arizona***

Exception	Case	Year
Public Safety	*New York* v. *Quarles*	1984
Impeachment of Testimony	*Harris* v. *New York*	1971
Purged Taint	*Wong Sun* v. *United States*	1963
Derivative Evidence	*Michigan* v. *Tucker*	1974
Resumed Questioning	*Michigan* v. *Mosley*	1975

The Public Safety Exception

The **public safety exception** to *Miranda* asserts that a suspect's incriminating statements made during custodial interrogation are admissible at trial if a threat to public safety requires an immediate interrogation, even if he or she has not been given the *Miranda* warnings.[85] In *New York* v. *Quarles,*[86] a woman approached two police officers at 12:30 AM, told them that she had just been raped by a black man, and that he had just entered a supermarket located nearby and that he had a gun. The officers observed the man, chased him through the aisles in the supermarket, and arrested him. One officer frisked Quarles and discovered that he was wearing an empty shoulder holster. After handcuffing Quarles, the officer asked him where the gun was. Quarles nodded in the direction of some empty cartons and said, "the gun is over there." The officer retrieved a loaded .38 caliber revolver from one of the cartons. He then placed Quarles under arrest, handcuffed him, and read him the *Miranda* warnings. A trial court ordered that all evidence of the gun be suppressed because Quarles was not given the *Miranda* warnings and was exposed to custodial interrogation when the officer asked him the location of the gun. The Supreme Court held that "there is a 'public safety' exception to the requirement that the *Miranda* warnings be given before a suspect's answers may be admitted into evidence . . ."[87] In these circumstances the social costs of providing the *Miranda* warnings outweighed the defendant's Fifth Amendment interests in order to "ensure that further damage to the public did not result from concealment of the gun in a public area."[88]

Impeachment

Although incriminating statements obtained in violation of a suspect's constitutional rights may not normally be used to convict a defendant at trial, such statements may be used for other limited purposes. One such purpose is for **impeachment,** which means to contradict a witness' trial testimony. For example, in *Harris* v. *New York,*[89] Harris was charged with selling heroin on two occasions. Police officers obtained incriminating statements about the crimes from Harris in violation of *Miranda*. At trial, Harris took the witness stand and denied making the sales. The prosecutor then read Harris's earlier confession to police in which he admitted making the heroin sales. The Supreme Court held that Harris's earlier statements could be used only to impeach his trial testimony. The Court stated that *Miranda* "cannot be perverted into a license to use perjury"[90] to mount a defense.[91]

Oregon v. *Hass*[92] presented a similar issue. A police officer arrested Hass and gave him the *Miranda* warnings. As he was being taken to the police station, Hass stated that he wished to speak with his attorney. The officer told Hass that he could telephone his attorney as soon as they reached the station. Hass then made incriminating statements, which appeared to have been taken in violation of *Miranda,* because he had asserted his right to counsel. At his trial on burglary charges, Hass testified that he did not commit the offense. The arresting officer then testified about Hass's incriminating statements made during the ride to the police station. The trial judge instructed the jury that the testimony was admissible solely for the purpose of impeaching Hass's credibility, not to prove that he had committed the offense. Hass was convicted of burglary. As in *Harris,* the Supreme Court held that Hass's prior inconsistent statements to the police officer could be used to impeach his credibility.

If a defendant's statements that are obtained in violation of *Miranda* are used to impeach trial testimony, he or she is entitled to have the judge give an instruction to the jury that the earlier confession may be used solely to show that the defendant's testimony is not credible, not to show that the defendant committed the charged offense. This may be asking too much from a juror, however. It may be unrealistic to assume that a juror will ignore an earlier confession and consider it solely to assess a defendant's credibility.

Using Silence to Impeach Later Testimony.   If, after a defendant has been given the *Miranda* warnings, he or she decides to remain silent, that fact may not be used to infer guilt. *Doyle* v. *Ohio*[93] held that "it would be fundamentally unfair and a deprivation of due process to allow the arrested person's silence to be used to impeach an explanation subsequently offered at trial."[94] A defendant's silence *before* he or she is arrested and given the *Miranda* warnings may, however, be used to impeach trial testimony. For example, in *Jenkins* v. *Anderson*[95] the defendant in a murder trial claimed self-defense at trial but did not tell the police before his arrest that he had acted in self-defense, although he had an opportunity to do so. The Supreme Court held that the defendant's silence before he was arrested could be used to impeach his testimony that he acted in self-defense.

The Purged Taint Exception

Chapter 3 discussed the fruit of the poisonous tree doctrine developed in *Wong Sun* v. *United States*[96] and the exclusionary rule of evidence. It observed that a confession obtained following an unlawful arrest may be admitted into evidence if the "taint" caused by the original illegality is somehow "purged." This is termed the **purged taint exception** to the exclusionary rule. *Brown* v. *Illinois*[97] developed a three-part test to be used to determine if the taint from an illegal arrest is purged sufficiently to allow the suspect's incriminating statements to be used at trial:

1. the amount of time that has elapsed between the arrest and the tainted confession;
2. whether extenuating circumstances exist (such as whether the suspect was given the *Miranda* warnings);
3. the extent and degree of police misconduct in the case.

In most circumstances, providing the suspect with the *Miranda* warnings will not purge the taint of an illegal arrest.[98] Moreover, if police officers' conduct is egregious it is highly unlikely that the taint caused by their illegal behavior will be purged. For example, suppose that police officers without probable cause arrest a suspect and jail him for three days, holding nonstop interrogation sessions but the suspect refuses to confess. After a three-hour break, he is given the *Miranda* warnings and signs a confession. In these circumstances it is unlikely that any combination of factors will purge the taint caused by the unlawful police behavior.

Suppose, however, that a suspect was arrested illegally and released almost immediately without being questioned by the police. Two weeks later the same individual comes voluntarily to police headquarters to answer questions about the same crime. He is given the *Miranda* warnings and makes incriminating statements. In these circumstances a court is likely to rule that the taint from the initial illegal arrest has been purged. First, a significant period of time has elapsed between the initial illegal arrest and the later confession. Second, the suspect was properly advised of his *Miranda* warnings. Third, the behavior of the police was not egregious. He was released immediately after the illegal arrest and his incriminating statements were not coerced.

Later cases indicate that it is somewhat difficult to purge the taint of a confession following an illegal arrest. In *Taylor* v. *Alabama*,[99] the Court held that a confession was tainted by an illegal arrest and could not be used as evidence at trial. Excerpts from this case are presented in Highlight 10.4.

New York v. *Harris*[100] presented a somewhat different situation, however. In *Harris,* police officers had probable cause to arrest the defendant but did not obtain an arrest warrant. This made the arrest unlawful. They arrested Harris at his apartment and advised him of his constitutional rights. Officers then took Harris to the police station where he confessed to a murder. At trial, Harris argued that the illegal arrest at his home tainted his later confession at the police station. The trial court admitted the confession and he was convicted. The Supreme Court held that the confession could be admitted into evidence because unlike the situation in *Brown* v. *Illinois,* where the defendant was arrested without probable cause, Harris's arrest was supported by probable cause.[101] It was therefore a lawful arrest that was technically defective. The Court held that the fruit of the poisonous tree doctrine applies only when a confession is "the product of illegal government activity."[102] Because Harris could have been lawfully arrested and taken to the police station and questioned, the police did not exploit the illegal entry into his home and the confession was properly admitted into evidence.

A final example should help to clarify the purged taint exception. Suppose a defendant is arrested lawfully and taken to the police station for questioning. The suspect is given the *Miranda* warnings but police officers forget to advise him or her of a right to have counsel present. The suspect confesses to a crime. Police officers realize their mistake immediately, however, and again give the suspect the *Miranda* warnings. The individual makes a second confession. May the second confession be used at trial, or is it the fruit of the original illegal confession? In *Oregon* v. *Elstad*,[103] the Supreme Court in similar circumstances held that the second confession may be used if it is "knowingly and intelligently made."[104] This rule would be unlikely to apply, however, if the suspect's first statement had been coerced.

Highlight 10.4

Taylor v. *Alabama,* **457 U.S. 687 (1982)**

 "[T]he State argues that the police conduct here was not flagrant or purposeful, and that we should not follow our decisions in *Brown* or *Dunaway* for that reason. However, we fail to see any relevant distinction between the conduct here and that in *Dunaway*. In this case, as in *Dunaway*, the police effectuated an investigatory arrest without probable cause, based on an uncorroborated informant's tip, and involuntarily transported petitioner to the station for interrogation in the hope that something would turn up. The fact that the police did not physically abuse petitioner, or that the confession they obtained may have been 'voluntary' for purposes of the Fifth Amendment, does not cure the illegality of the initial arrest. Alternatively, the State contends that the police conduct here argues for adopting a 'good faith' exception to the exclusionary rule. To date, we have not recognized such an exception, and we decline to do so here."

Derivative Evidence

Evidence discovered later as a result of a statement obtained in violation of *Miranda* is termed **derivative evidence.** For example, in *Michigan* v. *Tucker*[105] police officers investigating a rape case obtained statements from the defendant but failed to properly advise him of his constitutional rights. During the interrogation Tucker gave the police the name of a witness that would supposedly provide an alibi for him. When officers contacted this witness, however, he gave them information that incriminated Tucker. Tucker's statements to police were not used as evidence; however, the statements made by the witness were admitted, despite Tucker's objection. The Supreme Court held that the evidence derived from Tucker's statements, the information provided by the witness that incriminated Tucker, could be used as evidence.

    Michigan v. *Tucker* is an important qualification of *Miranda*. Under *Tucker,* evidence obtained from a witness who was discovered as a result of a defendant's statements without proper *Miranda* warnings, may be used at trial if a totality of the circumstances indicate that the taint has been purged from the initial incriminating statements. (See the discussion of the purged taint exception to the *Miranda* rule.)

Statements Obtained after Constitutional Rights Are Asserted

In *Michigan* v. *Mosley,*[106] the defendant in a robbery case, after being given his *Miranda* warnings, asserted his desire to remain silent. Police officers stopped questioning him and returned him to his cell. Several hours later, however, a different officer took him to another floor and, after giving Mosley the *Miranda* warnings again, questioned him again about a murder that had been committed during another robbery. The defendant made incriminating statements and he was convicted of robbery and murder. On appeal, the

Supreme Court held that the police did not violate Mosley's constitutional rights by resuming questioning. Here, the police had given the defendant the *Miranda* warnings, had waited a significant period of time before conducting a second interrogation, and had stopped immediately when the defendant had first asserted his right to remain silent.[107]

Arizona v. *Roberson* was considered earlier. In contrast to *Mosley,* Roberson, who was in police custody for approximately three days, had requested counsel but the request was not honored. In these circumstances the Supreme Court held that his later statements, which were obtained in the absence of counsel, could not be used as evidence.

The Effect of *Miranda* v. *Arizona* on Criminal Cases

Miranda v. *Arizona* was a 5 to 4 decision of the Warren Court. Since that time, some commentators have suggested that *Miranda* was a judicial mistake that effectively "handcuffed the cops."[108] Several early empirical studies of the *Miranda* rule's effect asserted that it had little impact on criminal prosecutions.[109] One scholar suggests, however, that many of the earlier studies are beset with methodological problems that threaten their accuracy.[110] Table 10.2, however, presents the results of a recent study, which concludes that *Miranda* v. *Arizona* has exerted a substantial impact on criminal prosecutions. The authors, who attempted to measure the effect of questioning success on the ultimate outcome of 172 criminal cases, concluded:

> Defendants whom police successfully questioned were less likely to receive concession in plea bargaining. Of suspects whom police successfully questioned, 30.6% pled to charges at the same level as initially filed, compared to only 15.4% for suspects invoking *Miranda* rights, 9.4% for suspects questioned unsuccessfully, and 10.8% for suspects not questioned. Along the same lines, defendants whom police successfully questioned were generally less likely to have charges dropped. Of suspects whom police successfully questioned, 9.6% either had charges dismissed or entered pleas in abeyance, as compared to 7.7% for suspects who invoked, 30.2% for suspects unsuccessfully questioned, and 21.6% for suspects not questioned.[111]

Cassell and Hayman's study indicates that *Miranda* v. *Arizona* continues to exert a significant impact on U.S. criminal cases. If police officers obtain incriminating statements from a suspect, "that individual is more likely to be convicted of more serious criminal charges. On the other side of the coin, if the police are unsuccessful, it appears the suspect is more likely to 'walk.'"[112]

The debate about *Miranda* v. *Arizona* may never be settled to everyone's satisfaction due to the competing interests represented in U.S. justice systems. Proponents of the *Miranda* rule will continue to assert that it represents a fundamental cornerstone of a commitment to due process of law. Opponents of the rule, on the other hand, will insist that it is an obstacle to effective law enforcement. In the final analysis, as one eminent legal scholar has suggested, the *Miranda* rule has exerted a highly positive impact on many different aspects of U.S. justice systems:

> A generation after *Miranda,* we know that the warnings work remarkably well, which is to say that the Fifth Amendment benefits society. *Miranda* led to the elimination of police

TABLE 10.2 Empirical Study of the Effects of *Miranda*

Result of Questioning	Outcomes																	
	Dismissed		Abeyance		Plea 3		Plea 2		Plea 1		Plea 0		Convicted		Acquitted		Total	
	No.	%	No.	%	No.	%	No.	%	No.	%	No.	%	No.	%	No.	%	No.	%
Invoked Rights	1	7.7%	0	0.0%	0	0.0%	1	7.7%	9	69.2%	2	15.4%	0	0.0%	0	0.0%	13	100%
Questioning Successful	3	4.8%	3	4.8%	0	0.0%	5	8.1%	30	48.4%	19	30.6%	2	3.2%	0	0.0%	62	100%
Questioning Unsuccessful	15	28.3%	1	1.9%	1	1.9%	8	15.1%	20	37.7%	5	9.4%	2	3.8%	1	1.9%	53	100%
Not Questioned	6	16.2%	2	5.4%	1	2.7%	4	10.8%	20	54.1%	4	10.8%	0	0.0%	0	0.0%	37	100%
Total	25	15.2%	6	3.6%	2	1.2%	18	10.9%	79	47.9%	30	18.2%	4	2.4%	1	0.6%	165	100%

Relation of Statements to Outcomes
(N = 172; 12 unavailable)

Table from Paul G. Cassell and Bret S. Hayman, "Police Interrogation in the 1990s," *UCLA Law Review*, Vol. 43, 1996, p. 912. [Originally published in 43 UCLA L. REV. 839. Copyright 1996, The Regents of the University of California. All Rights Reserved.]

inquisitions and of the third degree; it led too to a better educated and better trained police force that relies on the best evidence that can be found to support accusations of crime. Fewer convictions are reversed, and we are all freer because of *Miranda*.[113]

Compelling Waivers of the Privilege Against Self-Incrimination

A discussion of the Fifth Amendment privilege against self-incrimination would not be complete without considering the circumstances in which defendants and witnesses may be compelled to waive his or her privilege against self-incrimination and testify in a criminal case.

A Defendant's Right to Refuse to Testify

A defendant may not be forced to take the witness stand and provide self-incriminating testimony in a criminal case. Testimony is self-incriminating when an honest answer would tend to convict someone or provide evidence leading to a criminal conviction.[114] You may recall that O.J. Simpson declined to testify at his murder trial. This had certain strategic advantages for the defense. First, it prevented the prosecution from being able to cross-examine Simpson and delve into his past history of spousal abuse. Moreover, it eliminated the prosecution's opportunity to explore the numerous inconsistencies in O.J. Simpson's explanation of the events surrounding Nicole Brown Simpson's and Ronald Goldman's deaths.

The same protection did not extend to Simpson's civil trial for causing wrongfully the deaths of Nicole Brown Simpson and Ronald Goldman. In the civil trial, O.J. Simpson was forced to take the witness stand and testify about the events surrounding the deaths of these individuals. There was no violation of his Fifth Amendment privilege against self-incrimination because it was a civil trial and because the right to be free from double jeopardy would bar another criminal trial.

Another protection given to defendants who decline to testify in a criminal case is that prosecutors may not make any negative comment during the trial about the defendant's refusal. *Griffin* v. *California*[115] held that such comments violate the Fifth Amendment. A trial judge too may not make adverse comments about a defendant's refusal to testify[116] and a defendant has a right to insist on an instruction to the jury that the refusal may not give rise to an inference of guilt.[117]

A Witness's Right to Assert the Privilege

In *Allen* v. *Illinois*,[118] the Supreme Court held that a witness in a criminal case may assert the Fifth Amendment privilege against self-incrimination and cannot be compelled to answer incriminating questions. The prosecution may compel a witness to testify at trial or at a grand jury proceeding, however, by granting him or her **immunity** from prosecution. This means that the testimony may not be used to convict the individual of criminal charges. Once immunity is granted, however, the witness must testify because the testimony may no longer be used.

Two Types of Witness Immunity.   There are two different types of witness immunity. **Transactional immunity,** which gives a witness complete protection, provides that the individual may never be prosecuted for the crimes that he or she testifies about. It is granted to witnesses only in exceptional cases. One reason for giving a witness this type of immunity would be that the evidence that he or she is able to provide would be very difficult to obtain in any other way. Prosecutors have sometimes granted transactional immunity to witnesses testifying in cases involving top-level organized crime figures, or international terrorism. Often, such witnesses are themselves shady characters who may have committed heinous crimes including murder. Highlight 10.5 describes the testimony given by a witness in the World Trade Center bombing case in New York City.

Prosecutors are not required to grant a witness transactional immunity in order to compel their testimony. *Kastigar* v. *United States*[119] held that **use immunity** is sufficient to protect the Fifth Amendment privilege against self-incrimination. Use immunity, which is sometimes termed **derivative use immunity,** provides that a witness's *testimony* may not be used to convict him or her. In addition, the government is prevented from deriving any additional evidence from the testimony that could be used to bring a case against the witness.

To illustrate how use immunity works, suppose that John, a witness in a bank robbery case, testifies under a grant of use immunity that he shot and killed someone. The government could not use that testimony to prosecute John for the murder. If the government was able to prove its case without using the testimony, however, (for example, if there were five witnesses to the crime) the prosecution could proceed and John could be convicted of murder. Moreover, if John mentioned the name of someone who could provide additional evidence in the case, prosecutors would be prevented from getting additional evidence from that person to use in a case against John. In other words, they are prevented from *deriving* additional evidence from John's testimony.

Grants of Immunity Are Coextensive.   In the example above, if John was granted immunity from prosecution in one jurisdiction in return for his testimony in a murder case, that same testimony may not be used in another place to convict him of murder. To illustrate, if John was given immunity for his testimony in a murder case in the U.S. District Court for the Eastern District of Illinois, he could not later be prosecuted for the same crime in the U.S. District Court for the Northern District of Washington. In *Murphy* v. *Waterfront Commission,*[120] the Supreme Court held that a grant of immunity is **coextensive.** This means that the privilege against self-incrimination protects a state witness against incrimination under federal as well as state law and a federal witness under state as well as federal law. Likewise, a witness who testifies under a grant of immunity from one state may not be prosecuted by another state for the same offense by using his or her testimony in the first case.

The Mysterious Informant

He was tall, muscular and mysterious—an Egyptian Muslim who was fluent in Arabic and apparently well versed in the operational details of espionage and terrorism. He said he had been an officer in the Egyptian army and that he had been among those who guarded Anwar Sadat, Egypt's late president, when Sadat was assassinated by Muslim fundamentalists in 1981. And bit by bit, he insinuated himself into a select group of followers of Sheik Omar Abdel-Rahman, the blind Egyptian mullah, as they launched what the FBI now says was a conspiracy to bomb U.N. headquarters and other locations in New York. Who is Emad Salem and what exactly did he do? Salem is "one weird dude," says attorney William Kunstler, who represents one of the 11 defendants in the so-called Beta-cell case. "I trusted him," says Siddig Ibrahim Siddig Ali, the alleged ringleader of the Beta cell. "He played his role so cunningly."

What Siddig Ali and his lawyer hope to prove is entrapment—a sting operation, directed by the FBI and run by the mysterious Emad Salem, that went beyond the legally permissible bounds of investigative techniques. In an interview at the federal government's Metropolitan Correctional Center in New York City late last month, Siddig Ali claimed that Salem "kept pushing us and giving us money. He said, 'We must bomb America'." Siddig Ali's lawyer, Kunstler associate Ron Kuby, seized on the published revelation that Salem had surreptitiously taped his conversations with the FBI to suggest that the government's star witness was a "ruthless, consummate opportunist without any allegiance to any person or country except himself." More to the point, Kuby said, Salem's tapes "will show that this scheme was originated, generated and terminated by the FBI"—will show, in short, that Siddig Ali and his codefendants not only were bamboozled by the informer, but entrapped in a criminal conspiracy as well.

This is a tall order, and one that is arguably premature. Claiming entrapment or a clear pattern of government misconduct isn't easy, as defendants in the FBI's 1978 Abscam investigation of congressional corruption found out. The trial of Siddig Ali and his codefendants is still months away, and the defense lawyers have not yet seen all the evidence against their clients. And attorney Kuby has not heard the tapes of Salem's conversations with the FBI agents or seen a transcript of the tapes. (These tapes might contain "some little embarrassments," one source said, but they were probably "irrelevant" to the case.) So it is impossible for Kuby, Kunstler or anybody else to know just what Emad Salem said and did when he so adroitly led the defendants into the FBI's sting.

'Pretty good': And lead them he did. Salem was somehow able to convince Siddig Ali that the electronic gadget he put on Siddig Ali's phone was a countersurveillance device; it almost certainly was an FBI bug. Salem allegedly helped the defendants build their bombs and he apparently rented the apartment and attached warehouse in Queens that were allegedly used as a bomb factory. He was present on the night that the FBI swooped down, and he was able to record many hours of allegedly incriminating conversations among the defendants with a hidden body mike. On May 7, according to transcripts of those tapes, Salem smoothly led Siddig Ali into revealing his primary target. "I want the United Nations," Siddig Ali says in the transcript. "Your idea about the United Nations is an excellent idea," the informer replies. "He probed here and there and managed to fix clearly that the U.N. was a target," says Victoria Toensing, a former deputy U.S. attorney general. "He was pretty good."

But there is room for doubt. Like most informers, Salem seems to have had a murky past and tangled motives. Egyptian officials have denied he was ever a member of Sadat's bodyguard and reporters in New York have strange stories to tell. Among other details, they say, Salem was in the habit of showing reporters a macabre photo album that included pic-

(Continued)

(Concluded)

tures of people being tortured. "Salem boasted that he was a military explosives expert," Siddig Ali says. "As for allegations of this 'witches' brew' [a reference to the fuel-and-fertilizer mixture in the bombs] I know nothing of constructing bombs. Who made the witches' brew? Ask Mr. Salem." Others, meanwhile, have pointed out that Salem stands to earn a $500,000 reward for testifying in the case,

which hardly suggests high-minded heroism. All this could yet influence a jury that the FBI went a step too far, says Paul Marcus, an expert on the entrapment defense, particularly if the informer seems "sleazy." Salem, now in protective custody, will have his chance to be convincing to the jurors—and the case may depend on how well he acts the part.

From Melinda Liu, "The Mysterious Informant," p. 28. [From *Newsweek,* August 16, 1993, © 1993, Newsweek, Inc. All rights reserved. Reprinted by permission.]

Summary

Chapter 10 discusses constitutional rights under the Fifth and Sixth Amendments. *Miranda* v. *Arizona,* which was designed to protect a defendant's privilege against self-incrimination, has become one of the most important criminal procedure cases in U.S. history. In *Miranda,* the Supreme Court held that a defendant held for interrogation must be clearly informed of the right to remain silent and to consult with a lawyer during custodial interrogation.

The pre-*Miranda* standard for admitting confessions asserted that a confession must have been the product of a defendant's free will. The voluntariness test continues to be relevant in post-*Miranda* cases, because even if a suspect is given the *Miranda* warnings, the confession must still be voluntary. To determine if a confession is voluntary, a court will consider several factors including where the questioning takes place, whether *Miranda* warnings were given, and whether the police or the accused initiated the questioning. In addition, a court will consider a suspect's personal characteristics including age, drug addiction, psychological problems, physical condition, and lack of experience with the criminal justice system.

Even if a defendant's confession is found by an appellate court to be involuntary, there is still a chance that the conviction may stand. The harmless error doctrine provides that if the effect of admitting an involuntary confession at trial was harmless and did not prejudice the defendant's rights, the conviction will be upheld.

Miranda requires both custody and interrogation. If one of these essential elements is missing, police officers are not required to provide the *Miranda* warnings. It is a good police practice to read the *Miranda* warnings to a suspect. This reduces the possibility that the officer may fail to properly advise a suspect.

An individual is in police custody whenever he or she is deprived of the freedom of action in a significant way. Custody is more likely to be found when a suspect is placed in unfamiliar or potentially hostile surroundings.

Miranda's protections extend only to persons who are interrogated once they are in police custody. Express questioning is one form of interrogation as are police practices that are the "functional equivalent" of express questioning. In *Rhode Island* v. *Innis,* however, the Supreme Court took a restrictive view of what constitutes interrogation under *Miranda.*

A suspect may assert constitutional rights either by clearly indicating that he or she has decided to remain silent or wishes to speak with an attorney. In order to assert the constitutional rights, however, a suspect's request must be clear and unambiguous. The rule of *Edwards* v. *Arizona* asserts that if a suspect makes an unambiguous request for counsel, he or she must be allowed to have an attorney present when interrogation resumes.

The *Massiah* doctrine asserts that once a suspect has been indicted and formally charged with a crime, has retained counsel, and is released from custody, any statements he or she makes to an undercover agent who tries to elicit a confession are inadmissible at trial. Evidence obtained in this manner violates the defendant's right to counsel.

A suspect may waive his or her constitutional rights and agree to answer questions. The burden of proving that an accused had waived the constitutional rights, however, lies with the prosecution, which bears the heavy burden of proving that a waiver was voluntary and intelligent. A reviewing court will use a totality of circumstances approach to determine if a waiver was valid; however, a waiver need not be "wise to be intelligent." A waiver of constitutional rights need not be in writing, although obtaining a written waiver is a good law enforcement practice.

The Supreme Court has identified the following exceptions to the *Miranda* rule: the public safety exception, impeachment of a defendant's contradictory trial testimony, the purged taint exception, the derivative evidence exception, and an exception for statements made following an assertion of constitutional rights.

A recent empirical study indicates that *Miranda* v. *Arizona* has exerted a substantial impact on criminal prosecutions. The study's authors concluded that if police officers obtain incriminating statements from a suspect, the individual is more likely to be convicted of more serious criminal charges. If the police are unsuccessful, it appears that the suspect is more likely to "walk."

Chapter 10 concludes with a discussion of when the state may compel defendants and witnesses to waive their Fifth Amendment privilege against self-incrimination. A defendant may not be forced to take the witness stand in a criminal case. Likewise, a witness in a criminal case may assert the privilege against self-incrimination and refuse to answer incriminating questions. The prosecution may force a witness to testify, however, by granting him or her immunity from prosecution.

Review Questions

1. Why is *Miranda* v. *Arizona* sometimes described as a case that resulted in the marriage of the Fifth Amendment privilege against self-incrimination and the Sixth Amendment right to counsel?

2. Discuss the pre-*Miranda* standard for admitting a suspect's confession at trial. How did *Miranda* v. *Arizona* modify the legal standard for admitting confessions at trial? What must a police officer advise a suspect to satisfy *Miranda* v. *Arizona*? Why is a good police practice to *read* the warnings to a suspect before custodial interrogation?

3. Describe a situation in which a suspect's confession could not be used at trial, even if he or she has been given the *Miranda*

warnings by police officers. Specify the reasons that the confession could not be used.

4. Identify several factors that a court will consider to determine if a suspect's confession is voluntary. Briefly describe the harmless error doctrine.

5. Discuss two crucial factors that determine if police officers must give a suspect the *Miranda* warnings. Define the following concepts:
   a. custody
   b. interrogation

6. According to your text, the Supreme Court has eroded the *Miranda* doctrine by taking a restrictive view of what constitutes custodial interrogation. Identify and discuss several cases that have eroded the *Miranda* doctrine.

7. Discuss whether police officers are likely to be required to give a suspect the *Miranda* warnings during questioning in the following places:
   a. a police station
   b. a police car
   c. during on-the-scene questioning on the street
   d. while conducting a stop and frisk on the street
   e. when stopping a motorist for a traffic violation on a public street
   f. when questioning a defendant at his or her own home

8. According to the U.S. Supreme Court in *Rhode Island* v. *Innis,* both express questioning and police practices that are the "functional equivalent" of express questioning are forms of interrogation. Identify a police practice that may be the functional equivalent of express questioning. Why is it important if a police practice constitutes interrogation?

9. Discuss the rule of *Edwards* v. *Arizona.* How did *Minnick* v. *Mississippi* modify this rule?

10. According to your text, a suspect may waive his or her constitutional rights. What must the prosecution prove in order to admit a confession after such a waiver? How will a reviewing court determine if a suspect's waiver of constitutional rights is valid? Must a waiver of constitutional rights be in written form?

11. Describe the following exceptions to the *Miranda* rule:
    a. the public safety exception
    b. impeachment
    c. the purged taint exception
    d. derivative evidence
    e. statements obtained from later questioning following an assertion of constitutional rights

12. Discuss the effect of *Miranda* v. *Arizona* on criminal cases.

13. May a defendant in a criminal case be compelled to take the witness stand and testify? May a witness testifying in a criminal case assert his or her privilege against self-incrimination? Is there anything that a prosecutor can do to force a witness to testify, even though the responses may be self-incriminating?

14. Identify and discuss two different types of witness immunity in criminal cases. If you had to give incriminating testimony in a criminal case, which type of immunity would you prefer to have and why? Under current Supreme Court precedents, which type of immunity must a prosecutor give to a witness to force him or her to testify in a criminal case?

Issues for Analysis and Discussion

1. In *Miranda* v. *Arizona,* Chief Justice Earl Warren wrote that "the blood of the accused is not the only hallmark of an unconstitutional inquisition." Using Warren's language, explain this statement fully. Why does Chief Justice Warren believe that the custodial interrogation process poses great danger to a suspect's right to be free from self-incrimination?

2. Why did the Supreme Court in *Oregon* v. *Bradshaw* hold that the defendant had waived his right to the presence of counsel when he spoke with the police? Do you agree with the rule established in *Bradshaw*? Present an argument that the defendant had not validly waived his rights under the standard established in *Edwards* v. *Arizona.*

CASE EXCERPT: *MIRANDA* v. *ARIZONA*
SUPREME COURT OF THE UNITED STATES (1966)
384 U.S. 436

(This case was consolidated by the Court with three other cases that raised the issue of the admissibility of the defendants' confessions during custodial interrogation.) Ernesto Miranda was a suspect in a rape and kidnapping. He was arrested and taken to police headquarters for questioning. At the time, Miranda was 23 years old, indigent, and had little education. There was also a suggestion that he suffered from a serious mental disease. During custodial interrogation, detectives obtained a written confession from him, which was admitted into evidence at trial. Miranda was convicted of rape and kidnapping. The Arizona Supreme Court affirmed the conviction.

Mr. Chief Justice Warren delivered the opinion of the Court.

* * *

The cases before us raise questions which go to the roots of our concepts of American criminal jurisprudence: the restraints society must observe consistent with the Federal Constitution in prosecuting individuals for crime. More specifically, we deal with the admissibility of statements obtained from an individual who is subjected to custodial police interrogation and the necessity for procedures which assure that the individual is accorded his privilege under the Fifth Amendment to the Constitution not to be compelled to incriminate himself.

* * *

[*Escobedo* v. *Illinois*] has been the subject of judicial interpretation and spirited legal debate since it was decided two years ago. Both state and federal courts, in assessing its implications, have arrived at varying conclusions . . . We granted certiorari in these cases, in order to further explore some facets of the problems, thus exposed, or applying the privilege against self-incrimination to in-custody interrogation, and to give concrete constitutional guidelines for law enforcement agencies and courts to follow.

We start here, as we did in *Escobedo,* with the premise that our holding is not an innovation in

our jurisprudence, but is an application of principles long recognized and applied in other settings. We have undertaken a thorough re-examination of the *Escobedo* decision and the principles it announced, and we reaffirm it. That case was but an explication of basic rights that are enshrined in our Constitution—that "No person . . . shall be compelled to be a witness against himself," and that "the accused shall have the Assistance of Counsel"—rights which were put in jeopardy in that case through official overbearing. These precious rights were fixed in our Constitution only after centuries of persecution and struggle. And in the words of Chief Justice Marshall, they were secured "for ages to come, and . . . designed to approach immortality as nearly as human institutions can approach it."

* * *

Our holding will be spelled out with some specificity in the pages which follow but briefly stated it is this: the prosecution may not use statements, whether exculpatory or inculpatory stemming from custodial interrogation of the defendant unless it demonstrates the use of procedural safeguards effective to secure the privilege against self-incrimination. By custodial interrogation, we mean questioning initiated by law enforcement officers after a person has been taken into custody or otherwise deprived of his freedom of action in a significant way. (Footnote 4: This is what we meant in *Escobedo* when we spoke of an investigation which had focused on an accused.) As for the procedural safeguards to be employed, unless other fully effective means are devised to inform accused persons of their right of silence and to assure a continuous opportunity to exercise it, the following measures are required. Prior to any questioning, the person must be warned that he has a right to remain silent, that any statement he does make may be used as evidence against him, and that he has a right to the presence of an attorney, either retained or appointed. The defendant may waive effectuation of these rights, provided the waiver is made voluntarily, knowingly and intelligently. If, however, he indicated in any manner and at any stage of the process that he wishes to consult with an attorney before speaking there can be no questioning. Likewise, if the individual is alone and indicates in any manner that he does not wish to be interrogated, the police may not question him. The mere fact that he may have answered some questions or volunteered some statements on his own does not deprive him of the right to refrain from answering any further inquiries until he has consulted with an attorney and thereafter consents to be questioned.

The constitutional issue we decide in each of these cases is the admissibility of statements obtained from a defendant questioned while in custody or otherwise deprived of his freedom of action in any significant way. In each, the defendant was questioned by police officers, detectives, or a prosecuting attorney in a room in which he was cut off from the outside world. In none of these cases was the defendant given a full and effective warning of his rights at the outset of the interrogation process. In all the cases, the questioning elicited oral admissions, and in three of them, signed statements as well which were admitted at their trials. They all thus share salient features—

incommunicado interrogation of individuals in a police-dominated atmosphere, resulting in self-incriminating statements without full warnings of constitutional rights.

* * *

An understanding of the nature and setting of this in-custody interrogation is essential to our decisions today.

* * *

[T]he modern practice of in-custody interrogation is psychologically rather than physically oriented. As we have stated before . . . this Court has recognized that "coercion can be mental as well as physical, and that the blood of the accused is not the only hallmark of an unconstitutional inquisition." . . . Interrogation still takes place in privacy. Privacy results in secrecy and this in turn results in a gap in our knowledge as to what in fact goes on in the interrogation rooms. A valuable source of information about present police practices, however, may be found in various police manuals and texts which document procedures employed with success in the past, and which recommend various other effective tactics. These texts are used by law enforcement agencies themselves as guides. It should be noted that these texts professedly present the most enlightened and effective means presently used to obtain statements through custodial interrogation.

* * *

[R]epresentative samples of interrogation techniques [indicate that the] setting prescribed by the manuals and observed in practice [is] clear. In essence, it is this: To be alone with the subject is essential to prevent distraction and to deprive him of any outside support. The aura of confidence in his guilt undermines his will to resist. He merely confirms the preconceived story the police seek to have him describe. Patience and persistence, at times relentless questioning, are employed. To obtain a confession, the interrogator must "patiently maneuver himself or his quarry into a position from which the desired objective may be attained." When normal procedures fail to produce the needed result, the police may resort to deceptive stratagems such as giving false legal advice. It is important to keep the subject off balance, for example, by trading on his insecurity about himself or his surroundings. The police then persuade, trick, or cajole him out of exercising his constitutional rights.

Even without employing brutality, the "third degree" or the specific stratagems described above, the very fact of custodial interrogation exacts a heavy toll on individual liberty and trades on the weakness of individuals.

* * *

The principles announced today deal with the protection which must be given to the privilege against self-incrimination when the individual is first subjected to police interrogation while in custody at the station or otherwise deprived of his freedom in any significant way. . . .

Our decision is not intended to hamper the traditional function of police officers in investigating crime . . . When an individual is in custody on probable cause, the police may, of course, seek out evidence in the field to be used at trial against him. Such investigation may include inquiry of persons not under restraint. General on the scene questioning as to facts surrounding a crime or other general questioning of citizens in the fact-finding process is not affected by our holding. It is an act of responsible citizenship for individuals to give whatever information they may have to aid in law enforcement. In such situations the compelling atmosphere inherent in the process of in-custody interrogation is not necessarily present.

In dealing with statements obtained through interrogation, we do not purport to find all confessions inadmissible. Confessions remain a proper element in law enforcement. Any statement given freely and voluntarily without any compelling influence is, of course, admissible in evidence. The fundamental import of the privilege while an individual is in custody is not whether he is allowed to talk to the police without the benefit of warnings and counsel, but whether he can be interrogated. There is no requirement that police stop a person who enters a police station and states that he wishes to confess a crime, or a person who calls the police to offer a confession or any other statements he desires to make. Volunteered statements of any kind are not barred by the Fifth Amendment and their admissibility is not affected by our holding today.

To summarize, we hold that when an individual is taken into custody or otherwise deprived of his freedom by the authorities in any significant way and is subjected to questioning, the privilege against self-incrimination is jeopardized. Procedural safeguards must be employed . . . and unless other fully effective means are adopted to notify the person of his right of silence and to assure that the exercise of the right will be scrupulously honored, the following measures are required. He must be warned prior to any questioning that he has the right to remain silent, that anything he says can be used against him in a court of law, that he has the right to the presence of an attorney, and that if he cannot afford an attorney one will be appointed for him prior to any questioning if he so desires. Opportunity to exercise these rights must be afforded to him throughout the interrogation. After such warnings have been given, and such opportunity afforded him, the individual may knowingly and intelligently waive these rights and agree to answer questions or make a statement. But unless and until such warnings and waiver are demonstrated, no evidence obtained as a result of interrogation can be used against him.

CASE EXCERPT: *OREGON* V. *BRADSHAW*
THE SUPREME COURT OF THE UNITED STATES (1983)
462 U.S. 1039

During the investigation of the death of a person whose body had been found in his wrecked pickup truck, Bradshaw was questioned at the police station, where he was advised of his constitutional rights, and later arrested for furnishing liquor to the victim, a minor. Bradshaw denied the charges and asked for an attorney. Later, while being transferred from the police station to a jail, Bradshaw inquired of a police officer, "Well, what is going to happen to me now?" The officer answered that Bradshaw did not have to talk to him and Bradshaw said that he understood. The discussion continued about where Bradshaw was being taken and the offense with which he would be charged. The officer suggested that Bradshaw take a polygraph examination, which he did, after another reading of his constitutional rights. When the polygraph examiner told Bradshaw that he did not believe that Bradshaw was telling the truth, he recanted his earlier story and admitted that he had been driving the truck and that he had consumed a substantial amount of alcohol and had passed out at the wheel of the truck before it left the highway. Bradshaw was charged with first degree manslaughter, driving while under the influence of intoxicants, and driving while his license was revoked. His motion to suppress his statements admitting his involvement was denied, and he was found guilty after a bench trial. The Oregon Court of Appeals reversed, holding that the inquiry Bradshaw made of the police officer while being transferred to jail did not "initiate" a conversation with the officer, and that therefore the statements growing out of this conversation should have been excluded from evidence. The U.S. Supreme Court granted certiorari.

Justice Rehnquist delivered the opinion of the Court.

* * *

"[A]lthough we have held that after initially being advised of his *Miranda* rights, the accused may himself validly waive his rights and respond to interrogation, the Court has strongly indicated that additional safeguards are necessary when the accused asks for counsel; and we now hold that when an accused has invoked his right to have counsel present during custodial interrogation, a valid waiver of that right cannot be established by showing only that he responded to further police-initiated custodial interrogation even if he has been advised of his rights. We further hold that an accused, such as [the defendant], having expressed his desire to deal with the police only through counsel, is not subject to further interrogation by the authorities until counsel has been made available to him, unless the accused himself initiates further communication, exchanges, or conversations with the police."

Respondent's question in the present case, "Well, what is going to happen to me now?", admittedly was asked prior to respondent being "subject[ed] to further interrogation by the authorities." The Oregon Court of Appeals stated that it did not "construe defendant's question about what was going to happen to him to have been a waiver of his right to counsel, invoked only minutes before. . . ." The Court of

Appeals, after quoting relevant language from *Edwards,* concluded that "under the reasoning enunciated in *Edwards,* defendant did not make a valid waiver of his Fifth Amendment rights, and his statements were inadmissible."

We think the Oregon Court of Appeals misapprehended the test laid down in *Edwards.* We did not there hold that the "initiation" of a conversation by a defendant such as respondent would amount to a waiver of previously invoked right to counsel; we held that after the right to counsel had been asserted by an accused, further interrogation of the accused should not take place "unless the accused himself initiates further communication, exchanges, or conversations with the police." This was a prophylactic rule, designed to protect an accused in police custody from being badgered by police officers in the manner in which the defendant in *Edwards* was.

* * *

"If, as frequently would occur in the course of a meeting initiated by the accused, the conversation is not wholly one-sided, it is likely that the officers will say or do something that clearly would be 'interrogation.' In that event, the question would be whether a valid waiver of the right to counsel and the right to silence had occurred, that is, whether the purported waiver was knowing and intelligent and found to be so under the totality of the circumstances, including the necessary fact that the accused, not the police reopened the dialogue with the authorities."

* * *

Although ambiguous, the respondent's question in this case as to what was going to happen to him evinced a willingness and a desire for a generalized discussion about the investigation; it was not merely a necessary inquiry arising out of the incidents of the custodial relationship. It could

reasonably have been interpreted by the officer as relating generally to the investigation. That the police officer so understood it is apparent from the fact that he immediately reminded the accused that "you do not have to talk to me," and only after the accused told him that he "understood" did they have a generalized conversation. On these facts we believe that there was no violation of the *Edwards* rule.

Since there was no violation of the *Edwards* rule in this case, the next inquiry was "whether a valid waiver of the right to counsel and the right to silence had occurred, that is, whether the purported waiver was knowing and intelligent and found to be so under the totality of the circumstances, including the necessary fact that the accused, not the police, reopened the dialogue with the authorities." As we have said many times before, this determination depends "upon the particular facts and circumstances surrounding the case, including the background, experience, and conduct of the accused."

The state trial court made this inquiry and, in the words of the Oregon Court of Appeals, "found that the police made no threats, promises or inducements to talk, that defendant was properly advised of his rights and understood them and that within a short time after requesting an attorney he changed his mind without any impropriety on the part of the police. The court held that the statements made to the polygraph examiner were voluntary and the result of a knowing waiver of his right to remain silent."

We have no reason to dispute these conclusions, based as they are upon the trial court's first-hand observation of the witnesses to the events involved. The judgment of the Oregon Court of Appeals is therefore reversed, and the cause remanded for further proceedings.

It is so ordered.

Endnotes

1. *Malloy* v. *Hogan,* 378 U.S. 1 (1964).
2. *Escobedo* v. *Illinois,* 378 U.S. 478 (1964).
3. *Miranda* v. *Arizona,* 384 U.S. 436 (1966).
4. See Sandra M. Colatosti, "Despite Years of Erosion, It Still Provides the Best Balance Between the Interests of Law Enforcement and Those of the Criminal Suspect." 55 *Albany Law Review* pp. 255–291 (1991); Paul A. Nappi, "Miranda and the Rehnquist Court: Has the Pendulum Swung Too Far?" 30 *Boston College Law Review* pp. 523–571 (1989).
5. Supra, note 3 at 478.
6. For an excellent discussion of the Fifth Amendment see, Leonard W. Levy, *The Origins of the Fifth Amendment,* (New York, N.Y.: Macmillan, 1986).
7. *Spano* v. *New York,* 360 U.S. 315 (1959); Wayne R. LaFave and Jerold H. Israel, *Criminal Procedure,* 2d ed. (St. Paul, Minn.: West, 1992), p. 296.
8. *Brown* v. *Mississippi,* 297 U.S. 278 (1936).
9. Id. at 286.
10. Supra, note 7.
11. See also *Rogers* v. *Richmond,* 365 U.S. 534 (1961) (where police obtained the defendant's confession by pretending to arrest his sick wife. The statements were inadmissible).
12. Supra, note 3.
13. *Colorado* v. *Connelly,* 479 U.S. 157 (1986).
14. See George C. Thomas III, "A Philosophical Account of Coerced Self-Incrimination." 5 *Yale Journal of Law and the Humanities* pp. 79–112 (1993).
15. Robert A. Allison, "Custodial Interrogations," 84 *Georgetown Law Journal Twenty-Fifth Annual Review of Criminal Procedure* p. 869 (1996).
16. Id. at 869–870.
17. *Mincey* v. *Arizona,* 437 U.S. 385 (1978).
18. Id. at 398.
19. Id.
20. See *Ashcraft* v. *Tennessee,* 322 U.S. 143 (1944).
21. See John J. Henry, "Criminal Procedure— Application of the Harmless Error Rule to Miranda Violations." 14 *Western New England Law Review* pp. 109–144 (1992).
22. *Arizona* v. *Fulminante,* 499 U.S. 279 (1991).
23. But see Paul Marcus, "A Return to the 'Bright Line' Rule of Miranda." 35 *William and Mary Law Review* pp. 93–146 (1993).
24. *Illinois* v. *Perkins,* 496 U.S. 292 (1990).
25. *Colorado* v. *Prysock,* 453 U.S. 355 (1987).
26. See Julia C. Weissman, "Modern Confession Law After Duckworth v. Eagan: What's the Use of Explaining?" 66 *Indiana Law Journal* pp. 825–848 (1991).
27. *Duckworth* v. *Eagan,* 492 U.S. 195 (1989).
28. Id. at 198.
29. *Colorado* v. *Spring,* 479 U.S. 564 (1987).
30. Id.
31. See Richard A. Williamson, "The Virtues (and Limits) of Shared Values: The Fourth Amendment and Miranda's Concept of Custody." 21 *Search and Seizure Law Report* pp. 17–21 (1994).
32. *Stansbury* v. *California,* 114 S.Ct. 1526 (1994).
33. *California* v. *Beheler,* 463 U.S. 1121 (1983).
34. *Oregon* v. *Mathiason,* 429 U.S. 492 (1977).
35. See Mark A. Godsey, "When Terry Met Miranda: Two Constitutional Doctrines Collide." 22 *Search and Seizure Law Report* pp. 121–128 (1995).
36. *Berkemer* v. *McCarty,* 468 U.S. 420 (1984).
37. Id. at 439.
38. Id. at 420.
39. Id. at 442.
40. *Orozco* v. *Texas,* 394 U.S. 324 (1969).
41. *Beckwith* v. *United States,* 425 U.S. 341 (1976).
42. See Steve Finizio, "Prison Cells, Leg Restraints, and 'Custodial Interrogation': Miranda's Role in Crimes that Occur in Prison." 59 *University of Chicago Law Review* pp. 719–748 (1992).
43. *Mathis* v. *United States,* 391 U.S. 1 (1968).
44. *Minnesota* v. *Murphy,* 465 U.S. 420 (1984).
45. *Rhode Island* v. *Innis,* 446 U.S. 291 (1980).
46. Id. at 301.
47. See William A. Fragetta, "What Constitutes Interrogation?" 22 *Boston College Law Review* pp. 1177–1196 (1981).
48. Supra, note 45 at 302.
49. Id. at 303.
50. *Brewer* v. *Williams,* 430 U.S. 387 (1977); see also *Nix* v. *Wiliams,* 467 U.S. 431 (1984) (formulating the inevitable discovery exception to Miranda).
51. Id. at 300, n. 4.
52. See *Arizona* v. *Mauro,* 481 U.S. 520, 526 (1987).
53. *Arizona* v. *Mauro,* 481 U.S. 520 (1987).
54. Robert A. Allison, supra note 15 at 858–859.
55. *Estelle* v. *Smith,* 451 U.S. 454 (1981).
56. *Pennsylvania* v. *Muniz,* 496 U.S. 582 (1990).

57. See *United States* v. *Berisha,* 925 F.2d 791 (5th Cir. 1991); Robert A. Alleson, supra note 15 at 859.

58. See *Baxter* v. *Thomas,* 45 F.3d 1501 (11th Cir.), *cert denied,* 116 S.Ct. 385 (1995).

59. *United States* v. *Mandujano,* 425 U.S. 564 (1976).

60. *McNeil* v. *Wisconsin,* 501 U.S. 171 (1991).

61. Id. at 176.

62. See Craig R. Johnson, "Blurring a Line on Custodial Interrogation." *Wisconsin Law Review* pp. 1637–1667 (1992).

63. *Davis* v. *United States,* 114 S.Ct. 2350 (1994).

64. Id. at 2355.

65. *Michigan* v. *Jackson,* 475 U.S. 625 (1986).

66. *Edwards* v. *Arizona,* 451 U.S. 477 (1981).

67. Id. at 487.

68. Id. at 485.

69. *Minnick* v. *Mississippi,* 498 U.S. 146 (1990).

70. *Fare* v. *Michael C.,* 442 U.S. 707 (1979).

71. *Oregon* v. *Bradshaw,* 462 U.S. 1039 (1983).

72. *Arizona* v. *Roberson,* 486 U.S. 675 (1988).

73. *Massiah* v. *United States,* 377 U.S. 201 (1964).

74. *Maine* v. *Moulton,* 474 U.S. 159 (1985).

75. *United States* v. *Henry,* 447 U.S. 264 (1980).

76. *Kuhlman* v. *Wilson,* 477 U.S. 436 (1986).

77. See William T. Pizzi, "Waiver of Rights in the Interrogation Room: The Court's Dilemma." 23 *Connecticut Law Review* pp. 229–259 (1991).

78. Wayne R. LaFave and Jerold H. Israel, *Criminal Procedure,* 2d ed. (St. Paul, Minn.: West, 1992), p. 338.

79. *Colorado* v. *Connelly,* 479 U.S. 157 (1986).

80. *Fare* v. *Michael C.,* 442 U.S. 707 (1979).

81. *North Carolina* v. *Butler,* 441 U.S. 369 (1979).

82. Id. at 373.

83. *Connecticut* v. *Barrett,* 479 U.S. 523 (1987).

84. *Moran* v. *Burbine,* 475 U.S. 412 (1986); For an excellent discussion of these issues see Alleson, supra note 15 at 863.

85. See March Schuyler Reiner, "The Public Safety Exception to Miranda: Analyzing Subject Motivation." 93 *Michigan Law Review* pp. 2377–2407 (1995).

86. *New York* v. *Quarles,* 467 U.S. 649 (1984).

87. Id. at 655.

88. Id. at 657.

89. *Harris* v. *New York,* 401 U.S. 222 (1971).

90. Id. at 226.

91. See *Oregon* v. *Hass,* 420 U.S. 714 (1975).

92. *Oregon* v. *Hass,* 420 U.S. 714 (1975).

93. *Doyle* v. *Ohio,* 426 U.S. 610 (1976).

94. Id. at 618.

95. *Jenkins* v. *Anderson,* 447 U.S. 231 (1980).

96. *Wong Sun* v. *United States,* 371 U.S. 471 (1963).

97. *Brown* v. *Illinois,* 422 U.S. 590 (1975).

98. Id. at 603–604. See Robert B. Robards, "The Supreme Court has Another Bout With the Right to Counsel." 23 *Pacific Law Journal* pp. 1351–1388 (1992).

99. *Taylor* v. *Alabama,* 457 U.S. 687 (1982).

100. *New York* v. *Harris,* 495 U.S. 14 (1990).

101. See Alan C. Yarusko, "Brown to Payton to Harris: A Fourth Amendment Double Play by the Supreme Court." 43 *Case Western Reserve Law Review* pp. 253–286 (1992).

102. *New York* v. *Harris,* 495 U.S 14, 19 (1990).

103. *Oregon* v. *Elstad,* 470 U.S. 298 (1985).

104. Id. at 318.

105. *Michigan* v. *Tucker,* 417 U.S. 433 (1974).

106. *Michigan* v. *Mosley,* 423 U.S. 96 (1975).

107. See Marcy Strauss, "Reinterrogation." 22 *Hastings Constitutional Law Quarterly* pp. 359–404 (1995).

108. See Peter K. Lewis and Kenneth D. Peoples, *The Supreme Court and the Criminal Process* (Philadelphia, Pa.: W.B. Saunders, 1978), p. 8.

109. See John Medalie et al., "Custodial Police Interrogation in Our Nation's Capital: The Attempt to Implement Miranda." 66 *Michigan Law Review* pp. 1347–1422 (1967); Seeburger and Wettick, "Miranda in Pittsburgh: A Statistical Study." 1 *University of Pittsburgh Law Review* pp. 23–26.109 (1967).

110. George C. Thomas III, "Is Miranda a Real-World Failure? A Plea for More and Better Empirical Evidence." 43 *U.C.L.A. Law Review* pp. 821–837 (1996).

111. See Paul G. Cassell and Bret S. Hayman, "Police Interrogation in the 1990s: An Empirical Study of the Effects of Miranda." 43 *U.C.L.A. Law Review* p. 909 (1996).

112. Id. at 918.

113. Levy, supra note 6 at X–Xi.

114. *Hoffman* v. *United States,* 341 U.S. 479 (1951).

115. *Griffin* v. *California,* 380 U.S. 609 (1965); for an excellent discussion of these issues see Kimberly D. Ziropoulos, "Defendant's Right to Refuse to Testify." 84 *Georgetown Law Journal Twenty-Fifth Annual Review of Criminal Procedure* pp. 1215–1218 (1996).

116. *Lakeside* v. *Oregon,* 435 U.S. 333 (1978).

117. *Carter* v. *Kentucky,* 450 U.S. 288 (1981).

118. *Allen* v. *Illinois,* 478 U.S. 364 (1986).

119. *Kastigar* v. *United States,* 406 U.S. 441 (1972).

120. *Murphy* v. *Waterfront Commission,* 378 U.S. 52 (1964).

11 PRETRIAL IDENTIFICATION, THE RIGHT TO BE FREE FROM DOUBLE JEOPARDY, AND PROPERTY FORFEITURE PROCEEDINGS

Outline

Key Terms

Chapter 10 discussed the legacy of *Miranda* v. *Arizona* and the privilege against self-incrimination. Chapter 11 continues the discussion of pretrial criminal justice processes. Police officers frequently use identification procedures that are designed to help determine who committed a crime. Pretrial identification procedures are important because if a witness is unable to identify a suspect the case may not be brought to trial.

Another important constitutional protection is the right to be free from double jeopardy. The Fifth Amendment provides that no "person [shall] be subject for the same offence to be twice put in jeopardy of life or limb." According to Supreme Court precedents, the double jeopardy clause provides two independent constitutional protections for defendants in criminal proceedings. First, they may not be tried twice for the same offense. Second, they may not receive two punishments for the same crime. Double jeopardy concerns are raised most often before a second case involving the "same offense" is brought to trial.[1] These questions are therefore properly considered pretrial issues as well.

Pretrial Identification Procedures

Like cases involving custodial interrogations, pretrial identification proceedings may present Fifth, Sixth, and Fourteenth Amendment issues. One common Fifth Amendment issue is whether police officers violated a suspect's privilege against self-incrimination by requiring him or her to participate in a pretrial identification proceeding. Moreover, because suggestive identification proceedings may lead a witness to falsely identify a suspect, they may violate the Fifth and Fourteenth Amendments' due process guarantees. In addition, a defendant has a right to have an attorney present during some pretrial identification procedures. Therefore, the right to counsel may become an issue in a pretrial identification proceeding. Each of these topics is considered separately.

The Privilege Against Self-Incrimination

Self-incrimination issues may be raised when a defendant is required to produce evidence to enable police officers to conduct a criminal investigation. For example, in the O. J. Simpson murder case, Simpson was required to produce a DNA sample for comparison with those left at the crime scene. Highlight 11.1 describes the use of DNA in the investigatory process. One might argue that requiring a defendant to provide such evidence violates the privilege against self-incrimination because it involves using the suspect's own body chemistry to convict him or her.

Physical Evidence.   Physical evidence furnishes an often crucial link in the prosecution's case against a defendant. Defendants are sometimes asked to furnish evidence to be used for comparison with physical evidence left at a crime scene. Examples of such evidence may include blood, saliva, semen, hair, fingerprints, or voice recordings. The general rule is that prosecutors may require a defendant to furnish physical evidence to be used in an investigation. There is no violation of the privilege against self-incrimination because the evidence is neither **testimonial** nor

Highlight 11.1

DNA Use in Investigations

Defense attorneys still may challenge the validity of DNA evidence, as has been seen in the O. J. Simpson case, but it is fast becoming an accepted tool for identification, according to the American Chemical Society. DNA profiling compares deoxyribonucleic acid, the material genes are made of, retrieved from a crime scene with that taken from a suspect. The DNA can come from hair, blood, skin, saliva, semen, and other sources. Every individual's DNA is unique (except for that from identical siblings).

Fragments of DNA taken from the crime scene and from the suspect are compared. Generally speaking, if they match, they show that the suspect could be the criminal. Profiling techniques have different sample-size requirements. One method needs a blood stain the size of a dime, while a second requires just one percent of that amount. The first method can take a couple of months; the second, a few days.

While DNA profiling often is used to incriminate suspects, it also has liberated those who are innocent. In Virginia, for example, an individual was freed from prison in 1993 after DNA tests on old evidence showed he could not have committed a rape for which he had served almost seven years.

Data banks storing DNA profiles are becoming more common. The FBI and state and local crime labs are developing a national database of such profiles for convicted criminals so that samples taken from a new crime scene can be compared with DNA profiles already on file in order to track down a

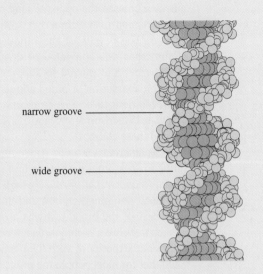

narrow groove ——————

wide groove ——————

possible suspect. The database will be used for missing persons cases as well.

There are concerns that DNA profiles could be abused, and some observers are disturbed by the government's access to such information. Congress has taken steps to protect privacy by limiting the use of the FBI's database to law enforcement and judicial purposes.

"DNA Evidence Gaining More Acceptance," *USA Today,* August 1995, p. 15. Reprinted by permission of the Society for the Advancement of Education.

Figure, "Three-Dimensional Configuration of DNA," *McGraw-Hill Encyclopedia of Science and Technology,* 7th Edition, Vol. 12, 1992, p.213. [Copyright © 1992. Reproduced with permission of the McGraw-Hill Companies.]

---

communicative. This means simply that the evidence itself does not testify or communicate. The distinction between testimonial and nontestimonial evidence is an important one. In *Doe* v. *United States,*[2] the Court defined a testimonial communication as one in which "an accused's communication must itself, explicitly or implicitly relate a factual assertion or disclose information."[3] As you will see, this principle provides little Fifth Amendment protection for nontestimonial physical evidence that is used solely for identification purposes.

Blood Tests. *Schmerber* v. *California*[4] illustrated the distinction between nontestimonial physical evidence that does not receive Fifth Amendment protection and testimonial and communicative evidence. In *Schmerber,* the defendant was arrested at a hospital where he was receiving treatment for injuries suffered in an automobile accident. After leaving a bar, Schmerber and a friend were injured when the car he was driving crossed the opposite lane of travel and struck a tree. At the direction of police officers, and over Schmerber's objections, a physician had extracted a sample of his blood. The results of the blood test were introduced as evidence at his trial and Schmerber was convicted of driving while under the influence of alcohol. At trial, Schmerber had moved to suppress the evidence of the blood test asserting that the forcible extraction of blood and its use as evidence violated his right to due process of law, his right to be free from unreasonable searches and seizures, his right to be free from self-incrimination, and his right to counsel. On appeal, the Supreme Court rejected these claims.

Schmerber's Fourth Amendment rights were not violated because "there was no time to seek out a magistrate and secure a warrant."[5] *Schmerber* may be distinguished from *Rochin* v. *California,*[6] where sheriff's deputies forced the defendant to swallow a stomach pumping solution and used the contents to convict him of drug offenses. In *Schmerber,* the blood test was a *reasonable* method of securing the evidence because "such tests are a commonplace occurrence in these days of periodic physical examinations and experience with them teaches that the quantity of blood extracted is minimal, and that for most people the procedure involves virtually no risk, trauma, or pain."[7]

The Supreme Court held too that the use of the blood as evidence did not violate Schmerber's Fifth Amendment privilege against self-incrimination. Justice William J. Brennan stated:

> History and a long line of authorities in lower courts have consistently limited [the privilege against self-incrimination's] protection to situations in which the State seeks to . . . [obtain] evidence against an accused through 'the cruel, simple expedient of compelling it from his own mouth. . . . In sum, the privilege is fulfilled only when the person is guaranteed the right to remain silent unless he chooses to speak in the unfettered exercise of his own will.[8]

The Court rejected too Schmerber's claim that extracting his blood and using it as evidence violated his Sixth Amendment right to counsel. Because Schmerber was not entitled to assert the Fifth Amendment privilege against self-incrimination, he had no right to counsel that was violated by the police.

It is interesting to note Justice Hugo Black's dissenting opinion in *Schmerber,* which presents a compelling argument against the proposition that the Fifth Amendment privilege against self-incrimination protects only testimonial and communicative evidence. Justice Black stated:

> [I]t seems to me that the compulsory extraction of [Schmerber's] blood for analysis so that the person who analyzed it could give evidence to convict him had both a "testimonial" and a "communicative" nature. The sole purpose of this project which proved to be successful was to obtain "testimony" from some person to prove that [Schmerber] had alcohol in his blood at the time he was arrested. And the purpose of the project was certainly

"communicative" in that the analysis of the blood was to supply information to enable a witness to communicate to the court and jury that [Schmerber] was more or less drunk.[9]

Although Justice Black's view of the Fifth Amendment privilege against self-incrimination is a compelling one, his position did not prevail. The Supreme Court has consistently held that prosecutors may require a defendant to furnish physical evidence to be used in a criminal investigation. There is no violation of the privilege against self-incrimination because the evidence is neither testimonial nor communicative. Under *Schmerber* and *Doe,* to determine if a communication is protected by the Fifth Amendment privilege against self-incrimination the courts must examine a police officer's reasons for requiring the communication—if the communication was to be used solely as an identifying personal characteristic, it is not protected. If, however, officers wish to use the *contents* of the suspect's response as evidence, the privilege against self-incrimination will protect the communication.

Chapter 10 discussed *Pennsylvania* v. *Muniz,*[10] a case in which police officers asked questions of an individual suspected of driving while under the influence of alcohol that were designed to test his mental functions. Using the test established in *Doe,* the Supreme Court held that although police officers may ask suspects routine booking questions without violating their privilege against self-incrimination, an officer's question to Muniz about the date of his sixth birthday sought a testimonial response. This was because an "incriminating inference of impaired mental faculties stemmed, not just from the fact that Muniz slurred his response, but also from a testimonial aspect of that response."[11]

Considered together, *Doe* and *Muniz* indicate that when police officers question suspects during pretrial investigations, most questions that they ask will be held to seek testimonial responses because "[t]here are very few instances in which a verbal statement, either oral or written, will not convey information or assert facts."[12] The Court has, however, identified at least one type of situation in which a defendant's verbal statement does not convey testimonial information.

Voice Samples. In *United States* v. *Dionisio,*[13] the Supreme Court held that a suspect may be compelled to appear before a grand jury and provide a voice sample for comparison with recordings that were being used as evidence. Addressing Dionisio's claim that compelling him to provide a voice sample violated his privilege against self-incrimination, the Court held that Dionisio had no legitimate Fifth Amendment right to refuse to produce the sample. Likewise, requiring Dionisio to provide a voice exemplar did not violate the Fourth Amendment because a person has no reasonable expectation of privacy in the sound of his or her voice. The Court stated:

> The physical characteristics of a person's voice, its tone and manner, as opposed to the content of a specific conversation, are constantly exposed to the public. Like a man's facial characteristics, or handwriting, his voice is repeatedly produced for others to hear. No person can have a reasonable expectation that others will not know the sound of his voice, any more than he can reasonably expect that his face will be a mystery to the world.[14]

The Court has extended *Dionisio*'s reasoning to require suspects to furnish physical evidence in other pretrial identification contexts as well. In *United States* v. *Wade,*[15] which will be discussed more fully later in this chapter, the Court held that no violation of the privilege against self-incrimination occurred where a suspect was compelled to stand in a police lineup and say "put the money in the bag." The Court stated that requiring Wade to speak these words did not compel him to provide testimonial evidence because "he was required to use his voice as an identifying physical characteristic, not to speak his guilt."[16]

Handwriting Samples.   *Gilbert* v. *California*[17] held that a suspect's privilege against self-incrimination is not violated by requiring him to produce handwriting samples. A suspect's handwriting is not testimonial evidence because, like his voice, it is simply an identifying physical characteristic.

Other Types of Pretrial Identification Procedures.   If evidence is to be used solely as an identifying physical characteristic, it is not protected by the privilege against self-incrimination. The courts have held that this principle applies to many different types of identification procedures, including: fingerprinting, examination of a suspect by X-rays or ultraviolet light, taking impressions of a suspect's teeth, or requiring a suspect to wear a hat, mask, wig, moustache, beard, or a tattoo.[18]

The Right to Counsel

A defendant's participation in pretrial identification procedures may implicate Sixth Amendment concerns as well. For example, suppose that police compel a defendant to appear in a pretrial lineup for identification purposes. Does he or she have a right to counsel's presence at the lineup? The answer to this question is "sometimes."

Lineups.   A **lineup** is a pretrial identification procedure that requires a suspect to appear and stand in a row of persons for observation by witnesses to a crime. The participants in the lineup may be asked to speak certain phrases or to wear outfits resembling those worn by the assailant. Witnesses or victims are asked to identify the perpetrator by selecting him or her from the candidates standing in the row. Other than the suspect, participants in a lineup often include jail inmates, police officers, or even citizens off the street who may volunteer to participate.

Lineup Composition.   The International Association of Chiefs of Police (IACP) has recommended the following guidelines for conducting lineups:

1. Lineups should consist of five or six people.
2. Suspects placed in a lineup should complete a waiver form, unless an attorney is present.
3. All persons participating in a lineup should be of comparable age, height, hair and skin color, gender, and race, to the suspect. If this is not possible, a lineup should be postponed until comparable individuals are found.
4. All persons participating in a lineup should wear similar types of clothing.
5. The suspect should be positioned in the lineup at random.

6. Individuals known to the witness should not be placed in the lineup.

7. If private citizens are asked to participate in a lineup, they should be asked to sign a written consent form indicating that they have not been arrested and are not being compelled to participate, and may leave at any time. Moreover, if juveniles are to participate in a lineup they must have permission from their parents.[19]

Figure 11.1 presents a form used by one police department to describe a lineup and ensure that it was conducted fairly. If the lineup is designed in a way that points to the accused, a trial court will not permit a witness to testify that he or she had identified the accused during the lineup. It may strike the witness's courtroom identification of the suspect as well because it was tainted by observing the defendant at the improper lineup. The IACP recommends the following steps to assure that lineups are conducted fairly:

1. Witnesses should view the lineup individually, so as to avoid a "contagion effect," where one witness's identification of a suspect may bias other witnesses' identifications.

2. All participants in the lineup should be given the same instructions and be asked to speak the same phrases.

3. While the lineup is being conducted, witnesses should be instructed not to comment on their identification of a suspect. Witnesses should be provided with a piece of paper and told to write down the number of any suspect he or she recognizes.

4. A lineup should be photographed. One photograph should provide a frontal view of the line up and another should provide a profile view. All persons in the lineup should be photographed together. If possible, color film should be used. These photographs may be introduced as evidence in court if it is later asserted that the lineup was biased.

5. One officer should advise the lineup participants of their rights and obtain the waivers, conduct the lineup, take all photographs, and question the witnesses following the lineup. Having one police officer perform all of these functions will limit the number of officers who will be required to testify at trial.[20]

The* Wade-Gilbert *Rule.   *United States* v. *Wade,* and *Gilbert* v. *California* formed what has become known as the ***Wade-Gilbert* rule,** which provides that a suspect has the right to the presence of counsel at a post-indictment lineup. If a suspect is exhibited to a witness at a post-indictment lineup conducted outside the presence of counsel, any identification must be excluded at trial. This means that the witness will not be allowed to testify that he or she previously identified the suspect during a police lineup. Moreover, the witness will even be prevented from testifying at trial that the defendant was the person who committed the crime, unless the prosecution can show by clear and convincing evidence that the in-court identification was not influenced, or tainted, by the improper lineup. For example, suppose that Jane, a rape victim, identified Paul as the rapist during a post-indictment police lineup conducted outside counsel's presence. On these facts solely, Jane would be prevented from testifying at

FIGURE 11.1

Lineup report form used by police department

DATE _____   CR # _____

LINE-UP REPORT

COMPLAINANT _____   OFFENSE NO. _____

OFFENSE _____   DATE _____

PERSON ARRESTED _____

DATE OF IDENTIFICATION _____   TIME _____

TEL. NO. _____   PLACE OF EMPLOYMENT _____

ADDRESS _____

POLICE IN ROOM WITH SUSPECTS _____

POLICE IN ROOM WITH WITNESS _____

LINE-UP CONDUCTED IN THE PRESENCE OF:

_____   _____
(Parent/Guardian)   (Attorney)

1	2	3	4	5	6

ONE WAY GLASS

RESULTS: _____

_____

_____

_____

_____

_____   INVESTIGATING OFFICER _____

Attached is a photograph of the line-up

trial that she had picked Paul out of the police lineup or that he was the person who had committed the crime. If, however, the prosecution could demonstrate by clear and convincing evidence that Jane and Paul knew each other well before the incident, her testimony is likely to be admitted at trial. Jane's courtroom identification of Paul would not be tainted by the improper lineup because she had independent knowledge of Paul's identity before the incident occurred.

United States *v.* Wade.   In *United States* v. *Wade,* the defendant, who was a suspect in a bank robbery, was exhibited to witnesses before trial at a post-indictment lineup in the absence of counsel. Each person in the lineup wore strips of tape and, at the direction of police officers, said something like "put the money in the bag." Two bank employees identified Wade as the robber. Wade's attorney moved to strike the bank officials' courtroom identifications on the grounds that conducting the lineup, without notice to and in the absence of counsel, violated Wade's Fifth Amendment privilege against self-incrimination and his Sixth Amendment right to counsel. The Supreme Court held that neither the lineup nor requiring Wade to wear the strips of tape or speak the words allegedly said by the robber violated his privilege against self-incrimination. Such evidence was neither testimonial nor communicative.

The Court further held, however, that requiring his participation in the post-indictment lineup violated his right to counsel. It noted that eyewitness identification during a lineup "is peculiarly riddled with innumerable dangers and variable factors which might seriously, even crucially, derogate from a fair trial."[21] The Court concluded:

> Since it appears that there is grave potential for prejudice, intentional or not, in the pretrial lineup, which may not be capable of reconstruction at trial, there can be little doubt that for Wade the post-indictment lineup was a critical stage of the prosecution at which he was "as much entitled to such aid [of counsel] . . . as at the trial itself."[22]

To summarize, the *Wade-Gilbert* rule requires that a defendant be allowed to have an attorney present at a post-indictment lineup for identification purposes.[23] This is because a post-indictment lineup is a critical stage of a criminal prosecution. In addition, if a defendant is required to appear at an identification proceeding held before a formal indictment is issued, he or she must be allowed to have an attorney present. This is because a preliminary hearing is an "adversary judicial criminal proceeding [where] the government [has] committed itself to prosecute."[24]

Counsel's Role at a Lineup.   In *United States* v. *Wade,* the government had argued that counsel's presence at a pretrial lineup would impede legitimate law enforcement interests. The Supreme Court asserted, however, that counsel's presence may aid law enforcement interests by "preventing the infiltration of taint in the prosecution's identification evidence,"[25] and may "assure a meaningful confrontation at trial."[26] Highlight 11.2 presents excerpts from *Wade* regarding counsel's role at a pretrial identification proceeding. The Supreme Court has not been completely clear on precisely what functions an attorney at a lineup should perform. Wade appears to indicate, however, that counsel's role is a limited one. An attorney may not disrupt the proceedings—

Highlight 11.2

United States v. *Wade,* 388 U.S. 218 (1967)

 "Since it appears that there is grave potential for prejudice, intentional or not, in the pretrial lineup, which may not be capable of reconstruction at trial, and since presence of counsel itself can often avert prejudice and assure a meaningful confrontation at trial, there can be little doubt that for Wade the post-indictment lineup was a critical stage of the prosecution at which he was 'as much entitled to such aid . . . as at the trial itself . . . Thus both Wade and his counsel should have been notified of the impending lineup and counsel's presence should have been a requisite to conduct of the lineup, absent an 'intelligent waiver.' . . .

Concern is expressed that the requirement will forestall prompt identifications and result in obstruction of the confrontations . . . [T]o refuse to recognize the right to counsel for fear that counsel will obstruct the course of justice is contrary to the basic assumptions upon which this Court has operated in Sixth Amendment cases . . . In our view counsel can hardly impede legitimate law enforcement; on the contrary, for the reasons expressed, law enforcement may be assisted by preventing the infiltration of taint in the prosecution's identification evidence. That result cannot help the guilty avoid conviction but can only help assure that the right man has been brought to justice."

---

he or she is present solely to ensure that the identification is fair and is not based on a biased presentation to the witness.[27] To this end, an attorney may take notes or otherwise record the lineup. Police officers conducting a proper lineup should welcome a defense attorney's presence because he or she may help to ensure that the identification is admissible at trial by eliminating suggestions that the procedure was biased.

Kirby *v.* Illinois.   The *Wade-Gilbert* rule provides that a suspect has a right to counsel's presence at a post-indictment lineup. *Kirby* v. *Illinois*[28] held that this rule does not require that a suspect be provided with counsel at a pre-indictment lineup. This means that counsel is not required in most cases when a suspect is arrested, taken to the police station, and placed in a lineup for identification purposes. Similarly, *Moore* v. *Illinois*[29] held that a victim who had identified an unrepresented defendant at a preliminary hearing should not have been allowed to testify at trial about her earlier identification of the suspect. Counsel need only be present at a lineup when "adversary judicial proceedings" have begun, "whether by way of formal charge, preliminary hearing, indictment, information, or arraignment."[30] This is because once these proceedings are initiated an accused is confronted with "the prosecutorial forces of organized society, and immersed in the intricacies of substantive and procedural law."[31]

Showup Identification Procedures.   In some situations it is more convenient for police officers to conduct a **showup** identification procedure rather than a lineup. A showup identification procedure involves a prompt confrontation between a victim or a witness and the arrested suspect, at or near the scene of the crime, at the police station, or at another location such as a hospital. Whenever possible, however, a lineup should be conducted because it is a less suggestive identification procedure.[32] During a showup, police officers will ask the victim or witness whether or not they can identify the suspect as the person who committed the crime. The general rule is that once adversary proceedings have commenced, an accused has the right to counsel at any confrontation between the suspect and a witness. Most often, however, showups are conducted *before* adversary proceedings have commenced in emergency situations where time is a critical factor. In these situations an accused has no right to counsel. Therefore, although a suspect has no right to have an attorney present, the proceeding must be conducted fairly and may not be improperly suggestive.

In *Kirby* v. *Illinois*,[33] on February 21, 1968, Willie Shard had reported to police that two men had robbed him of a wallet containing travelers checks and a social security card. The next day two police officers stopped Kirby who, when asked for identification, produced a wallet that contained Shard's property. When they arrived at the station, the officers learned of the robbery. A police car was dispatched to pick up Shard and bring him to the police station. Immediately upon entering the room where Kirby was seated, Shard identified him as one of the robbers. No lawyer was present. At trial, Shard described his identification of Kirby at the police station and identified him again as the robber. Kirby moved to suppress Shard's statements about the police station identification and his courtroom identification of Kirby as the robber. Kirby asserted that the *Wade-Gilbert* exclusionary rule should apply to identification testimony based upon the showup that took place before he had been indicted or otherwise formally charged with an offense. The Supreme Court held that a suspect has no right to counsel at such a proceeding because it is not a "critical stage" in the adversary process.

A showup that is improperly suggestive, however, is unfair and will violate due process of law. If police officers act in good faith, however, most showup procedures will be upheld by the courts. For example, in *Stovall* v. *Denno*,[34] a murder suspect was displayed to a seriously injured victim at a hospital. The victim identified the suspect, who was the only African-American in the room, and he was convicted of murder. The Supreme Court held that this showup was lawful and was not "so unnecessarily suggestive and conducive to irreparable mistaken identification" that it denied the suspect due process of law.[35] Because the victim's life was in jeopardy, the police were required to act quickly to attempt to identify the suspect.

Stovall suggests that a reviewing court will consider several factors in determining whether a showup was conducted properly, including:

1. Whether a true emergency justified conducting a showup.
2. Whether the police are acting in good faith or whether their conduct *suggested* that the suspect had committed the offense.
3. Whether a short amount of time has elapsed between the incident and the showup.
4. Whether the witness had a good opportunity initially to view the suspect.

The courts will use a totality of the circumstances test to determine if a witness's identification of a suspect at a showup is likely to be reliable. No single factor is controlling, and although a short time lapse between the incident and the identification does not automatically justify a showup, it is an important factor.[36]

Refusal to Cooperate or Participate in a Pretrial Identification Procedure. Suspects who refuse to furnish physical evidence or participate in an identification procedure may be held in contempt of court and jailed until they are willing to comply. Moreover, a prosecutor may comment at trial on a suspect's refusal to participate in a pretrial identification procedure. In *South Dakota* v. *Neville,*[37] Neville was stopped for driving under the influence of alcohol. Under South Dakota law, prosecutors were allowed to comment during trial on a suspect's refusal to submit to a test to determine blood alcohol content. The Supreme Court upheld the statute because a blood test does not require a suspect to provide testimonial and communicative evidence.

Photographic Displays.   Neither a suspect nor his or her attorney has a right to be present during a pretrial photographic display. In *United States* v. *Ash,*[38] an F.B.I. agent showed five black-and-white photographs of African-American males of generally the same age, height, and weight, to four witnesses to a bank robbery. One of these was a picture of Ash, who was a suspect in the case. All four witnesses made uncertain identifications of Ash's picture. At the time, Ash was not in custody and had not been charged. Later, an indictment was returned charging Ash with the bank robbery. Shortly before trial, an F.B.I. agent and the prosecutor showed five color photographs to the four witnesses who had previously identified the black-and-white photograph of Ash. Three of the witnesses selected Ash, but one was unable to make any selection. At trial, Ash asserted that the post-indictment photographic display violated his right to counsel. The Supreme Court held that the right to counsel does not apply to photographic displays, regardless of when they occur, because the accused has no right to be present. In response to Ash's argument that a suggestive photographic display might prejudice a witness's in-court identification of a suspect, the Court asserted that the display itself could be recreated at trial. This, in addition to the right to cross-examine prosecution witnesses, would serve as an adequate check against improper photographic displays.

Conducting Photographic Displays.   Police officers conducting photographic displays must ensure that the photographs used are not improperly suggestive. The rule is that photographic displays must be fair—officers may not arrange the display in such a way that it points to the accused. For example, suppose that the suspect in a burglary is a 6′2″ tall white male who weighs 180 pounds. Witnesses to the crime who had an opportunity to observe the suspect are brought to the police station and are shown a display containing five photographs, including the suspect's picture. The other individuals depicted in the photographs are all African-American males of various heights and weights. Such a display is clearly suggestive. If the prosecution attempted to introduce evidence about the identification, a court would hold it to be improperly suggestive and exclude testimony about the identification.

Another issue regarding photographic displays is the number of photographs that police officers should use. The courts have not established a clear rule. It is a good police practice to use at least seven pictures of individuals with similar physical characteristics in a photographic display for identification purposes.[39] Once again, however, the main issue is fairness. Therefore, it is often advisable to use a considerable number of photographs of individuals with similar physical characteristics rather than a small number of pictures of dissimilar persons. To determine if a photographic display was conducted in a fair manner, the courts will again use a totality of circumstances test and consider factors such as a witness's original opportunity to view a suspect. For example, suppose a witness was the victim of a personal assault and had the opportunity to view the perpetrator in close proximity for several minutes. A court is unlikely to suppress testimony about an identification resulting from a photographic display that contained the suspect's picture, even if it presented only a few photographs of other individuals.

The Court has even sanctioned an identification procedure that used a single photograph of a suspect and no others. In *Manson* v. *Brathwaite,*[40] two days after an illegal drug sale, a photograph of one suspect was shown to an undercover police officer, who had made the drug purchase. The officer identified the person in the photograph and testified that he had "no doubt whatsoever" that the individual was the seller. The defendant was convicted at trial. The Supreme Court held that under the circumstances of this case there was not a "very substantial likelihood of misidentification."[41] Therefore, the "evidence [was] for the jury to weigh," and "measure intelligently the weight of [the] identification testimony that [had] some questionable feature."[42]

Due Process Considerations. Due process of law requires that pretrial identification procedures be conducted in a fair manner. To use the Supreme Court's language, this means that an identification procedure cannot be "unnecessarily suggestive and conducive to irreparable misidentification."[43] All types of pretrial identification procedures are subject to due process constraints—they may not be biased or improperly suggest to witnesses that the accused committed a crime.[44] For example, a due process violation will occur if an African-American suspected of a crime is placed into a lineup with five white individuals.

Supreme Court precedents make it clear, however, that it is not easy for a defendant to establish a due process violation as a result of a pretrial identification procedure. In *Neil* v. *Biggers,*[45] a woman was assaulted in her poorly lit kitchen and was later taken from her house and was raped outdoors under a full moon. The victim gave police a description of the rapist. Approximately seven months after the crime, police officers conducted a one-person showup in which they brought the suspect before the victim, who stated that she was sure that he had committed the crime. He was convicted of rape at trial. On appeal, the Supreme Court held that the identification procedure was lawful. The central question was "whether under the 'totality of the circumstances' the identification was reliable even though the confrontation procedure was suggestive."[46] The Court held that although the showup was conducted in a suggestive manner, any prejudice that resulted was overcome by the reliability of the victim's identification of the suspect. The factors considered by the Court included: (1) the fact that the victim had viewed the rapist for between 15–30 minutes; (2) the lighting that enabled the victim to view her assailant; (3) the fact that the crime was a highly personal one; (4) the fact that there were no other witnesses to the crime; (5) the detailed description of the suspect that the victim had provided to police officers; and (6) the fact that the victim was certain of her identification of the suspect.[47]

Neil v. *Biggers* suggests that it is difficult to establish a due process violation as a result of the use of suggestive identification procedures. Even an identification obtained as a result of the use of suggestive identification procedures will be admissible if the circumstances surrounding the process provide a reason to believe that it is trustworthy.

If, however, a pretrial identification procedure is so inherently suggestive that it may lead to the likelihood of mistaken identification, a due process challenge may succeed. For example, in *Foster* v. *California*,[48] a robbery suspect was placed in a lineup with several shorter individuals, and only he wore clothing similar to that of the robber. When witnesses were unable to identify Foster, police officers conducted a one-person showup. When the witness's identification of Foster was still uncertain, police later conducted another lineup in which Foster was the only individual who had participated in the earlier proceedings. The Supreme Court held that these identification practices were so suggestive that they violated due process of law.

The Right to be Free from Double Jeopardy

Earlier portions of this chapter considered pretrial identification procedures. They observed that a suspect's constitutional rights may be violated during such identification proceedings. Another important constitutional issue is the Fifth Amendment right to be free from double jeopardy, which was applied to state proceedings in *Benton* v. *Maryland*.[49] The double jeopardy clause provides three independent protections. First, it does not permit a person to be retried for the same offense after a conviction. Second, it protects against reprosecution following an acquittal. Third, it protects against multiple punishments for the same offense. Double jeopardy issues pose some of the most challenging questions in U.S. criminal procedure.[50]

Five Basic Double Jeopardy Rules

There are five basic rules that are a key to understanding the right to be free from double jeopardy:

1. **Jeopardy attaches,** or may be asserted by a defendant, once the jury has been sworn in, or when the first witness takes his or her oath in a bench trial.
2. If a defendant moves for a **mistrial,** which means that some error has occurred that has biased the proceedings, he or she may not normally assert a double jeopardy claim at a second trial. For example, a mistrial would be declared if, after deliberating, a jury is unable to reach a verdict.

3. The prosecution may never appeal a defendant's acquittal. It may, however, appeal other decisions such as a judge's ruling that sets aside a jury's guilty verdict or a ruling on a motion to suppress evidence.

4. If a defendant appeals his or her conviction and it is overturned by an appellate court, normally the case may be retried. If, however, the appellate court overturns the conviction because there was insufficient evidence in the first trial, the case may not be retried.

5. The right to be free from double jeopardy applies only to bar a second trial for the "same offense." It does not bar later trials for different offenses.

One particularly challenging issue concerns how to determine if a second trial charges the "same offense" under the double jeopardy clause. For many years the Supreme Court has used a test developed in *Blockburger* v. *United States*.[51]

The Blockburger *Test*

Suppose that Bill steals a car and is riding around the City of Atlanta. Atlanta police officers apprehend Bill while he is driving the car and charge him with "joyriding" in violation of Georgia law. Bill pleads guilty at his arraignment and is sentenced to serve thirty days in jail and is fined $100. Three days after his release from jail, Macon police officers arrest Bill for automobile theft for the same incident that led to his conviction for joyriding. Before his second trial, Bill claims that his right to be free from double jeopardy should bar a second trial. May Bill be tried for automobile theft after his conviction for joyriding? The answer is no because joyriding is a **lesser included offense** of automobile theft.[52] This means that in order to prove automobile theft, the prosecution would have to prove all of the elements of joyriding as well.

A court will use the ***Blockburger* test** to determine if a defendant in a second trial is being tried for the same offense that he or she was tried for during the original trial. That test asks whether:

> Each of the offenses . . . requires proof of a different element. The applicable rule is that where the same act or transaction constitutes a violation of two distinct statutory provisions, the test to be applied to determine whether there are two offenses or only one, is whether each provision requires proof of a fact which the other does not.[53]

The *Blockburger* test is sometimes referred to as a **same evidence** double jeopardy test. In other words, if the prosecution will use the same evidence to prove the charges in both a first and second trial, the second trial is barred. This may be contrasted with a **same transaction** double jeopardy test, which a majority of the Supreme Court has not accepted. Under a same transaction test, the prosecution would be required to join at one trial all charges against a defendant that grow out of a single criminal episode.[54]

The *Blockburger* test focuses on the statutory *elements* of the charged offenses—if a second charged offense requires the prosecution to prove different statutory elements, a second trial may proceed. If, however, the offenses have the same statutory elements, a second trial is barred under the double jeopardy clause. For example, suppose that

Mary is convicted of assault and battery, but the victim later dies from complications resulting directly from the earlier assault. She is then charged with manslaughter for the same incident that led to her earlier conviction. A trial for manslaughter after the earlier assault and battery conviction based on the same incident would not violate the double jeopardy clause.[55] Under the *Blockburger* test, the crimes charged in the first and second trials are distinct offenses that have different statutory elements. The death of the injured person is the main element of manslaughter, but is no part of the assault and battery charge.

Grady *v.* Corbin *Developed a New Double Jeopardy Test*

In 1990, the Supreme Court briefly abandoned the *Blockburger* test in favor of a new double jeopardy test. Thomas Corbin drove his car across a double yellow line in New York, striking two oncoming vehicles and killing one person. His blood alcohol content was 0.19 percent. Corbin was cited to appear in traffic court on charges of driving while intoxicated and failing to keep to the right of the median. An assistant district attorney (ADA) began to gather evidence for a homicide prosecution as well. A second ADA who was assigned to conduct prosecutions in traffic court and did not know that the collision involved the death of another person, however, accepted Corbin's guilty pleas to driving while intoxicated and failing to keep to the right of the median. The judge sentenced Corbin to a $350 fine and revoked his driver's license for six months.

Two months later, a grand jury indicted Corbin for reckless manslaughter and other offenses based on the same incident. Corbin moved to dismiss the indictment on double jeopardy grounds. The trial court denied his motion, but the New York Court of Appeals reversed. The United States Supreme Court recognized that under the *Blockburger* test a second trial could have proceeded because the driving under the influence charge and the manslaughter charge had different statutory elements. The Court held, however, that the *Blockburger* test did not provide a defendant with sufficient protection in these circumstances because the same *conduct* would be used to prosecute both cases.[56] This was prohibited by the double jeopardy clause.

Grady v. *Corbin* established a new but short-lived "same conduct" double jeopardy test. In 1993, the Supreme Court overruled *Grady* v. *Corbin* and returned to the more familiar *Blockburger* same offense test.[57] The Supreme Court rarely overturns its decisions in a matter of a few years. In *United States* v. *Dixon*,[58] however, the Court held that *Grady* v. *Corbin*'s double jeopardy test was "wrong in principle" and was "wholly inconsistent with earlier Supreme Court precedent and with the clear common-law understanding of double jeopardy."[59] *United States* v. *Dixon*, therefore, returned double jeopardy analysis to the more familiar *Blockburger* test. Highlight 11.3 summarizes that rule.

The Dual Sovereignty Doctrine

The **dual sovereignty doctrine** denies double jeopardy protection to a defendant who, by a single criminal act, violates the laws of different jurisdictions. For example, in

Highlight 11.3

Summary of the *Blockburger* Test

***Blockburger v. United States*, 284 U.S. 302 (1932)**

"The applicable rule is that where the same act or transaction constitutes a violation of two distinct statutory provisions, the test to be applied to determine whether there are two offenses or only one, is whether each provision requires proof of a fact which the other does not."

Bartkus v. *Illinois*[60] the defendant was tried and acquitted in federal court of robbing a federally insured savings and loan. He was then tried and convicted on state bank robbery charges for the same offense and was sentenced to life imprisonment. The Supreme Court upheld Bartkus's state conviction, despite close cooperation between state and federal investigators.

In practice, successive federal and state prosecutions of the same defendant for the same crime are relatively uncommon.[61] The United States Department of Justice's *Petite* **policy** prevents the federal government from instituting a federal prosecution after a state prosecution based on substantially the same act, unless there is a compelling federal interest supporting the dual prosecutions.[62] The policy is designed to restrict prosecutorial discretion in order to promote efficient resource utilization and to protect defendants from the unfairness of multiple prosecutions and punishments for the same acts.[63]

The dual sovereignty principle applies to successive prosecutions by different states as well. *Heath* v. *Alabama*[64] held that "[t]o deny a state its power to enforce its criminal laws because another State has won the race to the courthouse would be a shocking and untoward deprivation of the historic right and obligation of the States to maintain peace and order within their confines."[65]

The dual sovereignty principle may not be used, however, to allow a juvenile to be tried in a later criminal trial for the same incident after he or she has been found to be delinquent in a juvenile court proceeding. This is a clear violation of the double jeopardy clause.[66]

The Collateral Estoppel Doctrine

Another interesting double jeopardy issue is the **collateral estoppel doctrine.** It provides that once an issue has been determined in a defendant's favor at trial, the same issue may not be relitigated by the prosecution hoping to get a more favorable outcome at a later trial. To illustrate, in *Ashe* v. *Swenson*,[67] six men who were playing poker in the basement of a home were robbed at gunpoint by several masked robbers. Ashe was charged at his first trial with robbing one of the victims, but the State's evidence was weak and he was found not guilty due to insufficient evidence. A short time later, Ashe was tried and convicted for robbing another poker player during the same incident. On appeal, the Supreme Court held that the doctrine of collateral estoppel, which is embodied in the Fifth Amendment double jeopardy clause, barred the second prosecution. That doctrine prevented Ashe's second prosecution because the jury in the first trial had determined by its verdict that he was not one of the robbers. In effect, the State was prevented from using the first trial as "a dry run for the second prosecution."[68]

The collateral estoppel doctrine is a fair and reasonable protection for defendants in criminal proceedings. It prevents a state from rehearsing its case against a defendant in order to attain a conviction in a later case. Allowing the State of Missouri to take multiple "pot shots" at Ashe in six different criminal trials would have been unfair. Neither the collateral estoppel doctrine nor the double jeopardy clause, however, will protect defendants who are facing both criminal and civil charges based on the same incident.

Double Jeopardy and Civil Proceedings

In general, the Fifth Amendment double jeopardy clause will not prevent a defendant from being sued civilly after he or she is found guilty.[69] Likewise, later administrative proceedings against a criminal defendant based on the same incident do not violate the double jeopardy clause. For example, suppose a medical doctor is convicted of sexually assaulting a patient and is sentenced to serve five years in prison. State authorities would be expected to revoke the individual's license to practice medicine. A license revocation proceeding following the individual's criminal trial would not violate the double jeopardy clause.

If, after a defendant has been found guilty and punished for a crime, a civil penalty is imposed that constitutes *punishment,* the double jeopardy clause is violated.[70] The general rule is that if the amount of the civil penalty is overwhelmingly disproportionate to the damages caused, it is punitive. In *Department of Revenue* v. *Kurth Ranch,*[71] the Supreme Court held that the double jeopardy clause prevented the State of Montana from imposing a punitive marijuana tax on the defendant following his conviction for various drug offenses. Recent precedents appear to indicate, however, that some types of civil sanctions do not constitute *punishment* under the double jeopardy clause.

Forfeiture Proceedings.   A **forfeiture proceeding** is a government action taken against property that is involved in some way with a defendant's unlawful activities. For example, one federal statute, the Comprehensive Drug Prevention and Control Act, provides for the forfeiture of a defendant's property that is used to facilitate illegal drug sales or is purchased with the proceeds from those sales.[72]

Property forfeiture laws have existed throughout U.S. history. For many years, however, they were not widely used by law enforcement authorities. In the 1970s, however, they experienced a revival with the passage of the **Racketeer Influence and**

Corrupt Organizations Act (RICO). Under this statute it is a violation of the law for any person,

> employed by or associated with any enterprise engaged in, or the activities of which affect, interstate or foreign commerce, to conduct or participate, directly or indirectly, in the conduct of such enterprise's affairs through a pattern of racketeering activity.[73]

Under the statute, racketeering activity may include murder, kidnapping, arson, robbery, bribery, extortion, and drug sales. In addition, there must be at least two instances of these activities over a 10-year period to constitute a pattern of racketeering activity.

Both the Comprehensive Drug Prevention and Control Act and RICO allow the government to initiate forfeiture proceedings against a defendant's property used to promote criminal activity or is produced by such activity. Moreover, many states have developed similar laws permitting property forfeiture actions against those suspected of committing serious crimes. With the proliferation of these laws the value of assets seized by the government has skyrocketed in recent years. Table 11.1 presents a summary of asset seizures by one federal agency, the Drug Enforcement Administration (DEA), between 1992 and 1994.

Forfeiture laws can be a powerful law enforcement tool. Proponents of these statutes believe that they constitute a powerful deterrent to illegal activities by denying criminals the fruits of their crimes. Forfeiture law opponents, on the other hand, believe that these laws are often misused by overly zealous law enforcement officials. Both federal law and the laws of many states may require that the proceeds from property seizures be used directly by law enforcement agencies to fund training programs or to purchase equipment. This may provide a financial incentive to pursue property forfeitures and lead to serious miscarriages of justice. Highlight 11.4 presents a discussion of the use of forfeiture laws by government authorities.

Legal challenges to modern forfeiture laws have advanced three primary theories: (1) that forfeiture statutes violate due process of law; (2) that they are cruel and unusual punishment or that they constitute an excessive fine; or (3) that forfeiture laws violate the double jeopardy clause. Defendants challenging these laws have met with only limited success.

Due Process of Law. In *United States* v. *Good Real Property*,[74] police officers seized approximately 89 pounds of marijuana and other contraband from Good's home. He pleaded guilty to state drug charges and was sentenced to one year in jail and was given a $1,000 fine. In addition, he forfeited $3,187 in cash found at the home. Approximately four years later, the federal government filed a forfeiture action seeking to seize Good's house and land because it had been used to commit a federal drug offense. A federal magistrate found probable cause to believe that Good's property was subject to forfeiture under the statute and authorized its seizure. The proceeding was held without notice to Good or his attorney. The property was then seized without notice or a further hearing. On appeal, the Supreme Court held that "[u]nless exigent circumstances are present, the Due Process Clause requires the Government to

TABLE 11.1   Asset Seizures by the Drug Enforcement Administration

By Type and Value of Asset Seized, Fiscal Years 1992–94

Type of Asset	1992		1993		1994	
	Number of Seizures	*Value*	*Number of Seizures*	*Value*	*Number of Seizures*	*Value*
Total	19,868	$874,889,400	16,895	$688,720,873	13,779	$649,705,121
Currency	8,344	267,820,145	7,014	250,469,017	6,617	316,312,836
Other financial instruments	741	154,834,673	588	50,703,447	463	47,048,668
Real property	1,712	320,631,938	1,565	255,157,081	910	171,925,045
Vehicles	5,948	57,065,862	4,737	48,787,715	3,780	39,009,342
Vessels	228	12,399,302	159	9,198,707	147	18,379,846
Aircraft	53	15,828,500	45	33,915,750	37	10,109,200
Other conveyance	278	2,146,124	323	4,333,503	196	1,814,528
Other	2,564	44,162,856	2,464	36,155,653	1,629	45,105,656

Kathleen Maguire and Ann L. Pastore, eds., *Sourcebook of Criminal Justice Statistics 1994,* U.S. Department of Justice, Bureau of Justice Statistics (Washington, D.C.: USGPO, 1995), p. 423.

afford notice and a meaningful opportunity to be heard before seizing real property subject to civil forfeiture."[75]

Simply because a defendant has a right to an adversary hearing *before* his or her property is forfeited, however, does not mean that the property will be retained. The federal forfeiture drug statute's burden of proof requires only that law enforcement officials establish *probable cause* to believe that the property was used to facilitate illegal drug activity.[76] If a defendant is already convicted of a crime, this is an easy standard to meet.

Right to be Free from Excessive Fines.   The Supreme Court has held that the Eighth Amendment's excessive fines clause applies to drug case forfeiture proceedings. The general rule is that a fine will be held to be excessive only if it is overwhelmingly disproportionate to the offense committed. *United States* v. *Halper*[77] held that a reviewing court was required to compare the amount of the fine with the sum that is necessary to compensate society and the government for the damages caused by the defendant. In *Halper,* the fine was held to be excessive when the defendant in a civil action was fined $130,000 for filing false medicaid claims for $585.

In *Austin* v. *United States,*[78] the defendant pleaded guilty to possessing cocaine with intent to distribute for selling two grams of cocaine. He was sentenced to seven years' imprisonment. The federal government then filed a forfeiture action against his mobile home and auto body shop. On appeal, the Supreme Court held that the excessive fines clause applies to drug case forfeiture proceedings because they serve retributive and deterrent purposes and constitute punishment.[79] The Court therefore remanded the case to the U.S. District Court to determine whether the forfeiture in this case was excessive.

Highlight 11.4

Highway Robbery

Hugh Grant is lucky he does not own a home in Hollywood. Under forfeiture laws in California, the British actor might have been asked to hand over his home and his car as part of any plea bargain. Instead, following his night out with Divine Brown on Sunset Boulevard, Grant's no-contest plea to lewd conduct resulted in a fine, probation, and an AIDS awareness seminar.

Years before Hugh Grant became a household name, John Bennis had a similar hankering one October day in 1988 and drove the family Pontiac down to a notorious stretch of Detroit's Eight Mile Road. This unfortunately caught the eye of the police.

Bennis was charged and convicted of gross indecency. Using a 1926 Michigan law, prosecutors moved to seize the Bennis family Pontiac. This proved too much for Bennis's wife, Tina, who felt she already had enough to cope with. She filed suit to get their car back. As she was not associated with the crime in the slightest way, she argued, her means of transportation should not be taken away.

Last November, the U.S. Supreme Court heard opening arguments in the Bennis case, which has become a cause celebre in the U.S., not so much because of its illicit beginnings, but because it represents one of the more outrageous incidents in the unparalleled "asset-seizure" bonanza sweeping America. [On March 4, the Supreme Court ruled 5–4 against Tina Bennis: She need not know that her car would be used in a crime in order for the state to seize it.-WPR]

Since 1984, when Congress passed the Comprehensive Crime Control Act, which vastly broadened the government's powers of seizure, the U.S. government has taken in more than $6 billion in an aggressive program of seizing the belongings of criminals facing conviction or already found guilty.

The new civil forfeiture laws suspend many legal precedents commonly associated with the Anglo-American tradition of law. Law-enforcement officials can seize property prior to charging an individual and can keep it even if the accused is not convicted. In addition, "guilty by association" takes on new meaning under some of the new forfeiture statutes. In 1993 alone, the U.S. Department of Justice took in more than $556 million. Its Office for Asset Forfeiture estimates that another $2 billion is in the pipeline. The department's shopping list goes way beyond such likely targets as houses, share portfolios, and private planes: It has extended to coin collections, kitchen coffee makers, and, in the case of a man accused of impersonating a psychiatrist, a pair of baby shoes.

But the easiest asset to get hold of remains cold hard cash. Knowing this, some rogue sheriff departments have turned stretches of U.S. freeway into virtual cash cows. "In Volusia County, Florida, sheriffs have been patrolling I-95 and stopping cars at random," says Roger Pilon of the Cato Institute, a Washington-based libertarian think tank. "If drivers are carrying any more than $1000 in cash, they [seize] it, using the argument that in this area it can only be dirty drug money."

Following the lead of the federal government, all 50 U.S. states have passed civil forfeiture laws. Although these laws were meant to give prosecutors and law-enforcement officials more weapons to go after criminals, especially those in the drug trade, the forfeiture boom turned out to provide an unexpected windfall for some financially strapped police departments.

In California, 90 percent of the $56 million seized in assets in 1991 was kept by law-enforcement authorities and used to pay for their own programs.

In the last 10 years, the U.S. Justice Department has transferred more than $1 billion in cash and property to 3,000 state and local agencies. According to the Cato Institute's Paul Roberts, "Increasing taxes is unpopular. But through forfeitures, the government can raise revenues and appear as moral crusaders."

(Continued)

(Concluded)

"It's turned into a real moneymaker for law-enforcement agencies," says Pilon. "The police get to act as judge and jury all rolled into one. Police departments are outfitting gymnasiums with the money. There have been cases recently of policemen driving around in BMWs seized from drug dealers."

Forfeiture law comes with a long, if somewhat dusty, tradition. For centuries, the English Crown raised revenue by collecting taxes on goods. If a ship's captain tried to evade customs duties, Crown agents could seize the vessel as well as its cargo. Like many other legal traditions, this branch of law was established in the U.S. with little change, even though it ignores the principle that people, rather than their property, commit crimes.

"It's been a rather sleepy backwater of American law," says Paul Levine of the National Association of Criminal Defense Lawyers (NACDL) in Washington. "It was the war on drugs which saw the use of forfeiture rise dramatically." On Capitol Hill, Chairman of the House Judiciary Committee Henry Hyde agrees: "The exigencies of the drug war have reviewed the hoary doctrines of Anglo-American forfeiture law like some jurisprudential Frankenstein monster."

Crime fighters see it differently. "It is a very valuable tool," says John Fuller of the Justice Department. "It sends a strong message to criminals, especially those trafficking in drugs."

Justice Department officials argue that drug lords and their employees regard doing time in jail as a regular aspect of their business, so going after the vast sums of money the drug lords accumulate is a much more severe deterrent. "If we are successful, the drug-trafficking organizations will wither and die," says Robert Bonner, the head of the Drug Enforcement Administration.

The asset-seizure boom has been so successful in the area of drug-related crime that agencies have extended its use to other areas of criminal activity. In California, 30 percent of asset seizures are in non-drug-related cases. Under the New Jersey law, Jacqueline Saravion lost her 1987 Oldsmobile because police said her son drove it to a local Sears, where he allegedly shoplifted a pair of pants and was stopped by a security guard.

Led by an unlikely coalition of conservatives and liberals, efforts are underway in Washington to change the forfeiture statutes. "Sadly, most of what appears to be an egregious abuse of police power is actually legal, because the current legislation gives way too much power to law-enforcement agencies," says Levine. The NACDL has joined with conservative groups to back a reform of the forfeiture laws sponsored by Representative Hyde.

The bill, which Levine says "has a good shot of passing," would realign the legal precedents of the current laws. It would also shift the burden of proof back to the state, appoint free legal counsel for indigents, protect innocent property owners, and extend the deadline for forfeiture challenge from 10 to 60 days.

"For 200 years, this area of law was hardly used or challenged," Levine says. "Suddenly, its use rose dramatically. It makes sense to sort this branch of law out and make it consistent with the respect afforded individual liberty and property rights we are now accustomed to."

From David Hay, "Highway Robbery," *World Press Review,* 43:6, June 1996, p. 28. Reprinted by permission of the author.

Double Jeopardy Issues in Forfeiture Cases.   Property forfeiture proceedings in illegal drug cases present interesting double jeopardy questions as well. *Witte* v. *United States*[80] held that the double jeopardy clause's protection against multiple punishments prevents the government from "punishing twice, or attempting a second time to punish criminally for the same offense."[81] In 1996, *Bennis* v. *Michigan*[82] held, however, that property forfeiture proceedings directed against even innocent property owners do not constitute multiple punishment under the double jeopardy clause. In that case the wife of a man convicted of "gross indecency" for consorting with a prostitute challenged Michigan's forfeiture law. The car had been seized as a "public nuisance" after the husband used it during an encounter with the prostitute. The Supreme Court held:

> The Bennis automobile, it is conceded, facilitated and was used in criminal activity. A long and unbroken line of cases holds that an owner's interest in property may be forfeited by reason of the use to which the property is put, even though the owner did not know that it was to be put to such use.[83]

Even more recently *United States* v. *Ursery*,[84] held that "[f]orfeitures serve a variety of purposes, but are designed primarily to confiscate property used in violation of the law, and to require disgorgement of the fruits of illegal conduct."[85] The Court emphasized that property forfeitures are separate civil *sanctions* that are remedial in nature and do not constitute *punishment* for double jeopardy purposes.

The following rules emerge from the Supreme Court's drug forfeiture cases:

1. Defendants in property forfeiture proceedings must be given due process safeguards, which include notice and an adversary hearing.
2. The Eighth Amendment's protection against excessive fines applies to property forfeiture proceedings.
3. A property forfeiture proceeding following the imposition of punishment for a criminal conviction does not violate the Fifth Amendment's Double Jeopardy Clause.

Summary

Chapter 11 discusses pretrial identification procedures and the right to be free from double jeopardy. Like cases involving custodial interrogations, pretrial identification proceedings may present Fifth, Sixth, and Fourteenth Amendment issues. Fifth Amendment issues include whether compelling a suspect to participate in a pretrial identification proceeding violated his privilege against self-incrimination. If the identification proceeding is improperly suggestive it will violate the Fifth and Fourteenth Amendments' due process guarantees. In addition, a defendant has a right to counsel during some pretrial identification procedures.

Self-incrimination issues may be raised when a defendant is required to produce evidence for a criminal investigation. One might argue that requiring a defendant to provide evidence such as bodily fluids or hair for comparison with those left at a crime scene violates the privilege against self-incrimination because it involves using the suspect's own body chemistry to gain a conviction. The Supreme Court has rejected this argument, however, because such physical evidence is neither testimonial nor communicative.

A suspect's participation in pretrial identification procedures may implicate Sixth Amendment concerns as well. Under the *Wade-Gilbert* rule, a suspect has a right to counsel at a post-indictment lineup for identification purposes. Counsel need only be present, however, when adversary judicial proceedings have begun, whether by way of formal charge, preliminary hearing, indictment, information, or arraignment. If a suspect is exhibited to a witness at a post-indictment lineup conducted outside the presence of counsel, any identification must be excluded at trial.

Another type of pretrial identification procedure, termed a showup, involves a prompt confrontation between a witness and the arrested suspect at or near the crime scene, at the police station, or at another location such as a hospital. Once adversary proceedings have commenced, an accused should be given the opportunity to have counsel present at any confrontation with a witness.

Neither a suspect nor his or her attorney has a right to be present during a pretrial photographic display because such a display may be recreated easily at trial. Like lineups and showups, photographic displays may not be improperly suggestive and may not be arranged in such a way that they point to the accused.

Due process of law requires that all types of pretrial identification procedures be conducted in a fair manner. It is not easy, however, for a defendant to establish a due process violation. Even if an identification is obtained as a result of suggestive procedures it will be admissible at trial if the circumstances surrounding the process provide a reason to believe that it is trustworthy. If, however, pretrial identification procedures are so inherently suggestive that they may lead to the likelihood of mistaken identification, a due process challenge may succeed.

The Fifth Amendment right to be free from double jeopardy provides three independent protections. First, it does not allow a person to be retried for the same offense after a conviction. Second, it protects against reprosecution following an acquittal. Third, it protects against multiple punishments for the same offense.

Courts will use the *Blockburger* test to determine if a defendant in a second trial is being tried for the same offense that he or she was tried for during the original trial. The *Blockburger* test focuses on the statutory elements of the charged offenses—if a second charged offense requires the prosecution to prove different statutory elements, a second trial may proceed. If, however, a defendant by a single criminal act violates the laws of different jurisdictions, the dual sovereignty doctrine will permit both jurisdictions to convict and punish the individual.

Another double jeopardy issue is the collateral estoppel doctrine. It provides that once an issue has been determined in a defendant's favor at trial, the same issue may not be relitigated by the prosecution hoping to get a more favorable outcome at a later trial.

The double jeopardy clause will not prevent a defendant from being sued civilly after he or she is found guilty for a criminal act. Likewise, later administrative proceedings against a criminal defendant based on the same incident do not violate the double jeopardy clause.

Forfeiture proceedings, which are government actions taken against property that is involved in some way with a defendant's unlawful activities, sometimes raise double jeopardy issues. In recent years, most challenges to these laws have been unsuccessful.

Review Questions

1. Discuss how Fifth Amendment privilege against self-incrimination issues may arise during the pretrial identification process.

   a. The Supreme Court has held that prosecutors may require a defendant to furnish physical evidence such as hair or voice samples to be used in an investigation. Present arguments for and against the proposition that requiring a defendant to provide such evidence violates the privilege against self-incrimination.

2. The Supreme Court has held that the Fifth Amendment privilege against self-incrimination protects an accused from having to furnish evidence that is either testimonial or communicative. What implications does this have for the pretrial identification process?

3. Discuss whether the Fifth Amendment privilege against self-incrimination would protect an individual from having to furnish the following types of evidence to police investigators:
   a. blood samples
   b. voice samples
   c. handwriting samples
4. Present the IACP's guidelines for conducting lineups. What may a prosecutor do if a defendant refuses to furnish physical evidence or participate in a pretrial identification procedure?
5. What is the *Wade-Gilbert* rule?
6. Describe the proper role of an attorney at a pretrial lineup for identification purposes.
7. What is a showup identification procedure? Discuss several factors that a court would consider to determine if a showup was conducted properly.
8. Discuss the Supreme Court's holding in *United States* v. *Ash.*

9. Describe a situation in which a defendant is likely to challenge a pretrial identification procedure based on due process of law. How may law enforcement officers prevent successful due process challenges to pretrial identification procedures?
10. Describe three protections provided by the Fifth Amendment's double jeopardy clause. Identify five basic rules that are a key to understanding the right to be free from double jeopardy.
11. Discuss the *Blockburger* "same offense" test. How did *Grady* v. *Corbin* change that test? What is the current legal status of the *Blockburger* test?
12. Describe the dual sovereignty doctrine. How does the Petite policy impact this doctrine?
13. Discuss the collateral estoppel doctrine. Illustrate how this doctrine works by using the facts in *Ashe* v. *Swenson.*
14. What is a civil forfeiture proceeding? Identify three rules that emerge from the Supreme Court's recent civil forfeiture decisions.

Issues for Analysis and Discussion

1. In *United States* v. *Wade,* the Supreme Court stated: "The rule sought by the State here, however, would make the trial no more than an appeal from the interrogation." What rule did the state request in *Wade?* Why did the Court assert that adoption of this rule would have made a trial "no more than an appeal from [an] interrogation"? Do you agree with the Court's decision, or would you advocate a contrary rule?

2. In *Department of Revenue* v. *Kurth Ranch,* the Supreme Court held that a Montana law that authorized a tax on the possession of illegal drugs was unconstitutional. According to the Supreme Court, what changes could be made to the Montana law to make it constitutional? When does a "tax" violate the Fifth Amendment's double jeopardy clause?

Case Excerpt: *United States v. Wade*
Supreme Court of the United States (1967)
388 U.S. 218

Wade was indicted for robbery of a federally insured bank, and an attorney was appointed to represent him. Without notice to Wade's attorney, an F.B.I. agent arranged to have two bank employees observe a lineup of Wade and five or six other individuals. The persons in the lineup were required, like the robber, to wear strips of tape on their faces and to say, "Put the money in the bag." The witnesses identified Wade as the robber. At Wade's trial in federal court, both witnesses identified Wade. Defense counsel's motion to strike the courtroom identification was denied and Wade was convicted. The U.S. Court of Appeals reversed because the lineup without Wade's attorney violated his Sixth Amendment right to counsel. The U.S. Supreme Court granted certiorari.

Mr. Justice Brennan delivered the opinion of the Court.

* * *

The question here is whether courtroom identifications of an accused at trial are to be excluded because the accused was exhibited to the witnesses before trial at a post-indictment lineup conducted for identification purposes without notice to and in the absence of the accused's appointed counsel.

* * *

Neither the lineup itself nor anything shown by this record that Wade was required to do in the lineup violated his privilege against self-incrimination.

* * *

We have no doubt that compelling the accused merely to exhibit his person for observation by a prosecution witness prior to trial involves no compulsion of the accused to give evidence having testimonial significance. It is the compulsion of the accused to exhibit his physical characteristics, not compulsion to disclose any knowledge he might have. It is no different from compelling Schmerber to provide a blood sample or Holt to wear the blouse, and, as in those instances, is not

within the cover of the privilege. Similarly, compelling Wade to speak within hearing distance of the witnesses, even to utter words purportedly uttered by the robber, was not compulsion to utter statements of a "testimonial" nature; he was required to use his voice as an identifying physical characteristic, not to speak his guilt.

* * *

The fact that the lineup involved no violation of Wade's privilege against self-incrimination does not, however, dispose of his contention that the courtroom identifications should have been excluded because the lineup was conducted without notice to and in the absence of his counsel. Our rejection of the right to counsel claim in *Schmerber* rested on our conclusion in that case that "[n]o issue of counsel's ability to assist petitioner in respect of any rights he did possess is presented." In contrast, in this case it is urged that the assistance of counsel at the lineup was indispensable to protect Wade's most basic right as a criminal defendant—his right to a fair trial at which the witnesses against him might be meaningfully cross-examined.

* * *

[T]oday's law enforcement machinery involves critical confrontations of the accused by the prosecution at pretrial proceedings where the results might well settle the accused's fate and reduce the trial itself to a mere formality. In recognition of these realities of modern criminal prosecution, our cases have construed the Sixth Amendment guarantee to apply to "critical" stages of the proceedings. The guarantee reads: "In all criminal prosecutions, the accused shall enjoy the right . . . to have the Assistance of Counsel *for his defence.*" The plain wording of this guarantee thus encompasses counsel's assistance whenever necessary to assure a meaningful "defence."

As early as *Powell* v. *Alabama,* supra, we recognized that the period from arraignment to trial was "perhaps the most critical period of the proceedings . . ." during which the accused "requires the guiding hand of counsel . . . ," if the guarantee is not to prove an empty right. That principle has since been applied to require the assistance of counsel at the type of arraignment . . . where certain rights might be sacrificed or lost. "What happens there may affect the whole trial. Available defenses may be irretrievably lost, if not then and there asserted."

* * *

The rule sought by the State here, however, would make the trial no more than an appeal from the interrogation; and the 'right to use counsel at the formal trial [would be] a very hollow thing [if], for all practical purposes, the conviction is already assured by pretrial examination' . . . 'One can imagine a cynical prosecutor saying: "Let them have the most illustrious counsel, now. They can't escape the noose. There is nothing that counsel can do for them at trial.'"

* * *

In sum, the principle of *Powell* v. *Alabama* and succeeding cases requires that we scrutinize

any pretrial confrontation of the accused to determine whether the presence of his counsel is necessary to preserve the defendant's basic right to a fair trial as affected by his right meaningfully to cross-examine the witnesses against him and to have effective assistance of counsel at the trial itself. It calls upon us to analyze whether potential substantial prejudice to defendant's rights inheres in the particular confrontation and the ability of counsel to held avoid that prejudice.

The Government characterizes the lineup as a mere preparatory step in the gathering of the prosecution's evidence, not different—for Sixth Amendment purposes—from various other preparatory steps, such as systematized or scientific analyzing of the accused's fingerprints, blood sample, clothing, hair, and the like. We think there are differences which preclude such stages being characterized as critical stages at which the accused has the right to the presence of counsel. Knowledge of the techniques of science and technology is sufficiently available, and the variables in techniques few enough, that the accused has the opportunity for a meaningful confrontation of the Government's case at trial thought the ordinary process of cross-examination of the Government's expert witness and the presentation of the evidence of his own experts. The denial of a right to have his counsel present at such analyses does not therefore violate the Sixth Amendment; they are not critical stages since there is minimal risk that his counsel's absence at such stages might derogate from his right to a fair trial.

But the confrontation compelled by the State between the accused and the victim or witnesses to a crime to elicit identification evidence is peculiarly riddled with innumerable dangers and variable factors which might seriously, even crucially, derogate from a fair trial. The vagaries of eyewitness identification are well-known; the annals of criminal law are rife with instances of mistaken identification. Mr. Justice Frankfurter once said: "What is the worth of identification testimony even when uncontradicted? The identification of strangers is proverbially untrustworthy. The hazards of such testimony are established by a formidable number of English and American trials. These instances are recent—not due to the brutalities of ancient criminal procedure." A major factor contributing to the high incidence of miscarriage of justice from mistaken identification has been the degree of suggestion inherent in the manner in which the prosecution presents the suspect to witnesses for pretrial identification. A commentator has observed that "[t]he influence of improper suggestion upon identifying witnesses probably accounts for more miscarriages of justice than any other single factor—perhaps it is responsible for more such errors than all other factors combined." Suggestion can be created intentionally or unintentionally in many subtle ways. And the dangers for the suspect are particularly grave when the witness's opportunity for observations was insubstantial, and thus his susceptibility to suggestion the greatest.

Moreover, "[i]t is a matter of common experience that, once a witness has picked out the accused at the lineup, he is not likely to go back on his word later on, so that in practice the issue of identity may (in the absence of other relevant evidence) for all practical purposes be determined there and then, before the trial."

The pretrial confrontation for purpose of identification may take the form of a lineup, also known as "identification parade" or "showup," as in the present case, or presentation of the suspect alone to the witness as in *Stovall* v. *Denno*. It is obvious that risks of suggestions attend either form of confrontation and increase the dangers inhering in eyewitness identification. But as is the case with secret interrogations, there is serious difficulty in depicting what transpires at lineups and other forms of identification confrontations: "Privacy results in secrecy and this in turn results in a gap in our knowledge as to what in fact goes on." For the same reasons, the defense can seldom reconstruct the manner and mode of lineup identification for judge or jury at trial. Those participating in a lineup with the accused may often be po-

lice officers; in any event, the participants' names are rarely recorded or divulged at trial. The impediments to an objective observation are increased when the victim is the witness. Lineups are prevalent in rape and robbery prosecutions and present a particular hazard that a victim's understandable outrage may excite vengeful or spiteful motives. In any event, neither witnesses nor lineup participants are apt to be alert for conditions prejudicial to the suspect. And if they were, it would likely be of scant benefit to the suspect since neither witnesses nor lineup participants are likely to be schooled in the detection of suggestive influences. Improper influences may go undetected by a suspect, guilty or not, who experiences the emotional tension which we might expect in one being confronted with potential accusers. Even when he does observe abuse, if he has a criminal record he may be reluctant to take the stand and open up the admission of prior convictions. Moreover, any protestations by the suspect of the fairness of the lineup made at trial are likely to be in vain; the jury's choice is between the accused's unsupported version and that of the police officers present. In short, the accused's inability effectively to reconstruct at trial any unfairness that occurred at the lineup may deprive him of his only opportunity meaningfully to attack the credibility of the witness's courtroom identification.

* * *

Since it appears that there is grave potential for prejudice, intentional or not, in the pretrial lineup, which may not be capable of reconstruction at trial, and since presence of counsel itself can often avert prejudice and assure a meaningful confrontation at trial, there can be little doubt that for Wade the post-indictment lineup was a critical stage of the prosecution at which he was "as much entitled to such aid [of counsel] . . . as at the trial itself." Thus both Wade and his counsel should have been notified of the impending lineup, and counsel's presence should have been a requisite to conduct of the lineup, absent "intelligent waiver." . . . We leave open the question whether the presence of substitute counsel might not suffice where notification and presence of the suspect's own counsel would result in prejudicial delay. And to refuse to recognize the right to counsel for fear that counsel will obstruct the course of justice is contrary to the basic assumptions upon which this Court has operated in Sixth Amendment cases. We rejected similar logic in *Miranda* v. *Arizona* concerning presence of counsel during custodial interrogation: "[A]n attorney is merely exercising the good professional judgement he has been taught. This is not cause of considering the attorney a menace to law enforcement. He is merely carrying out what he is sworn to do under his oath—to protect to the extent of his ability the right of his client. In fulfilling this responsibility the attorney plays a vital role in the administration of criminal justice under our Constitution."

In our view counsel can hardly impede legitimate law enforcement; on the contrary, for the reasons expressed, law enforcement may be assisted by preventing the infiltration of taint in the prosecution's identification evidence. That result cannot help the guilty avoid conviction but can only help assure that the right man has been brought to justice.

* * *

The judgment of the Court of Appeals is vacated and the case is remanded to that court with direction to enter a new judgment vacating the conviction and remanding the case to the District Court for further proceedings consistent with this opinion.

Case Excerpt: *Department of Revenue of Montana v. Kurth Ranch*
Supreme Court of the United States (1994)
114 S.Ct. 994

A Montana law imposed a tax on the possession and storage of dangerous drugs. A taxpayer had no obligation to pay any tax unless he or she was arrested. The members of a Montana family operated a farm at which marijuana was grown. Police officers raided the farm, arrested family members, and confiscated marijuana plants and other contraband. In a criminal proceeding several family members entered into a plea agreement on the drug charges and were sentenced. In a separate civil proceeding, Montana's department of revenue applied the drug tax law and ultimately attempted to collect almost $900,000 in taxes on the marijuana. At the same time the family had filed a bankruptcy petition in federal court in which they had objected to the department's claim for drug taxes and challenged the constitutionality of the tax. The Bankruptcy Court ruled that most of the drug tax assessment was invalid as a matter of state law and, although one assessment of $181,000 on 1,811 ounces of marijuana was authorized under the statute, that assessment was invalid under the Double Jeopardy Clause, because the statute's purpose was to impose punishment rather than to recover law enforcement costs. The U.S. District Court and the U.S. Court of Appeals both affirmed. The U.S. Supreme Court granted certiorari.

Mr. Justice Stevens delivered the opinion of the Court.

* * *

This case presents the question whether a tax on the possession of illegal drugs assessed after the State has imposed a criminal penalty for the same conduct may violate the constitutional prohibition against multiple punishments for the same crime.

* * *

[*United States* v.] *Halper* decided that the legislature's description of a statute as civil does not foreclose the possibility that it has a punitive character. We also recognized in *Halper* that a so-called civil "penalty" may be remedial in character if it merely reimburses the government for its actual costs arising from the defendant's criminal conduct. . . . *Halper* did not, however, consider whether a tax may similarly be characterized as punitive.

Criminal fines, civil penalties, civil forfeitures, and taxes all share certain features: They generate government revenues, impose fiscal burdens on individuals, and deter certain behavior. All of these sanctions are subject to constitutional constraints. A government may not impose criminal fines without first establishing guilt by proof beyond a reasonable doubt. A defendant convicted and punished for an offense may not have a nonremedial civil penalty imposed against him for the same offense in a separate proceeding. A civil forfeiture may violate the Eighth Amendment's proscription against excessive fines. And a statute imposing a tax on unlawful conduct may be invalid because its reporting requirements compel taxpayers to incriminate themselves.

As a general matter, the unlawfulness of an activity does not prevent its taxation. Montana no doubt could collect its tax on the possession of marijuana, for example, if it had not previously punished the taxpayer for the same offense, or indeed if it had assessed the tax in the same proceeding that resulted in his conviction. Here, we ask only whether the tax has punitive characteristics that subject it to the constraints on the Double Jeopardy Clause.

Although we have never held that a tax violated the Double Jeopardy Clause, we have assumed that one might. In the context of other constitutional requirements, we have repeatedly examined taxes for constitutional validity. We have cautioned against invalidating a tax simply because its enforcement might be oppressive or because the legislature's motive was somehow suspect. Yet we have also recognized that "there comes a time in the extension of the penalizing features of the so-called tax when it loses its character as such and becomes a mere penalty with the characteristics of regulation and punishment." That comment, together with *Halper*'s unequivocal statement that labels do not control in a double jeopardy inquiry, indicates that a tax is not immune from double jeopardy scrutiny simply because it is a tax. . . . [A]t some point, an exaction labeled as a tax approaches punishment, and our task is to determine whether Montana's drug tax crosses that line.

* * *

In this case, the tax assessment not only hinges on the commission of a crime, it also is exacted only after the taxpayer has been arrested for the precise conduct that gives rise to the tax obligation in the first place. Persons who have been arrested for possessing marijuana constitute the entire class of taxpayers subject to the Montana tax. . . . A tax on "possession of goods that no longer exist and that the taxpayer never lawfully possessed has an unmistakable punitive character. This tax, imposed on criminals and no others, departs so far from normal revenue laws as to become a form of punishment.

Taken as a whole this drug tax is a concoction of anomalies, too far-removed in crucial respects from a standard tax assessment to escape characterization as punishment for the purpose of Double Jeopardy analysis.

* * *

This drug tax is not the kind of remedial sanction that may follow the first punishment of a criminal offense. Instead, it is a second punishment within the contemplation of a constitutional protection that has "deep roots in our history and jurisprudence," and therefore must be imposed during the first prosecution or not at all. The proceeding Montana initiated to collect a tax on the possession of drugs was the functional equivalent of a successive criminal prosecution that placed the Kurths in jeopardy a second time "for the same offense."

The judgment of the Court of Appeals is affirmed.

Endnotes

1. See *Abney* v. *United States,* 431 U.S. 651 (1977).
2. *Doe* v. *United States,* 487 U.S. 201 (1988).
3. Id. at 210.
4. *Schmerber* v. *California,* 384 U.S. 757 (1966).
5. Id. at 771.
6. *Rochin* v. *California,* 342 U.S. 165 (1952).
7. Supra, note 4 at 771.
8. Id. at 762–763.
9. Id. at 774.
10. *Pennsylvania* v. *Muniz,* 496 U.S. 582 (1990).
11. Id. at 599.
12. Supra, note 2 at 213.
13. *United States* v. *Dionisio,* 410 U.S. 1 (1973).
14. Id. at 14.
15. *United States* v. *Wade,* 388 U.S. 218 (1967).
16. Id. at 222–223; see Wallace W. Sherwood, "The Erosion of Constitutional Safeguards in the Area of Eyewitness Identification." 30 *Howard Law Journal* pp. 439–479 (1987).
17. *Gilbert* v. *California,* 388 U.S. 263 (1967).
18. Wayne R. LaFave and Jerold H. Israel, *Criminal Procedure,* 2d ed. (St. Paul, Minn.: West, 1992), p. 356.
19. International Association of Chiefs of Police, "Eyewitness Identification." *Legal Points* (Gaithersburg, MD: IACP Police Legal Center, 1975), p. 1.
20. Id. at 1–2.
21. *United States* v. *Wade,* 388 U.S. 218 (1967); see Garrett L. Berman and Brian L. Cutter, "Effects of Inconsistencies in Eyewitness Testimony on Mock-Juror Decision Making." 81 *Journal of Applied Psychology* pp. 170–177 (1996).
22. Id. at 236–237.
23. See A.M. Levi and Noam Jungman, "The Police Lineup: Basic Weaknesses, Radical Solutions." 22 *Criminal Justice and Behavior* pp. 347–372 (1995).
24. *Moore* v. *Illinois,* 434 U.S. 220, 228 (1977).
25. *United States* v. *Wade,* 388 U.S. 218, 238 (1967).
26. Id. at 239.
27. See Neil Coman McCabe, "The Right to a Lawyer at a Lineup: Support from State Courts and Experimental Psychology." 22 *Indiana Law Review* pp. 905–938 (1989); supra note 18 at 365.
28. *Kirby* v. *Illinois,* 406 U.S. 682 (1972).
29. *Moore* v. *Illinois,* 434 U.S. 220 (1977).
30. Id. at 226.
31. Id. at 228.
32. Charles H. Whitebread and Christopher Slobogin, *Criminal Procedure,* 2d ed. (Mineola, NY: Foundation, 1986), p. 435.
33. Supra, note 28.
34. *Stovall* v. *Denno,* 388 U.S. 293 (1967).
35. Id. at 302.
36. Supra note 32 at 436.
37. *South Dakota* v. *Neville,* 459 U.S. 553 (1983).
38. *United States* v. *Ash,* 413 U.S. 300 (1973).
39. Supra note 32 at 439.
40. *Manson* v. *Brathwaite,* 432 U.S. 98 (1977).
41. Id. at 116.
42. Id.
43. *Stovall* v. *Denno,* 388 U.S. 293, 302 (1967).
44. See Benjamin E. Rosenberg, "Rethinking the Right to Due Process in Connection with Pretrial Procedures: An Analysis and a Proposal." 79 *The Kentucky Law Journal* pp. 259–316 (1991).
45. *Neil* v. *Biggers,* 409 U.S. 188 (1972).
46. Id. at 199.
47. Id. at 200–201.
48. *Foster* v. *California,* 394 U.S. 440 (1969).
49. *Benton* v. *Maryland,* 395 U.S. 784 (1969).
50. In *Albernaz* v. *United States,* 450 U.S. 333, 343 (1981), Justice William Rehnquist stated: "While the double jeopardy clause itself simply states that

no person shall 'be subject for the same offense to be twice put in jeopardy of life or limb,' the decisional law in the area is a veritable Sargasso Sea which could not fail to challenge the most intrepid judicial navigator."

51. *Blockburger* v. *United States,* 284 U.S. 299 (1932).

52. See *Brown* v. *Ohio,* 432 U.S. 161 (1977).

53. Supra, note 51.

54. See *Ashe* v. *Swenson,* 397 U.S. 436 (1970).

55. See *Diaz* v. *United States,* 223 U.S. 442 (1911).

56. See Thomas J. Hickey, "Double Jeopardy After Grady v. Corbin." 28 *Criminal Law Bulletin* pp. 3–31 (1992).

57. See Thomas J. Hickey, "Double Jeopardy After United States v. Dixon." 30 *Criminal Law Bulletin* pp. 346–365 (1994); David McCune, "What Does 'Same Offense' Really Mean?" 48 *Arkansas Law Review* pp. 709–753 (1995).

58. *United States* v. *Dixon,* 113 S.Ct. 2856 (1993).

59. Id. at 2860.

60. *Bartkus* v. *Illinois,* 359 U.S. 121 (1959).

61. See William G. Ross, "The Perils of Selective Abandonment of Dual Sovereignty." 26 *Cumberland Law Review* pp. 57–61 (1995).

62. United States Attorney's Manual, 9-2.142(A) 19 (1988).

63. See *Rinaldi* v. *United States,* 434 U.S. 22, 24 n. 5 (1977).

64. *Heath* v. *Alabama,* 474 U.S. 82 (1985).

65. Id. at 92–93.

66. *Breed* v. *Jones,* 421 U.S. 519 (1975).

67. *Ashe* v. *Swenson,* 397 U.S. 436 (1969).

68. Id. at 446–447.

69. *One Lot Emerald Cut Stones and One Ring* v. *United States,* 409 U.S. 232 (1972).

70. *United States* v. *Halper,* 490 U.S. 435 (1980).

71. *Department of Revenue* v. *Kurth Ranch,* 114 S.Ct. 1937 (1994).

72. 21 U.S.C. Section 881 (a)(7).

73. 18 U.S.C.A. Section 1961 et seq.

74. *United States* v. *Good Real Property,* 114 S.Ct. 492 (1993).

75. Id. at 505.

76. See James D. Tolliver, "The Burden of Proof in Criminal Forfeiture Proceedings Under 21 U.S.C. Section 853." 43 *Mercer Law Review* pp. 1329–1343 (1992).

77. *United States* v. *Halper,* 490 U.S. 435 (1989).

78. *Austin* v. *United States,* 113 S.Ct. 2801 (1993).

79. See Robin M. Sackett, "The Impact of Austin v. United States: Extending Constitutional Protections to Claimants in Civil Forfeiture Proceedings." 24 *Golden Gate University Law Review* pp. 495–522 (1994).

80. *Witte* v. *United States,* 115 S.Ct. 2199 (1995).

81. Id. at 2204.

82. *Bennis* v. *Michigan,* 116 S.Ct. 994 (1996).

83. Id. at 998.

84. *United States* v. *Ursery,* 116 S.Ct. 2135 (1996); companion case: *United States* v. *$405,089.23 in U.S. Currency.*

85. Id. at 4570.

12 A DEFENDANT'S RIGHTS AT TRIAL

Outline

Key Terms

Chapter 11 concluded the discussion of defendants' rights during the pretrial investigatory process. Those rights originated in several different constitutional amendments: the Fifth Amendment privilege against self-incrimination and right to due process of law, the Sixth Amendment right to counsel, and the Fourteenth Amendment's due process clause. Chapter 12 shifts the focus of this study to a defendant's constitutional rights during trial, which are grounded primarily in the Sixth Amendment. A defendant's right to have each element of a criminal charge proved beyond a reasonable doubt, guaranteed by the due process clauses of the Fifth and Fourteenth Amendments, and the Eighth Amendment right to be free from excessive bail are discussed as well.

Sixth Amendment Rights at Trial

The Sixth Amendment is an essential source of constitutional rights for a defendant facing a criminal trial. These include the following protections:

1. the right to a speedy trial;
2. the right to a public trial;
3. the right to a trial by an impartial jury;
4. the right to be informed of the nature of the criminal charges;
5. the right to confront adverse witnesses;
6. the right to compulsory process for obtaining witnesses; and
7. the right to counsel.

Each of these essential safeguards will be considered separately.

The Right to a Speedy Trial

A defendant in a criminal case has the right to a speedy trial. This protection is designed to ensure that the defendant is not confined for a prolonged period before trial and that the case is tried while the evidence is fresh. The right to a speedy trial is guaranteed by federal and state statutes as well as the U.S. Constitution.

The Speedy Trial Act

18 U.S.C. Sections 3161–3174, the federal **Speedy Trial Act,** contains two separate time provisions. First, not more than 30 days may elapse between the time a suspect is arrested until the time he or she is indicted on criminal charges. Second, once a defendant is formally charged, his or her trial must usually begin within 70 days. These time limitations are highly flexible, however, and contain many exceptions. In addition, if the time provisions of this statute are violated, a trial court judge may dismiss the case **without prejudice,** meaning that the same charges may be refiled against the defendant at a future time. There is no violation of a defendant's right to be free from double jeopardy because that right attaches only when a trial has actually started.

Most states have statutes that specify permissible time periods for bringing criminal cases to trial. These too are flexible and give a trial judge substantial discretion in deciding whether to dismiss a criminal case.[1]

The Constitutional Standard

The Supreme Court has not provided a clear rule to determine when a defendant's right to a speedy trial is violated. Rather, in *Barker* v. *Wingo,*[2] it developed a four-part balancing test. The factors a trial court must consider include:

1. the length of the delay;
2. the reason for the delay;
3. whether the defendant had asserted his right to a speedy trial;
4. whether the delay caused any prejudice to the defendant.

First, there must be a significant time delay between the time a defendant is arrested or indicted and when he or she is brought to trial. If that time period is exceedingly long, a court will presume that the delay has prejudiced the defendant's case.[3]

Second, a trial court will consider the reason for the delay. If prosecutors intentionally cause the delay to gain some advantage in the case, it will be easier for the defendant to establish a speedy trial violation. Highlight 12.1 describes the Medgar Evers murder case. Byron De La Beckwith, the defendant, was convicted in 1990, approximately 30 years after murder charges were filed originally. Although the speedy trial issues in this case have yet to be decided by an appellate court, state prosecutors admitted that a jury in 1990 was more likely to convict the defendant than the jury that heard the case originally in 1960. The earlier trial had resulted in a hung-jury mistrial. Whether or not this type of tactical advantage is proper legally remains to be determined by the appellate courts.

A defendant's speedy trial claim will not succeed if he or she was responsible for a delay in the case. For example, if a defendant is charged with bank robbery and eludes capture by the police for several years, a speedy trial claim will not succeed. Likewise, in one case a defendant caused a 10-year delay between his indictment on drug charges and his trial by remaining in another country under an assumed name. The reviewing court held that because the defendant caused the delay, the government did not violate his right to a speedy trial.[4]

Third, a court will consider whether a defendant strenuously asserted his or her right to a speedy trial. A defendant must make a clear assertion of the right in a timely way. For example, a defendant who waives the right to a speedy trial or agrees to continuances will not succeed on a speedy trial claim.

Fourth, it will be difficult to establish a speedy trial violation unless actual prejudice results from a delay in the proceedings. In *Barker* v. *Wingo,* the Supreme Court held that such prejudice may include: (1) a lengthy period of pretrial incarceration; (2) anxiety, stress, and concern; and (3) an adverse impact on the defendant's ability to prepare a defense.

Beckwith v. *State of Mississippi* **615 So.2d 1134 (Miss. Supreme Court, 1992)**

HAWKINS, Presiding Justice, for the Court:

Medgar Evers, a black civil rights activist and leader in the turbulent 1950s–1960s civil rights struggles, was murdered at his home in Jackson June 12, 1963. Byron De La Beckwith, a vocal pro-segregationist and white supremacist in this State, was arrested June 23 and indicted for Evers' murder at the July, 1963, term of the grand jury of Hinds County. He stood trial in February, 1964, and following a hung jury, a mistrial was ordered by the circuit judge February 7. He again stood trial in April, and following another hung jury, the circuit judge declared a mistrial April 17, 1964. Until his second trial, Beckwith had been incarcerated without bail.

Following his second trial Beckwith was released on $10,000 bail. He ran a markedly unsuccessful campaign for Lieutenant Governor in 1967. The district attorney prosecuting the case did not seek re-election, and his successor on March 10, 1969, moved the court to enter a *nolle prosequi* of the indictment. The three circuit judges of the Seventh Circuit Court District signed the order granting a *nolle prosequi*. There was no objection by the defense to the entry of the *nolle prosequi*.

Over the years this case has received considerable public attention by the press, but no further effort was made by the State to initiate criminal proceedings against Beckwith until the December, 1990, term of the Hinds County grand jury when he again was indicted for murder. Beckwith, then living in Tennessee, following an extradition contest in the Tennessee courts, was extradited to Mississippi and incarcerated in a Hinds County jail.

His request for bail was denied by the circuit judge, and affirmed on appeal by this Court's order of March 25, 1992. He has been in jail in this State since October, 1991.

In April 1992, he sought dismissal of the indictment against him on three constitutional grounds.

The circuit court on August 4, 1992, denied his motion, and Beckwith then petitioned this Court for an interlocutory appeal, pursuant to our Rule 5, Mississippi Supreme Court Rules. This Court by August 26, 1992, Order granted an interlocutory appeal.[1]

There should be no necessity to emphasize the obvious: This case is not before us from a final conviction. It is before us on an interlocutory appeal in which Beckwith claims a Constitutional right not to even be put to trial, seeking this Court to intervene in circuit court criminal trial proceedings instituted by the State of Mississippi, stop them, and order his discharge.

This Court does not equate the right not to be wrongfully convicted as somehow giving a defendant a right not to be put to trial at all. We adhere to the wisdom stated by the United States Supreme Court in *Cobbledick v. United States,* 309 U.S. 323 at 325, 60 S.Ct. 540 at 541, 84 L.Ed. 783 at 785 (1940):

An accused is entitled to scrupulous observance of constitutional safeguards. But encouragement of delay is fatal to the vindication of the criminal law. *Bearing the discomfiture and cost of a prosecution for crime even by an innocent person is one of the painful obligations of citizenship.* The correctness of a trial court's rejection even of a constitutional claim made by the accused in the process of prosecution *must await his conviction* before its reconsideration by an appellate tribunal. (Emphasis added.)

On his appeal Beckwith seeks the dismissal of the indictment and his discharge from custody on three grounds:

(1) Denial of a speedy trial. "In all criminal prosecutions, the accused shall enjoy the right to a speedy and public trial, by an impartial jury of the State and district wherein the crime shall have been committed. . . ." Amendment 6, U.S. Constitution. "In all criminal prosecutions the accused shall have a right to a . . . speedy and public trial by an impartial

(Continued)

(Concluded)

jury of the county where the offense was committed. . . ." Art. 3 § 26, Mississippi Constitution.

(2) Denial of due process. "No person shall be . . . deprived of life, liberty or property, without due process of law. . . ." Amendment 5, U.S. Constitution.

(3) Double jeopardy. "[N]or shall any person be subject for the same offense to be twice put in jeopardy of life or limb. . . ." Amendment 5, U.S. Constitution.

We find much wisdom in the principles enunciated in the Federal Courts on questions such as those raised here, and today hold that in applying Rule 5 to any attempted interlocutory appeal in which a defendant seeks to have all criminal charges against him dismissed and for his final discharge, we will adhere to the same principles and criteria of the Federal Courts.

The interlocutory appeal granted Beckwith in this case was not based upon any Constitutional mandate or statute giving him any such right, but solely upon a rule promulgated by this Court. While Beckwith's indictment, arrest and anticipated trial may raise serious and troubling Constitutional questions, he clearly has no Constitutional or statutory right to an *interlocutory appeal*.

After mature consideration we have concluded that the first two grounds asserted by Beckwith afford no basis for an interlocutory appeal, and decline to address them. We do address the final ground and find it without merit.

_____

1. Rule 5 states in pertinent part:

(a) **Petition for Permission to Appeal.** An appeal from an interlocutory order may be sought if the order grants or denies certification by the trial court that a substantial basis exists for a difference of opinion on a question of law as to which appellate resolution may:

(1) Materially advance the termination of the litigation and avoid exceptional expense to the parties; or

(2) Protect a party from substantial and irreparable injury, or

(3) Resolve an issue of general importance in the administration of justice.

In most cases, a defendant must demonstrate actual prejudice to establish a violation of his or her right to a speedy trial. If a delay between a defendant's indictment and trial is extensive, however, he or she may not be required to demonstrate prejudice. In *Doggett* v. *United States,*[5] the Supreme Court held that an eight-and-a-half-year delay between a defendant's indictment and his trial violated the Sixth Amendment, even without a showing of actual prejudice resulting from the delay.[6]

The Right to Bail

A question that sometimes arises in the context of speedy trial issues is whether an accused has a right to bail. The constitutional issue presented in these cases is whether an accused who is denied bail and is forced to remain in jail pending trial is being punished before he or she has been convicted of a crime.

The Eighth Amendment provides that an accused has a right to be free from *excessive* bail. U.S. courts have not interpreted this provision to provide a generalized right to bail. In *Stack* v. *Boyle,*[7] the Supreme Court held that excessive bail is that amount that is higher than reasonably necessary to guarantee a defendant's appearance at trial. The Supreme Court, however, has given state courts great leeway to determine precisely what level of bail is appropriate in a particular case.

Preventive Detention.   In deciding whether to grant bail to a defendant, trial courts sometimes face a serious dilemma. Even if the evidence in a particular case weighs heavily against the accused, the individual is innocent technically until he or she is convicted at trial. In some cases an accused person would present a serious threat to the community if he or she were released pending trial. For example, suppose that the police arrest a suspect who is believed to be a serial rapist. The evidence in the case strongly points to the accused. Suppose further that state law provides for bail in all cases except murder. The judge in this case faces a problem: the accused who has not yet faced trial is innocent legally and has a right to bail; however, the individual poses a serious threat to community safety. Faced with this dilemma many trial judges have set bail at such a high level that the accused could not possibly gain pretrial release. For example, a trial judge who sets bail at $1,000,000 for an indigent defendant has effectively determined that he or she will remain in jail until a trial is completed. The practice of setting bail at a high level to ensure that a defendant could not possibly gain release and victimize the community is termed **preventive detention.** This practice occurred for many years in U.S. justice systems. Without a statutory basis, however, its legal status was questionable.

Bail Reform Act of 1984.   The federal Bail Reform Act of 1984, 18 U.S.C. Sections 3141–3150 (1994), allows a judge to detain an arrested person before trial if the prosecution shows by clear and convincing evidence that if the accused is released, he or she would present a danger to the community.[8] Many states have modeled statutes after the Bail Reform Act of 1984, and now permit preventive detention if an accused presents a threat to the community. In *United States* v. *Salerno,*[9] the Supreme Court upheld the preventive detention section of the Bail Reform Act of 1984. It further held that detaining an accused before trial is a regulatory measure rather than punishment and does not violate due process of law or the Eighth Amendment.

The Right to a Public Trial

In re Oliver[10] held that a defendant has a right to a public trial. The defendant may request a closed proceeding. Because this request may sometimes conflict with the right of the public and the press to attend a criminal trial, however, it will not be granted unless there is a compelling reason to close the proceedings. There are two ways to view the right to a public trial: (1) the right of the public and the press to attend a trial; and (2) the defendant's right to have members of the public present at his or her trial.[11]

The First Amendment protects the right of the public and the press to attend a criminal trial. In *Waller* v. *Georgia,*[12] the Supreme Court identified several interests that are served by allowing the public to be present at criminal trials, including: ensuring public confidence in the judicial system, allowing members of the public to react to crimes, public oversight of judges and prosecutors, allowing those with evidence to bring it to the attention of the court, and making witnesses more hesitant to commit perjury.

A trial judge may not entirely close a trial unless it is very clear that the public's presence would compromise a defendant's right to a fair trial.[13] A judge may, however, close portions of a trial if there is a compelling state interest that outweighs the public's right to be present.[14] For example, many states have passed laws that allow a judge to close portions of a trial where a juvenile is likely to give highly sensitive testimony in a case involving rape, sexual assault, or child abuse. Highlight 12.2 presents an example of one such statute.

In addition, a defendant has a Sixth Amendment right to have members of the public present at his or her trial. This protection is designed to ensure that a trial is conducted fairly and to permit public scrutiny of the judicial process.

The Right to a Trial by an Impartial Jury

Duncan v. *Louisiana*[15] held that the right to a trial by an impartial jury is fundamental and applies to all trials for nonpetty criminal[16] offenses. *Baldwin* v. *New York*[17] held that a petty offense is one that is punishable by a possible jail sentence exceeding six months. The Supreme Court recently reaffirmed this principle in *Lewis* v. *United States*.[18] In theory, the six-month standard is a flexible rule. In *Blanton* v. *City of North Las Vegas,*[19] the Supreme Court held that if the possible punishment for a crime is less than six months but additional sanctions are so severe that they reflect the legislature's determination that the offense is a serious one, a defendant may still have a right to a jury trial.[20] In practice, however, trial courts closely follow the six-month rule.

Somewhat surprisingly, very few states give a defendant an unconditional right to a **bench trial,** a case decided by a judge without a jury. One reason that many states do not provide the right to a bench trial is that prosecutors have a clear interest in maintaining the role of the jury in U.S. justice systems.[21]

Waiving the Right to a Jury Trial

A defendant may waive the right to a jury trial in a criminal case. In *Singer* v. *United States,*[22] the Supreme Court held that such a waiver must be voluntary, knowing, and intelligent. Before accepting a waiver of a jury trial, trial judges should advise the defendant about the potential consequences of such a waiver.

Jury Size

The Constitution does not specify a particular size for juries in criminal cases. Although juries in federal criminal trials must comprise twelve persons,[23] the Supreme Court has been more flexible about allowing the states to develop their own rules for determining the size of juries. *Williams* v. *Florida,*[24] held that the Sixth Amendment permitted a jury composed of six members in a criminal case. A five-person jury is not permitted, however.[25] A jury of at least six persons is needed to ensure both an effective discussion of the case and that the jury is an effective cross-section of the community.[26]

Highlight 2.2

Ann. Code of Maryland, Section 9–102
Testimony of Victim in Child Abuse Case
by Means of Closed Circuit Television

§ 9-102. Testimony of victim in child abuse case by means of closed circuit television.

(a) *Conditions.*—In a case of abuse of a child as defined in § 5-701 of the Family Law Article or Article 27. § 35A of the Code, a court may order that the testimony of a child victim be taken outside the courtroom and shown in the courtroom by means of closed circuit television if:

(1) The testimony is taken during the proceeding; and

(2) The judge determines that testimony by the child victim in the defendant's presence will result in the child suffering serious emotional distress such that the child cannot reasonably communicate.

(b) *Location of certain persons; questioning of child.*—(1) Only the following persons may be in the room with the child when the child testifies by closed circuit television:

(i) The prosecuting attorney;

(ii) The attorney for the defendant;

(iii) The operators of the closed circuit television equipment; and

(iv) Unless the defendant objects, any person whose presence, in the opinion of the court, contributes to the well-being of the child, including a person who has dealt with the child in a therapeutic setting concerning the abuse.

(2) During the child's testimony by closed circuit television, the judge and the defendant shall be in the courtroom.

(3) The judge and the defendant shall be allowed to communicate with the persons in the room where the child is testifying by any appropriate electronic method.

(4) Only the prosecuting attorney, the attorney for any defendant, and the judge may question the child.

(c) *Examination by judge.*—(1) In determining whether testimony by the child victim in the defendant's presence will result in the child suffering serious emotional distress such that the child cannot reasonably communicate, the judge may observe and question the child either inside or outside the courtroom and hear testimony of a parent or custodian of the child or any other person, including a person who has dealt with the child in a therapeutic setting.

(2) (i) Except as provided in subparagraph (ii) 2 of this paragraph, any defendant, any defendant's attorney, and the prosecutor shall have the right to be present when the judge hears testimony on whether to allow a child victim to testify by closed circuit television.

(ii) If the judge decides to observe or question the child in connection with the determination to allow closed circuit television:

1. Any defendant's attorney and the prosecutor shall have the right to be present; and

2. The judge may not permit a defendant to be present.

(d) *Applicability.*—The provisions of this section do not apply if the defendant is an attorney pro se.

(e) *Identification of defendant.*—This section may not be interpreted to preclude, for purposes of identification of a defendant, the presence of both the victim and the defendant in the courtroom at the same time.

(f) *Two-way closed circuit television prohibited.*—This section may not be interpreted to permit the use of two-way closed circuit television or any other procedure that would result in the child being exposed to the defendant. (1985. chs. 495, 499; 1988, ch. 6, § 1; 1992, ch. 469.)

Unanimous Verdicts

Defendants in federal criminal trials have a right to a unanimous verdict. Once again, however, the rule is more flexible in state criminal proceedings. *Apodaca* v. *Oregon*[27] upheld a defendant's conviction based on a vote to convict by 10 members of a 12-person jury. Likewise, *Johnson* v. *Louisiana*[28] upheld a conviction based on 9 votes of a 12-person jury. In *Burch* v. *Louisiana,*[29] the Supreme Court held, however, that a conviction based on the votes of five members of a six-person jury violated the defendant's right to a jury trial. The less-than-unanimous verdict principle has not been applied to state capital cases, which carry a possible death penalty or life imprisonment.[30]

Selecting a Jury

In most states, juries are randomly selected from some type of standard official list, such as a list of registered voters or a list of persons with driver's licenses. In *Taylor* v. *Louisiana,*[31] the Supreme Court held that such a list must present a fair cross-section of the community. The general list is termed a **venire.** Once a list of possible jurors is chosen, the individuals receive a subpoena to appear in court. Individuals who present an important reason, such as a personal illness, will be excused from jury service. The remaining persons will become a **jury pool,** from which jurors will be chosen for individual cases.

Voir Dire Examination

Once the prospective jurors are selected, a trial court will conduct a **voir dire examination,** during which the court or defense attorneys and prosecutors will pose questions to potential jurors. The purpose of a voir dire examination is to ensure that potential jurors are not biased. In general, trial judges have broad discretion to conduct a voir dire examination and determine the types of questions to be asked. If there is a significant likelihood that racial prejudice may impact a case, however, due process of law requires that prospective jurors be questioned on the issue of possible racial bias. In some jurisdictions the judge or lawyers will question the prospective jurors as a group; in other places jurors are questioned individually.

A **challenge for cause** may be used to exclude any juror who is biased or who is disqualified by law from serving on a jury in a particular case. For example, if a potential juror is related to the defendant or has a financial interest in the outcome of the case, he or she would be excluded for cause.

A **peremptory challenge** may be used by either the defense or the prosecution to exclude *any* potential juror. The party challenging the juror need not specify a reason for the exclusion. The number of peremptory challenges is determined normally by the seriousness of the charged offense. For example, in federal death penalty cases both the defense and the prosecution may exercise 20 peremptory challenges. Highlight 12.3 presents Federal Rule of Criminal Procedure 24(b), which regulates the use of peremptory challenges in federal criminal trials.

Highlight 12.3

Fed. R. Crim. P. 24(b)

Rule 24. Trial Jurors

(a) Examination. The court may permit the defendant or the defendant's attorney and the attorney for the government to conduct the examination of prospective jurors or may itself conduct the examination. In the latter event the court shall permit the defendant or the defendant's attorney and the attorney for the government to supplement the examination by such further inquiry as it deems proper or shall itself submit to the prospective jurors such additional questions by the parties or their attorneys as it deems proper.

(b) Peremptory challenges. If the offense charged is punishable by death, each side is entitled to 20 peremptory challenges. If the offense charged is punishable by imprisonment for more than one year, the government is entitled to 6 peremptory challenges and the defendant or defendants jointly to 10 peremptory challenges. If the offense charged is punishable by imprisonment for not more than one year or by fine or both, each side is entitled to 3 peremptory challenges. If there is more than one defendant, the court may allow the defendants additional peremptory challenges and permit them to be exercised separately or jointly.

(c) Alternate jurors. The court may direct that not more than 6 jurors in addition to the regular jury be called and impanelled to sit as alternate jurors. Alternate jurors in the order in which they are called shall replace jurors who, prior to the time the jury retires to consider its verdict, become or are found to be unable or disqualified to perform their duties. Alternate jurors shall be drawn in the same manner, shall have the same qualifications, shall be subject to the same examination and challenges, shall take the same oath and shall have the same functions, powers, facilities and privileges as the regular jurors. An alternate juror who does not replace a regular juror shall be discharged after the jury retires to consider its verdict. Each side is entitled to 1 peremptory challenge in addition to those otherwise allowed by law if 1 or 2 alternate jurors are to be impanelled, 2 peremptory challenges if 3 or 4 alternate jurors are to be impanelled, and 3 peremptory challenges if 5 or 6 alternate jurors are to be impanelled. The additional peremptory challenges may be used against an alternate juror only, and the other peremptory challenges allowed by these rules may not be used against an alternate juror.

(Amended July 1, 1966; Aug. 1, 1987.)

Some attorneys have used social science research and jury selection teams to assist them in the jury selection process. Highlight 12.4 presents a description of the techniques used by the O.J. Simpson defense team to screen potential jurors and decide how to use peremptory challenges. Figure 12.1 presents portions of the questionnaire used to screen potential jurors in the Simpson case.

In the typical criminal or civil case, however, attorneys exercise these challenges based on common sense and their own intuition about whether particular types of individuals will be sympathetic to their client's case. To illustrate, suppose that you were an attorney for the state's division of child welfare who was prosecuting a civil paternity case against a 22-year-old male who had denied fathering an illegitimate child. The relevant jury pool contains seven women and eight men. Several of the women are middle-aged, married, and have children and grandchildren. The state's attorney

Highlight 12.4

Star Rising for Simpson Jury Consultant

 Lately, business opportunities have been flowing into the Pasadena, Calif., office of trial consultant Jo-Ellan Dimitrius. Criminal defendants and major corporate litigants alike are eager to hire the woman who seemingly had helped seat a jury of police skeptics and O.J. Simpson sympathizers in the so-called trial of the century.

It wasn't just social science wizardry that got Dimitrius the jury she wanted, though. It helped that the jury pool was from Los Angeles County, where sentiment was on Simpson's side. Another factor in her favor: The prosecution declined jury selection advice from its pro bono consultant, Donald Vinson of DecisionQuest in Torrance, Calif.

Admirers of a Football Great

In the end, the jury consisted of eight black women, one black man, two white women and one Hispanic man. Their answers to voir dire questionnaires prepared by both consultants suggest many admired Simpson and could be suspicious of police.

Among the findings were that 75 percent believed Simpson was unlikely to murder because he excelled at football and 42 percent thought it was OK to use physical force on a family member.

Dimitrius knew the jury pool would be favorable even before she was hired because of an informal survey she took of about 100 people in Los Angeles County using randomly generated numbers.

"Sentiment was generally very supportive of O.J.," says Dimitrius, a former college professor with a Ph.D. in government and criminology. "While there were some people who thought he might have done it, a tremendous amount of people said they hoped he didn't do it."

Dimitrius and her company, Forensic Technologies International, surveyed 1,600 people by telephone to learn about attitudes of population segments toward Simpson and trial evidence. She also wrote juror questionnaires and prepared exhibits for the defense throughout the trial.

One important survey finding, Dimitrius says, "was that black females were much more neutral on the issue of abuse and domestic violence than perhaps a white female would be." She speculates that more males would have been selected for the jury if the prosecution had followed DecisionQuest's advice. "But given the makeup of the jury pool, there would be no difference racewise" in the jury.

Vinson, who has a Ph.D. in market research and sociology, is more equivocal in discussing what his advice would have been. "I had come to the conclusion that there were certain kinds of jurors, based on race and gender—and I really don't want to go beyond that—who were simply not willing to entertain the notion that O.J. Simpson could conceivably be guilty of this crime," he says. "I believe those kinds of people ultimately found their way onto this jury."

Dimitrius admits part of her job is to use "some sort of stereotypes" in developing the profile of jurors she wants. But she also is interested in getting potential jurors to reveal their predispositions. She wanted to know what potential jurors had heard and read, and if they could put that aside.

Lessons Learned

Both Dimitrius and Vinson say the trial has taught them some important lessons. One lesson for Dimitrius

(Continued)

(Concluded)

is that it's unfair to sequester jurors for so long. Another is that cameras in courts are detrimental because the public makes a judgment based on information the jury does not have.

For the rejected Vinson, whose company nonetheless donated $1 million in trial exhibits to the prosecution, the lesson is about the importance of jury consultants, "I can't imagine anyone with any sense of professional responsibility to a client moving ahead with an important case without undertaking jury research," he says.

From Marc Davis and Kevin Davis, "Star Rising for Jury Consultant," *American Bar Association Journal*, December 1995, p. 14. [Reprinted by permission of the American Bar Association Journal.]

may be tempted to conclude that these individuals are likely to be sympathetic to his case and would be unlikely to exclude them with peremptory challenges. Likewise, the state's attorney may believe that older, stable males with a strong family orientation would be favorably disposed to his case. He would therefore be unlikely to use preemptory challenges to dismiss these types of individuals as well. In contrast, assume that the jury pool contained one 18-year-old male dressed in blue jeans with the outline of a smokeless tobacco can protruding from his back pocket, who was wearing a t-shirt and a baseball cap. Based on common and possibly inaccurate stereotypes, the state's attorney may exercise a peremptory challenge to eliminate this individual based upon a hunch that his youth, gender, and appearance would suggest that he is more likely to be sympathetic to the defendant.

Equal Protection Issues.   One important rule that governs peremptory challenges is that they may not be used in a racially discriminatory fashion in either civil[32] or criminal cases. If a prosecutor uses peremptory challenges in a racially discriminatory manner, it will violate the defendant's right to equal protection of law. For example, suppose that an African-American defendant is charged with robbery. Assume that the jury pool contains 18 persons, 6 African-Americans and 12 whites. Following voir dire, the prosecutor uses his six peremptory challenges to remove all of the African-Americans from the list of possible jurors. The prosecutor's use of peremptory challenges in this way is likely to be held to be a violation of equal protection of law.

In *Batson* v. *Kentucky,*[33] the Supreme Court developed a three-part test to determine if the use of peremptory challenges violates equal protection of law. The defendant may establish a claim of purposeful discrimination by showing:

1. That the defendant is a member of a recognized *racial* group. These groups would include, among others, African-Americans, Native Americans, and Hispanics, but not Italian-Americans, Irish-Americans, young persons, the elderly, or obese persons. In 1994, the Supreme Court expanded *Batson* to include gender-based discrimination. *J.E.B.* v. *Alabama ex rel. T.B.*[34] held that the use of peremptory challenges to exclude potential jurors based on their gender violates equal protection of law.

2. That the group's members have been excluded from the jury.

3. That the circumstances of the case raise an inference that the exclusion of these individuals was based on race. If the defendant satisfies the above requirements, the

FIGURE 12.1

Simpson juror questionnaire excerpts

1. Have you seen television coverage, other than appearances in court, of any of the lawyers for the defense?

   No 1   Yes 2

2. Have you seen television coverage, other than appearances in court, of any of the lawyers for the prosecution?

   No 1   Yes 2

3. Which of the following best describes how you feel about the media coverage, overall?

Extremely biased in favor of the defense	Somewhat biased in favor of the defense	Basically fair to both sides	Somewhat biased in favor of the prosecution	Extremely biased in favor of the prosecution
1	2	3	4	5

4. If you have discussed this case with friends and/or relatives, do your friends/relatives, overall, seem to lean toward thinking that O. J. Simpson is:

Not guilty	Probably not guilty	Not sure	Probably guilty	Guilty
1	2	3	4	5

5. Have you ever seen O. J. Simpson in any form of advertising [Hertz commercials, orange juice ads]?

   No 1   Yes 2

6. Have you ever seen O. J. Simpson on TV [as a football player] or in the movies [Naked Gun, Roots]?

   No 1   Yes 2

7. Based upon your feelings toward O. J. Simpson, are you inclined to believe him guilty of the crimes with which he has been acquitted?

   No 1   Yes 2

8. Based upon your feelings toward O. J. Simpson, are you inclined to believe him not guilty of the crimes with which he has been charged?

   No 1   Yes 2

   Did you hold the prosecution to a higher standard than is legally required because the defendant is:

African-American	No	1	Yes 2
Wealthy	No	1	Yes 2
Famous	No	1	Yes 2

Figure 12.1—*continued*

9. Have you or has someone you know had any contact with a family violence program, a battered women's shelter, or attended any programs concerning family or domestic violence?

No   1   Yes   2

10. How big a problem do you think racial discrimination against African-Americans is in Southern California:

Very serious problem	somewhat serious	not too serious	not at all serious	not a problem
5	4	3	2	1

11. If you were selected as juror in this case, would you base your decision on the defendant's guilt or innocence solely on the evidence presented to you during trial?

No   1   Yes   2

12. If you were selected as a juror in this case, would you set aside any personal feelings you may have about the defendant, positive or negative, and rely solely and exclusively on the evidence presented to you in court to decide this case?

No   1   Yes   2

Please state your personal belief regarding each statement using the scales listed after each item.

13. "A defendant is innocent until proven guilty beyond a reasonable doubt."

Strongly disagree	disagree somewhat	no opinion	agree somewhat	strongly agree
1	2	3	4	5

14. "If the prosecution goes to the trouble of bringing someone to trial, the person is probably guilty."

Strongly disagree	disagree somewhat	no opinion	agree somewhat	strongly agree
1	2	3	4	5

15. "The testimony of law enforcement officers is not entitled to any greater or lesser weight merely because they are law enforcement officers."

Strongly disagree	disagree somewhat	no opinion	agree somewhat	strongly agree
1	2	3	4	5

16. "Regardless of what the law says, a defendant in a criminal trial should be required to prove his or her innocence."

Strongly disagree	disagree somewhat	no opinion	agree somewhat	strongly agree
1	2	3	4	5

Figure 12.1—*concluded*

---

17. "People who make a lot of money are treated better by our court system than other people."

Strongly disagree	disagree somewhat	no opinion	agree somewhat	strongly agree
1	2	3	4	5

18. "Do you agree that a defendant in a criminal case should testify or produce some evidence to prove that he or she is not guilty?"

Strongly disagree	disagree somewhat	no opinion	agree somewhat	strongly agree
1	2	3	4	5

19. Have you followed any criminal cases in the media?

	No	1	Yes	2
If so, which ones				
Menendez	No	1	Yes	2
Reginald Denny Beating case	No	1	Yes	2
Rodney King	No	1	Yes	2

---

burden then shifts to the prosecution to demonstrate that the challenges were not based on racial factors.[35]

Defendants too may not use peremptory challenges in a racially discriminatory manner. In *Georgia* v. *McCollum,*[36] the Supreme Court held that the Constitution prohibits a criminal *defendant* from "engaging in purposeful discrimination on the ground of race in the exercise of peremptory challenges."[37]

The Right to be Informed of the Nature of Criminal Charges

An accused person must be given notice of the charges against him or her. The Federal Rules of Criminal Procedure require that the charging document, an **indictment,** contain a "plain . . . written statement of the essential facts constituting the offense charged."[38] The reason for this rule is that a person must know the nature of the accusation in order to prepare an effective defense and, if appropriate, enable him or her to assert a double jeopardy claim.[39] Figure 12.2 presents a copy of an indictment in a criminal case.

In addition, an accused must be given sufficient time to prepare a defense to criminal charges. What constitutes sufficient time varies substantially with the type of crime that is charged. Clearly, more complex cases will take significantly more time to prepare than simple ones. A trial judge has broad discretion to grant a continuance in a criminal case if he or she believes that the defense has not had sufficient time to prepare for trial.

FIGURE 12.2

Indictment

```
                IN THE SUPERIOR COURT FOR THE
     STATE OF RHODE ISLAND AND PROVIDENCE PLANTATIONS
                       NEWPORT COUNTY




STATE OF RHODE ISLAND


v.                                      IND. NO. X


John Doe



    The Newport County Grand Jury of the State of Rhode
Island and Providence Plantations charges:
    That John Doe, of the State of Maine, on or about the
19th day of January, 1992, at Tiverton, in the county of
Newport, did murder J. Smith, in violation of §11-23-1 of
the General Laws of Rhode Island, 1956, as amended
(Reenactment of 1981).
```

```
_____
ASSISTANT ATTORNEY GENERAL
```

FIGURE 12.2—*concluded*

STATE OF RHODE ISLAND AND PROVIDENCE PLANTATIONS

STATE OF RHODE ISLAND   Providence, S. C.
v.   Criminal Information No. V
John Doe

<u>CRIMINAL INFORMATION</u>

The Attorney General of the State of Rhode Island charges: That John
Doe, of Providence County, on or about the 9th day of August, 1992, in
the County of Providence, did unlawfully, with knowledge and intent
possess a controlled substance, to wit, the chemical equivalent of a
preparation of coca leaves in a form known as Cocaine, as set forth in
Schedule II of §21-28-2.08 of the General Laws, as amended, in
violation of §21-28-4.01(C) (1) (a) of the General Laws of Rhode
Island, 1956, as amended (Reenactment of 1989).
                            COUNT 2
That John Doe, of Providence County, on or about the 9th day of August,
1992, in the County of Providence, did unlawfully, with knowledge and
intent possess a controlled substance, to wit, Heroin, as set forth in
Schedule I, of §21-28-2.08 of the General Laws, as amended, in
violation of §21-28-4.01 (C) (1) (a) of the General Laws of Rhode
Island, 1956, as amended (Reenactment of 1989).
                            COUNT 3
That John Doe, of Providence County, on or about the 9th day of August,
1992, in the County of Providence, did operate a motor vehicle while
knowingly having in said motor vehicle or in his possession a controlled
substance, to wit, Cocaine and Heroin, as defined in Rhode Island
General Laws Section §21-28-1.02, in violation of §31-27-2.4 of the
General Laws of Rhode Island, 1956, as amended (Reenactment of 1994).
                            COUNT 4
That John Doe, of Providence County, on or about the 9th day of August,
1992, in the County of Providence, did operate a vehicle in this state
while under the influence of intoxicating liquor, and/or drugs, in
violation of §31-27-2 of the General Laws of Rhode Island, 1956, as
amended (Reenactment of 1994).
                            COUNT 5
That John Doe, of Providence County, on or about the 9th day of August,
1992, at Smithfield, in the County of Providence, did assult J. Jones
in violation of §11-5-3 of the General Laws of Rhode Island, 1956, as
amended (Reenactment of 1994).
                            COUNT 6
That John Doe, of Providence County, on or about the 9th day of August,
1992, in the County of Providence, did use force in resisting a legal
arrest by a peace officer, to wit, in violation of §12-7-10 of the
General Laws of Rhode Island, 1956, as amended (Reenactment of 1994).

Against the form of the statute in such case made and provided and
against the peace and dignity of the state.

Special Assistant Attorney General
Designated by the Attorney General

The Right to Confront and Cross-Examine Adverse Witnesses

The Sixth Amendment's confrontation clause guarantees a criminal defendant the right to physically confront and cross-examine adverse witnesses. The right to confront an adverse witness is designed to ensure the fairness of the proceedings.[40] Similarly, the right to cross-examine adverse witnesses is designed to guarantee that testimonial evidence will be tested vigorously.

A defendant's right to confront adverse witnesses is not absolute, however. A defendant may waive this right if he or she is voluntarily absent, or intentionally disrupts the proceedings.[41] Moreover, in some circumstances the right to a face-to-face confrontation with adverse witnesses is outweighed by important social interests.

Cases Involving Child Victims

Maryland v. *Craig*[42] presented the issue of whether the confrontation clause prohibited a child witness in a child sexual abuse case from testifying by one-way closed circuit television against a defendant at trial, outside the defendant's physical presence.[43] Sandra Craig had been charged with committing various sexual offenses against a six-year-old girl who had attended a preschool that Craig owned and operated. Under Maryland law, a trial judge could permit a juvenile child abuse victim to testify by closed circuit television if the judge "determined that testimony by the child victim in the courtroom will result in the child suffering serious emotional distress such that the child cannot reasonably communicate."

Once the determination was made, the child witness, prosecutor, and defense counsel would withdraw to a separate room, while the judge, jury, and defendant remained in the courtroom. The child witness was then examined and cross-examined in the separate room, while a video monitor recorded and displayed the child's testimony to those in the courtroom. During this time the child could not see the defendant, who remained in electronic contact with her attorney. Objections could be made and ruled on as if the witness was actually testifying in the courtroom.

In *Craig,* the State presented expert testimony that the victim, as well as several other children who were allegedly abused by Craig, would have suffered serious emotional distress such that they would not have been able to communicate if they had been required to testify in the courtroom. Over Craig's objection the children testified via one-way closed circuit television after the trial judge found that the children would experience emotional distress and that Craig still retained the essence of the right to confrontation.

On appeal, the Supreme Court distinguished this case from an earlier precedent, *Coy* v. *Iowa,*[44] which had held on the facts of that case that a defendant had a right to a face-to-face confrontation with a child sexual abuse victim. In *Coy,* the trial court had used a screen that prevented two child abuse victims from viewing the defendant as they testified against him. The Supreme Court held that because the trial judge in *Coy* had not made particularized findings that the child required special protection, the procedure violated the confrontation clause.

In *Maryland* v. *Craig,* however, the trial judge had made specific findings that the child witnesses would be harmed by viewing the defendant. The Supreme Court stated:

> Thus, though we affirm the importance of face-to-face confrontation with witnesses appearing at trial, we cannot say that such confrontation is an indispensable element of the Sixth Amendment's guarantee of the right to confront one's accusers. . . . Accordingly, we hold that, if the State makes an adequate showing of necessity, the state interest in protecting child witnesses from the trauma of testifying in a child abuse case is sufficiently important to justify the use of a special procedure that permits a child witness in such cases to testify at trial against a defendant in the absence of face-to-face confrontation with the defendant.[45]

Maryland v. *Craig* is an important precedent, which requires trial courts to balance a defendant's interests in confronting adverse witnesses with society's interests in protecting the victims of child abuse.[46] Another issue that implicates the right to confront and cross-examine adverse witnesses is the use of hearsay evidence.

Hearsay Evidence.   A deceptively simple definition of **hearsay evidence** is an out-of-court statement that is offered for the truth of what it asserts. The use of hearsay evidence may raise Sixth Amendment issues because an accused has no opportunity to confront and cross-examine at trial the witness who made the statement.[47] For example, suppose that Jane wants to prove that Bill ran a red light and she calls Bob to testify that he heard but did not see the accident that resulted. Bob, however, heard a bystander who had observed the accident say at the time "Bill's car ran a red light." If Bob is called to testify that he heard the bystander say that Bill ran a red light, Bob's testimony would be hearsay because it is offered to prove at trial that Bill ran a red light.[48] Unless an exception to the hearsay rule applies to allow the testimony, it would be inadmissible. One of the chief reasons for this rule is that it denies the accused person the opportunity to confront and cross-examine the person who made the statement.

There are several recognized exceptions to the hearsay rule in U.S. legal systems. These include dying declarations, co-conspirator statements, business records, excited utterances, agency admissions, statements made for purposes of medical diagnosis, past recorded recollections, statements about the declarant's state of mind, and statements against the declarant's penal interest. A detailed treatment of these exceptions is beyond the scope of this text.[49] An example should, however, help to illustrate their possible importance in criminal cases. Suppose that during a domestic argument, Paul takes a handgun and shoots Sally. When police officers arrive at the scene, Sally is close to death. She realizes this and tells officers that Paul was the person who shot her. Sally's statements to police would constitute a **dying declaration,** which is a recognized exception to the hearsay rule of evidence. If the officers were called as witnesses at trial, they would be allowed to testify that Sally had told them that Paul shot her, even if Sally had died and could not be cross-examined. Dying declarations are one of several important exceptions to the hearsay rule and are powerful evidence at a criminal trial.

Statements by Children to Authorities.   Another issue involving the hearsay rule is whether an abused child's statements made to a psychologist, physician, or police officers may be admitted into evidence at trial. In *Ohio* v. *Roberts,*[50] the Supreme Court held that hearsay statements may be admitted into evidence if the prosecution establishes that the person who originally made the statement is unavailable at trial and that the statement is sufficiently reliable. A statement's reliability may be inferred if it falls within a traditional and firmly rooted exception to the hearsay rule. Moreover, as in *Maryland* v. *Craig,* a child witness may be traumatized by the prospect of having to testify in front of the accused. Therefore a trial court may rule that the child is "unavailable" for hearsay rule purposes.

In *Idaho* v. *Wright,*[51] the defendant was charged with sexually abusing a child. The Supreme Court was asked to decide whether the admission at trial of certain hearsay statements made by a two-and-a-half-year old victim to a physician violated the defendant's rights to confront adverse witnesses. The Court held that although the young victim was unavailable at trial because her age rendered her incapable of testifying, the statements did not fall within a traditional exception to the hearsay rule. Moreover, they did not contain sufficient and "particularized guarantees of trustworthiness"[52] to render them admissible in this case. The Court declined to develop a mechanical rule for determining when a child's hearsay statements would have sufficient particularized guarantees of trustworthiness to be admitted into evidence. Some of the factors to be considered include:

1. whether the child's statements were spontaneous and were repeated;
2. whether the child's language describing the incident could be expected of a child of his or her age;
3. and a lack of incentive to be untruthful.[53]

If, however, a child's statements fall within a traditionally recognized exception to the hearsay rule, they may be admitted into evidence. In *White* v. *Illinois,*[54] the Supreme Court held that the prosecution need not make an additional showing that the admission of the hearsay testimony is necessary to protect the child's physical and psychological well-being.

The rule that emerges from these cases is that a child abuse victim's hearsay statements may be admitted into evidence if they fall within a recognized exception to the hearsay rule of evidence. Moreover, even if they do not qualify under one of these exceptions, they may be admitted if they contain particularized guarantees of trustworthiness. Although the Supreme Court has provided some general guidelines, the issue of precisely what constitutes a particularized guarantee of trustworthiness awaits clarification by the courts. If, however, a child's hearsay statements contain a graphic description of the alleged abuse, or other guarantees of trustworthiness, they are more likely to be admitted into evidence.[55]

The Right to Compulsory Process for Obtaining Witnesses

Under the Sixth Amendment's compulsory process clause, defendants have a right to present the testimony of witnesses for the defense and to require them to attend the trial. The general rule is that defendants must be able to present a witness's testimony if it is relevant and favorable. Moreover, states may not develop laws or procedural rules that arbitrarily limit a defendant's ability to procure the testimony of favorable witnesses.[56] For example, in *Washington* v. *Texas,*[57] the Supreme Court declared unconstitutional a law that prevented alleged accomplices from testifying for each other. This is because accomplices can provide relevant testimony regarding events about which they had personal information.

Moreover, the states may not use procedural rules to defeat the ends of justice. In *Chambers* v. *Mississippi,*[58] the defendant was not permitted to call a witness because the testimony to be presented was hearsay. The witness would have given testimony that was favorable to Chambers. The Supreme Court held that the State of Mississippi could not apply its hearsay evidence rule "mechanistically to defeat the ends of justice."[59]

The Right to Counsel

The Sixth Amendment guarantees the right to counsel. Chapters 10 and 11 discussed a suspect's right to counsel during critical pretrial phases of the investigative process. This chapter, in contrast, changes the focus to the right to counsel during trial.

The right to counsel, which has a long history in U.S. legal systems, was recognized by 12 of the original 13 American colonies. Some of the most famous cases that the U.S. Supreme Court has ever decided have involved the Sixth Amendment right to counsel.

Counsel in Capital Cases

In 1932, *Powell* v. *Alabama*[60] presented the case of the "Scottsboro Boys." The trial record showed that the defendants and several other African-Americans were riding on a freight train that traveled through Alabama. On the same train were several white boys and girls. A fight took place between the white and black youths and the white boys were thrown off the train. A message was sent ahead reporting the fight and asking that the African-Americans be removed from the train. Two girls testified that each of them was assaulted by six different African-Americans and identified the defendants as the perpetrators.

Before the train reached Scottsboro, Alabama, a sheriff's posse seized the defendants and two other African-Americans. Both girls and the African-Americans were taken to Scottsboro. Word of their coming and of the alleged assault had preceded them, and they were met at Scottsboro by a large crowd. The proceedings took place in an atmosphere of great hostility. The trial record did not disclose the defendants' ages, except that one youth was 19 years old; however, it clearly indicated that most, if not all, of them were youthful, and they were constantly referred to as "the boys." All of the defendants were illiterate and were residents of other states.

Ozzie Powell and two other African-American defendants were charged in an Alabama state court with raping the two white girls. When the defendants requested counsel, the trial judge had "appointed all members of the bar" for the "purpose of arraigning the defendants." The defendants pleaded not guilty to the charges, were convicted by different juries on the same day, and were sentenced to death.

Highlight 12.5

Quotation from *Powell* v. *Alabama*

 Even the intelligent and educated layman has small and sometimes no skill in the science of law. If charged with crime, he is incapable, generally, of determining for himself whether the indictment is good or bad. . . . He requires the guiding hand of counsel at every step in the proceeding against him. Without it, though he be not guilty, he faces the danger of conviction because he does not know how to establish his innocence.[61]

On appeal, the U.S. Supreme Court concluded that the defendants had been denied their right to counsel and reversed the judgments. In a now famous passage presented in Highlight 12.5, Justice Sutherland discussed the problems that defendants face when they are forced to defend against criminal charges without a lawyer.

The rule that emerged from this case is that defendants charged with capital crimes in state court have a Sixth Amendment right to counsel. In the years since *Powell* v. *Alabama,* the Supreme Court has greatly expanded this principle.

Counsel in Felony Cases

In 1942, the Court held in *Betts* v. *Brady*[62] that indigent defendants in state felony proceedings had no right to appointed counsel. An **indigent defendant** is one who cannot afford to retain private counsel.[63]

Another famous case, *Gideon* v. *Wainright,*[64] in 1963, reversed *Betts* v. *Brady* and held that indigent defendants have a fundamental right to appointed counsel in state felony cases. The Court stated, "reason and reflection require us to recognize that in our adversary system of criminal justice, any person haled into court, who is too poor to hire a lawyer, cannot be assured a fair trial unless counsel is provided for him."[65] *Gideon* held too that if a defendant is entitled to counsel at trial and counsel is not provided, his or her conviction must be reversed. *Gideon*'s impact on U.S. justice systems is difficult to overestimate.

Counsel in Misdemeanor Cases

Indigent defendants in many misdemeanor cases have a right to appointed counsel. In *Argersinger* v. *Hamlin*[66] the Supreme Court was asked to decide whether prosecutions punishable by imprisonment for less than six months could be tried without a lawyer being appointed to represent the accused. Jon Argersinger, an indigent defendant, was convicted in Florida state court of carrying a concealed weapon, a crime punishable by imprisonment up to six months, a $1,000 fine, or both. At trial Argersinger requested counsel, but the request was denied. He was convicted and sentenced to serve 90 days in jail. The Florida Supreme Court affirmed his conviction and held that the Sixth Amendment right to counsel extended only to trials for nonpetty offenses punishable by more than six months' imprisonment.

The U.S. Supreme Court held that the "problems associated with misdemeanor and petty offenses often require the presence of counsel to insure the accused a fair trial."[67] The Court went on to formulate a clear rule regarding the Sixth Amendment right to counsel in misdemeanor cases: "[A]bsent a knowing and intelligent waiver, no person may be imprisoned for any offense, whether classified as petty, misdemeanor, or felony, unless he was represented by counsel at his trial . . ."[68]

Argersinger v. *Hamlin* stated a bright line rule that trial courts must follow in misdemeanor and petty offense cases—if the accused is to be imprisoned upon conviction of a misdemeanor or petty offense, his or her request for counsel must be granted. As the Supreme Court stated:

> Under the rule we announce today, every judge will know when the trial of a misdemeanor starts that no imprisonment may be imposed, even though local law permits it, unless the accused is represented by counsel. He will have a measure of the seriousness and gravity of the offense and therefore know when to name a lawyer to represent the accused before the trial starts.[69]

In 1979, *Scott* v. *Illinois*[70] further clarified *Argersinger.* It held that counsel is required only when a sentence of confinement is *imposed* in a misdemeanor case. An indigent defendant has no right to appointed counsel in a misdemeanor case when a jail sentence is authorized under a particular statute but is not imposed.

State criminal courts take *Argersinger*'s rule seriously. For example, the State of Vermont's court rules provide for an immediate appeal to the Vermont Supreme Court of a trial judge's decision not to appoint counsel for a defendant in a misdemeanor case.[71] Significantly, many of these cases involve defendants who are charged with driving under the influence of alcohol. Alcohol-related offenses in the United States have reached epidemic proportions. Table 12.1 presents the results of a 1993 United States Department of Justice survey of state arrests for alcohol-related offenses.

Counsel on Appeal

Douglas v. *California*[72] held that indigent defendants have a right to counsel on their first appeal of a criminal conviction. The laws of many states give a defendant an automatic right to a first appeal of a criminal conviction to an appellate court. This is termed **mandatory review** because the appellate court *must* agree to hear the case. Appellate courts are not normally obliged to hear an appeal of a criminal case once an initial appeal has concluded. In some circumstances, however, an appellate court may in its discretion decide to hear an appeal of a criminal case after a first appeal has concluded. This is termed **discretionary review.** In *Ross* v. *Moffit*,[73] the Supreme Court held that the U.S. Constitution does not require a state to appoint counsel for an indigent defendant during later discretionary appeals.[74]

TABLE **12.1**   **Arrests for Alcohol-Related Offenses**

By Offense and State, 1993

State	Total alcohol-related arrests	Driving under influence	Liquor law violations	Drunkenness	Disorderly conduct	Vagrancy
Total	2,926,037	1,221,503	413,831	606,984	658,962	24,757
Alabama	49,980	19,708	9,149	15,653	5,260	210
Alaska	8,526	5,366	2,178	4	978	NA
Arizona	70,281	25,980	22,853	NA	20,397	1,051
Arkansas	51,959	19,567	3,822	21,120	6,812	638
California	390,365	230,329	15,702	125,778	14,004	4,552
Colorado	64,720	28,920	15,834	493	18,274	1,199
Connecticut	39,884	10,503	1,704	8	27,163	506
Delaware	994	NA	339	170	443	42
District of Columbia	10,878	3,560	46	NA	7,272	NA
Florida	77,555	36,969	20,698	NA	19,888	NA
Georgia	108,346	52,048	12,148	12,776	31,156	218
Hawaii	7,556	5,177	1,076	NA	1,303	NA
Idaho	16,111	10,475	4,042	102	1,479	13
Illinois	81,156	10,716	7,572	575	62,248	45
Indiana	51,723	18,106	8,938	17,619	7,051	9
Iowa	35,485	13,611	9,832	7,818	4,199	25
Kansas[a]	NA	NA	NA	NA	NA	NA
Kentucky	46,249	16,516	1,731	19,809	8,192	1
Louisiana	32,823	11,847	1,100	8,950	10,271	655
Maine	9,903	6,864	1,489	18	1,532	NA
Maryland	34,342	23,198	5,094	21	5,749	280
Massachusetts	33,419	12,471	3,060	7,927	9,896	65
Michigan	87,437	46,380	18,510	347	21,835	365
Minnesota	59,609	32,261	15,345	NA	11,798	205
Mississippi	19,754	6,388	1,885	6,061	5,409	11
Missouri	39,826	22,692	6,247	1,499	8,780	608
Montana	4,738	2,043	1,803	NA	892	NA
Nebraska	23,500	12,009	7,501	NA	3,980	10
Nevada	14,027	6,236	3,411	533	2,949	898
New Hampshire	9,478	4,672	2,235	1,448	1,022	101
New Jersey	70,711	24,640	8,391	40	37,188	454
New Mexico	15,385	9,612	3,295	489	1,981	8
New York	114,297	36,735	14,388	NA	53,849	9,325
North Carolina	96,675	70,863	10,492	NA	15,166	154
North Dakota	6,845	2,402	3,003	328	1,112	NA
Ohio	83,272	27,282	16,460	19,382	19,447	701

TABLE 12.1 *concluded*
By Offense and State, 1993

State	Total alcohol-related arrests	Driving under influence	Liquor law violations	Drunkenness	Disorderly conduct	Vagrancy
Oklahoma	61,423	24,635	5,062	29,224	2,502	NA
Oregon	39,714	21,067	13,942	NA	4,705	NA
Pennsylvania	114,867	27,521	16,620	19,673	50,714	339
Rhode Island	6,694	2,309	1,277	43	3,060	5
South Carolina	60,384	18,445	9,761	14,879	17,094	205
South Dakota	14,256	5,501	6,303	276	2,176	NA
Tennessee	60,834	22,111	4,052	25,742	8,779	150
Texas	341,441	101,978	21,550	180,965	35,890	1,058
Utah	28,881	7,812	9,556	7,407	3,945	161
Vermont	1,125	955	115	2	53	NA
Virginia	106,715	35,304	14,053	47,668	9,689	1
Washington	56,344	38,785	12,843	59	4,397	260
West Virginia	22,282	9,080	1,095	10,114	1,962	31
Wisconsin	131,916	35,073	32,813	267	63,570	193
Wyoming	11,352	4,781	3,416	1,697	1,453	5

Note: These data are compiled from the Federal Bureau of Investigation's Uniform Crime Reporting Program. The data presented in this table differ from those presented in the U.S. Department of Justice, Federal Bureau of Investigation, *Crime in the United States, 1993* (Washington, DC: USGPO, 1994). This is because this table includes data processed by the Federal Bureau of Investigation after the cut off date for that publication. "In many States where drunkenness and/or vagrancy are not treated as criminal actions, these categories are not permissible causes of arrest. In one respect, these data may be considered conservative estimates of alcohol-related arrests. Arrests are classified by a single offense, using a hierarchical rule. Consequently, crimes committed while intoxicated are categorized under the primary offense. On the other hand, 'driving under the influence' includes impairment due to any type of drug; it is not limited to impairment due to alcohol".

[a]Complete data for 1993 were not available for Kansas.

Source: Table adapted by SOURCEBOOK staff from table provided by the U.S. Department of Health and Human Services, National Institute on Alcohol Abuse and Alcoholism.

Citation: Kathleen Maguire and Ann L. Pastore, eds., *Sourcebook of Criminal Justice Statistics 1994* U.S. Department of Justice, Bureau of Justice Statistics (Washington, D.C.: USGPO, 1995), p. 412.

Waiving the Right to Counsel

Defendants may choose to proceed without counsel in criminal cases. Defendants who represent themselves are said to proceed **pro se.** *Faretta* v. *California,*[75] held that a state may not "constitutionally hale a person into its criminal courts and there force a lawyer upon him, even when he wants to conduct his own defense."[76] A waiver of the right to counsel must be knowing and intelligent, however. This does not mean that a waiver must be "wise" to be intelligent. In *Patterson* v. *Illinois,*[77] the Supreme Court held that it means a trial court judge must make a careful inquiry into the defendant's understanding of the right to counsel and his or her knowledge of the problems associated with self-representation. A trial judge may ask a defendant who is contemplating self-representation numerous questions designed to test his or her awareness of the statutory elements of the charges, the penalties associated with conviction, and will often advise the defendant of the advantages of legal representation. If the defendant still wishes to proceed pro se, he or she must be permitted to do so.

A trial judge sometimes faces an uphill battle with a defendant who insists upon self-representation. To ensure that a defendant's waiver of counsel is knowing and intelligent, an experienced trial judge may even make the following type of statement on the record: "You need a lawyer; you do not have the education or training needed to conduct an effective defense to the charges in this case. Although you have the right to represent yourself, I would strongly advise you not to do so." In addition, even most lawyers retain an attorney if they are charged with crimes or are personally involved in a civil lawsuit. Among lawyers, there is a saying that an attorney who represents himself or herself has a fool for a client.[78]

The Use of Standby Counsel.   In serious criminal cases when a defendant has asserted his or her right to self-representation, a trial judge will sometimes appoint **standby counsel** to assist in the proceedings. A standby counsel is an attorney appointed by the court who assists a pro se defendant with various aspects of the trial process. In *McKaskle* v. *Wiggens*,[79] the Supreme Court held that a trial court's decision to appoint standby counsel does not violate a defendant's right to self-representation, even if the defendant objects to the attorney's presence.[80]

Ineffective Assistance of Counsel

The Sixth Amendment guarantees a defendant the right to the effective assistance of counsel. In practice, however, it is quite difficult for a defendant to have his or her conviction reversed by an appellate court based on a violation of the right to the effective assistance of counsel. In *Strickland* v. *Washington*,[81] the Supreme Court held that in order to establish a violation of this right the defendant must show:

1. that the lawyer's conduct was below that of a reasonable attorney; and
2. that the attorney's poor performance resulted in an unreliable or unfair outcome in the case.[82]

A defendant must satisfy both parts of this test. If he or she is unable to make either showing, the appeal will fail. An appeal based on an ineffective assistance of counsel claim may succeed, however, if an attorney's performance is clearly below professional standards and results in harm to the defendant.[83] For example, suppose that Susan, a defendant in a criminal case, claims that she was visiting relatives in a different state at the time of the offense. Her attorney, however, fails to interview and investigate the witnesses that would establish Susan's alibi claim and she is convicted. Susan may prevail on appeal if she can establish that a reasonable attorney would have interviewed these witnesses, and that if they had testified she was likely to be acquitted of the charges.[84]

The Right to Proof Beyond a Reasonable Doubt

In re Winship[85] held that a defendant in a criminal case has the right to have each element of the crime proved beyond a reasonable doubt. The prosecution's failure to prove any element of the charged crime will result in an acquittal. For example, suppose that John is charged with burglary in a state that uses the old common law definition of this offense. The prosecution must prove each of the elements of this crime, including:

1. a breaking and entering;
2. in the nighttime;
3. of an occupied dwelling house of another;
4. with the intent to commit a felony.

If the prosecutor fails to show that the offense was committed during the nighttime, John may not be convicted of burglary. He may, however, be convicted of a lesser-included offense, such as breaking and entering, which may be easier to prove because at common law it did not require the prosecution to prove that the intrusion occurred during the nighttime.

When a Defendant Must Carry the Burden of Proof

An **affirmative defense** to criminal charges requires a defendant to carry the burden of establishing a particular defense. Affirmative defenses to criminal charges are governed by state and federal law and vary considerably among different jurisdictions, although some general observations are possible. The most common affirmative defenses include insanity, self-defense, and alibi. When a defendant uses one of these defenses, he or she must make a showing that the defense applies to the particular facts of the case. The burden then shifts to the prosecution to prove beyond a reasonable doubt that the defense should not apply. For example, suppose that Bob, who is charged with manslaughter in North Carolina, uses an alibi defense and maintains that he was in Florida at the time of the offense. If Bob introduces evidence to show that he was in Florida at the time of the offense, the burden would shift to the prosecution to disprove Bob's alibi defense. If the prosecution is able to show that Bob's alibi witness had lied and that Bob was not in Florida at the time of the offense, it may carry the burden of disproving Bob's alibi defense beyond a reasonable doubt.

Likewise, if Bob attempted to use an insanity defense to a manslaughter charge, in many states he would be required to show substantial evidence of his insanity. The burden would then shift to the prosecution to prove beyond a reasonable doubt that Bob was sane at the time the offense occurred.

At this point it is appropriate to discuss briefly the insanity defense in criminal cases. Several different tests have been used in various states to determine if a defendant was legally insane at the time of an offense. Some states use the **M'Naghten test.** This test asks whether the defendant was able to determine right from wrong at the time of the offense. A second and more widely used insanity test was developed by the American Law Institute. The **ALI test** asks whether the defendant lacked the substantial capacity

"To appreciate the wrongfulness of his or her conduct or to conform his or her conduct to the requirements of law." Another insanity test that is used in a small minority of states is the **irresistible impulse test.** This test asserts that a defendant's actions will be excused if as a consequence "of a mental disease or defect he or she did not know the nature or quality of his act; or he did not know that what he was doing is wrong; or he did not have the ability to control his conduct even if he knew that what he was doing was wrong."[86] A final insanity test is termed the **Durham test.** This test asks simply whether a defendant's actions at the time of the offense were the product of a mental disease or defect.

Many popular myths surround the insanity defense.[87] One common misconception is that it is used frequently in criminal cases. One study indicates that defendants use this defense in only a very small percentage of criminal cases, and an even smaller percentage of insanity claims actually succeed.[88]

Another common misconception is that defendants who successfully use an insanity defense somehow escape punishment for their crimes. A recent study does not support this conclusion. Based on a comparison of the periods of confinement of defendants who successfully used an insanity defense with those who were unsuccessful, the researcher's findings indicate that the groups had similar lengths of incarceration.[89]

Incompetence to Stand Trial

An issue related to the insanity defense is a defendant's competence to stand trial. The two issues are distinct, however, because a defendant who was legally insane at the time a crime was committed may still be competent to stand trial. Likewise, a defendant who was sane at the time of an offense may later become incompetent to stand trial. The Supreme Court has held that a criminal defendant must have the ability to consult with a defense lawyer and assist in his or her defense. Moreover, the defendant must be able to understand the nature of the proceedings.

In most cases when a defendant asserts that he or she is incompetent to stand trial, a **competency hearing** will be held. A trial court will use a totality of circumstances test at such a hearing and will consider factors including a defendant's irrational behavior. Psychiatric experts are appointed frequently by the courts to determine a defendant's ability to stand trial. If a defendant is found to be legally incompetent, he or she may not be compelled to stand trial and may be committed to a mental institution for a reasonable period. In federal cases, that period may not exceed four months or the government must release the defendant or file civil commitment proceedings.

Guilty Pleas

A defendant who enters a guilty plea admits that he or she committed a charged offense. In *Parke* v. *Riley,*[90] the Supreme Court held that a guilty plea must be made in a knowing and voluntary manner because by pleading guilty a defendant waives many important constitutional rights. These include the right to a jury trial, the right to challenge the admission of evidence as the product of an unlawful search and seizure or a *Miranda* violation, the privilege against self-incrimination, and the right to confront and cross-examine adverse witnesses.[91]

The vast majority of criminal convictions in the United States are obtained as a result of guilty pleas. Defendants may plead guilty to criminal charges for any number of reasons, but most do so in exchange for some kind of favorable action by the state. This somewhat controversial practice is termed **plea bargaining.** A plea bargain is essentially a contract between the prosecution and the defendant that promises to reduce charges, agree to a particular sentence, or to forgo additional opportunities for prosecution. As a contract, a plea agreement may not be breached by either party.[92]

If a defendant breaches a plea bargain agreement, the prosecution is free to bring any charges it is able to sustain, including more serious charges than those discussed during plea negotiations. In *Ricketts* v. *Adamson,*[93] the defendant, who had been allowed to plead guilty to a second-degree murder charge, breached a plea agreement to testify against other defendants. Prosecutors then reinstated a first-degree murder charge against him. The Supreme Court upheld his subsequent conviction for first-degree murder because he had breached the earlier plea agreement.

The Supreme Court has held too that if the prosecution breaches a plea agreement a defendant is free to withdraw his or her guilty plea and proceed to trial. In *Santobello* v. *New York,*[94] the defendant entered a guilty plea based on a prosecutor's promise to make no sentencing recommendation to the judge. Prior to sentencing, a new prosecutor who had taken over the case recommended, and the trial judge imposed, the maximum sentence for the crime. The Supreme Court held that if the prosecution breaches a plea agreement, the defendant must be allowed to withdraw the plea and proceed to trial. In some cases, a trial judge may order the prosecution to comply with an earlier plea agreement. This is termed **specific performance,** a legal remedy usually associated with civil contract cases.

Prosecutors have great discretion in the plea bargaining process. Often they will threaten to file more serious criminal charges against a defendant if he or she does not plead guilty. In *Bordenkircher* v. *Hayes,*[95] the Supreme Court held that such threats are permissible if a defendant refuses to plead guilty, provided that the threatened charges are supported by probable cause. Likewise, *Parker* v. *North Carolina*[96] held that a defendant's guilty plea to capital murder charges, under a state law providing that defendants who pleaded guilty could not be sentenced to death, was voluntary even though it was influenced by his desire to avoid the death penalty.

Normally, a trial judge will comply with a plea agreement between a defendant and the prosecution. Sometimes, however, a judge will reject a plea bargain agreement. When this occurs a defendant is free to withdraw his or her guilty plea and proceed to trial.

Plea bargaining is a controversial practice in U.S. justice systems.[97] Some commentators have suggested that it is a necessary evil—without it U.S. court systems would be unable to handle the huge volume of criminal cases. The evidence suggests, however, that this has not happened in jurisdictions that have abolished plea bargaining.[98]

Summary

Chapter 12 discusses defendants' constitutional rights during trial, which are primarily grounded in the Sixth Amendment. The right to a speedy trial is designed to ensure that the defendant is not confined for a prolonged period before trial and that the case is tried while the evidence is fresh.

The Sixth Amendment guarantees the right to a public trial as well. There are two ways to view the right to a public trial: (1) the right of the public and the press to attend a trial; and (2) the defendant's right to have members of the public present at his or her trial. A trial judge may not completely close a criminal trial unless it is very clear that the presence of the public would compromise a defendant's right to a fair trial. A judge may, however, close portions of a trial if there is a compelling state interest that outweighs the right of the public to be present. In addition, a defendant has a Sixth Amendment right to have members of the public present at his or her trial. This protection is designed to ensure that a trial is conducted fairly and to permit public scrutiny of the judicial process.

In addition, an accused has the right to a trial by an impartial jury. *Duncan* v. *Louisiana* held that the right to a trial by an impartial jury is fundamental and applies to all trials for nonpetty criminal offenses. A nonpetty offense is one that is punishable by a jail sentence exceeding six months.

The Constitution does not specify a particular size for juries in criminal cases. Although juries in federal criminal cases must be composed of twelve persons, the Supreme Court has been more flexible about allowing the states to develop their own rules for determining the size of juries.

Defendants in federal criminal trials have a right to a unanimous verdict. Once again, however, the rule is more flexible in state criminal proceedings.

Once prospective jurors are selected, a trial court will conduct a voir dire examination, during which the court or defense attorneys and prosecutors will pose questions to potential jurors. A challenge for cause may be used to exclude any juror who is biased or who is disqualified by law from serving on a jury in a particular case. A peremptory challenge may be used by either the defense or the prosecution to exclude any potential juror. The party challenging the juror need not specify a reason for the exclusion. Peremptory challenges may not be used in a racially discriminatory fashion.

An accused person must be given notice of the charges against him or her. A charging document, or indictment, must contain a plain and definite written statement of the essential facts constituting the offense charged.

The Sixth Amendment's confrontation clause guarantees a criminal defendant the right to confront physically and cross-examine adverse witnesses. These rights are designed to ensure the fairness of the proceedings and to ensure that evidence is tested vigorously.

Under the Sixth Amendment's compulsory process clause, defendants have a right to present the testimony of witnesses for the defense and to require them to attend the trial. Defendants must be able to present a witness's testimony if it is relevant and favorable.

The Sixth Amendment provides a defendant with the right to counsel in capital and felony cases. In misdemeanor cases, if an accused will be imprisoned upon conviction of a misdemeanor or petty offense, a trial court must grant his or her request for counsel. An indigent defendant has a right to counsel on his or her first appeal of a criminal conviction but does not have the same right during later discretionary appeals.

A criminal defendant may decide to proceed without counsel. Defendants who represent themselves are said to proceed pro se. A waiver of counsel must be knowing and intelligent, however.

An accused has the right to the effective assistance of counsel as well. In practice, however, it is difficult for a defendant to have a conviction reversed by an appellate court based on a violation of this right.

When a defendant is charged with a crime, the state must prove each element of the offense beyond a reasonable doubt. The prosecution's failure to prove any element of the charged crime will result in an acquittal.

An affirmative defense to a criminal charge requires a defendant to carry the burden of establishing a particular defense. The most common affirmative defenses include insanity, self-defense, and alibi. When a defendant uses one of these defenses, he or she must make a showing that the defense applies to the particular facts of the case. The burden then shifts to the prosecution to prove beyond a reasonable doubt that the defense should not apply.

Several different tests have been used in various states to determine if a defendant was legally insane at the time of an offense. The M'Naghten test asks whether the defendant was able to determine right from wrong at the time of the offense. The ALI test asks whether the defendant lacked the substantial capacity "either to appreciate the wrongfulness of his or her conduct or to conform his or her conduct to the requirements of law." The irresistible impulse test asserts that a defendant's actions will be excused if "as a result of a mental disease or defect he or she did not know the nature or quality of his act; or he did not know that what he was doing is wrong; or he did not have the ability to control his conduct even if he knew that what he was doing was wrong." The Durham test asks simply whether a defendants actions at the time of the offense were the product of a mental disease or defect. These different tests have been used in various states to determine if a defendant is legally insane at the time of an offense.

A related issue is a defendant's competence to stand trial. A defendant who was legally insane at the time a crime was committed may still be competent to stand trial. Likewise, a defendant who was sane at the time of an offense may later become incompetent to stand trial.

The vast majority of criminal convictions in the United States are obtained as a result of guilty pleas. A guilty plea must be made in a knowing and voluntary manner because by pleading guilty a defendant waives many important constitutional rights. Defendants may plead guilty to criminal charges for any number of reasons, but most do so in exchange for some kind of favorable action by the state. This practice is termed plea bargaining, which is a controversial practice in U.S. justice systems.

Review Questions

1. Identify and discuss several factors that a court will use to determine if a defendant's right to a speedy trial has been violated. Which of these factors weighs most heavily in a trial judge's analysis?

2. Does a defendant have a constitutional right to bail in a criminal case? Define excessive bail. Outline the present constitutional status of preventive detention.

3. Discuss the right to a public trial. In what circumstances may a trial judge close portions of a criminal trial? How is the First Amendment implicated when a trial judge decides to close portions of a criminal trial?

4. When does a defendant in a criminal case have a right to trial by jury? What are the requirements for waiving the right to a jury trial?

5. Discuss the rules that the Supreme Court has developed regarding the size of juries. Must jury verdicts be unanimous?

6. Define the following terms:
   a. venire
   b. jury pool
   c. voir dire examination
   d. challenge for cause
   e. peremptory challenge

7. Discuss the Supreme Court's ruling in *Batson* v. *Kentucky*. How did *J.E.B.* v. *Alabama ex rel. T.B.* expand *Batson*'s holding?

8. What is the purpose of an indictment document in a criminal case?

9. Why does a defendant in a criminal case have a right to physically confront and cross-examine adverse witnesses? When may this right be suspended in child abuse cases?

10. What is hearsay evidence? Why does the use of hearsay evidence implicate a defendant's right to confront and cross-examine adverse witnesses?

11. Outline the scope of an indigent person's right to counsel in the following types of cases:
    a. capital cases
    b. felony cases
    c. misdemeanor cases
    d. petty offenses that may not result in confinement
    e. appeals of criminal cases

12. Discuss the Supreme Court's rationale for requiring the states to provide counsel for indigent defendants in criminal cases. (Be sure to refer to relevant case law in completing your answer.)

13. When may a defendant waive his or her right to counsel and proceed pro se in a criminal case? What is a "standby counsel?"

14. Why is it difficult to establish that an accused has received ineffective assistance of counsel in a criminal case?

15. A defendant has a right to have each element of a crime proved beyond a reasonable doubt. Provide an example to illustrate this principle.
    a. What is an affirmative defense to criminal charges?

16. Identify several different tests that have been used in various states to determine if a defendant was legally insane at the time of an offense.

17. Discuss the practice of plea bargaining in U.S. justice systems.
    a. When may a defendant withdraw a guilty plea?
    b. What will happen if a prosecutor breaches a plea bargain agreement?
    c. What will happen if a trial judge rejects a plea bargain agreement?

Issues for Analysis and Discussion

1. In *Gideon* v. *Wainright,* the Supreme Court held that *Betts* v. *Brady* was "an anachronism when handed down." Outline the Supreme Court's reasons for holding that *Betts* was incorrectly decided.

2. In *J.E.B.* v. *Alabama ex rel T.B.,* Justice Blackmun wrote that "gender, like race, is an unconstitutional proxy for juror competence and impartiality." Explain this statement fully. Do you agree with the Court's holding in this case? Develop an argument that gender should be treated differently from race in these cases.

CASE EXCERPT: *GIDEON* V. *WAINRIGHT*
SUPREME COURT OF THE UNITED STATES
372 U.S. 335 (1963)

Clarence Earl Gideon was convicted of breaking and entering a building with the intent to commit a misdemeanor. Because Gideon was indigent, he asked that the court appoint an attorney to represent him. The court denied his request because under *Powell* v. *Alabama* and Florida law, appointed counsel was required only in capital cases. At trial, Gideon was convicted and was sentenced to serve five years in prison. The Florida Supreme Court denied Gideon's appeal and the U.S. Supreme Court granted certiorari.

Mr. Justice Black delivered the opinion of the Court.

* * *

I

Since the facts and circumstances of [*Betts* v. *Brady* and *Gideon* v. *Wainright*] are so nearly indistinguishable, we think the *Betts* v. *Brady* holding if left standing would require us to reject Gideon's claim that the Constitution guarantees him the assistance of counsel. Upon full reconsideration we conclude that *Betts* v. *Brady* should be overruled.

II

The Sixth Amendment provides, "In all criminal prosecutions, the accused shall enjoy the right . . . to have the Assistance of Counsel for his defence." We have construed this to mean that in federal courts counsel must be provided for defendants unable to employ counsel unless the right is competently and intelligently waived. Betts argued that this right is extended to indigent defendants in state courts by the Fourteenth Amendment. In response the Court stated that, while the Sixth Amendment laid down "no rule for the conduct of the States, the question recurs whether the constraint laid by the Amendment upon the national courts expresses a rule so fundamental and essential to a fair trial, and so, to due process of law, that it is made obligatory upon the States by the Fourteenth Amendment." . . . In order to decide whether the Sixth Amendment's guarantee of counsel is of this fundamental nature, the Court in *Betts* set out and considered "[r]elevant data on the subject . . . afforded by constitutional and statutory provisions subsisting in the colonies and the States prior to the inclusion of the Bill of Rights in the national Constitution, and in the constitutional, legislative and judicial history of the States to the present date." . . . On the basis of this historical data the Court concluded that "appointment of counsel is not a fundamental right, essential to a fair trial." It was for this reason the *Betts* Court refused to accept the contention that the Sixth Amendment's guarantee of counsel for indigent federal defendants was extended to or, in the words of that Court, "made obligatory upon the States by the Fourteenth Amendment." Plainly, had the Court concluded that appointment of counsel for an indigent criminal defendant was "a fundamental right, essential to a fair trial," it would have held that the Fourteenth Amendment requires appointment of counsel in a state court, just as the Sixth Amendment requires in a federal court.

We accept *Betts* v. *Brady's* assumption, based as it was on our prior cases, that a provision of the Bill of Rights which is "fundamental and essential to a fair trial" is made obligatory upon the States by the Fourteenth Amendment.

We think the Court in *Betts* was wrong, however, in concluding that the Sixth Amendment's guarantee of counsel is not one of these fundamental rights. Ten years before *Betts* v. *Brady,* this Court, after full consideration of all the historical data examined in *Betts,* had unequivocally declared that "the right to the aid of counsel is of this fundamental character." . . . While the Court at the close of its Powell opinion did by its language, as this Court frequently does, limit its holding to the particular facts and circumstances of that case, its conclusions about the fundamental nature of the right to counsel are unmistakable.

* * *

The fact is that in deciding as it did—that "appointment of counsel is not a fundamental right, essential to a fair trial"—the Court in *Betts* v. *Brady* made an abrupt break with its own well-considered precedents. In returning to these old precedents, sounder we believe than the new, we but restore constitutional principles established to achieve a fair system of justice. Not only these precedents but also reason and reflection require us to recognize that in our adversary system of criminal justice, any person haled into court, who is too poor to hire a lawyer, cannot be assured a fair trial unless counsel is provided for him. This seems to us to be an obvious truth. Governments, both state and federal, quite properly spend vast sums of money to establish machinery to try defendants accused of crime. Lawyers to prosecute are everywhere deemed essential to protect the public's interest in an orderly society. Similarly, there are few defendants charged with crime, few indeed, who fail to hire the best lawyers they can get to prepare and present their defenses. That government hires lawyers to prosecute and defendants who have the money hire lawyers to defend are the strongest indications of the widespread belief that lawyers in criminal courts are necessities, not luxuries. The right of one charged with crime to counsel may not be deemed fundamental and essential to fair trials in some countries, but it is in ours. From the very beginning, our state and national constitutions and laws have laid great emphasis on procedural and substantive safeguards designed to assure fair trials before impartial tribunals in which every defendant stands equal before the law. This noble ideal cannot be realized if the poor man charged with crime has to face his accusers without a lawyer to assist him.

* * *

This Court in *Betts* v. *Brady* departed from the sound wisdom upon which the Court's holding in *Powell* v. *Alabama* rested. Florida, supported by two other States, has asked that *Betts* v. *Brady* be left intact. Twenty-two States, as friends of the Court, argue that Betts was "an anachronism when handed down" and that it should now be overruled. We agree.

The judgment is reversed and the cause is remanded to the Supreme Court of Florida for further action not inconsistent with this opinion.

Reversed.

Case Excerpt: *J.E.B.* v. *Alabama ex rel. T.B.*
Supreme Court of the United States
114 S.Ct. 1419 (1994)

At J.E.B.'s paternity and child support trial, the prosecutor used 9 of its 10 peremptory challenges to remove male jurors. The court empaneled an all-female jury after rejecting J.E.B.'s claim that the logic and reasoning of *Batson* v. *Kentucky* applied to using peremptory challenges based on gender. In *Batson* the Supreme Court had held that the Equal Protection Clause of the Fourteenth Amendment prohibits the use of peremptory challenges based on race. The jury found J.E.B. to be the father of the child and the trial court ordered him to pay child support. The Alabama Court of Appeals affirmed. The U.S. Supreme Court granted certiorari.

Mr. Justice Blackmun delivered the opinion of the Court.

* * *

In *Batson* v. *Kentucky,* this Court held that the Equal Protection Clause of the Fourteenth Amendment governs the exercise of peremptory challenges by a prosecutor in a criminal trial. The Court explained that although a defendant has "no right to a 'petit jury composed in whole or in part of persons of his own race,'" the "defendant does have the right to be tried by a jury whose members are selected pursuant to nondiscriminatory criteria." Since Batson, we have reaffirmed repeatedly our commitment to jury selection procedures that are fair and nondiscriminatory. We have recognized that whether the trial is criminal or civil, potential jurors, as well as litigants, have an equal protection right to jury selection procedures that are free from state-sponsored group stereotypes rooted in, and reflective of, historical prejudice.

Although premised on equal protection principles that apply equally to gender discrimination, all our recent cases defining the scope of Batson involved alleged racial discrimination in the exercise of peremptory challenges. Today we are faced with the question whether the Equal Protection Clause forbids intentional discrimination on the basis of gender, just as it prohibits discrimination on the basis of race. We hold that gender,

like race, is an unconstitutional proxy for juror competence and impartiality.

* * *

We granted certiorari to resolve a question that has created a conflict of authority—whether the Equal Protection Clause forbids peremptory challenges on the basis of gender as well as on the basis of race. Today we reaffirm what, by now should be axiomatic: Intentional discrimination on the basis of gender by state actors violates the Equal Protection Clause, particularly where, as here, the discrimination serves to ratify and perpetuate invidious, archaic, and overbroad stereotypes about the relative abilities of men and women.

* * *

While the prejudicial attitudes toward women in this country have not been identical to those held toward racial minorities, the similarities between the experiences of racial minorities and women, in some contexts, "overpower those differences." . . . Certainly, with respect to jury service, African-Americans and women share a history of total exclusion, a history which came to an end for women many years after the embarrassing chapter in our history came to an end for African-Americans.

We need not determine, however, whether women or racial minorities have suffered more at the hands of discriminatory state actors during the decades of our Nation's history. It is necessary only to acknowledge that "our Nation has had a long and unfortunate history of sex discrimination," a history which warrants the heightened scrutiny we afford all gender-based classifications today. Under our equal protection jurisprudence, gender-based classifications require "an exceedingly persuasive justification" in order to survive constitutional scrutiny.

* * *

Discrimination in jury selection, whether based on race or on gender, causes harm to the litigants, the community, and the individual jurors who are wrongfully excluded from participation in the judicial process. The litigants are harmed by the risk that the prejudice which motivated the discriminatory selection of the jury will infect the entire proceedings. The community is harmed by the State's participation in the perpetuation of invidious group stereotypes and the inevitable loss of confidence in our judicial system that state-sanctioned discrimination in the courtroom engenders.

When state actors exercise peremptory challenges in reliance on gender stereotypes, they ratify and reinforce prejudicial views of the relative abilities of men and women. Because these stereotypes have wreaked injustice in so many other spheres of our country's public life, active discrimination by litigants on the basis of gender during jury selection "invite cynicism respecting the jury's neutrality and its obligation to adhere to the law." The potential for cynicism is particularly acute in cases where gender-related issues are prominent, such as cases involving rape, sex-

ual harassment, or paternity. Discriminatory use of peremptory challenges may create the impression that the judicial system has acquiesced in suppressing full participation by one gender or that the "deck has been stacked" in favor of one side. . . . All persons, when granted the opportunity to serve on a jury have the right not to be excluded summarily because of discriminatory and stereotypical presumptions that reflect and reinforce patterns of historical discrimination.

* * *

Equal opportunity to participate in the fair administration of justice is fundamental to our democratic system. It not only furthers the goals of the jury system. It reaffirms the promise of equality under the law—that all citizens, regardless of race, ethnicity, or gender, have the chance to take part directly in our democracy. When persons are excluded from participation in our democratic processes solely because of race or gender, this promise of equality dims, and the integrity of our judicial system is jeopardized.

In view of these concerns, the Equal Protection Clause prohibits discrimination in jury selection on the basis of gender, or on the assumption that an individual will be biased in a particular case for no reason other than the fact that the person happens to be a woman or happens to be a man. As with race, the "core guarantee of equal protection, ensuring citizens that their State will not discriminate . . . would be meaningless were we to approve the exclusion of jurors on the basis of such assumptions, which arise solely from the jurors' [gender]."

The judgment of the Court of Civil Appeals of Alabama is reversed and the case is remanded to that court for further proceedings not inconsistent with this opinion.

It is so ordered.

Endnotes

1. See Thomas P. Schneider and Robert C. Davis, "Speedy Trial Homicide Courts: Justice in Milwaukee Stops Spinning Its Wheels." 9 *Criminal Justice* pp. 24–29 (1995).
2. *Barker* v. *Wingo,* 407 U.S. 514 (1972).
3. For an excellent analysis of a defendant's right to a speedy trial considering these factors, see Steven D. Feldman, "Speedy Trial." 84 *The Georgetown Law Journal Twenty-Fifth Annual Review of Criminal Procedure* pp. 1025–1028 (1996). This source provides a comprehensive analysis of the federal case law in this area as well.
4. See *United States* v. *Blanco,* 861 F.2d 773 (2d Cir. 1988).
5. *Doggett* v. *United States,* 505 U.S. 647 (1992); Feldman, supra note 3 at 1028.
6. See Timothy J. Searight, "The Sixth Amendment Right to a Speedy Trial: Applying Barker v. Wingo After United States v. Doggett." 22 *Western State University Law Review* pp. 61–74 (1994).
7. *Stack* v. *Boyle,* 342 U.S. 1 (1951).
8. 18 U.S.C. Section 3142(e), (f) (1994).
9. *United States* v. *Salerno,* 481 U.S. 739 (1987).
10. *In re Oliver,* 333 U.S. 257 (1948).
11. Christopher K. DeScherer and David L. Fogel, "Sixth Amendment at Trial." 84 *The Georgetown Law Journal Twenty-Fifth Annual Review of Criminal Procedure* p. 1224 (1996).
12. *Waller* v. *Georgia,* 467 U.S. 39 (1984).
13. See Jack B. Harrison, "How Open is Open? The Development of the Public Access Doctrine Under State Open Court Provisions." 60 *University of Cincinnati Law Review* pp. 1307–1334 (1992).
14. See *Press-Enterprise Co.* v. *Superior Court* (*Press Enterprise I*), 464 U.S. 501 (1984).
15. *Duncan* v. *Louisiana,* 391 U.S. 145 (1968).
16. The Supreme Court has held that juveniles facing delinquency adjudication proceedings have no right to a jury trial. See *McKeiver* v. *Pennsylvania,* 403 U.S. 528 (1971).
17. *Baldwin* v. *New York,* 399 U.S. 66 (1970).
18. *Lewis* v. *United States,* 116 S.Ct. 2163 (1996).
19. *Blanton* v. *City of North Las Vegas,* 489 U.S. 538 (1989).
20. See David C. Owen, "Striking Out Juveniles; A reexamination of the Right to a Jury Trial in Litigation of California's Three Strikes Legislation." 29 *University of California Davis Law Review* pp. 437–464 (1996); Joseph J. Sklansky, "Right to a Jury Trial." 84 *The Georgetown Law Journal Twenty-Fifth Annual Review of Criminal Procedure* pp. 1140 (1996).
21. Wayne R. LaFave and Jerold H. Israel, *Criminal Procedure,* 2d ed. (St. Paul, Minn.: West, 1992), p. 961.
22. *Singer* v. *United States,* 380 U.S. 24 (1965).
23. Fed. R. Crim. P. 23(b).
24. *Williams* v. *Florida,* 399 U.S. 78 (1970).
25. *Ballew* v. *Georgia,* 435 U.S. 223 (1978).
26. See Gail Diane Cox, "Bigger is Better?" 12 *The National Law Journal* p. 6 (December 18, 1989).
27. *Apodaca* v. *Oregon,* 406 U.S. 404 (1972).
28. *Johnson* v. *Louisiana,* 406 U.S. 356 (1972).
29. *Burch* v. *Louisiana,* 441 U.S. 130 (1979).
30. See Robert T. Roper, "Jury Size and Verdict Consistency: A Line Has to be Drawn Somewhere." 14 *Law and Society Review* pp. 978–995 (1980).
31. *Taylor* v. *Louisiana,* 419 U.S. 522 (1975).
32. See *Edmonson* v. *Leesville Concrete Co.,* 500 U.S. 614 (1991).
33. *Batson* v. *Kentucky,* 476 U.S. 79 (1986).
34. *J.E.B.* v. *Alabama ex rel. T.B.,* 114 S.Ct. 1419 (1994); see Brian A. Howie, "A Remedy Without a Wrong: J.E.B. and the Extension of Batson to Sex Based Peremptory Challenges." 52 *Washington and Lee Law Review* pp. 1725–1770 (1996); David Hricik and Matthew P. Eastus, "Batson, J.E.B., and Pucket: A Step-by-Step Guide to Making and Challenging Peremptory Challenges in Federal Court." 37 *South Texas Law Review* pp. 127–159 (1996).
35. Joseph J. Sklansky, "Right to a Jury Trial." 84 *The Georgetown Law Journal Twenty-Fifth Annual Review of Criminal Procedure* pp. 1157–1160 (1996).
36. *Georgia* v. *McCollum,* 505 U.S. 42 (1992).
37. Id. at 44; see Stephen R. DiPrima, "Selecting a Jury in Federal Criminal Trials After Batson and McCollum." 95 *Columbia Law Review* pp. 888–928 (1995).
38. Fed. R. Crim. P. 7(c)(1).
39. Luisa Caro and Alan S. Marzilli, "Indictments." 84 *The Georgetown Law Journal Twenty-Fifth Annual Review of Criminal Procedure* pp. 942 (1996).

40. See Randolph N. Jonakait, "The Origins of the Confrontation Clause: An Alternative History." 27 *Rutgers Law Journal* pp. 77–168 (1995).

41. Supra, note 11 at 1231.

42. *Maryland* v. *Craig,* 497 U.S. 836 (1990).

43. See Ralph H. Kohlmann, "The Presumption of Innocence: Patching the Tattered Cloak After Maryland v. Craig." 27 *St. Mary's Law Review* pp. 389–421 (1996).

44. *Coy* v. *Iowa,* 487 U.S. 1012 (1988).

45. *Maryland* v. *Craig,* 497 U.S. 836, 849–850 (1990).

46. See Bryan H. Wildenthal, "The Right of Confrontation, Justice Scalia, and the Power and Limits of Textualism." 48 *Washington and Lee University Law Review* pp. 1323–1392 (1991).

47. See Charles R. Nesson and Yochai Benkler, "Constitutional Hearsay: Requiring Foundational Testing and Corroboration Under the Confrontation Clause." 81 *Virginia Law Review* pp. 149–174 (1995).

48. This example is taken from Christopher B. Mueller and Laird C. Kirkpatrick, *Evidence Under the Rules* (Boston, Mass.: Little, Brown, 1988), p. 115.

49. For a comprehensive discussion of these exceptions to the hearsay rule of evidence see, id. at 183–486.

50. *Ohio* v. *Roberts,* 448 U.S. 56 (1980).

51. *Idaho* v. *Wright,* 497 U.S. 805 (1990); For an excellent discussion of these issues see Christopher K. DeScherer and David L. Fogel, "Compulsory Process." 84 *The Georgetown Law Journal Twenty-Fifth Annual Review of Criminal Procedure* pp. 1237–1239 (1996).

52. Id. at 815.

53. See Robert P. Mosteller, "Remaking Confrontation Clause and Hearsay Doctrine Under the Challenge of Child Sexual Abuse Prosecutions." 1993 *University of Illinois Law Review* pp. 691–807 (1993).

54. *White* v. *Illinois,* 502 U.S. 346 (1992).

55. Cf. *United States* v. *N.B.,* 59 F.3d 771 (8th Cir. 1995).

56. Supra note 51 at 1243–1248.

57. *Washington* v. *Texas,* 388 U.S. 14 (1967).

58. *Chambers* v. *Mississippi,* 410 U.S. 284 (1973).

59. Id. at 302.

60. *Powell* v. *Alabama,* 287 U.S. 45 (1932).

61. Id. at 69.

62. *Betts* v. *Brady,* 316 U.S. 455 (1942).

63. See Pascal F. Calogero, Jr., "The Right to Counsel and Indigent Defendants." 41 *Loyola Law Review* pp. 265–278 (1995).

64. *Gideon* v. *Wainright,* 372 U.S. 335 (1963).

65. Id. at 344.

66. *Argersinger* v. *Hamlin,* 407 U.S. 25 (1972).

67. Id. at 36–37.

68. Id. at 37.

69. Id. at 40.

70. *Scott* v. *Illinois,* 440 U.S. 367 (1979).

71. See Vermont R. Crim. P. 44.

72. *Douglas* v. *California,* 372 U.S. 353 (1963).

73. *Ross* v. *Moffit,* 417 U.S. 600 (1974).

74. See Michael J. Stacchini, "Narrowing the Sixth Amendment Guarantee of Counsel." 75 *Boston University Law Review* pp. 1233–1256 (1995).

75. *Faretta* v. *California,* 422 U.S. 806 (1975).

76. Id. at 807.

77. *Patterson* v. *Illinois,* 487 U.S. 285 (1988).

78. See John F. Decker, "The Sixth Amendment Right to Shoot Oneself in the Foot: An Assessment of the Guarantee of Self-Representation Twenty Years After Faretta." 6 *Seton Hall Constitutional Law Journal* pp. 483–598 (1996).

79. *McKaskle* v. *Wiggens,* 465 U.S. 168 (1984).

80. See Teresa A. Scott, "The Role of Standby Counsel: The Road From Faretta to Wiggens." *Howard Law Journal* pp. 1799–1811 (1984).

81. *Strickland* v. *Washington,* 466 U.S. 688 (1984).

82. Bonnie Dunninger and Andrew S. Locker, "Right to Counsel." 84 *The Georgetown Law Journal Twenty-Fifth Annual Review of Criminal Procedure* pp. 1126–1127 (1996).

83. See Jennifer N. Foster, "Using Hindsight to Evaluate Prejudice in Claims of Ineffective Assistance of Counsel." 72 *North Carolina Law Review* pp. 1369–1398 (1994).

84. See *Bryant* v. *Scott,* 28 F.3d 1411 (5th Cir. 1994).

85. *In re Winship,* 397 U.S. 358 (1970).

86. For an excellent discussion of these issues, see Rolando V. delCarmen, *Criminal Procedure Law and Practice,* 3d ed. (Belmont, Cal.: Wadsworth, 1995), pp. 394–395.

87. See Normal J. Finkel and Christopher Slobogin, "Insanity, Justification, and Culpability: Toward a Unifying Schema." 19 *Law and Human Behavior* pp. 447–464 (1995).

88. See Karla L. Leeper and Jon Burschke, "The Prevalence of the Abuse Excuse: Media Hype of Cause for Concern." 17 *Communication and the Law* pp. 47–65 (1995).

89. Eric Silver, "Punishment or Treatment? Comparing the Lengths of Confinement of Successful and

Unsuccessful Insanity Defendants." 19 *Law and Human Behavior* pp. 375–388 (1995).

90. *Parke* v. *Riley,* 113 S.Ct. 517 (1992).

91. Angili Soni and Michael E. McCann, "Consequences of a Plea." 84 *The Georgetown Law Journal Twenty-Fifth Annual Review of Criminal Procedure* p. 1049 (1996).

92. See Robert E. Scott and William J. Stuntz, "Plea Bargaining as Contract." 101 *Yale Law Journal* pp. 1909–1968 (1992).

93. *Ricketts* v. *Adamson,* 483 U.S. 1 (1987).

94. *Santobello* v. *New York,* 404 U.S. 257 (1971).

95. *Bordenkircher* v. *Hayes,* 434 U.S. 357 (1978).

96. *Parker* v. *North Carolina,* 397 U.S. 790 (1970).

97. See Stephen J. Schulhofer, "Plea Bargaining as a Disaster." 101 *Yale Law Journal* pp. 1979–2009 (1992).

98. Teresa White Carns and John Kruse, "A Reevaluation of Alaska's Plea Bargaining Ban." 8 *Alaska Law Review* pp. 27–69 (1991).

13 A Defendant's Rights Following Conviction— Sentencing, Appeals, and Habeas Corpus Review

---

Outline

Key Terms

affirm,   390

bifurcated trial,   377

collateral attack on sentencing,   393

concurrent sentence,   381

consecutive sentence,   381

contemporaneous objection rule,   390

corporal punishment,   388

felony-murder doctrine,   376

habeas corpus lawsuit,   393

harmless error rule,   391

mitigating factors,   378

parole,   384

plain error rule,   390

probation,   387

proportionality principle,   376

remand,   391

reverse ,   390

rules of appellate procedure,   390

sentencing disparity,   384

sentencing enhancement,   381

writ of habeas corpus,   393

Earlier chapters have considered a defendant's procedural rights before and during a criminal trial. Chapter 13 shifts our focus to a defendant's rights once he or she has been convicted of a crime. It therefore considers three important post-conviction processes: sentencing, appeals, and habeas corpus review. Each of these processes will be discussed separately.

Sentencing

Once a defendant is convicted, a sentence must be imposed. The primary responsibility for setting the range of possible sentences belongs to the legislatures, which specify appropriate sentences for particular crimes. Legislative discretion to direct sentencing is limited by the Eighth Amendment's cruel and unusual punishment clause, however, which provides: "[e]xcessive bail shall not be required, nor excessive fines imposed, nor cruel and unusual punishments inflicted."

The cruel and unusual punishment clause is binding on state proceedings through the Fourteenth Amendment's due process clause. In *Robinson* v. *California,*[1] the Supreme Court held unconstitutional a California statute that made it a crime to "be addicted to the use of narcotics." The Court further held that the Eighth Amendment's cruel and unusual punishment clause was binding on state proceedings. Excerpts from *Robinson* v. *California* are presented in Highlight 13.1.

Robinson's reasoning may be extended to any law that attempts to make a *status* unlawful. The problem is that a statute that attempts to outlaw a status does not require the accused to commit a criminal act. For example, a law that attempts to make it a crime to have AIDS, or to be afflicted with venereal disease, is clearly unconstitutional.[2] In contrast, statutes that make it unlawful to commit sodomy or to be intoxicated in a public place are constitutional because such laws criminalize *conduct,* not a person's status.[3]

The Supreme Court has identified three factors that may render a punishment a violation of the Eighth Amendment's cruel and unusual punishment clause:

1. if the punishment inflicts unnecessary or wanton pain;
2. if it is unacceptable in society;
3. if it is excessive or grossly disproportionate to the offense.

Several major types of penal sanctions are lawful in U.S. justice systems. These include the death penalty (capital punishment), incarceration in a prison or jail, fines, and conditional freedom in the community (probation).

The Death Penalty

Capital punishment is the most controversial form of punishment in U.S. justice systems. In 1995, there were 2,960 men and 49 women awaiting execution in the United States.[4] There are many arguments for and against the death penalty,[5] although an extended discussion of these issues is beyond the scope of this text. Highlight 13.2 presents a synopsis of these arguments.

Highlight 13.1

Robinson v. *California,* 370 U.S. 660, 666-668 (1962)

 It is unlikely that any State at this moment in history would attempt to make it a criminal offense for a person to be mentally ill, or a leper, or to be afflicted with a venereal disease. A State might determine that the general health and welfare require that the victims of these and other human afflictions be dealt with by compulsory treatment, involving quarantine, confinement, or sequestration. But, in light of contemporary human knowledge, a law which made a criminal offense of such a disease would doubtless be universally thought to be an infliction of cruel and unusual punishment. . . .

We cannot but consider the statute before us as of the same category. In this Court counsel for the State recognized that narcotic addiction is an illness. Indeed, it is apparently an illness which may be contracted innocently or involuntarily. We hold that a state law which imprisons a person thus afflicted as a criminal, even though he had never touched any narcotic drug within the State or been guilty or any irregular behavior there, inflicts a cruel and unusual punishment in violation of the Fourteenth Amendment. To be sure, imprisonment of ninety days is not, in the abstract, a punishment which is either cruel or unusual. But the question cannot be considered in the abstract. Even one day in prison would be a cruel and unusual punishment for the "crime" of having a common cold.

We are not unmindful that the vicious evils of the narcotics traffic have occasioned the grave concern of government. There are, as we have said, countless fronts on which those evils may be legitimately attacked. We deal in this case only with an individual provision of a particularized local law as it has so far been interpreted by the California courts.

Reversed.

Constitutionality.   In 1976, *Gregg* v. *Georgia*[6] held that the death penalty is permitted by the U.S. Constitution. This proposition is subject to several important restrictions, however. First, it may not inflict unnecessary pain. *Enmund* v. *Florida*[7] held that a sentence inflicts unnecessary pain if it fails to further important social goals of retribution or deterrence. U.S. Courts have upheld several different forms of execution against challenges that they inflict unnecessary pain. Presently, the following modes of execution are permitted in the United States: electrocution, the gas chamber, lethal injection, hanging, and a firing squad.[8] If a state tried to use a more extreme form of execution, it is likely to be held unconstitutional. For example, suppose that a state's legislature passed a law requiring that convicted murderers be starved to death. Such a form of execution is likely to be held unconstitutional because it inflicts unnecessary pain and a lingering death. Moreover, in considering the factors that may render a punishment a violation of the Eighth Amendment, this mode of execution is likely to be unacceptable to a majority of the members of society.

Another constitutional limitation on capital punishment in U.S. justice systems is that it may be imposed solely for murder. In *Coker* v. *Georgia,*[9] the Supreme Court

---

Highlight 13.2

Synopsis of Arguments For and Against the Death Penalty

Arguments for Capital Punishment

The major arguments in support of the death penalty are that (1) the Bible upholds this form of punishment ("He who kills a man shall be put to death." Leviticus 24:7); (2) it has a deterrent effect on murder and other serious crimes; (3) most states and the majority of nations provide for the death penalty; (4) certainty of punishment is an essential ingredient of deterrence; (5) it costs more to keep a man in prison for a long term than to execute him; (6) rehabilitation is not an effective substitute for the death penalty; (7) a life sentence is usually not for one's natural life, but rather for a varied term of years; (8) society has a right to seek revenge for vicious crimes; (9) intricate legal safeguards virtually preclude the execution of innocent persons; and (10) it is not "cruel and unusual" punishment.

Arguments Against Capital Punishment

Opponents of capital punishment argue that (1) it violates the Biblical commandment, "Thou shall not kill"; (2) it is not an effective (or measurable) deterrent to murder or other serious crimes; (3) it has been disproportionately imposed on the poor and nonwhite; (4) the per capita cost of exccution is higher than imprisonment; (5) it is a primitive notion rooted in revenge; (6) innocent men could be executed; (7) a civilized society upholds the sanctity of human life; (8) paroled and pardoned murderers are the least likely to recidivate; (9) it undermines rehabilitative and other penologic goals; (10) it is unthinkable that death, as a legal sentence, should be subject to human discretion; and (11) it is "cruel and unusual" punishment.

[Excerpts from *The Supreme Court and the Criminal Process: Cases and Comments* by Peter W. Lewis and Kenneth D. Peoples, copyright © 1978 by Holt, Rinehart and Winston, reprinted by permission of the publisher.]

---

held that the death penalty for the crime of rape was "grossly disproportionate" to offense. This is termed the **proportionality principle.** The Court has also held that the states may not impose the death penalty for the crimes of robbery and kidnapping.[10]

Capital punishment will be held to violate the proportionality principle[11] if it is applied to certain groups of people, regardless of the crimes they commit.[12] In *Thompson* v. *Oklahoma,*[13] the Supreme Court in a plurality opinion held that a state may not impose the death penalty on an individual who was fifteen years of age when he committed murder. *Stanford* v. *Kentucky,*[14] held that this same principle does not apply to defendants who were sixteen years of age when they committed their crimes.[15] Moreover, in *Tison* v. *Arizona,* the Supreme Court held that defendants who are charged with felony-murder may receive the death penalty only if they intend to kill or show "reckless disregard for human life."[16] The **felony-murder doctrine** permits any person who joins in the commission of a felony that results in death to be charged with murder even if the death was unintended. Many states limit the application of the felony-murder doctrine to a limited category of the most dangerous types of crimes.

In *Perry* v. *Lynaugh,*[17] the Supreme Court held that a mentally retarded person may foster the criminal intent necessary to merit capital punishment. A person may not, however, be executed if he or she becomes insane prior to execution.[18] The reason

Source: UPI/Corbis Bettmann

for this rule is that a person should know why he or she is being punished, and a sane individual may be able to establish his or her innocence or provide some other legitimate reason why the execution should not take place.

Death Penalty Laws.   Imposing the death penalty is an awesome responsibility. Consequently, the Supreme Court has required that the death penalty sentencing process be even more reliable than the traditional sentencing process.[19] To lessen the risk that the death penalty will be imposed mistakenly, the Court has placed two general requirements on the capital sentencing process. First, a state's legislature must develop a statute that restricts the sentencer's discretion. This narrows the group of persons that a judge or jury may find to be eligible for the death penalty and justifies the imposition of a more severe sentence on the defendant than on others found guilty of murder. Second, a state may not limit the sentencer's consideration of any relevant evidence that may mitigate against imposing the death penalty in the particular case.[20]

Restricting the Eligible Group of Persons.   Some states require that the trial be separated from the sentencing proceeding. This is termed a **bifurcated trial.** At the sentencing hearing, the sentencer must restrict the group of persons eligible to receive the death penalty by determining if aggravating factors are present. These are circumstances that make the particular crime so heinous that the defendant merits the death penalty.[21] The sentencer must find at least one aggravating factor in order to sentence a defendant to death. Highlight 13.3 presents the State of California's list of aggravating factors that the sentencer may consider in determining if a particular defendant merits the death penalty. Page 380 presents a photograph of Polly Klaas, a child murder victim. Richard Allen Davis was sentenced to death for her murder. In that case the jury found that Davis had murdered Polly Klaas following a sexual assault. This was an aggravating factor that justified the imposition of the death penalty.

Mitigating Factors.   State death penalty laws must allow the sentencer to consider *any* evidence that may mitigate against imposing the death penalty in the particular case, such as a defendant's past history of mental impairment and childhood abuse.[22] These are termed **mitigating factors.** In the Polly Klaas murder case, Richard Allen Davis's attorney introduced evidence at the sentencing phase of the trial that indicated the defendant had been abused as a child. Apparently the jury did not find this evidence highly persuasive because it recommended that Richard Allen Davis be sentenced to death in the gas chamber.

Qualified Jurors in Death Penalty Cases.   Suppose that a person were unalterably opposed to capital punishment for religious or moral reasons and could not vote to impose it under any circumstances. Or, suppose that someone believed so strongly in the death penalty that he or she would vote to impose a death sentence for every defendant who was convicted of murder, regardless of the circumstances. Should either of these types of individuals be permitted to participate as a juror in a death penalty case? In *Wainright* v. *Witt,*[23] the Supreme Court held that members of a potential jury who are unalterably opposed to the death penalty may be excused by a challenge for cause. This is because a state has a legitimate interest in maintaining its death penalty statute.[24] Likewise, potential jurors who would always vote for the death penalty and could not individualize a death penalty decision may be excused by a challenge for cause as well.[25]

Given the preceding rules, one issue that may be raised is whether a jury will be biased toward imposing the death penalty, if all potential jurors on a jury panel who are opposed to the death penalty are excused. The Supreme Court rejected this argument, however, in *Lockhart* v. *McCree.*[26]

Federal Death Penalty Law.   In 1994, the U.S. Congress passed a new federal death penalty law.[27] The Act allows the death penalty for nine federal crimes, including the assassination of high-ranking government personnel. As of this writing, no person has yet been executed based on this statute.

Incarceration

A period of incarceration in a jail or a prison is imposed often as a penalty for a crime. The difference between the two types of facilities is significant. Jails typically hold

---

Highlight 13.3

California's Death Penalty Statute
Cal. Pen. Code Section 190.3

 If the defendant has been found guilty of murder in the first degree, and a special circumstance has been charged and found to be true, or if the defendant may be subject to the death penalty after having been found guilty of violating subdivision (a) of Section 1672 of the Military and Veterans Code or Sections 37, 128, 219, or 4500 of this code, the trier of fact shall determine whether the penalty shall be death or confinement in state prison for a term of life without the possibility of parole. In the proceedings on the question of penalty, evidence may be presented by both the people and the defendant as to any matter relevant to aggravation, mitigation, and sentence including, but not limited to, the nature and circumstances of the present offense, any prior felony conviction or convictions whether or not such conviction or convictions involved a crime of violence, the presence or absence of other criminal activity by the defendant which involved the use or attempted use of force or violence or which involved the express or implied threat to use force or violence, and the defendant's character, background, history, mental condition and physical condition.

However, no evidence shall be admitted regarding other criminal activity by the defendant which did not involve the use or attempted use of force or violence or which did not involve the express or implied threat to use force or violence. As used in this section, criminal activity does not require a conviction.

However, in no event shall evidence of prior criminal activity be admitted for an offense for which the defendant was prosecuted and acquitted. The restriction on the use of this evidence is intended to apply only to proceedings pursuant to this section and is not intended to affect statutory or decisional law allowing such evidence to be used in any other proceedings.

Except for evidence in proof of the offense or special circumstances which subject a defendant to the death penalty, no evidence may be presented by the prosecution in aggravation unless notice of the evidence to be introduced has been given to the defendant within a reasonable period of time as determined by the court, prior to trial. Evidence may be introduced without such notice in rebuttal to evidence introduced by the defendant in mitigation.

The trier of fact shall be instructed that a sentence of confinement to state prison for a term of life without the possibility of parole may in future after sentence is imposed, be commuted or modified to a sentence that includes the possibility of parole by the Governor of the State of California.

In determining the penalty, the trier of fact shall take into account any of the following factors if relevant:

(a) The circumstances of the crime of which the defendant was convicted in the present proceeding and the existence of any special circumstances found to be true pursuant to Section 190.1.

(b) The presence or absence of criminal activity by the defendant which involved the use or attempted use of force or violence or the express or implied threat to use force or violence.

(c) The presence or absence of any prior felony conviction.

(d) Whether or not the offense was committed while the defendant was under the influence of extreme mental or emotional disturbance.

(e) Whether or not the victim was a participant in the defendant's homicidal conduct or consented to the homicidal act.

(f) Whether or not the offense was committed under circumstances which the defendant reasonably believed to be a moral justification or extenuation for his conduct.

(g) Whether or not defendant acted under extreme duress or under the substantial domination of another person.

(Continued)

(Concluded)

(h) Whether or not at the time of the offense the capacity of the defendant to appreciate the criminality of his conduct or to conform his conduct to the requirements of law was impaired as a result of mental disease or defect, or the affects of intoxication.

(i) The age of the defendant at the time of the crime.

(j) Whether or not the defendant was an accomplice to the offense and his participation in the commission of the offense was relatively minor.

(k) Any other circumstance which extenuates the gravity of the crime even though it is not a legal excuse for the crime.

After having heard and received all of the evidence, and after having heard and considered the arguments of counsel, the trier of fact shall consider, take into account and be guided by the aggravating and mitigating circumstances referred to in this section, and shall impose a sentence of death if the trier of fact concludes that the aggravating circumstances outweigh the mitigating circumstances. If the trier of fact determines that the mitigating circumstances outweigh the aggravating circumstances the trier of fact shall impose a sentence of confinement in state prison for a term of life without the possibility of parole.

(Added by § 8 of Initiative Measure approved Nov. 7, 1978.)

Source: Reuters Corbis-Bettmann

persons awaiting trial and those convicted of minor offenses or misdemeanors. The penalties for these offenses normally do not exceed incarceration for more than one year. Prisons typically house persons convicted of felonies, who are sentenced to serve more than one year in prison.

Often, defendants are convicted of multiple offenses. In most states, a judge may determine if a defendant is to serve a **concurrent sentence** or a **consecutive sentence.** Concurrent sentences are served at the same time. For example, suppose that a defendant was convicted of committing two burglaries and received a sentence of five years' imprisonment on each charge. In most jurisdictions, the sentencing judge, at his or her discretion, could sentence the defendant to serve the terms concurrently, meaning that the defendant would have served his or her entire term of incarceration after five years. If, however, the judge decided to impose consecutive sentences, the five-year terms would be "stacked"—after the defendant had served the first five-year term he or she would then be required to serve the second five-year sentence. A trial judge may consider any number of factors in deciding which sentence to impose, including the defendant's prior record and whether he or she shows remorse for the criminal behavior. Moreover, in *United States* v. *Watts,*[28] the Supreme Court held that during a trial's sentencing phase a judge may even consider a defendant's past acquitted conduct, as long as the prosecution proves the earlier behavior by a preponderance of the evidence. The prior conduct may then be used to decide whether to impose a more stringent penalty. This is termed a **sentencing enhancement,** which does not violate the Fifth Amendment's double jeopardy clause because, according to the Supreme Court, it does "not punish a defendant for crimes of which he was not convicted, but rather increase[s] his sentence because of the manner in which he committed the crime of conviction."[29]

Trial judges have substantial discretion during the sentencing process, and will sometimes state the reasons for deciding to impose a particular sentence. Highlight 13.4 presents a transcript of a sentencing colloquy in a federal case from the Territory of New Mexico, *United States* v. *Gonzales,* in 1881.

There are several different approaches to sentences of incarceration. These include determinate (fixed) sentencing, mandatory sentencing, presumptive sentencing, and indeterminate sentencing. Table 13.1 illustrates the differences among these approaches.

United States justice systems sentence many persons to terms of confinement. In fact, the U.S. prison population has been increasing at an alarming rate. According to the U.S. Bureau of Justice Statistics (BJS), 114,579 persons are serving sentences of incarceration in U.S. correctional facilities in 1996.[30] That number is projected to increase to 133,534 by the year 2000.[31]

The Eighth Amendment's cruel and unusual punishment clause is important to those already incarcerated in jails and prisons throughout the United States as well. The Supreme Court has held that the conditions in a state's prison system or jails may not be such that they violate inmates' basic constitutional rights. Moreover, inmates lose only those rights that are inconsistent with their status as prisoners. Therefore, they retain many basic rights including: safe and tolerable living conditions, access to the courts, worship, and other rights consistent with their status as prisoners.[32]

Highlight 13.4

United States v. *Gonzales* (1881), United States District Court, New Mexico Territory Sessions

 Jose Manuel Miguel Xavier Gonzales, in a few short weeks it will be spring. The snows of winter will flee away. The ice will vanish. And the air will become soft and balmy. In short, Jose Manuel Miguel Xavier Gonzales, the annual miracle of the years will awaken and come to pass, but you won't be there.

The rivulet will run its soaring course to the sea. The timid desert flowers will put forth their tender shoots. The glorious valleys of this imperial domain will blossom as the rose. Still, you won't be here to see.

From every tree top some wild woods songster will carol his mating song. Butterflies will sport in the sunshine. The busy bee will hum happy as it pursues its accustomed vocation. The gentle breeze will tease the tissels of the wild grasses, and all nature, Jose Manuel Miguel Xavier Gonzales, will be glad but you. You won't be here to enjoy it because I command the sheriff or some other officers of the country to lead you out to some remote spot, swing you by the neck from a knotting bough of some sturdy oak, and let you hang until you are dead.

And then, Jose Manuel Miguel Xavier Gonzales, I further command that such officer or officers retire quickly from your dangling corpse, that vultures may descend from the heavens upon your filthy body until nothing shall remain but bare, bleached bones of a cold-blooded, copper-colored, blood-thirsty, throat-cutting, chili-eating, sheep-herding, murdering son-of-a-bitch.

On the other hand, prison authorities must be able to maintain order and discipline. In *Sandin* v. *O'Conner*,[33] the Supreme Court held that the federal courts should be flexible and show deference to state prison officials who face a difficult task. Prison inmates' constitutional rights may be limited by corrections administrators if there is a good reason to justify a particular restriction.[34] For example, inmates' violent behavior must be controlled. If prison administrators institute a program of unannounced cell searches designed to discover contraband and weapons, it will be upheld by the courts even if it infringes on inmates' privacy rights.[35]

In *Bell* v. *Wolfish*,[36] the Supreme Court upheld the following institutional rules that were developed by correctional administrators at New York City's Metropolitan Correctional Center to govern inmate conduct: (1) a prohibition against receiving personal packages from outside the institution; (2) a rule allowing inmates to receive books and magazines only if they were sent directly by a publisher; (3) a rule requiring body cavity searches of inmates following contact visits with outsiders; (4) a program of unannounced cell searches; and (5) the practice of placing two inmates in a cell designed for one (double bunking). The Court held that all of these measures were justified by the "need to maintain order and institutional security."[37] Moreover, the challenge to these rules was brought by inmates who were awaiting trial, pretrial detainees. These inmates had not yet been convicted of a criminal offense. One would expect that the administrative restrictions that may be placed on the behavior of convicted offenders would be even greater than those that were placed on pretrial detainees in *Bell* v. *Wolfish*.

TABLE 13.1 **Different Approaches to Sentencing**

Approach	Term of Confinement	Penal Rationale
Determinate	Legislature fixes term; judge cannot modify	Punishment and retribution
Mandatory	Legislature fixes term; judge may suspend, or impose probation	Punishment, but some individual treatment
Presumptive	Legislature fixes usual sentence; judge may modify but must specify reasons for deviation	Punishment, individual treatment
Indeterminate	No fixed term; corrections experts release individual when rehabilitated	Individual treatment, rehabilitation

Eighth Amendment Challenges to Sentences of Imprisonment.   Sentences of incarceration are subject to most of the same restrictions that bind capital sentences—they must not inflict unnecessary or wanton pain, and must be acceptable to society. The Supreme Court has given congress and state legislatures great flexibility, however, to determine appropriate terms of confinement for specific crimes. In 1983, *Solem* v. *Helm*[38] set aside a sentence of life imprisonment without the possibility of parole because it was disproportionate under the Eighth Amendment. The defendant had been convicted under a South Dakota recidivist statute for successive offenses that included three convictions of burglary, one of obtaining money by false pretenses, one of grand larceny, one of third-offense driving while intoxicated, and one of writing a bad check with intent to defraud. The Supreme Court held that because the sentence was disproportionate to the offenses, it violated the Eighth Amendment.

In 1991, however, in *Harmelin* v. *Michigan*[39] the Court reversed *Solem* v. *Helm* because it "was simply wrong."[40] Harmelin was convicted of possessing 672 grams of cocaine and was sentenced to a mandatory term of life in prison without the possibility of parole. On appeal, he claimed that his sentence was cruel and unusual punishment because it was disproportionate to the offense and because the sentencing judge was required to impose it, without taking into account the particularized circumstances of the crime and the criminal. The Supreme Court held that "the Eighth Amendment is not a ratchet, whereby a temporary consensus on leniency for a particular crime fixes a permanent constitutional maximum, disabling the States from giving effect to altered beliefs and responding to changed social conditions . . . ."[41] Further, the Court refused to extend proportionality analysis, which is used in death penalty cases, to cases involving sentences of imprisonment because "the Eighth Amendment contains no proportionality guarantee."[42]

The cases discussed above involved defendants who were sentenced to terms of incarceration under valid state and federal sentencing laws. They indicate that an appeal of a sentence of imprisonment based on the Eighth Amendment's cruel and unusual punishment clause is unlikely to succeed because the Supreme Court will defer normally to a legislature's judgment of what constitutes an appropriate punishment for a particular crime.[43] There remains a possibility, however, that a defendant's sentence may be so outrageous that it constitutes cruel and unusual punishment. For example, if a defendant were sentenced to five years' imprisonment for jaywalking, a Supreme Court majority is likely to hold that it violates the Eighth Amendment, even if the sentence were authorized by state law.[44]

The Federal Sentencing Guidelines.   Historically, one of the major criticisms of sentencing policies in U.S. justice systems has been a lack of consistency. Similar defendants, who may have committed virtually identical offenses, have received wildly different sentences for their crimes in different jurisdictions and sometimes even within the same jurisdiction. This phenomenon is termed **sentencing disparity.** Sentencing disparity offends U.S. ideals of fair treatment under the law. If everything else is equal, two persons who commit the same offense should receive a similar punishment.

The Federal Sentencing Guidelines, which were designed in part to eliminate sentencing disparity, specify definite sentences for specific federal crimes.[45] The Guidelines contain a sentencing table with 43 offense levels and six criminal history categories. The Supreme Court, in *Mistretta* v. *United States,*[46] upheld the constitutionality of the Federal Sentencing Guidelines.

In applying the Sentencing Guidelines, a judge must first determine the applicable offense level. Next, he or she will determine the defendant's criminal history. The highest criminal history category is termed "career offenders." As you would expect, these offenders receive the most stringent sentences. Under the Guidelines, an offender is classified as a career offender if (1) he or she was at least eighteen years of age at the time of the offense; (2) the charged offense is a crime of violence or one involving a controlled substance; and (3) if he or she has at least two prior felony convictions for similar crimes.[47] Next, the sentencing judge determines the defendant's sentence by selecting the range in the Guidelines table that is appropriate for the specific offense level and the defendant's criminal history category. Table 13.2 presents a federal sentencing guidelines table.

A simple example will help to illustrate how this sentencing table works. Suppose that Paul, a career offender with a prior conviction for importing marijuana, is convicted of conspiracy to distribute two tons of cocaine that he had attempted to import from a South American country. In the past, Paul has served separate prison terms of five years and three years for various felony drug offenses. He was released from a federal prison last year. Based on the quantity of the cocaine involved in this case, and assuming that there are no aggravating or mitigating factors, Paul's base offense level is 36.[48] Because Paul satisfies the "Career Offender" criteria, his criminal history category would be Category VI.[49] Using the sentencing table presented in Table 13.2, at a base level offense of 36, with a Level VI criminal history, Paul would receive 324–405 months (27–33 years) in federal prison.

Although the Federal Sentencing Guidelines appear to have reduced sentencing disparity, they have received substantial criticism. Opponents of the Guidelines argue that they often mandate excessively long prison terms for nonviolent offenders and effectively eliminate judicial discretion.

Parole is Abolished Under the Federal Guidelines.   **Parole** is a process in which convicted offenders who have served part of their prison sentences may be released

TABLE **13.2**   **Sentencing Guidelines Sentencing Table**

Offense Level	Criminal History Category					
	I *0 or 1*	*II* *2 or 3*	*III* *4, 5, 6*	*IV* *7, 8, 9*	*V* *10, 11, 12*	*VI* *13 or more*
1	0–1	0–2	0–3	0–4	0–5	0–6
2	0–2	0–3	0–4	0–5	0–6	1–7
3	0–3	0–4	0–5	0–6	2–8	3–9
4	0–4	0–5	0–6	2–8	4–10	6–12
5	0–5	0–6	1–7	4–10	6–12	9–15
6	0–6	1–7	2–8	6–12	9–15	12–18
7	1–7	2–8	4–10	8–14	12–18	15–21
8	2–8	4–10	6–12	10–16	15–21	18–24
9	4–10	6–12	8–14	12–18	18–24	21–27
10	6–12	8–14	10–16	15–21	21–27	24–30
11	8–14	10–16	12–18	18–24	24–30	27–33
12	10–16	12–18	15–21	21–27	27–33	30–37
13	12–18	15–21	18–24	24–30	30–37	33–41
14	15–21	18–24	21–27	27–33	33–41	37–46
15	18–24	21–27	24–30	30–37	37–46	41–51
16	21–27	24–30	27–33	33–41	41–51	46–57
17	24–30	27–33	30–37	37–46	46–57	51–63
18	27–33	30–37	33–41	41–51	51–63	57–71
19	30–37	33–41	37–46	46–57	57–71	63–78
20	33–41	37–46	41–51	51–63	63–78	70–87
21	37–46	41–51	46–57	57–71	70–87	77–96
22	41–51	46–57	51–63	63–78	77–96	84–105
23	46–57	51–63	57–71	70–87	84–105	92–115
24	51–63	57–71	63–78	77–96	92–115	100–125
25	57–71	63–78	70–87	84–105	100–125	110–137
26	63–78	70–87	78–97	92–115	110–137	120–150
27	70–87	78–97	87–108	100–125	120–150	130–162
28	78–97	87–108	97–121	110–137	130–162	140–175
29	87–108	97–121	108–135	121–151	140–175	151–188
30	97–121	108–135	121–151	135–168	151–188	168–210
31	108–135	121–151	135–168	151–188	168–210	188–235
32	121–151	135–168	151–188	168–210	188–235	210–262
33	135–168	151–188	168–210	188–235	210–262	235–293
34	151–188	168–210	188–235	210–262	235–293	262–327
35	168–210	188–235	210–262	235–293	262–327	292–365
36	188–235	210–262	235–293	262–327	292–365	324–405
37	210–262	235–293	262–327	292–365	324–405	360–life
38	235–293	262–327	292–365	324–405	360–life	360–life
39	262–327	292–365	324–405	360–life	360–life	360–life

TABLE 13.2   *concluded*

Offense Level	Criminal History Category					
	I *0 or 1*	*II* *2 or 3*	*III* *4, 5, 6*	*IV* *7, 8, 9*	*V* *10, 11, 12*	*VI* *13 or more*
40	292–365	324–405	360–life	360–life	360–life	360–life
41	324–405	360–life	360–life	360–life	360–life	360–life
42	360–life	360–life	360–life	360–life	360–life	360–life
43	life	life	life	life	life	life

Application Notes:

1. The Offense Level (1–43) forms the vertical axis of the Sentencing Table. The Criminal History Category (I–VI) forms the horizontal axis of the Table. The intersection of the Offense Level and Criminal History Category displays the Guideline Range in months of imprisonment. "Life" means life imprisonment. For example, the guideline range applicable to a defendant with an Offense Level of 15 and a Criminal History Category of III is 24–30 months of imprisonment.

2. In rare cases, a total offense level of less than 1 or more than 43 may result from application of the guidelines. A total offense level of less than 1 is to be treated as an offense level of 1. An offense level of more than 43 is to be treated as an offense level of 43.

3. The Criminal History Category is determined by the total criminal history points from Chapter Four, Part A. The total criminal history points associated with each Criminal History Category are shown under each Criminal History Category in the Sentencing Table.

into the community under the supervision of parole authorities. The new Federal Sentencing Guidelines were established pursuant to the Sentencing Reform Act of 1984.[50] That law requires a convicted offender to serve the entire term of his or her sentence. For offenders sentenced under the Federal Sentencing Guidelines, parole is no longer an option. In some cases, however, federal inmates may be released into the community before they have served their entire sentences. The federal corrections system continues to permit selected inmates to participate in furlough programs that require them to work, attend school, or participate in various other activities.

Fines

Most of us at one time or another have paid a fine for parking violations, motor vehicle infractions, or various other minor offenses. For most such offenses, legislative bodies set a range of possible fines. Judges have discretion to levy fines within the range set by the legislature.

The Eighth Amendment's text prohibits excessive fines. In general, the Supreme Court has deferred to the legislature and has provided little guidance about precisely what constitutes an excessive fine. It is clear, however, that the Constitution will not permit imposing a more stringent punishment on a poor person than on a wealthier one.[51] In *Williams* v. *Illinois,*[52] the defendant was convicted of a minor theft offense.

Williams was sentenced to prison for one year, a $500 fine, and court costs of $5. Williams was unable to pay the $505 fine, and he was held in jail for an additional 101 days *beyond the maximum term* authorized for theft. The Supreme Court held that the State of Illinois had violated the Fourteenth Amendment's equal protection clause by holding Williams beyond the maximum term allowed by law for the offense because he could not pay the fine. The Court stated:

> [O]nce the State has defined the outer limits of incarcerations necessary to satisfy its phenological interests and policies, it may not then subject a certain class of convicted defendants to a period of imprisonment beyond the statutory maximum solely by reason of their indigency.[53]

Williams means that an indigent defendant may not be sentenced to an *additional* term of incarceration beyond the statutory maximum because he or she is unable to pay a fine. An indigent defendant may, however, be sentenced to an additional term of confinement due to his or her inability to pay a fine as long as the period of incarceration falls within the maximum term allowed by the statute for the particular offense. For example, suppose that Joan, who is indigent, is convicted of shoplifting and is sentenced to 30 days in jail and a $200 fine. She is unable to pay the fine. The statutory maximum term for shoplifting in that state is a six-month jail sentence and a $1,000 fine. The state has a law that provides that an inmate may be required to serve jail time in lieu of a fine at a rate of $20 per day. In these circumstances, Joan may be required lawfully to spend an additional 10 days in jail due to her inability to pay her fine. This is because her total period of confinement (40 days) would not exceed the statutory maximum period of six months in jail.

Conditional Freedom in the Community

Another type of penal sanction that is used often in U.S. justice systems is conditional freedom in the community, or **probation.** It is a sentence that requires the supervised and conditional release into the community of a person convicted of a crime. Most convicted offenders are placed on some form of probation. According to the U.S. Justice Department, 1,084,882 offenders were serving sentences of probation in 1993.[54] Often, different forms of conditional freedom are combined. For example, shock probation and electronic monitoring of an offender sentenced to home confinement are increasingly frequent penal alternatives.

An important point about probation is that it involves the *conditional* release of an offender into the community—in order to be eligible to receive probation, an offender must agree to abide by specified contractual terms. A typical probationer's conditions of probation may include:

1. Refraining from drug and alcohol usage.
2. Agreement to submit to drug and alcohol testing.
3. Agreement not to go to bars and other places where alcohol is served.
4. Attendance at regular meetings with probation officers.
5. Not committing additional violations of the law.
6. Making restitution to the victim.

7. Agreement not to associate with criminals or former offenders.
8. Agreement to remain employed and to support his or her dependents.
9. Agreement not to leave the jurisdiction without a probation officer's permission;
10. Attendance at regular meeting of Alcoholic's Anonymous or other alcohol or drug treatment programs.

The terms of a probation agreement must be lawful and reasonably related to the offender's prospects for rehabilitation. Sentencing judges have substantial discretion to fashion appropriate probation conditions, however, and their determinations are rarely overturned by appellate courts.

It is important to note that a probation agreement is a contract between the probationer and corrections authorities. If a probationer breaks the probation contract, it may be terminated and he or she may be sentenced to a term of confinement.

A convicted offender has no constitutional right to probation. Rather, probation is a privilege. Even so, *Gagnon* v. *Scarpelli*[55] held that a probationer has certain procedural rights if probation authorities are seeking to revoke his or her probation:

1. Written notice of the alleged violation of the terms of probation.
2. Disclosure of the evidence against the probationer.
3. An opportunity to be heard in person and to present witnesses and documentary evidence.
4. A limited right to confront and cross-examine adverse witnesses.
5. A neutral and detached hearing body.
6. A written record of the evidence relied upon and the reasons for revoking probation.[56]

Gagnon v. *Scarpelli* did not require that an offender facing revocation of his or her probation be provided with counsel. The Court held that the "need for counsel must be made on a case-by-case basis in the exercise of a sound discretion by the state authority charged with responsibility for administering the probation and parole system."[57] Thus, counsel should be provided for an indigent defendant if the issues in a probation revocation case are complex or if he or she is unable to effectively present the case.

Corporal Punishment

Corporal punishment, or physical punishment, is not a lawful sentence for conviction of a crime in the United States.[58] In 1994, the issue of corporal punishment received widespread public attention when Michael Fay (see photo) was convicted of public vandalism in Singapore and was sentenced to receive six cane strokes. The sentence was later reduced to four strokes, after President Clinton appealed to the Government of Singapore.

Civil libertarians have criticized the corporal punishment process as a barbaric anachronism that has no place in U.S. justice systems. At least one well-known

Source: Reuters Corbis-Bettmann

criminologist, however, has argued that corporal punishment may be a better punishment method than traditional forms of imprisonment.[59]

The use of corporal punishment is unlawful in prisons as well. In 1968, in *Jackson v. Bishop,*[60] the U.S. Court of Appeals held that whipping prisoners violated the Eighth and Fourteenth Amendments. *Jackson*'s rationale for eliminating corporal punishment has been followed consistently by courts and legislatures that have outlawed these practices in U.S. penal institutions.[61]

Appeals

Convicted offenders may appeal their criminal convictions. Every state, by statute, provides for some type of appellate review of criminal cases. The Supreme Court has never held, however, that a convicted state offender has a *constitutional right* to an appeal of a criminal conviction. In fact, it has suggested in dictum that there is no such right.[62]

On appeal, attorneys for the defense and prosecution present arguments based on strictly legal issues—they do not relitigate the facts of a case, such as whether an accused was present in the state when the crime was committed. Appeals determine whether a trial judge committed some error. Examples of possible appellate issues include whether evidence obtained by police officers who had searched a suspect's car was improperly admitted, whether a confession was taken in violation of a suspect's *Miranda* warnings, or whether an accused was tried a second time for the same offense in violation of his or her right to be free from double jeopardy.

Because often technical legal issues are raised, it would be very difficult for even highly educated and sophisticated defendants to present an effective appeal. Consequently, in *Douglas* v. *California*,[63] the Supreme Court held that if a state's law grants an indigent offender a right to appeal a conviction, he or she must be provided with counsel for a *first* appeal. *Ross* v. *Moffit*[64] held that this same principle does not apply to later discretionary appeals, however. Moreover, *Griffin* v. *Illinois*[65] established that a state must pay for the cost of transcripts for the first appeal of a criminal conviction by an indigent person.

In order to file an appeal, attorneys must pay very close attention to the procedural rules of the jurisdiction where the case was tried. One rule that is important in all states and in the federal system is termed the **contemporaneous objection rule,** or timely objection requirement. This rule holds that in order to preserve an issue for a later appeal, an attorney must state an objection to admission of challenged evidence at a pretrial hearing or at the trial itself. If a proper objection is not made in a timely way, the issue may not be raised in a later appeal. A state's rules for filing appeals, often termed **rules of appellate procedure,** specify time limitations for filing motions and other documents, detail the form that such documents must use, and prescribe other rules that attorneys must follow closely. The failure to comply precisely with these rules may completely bar the appeal or result in dismissal of the case. For example, the Commonwealth of Pennsylvania requires that a notice that a defendant will appeal, termed a notice of appeal, must be filed within 30 days from the time that he or she is sentenced.[66]

An attorney's mistakes may not be fatal to a defendant's case in some circumstances, however. Many states and the federal government have developed a rule designed to prevent a convicted defendant from being penalized by the negligence or incompetence of his or her attorney. The **plain error rule** is an exception to the timely objection requirement, which permits a defendant to appeal an issue that was not raised properly at trial, if it affects his or her important constitutional rights.[67] For example, suppose that an attorney does not comply with a jurisdiction's contemporaneous objection rule and fails to object to the admission of a confession even though it was clearly obtained in violation of a defendant's rights. At the discretion of the appellate court, the defendant may still be permitted to appeal the admission of the confession, even though his or her attorney failed to object to the confession at trial. This rule is designed to prevent miscarriages of justice and to prevent defendants from being penalized for their attorneys' errors.

When appellate courts decide cases they may **affirm** the decision of a trial court, which means that the original decision stands. Sometimes an appellate court will **reverse** a decision of a lower court, which means that the lower court's decision is no longer binding on the parties. In some cases an appellate court may affirm a portion of a trial court's decision, but may reverse other parts of the same decision. In cases where trial courts have committed serious errors that have prejudiced a defendant's rights an appellate court may order that the case be dismissed. More often, however, if a decision is reversed by an appellate court it will **remand** the case, which means that it is returned to the trial court and may be retried.

This text's focus on cases that criminal defendants have successfully appealed may convey the impression that it is easy to win an appeal of a criminal case. That conclusion is wrong. The original verdict of the trial court is affirmed in the vast majority of appeals that come before appellate courts. One reason it is so difficult for a defendant to win an appeal in a criminal case is the harmless error rule.

The Harmless Error Rule

The **harmless error rule** provides that a trial judge's error in a criminal case may not be the basis for a reversal of a defendant's conviction unless it affects his or her *important* or *substantial* rights.[68] *Chapman* v. *California*[69] stated that the rationale for the harmless error rule was to prevent overturning convictions "for small errors . . . that have little, if any, likelihood of having changed the result of the trial."[70] This rule makes it more difficult for defendants to prevail on appeal. The harmless error rule requires an appellate court to undertake a two-part analysis: first, it must determine if an error was made during trial; second, if there was an error, the appellate court must determine if it affected a substantial right of the defendant.[71]

The Supreme Court has held that some types of errors in a criminal trial are subject to harmless error analysis, whereas other types of errors are so serious that they require an automatic reversal of a defendant's conviction. In *Chapman,* the Court identified three types of errors that require an automatic reversal: (1) using a coerced confession against a defendant in a criminal trial; (2) depriving a defendant of counsel; and (3) trying a defendant before a biased judge. Later cases indicate that other types of errors may require an automatic reversal of a defendant's conviction as well. These include violations of the right to a public trial, and the right to represent oneself at trial.

In 1991, *Arizona* v. *Fulminante,*[72] presented an important harmless error analysis issue. In this rather complex case, Fulminante was suspected of murdering his 11-year-old stepdaughter, who had been strangled and shot, after he had sexually assaulted her. While he was awaiting trial in a federal correctional facility, he was befriended by another inmate, who had posed as an organized crime figure, but was a paid F.B.I. informant. Fulminante feared being assaulted by other inmates for his alleged crime. The informant told Fulminante that the only way he could protect him was if Fulminante told him whether he had committed the crime. Fulminante admitted that he had assaulted and murdered the child-victim. Fulminante made a second confession to a woman, who later became the informant's wife, as well. Fulminante's confessions were admitted into evidence at his murder trial over defense objections that the confessions had been coerced, and he was convicted.

The Arizona Supreme Court held that Fulminante's confession to the government informant had been coerced. It therefore remanded the case for a new trial without the tainted confession.

The U.S. Supreme Court granted certiorari and affirmed the judgment of the Arizona Supreme Court. It held first that Fulminante's confession to the informant had been coerced. Further, the admission at a state criminal trial of a defendant's coerced confession is subject to harmless error analysis. The prosecution, however, bears the burden of proving beyond a reasonable doubt that the error was harmless. Here, it did not meet that heavy burden. Therefore, the admission of Fulminante's first confession to the informant was not harmless error. The case was remanded to the trial court for a new trial without the tainted confession.

Arizona v. *Fulminante* expanded the harmless error doctrine substantially. Even when a defendant's coerced confession is improperly admitted at trial, the error is subject to harmless error analysis. The Supreme Court, based on its analysis of the totality of the circumstances in that case, held that Fulminante was entitled to a new trial because his confession had been coerced. Later cases may arise, however, in which an appellate court may determine that a coerced confession constitutes harmless error.

Enhanced Charges Following a Successful Appeal

Suppose that a defendant who is convicted at trial wins a reversal of his conviction on appeal. May the state try the defendant for the same offense in another criminal trial? The answer is yes, unless the reversal was based on the fact that the first conviction was based on insufficient evidence. If a defendant prevails on appeal, a second trial does not normally violate his or her right to be free from double jeopardy.[73] In a second trial after a successful appeal, however, a defendant's conviction in the first trial forms a baseline; he or she may not be charged with a greater offense in a second trial. For example, in *Price* v. *Georgia,*[74] the defendant was charged in his first trial with first-degree murder, but was convicted of second-degree murder. He successfully appealed his conviction. At a second trial, the state again charged Price with first-degree murder, but he was convicted again of second-degree murder. On appeal, the Supreme Court held that the highest offense that the State should have charged the defendant within his second trial was second-degree murder. It remanded the case for a new trial based on that offense.

An Increased Sentence Following a Successful Appeal

Suppose a defendant is convicted at trial of auto theft and is sentenced to five years' imprisonment. The state's auto theft statute allowed the trial judge to sentence the defendant to a term of imprisonment from one to ten years. His conviction is reversed on appeal and at a second trial the same auto theft charges are reinstated and he is convicted again. This time the trial judge sentences the defendant to ten years' imprisonment. Does imposing a greater sentence upon reconviction violate the Constitution? In *North Carolina* v. *Pearce,*[75] the Supreme Court held that a trial judge may impose a greater sentence at a second trial, as long as it is within the range allowed by state law.[76]

The same rule does not appear to apply to death penalty cases, however. *Bullington* v. *Missouri*[77] held that if a defendant's conviction is reversed after a jury has recommended against imposing the death penalty, the Fifth Amendment's double jeopardy clause bars a death sentence at a later trial on the same charges. The Court held that a contrary holding would make a possible death sentence the cost of an appeal.

Habeas Corpus Review

When prisoners' state appeals are exhausted, they may challenge the legality of their confinement under federal law. This type of legal challenge is termed a **collateral attack on sentencing.** Such an action alleges that the individual is being confined in violation of one or more of his or her basic federal constitutional rights. This is a complex area of the law and only a brief overview of the process will be presented here.

A collateral attack on a prisoner's sentence often proceeds as follows: a prison inmate alleges that a basic error occurring at his or her trial was not corrected on appeal. For example, he or she may assert that evidence was improperly admitted at trial. The inmate further asserts that the appellate court sustained or refused to correct the trial court's mistake. The inmate alleges that because of the errors of these courts, who had failed to protect his or her constitutional rights, the detention is unlawful.

Chapter 1 discussed the **writ of habeas corpus.** A writ of habeas corpus is a court order directed to a government official to produce an incarcerated person before the court to determine if the person is being held lawfully. The "great writ" is a fundamental right provided in the U.S. Constitution. One of the principal modes of collateral attack is termed a **habeas corpus lawsuit,** which is a civil proceeding that asserts that a prisoner is being held unlawfully and asks a reviewing court to order his or her release. The right to a writ of habeas corpus is provided by all the states and by the federal constitution. Most habeas corpus lawsuits, however, are brought by state prison inmates using federal law in federal court, alleging an error in the state proceedings that resulted in their confinement.[78] As a consequence of federal habeas corpus lawsuits, a state prison inmate has two basic avenues of review for his or her conviction—the traditional state appeals process, and if that does not succeed, federal habeas corpus review.[79]

There are four basic requirements for a federal habeas corpus lawsuit by a state prisoner:

1. The state's appeals process must be exhausted.
2. The prisoner must be in custody.
3. The custody must be in violation of federal law.
4. The prisoner must file a sworn written complaint detailing the facts of the illegal detention.[80]

Many inmates have filed these lawsuits in the federal courts, and the number of federal habeas corpus actions brought by state prisoners has skyrocketed. In recent years, however, the Supreme Court has moved to restrict the number of habeas corpus lawsuits.[81]

Case Law on Federal Habeas Corpus Review

Stone v. *Powell,*[82] restricted the scope of federal habeas corpus review in Fourth Amendment cases. The Supreme Court held that if a state prisoner has had a full and fair opportunity to litigate a Fourth Amendment claim in state proceedings, he or she is not entitled to raise the issue again in a federal habeas corpus proceeding. In *Withrow* v.*Williams,*[83] the Court held that this same principle does not apply to violations of a suspect's *Miranda* rights, however, because Fifth Amendment claims threaten the integrity of the trial process.[84]

More recently, the Supreme Court has adopted in federal habeas corpus cases a principle that is comparable to the harmless error rule in the appeals process. *Brecht* v. *Abrahamson*[85] held that a state prisoner may prevail in a federal habeas corpus action only if the violation of his or her rights in state court had a substantial "effect . . . in determining the jury's verdict."[86] The type of violation that exerts an injurious effect on a jury's verdict was illustrated in *Kyles* v. *Whitley*.[87] In that case the Supreme Court held that a prosecutor's failure to disclose evidence favorable to the defense supported granting a prisoner's claim for federal habeas corpus relief.

The Supreme Court's decision in *Herrera* v. *Collins*[88] presented a substantial blow to state prisoners who file federal habeas corpus actions.[89] Herrera, who was convicted of capital murder of a police officer, exhausted his state remedies and sought federal habeas corpus review of his claim that newly discovered evidence proved his innocence. The U.S. District Court granted a stay of execution pending a hearing, but the U.S. Court of Appeals ruled in favor of the State of Texas and vacated the stay. The Supreme Court held that Herrera's claim of actual innocence based on newly discovered evidence is not an appropriate ground for federal habeas corpus relief, absent a showing that the original trial was tainted with some form of constitutional error. The Court stated:

> Claims of actual innocence based on newly discovered evidence have never been held to state a ground for federal habeas relief absent an independent constitutional violation occurring in the underlying criminal proceeding. . . . This rule is grounded in the principle that federal habeas corpus courts sit to ensure that individuals are not imprisoned in violation of the Constitution—not to correct errors of fact.[90]

Herrera indicates that in order to prevail in a federal habeas corpus action, a state inmate must normally demonstrate that some type of constitutional error tainted the original trial. Moreover, if no state relief had been available to review Herrera's claim of actual innocence, federal habeas corpus relief would have been an appropriate remedy to prevent his execution. Here, however, the state of Texas had provided Herrera with multiple opportunities for appellate review of his claims, which were found to lack merit. Therefore, Herrera did not meet the high showing necessary to establish a constitutional violation in this case.

State prisoners appear to have no Sixth Amendment right to the assistance of counsel in federal habeas corpus proceedings as well.[91] Moreover, because many state prisoners have filed successive federal habeas corpus petitions, the Supreme Court has made it relatively easy for U.S. District Courts to dismiss these actions. In *Schlup* v. *Delo*,[92] the Supreme Court held that the "ends of justice" require a state prisoner who files a successive habeas corpus claim to demonstrate that some constitutional violation by state authorities is likely to have resulted in a wrongful conviction. This is a very difficult standard to meet.

The U.S. Congress appears determined to restrict the volume of habeas corpus petitions filed in federal court. Recently, it passed the Antiterrorism and Effective Death

Penalty Act of 1996.[93] Title I of the Act requires dismissal of a claim presented in a state prisoner's second or successive federal habeas application if the claim was also presented in a prior application.[94] Moreover, to succeed in a successive federal habeas corpus application, a state prisoner must demonstrate that "the facts underlying the claim, if proven and viewed in light of the evidence as a whole, would be sufficient to establish by clear and convincing evidence that, but for the constitutional error, no reasonable factfinder would have found the applicant guilty of the underlying offense."[95] The statute presents additional impediments to successive federal habeas corpus actions as well.[96]

In *Felkner* v. *Turpin*,[97] a state prisoner challenged the Act's provisions restricting successive habeas corpus petitions, asserting that Congress had suspended the writ of habeas corpus, in violation of Article I, Section 9, of the U.S. Constitution. The prisoner also maintained that the new law deprived the Supreme Court of appellate jurisdiction under Article III, Section 2 of the Constitution. The Supreme Court upheld the Title I's new requirements for granting habeas corpus relief to state prisoners because the law did not amount to a suspension of the writ of habeas corpus and did not disturb the Court's appellate jurisdiction.

The preceding cases indicate that the Supreme Court and Congress are determined to restrict the tide of federal habeas corpus lawsuits filed by state prisoners.[98] At best, those filing successive habeas corpus petitions in federal court will face an uphill battle.

Summary

Chapter 13 focuses on a defendant's rights once he or she has been convicted of a crime. Three post-conviction processes are discussed: sentencing, appeals, and post-conviction relief in the form of habeas corpus review.

Once a defendant is convicted, a sentence must be imposed. The primary responsibility for setting the range of possible sentences belongs to the legislatures, which specify appropriate sentences for particular crimes. Legislative discretion to direct sentencing is limited by the Eighth Amendment's cruel and unusual punishment clause, however. This clause is binding on state proceedings through the Fourteenth Amendment's due process clause.

Three different factors may render a punishment a violation of the cruel and unusual punishment clause: (1) if the punishment inflicts unnecessary or wanton pain; (2) if it is unacceptable in society; (3) if it is excessive or grossly disproportionate to the offense.

Several major types of penal sanctions are lawful in U.S. justice systems. These include the death penalty, incarceration in a prison or jail, fines, and conditional freedom in the community.

The death penalty is the most controversial form of punishment in U.S. justice systems. This penalty is permitted by the U.S. Constitution; however, it may not inflict unnecessary pain and suffering. Presently, the following modes of execution are permitted in various states: electrocution, the gas chamber, lethal injection, hanging, and a firing squad. In addition, the death penalty may be imposed solely for murder. Moreover, capital punishment may be disproportionate when applied to certain groups of people, regardless of the crimes they commit.

To lessen the risk that the death penalty will be imposed mistakenly, the Supreme Court has required that the death penalty sentencing process be even more reliable than the traditional sentencing process. It has placed two general requirements on the capital sentencing process: first, a state must restrict the sentencer's discretion in an effort to narrow the group of persons eligible for the death penalty and justify the imposition of a more severe sentence on the defendant than on others found guilty of murder; second, a state may not limit the sentencer's consideration of any relevant evidence that may mitigate against imposing the death penalty in a particular case.

Incarceration is another form of punishment in U.S. justice systems. There are several different approaches to sentences of incarceration. These include determinate sentencing, mandatory sentencing, presumptive sentencing, and indeterminate sentencing. The Eighth Amendment's cruel and unusual punishment clause is important to those already incarcerated in jails and prisons throughout the United States. The conditions in a state's prison system or jails may not be such that they violate inmates' basic constitutional rights. Moreover, inmates lose only those rights that are inconsistent with their status as prisoners. They retain many basic rights, including: safe and tolerable living conditions, access to the courts, worship, and other rights consistent with their status as prisoners. On the other hand, prison authorities must be able to maintain order and discipline. Therefore, the federal courts will show deference to state prison officials, and inmates' constitutional rights may be limited by corrections administrators, if there is a good reason to justify a particular restriction.

Sentences of incarceration are subject to many of the same restrictions that bind capital sentences—they must not inflict unnecessary pain and must be acceptable to society. The Supreme Court has given Congress and state legislatures great flexibility, however, to determine appropriate terms of confinement.

Sentencing disparity describes a phenomenon in which similar defendants, who may have committed virtually identical offenses, have received wildly different sentences for their crimes. The Federal Sentencing Guidelines specify definite sentences for specific federal crimes.

Another type of penal sanction in U.S. justice systems is a fine. The Eighth Amendment's text prohibits excessive fines. In general, the Supreme Court has deferred to the legislature and has provided little guidance about precisely what constitutes an excessive fine. The Constitution will not permit imposing a more stringent punishment on a poor person than on a wealthier one. Moreover, an indigent person may not be sentenced to an additional term of incarceration beyond the statutory maximum because he or she is unable to pay a fine.

Still another type of penal sanction that is used often in U.S. justice systems is conditional freedom in the community (probation). Because probation involves a conditional release into the community, an offender must agree to abide by specific contractual terms, which must be lawful and reasonably related to his or her prospects for rehabilitation. If a probationer breaks the probation contract, it may be terminated and he or she may be sentenced to a term of confinement.

Corporal, or physical punishment, is not a lawful sentence for conviction of a crime in the United States. It is not permitted as a disciplinary method in prisons as well.

Chapter 13 considers the appeals process. Every state, by statute, provides for some type of appellate review of criminal cases. The Supreme Court has never held, however, that a convicted state offender has a constitutional right to appeal a criminal conviction. On appeal, attorneys for the defense and prosecution present arguments based on strictly legal issues—they do not relitigate the facts of a case. Appeals determine whether a trial judge committed some error.

It is difficult for a defendant to prevail on appeal. One reason that it is difficult to win is the harmless error rule. This rule provides that a trial judge's error in a criminal case may not be the basis for a reversal of a defendant's conviction, unless it affects his or her important or substantial rights. If a defendant does prevail on appeal, a second trial for the same offense does not violate his or her right to be free from double jeopardy.

When prisoners' state appeals are exhausted, they may challenge the legality of their confinement under federal law. This type of legal challenge is termed a collateral attack on sentencing. One of the principal modes of collateral attack is termed a habeas corpus lawsuit, which asserts that a prisoner is being held unlawfully and asks a reviewing court to order his or her release. Most habeas corpus lawsuits are brought by state prison inmates in federal court, alleging an error in the state proceedings that resulted in their confinement.

The Supreme Court has narrowed the scope of federal habeas corpus review of state convictions in recent years. A state prisoner may prevail in a federal habeas corpus action only if the violation of his or her rights in state court had a substantial and injurious effect in determining the jury's verdict.

Review Questions

1. Discuss the significance of *Robinson* v. *California.* Suppose that you were an attorney for a state legislator who was contemplating introducing a bill that would make it a crime to "be infected with H.I.V. (AIDS)." What advice would you give regarding the possible constitutional issues surrounding this bill?
2. Present and discuss several factors that may render a punishment a violation of the Eighth Amendment's cruel and unusual punishment clause.
   a. Discuss the present legal status of the death penalty.
3. To lessen the risk that the death penalty will be mistakenly or arbitrarily imposed, the Supreme Court has placed two general requirements on the capital sentencing process. Identify and discuss these requirements.
   a. When may an attorney use a challenge for cause to disqualify a potential juror in a death penalty case?
4. Define the following terms:
   a. concurrent sentence
   b. consecutive sentence
   c. determinate sentence
   d. mandatory sentence
   e. presumptive sentence
   f. indeterminate sentence

5. Prison inmates "lose only those constitutional rights that are inconsistent with their status as prisoners."
   a. Identify several constitutional rights that prison inmates retain during incarceration.
   b. Identify several constitutional rights that prison inmates lose during incarceration.
   c. Present the Supreme Court's holding in *Bell* v. *Wolfish.*
6. Discuss the significance of *Harmelin* v. *Michigan.* Why is it important that the Eighth Amendment's cruel and unusual punishment clause provides no "proportionality guarantee?"
7. Identify several factors that are used in the Federal Sentencing Guidelines to determine an offender's sentence. What factors would be used to determine if an individual is a "career offender?"
8. When may an indigent defendant be sentenced to an additional term of confinement due to his or her inability to pay a fine?
9. According to your text, a probation agreement constitutes a "contract" between the probationer and the state. Discuss the significance of the fact that this agreement is a contract. Identify several typical conditions of probation.
   a. What procedural rights does a probationer have in a probation revocation proceeding?

10. Distinguish an "appeal" from a trial.
    a. What is the purpose of the "contemporaneous objection rule?"
11. What happens to a case when an appellate court:
    a. "affirms" the lower court's decision?
    b. "reverses" the lower court's decision?
    c. "remands" the lower court's decision?
12. Identify and discuss the following terms:
    a. plain error rule
    b. harmless error rule
13. Suppose a defendant who is convicted at trial wins a reversal of his or her conviction on appeal.
    a. May the state try the defendant for the same offense in another criminal trial?
    b. If so, may the defendant in a second trial be charged with a more serious offense than he or she was convicted for during the first trial?

    c. May a defendant in a second trial who had prevailed in an appeal of a first conviction be sentenced to a longer period of confinement than he or she originally received after the first trial?
    d. Suppose a defendant's conviction is reversed in a capital case after a jury had recommended against imposing the death penalty. May he or she receive a death sentence after a second trial?
14. Discuss the following terms:
    a. collateral attack on sentencing
    b. habeas corpus lawsuit
15. How has the Supreme Court restricted the scope of federal habeas corpus lawsuits in recent years? Be sure to use case law to support your answer.

Issues for Analysis and Discussion

1. In *Harmelin* v. *Michigan,* the Supreme Court held that the Eighth Amendment contains no "proportionality guarantee." Discuss the significance of this holding. Does this principle apply in *all* cases? Identify Justice Scalia's principal reason for asserting that the Eighth Amendment should not provide a proportionality guarantee.

2. In *Herrera* v. *Collins,* Chief Justice Rehnquist asserted that "due process does not require that every conceivable step be taken, at whatever cost, to eliminate the possibility of convicting an innocent person." Present several arguments that Rehnquist uses to support this proposition. Do you believe that this holding is justified in death penalty cases?

CASE EXCERPT: *HARMELIN* V. *MICHIGAN*
SUPREME COURT OF THE UNITED STATES
501 U.S. 956 (1991)

Harmelin was convicted under Michigan law of possessing more than 650 grams of cocaine and sentenced to a mandatory term of life in prison without the possibility of parole. The Michigan Court of Appeals affirmed his sentence, rejecting his argument that the sentence was "cruel and unusual" within the meaning of the Eighth Amendment. On appeal to the U.S. Supreme Court, Harmelin alleged that his sentence was cruel and unusual punishment because it was significantly disproportionate to the crime he committed, and because the sentencing judge was required by statute to impose it, without taking into account the particularized circumstances of the crime and of the criminal.

Mr. Justice Scalia delivered the opinion of the Court.

* * *

In *Rummel* v. *Estelle,* we held that it did not constitute "cruel and unusual punishment" to impose a life sentence, under a recidivist statute, upon a defendant who had been convicted, successively, of fraudulent use of a credit card to obtain $80 worth of goods or services, passing a forged check in the amount of $28.36, and obtaining $120.75 by false pretenses. We said that "one could argue without fear of contradiction by any decision of this Court that for crimes concededly classified and classifiable as felonies, that is, as punishable by significant terms of imprisonment in a state penitentiary, the length of the sentence actually imposed is purely a matter of legislative prerogative." We specifically rejected the proposition asserted by the dissent, that unconstitutional disproportionality could be established by weighing three factors: (1) the gravity of the offense compared to severity of the penalty; (2) penalties imposed within the same jurisdiction for similar crimes, and (3) penalties imposed in other jurisdictions for the same offense. A footnote in the opinion, however, said: "This is not to say that a proportionality principle would not come into play in the extreme example mentioned by the dissent, . . . if a legislature made overtime parking a felony punishable by life imprisonment."

* * *

It should be apparent from the above discussion that our 5-to-4 decision eight years ago in *Solem* [v. *Helm*] was scarcely the expression of clear and well accepted constitutional law. We have long recognized, of course, that the doctrine of stare decisis is less rigid in its applications to constitutional precedents, and we think that to be especially true of a constitutional precedent that is both recent and in apparent tension with other decisions. Accordingly, we have addressed anew, and in greater detail, the question whether the Eighth Amendment contains a proportionality guarantee—with particular attention to the background of the Eighth Amendment . . . and to the understanding of the Eighth Amendment before the end of the 19th century (which Solem discussed not at all). We conclude from this examination that Solem was simply wrong; the Eighth Amendment contains no proportionality guarantee.

* * *

The language bears the construction, however—and here we come to the point crucial to resolution of the present case—that "cruelty and unusualness" are to be determined not solely with reference to the punishment at issue ("Is life imprisonment a cruel and unusual punishment?") but with reference to the crime for which it is imposed as well ("Is life imprisonment cruel and unusual punishment for possession of unlawful drugs?"). The latter interpretation would make the provision a form of proportionality guarantee. The arguments against it, however, seem to us conclusive.

First of all, to use the phrase "cruel and unusual punishment" to describe a requirement of proportionality would have been an exceedingly vague and oblique way of saying what Americans were well accustomed to saying more directly. The notion of "proportionality" was not a novelty (though then as now there was little agreement over what it entailed).

We think it enough that those who framed and approved the Federal Constitution chose, for whatever reason, not to include within it the guarantee against disproportionate sentences that some State Constitutions contained. It is worth noting, however, that there was good reason for that choice—a reason that reinforces the necessity of overruling Solem. While there are relatively clear historical guidelines and accepted practices that enable judges to determine which *modes* of punishment are "cruel and unusual," *proportionality* does not lend itself to such analysis. Neither Congress nor any state legislature has ever set out with the objective of crafting a penalty that is "disproportionate"; yet as some of the examples mentioned above indicate, many enacted dispositions seem to be so—because they were made for other times or other places, with different social attitudes, different criminal epidemics, different public fears, and different prevailing theories of penology. This is not to say that there are no absolutes; one can imagine extreme examples that no rational person, in no time or place, could accept. But for the same reason these examples are easy to decide, they are certain never to occur. The real function of a con-

stitutional proportionality principle, if it exists, is to enable judges to evaluate a penalty that *some* assemblage of men and women *has* considered proportionate—and to say that it is not. For that real-world enterprise, the standards seem so inadequate that the proportionality principle becomes an invitation to imposition of subjective values.

* * *

Petitioner claims that his sentence violates the Eighth Amendment for a reason in addition to its alleged disproportionality. He argues that it is "cruel and unusual" to impose a mandatory sentence of such severity, without any consideration of so-called mitigating factors such as, in his case, the fact that he had no prior felony convictions. He apparently contends that the Eighth Amendment requires Michigan to create a sentencing scheme whereby life in prison without the possibility of parole is simply the most severe of a range of available penalties that the sentencer may impose after hearing evidence in mitigation and aggravation.

As our earlier discussion should make clear, this claim has no support in the text and history of the Eighth Amendment. Severe, mandatory penalties may be cruel, but they are not unusual in the constitutional sense, having been employed in various forms throughout our Nation's history. As noted earlier, mandatory death sentences abounded in our first Penal Code. They were also common in the several States—both at the time of the founding and throughout the 19th Century. There can be no serious contention then, that a sentence which is not otherwise cruel and unusual becomes so simply because it is "mandatory."

Petitioner's "required mitigation" claim, like his proportionality claim, does find support in our death penalty jurisprudence. We have held that a capital sentence is cruel and unusual under the Eighth Amendment if it is imposed without an individualized determination that punishment is "appropriate"—whether or not the sentence is "grossly disproportionate." Petitioner asks us to extend this so-called "individualized capital-sentencing doctrine," to an "individualized mandatory life in prison without parole sentencing doctrine." We refuse to do so.

Our cases creating and clarifying the "individualized capital sentencing doctrine" have repeatedly suggested that there is no comparable requirement outside the capital context, because of the qualitative difference between death and all other penalties.

* * *

It is true that petitioner's sentence is unique in that it is the second most severe known to the law; but life imprisonment *with* possibility of parole is also unique in that it is the third most severe. And if petitioner's sentence forecloses some "flexible techniques" for later reducing his sen-

tence, it does not foreclose all of them, since there remain the possibilities of retroactive legislative reduction and executive clemency. In some cases, moreover, there will be negligible difference between life without parole and other sentences of imprisonment—for example, a life sentence with eligibility for parole after 20 years, or even a lengthy term sentence without eligibility for parole, given to a 65-year-old man. But even where the difference is the greatest, it cannot be compared with death. We have drawn the line of required individualized sentencing at capital cases, and see no basis for extending it further.

The judgement of the Michigan Court of Appeals is Affirmed.

CASE EXCERPT: *HERRERA V. COLLINS*
SUPREME COURT OF THE UNITED STATES
113 S.Ct. 853 (1993)

On the basis of proof which included two eyewitness identifications, numerous pieces of circumstantial evidence, and Herrera's handwritten letter impliedly admitting his guilt, Herrera was convicted of the capital murder of a police officer and was sentenced to death in January 1982. After pleading guilty, in July 1982, to the related capital murder of another police officer, Herrera unsuccessfully challenged the conviction for the murder of the first police officer on direct appeal and in two collateral proceedings in the Texas state courts, and in a federal habeas corpus petition. Ten years after his conviction, he urged in a second federal habeas proceeding that newly discovered evidence demonstrated that he was "actually innocent" of both murders, and that the Eighth Amendment's prohibition against cruel and unusual punishment and the Fourteenth Amendment's due process guarantee forbid his execution. He supported his claim with affidavits tending to show that his now-dead brother had committed the murders. The U.S. District Court granted his request for a stay of execution so that he could present his actual innocence claim and the supporting affidavits in state court. The Court of Appeals vacated the stay and held that the claim was not appropriate for federal habeas corpus review absent an accompanying federal constitutional violation. The U.S. Supreme Court granted certiorari.

Chief Justice Rehnquist delivered the opinion of the Court.

* * *

A person when first charged with a crime is entitled to a presumption of innocence, and may insist that his guilt be established beyond a reasonable doubt. Other constitutional provisions also have the effect of ensuring against the risk of convicting an innocent person. All of these constitutional safeguards, of course, make it more difficult for the State to rebut and finally overturn the presumption of innocence which attaches to every criminal defendant. But we have also observed that "due process does not require that every conceivable step be taken, at whatever cost, to eliminate the possibility of convicting an innocent person." To conclude otherwise would all but paralyze our system for enforcement of the criminal law.

Once a defendant has been afforded a fair trial and convicted of the offense for which he has been charged, the presumption of innocence disappears. Here, it is not disputed that the State met its burden of proving at trial that petitioner was guilty of the capital murder of Officer Carrisalez beyond a reasonable doubt. Thus, in the eyes of the law, petitioner does not come before the Court as one who is "innocent," but on the contrary as one who had been convicted by due process of law of two brutal murders.

* * *

Claims of actual innocence based on newly discovered evidence have never been held to state a ground for federal habeas relief absent an independent constitutional violation occurring in the underlying state criminal proceeding. . . . This rule is grounded in the principle that federal habeas courts sit to ensure that individuals are not imprisoned in violation of the Constitution—not to correct errors of fact.

More recent authority construing federal habeas statutes speaks in a similar vein. "Federal courts are not forums in which to relitigate state trials." The guilt or innocence determination in state criminal trials is "a decisive and portentous event." "Society's resources have been concentrated at that time and place in order to decide, within the limits of human fallibility, the question

of guilt or innocence of one of its citizens." Few rulings would be more disruptive of our federal system than to provide for federal habeas review of free-standing claims of actual innocence.

* * *

This is not to say that our habeas jurisprudence casts a blind eye towards innocence. In a series of cases culminating with *Sawyer* v. *Whitley* decided last term, we have held that a petitioner otherwise subject to defenses of abusive or successive use of the writ may have his federal constitutional claim considered on the merits if he makes a proper showing of actual innocence. This rule, or fundamental miscarriage of justice exception is grounded in the "equitable discretion" of habeas courts to see that federal constitutional errors do not result in the incarceration of innocent persons. But this body of our habeas jurisprudence makes clear that a claim of "actual innocence" is not itself a constitutional claim, but instead a gateway through which a habeas petitioner must pass to have his otherwise barred constitutional claim considered on the merits.

Petitioner in this case is simply not entitled to habeas relief based on the reasoning of this line of cases. For he does not seek excusal of a procedural error so that he may bring an independent constitutional claim challenging his conviction or sentence, but rather argues that he is entitled to habeas relief because newly discovered evidence shows that his conviction is factually incorrect. The fundamental miscarriage of justice exception is available only where the prisoner supplements his constitutional claim with a colorable showing of factual innocence. We have never held that it extends to freestanding claims of actual innocence. Therefore, the exception is inapplicable here.

Alternatively, petitioner invokes the Fourteenth Amendment's guarantee of due process of law in support of his claim that his showing of actual innocence entitles him to a new trial, or at least to a vacation of his death sentence. "[B]ecause the States have considerable expertise in matters of criminal procedure and the criminal process is grounded in centuries of common-law tradition," we have "exercis[ed] substantial deference to legislative judgments in this area." Thus, we have found the criminal process lacking only where it " 'offends some principle of justice so rooted in the traditions and conscience of our people as to be ranked as fundamental.' " "Historical practice is probative of whether a procedural rule can be characterized as fundamental."

The Constitution itself, of course, makes no mention of new trials. New trials in criminal cases were not granted in England until the end of the 17th Century. And even then, they were available only in misdemeanor cases, though the writ of error coram nobis was available for some errors in felony cases.

* * *

The early federal cases adhere to the common-law rule that a new trial may be granted only during the terms of court in which the final judgment was entered.

* * *

The American Colonies adopted the English common law on new trials. Thus, where new trials were available, motions for such relief typically had to be filed before the expiration of the term during which the trial was held.

As the foregoing discussion illustrates, in state criminal proceedings the trial is the paramount event for determining the guilt or innocence of the defendant. Federal habeas review of state convictions has traditionally been limited to claims of constitutional violations occurring in the course of the underlying state criminal proceedings. Our federal habeas cases have treated claims of "actual innocence," not as an independent constitutional claim, but as a basis upon which a habeas petitioner may have an independent constitutional claim considered on the merits, even though his habeas petition would otherwise be regarded as successive or abusive. History shows that the traditional remedy for claims of innocence based on new evidence, discovered too late in the day to file a new trial motion, has been executive clemency.

We may assume, for the sake of argument in deciding this case, that in a capital case a truly persuasive demonstration of "actual innocence" made after trial would render the execution of a defendant unconstitutional, and warrant federal habeas relief if there were no state avenue open to process such a claim. But because of the very disruptive effect that entertaining claims of actual innocence would have on the need for finality in capital cases, and the enormous burden that having to retry cases based on often stale evidence would place on the States, the threshold showing for such an assumed right would necessarily be extraordinarily high. The showing made by petitioner in this case falls far short of any such threshold. . . . [C]oming 10 years after petitioner's trial, this showing of innocence falls far short of that which would have to be made in order to trigger the sort of constitutional claim which we have assumed, arguendo, to exist.

The judgment of the Court of Appeals is Affirmed.

Endnotes

1. *Robinson* v. *California,* 370 U.S. 660 (1962).
2. See Juliette Smith, "Arresting the Homeless for Sleeping in Public: A Paradigm for Expanding the Robinson Doctrine." 29 *Columbia Journal of Law and Social Problems* pp. 293–335 (1996).
3. *Powell* v. *Texas,* 392 U.S. 514 (1968).
4. Randall Coyne and Lyn Entzeroth, *Capital Punishment and the Judicial Process* (Durham, N.C.: Carolina Acad. Press, 1994), p. 55. This work presents an excellent and comprehensive discussion of legal issues and capital punishment.
5. For an excellent synopsis of arguments for and against capital punishment, see Sue Titus Reid, *Crime and Criminology,* 8th ed. (Madison, WI: Brown & Benchmark, 1994), pp. 103–104.
6. *Gregg* v. *Georgia,* 428 U.S. 153 (1976).

7. *Enmund* v. *Florida,* 458 U.S. 782 (1982).

8. See Peter S. Adolf, "Killing Me Softly: Is the Gas Chamber, or Any Other Method of Execution "Cruel and Unusual Punishment?" 22 *Hastings Constitutional Law Quarterly* pp. 815–866 (1995); Robert J. Sech, "Hang'em High: A Proposal for Thoroughly Evaluating the Constitutionality of Execution Methods." 30 *Valparaiso University Law Review* pp. 381–420 (1995).

9. *Coker* v. *Georgia,* 433 U.S. 584 (1977).

10. See *Enmund* v. *Florida,* 458 U.S. 782 (1982).

11. See Steven Grossman, "Proportionality in Non-Capital Sentencing: The Supreme Court's Tortured Approach to Cruel and Unusual Punishment." 84 *The Kentucky Law Journal* pp. 107–172 (1995).

12. Krista DeLargy and John P. Nolan, "Capital Punishment." 84 *The Georgetown Law Journal Twenty-Fifth Annual Review of Criminal Procedure* pp. 1326–1352, 1329 (1996). This voluminous review is without question one of the best resources available on U.S. procedural law. Portions of this discussion of capital punishment have relied heavily on this work.

13. *Thompson* v. *Oklahoma,* 487 U.S. 815 (1988).

14. *Stanford* v. *Kentucky,* 492 U.S. 361 (1989).

15. See Jason D. Sanabria, "Do Prisoners Have Any Rights Left Under the Eighth Amendment?" 16 *Whittier Law Review* pp. 1113–1153 (1995).

16. *Tison* v. *Arizona,* 481 U.S. 137, 157–158 (1987).

17. *Perry* v. *Linaugh,* 492 U.S. 302 (1989).

18. *Ford* v. *Wainright,* 477 U.S. 399 (1986); DeLargy and Nolan, supra note 12, at 1330.

19. DeLargy and Nolan, supra note 12, at 1331.

20. Id. at 1331–1332.

21. Id. supra note 12, at 1332.

22. Id. at 1337.

23. *Wainright* v. *Witt,* 469 U.S. 412 (1985);DeLargy and Nolan, supra note 12, at 1348.

24. See Christopher R. Drahozal, "*Wainright* v. *Witt* and Death Qualified Juries: A Changed Standard but an Unchanged Result." 71 *Iowa Law Review* pp. 1187–1208 (1986); DeLargy and Nolan, supra note, 12 at 1348.

25. *Morgan* v. *Illinois,* 504 U.S. 719 (1992); DeLargy & Nolan, supra note 12 at 1349.

26. *Lockhart* v. *McCree,* 476 U.S. 162 (1986); see Ian Thomas Moar, "Death Qualified Juries in Capital Cases: The Supreme Court's Decision in Lockhart v. McCree." 19 *Columbia Human Rights Law Review* pp. 369–397 (1988); DeLargy and Nolan, supra note 12, at 1349.

27. 18 U.S.C. Sections 3591–3598 (1994).

28. *United States* v. *Watts,* 136 L.Ed 2d 554 (1997).

29. Id. at 97.

30. United States Department of Justice, Bureau of Justice Statistics, *Sourcebook of Criminal Justice Statistics—1994* (Washington, D.C.: U.S. Govt. Printing Office, 1995), p. 537.

31. Id.

32. A thorough treatment of inmate rights is beyond the scope of this text. For an excellent short treatment of the rights of prison inmates see Sue Titus Reid, *Criminal Justice,* 4th ed. (Madison, WI.: Brown & Benchmark, 1996), pp. 394–429.

33. *Sandin* v. *O'Conner,* 115 S.Ct. 2293 (1995).

34. See Melvin Gutterman, "The Contours of Eighth Amendment Prison Jurisprudence: Conditions of Confinement." 48 *Southern Methodist University Law Review* pp. 373–407 (1995).

35. *Hudson* v. *Palmer,* 468 U.S. 517 (1984).

36. *Bell* v. *Wolfish,* 441 U.S. 520 (1979).

37. Id. at 561; see Alexander Williams, Jr., "Court-Ordered Prison Reform—An Argument for Restraint." 34 *Howard Law Journal* pp. 559–566 (1991).

38. *Solem* v. *Helm,* 463 U.S. 277 (1983).

39. *Harmelin* v. *Michigan,* 111 S.Ct. 2680 (1991).

40. Id. at 2686.

41. Id. at 2699.

42. Id. at 2686; see Scott K. Petersen, "The Punishment Need Not Fit the Crime: Harmelin v. Michigan and the Eighth Amendment." 20 *Pepperdine Law Review* pp. 747–794 (1993).

43. See Kelly A. Patch, "Is Proportionate Sentencing Merely Legislative Grace?" 1992 *Wisconsin Law Review* pp. 1697–1724 (1992).

44. In separate concurring opinion in *Harmelin,* three Justices emphasized that even though the Eighth Amendment does not require a strict proportionality between the offense and the punishment, it prohibits sentences that are "grossly disproportionate" to the crime. *Harmelin* v. *Michigan,* 111 S.Ct. 2680, 2705 (1991).

45. A comprehensive review of the federal sentencing guidelines is beyond the scope of this text. For an excellent and comprehensive review of legal issues

and the sentencing guidelines, see David Leibsohn, Kiersten Boyce, and James M. Moakley, "Sentencing Guidelines." 84 *Georgetown Law Journal Twenty-Fifth Annual Review of Criminal Procedure* pp. 1261–1309 (1996).

46. *Mistretta* v. *United States,* 488 U.S. 361 (1989).
47. Leibsohn et al., supra note 45, at 1275–1276.
48. United States Sentencing Commission, *Federal Sentencing Guideline Manual,* Drug Quantity Table, "Controlled Substances and Quantity." p. 58 (October 1987).
49. Id. at 207.
50. 18 U.S.C. Sections 3551–3673, 28 U.S.C. Sections 991–998 (1994).
51. *Tate* v. *Short,* 401 U.S. 395 (1971).
52. *Williams* v. *Illinois,* 399 U.S. 235 (1970).
53. Id. at 241–242.
54. United States Department of Justice, supra note 30, at 526.
55. *Gagnon* v. *Scarpelli,* 411 U.S. 778 (1973).
56. Parolees facing parole revocation proceedings have similar procedural rights. See *Morrissey* v. *Brewer,* 408 U.S. 471 (1972).
57. *Gagnon* v. *Scarpelli,* 411 U.S. 778, 790 (1973).
58. See Daniel E. Hall, "When Caning Meets the Eighth Amendment: Whipping Offenders in the United States." 4 *Widener Journal of Public Law* pp. 403–460 (1995).
59. Graeme Newman, *Just and Painful: A Case for the Corporal Punishment of Criminals.* (New York, NY: Macmillan, 1983).
60. *Jackson* v. *Bishop,* 404 F.2d 571 (8th Cir. 1968).
61. John W. Palmer, *Constitutional Rights of Prisoners,* 3d ed. (Boston, MA: Anderson, 1985), p. 23.
62. *Ross* v. *Moffit,* 417 U.S. 600, 606 (1974).
63. *Douglas* v. *California,* 372 U.S. 353 (1963).
64. *Ross* v. *Moffit,* 417 U.S. 600 (1974).
65. *Griffin* v. *Illinois,* 351 U.S. 12 (1956).
66. Pa. R. Crim. P. 1410 A(3) (1994).
67. See Girardeau A. Spann, "A Functional Analysis of the Plain-Error Rule." 71 *Georgetown Law Journal* pp. 945–989 (1983).
68. See Shawn O. Miller, "Harmful Error: The Expansion of the Harmless-Error Rule." 12 *Northern Illinois University Law Review* pp. 435–462 (1992).
69. *Chapman* v. *California,* 386 U.S. 18 (1967).
70. Id. at 22; For a comprehensive discussion of these issues see Jennifer Calabrese and Craig A. Gothery,

"Harmless Error." 84 *The Georgetown Law Journal Twenty-Fifth Annual Review of Criminal Procedure* pp. 1385–1389 (1996).
71. See Daniel J. Meltzer, "Harmless Error and Constitutional Remedies." 61 *University of Chicago Law Review* pp. 1–39 (1994).
72. *Arizona* v. *Fulminante,* 499 U.S. 279 (1991).
73. *Justices of Boston Municipal Court* v. *Lydon,* 466 U.S. 294 (1984).
74. *Price* v. *Georgia,* 398 U.S. 323 (1970).
75. *North Carolina* v. *Pearce,* 395 U.S. 711 (1969).
76. See Jonathan D. Youngwood, "The Presumption of Judicial Vindictiveness in Multi-Count Resentencing." 60 *University of Chicago Law Review* pp. 725–756 (1993).
77. *Bullington* v. *Missouri,* 451 U.S. 430 (1981).
78. 28 U.S.C. Sections 2241–2255 (1988); See Victor Eugene Flango and Patricia McKenna, "Federal Habeas Corpus Review of State Court Convictions." 31 *Case Western Reserve Law Review* pp. 237–275 (1995).
79. Peter W. Lewis and Kenneth D. Peoples, *The Supreme Court and the Criminal Process* (Philadelphia, PA: W.B. Saunders, 1978), p. 1042.
80. Id. at 1043.
81. See Michael T. Navigato, "State Prisoners Take Notice—Federal Habeas Corpus Review is Limited by Concepts of Federalism." 18 *Ohio Northern University Law Review* pp. 939–949 (1992).
82. *Stone* v. *Powell,* 428 U.S. 465 (1976); Nicole Veilleux, Jonathan A. Friedman, and Andrew S. Williamson, "Habeas Relief for State Prisoners." 84 *Georgetown Law Journal Twenty-Fifth Annual Review of Criminal Procedure* pp. 1408 (1996).
83. *Withrow* v. *Williams,* 113 S.Ct. 1745 (1993).
84. See Carole J. Yanofsky, "The Supreme Court's Surprising Refusal to Stone Miranda." 44 *American University Law Review* pp. 323–359 (1944).
85. *Brecht* v. *Abrahamson,* 113 S.Ct. 1710 (1993).
86. Id. at 1714; see J. Thomas Sullivan, "The 'Burden' of Proof in Federal Habeas Corpus Litigation." 26 *The University of Memphis Law Review* pp. 205–255 (1995).
87. *Kyles* v. *Whitley,* 115 S.Ct. 1555 (1995).
88. *Herrera* v. *Collins,* 113 S.Ct. 853 (1993).
89. See Tara L. Swafford, "Responding to Herrera v. Collins: Ensuring that Innocents are not Executed." 45 *Case Western Reserve Law Review* pp. 603–639 (1995).
90. *Herrera* v. *Collins,* 1135 Ct. 853, 860 (1993).

91. Veilleux, supra note 82 at 1444. See *Hunt* v. *Nuth,* 57 F.3d 1327 (4th Cir. 1995), *cert denied,* 116 S.Ct. 724 (1996).

92. *Schulp* v. *Delo,* 115 S.Ct. 851 (1995).

93. Pub. L. 104–132, 110 Stat. 1217.

94. Id. at Section 106(b)(1).

95. Id. at Sections 1220–1221.

96. For example, the law provides that in a second or successive habeas corpus application, a claim that was not presented in the prior case shall be dismissed, unless the applicant shows that the claim relies on a new rule of constitutional law, made retroactive to cases on collateral review by the Supreme Court that was previously unavailable.

97. *Felkner* v. *Turpin,* 135 L.Ed. 2d. 827 (1996).

98. See Joseph M. Ditkoff, "The Ever More Complicated Actual Innocence Gateway to Habeas Review." 18 *Harvard Journal of Law & Public Policy* pp. 889–903 (1995).

APPENDIX
SELECTED U.S. CONSTITUTIONAL AMENDMENTS

Amendment I

[Ratified 1791]   Congress shall make no law respecting an establishment of religion, or prohibiting the free exercise thereof; or abridging the freedom of speech, or of the press; or the right of the people peaceably to assemble, and to petition the Government for a redress of grievances.

Amendment II

[Ratified 1791]   A well regulated Militia, being necessary to the security of a free State, the right of the people to keep and bear Arms, shall not be infringed.

Amendment III

[Ratified 1791]   No Soldier shall, in time of peace be quartered in any house, without the consent of the Owner, nor in time of war, but in a manner to be prescribed by law.

Amendment IV

[Ratified 1791]   The right of the people to be secure in their persons, houses, papers, and effects, against unreasonable searches and seizures, shall not be violated, and no Warrants shall issue, but upon probable cause, supported by Oath of affirmation, and particularly describing the place to be searched, and the persons or things to be seized.

Amendment V

[Ratified 1791]   No person shall be held to answer for a capital, or otherwise infamous crime, unless on a presentment or indictment of a Grand Jury, except in cases arising in the land or naval forces, or in the Militia, when in actual service in time of War or public danger; nor shall any person be subject for the same offence to be twice put in jeopardy of life or limb; nor shall be compelled in any criminal case to be a witness against himself, nor be deprived of life, liberty, or property, without due process of law; nor shall private property be taken for public use, without just compensation.

Amendment VI

[Ratified 1791]   In all criminal prosecutions, the accused shall enjoy the right to a speedy and public trial, by an impartial jury of the State and district wherein the crime shall have been committed, which district shall have been previously ascertained by law, and to be informed of the nature and cause of the accusation; to be confronted with the witnesses against him; to have compulsory process for obtaining Witnesses in his favor, and to have the Assistance of Counsel for his defense.

Amendment VII

[Ratified 1791]   In Suits at common law, where the value in controversy shall exceed twenty dollars, the right of trial by jury shall be preserved, and no fact tried by a jury, shall be otherwise re-examined in any Court of the United States, than according to the rules of the common law.

Amendment VIII

[Ratified 1791]   Excessive bail shall not be required, nor excessive fines imposed, nor cruel and unusual punishments inflicted.

Amendment IX

[Ratified 1791]   The enumeration in the Constitution, of certain rights, shall not be construed to deny or disparage others retained by the people.

Amendment X

[Ratified 1791]   The powers not delegated to the United States by the Constitution, nor prohibited by it to the States, are reserved to the States respectively, or to the people.

Amendment XIV

[Ratified 1868]   *Section 1.* All persons born or naturalized in the United States and subject to the jurisdiction thereof, are citizens of the United States and of the State wherein they reside. No State shall make or enforce any law which shall abridge the privileges or immunities of citizens of the United States; nor shall any State deprive any person of life, liberty, or property, without the due process of law; nor deny to any person within its jurisdiction the equal protection of the laws.